Kyrgyzstan

the Bradt Travel Guide

Laurence Mitchell

edition
3

www.bradtguides.com

Bradt Travel Guides Ltd, UK
The Globe Pequot Press Inc, USA

Bishkek: a selection of interesting sights and the best choice of hotels and restaurants in the country
pages 87–122

KAZAKHSTAN

Ala-Archa & Alamedin valleys: excellent hiking close to the Kyrgyz capital
pages 123–7

Kara-Balta

BISH

Sary-Chelek Biosphere Reserve: pristine blue lakes surrounded by wild fruit forests and rocky crags
pages 263–5

Talas

Chui

Talas

Toktogul Reservoir

Toktogul

Chatkal

Sary-Chelek Biosphere Reserve

Arkyt

Kara-Köl

Min-K

Narin

Jalal-Abad

Kazarr

Ala-Buka

Kerben

Tash-Kömür

Arslanbob

Na

UZBEKISTAN

Ortok

Arslanbob: charming Uzbek village and summer resort surrounded by mountain peaks and the world's largest walnut forests
pages 251–9

Jalal-Abad

Özgön

Kara-Daria

Osh

Gulcha

Sülüktü

Batken

Sokh (UZB)

Kyzyl-Kiya

Osh

Isfana

Vorukh (TAJ)

Batken

Shakhimardan (UZB)

Sary-Tash

Irkeshtam

Daroot-Korgon

Kyzyl-Suu

Lenin 7,134m

Kyzyl-Art Pass 4,280m

TAJIKISTAN

Osh: Kyrgyzstan's 5,000-year-old second city, with a Muslim pilgrimage site and fascinating ancient bazaar
pages 269–77

AFGHANISTAN

Karakol: an enjoyable small city
and important trekking centre
pages 171–80

Lake Issyk-Kul: lakeside beaches with
a beautiful mountainous backdrop
pages 145–9

Karakol & Altyn Arashan valleys:
gorgeous scenery and superb trekking
opportunities close to Karakol
pages 181–5

Tokmok

Tamchy   Cholpon-Ata   Tyup

Balykchy   Lake   Karakol
                Issyk-Kul
                            Kyzyl-Suu

                                        Khan Tengri
                                        6,995m ▲
                                        Pobedy
                                        7,439m ▲

Kochkor
Bokonbaevo   Tamga   Barskoon
                                Issyk-Kul

                Naryn
Naryn

Baetov   N a r y n

At-Bashy   Central Tien Shan: central Asia's highest mountains –
                                    glaciers, heli-skiing and serious mountaineering
                                    pages 189–93

                Ak-Sw

Lake

Torugart Pass   Tash Rabat: Kyrgyzstan's most intriguing monument
3,752m   sits high in the mountains near the Chinese border
                     pages 236–7

Saimaluu-Tash petroglyphs: outdoor gallery of
mysterious rock paintings set high on a mountain top
pages 249–50

                                    N

                                    Bradt

CHINA

0   100km
0   100 miles

KEY

Capital   ■
Town   ●
Village   ○
Mountain peak   ▲
Ancient site   ∴
National park/reserve ●
Road   ══════
Railway   ┅┅┅┅┅

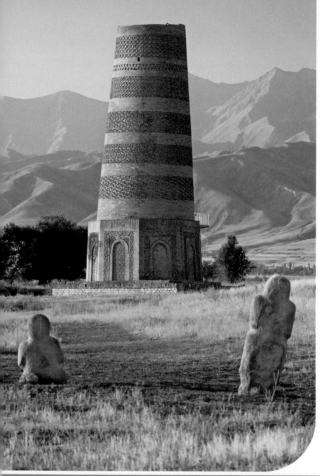

Kyrgyzstan Don't miss...

Silk Road treasures
Burana Tower in the Chui Valley is, in fact, a minaret, and all that remains of the former Karakhanid city of Balasagun
(P/S) pages 132–4

Staying in a *jailoo* yurt
Bel-Tam yurt camp on the shore of Lake Issyk-Kul gives a taste of the traditional Kyrgyz way of life
(LM) page 202

Arslanbob region

This region in the Jalal-Abad Province, in the shadow of the Fergana mountain range, is home to a vast relic walnut forest
(LM) pages 251–9

Hiking in the mountains south of Karakol

There are numerous options for summer hiking in the beautiful mountain valleys that lie south of Karakol
(AP/AWL)
pages 187–9

Karakol Sunday animal market

Held on the edge of town early every Sunday morning, this animal bazaar attracts people from all over the Karakol region (LM)
pages 179–80

Kyrgyzstan in colour

above   The red sandstone rock formation of Jeti-Ögüz ('Seven Bulls') south of Lake Issyk-Kul takes its name from a famous Kyrgyz legend (IV/AWL) pages 185–7

left   A *jailoo* yurt camp approaching the Torugart Pass on the route to China (JS/AWL) pages 238–41

below   Lake Issyk-Kul, whose name means 'warm lake' in Kyrgyz because it never freezes, is the second-largest alpine lake in the world (N/S) pages 145–9 *above* The Barskoon Valley leads from the southeast shore of Lake Issyk-Kul up to a 4,021m-high **pass** (EM/S) pages 196–7

right The small waterfall at Arslanbob is a popular attraction for Uzbek visitors to the village in **summer** (LM) page 255

below Lake Ala-Köl in the Central Tien Shan makes a scenic stopping point when trekking in the Karakol Valley (ED/S) page 188

We're 40...
how did that happen?

How did it all happen? George (my then husband) and I wrote the first Bradt guide – about hiking in Peru and Bolivia – on an Amazon river barge, and typed it up on a borrowed typewriter. We had no money for the next two books so George went to work for a printer and was paid in books rather than money.

Forty years on, Bradt publishes over 200 titles that sell all over the world. I still suffer from Imposter Syndrome – how did it all happen? I hadn't even worked in an office before! Well, I've been extraordinarily lucky with the people around me. George provided the belief to get us started (and the mother to run our US office). Then, in 1977, I recruited a helper, Janet Mears, who is still working for us. She and the many dedicated staff who followed have been the foundations on which the company is built. But the bricks and mortar have been our authors and readers. Without them there would be no Bradt Travel Guides. Thank you all for making it happen.

Hilary Bradt

Celebrate our anniversary and get a 40% discount on all titles with the code BRADT40.

Available from www.bradtguides.com

AUTHOR

Laurence Mitchell is a travel writer and photographer with an interest in forgotten places, border zones and territories in transition. After completing a degree in environmental science and pursuing a varied career that has included teaching English in rural Sudan, clerical work and surveying historic farm buildings, he retrained as a geography teacher, which he pursued for 12 years before swapping it for the uncertainties of full-time travel writing and photography. As well as writing guidebooks for Bradt including *Serbia*, *Slow Travel Norfolk* and *Slow*

Travel Suffolk, he has contributed to publications that include *Walk*, *hidden europe*, *Geographical*, *Discover Britain* and *Russian Life*. He is a member of the British Guild of Travel Writers and the Outdoor Writers and Photographers Guild. His website can be found at www.laurencemitchell.com and blog at http://eastofelveden. wordpress.com.

AUTHOR'S STORY

My first experience of Kyrgyz culture was not in Kyrgyzstan itself but across the border in Xinjiang Province in China, where I stayed in a yurt on the way to Pakistan via the Karakoram Highway. What I discovered when I finally visited the republic a few years later was a newly independent country that was far more than just the sum of its parts. If Russia, as Churchill famously claimed, is 'a riddle wrapped in a mystery inside an enigma', then Kyrgyzstan is a central Asian *matryoshka* doll of interwoven Turkic, Mongol and Slavic cultures that has been coloured by successive shamanistic, Islamic and communist traditions.

Getting around the country to do research was not always easy. One fateful share taxi ride from Talas to Jalal-Abad took around 16 hours, rather than the seven I had been promised. This was partly due to the driver's insistence on frequent stops for tea and *shashlyk*, but mostly because of the poor quality, water-diluted petrol that he had filled the car with. At first, the taxi would stall when going up the steeper hills; later on, it could hardly manage on the flat – in a country where 90% of the terrain is mountainous this is not a good thing. I have vivid memories of pushing the taxi at two in the morning along a coal-black road just north of Jalal-Abad while overloaded trucks whistled past in the dark. My pushing accomplice was a customs officer from Batken Province who kept laughing maniacally into the night and repeatedly shouting '*Ekstrim turizm, da*? Ha! Ha!' at me. Happy days! Such occasional unpredictability is all part of the experience but, on the whole, things tend to work out and most travel in Kyrgyzstan is as adventurous as you would like it to be.

PUBLISHER'S FOREWORD   *Adrian Phillips, Managing Director*

I settled down to read the first edition of this book in happy anticipation. Laurence Mitchell is a trusted Bradt author who had already written our guide to Serbia (and who has since covered places closer to home in his Slow Travel Guides to Norfolk and Suffolk), so I knew he'd have done a great job. His *Kyrgyzstan* guide was all that I hoped for: carefully researched, well written, and full of interest and surprises. It's been thoroughly updated for this third edition, of course – and, most importantly, it makes you want to go to Kyrgyzstan.

Third edition published February 2015
First published January 2008

Bradt Travel Guides Ltd, IDC House, The Vale, Chalfont St Peter, Bucks SL9 9RZ, England
www.bradtguides.com
Print edition published in the USA by The Globe Pequot Press Inc, PO Box 480, Guilford, Connecticut 06437-0480

Text copyright © 2015 Laurence Mitchell
Maps copyright © 2015 Bradt Travel Guides Ltd
Illustrations copyright © 2015 Individual photographers (see below)
Project Manager: Laura Pidgley
Cover image research: Pepi Bluck, Perfect Picture

ISBN 13: 978 1 84162 856 1
e-ISBN: 978 1 78477 114 0 (ePub)
e-ISBN: 978 1 78477 214 7 (mobi)

British Library Cataloguing in Publication Data
A catalogue record for this book is available from the British Library

Photographs Alamy: ESCUDERO Patrick/hemis.fr (EP/H/A), Kyrgyzstan (K/A); AWL Images: Aurora Photos (AP/AWL), Ivan Vadovan (IV/AWL), Jane Sweeney (JS/AWL), Paul Harris (PH/AWL); Laurence Mitchell (LM); Shutterstock: Djusha (D/S), Dmitri Gomon (DG/S), Evgeny Dubinchuk (ED/S), elena moiseeva (EM/S), Elena Mirage (ELM/S), Idea Studio (IS/S), Novoselov (N/S), Nikita Maykov (NM/S), PavelSvoboda (P/S), Paul Reeves Photography (PRP/S), Pikoso.kz (PS/S), Radiokafka (R/S), Tracing Tea (TT/S); SuperStock (SS)
Front cover Eagle-hunter, Issyk-Kul (K/A)
Back cover A procession of stone wheels at Burana Tower (P/S); Ala-Kol Lake (IS/S)
Title page Jeti-Ögüz rock formation (IV/AWL); Food yurts flying the Kyrgyzstan flag close to Broken Heart rock in Jeti-Ögüz valley (LM); Children in Altyn Arashan valley (SS)

Maps David McCutcheon FBCart.S; colour map base by Nick Rowland FRGS

Typeset from the author's disk by Wakewing and Ian Spick, Bradt Travel Guides Ltd
Production managed by Jellyfish Print Solutions; printed in India
Digital conversion by www.dataworks.co.in

Acknowledgements

My thanks go to all the team at Bradt for seeing this through to its third edition, in particular Rachel Fielding, Laura Pidgley and Deborah Gerrard. In Kyrgyzstan my gratitude goes to the following for their generous help and support: Ernist Djumagulov, Ines Beyer, Asylbek Rajiev, Taalai Janybekov and family, Hayat Tarikov, Talant Toksonbaev, Bekbolot Builashov, Artyk Kulubaev, Gulira Kenjekaraeva, Azamat Asanov, Aida Kydyrgycheva, Saltanat Kadyrkulova, Janybek Sariev, Mir Bazarov, and Tamara and Askar at Tamga. For this third edition I would also like to thank the following correspondents for their valuable contributions and feedback: Gilad Allon, Anna Bauer, Pasi Hannonen, Alice Harrison, Gerrit Heij, Felix Lampadius, Achim Pfriender, David Stein and Jacos Van Zelst. I am also indebted to Dennis Keen for sharing his broad knowledge of eagle-hunting in Kyrgyzstan, Eric Straw for his advice on self-drive car hire and Hazel Adamson for her contribution on setting up a yurt camp.

UPDATES WEBSITE AND FEEDBACK REQUEST

At Bradt Travel Guides we're aware that guidebooks start to go out of date on the day they're published – and that you, our readers, are out there in the field doing research of your own. You'll find out before us when a fine new family-run hotel opens or a favourite restaurant changes hands and goes downhill. So why not write and tell us about your experiences? Contact us on ✆ 01753 893444 or e info@bradtguides.com. We will forward emails to the author who may post updates on the Bradt website at www.bradtupdates.com/kyrgyzstan. Alternatively you can add a review of the book to www.bradtguides.com or Amazon.

Contents

LIST OF MAPS

Introduction

In the last edition of this book I wrote that before the spring of 2010 few had heard of Kyrgyzstan. In that fateful year the country achieved momentary fame for all the wrong reasons when violent protests in Bishkek, Osh and other cities brought this small central Asian country to our television screens for a short while. Thankfully things have settled down since then and the country has gone back to its previous state of quiet obscurity.

Say 'Kyrgyzstan' to most people and there may be a flicker of recognition, but it is usually for the wrong reason. Sometimes, the country becomes confused with Kurdistan in people's minds, but it is probably the suffix '-stan' that causes well-meaning friends and family to ask 'Will it be safe?' Of course, '-stan' may have a whiff of danger about it, but it just means 'country of…' in Persian, in the same way that '-land' does for countries like Finland, Switzerland, England and Scotland. You could always try saying Kyrgyz Republic instead, as that is the country's official name, but that might bring even blanker looks.

As for describing where Kyrgyzstan is, saying it is north of Tajikistan, west of Xinjiang doesn't really help in most cases. In terms of the mental maps that people carry around in their heads, central Asia is pretty much terra incognita for most and Kyrgyzstan might as well be Ruritania. So why is the country so little known? Part of the reason is that just over two decades ago the country did not exist at all, and was merely a far-flung autonomous region of the vast, crumbling USSR. Then, in 1991, just like its immediate neighbours, it found itself suddenly independent and, as no such country had ever existed in the pre-Soviet period, having to invent itself. The present country's boundaries were drawn up in the 1920s by Stalin, whose aim was to divide and rule in Soviet central Asia. The notion was for an autonomous Kyrgyz republic within the USSR, but what resulted was only an approximation and, although ethnic Kyrgyz currently make up around two-thirds of the population, the country is a mosaic of ethnicities that includes Russians, Uzbeks, Dungans, Uyghurs, Tajiks and Tatars.

All that the visitor really needs to know is that Kyrgyzstan is an outdoors sort of place; that is, if you prefer to spend your time looking at beautiful buildings and drinking espresso in chic cafés then this may not be your ideal destination. If you enjoy trekking, horseriding, birdwatching, camping and visiting remote prehistoric sites, then it most certainly is. The Kyrgyz landscape is magnificent and hugely varied, and Swiss, Scots, Canadians, Italians and even Israelis can all be heard to exclaim that, in places, the scenery reminds them of their homeland. This is no exaggeration as the country has it all – alpine lakes, fast-flowing rivers, arid steppes, snow-capped peaks, conifer forests, agricultural plains, rolling meadows and vast walnut forests. But, if there is one physical characteristic that stands out above all else, it is mountains: 90% of Kyrgyzstan lies above

1,500m and the country's topography is dominated by the various ranges of the Tien Shan system.

The beauty of Kyrgyzstan for visitors is that it has a bit of everything: nomadic traditions, central Asian mystique, Soviet-era trappings, a few spectacular prehistoric and Silk Road sites and, above all else, a culture that can best be described as a palimpsest, and over the centuries has absorbed the influence of shamanism, Zoroastrianism, Sufism and communism to become something entirely unique.

A visit to Kyrgyzstan is as adventurous as you would like it to be, which can mean everything from lazing on a beach at Lake Issyk-Kul to glacier walking in the Central Tien Shan. The low prices, hospitable people and gorgeous scenery are simply a bonus. Now that there is a visa-free regime and relatively inexpensive daily flights from Europe, there has never been a better time to come and see this beautiful country. For all those who come and see, *Ak-Jol*!

A BRIEF NOTE ON TRANSLITERATION

There are many variations on the standard Latin spelling of Kyrgyz words and place names, depending on whether this has been done entirely phonetically or by transliteration from either Russian or Kyrgyz Cyrillic spellings. I have done my best to be consistent, either by adopting the commonest written form in normal use or by making a direct transliteration of the standard Kyrgyz Cyrillic form, hence Jalal-Abad rather than Dzhalal-Abad and Özgön rather than Uzgen.

I have used the word **Kyrgyz** in a very broad sense, not just to relate to that which is ethnically Kyrgyz but also to describe things that pertain to the modern Kyrgyz Republic, ie: a Kyrgyz travel agency (which may well be staffed by ethnic Russians and Dungans) rather than a Kyrgyzstani travel agency, which, although strictly correct, simply does not sound right. I have also done the same with my use of the words Uzbek and Tajik.

MAPS

Keys and symbols Maps include alphabetical keys covering the locations of those places to stay, eat or drink that are featured in the book. Note that regional maps may not show all hotels and restaurants in the area: other establishments may be located in towns shown on the map.

Grids and grid references Several maps use grid lines to allow easy location of sites. Map grid references are listed in square brackets after the name of the place or sight of interest in the text, with page number followed by grid number, eg: [102 A3].

SEND US YOUR SNAPS!

We'd love to follow your adventures using our *Kyrgyzstan* guide – why not send us your photos and stories via Twitter (@BradtGuides) and Instagram (@bradtguides) using the hashtag #kyrgyzstan. Alternatively, you can upload your photos directly to the gallery on the Kyrgyzstan destination page via our website (*www.bradtguides.com*).

Part One

GENERAL INFORMATION

KYRGYZSTAN AT A GLANCE

Official name Kyrgyz Republic

Location Landlocked in central Asia, bordered by Kazakhstan to the north, China to the east and southeast, Uzbekistan to the west and Tajikistan to the southwest

Size/area 198,500km² (about the same as England, Wales and Scotland combined or Nebraska, USA)

Climate Dry continental to polar (Tien Shan); subtropical in the southwest (Fergana Valley); temperate in northern foothill zone

Status Republic headed by president, government headed by prime minister

Head of state President Almazbek Atambayev

Head of government Prime Minister Djoomart Otorbaev

Independence Declared from Soviet Union on 31 August 1991

Population Approximately 5.8 million (2014 estimate); Kyrgyz 72.6%, Uzbeks 14.4%, Russians 6.4%, others 6.6%

Life expectancy Male 65.9 years, female 74.5 years (2014 estimate)

Capital Bishkek, estimated population about 900,000

Other main towns Osh, Naryn, Jalal-Abad, Karakol, Talas

Economy Livestock, agriculture, mining, hydro-electric energy, recycled metal, tourism

GDP US$14.3 billion, equivalent to US$2,500 per capita per annum

Languages Official languages are Kyrgyz and Russian; also Uzbek, Uyghur, Dungan and others

Adult literacy rate Claimed to be 99.2% (2009 estimate)

Religion Sunni Islam, Orthodox Christian, animistic beliefs

Ethnic diversity Kyrgyz dominate in the north with Russians, other Slavs and Dungans forming sizeable minorities; many Uzbeks in the south form the majority in some regions

Currency Kyrgyz som; US$1 = 57som, €1 = 72som, £1 = 90som (November 2014)

International telephone code 996

Time GMT+5

Electrical voltage 220V, 50Hz, standard two-pin round-prong plug

Flag Red with a yellow *tunduk* (yurt roof piece) in centre surrounded by a 40-rayed sun

Coat of arms Rising sun over mountain and lake within the wings of a spread eagle

Public holidays See pages 77–8.

1

Background Information

GEOGRAPHY

Kyrgyzstan is a landlocked country located at the heart of central Asia. It is surrounded by the former USSR territories of Kazakhstan, Uzbekistan and Tajikistan to the north, west and southwest respectively, with China lying to the east. At just under 200,000km² the republic is a little smaller in area than the UK minus Northern Ireland, or the state of Nebraska in the USA. Kyrgyzstan's territory extends roughly 900km from east to west and 410km from north to south.

MOUNTAINS The country is extremely mountainous, with 90% of the land area above 1,500m in elevation above sea level and 71% above 2,000m. The country's average elevation is 2,750m. This mountainous character has led Kyrgyzstan to be known as the 'Switzerland of central Asia' on occasion, although the comparison does not extend much beyond physical geography.

The majority of Kyrgyzstan's mountain ranges belong to the Tien Shan system, the legendary Celestial Mountains of Chinese folklore. This mountain chain stretches west to east well beyond the political borders of Kyrgyzstan, from just to the east of Tashkent in Uzbekistan, almost as far as Ürümqi in China's Xinjiang Province. The eastern end of the range, made of mostly crystalline and sedimentary rock, is its oldest part, created during the Palaeozoic era 540–250 million years ago; the western end is of softer and younger metamorphic rock. Within Kyrgyzstan itself the Tien Shan system is divided into several subsidiary ranges, including those of Kungey and Terskey Ala-Too which frame Lake Issyk-Kul north and south, the Kyrgyz Ala-Too south of Bishkek, the Fergana range in the southwest which hems in the Fergana Valley, and the Chatkal range in the far west which extends into Uzbekistan.

Many of the mountain peaks are perennially covered with snow and ice in the form of glaciers, the largest being the 62km-long Inylchek Glacier in the Central Tien Shan – in the far east of the country near the borders with Kazakhstan and China – which is one of the world's longest. Altogether there are estimated to be 6,500 distinct glaciers in the country that together hold a store of 650km³ of water and cover a total of 4% of the land area: a quantity such that, if it were to melt, it would cover the entire surface area of Kyrgyzstan with water to a depth of 3m.

The highest mountain peaks also lie in the Central Tien Shan range: Jengish Chokusu, formerly known as Pik Pobedy, is both Kyrgyzstan's and the Tien Shan's highest peak, standing at 7,439m on the border with China. Nearby, the slightly lower peak of Khan Tengri, on the border with Kazakhstan, reaches 7,010m and is considered by geologists to be the world's most northerly 7,000m summit. Kyrgyzstan's other major mountain ranges are the Pamir range in the far south, which it shares with Tajikistan and China's Xinjiang Province, and the Pamir Alay range, which separates the Pamir and Tien Shan ranges. In comparison, the Pamirs are older, more rounded mountains that lack the rugged peaks of the Tien Shan range, but only the most northerly range of the Pamir system – the Zaalaysky Ridge – is within Kyrgyzstan; the rest lie firmly in Tajikistan and China. Here there are high passes through to China and Tajikistan, with Peak Lenin at 7,134m, the second highest peak in the Pamir range, marking the frontier with Tajikistan. The southwest sector of the country that extends an arm beneath the Fergana Valley is dominated by the Pamir Alay range, a high range of 5,000m peaks that extends into the Turkestan ridge and has the aptly named 5,509m Piramida Chokusu (Pyramid Peak) marking the border with Tajikistan.

VALLEYS Enclosed in a pincer grip between the Pamir Alay and the Fergana range of the Tien Shan is the low-lying Fergana Valley, a farming region of which Kyrgyzstan has a share, along with Uzbekistan and Tajikistan. Here you will find the country's lowest point at 401m, in Kulundy village, in Batken Province in the southwest. The Fergana Valley, along with the relatively flat Chui and Talas valleys in the north, comprise the only really suitable terrain for large-scale agriculture in the entire country.

WATERWAYS AND LAKES Kyrgyzstan has no navigable waterways and the majority of rivers are small, rapid run-off streams and tributaries of the Syr Darya system. These rivers flow into Uzbekistan and have their source in the Tien Shan near the Chinese border, the exception to this being the Chui River of northern Kyrgyzstan, which arises in northern Kazakhstan. The River Naryn is Kyrgyzstan's longest at 535km in length; other major rivers include the Talas in the west, the Chui in the north, Sary-Jaz in the east and the Chatkal River in the extreme west, which flows into Uzbekistan.

None of these rivers flow into the country's principal lake, Lake Issyk-Kul (meaning 'warm lake') in Kyrgyzstan's northeast, which is the third largest body of water in central Asia, after Lake Balkash and the rapidly shrinking Aral Sea. Standing at an altitude of 1,606m above sea level, it qualifies as the second largest alpine lake in the world after Lake Titicaca in Peru/Bolivia. As well as covering a large area, being approximately 180km long and 60km wide, Lake Issyk-Kul is also very deep – up to 668m in places. The country's second and third largest lakes are higher still, but far smaller in both size and volume: Song-Köl at 3,016m in central Kyrgyzstan and Chatyr-Köl at 3,530m near the Torugart Pass into China, both of which belong to the Naryn River basin.

At around the same elevation as Lake Chatyr-Köl is Lake Merzbacher at the Inylchek Glacier in the Central Tien Shan: a rare geographical phenomenon that appears and disappears over a short period of time each summer. In contrast, the small jewel-like Lake Sary-Chelek in the southwest, at the modest altitude of just 1,873m, is considered by many to be one of Kyrgyzstan's most beautiful. A manmade lake, the Toktogul Reservoir lies in the valley between the Ala-Too and Fergana ranges in the west of the country and is an important source of both drinking water and hydro-electrical power.

CLIMATE

Kyrgyzstan's climate is partly influenced by its mountains and partly by its continental location far from any ocean. For the most part it is continental, with cold winters and warm summers. In the lowlands, the temperature ranges between −4°C and −6°C in January and between 16°C and 24°C in July. The coldest temperatures are in the mountain valleys where −30°C is not uncommon and a record of −53.6°C has been measured, although −14°C to −20°C is more usual. In the Fergana Valley, the average temperature in July is around 27°C, although temperatures frequently reach the low 40s. Even in the summer, temperatures may drop as low as −10°C at night on the mountain peaks. Of the major urban centres, Naryn has by far the most extreme climate, with an average minimum temperature in January of −19°C and an average maximum July temperature of 25°C. Both Bishkek and Osh have much milder winter temperatures but warmer summers. Generally temperatures are far less extreme in the region of Lake Issyk-Kul, where the presence of a large body of nonfreezing, slightly saline water has a moderating influence on the local climate.

Rainfall is generally fairly low throughout the country – as little as 100mm per annum on the southwest shore of Lake Issyk-Kul, to around 2,000mm in the mountains above the Fergana Valley. The national average is 380mm, with March to May and October and November usually the wetter months. There is sometimes heavy snowfall in winter. Clear skies are common and Kyrgyzstan averages more than 300 sunny days per year. Recent years have seen a number of unusual climatic events, which are possibly linked with worldwide climate change and glaciers receding. droughts in the Fergana Valley and elsewhere, low winter snowfall, unusually heavy rain in the spring and an increase in the water level of Lake Issyk-Kul, despite a preceding trend in which the water level was dropping.

NATURAL HISTORY AND CONSERVATION

With a wide variety of habitats, which range from temperate grasslands to high mountain meadows, and conifer forests to cold steppes, Kyrgyzstan has an immense wealth of both flora and fauna. Overall, Kyrgyzstan has about 3% of the total animal species and 2% of the flora found in the world – an impressive figure for a small country that occupies just 0.13% of the world's land area. More importantly, with some highly specialised natural habitats, the country is also home to some of the world's scarcest species, particularly mammals.

FLORA Kyrgyzstan has at least 4,500 species of plant in total, of which 125 species are endemic and 300 are considered to be endangered. The country's extensive **forests** are particularly noteworthy, with large tracts of spruce, juniper (*archa*), pine, maple, poplar-willow, rowan and birch.

Jalal-Abad Province has the greatest percentage of forest cover (9%), which includes a large expanse of walnut forest in the region of Arslanbob; this is followed by Osh (5.1%), Talas (3.6%), Issyk-Kul (2.7%), Naryn (2.2%) and Chui (2.1%). Overall, 4.2% of the country (about 843,000ha) is estimated to be covered by woodland.

Kyrgyzstan's natural forests contain a total of 120 woody species. On the northern mountain ranges the most significant species are spruce (*Picea schrenkiana*), Tien Shan fir (*Pinus schrenkiana*), several junipers (*Juniperus* spp), rowan (*Sorbus tianschanica*) and birch (*Betula* spp), along with bushy scrub of barberry (*Berberis* spp), wild rose (*Rosa* spp) and buckthorn (*Hippophae rhamnoides*), among others. In the western Tien Shan range, in the more protected, drier areas, pistachio (*Pistacia vera*) is present in significant quantities, as is wild almond (*Prunus amygdalus communis*). In the wetter mountain areas, particularly on the southern slopes north of the Fergana Valley in Jalal-Abad Province, stand some of the world's most significant relic forests of walnut (*Juglans regia*), along with stands of wild fruit trees such as apple (*Malus* spp), cherry and plum (*Prunus* spp), and hardwoods such as maple (*Acer turkestanica*).

Unfortunately, some of Kyrgyzstan's forests, particularly its relic walnut forests in the south, are ageing faster than they are regenerating and the overmature forests are susceptible to damage from pests and diseases.

As well as its forests, Kyrgyzstan is also well known throughout central Asia for the variety of valuable medicinal herbs that are found in its meadows and valleys – around 200 in all. These include plants such as plantain (*Plantago* spp), Jerusalem sage (*Phlomis* spp), wormwood (*Artemisia* spp) and *Ephedra* species. Some of the most spectacular flora is found at altitudes of 3,000m or higher, where, in high alpine meadows, edelweiss (*Leontopodium alpinum*) is common, as are crocuses, anemones, asters, wild onions (*Allium* spp), tulips including Greig's tulip (*Tulipa greigii*) and Kaufmann's tulip (*Tulipa kaufmanniana*), and poppies (*Papaver* spp).

FAUNA Kyrgyzstan has well over 500 species of vertebrates and more than 3,000 types of insect, which include 60 species of dragonfly, 86 of butterfly, 33 of bee, 86 of ant and 250 of cicada. Reptiles are well represented too, with 28 species of tortoise, snake and lizard. Seventy-five different species of fish can be found in the various lakes, reservoirs and rivers of the country, with many of these in Kyrgyzstan's largest body of water, Lake Issyk-Kul, which has carp, trout, *osman*, bream, pike-perch and many other species (see page 153). Many of the species are endemic either to the central Asian region or to Kyrgyzstan in particular.

Birds Of the vertebrates, birds make up 368 of the 500 species. Raptors and waterbirds are particularly well represented, with the saker falcon (*Falco cherrug*), golden eagle (*Aquila chrysaetos*), lammergeier (*Gypaetus barbatus*) and white-tailed eagle (*Haliaeetus albicilla*) among the former group, and geese (*Anser* spp), swans (*Cygnus* spp) and pelicans (*Pelecanus* spp) among the latter. Lake Issyk-Kul is good for many breeding birds such as Kentish plover (*Charadrius alexandrinus*), snipe (*Gallinago gallinago*), little bittern (*Ixobrychus minutus*), ferruginous duck (*Aythya nyroca*) and paddyfield (*Acrocephalus agricola*) and Cetti's warblers (*Cettia cetti*).

As well as avifauna typical of mountains and lakes, birds that favour a dry steppe habitat, such as bustards and steppe eagles (*Aquila rapax*), may also be found in appropriate locations. Other rare raptors that may be seen include imperial eagles (*Aguilla heliaca*) and black vultures (*Aegypius monarchus*).

The mountains hold a mixture of Himalayan and western palaearctic passerines such as the white-winged crossbill (*Loxia leucoptera*), black-throated (*Prunella atrogularis*) and Himalayan accentor (*Prunella himalayana*), and Güldenstädt's (*Phoenicurus erythrogaster*) and Eversmann's redstart (*Phoenicurus erythronotus*).

Migratory birds such as cranes (*Grus grus*) and ibisbills (*Ibidorhyncha struthersii*) are found at upland lake locations like Song-Köl and Chatyr-Köl, and many wildfowl spend the winter on the nonfreezing waters of Lake Issyk-Kul. In spring and autumn, a large number of migratory birds pass through Kyrgyzstan and, at this time, a wealth of migratory species such as larks, buntings, thrushes and raptors appear in farmland and even in city parks. Another migratory species is demoiselle crane (*Grus virgo*), which breeds in small numbers in Kyrgyzstan, in the foothills near Lake Issyk-Kul, but which is present in large numbers on passage.

For more information on birding in Kyrgyzstan see www.centralasianbirding.com or www.fatbirder.com.

Mammals Altogether there are 83 species of mammals to be found, with the high spruce forests of mountain valleys such as Suusamyr providing an ideal habitat for the brown bear (*Ursus arctos*) and Altai maral (*Cervus canadensis canadensis*). The bare mountain ridges and valleys are home to red foxes (*Vulpes vulpes*), grey wolves (*Canus lupus*), weasels and stoats (*Mustela* spp), wild boar (*Sus scrofa*), Siberian roe deer (*Capreolus pygargus*), mountain hare (*Lepus timidus*), Siberian ibex (*Capra sibirica*), steppe polecat (*Mustela eversmannii*) and marmots (*Marmota* spp), which are common, while the dry, open steppe has goitered gazelle (*Gazella subgutturosa*) and corsac fox (*Vulpes carsac*). The rarest and most elusive mammal in the country is the snow leopard (*Uncia uncia*), which survives at altitude in small numbers in the Tien Shan, although it is notoriously difficult to see. The giant marmot, Menzbier's marmot (*Marmota menzbieri*), is also restricted to the Tien Shan region. Another rare, high-altitude speciality is the Marco Polo sheep (*Ovis ammon polii*), which, like the snow leopard, appears in Kyrgyzstan's Red Data Book (see below).

CONSERVATION ISSUES
Endangered species According to Kyrgyzstan's Red Data Book report of 1985, 15% of mammals and 10% of the plant species in the country were threatened to the point of extinction – and many considered this figure to be a serious underestimate. Altogether, 13 mammals, 32 birds, 71 plants, three reptiles, two fish and 19 species of insect were listed. By the time the second edition was published in 2006 this list had lengthened to include a total of 23 mammals, 57 birds, 83 plants, eight reptiles, seven fish and 18 species of insect, as well as four fungi and two amphibians.

Threatened mammals include maral (*Cervus canadensis canadensis*), snow leopard (*Uncia uncia*), the Eurasian otter (*Lutra lutra*), Tien Shan brown bear (*Ursus arctos isabellinus*), Tien Shan mountain sheep (*Ovis ammon*) and Marco Polo sheep (*Ovis ammon polii*). Some of the Kyrgyzstan animals that appear in Kyrgyzstan's Red Data Book are the snow leopard, Menzbier's marmot, goitered gazelle (*Gazella subgutturosa*) and grey monitor lizard (*Varanus griseus*).

Deforestation It is estimated that Kyrgyzstan's forest cover has been reduced by at least 50% over the past 30 years. Historically, it was undoubtedly much greater. Much timber was felled during World War II and centuries of uncontrolled grazing have taken their toll. Southern forests in particular are threatened by deforestation, either as felling for building and firewood or for conversion into arable land. Pests such as gypsy moths also wreak considerable damage. Attempts at reforestation have generally met with little success as young trees are highly vulnerable in Kyrgyzstan's unforgiving climates, and few survive transplanting.

Mining One of the most acute problems facing Kyrgyzstan's natural environment is **uranium exploration**, a legacy of the Soviet period. In 1999 there were 36 uranium tailings sites and 25 uranium mining sites in the country. Apart from the obvious problems concerned with dealing with such a hazardous substance, many of the mines are located in areas prone to earthquakes and landslides, and close to river basins that are important sources of drinking and irrigation water. The worst problems occur in the south of the country in the Mailuu-Suu region where, according to a report in 2004, two million cubic metres of radioactive waste is being stored in 23 dumps and 13 tailings in the area. Because of a lack of finance, local authorities are unable to secure the dumps properly and they remain highly

1

vulnerable to floods or tectonic activity. In recent years, majority shares of existing mines at Kara-Balta and Mailuu-Suu have been sold off to foreign companies, and exploration licences have been granted to international mining companies such as Monara (Australia) and Uranium One (Canada).

In addition to uranium mines, there are other mining operations at work in Kyrgyzstan which cause great environmental concern. Most notable among these is the Kumtor gold mine in the Barskoon Valley of Issyk-Kul Province, which has caused alarming spillages of toxic chemicals such as cyanide in the past (see page 199). Including gold and uranium, Kyrgyzstan has more than 230 mining facilities that produce more than 600 million cubic metres of toxic waste annually.

National parks and conservation areas Kyrgyzstan has a network of 83 officially protected areas which include six state reserves (*zapovedniki*), six national and 'natural' parks and 67 nature parks (*zakazniki*) – these are divided into 'forest', 'botanical', 'geological', 'multi-use' and 'hunting' – and two biosphere reserves that are recognised by UNESCO. Together, these cover a total area of 777,300ha or 3.9% of the total land area.

Unfortunately, many of these protected areas are too small to maintain viable populations of plants or wildlife within their boundaries, and are generally too widely dispersed and lack connecting wildlife corridors. Further problems are created by uncontrolled hunting and grazing. Despite considerable international interest in the area, there is a lack of funds to provide adequate management and control. The protected areas come under the jurisdiction of the Kyrgyzstan government's Department of Protected Areas, but this is thought to have little real authority, as other objectives are frequently imposed, such as firewood collecting or livestock grazing, for the purpose of revenue generation.

State reserves (zapovedniki) State reserves were established for nature conservation and scientific research, and allow only restricted public access. The six *zapovedniki* established in Kyrgyzstan are, in chronological order: Issyk-Kul (established 1948), Sary-Chelek (1959), Besh-Aral (1979), Naryn (1983), Karatal-Japyryk (1994) and Sarychat-Ertash (1995).

The **Issyk-Kul State Reserve** (page 147), occupying some 19,000ha, now forms part of the larger biosphere reserve. It was the first protected territory to be set up in Kyrgyzstan and was founded to preserve the habitat of wintering waterfowl in the Lake Issyk-Kul region. The **Issyk-Kul Biosphere Reserve** (page 147) occupies 43,100km^2 and has a large variety of ecosystems represented within its boundaries that range from near desert to alpine tundra. It is home to several species of flora and fauna that are seriously endangered, including Marco Polo sheep, Siberian ibex, Tien Shan brown bear and the snow leopard. The reserve was designated an official Ramsar Wetland Site in 2003.

Sary-Chelek Biosphere Reserve (page 263) is located in the west of Kyrgyzstan on the southern spurs of the Chatkal range. The reserve covers an area of 23,868ha and varies in altitude from 1,200m to over 4,000m above sea level. The reserve was originally established in 1959 to preserve the forests and mountain landscapes that surround Lake Sary-Chelek. It was declared a Biosphere Reserve in 1979. The reserve has more than a thousand species of plant within its boundaries, which include many wild varieties of commercially important plants such as apples, cherries and plums. Roughly a third of the protected area is forest, but there are also meadows, lakes, steppes and rocky areas.

Besh-Aral State Reserve (page 267) is in the southwest of the Jalal-Abad Province next to the border with Uzbekistan. It was established to preserve the forests of the Chatkal Valley and to protect the habitat of the Menzbier's marmot and certain wild tulips – Greig's tulip and Kaufmann's tulip.

Naryn State Reserve (page 231) was founded to protect a range of coniferous forests and alpine meadows in Naryn Province.

Karatal-Japyryk Reserve (page 224) consists of three separate areas within Naryn Province that constitute a total of 72,000ha: a forested area south of Lake Song-Köl, Lake Song-Köl itself and Lake Chatyr-Köl, south of Tash Rabat, close to the Chinese frontier.

Sarychat-Ertash Reserve (page 147) lies in Issyk-Kul Province and has 72,000ha of high-altitude mountain habitats.

National parks National parks were formed with the intent of preserving the natural environment while making it available for recreational use and so, in terms of protection for wildlife, are lower in the hierarchy than state reserves. So-called 'natural' parks also fulfil the same function. Together, they make up a protected area of 238,697ha.

Ala-Archa National Park (page 123) was founded in 1976 to protect parts of the Ala-Archa River valley that lie close to the capital of Bishkek. The national park extends for 15km along the valley at an altitude that ranges from 1,500m to 2,240m.

Chong-Kemin National Park (page 135) was founded in 1997 along the Chong-Kemin River valley. The park, which contains both hunting and botanical reserves and the mausoleum of Shabdan Baatyr, was set up with the aim of preserving the diversity of fauna and flora within its environs.

Kyrgyzstan's natural parks include: Karakol Natural Park (page 147), which was founded in 1997 and has a total area of 38,256ha, 4,767ha of which are forest; Kyrgyz Ata Natural Park (page 273) in Osh Province, founded in 1992, has 1,172ha of natural *archa* (juniper) forest; and Kara-Shoro Natural Park (page 281) in Osh Province, which was established in 1996 and has 823ha of forest within 8,450ha of mostly pasture.

Reserves (zakazniki) Reserves are the most numerous of the specially protected areas. In these reserves, which aim to preserve unique sites and habitats and provide recreational activities, only limited types of economic activities are permitted. There are 52 such protected reserves in the Kyrgyz Republic, occupying 289,200ha in total and making up more than half of the area of the protected territories. Many of the reserves are relatively recent designations. They include: Padysha-Ata State Reserve (page 263) in Jalal-Abad Province; Saimaluu-Tash State Park (page 249), established in 2001 in eastern Jalal-Abad Province along the Kurart Valley, in an area famous for its mountain-top petroglyphs and also important for biodiversity; and the 10,448ha Salkyn-Tör State Park (page 231) in Naryn Province, also established in 2001, which is dedicated to re-establishing the Tien Shan maral, in addition to providing a recreational centre for the local population.

HISTORY

PREHISTORY The history of the tract of land that is now the Kyrgyz Republic stretches back to long before the territory was occupied by nomadic Kyrgyz, crop-growing Uzbeks or colonising Russians, the republic's present-day occupants. The earliest evidence of settlement comes from Tosor on the southern shore of Lake

Issyk-Kul, where evidence of human occupation has been found that dates back to the Palaeolithic period of 40,000 years ago or more. Most other archaeological evidence is of a much later date. Prehistoric petroglyphs have been found at various sites around the country, most famously at Saimaluu-Tash and Cholpon-Ata, which point to a continuous and widespread occupation of the territory in the period between the Bronze Age of about 2000BC to around AD500. Excavations around Lake Issyk-Kul have revealed evidence of sunken cities by the lake that date from this time and a number of artefacts from various periods have been found, including a Greek amphora which dates from the time of Alexander the Great, 2,500 years ago.

ARRIVAL OF THE SAKA TRIBES During the 1st millennium BC it has been documented that Sogdian, Bactrian and Khorezm peoples were present in the region, and it is known that the city of Osh in the Fergana Valley in the south was founded in this period, sometime around 1000BC. However, it is the Saka, a warrior clan normally considered to be a branch of the Scythians, who were the first notable residents to have been recorded in the region and who lived here from about the 6th century BC to the 5th century AD. Pushed eastward by other Iranian tribes to the west, the Saka would have occupied much of central Asia by the 1st millennium BC, and what is now Kyrgyzstan would have been at the southeast of their territory. The Saka practised both settled agriculture and herding, and were known for their creative skills with metal, particularly gold. They are responsible for the large number of burial mounds (*kurgani*) seen in the north of the country.

Although Alexander the Great conquered great tracts of central Asia with his Macedonian armies, he did not succeed in conquering the Saka. They were eventually absorbed into the Kushan Empire, a state that stretched from the Fergana Valley south to central India, the Kushan being an Indo-European people who came from western China and practised Zoroastrianism and later Buddhism.

The Kushan Empire collapsed when the region came under the attack of marauding Huns who arrived in the area in the 4th century. As the Hun Empire eventually collapsed under the strain of its own ambition (they had marched west and almost conquered Rome), the power vacuum was filled by Tocharians who, in turn, were replaced by Turkic tribes.

THE WESTERN TURKIC KHANATE From the 6th century AD onward the region came under the control of various Turkic alliances. At this time there was a sizeable population living on the shores of Lake Issyk-Kul, and settlements such as Balasagun (near Tokmok in the Chui Valley) and Barskoon (on the southern shore of Lake Issyk-Kul) thrived on trade from the Silk Road. The Turkic khanate was split into two factions at this time; the western Turkic khanate was most probably based at Suyab in the Chui Valley, where it was able to prosper from its pivotal position on the Silk Road, while the eastern khanate controlled Mongolia until it was defeated by the Chinese in around AD630. The western khanate established political and commercial links with the Sogdians of Persian origin who had settled in the region to farm and trade, and a number of prosperous towns developed and flourished in the Chui Valley region. One such town was Navekat (now Krasnaya Rechka), where Buddhists, Zoroastrians and Nestorian Christians peacefully coexisted under the protection of the western Turkic khanate.

THE ARRIVAL OF ISLAM Islam first came to the central Asian region in AD651 when Arab armies captured Merv in present-day Turkmenistan. The proselytising

Arab invasion advanced east to the city-states of Bokhara, Samarkand and Fergana in the early 8th century, where they were resisted and successfully repelled by the Sogdian and Turkic inhabitants. Taking advantage of the disruption caused by the aftermath of the Arab invasion, the Chinese chose to invade the territories of the Turkic khanate in the Fergana Valley. Rather than be defeated and forced to succumb to Chinese expansion, the Sogdians and Turks made a strategic turnaround which was probably based more on pragmatism than ideology – and joined forces with the same Arab armies that they had just repelled. In AD751, a decisive battle was fought near the modern-day city of Taraz in Kazakhstan, just over the present-day Kyrgyzstan border, on the banks of the Talas River. The combined might of the Turkic khanate and its new-found Arab allies proved too much for the invaders and the Tang Chinese army was driven from central Asia for good. Chinese expansionism in the region had been halted and Islam became the major religious voice.

THE KARAKHANIDS The Arabs did not remain in the region for long and by the middle of the 8th century had been ousted by a new Persian dynasty founded by a Zoroastrian noble who had converted to Islam – that of the Samanids – and whose spiritual and political base was in Bokhara.

The Samanids themselves were dislodged from power in the 10th century, this time by the Karakhanids, a Turkic people related to the Uyghurs of Chinese Turkestan. The Karakhanids were a cultured people who had firmly embraced Islam at the outset and would prove to be the ones to ensure the religion had a foothold in the region for good. They took over Bokhara from the Samanid dynasty and maintained the city as a centre for Islamic study, while developing three Silk Road cities to serve as their power base in the region: Balasagun in the Chui Valley, Özgön on the edge of the Fergana Valley and Kashgar in Chinese Turkestan (Xinjiang).

In the mid-11th century, another Turkic group from the lower reaches of the Syr Darya, the Seljuks, conquered the entire central Asian region and established their capital in Merv, in what is now Turkmenistan. The Karakhanids, whose strength had been reduced by now by constant internecine warfare, were reduced to the role of vassals, while the Seljuks would expand westward to conquer Anatolia, until they too would fall into decline at the beginning of the 13th century.

ENTER THE KYRGYZ ... AND THE MONGOLS While various Turkic and Persian peoples had been struggling to hold on to power in central Asia, the early Kyrgyz tribes had been living a nomadic life to the north in the upper Yenisey Valley of southern Siberia, between Lake Baikal and the Altai Mountains. According to Tang dynasty (AD618–907) Chinese sources, these Kyrgyz tribes were described as fair-skinned, green-eyed and red-haired people ('black hair', the chronicler explains, was considered an evil omen among them), with a mixture of European and Mongol features – not generally the physical characteristics associated with the Kyrgyz of today, but perhaps an accurate description of their appearance before they started to widely intermingle with other Turkic and Mongol peoples in the region.

The Kyrgyz tribes had originally inhabited the region that is now northwest Mongolia. During the 4th and 3rd centuries BC Kyrgyz bands were actively raiding Chinese territory and became part of the 'barbarian' impetus that led to the Great Wall of China being constructed as a defensive measure. The Kyrgyz warriors achieved a fierce reputation and became well known in the region as both great fighters and traders.

In the centuries that followed some Kyrgyz tribes moved northward to inhabit the Yenisey Valley of southern Siberia. The first Kyrgyz state, the Kyrgyz khanate, which existed between the 6th and the 13th centuries, went on the offensive in AD840 and swept through central Mongolia to destroy the Uyghur khanate that was based in the region. They were routed a century later by the Khitan khanate and this precipitated a drift southward towards the Tien Shan and their present-day territories. There is little agreement as to exactly when the Kyrgyz first started to arrive in the Tien Shan region in any appreciable number: some sources suggest it may have been as early as the 10th century, while others put the date much later. In all probability it was most likely a gradual migration that became accelerated in the 13th century by the emergence of the Mongol Empire under the leadership of the warlord Genghis Khan. The Kyrgyz that remained in the Yenisey Valley in the north are believed to have largely complied with the demands of the invading Mongols, whereas those who had migrated to the Tien Shan fought the Mongol invaders fiercely in order to maintain their identity.

Genghis Khan's Mongol Empire had emerged in the early years of the 13th century. From his Mongolian stronghold, Genghis Khan and his mounted warriors staged a succession of ferocious attacks on central Asia in 1219 and, within the space of just two years, all of central Asia's cities of culture and learning – Samarkand, Bokhara, Khiva and Merv – had been overpowered and razed to the ground. The Kyrgyz tribes that initially offered resistance to the attacks suffered devastating defeats at the hands of the Mongols and chose instead to offer allegiance in order to survive. Their territory in the Yenisey region was occupied by Genghis Khan's oldest son, Jochi, without any further opposition. Following Genghis Khan's death in 1227, his conquered lands were divided up, and the younger of his two sons, Chaghatai, inherited the territory that is now Kyrgyzstan. The Kyrgyz would continue to remain vassals of the Mongols and the Golden Horde until the end of the 14th century.

TAMERLANE AND OYRATS By the 15th–16th century the Kyrgyz had settled in large numbers in their new home that is present-day Kyrgyzstan. The domination of the Kyrgyz by the Golden Horde ended in 1510, but their freedom was lost again in 1685 when Mongol Buddhist Oyrats of the Zhungarian Empire (sometimes referred to as Kalmyks – those Oyrats who later migrated west from central Asia) forced many Kyrgyz to escape south into what is now Tajikistan. In 1758 the Oyrats were defeated by the Manchu Qing dynasty, which had seized the opportunity to invade during an internal dispute over Oyrat succession.

As a result, the Kyrgyz automatically became nominal subjects of the Chinese. The Manchus by and large allowed the Kyrgyz to follow their nomadic ways in peace, but in the early 19th century those living in the southern territory of the present-day Kyrgyz Republic suddenly found themselves as feudal subjects of the far more demanding Uzbek Kokand khanate. By the 1820s the Kokand khanate's power reached into most of what is today's Kyrgyzstan and the khanate built a chain of fortresses to protect its Silk Road trade interests, including one at Pishpek in the Chui Valley. Reeling under the impact of high taxation, enforced military conscription and harsh penalties imposed by Kokand, Kyrgyz protests against the khanate were frequent and fervent; so, too, were the cruel punishments and violent repression meted out by their Uzbek masters.

RUSSIAN TSARIST RULE Russians first arrived in the area as Tsarist empire-builders in the early part of the 19th century and soon made their influence felt. To stamp their presence in the region they built their own fortress at the tiny settlement of Pishpek in the Chui Valley, where the Kokand khanate had already established a base, and which would later expand and develop to become Bishkek, the Kyrgyz capital. The Russians eventually defeated the forces of the Kokand khanate at Tashkent in 1865, and then went on to conquer their capital Kokand, transforming the once powerful khanate into a Russian vassal state.

Most Kyrgyz in the region were pragmatic in their attitude towards accepting Russian protection, which they saw as the lesser of two evils when compared with the corrupt and cruel rule they had been subjected to under the Kokand khanate. The Russians went on to annex the entire territory for the Tsar and the Russian Empire in 1876. The Kyrgyz peoples had been brought under Russian control for the first time.

In the latter years of the 19th century, Russians and other Slavic peoples, such as Ukrainians, started to arrive in the area in large numbers. The first settlers, mostly Cossacks, came to the region in the 1860s, encouraged by the Tsarist wish to populate the region with its own people in order to establish a Russian presence along the Chinese frontier. The new settlers inevitably took the best and most fertile land for themselves, appropriating land that had previously belonged to the nomadic Kyrgyz population as seasonal grazing. As a result, the local Kyrgyz soon became resentful of the new Russian influx, even if, in general terms, life under Tsarist control was vaguely preferable to the cruelties of Kokand rule. For the Russians settling in the region it was quite a different matter: this was the equivalent of the promised land, as many of the new settlers were landless peasants who had recently been released from serfdom in European Russia or Siberia. The offer of free land and building materials in exchange for populating this frontier zone in the name of the Tsar was too good to turn down.

In 1877–78, the population of the territory was swelled further when Chinese Hui Muslim refugees started to arrive in large numbers from across the Tien Shan, following uprisings in the Chinese provinces of Xinjiang, Gansu and Shaanxi, in which the Han Chinese authorities had meted out brutal repression on the local Hui Muslim population, following the insurrection of the Dungan revolt. Another wave of Hui and Uyghur migration followed in the early 1880s, when Hui and Uyghur people of the Chinese Turkestan border region were allowed to move into Russian territories following the withdrawal of Russian troops in the zone.

In 1916, in the dying throes of an empire that had been caught up in World War I, a widespread rebellion took place in the region against the Russian authorities. The rebellion had been triggered by the imposition of a military draft for non-Russian central Asians, requiring them to assist the war effort in Europe by building roads and producing food. By August of that year, the rebellion reached the Kyrgyzstan region. The insurrection, which had arbitrarily killed many Russian civilians as well as bona fide military targets, was brutally suppressed by the authorities and, in October 1916, a mass exodus of Kyrgyz left for China over the high passes of the Tien Shan. Between 25 June 1916 and October 1917 it is estimated that 1½ million central Asians died. It is thought that 41% of the Kyrgyz population in the north of the country were killed and another 120,000 people fled to China, a large proportion of whom died along the way as the victims of winter cold or banditry.

THE EARLY SOVIET PERIOD The October Revolution that took place in Moscow and St Petersburg in 1917 (which was actually in November by today's Western calendar) was slow to make an immediate impact in this far-flung corner of the former Russian Empire. However, on New Year's Day in 1918, Bolsheviks seized power in Pishpek, the provisional government was overthrown and Soviet power was established in the region, with local revolutionary firebrand Aleksei Ivanitsyn at the helm. This triggered a counter-revolution in the territory, initiated in the small town of Belovodsk just to the west of Bishkek, at the end of the same year, but this was easily defeated within a few days by summoning troops from nearby Vyernyi (Almaty) in what is now Kazakhstan.

In 1922 the territory of Kirgizia, as it was then known, became part of the Turkestan Autonomous Soviet Socialist Republic (Turkestan ASSR) within the Russian Soviet Federated Socialist Republic (RSFSR). The Kara-Kyrgyz Autonomous Oblast was established within the RSFSR in October 1924, to be renamed as the Kyrgyz Autonomous Oblast in the following year. Up until that time, Kara-Kyrgyz ('Black Kyrgyz') had been a term that had been used to distinguish the Kyrgyz (the Kara-Kyrgyz) from the Kazakhs (then also confusingly referred to as Kyrgyz), a division that was as much about geographical location – mountain- or steppe-dwelling – as it was about ethnicity.

The creation of the Kyrgyz Autonomous Oblast involved the drawing up of some rather eccentric political boundaries, particularly in the Fergana Valley, as part of Stalin's divide-and-rule approach. Stalin himself may well have had direct involvement in the drawing up of the boundaries, as he was chairman of the Minorities Committee that had instigated this spurious nation-building. These jigsaw-like ethnic and political demarcations continue to have repercussions to this day and have proved disastrous for trade and the free movement of people in the post-independence period (see page 287).

The Soviet partitioning of central Asia that took place at this time had been inspired by a wish to create 'nations' largely based on linguistic differences. The fear in the region for the authorities was the double-edged sword of Islam, which was practised by all five central Asian nationalities, and pan-Turkic revolt as four of the five nations were peopled by inhabitants of Turkic stock. The introduction of these slightly bogus national divisions was intended to weaken the bonds of Islam and pan-Turkism in the region, and dilute the threat posed to the larger Soviet state.

Widespread land reforms started to take place around this time. In many cases this worked to the advantage of Kyrgyz as some of the land originally taken by Russian settlers was redistributed back into Kyrgyz hands – an astute move by the authorities and a clever way of assuaging the understandable anti-Russian sentiment that had previously been prevalent in the country. Rapid economic and social development took place; free, universal education was introduced and levels of literacy started to increase dramatically, albeit from a very low base. To encourage the educational advancement of the Kyrgyz people, it was important that literacy in the Kyrgyz language be encouraged. An Arabic-based script for the Kyrgyz language was introduced in 1923 but this was replaced by a Latin script just five years later, which remained until 1940, when the modified Cyrillic alphabet still in use today was adopted.

In the Soviet mould, of course, education meant far more than a simple matter of raising literacy levels. It was necessary to introduce the creed of Marxism-Leninism as a suitable ideological replacement for the rather syncretic version of Islam that the Kyrgyz had adopted. It was essential to repackage national culture as socialism with a Kyrgyz twist – to inaugurate a new hierarchy of identity in which Marxism-Leninism and the Soviet state were positioned above any form of religious or tribal identity. This transition required the use of propaganda in myriad forms. One such vehicle for propaganda was the Society of the Godless (later known as the Union of Belligerent Atheists), a movement consisting of workers, peasants, students and intelligentsia, which was dedicated to eradicating religious beliefs that were not conducive to the Soviet ideal.

At the same time the propagandising of socialist 'good practice' was also encouraged, and one particular group of young, idealistic volunteers travelled across the territories of the USSR to Soviet Kyrgyzstan to work and spread the socialist message. In 1925 the first **Interhelpa** volunteers started to arrive in Bishkek – volunteers from eastern Europe who formed workers' collectives dedicated to building socialism in Soviet Kyrgyzstan and improving the country's infrastructure. Interhelpa involved themselves in projects such as setting up factories to produce textiles and furniture, building power stations, constructing Bishkek's *Dom Druzhby* (Friendship House), the first seat of the republic's government, and building Bishkek's first housing estate, which became known as Workers Town (*Rabochiy Gorodok*). The first group of volunteers to arrive were from Czechoslovakia and included the family of Alexander Dubček, who would go on to become Czechoslovakian president during the Prague Spring of 1968.

As determined volunteers, they were highly successful and by 1934 Interhelpa was producing 20% of Soviet Kyrgyzstan's total industrial output. Interhelpa brigades continued coming to the Kyrgyz ASSR to work as doctors, teachers and builders, and perform revolutionary good works until the onset of the Great Patriotic War (World War II) in 1941 introduced far more urgent priorities. The co-operative was finally liquidated in 1943, after many of its members had been persecuted in the purges of the 1930s and declared enemies of the state by Stalin.

The year 1926 brought yet another change of name and the republic became known as the Autonomous Socialist Soviet Republic of Kyrgyzstan. This, in turn, would be changed to the Kyrgyz Soviet Socialist Republic (Kyrgyz SSR) in 1936, when it would become established as a full union republic within the USSR. In the same year, 1926, the capital Pishpek was also renamed Frunze, in honour of the Bolshevik general, Mikhail Frunze, who had been born in the city and had died the year before.

THE BASMACHI MOVEMENT In the early years of the Soviet period, an Islamic guerrilla movement known as the Basmachi started to gain sway in the region. It had begun in 1916 as a protest against the Russian Empire, when the Tsarist government ceased to exempt Muslims from compulsory military service. This revolt had led to brutal massacres and the forced exodus of many Kyrgyz from the region.

Following the October Revolution of 1917, anti-Russian rebellion continued to foment in the Fergana Valley, an ethnic Uzbek region that was traditionally a bastion of conservative Islam, and today belongs mostly to Uzbekistan but partly to the Kyrgyz Republic and Tajikistan. In the period 1918–19 the Basmachi seized the southern Uzbek-dominated strongholds of Osh and Jalal-Abad, and the movement was even supported by Russian settlers from the region for a short period. (The same settlers deserted the cause later on when Mikhail Frunze, head of Lenin's newly appointed Tashkent Commission, negotiated with them and offered food supplies in exchange for defection.)

Over the next few years, Basmachi revolt spread throughout the Uzbek and Tajik territories from its Fergana source, with some groups receiving support from both British and Turkish intelligence services. Advances were made for the cause when the movement was joined by the charismatic leader Enver Pasha in May 1922, but support started to founder when he was killed in August of the same year. Lacking firm leadership, the movement had mostly died out by the time the Kyrgyz ASSR was established in 1926, but activity continued intermittently throughout the region until 1934, when the last seats of Basmachi power, in this case within the Kyrgyz ASSR itself, were destroyed.

POLITICAL REPRESSION AND SOCIAL CHANGE As well as dissent that came from a religious background, politically different points of view were badly tolerated, too. This was a one-party state, with the Kyrgyz Communist Party as the only legal representation, and the unwavering imposition of Stalin's hard-line policies meant the new regime would brook no dissent. As a consequence, as elsewhere in the USSR during this dark period, many questioning intellectuals 'disappeared' overnight or were summarily executed; many more were arrested and imprisoned in the barbaric conditions of prison camps that almost guaranteed an early grave.

The repression and purges in the Kyrgyz ASSR/SSR, as elsewhere in the Soviet Union, reached their nadir during the mid-1930s. One such incident in the Kyrgyz SSR, which was not revealed until many years later, was the 1937 massacre at Chong-Tash near Bishkek, in which some 140 prominent political figures were assassinated in secret. This included almost all of the Kyrgyz SSR's regional government and the father of Kyrgyz novelist Chingiz Aitmatov (see page 45).

Meanwhile, the land reform programme, which had begun immediately after the creation of the Kyrgyz ASSR and which had pleased many Kyrgyz as they regained previously confiscated territory, went a stage further in the years 1928–32 when mass collectivisation was introduced. This decreed that all farmland – both arable and pasture – be taken under state control to be worked as collective farms supervised by an autonomous local committee. The nomadic or semi-nomadic practices of the Kyrgyz pastoralists no longer had a role to play and the herders had to learn to adapt to a settled way of life. This proved traumatic in the extreme for many Kyrgyz, to whom the freedom of a nomadic existence meant everything. Not only were they forcibly settled, many also became disenfranchised by the process as the collective farms were more often than not headed by ethnic Russians. This enforced transition to a collectivised – and perhaps more importantly, settled – way of life, which was alien to the nomadic Kyrgyz spirit, inspired some to escape over the mountains into China. Others, rendered powerless by the hand of the state machine, merely slaughtered their herds in defiance.

THE GREAT PATRIOTIC WAR 1941–45 Many Kyrgyz, along with other indigenous central Asians, were enrolled to fight in the campaign against the Nazis. Some of these, sensing little difference between Nazi and Stalinist repression, or perhaps out of mere pragmatism, defected at the front to the German side; but many more joined the ranks of the German army's Muslim Turkic division, the **Turkestan Legion**, as captured prisoners of war, having little choice in the matter. Many of those who survived would inevitably be branded as 'traitors of the motherland' on their return and end up in Soviet prison camps.

During the war much of the Soviet Union's armament-producing industry shifted base to new factories in central Asia, and specifically Kyrgyzstan, well away from the theatre of war and German bombs in European Russia.

It was not only the factories of the Soviet war machine that were moved eastward in this period. During the war years all of the major film studios from Moscow, Leningrad and Kiev, as well as film-makers such as Sergei Eisenstein, were evacuated to central Asia, where they could help the war effort (by way of propaganda) in safety. Large numbers of Axis prisoners of war ended up in camps in central Asia, where they were used through enforced labour to build roads and railways, or to work in farming, forestry or mining. Others were enlisted for construction projects in the Kyrgyz capital – Bishkek's railway station was built by German POWs in 1946.

THE LATE SOVIET PERIOD Following the movement of much of the Soviet Union's war machine to the region during World War II, Kyrgyzstan was set, along with its other central Asian neighbours, for further industrialisation in the period that followed. More Russians moved to the region as managers, engineers and technicians, continuing the earlier tradition in which Europeans took the best, and more highly qualified, positions.

Kyrgyzstan's isolated geographical position, well away from the prying eyes of the West, encouraged the Soviet Union to locate some of its most militarily sensitive and politically secretive activities in the republic. Lake Issyk-Kul, well off the permitted circuit for even those lucky enough to get tourist visas, was used as a secret base for the testing of naval weapons, while the mining of uranium for use in nuclear weapons was carried out at Mailuu-Suu, near the Fergana Valley, leaving a horrendous environmental legacy for subsequent generations to deal with.

There were serious riots in the capital in 1967, following an incident in which widespread resentment against the police made itself known. The incident, which was precipitated by a drunken soldier being beaten up by a group of policemen, ended in widespread street rioting, a mass march on the KGB headquarters and police officers dragged from their cars to be beaten up by protesters. It was quelled with the support of the army and KGB units, and the blame attributed to Chinese agitators.

The period of the 1970s and 1980s that followed was considered by many to be Soviet Kyrgyzstan's 'golden period'. After decades of Stalinist repression, followed by economic hardships, there were now goods in the shops and full employment. Hunger had finally been banished and a number of grandiose building projects were taking place in Frunze (Bishkek) that exuded confidence and pride in Kyrgyzstan's modest, but valued, place within the Soviet Union.

It was during this period that the White House, the Philharmonic building, the National Library and Ala-Too Square were constructed in the capital, despite an increasing lack of decent workers' housing in the city. By 1988, the housing shortage had become so acute that the mere rumour that homeless victims of an Armenian earthquake were to be allocated housing in the capital prompted mass demonstrations calling for the government to resign.

The spirit of *glasnost* that took hold further west in the USSR during the late 1980s had very little influence on provincial Kyrgyz political life, and in 1990 the Kyrgyz Communist Party leadership firmly opposed changes to the Soviet constitution that allowed non-Communists to participate in politics. However, there were more immediate concerns at that time, which were ethnically rather than politically based. Ethnic tensions were surfacing in the south, where Uzbeks formed the majority group. A state of emergency and curfew was announced in June, when violent inter-ethnic conflict between Uzbeks and Kyrgyz took place in and around Osh and Özgön. The clashes, which were not pacified until August, had been sparked by disputes over the perennial problem of land access and housing issues. The conflict left up to a thousand victims dead in a horrifying bloodbath that shocked everybody with both its spontaneity and ferocity.

INDEPENDENCE In October of 1990, the same year as the Uzbek-Kyrgyz inter-ethnic strife in the south, Askar Akayev, a physicist academic in favour of reform, was elected by the legislature to the newly created post of president.

Akayev had been elected as a compromise candidate in a role that was designed to be wholly symbolic and without any serious political clout but, responding to the zeitgeist of *glasnost* and *perestroika* that was taking place in Moscow, he immediately introduced new government structures and appointed a new government of fellow reform-minded members. In December of the same year, the republic was renamed Kyrgyzstan (it had been known as Kirgizia in Soviet times and would be retitled the Kyrgyz Republic in 1993). Wishing to extend this new Kyrgyz identity a stage further, the capital Frunze was renamed Bishkek in February 1991.

Just as the August putsch was taking place, unsuccessfully, in Moscow, a coup attempted to remove Akayev from power on 19 August 1991. This failed, and the following week both Akayev and his vice-president German Kuznetsov announced they would be resigning from the Communist Party of the Soviet Union; the entire politburo and secretariat immediately followed suit. The Supreme Soviet declared independence from the USSR on 31 August. Akayev announced that Kyrgyz would become the new official language of state and dissolved the Communist Party, seizing its assets and declaring it, temporarily at least, illegal.

In October 1991, Akayev was voted in for another presidential term, with 95% of the vote in an election in which he ran unopposed. On 21 December 1991 Kyrgyzstan acceded to the newly formed Commonwealth of Independent States (CIS) and the following year Kyrgyzstan became a member of both the United Nations and the OSCE.

Shortly after the initial period of independence, Akayev started to come under scrutiny because of allegations of corruption against some of his close associates. This required him to dismiss his first government in 1993 and call upon a former communist prime minister, Apas Djumagulov, to form a new one. Several referendums followed over the next couple of years that made changes to the constitution.

In December 1995, Akayev was re-elected for a further five-year term in elections that were considered fair overall. However, the parliamentary elections that took place in early 2000, and the presidential one that occurred later that same year, were seen as badly flawed and declared invalid by international observers.

THE BATKEN INSURGENCIES 1999–2000 The Batken region in Kyrgyzstan's remote southwestern arm was, and still remains, the part of the country most distant from Bishkek in both geographical and political terms. It is a region that is surrounded on three sides by the neighbouring states of Uzbekistan and Tajikistan and is also the home of six Uzbek and Tajik territorial enclaves that lie politically landlocked within Kyrgyz territory (see page 288).

For a number of reasons, mainly a sense of neglect by central government but also because of ethnic differences and its precarious geographical position, Batken was the region where political unrest was most likely to emerge in the new republic. This came to fruition in 1999 when incursions into the Batken region were made by fighters of the Islamic Movement of Uzbekistan (IMU), who were waging a low-scale war against the might of Islam Karimov's Uzbek forces in the Fergana Valley. (The IMU, in some ways similar to the Basmachi rebels of the 1920s and 1930s, were mostly young Muslim Uzbeks who were fighting to establish an Islamic state in Uzbekistan's Fergana Valley, where the majority of them had originally come from. They had trained and fought in Afghanistan, where they had possibly been supported by the Taliban and other Islamic rebel groups. Having left their Afghanistan and Tajikistan bases, their route back home led across Kyrgyzstan's southwestern Batken region.)

The first so-called 'incident' took place in 1999, when a group of IMU fighters kidnapped a group of Japanese geologists who were working in the mountains of the southwest. Some sporadic fighting took place before negotiations were initiated. The hostages were eventually released and the IMU rebels withdrew to their bases in Tajikistan.

In response to these incursions, President Akayev created a new regional administration for Batken (the region had previously been part of Osh Province) in addition to tightening up border controls. The Uzbek government's reaction in Tashkent was altogether more hard line, launching air attacks on suspected bases within Kyrgyzstan and laying minefields along the border, which killed a number of innocent civilians going about their daily lives.

The insurgents returned the following year, and a number of skirmishes took place between the IMU and Kyrgyz government forces. This time, it was groups of climbers in the region who were captured. One group of four young American climbers managed to escape from their captors, while the others were eventually released. In total, 49 Kyrgyz soldiers died in combat during the incidents of 1999 and 2000. Since then there have been no more armed incursions recorded in the region, apart from an incident in May 2006 when a Tajik border post was attacked, resulting in two fatalities, although evidence suggests this was more likely connected with a drug-running operation than with Islamic militants.

THE AKSU INCIDENT In January 2002, Azimbek Beknazarov, a deputy in the Jogorku Kenesh parliament, was arrested on charges of corruption and abuse of power. His supporters claimed that the arrest had been politically motivated and engineered by President Akayev as a means of removing an opponent who had been critical of his ceding Kyrgyz territory in the high Tien Shan to China. Following his conviction, a large group of Beknazarov's supporters gathered to march to the court where he was to be sentenced in order to protest against the decision. The road to the court was blocked by the police, and a confrontation ensued in which six protesters were killed by gunfire and even more injured. The authorities claimed the initial gunfire had come from the crowd, whereas the protesters observed that the police had fired indiscriminately into the crowd in panic. The government opened an investigation into the incident but, while the elected commission was making enquiries, more protests started up around the country demanding Beknazarov's release. A month later, the commission released their report that found the police and local authorities were at fault. Some local officials were arrested and jailed but were later released under an amnesty.

Weakened by the controversy created by the incident, the government fell and a new prime minister, Nikolai Tanaev, was appointed, although Askar Akayev still remained in place as president. Protests continued but somehow the new government managed to survive, despite the tensions building up throughout the country.

THE TULIP REVOLUTION The parliamentary elections of 2005 were seen as an improvement on those held in 2000 but they still fell short of the mark. The opposition, which had won just a few seats, claimed the election had been rigged and, as a result, sporadic protests against the perceived fraud of Akayev and his associates erupted around the country. These escalated into more widespread protests, particularly in the south, that called for the government to stand down. Government buildings in Osh and Jalal-Abad were seized by angry protesters, and the whole of the south went over to the opposition and beyond government control.

Following this, on 24 March 2005, a demonstration of 15,000 pro-opposition protesters took to the streets of the capital to call for President Akayev's resignation. The main government building was occupied and Akayev fled, first to Kazakhstan, then Moscow, claiming he had decided to leave in order to prevent civil war breaking out. He resigned his office on 4 April and this was ratified by the Kyrgyz parliament on 11 April.

1

The Kyrgyz parliament appointed the former prime minister, Kurmanbek Bakiyev, as acting president at the head of an interim government. On 1 September 2005 Feliks Kulov was appointed as prime minister, a role he kept for just over a year, until he resigned with his government on 19 December 2006 in a move to accelerate the holding of parliamentary elections and push through reforms.

Azimbek Beknazarov, who had long been a sworn enemy of Akayev and had been at the heart of the Aksu incident in 2002, was appointed prosecutor general of the Kyrgyz Republic, and immediately waged a campaign against Akayev and his family, seeking a return of the fortune they had amassed. He resigned from this position a few months later, when his own reputation came under scrutiny following allegations of corruption.

Following the collapse of Akayev's rule, the immediate aftermath was a brief period of rioting and looting, in which foreign-owned concerns such as big department stores were targeted, partly out of resentment and partly because the goods they contained were normally beyond the means of the vast majority of Kyrgyzstan's citizens. The looting soon abated and ceased completely after the second night, hindered as much by bad weather as active policing.

The Tulip Revolution was so named because of the tulips many of the demonstrators carried on the protests to signify their peaceful intent; many others carried daffodils and so Daffodil Revolution might well have been an equally appropriate sobriquet.

KYRGYZSTAN POST-TULIP REVOLUTION Even after the revolution, political stability in Kyrgyzstan seemed to remain elusive, with various factions, some allegedly linked to organised crime, jostling for a share of power. Of the 75 members of the new government that was elected in March 2005, three were assassinated soon afterwards, with another killed in May 2006 shortly after winning his brother's seat in a by-election. All four victims were said to have links with disreputable business interests. A further political crisis ensued in 2006 as thousands demonstrated in a series of protests in Bishkek. Bakiyev was accused of reneging on his promised constitutional reforms to limit presidential power as well as failing to eradicate crime and corruption. A new prime minister, Azim Isabekov, was approved by parliament on 29 January 2007 to replace Feliks Kulov, who had resigned the month before, but he, too, was forced to resign after just three months, having dismissed a number of ministers in an attempt to incorporate new people in the government. Spring 2007 saw another brief period of rioting in the capital with mass demonstrations calling for President Bakiyev's resignation.

Bakiyev hung on in power but incensed the authorities in Russia when, in June 2009, he reneged on a promise to expel the US military from Manas Air Base near Bishkek. In April 2010, various Russian media – newspapers, television and radio – quite possibly with backing from the Kremlin, accused Bakiyev of corruption and nepotism. Accusations of economic mismanagement were redirected by Bakiyev on to his cabinet, but his strategy of sacking all of them backfired, as did his misplaced comments suggesting Kyrgyzstan was a country not suited to a democratic system.

Widespread dissatisfaction with Bakiyev, coupled with a dramatic increase in gas prices, drove the country into riot mode. The first demonstrations in Talas soon turned violent and spread almost immediately to Bishkek, as large crowds protested angrily against what they perceived to be endemic corruption. A state of emergency was announced on 7 April but by now the protests had reached critical mass. The riots became increasingly violent, as heavily armed mobs fought with police, leaving an estimated 80 casualties and hundreds seriously injured. Bakiyev was smuggled from the White House in order to flee temporarily to his native southern Kyrgyzstan, before going to Kazakhstan on 15 April and, later, exile in Belarus, allegedly taking with him millions of dollars in cash and state funds sequestered in foreign bank accounts.

Rosa Otunbayeva, a former foreign minister and one-time ambassador to the UK, was appointed as interim president by the opposition, but the revolution was not yet over. With most police too afraid to show their faces for fear of being beaten up, widespread looting took place in Bishkek in the aftermath of the bloody demonstrations.

In June 2010, further rioting took place in the southern cities of Jalal-Abad and Osh. Although exactly what instigated these riots still remains unclear – both faithful Bakiyev supporters and Islamist rebels have been blamed – these turned out to be even more serious than those in the capital, leaving a death toll in the hundreds and resulting in the flight of tens of thousands of Uzbeks over the border to Uzbekistan. Otunbayeva put the blame firmly on the activities of the Bakiyev family and vehemently denied Kyrgyz troops had supported – or at least turned a blind eye to – the large-scale killing of ethnic Uzbeks by Kyrgyz gangs in Osh. Feeling that she had lost control of the country Otunbayeva asked Russia to send troops to help calm the turmoil but this request was firmly declined by President Medvedev. The riots eventually settled, but not until enormous loss of life and extensive damage to private property had taken place in the main cities of the south. The clashes left an estimated 300,000 internally displaced, in addition to 75,000 who had fled over the border to neighbouring Uzbekistan. Most of these refugees and internally displaced persons returned to their place of origin by the end of the same year. Since 2010 the UN Refugee Agency has been helping the Kyrgyzstan government to reintegrate people displaced by the conflict.

GOVERNMENT AND POLITICS

The Kyrgyz Republic is technically a semi-presidential representative democracy in which the president is the head of state and the prime minister the head of government. In this system, the government exercises executive power while legislative power lies in the hands of both government and parliament.

Following independence from the USSR in 1991, Kyrgyzstan's first president, Askar Akayev, announced his full commitment to the process of political reform and, as a result, received enthusiastic backing from the IMF and other Western donors who were keen to see the new republic's transition from centrally planned communist colony to free-market economy.

A scandal emerged in 1993 when close associates of Akayev, including the prime minister, Tursunbek Chyngyshev, were accused of corruption. Chyngyshev was dismissed, along with the government, and Akayev called upon Apas Djumagulov, who had been the last communist premier, to form a new government. A referendum was held in January 1994 to ask for a renewed mandate for Akayev to complete his term of office and he achieved this with 96.2% of the vote.

In May 1993, a new constitution was passed by parliament but, in 1994, parliament failed to achieve a quorum for its last scheduled session before the expiration of its term and Akayev was accused of having manipulated a boycott. The president announced another referendum for October 1994 that proposed two changes to the constitution: one that would permit amendment of the constitution by referendum, and a second that created a parliament with two legislative chambers called the

1

Jogorku Kenesh. Elections took place in February 1995 for the new parliament, which were championed as being free and fair by international observers despite a few polling-day irregularities. On 24 December 1995, Akayev was re-elected for another five-year term and in February 1996 a referendum amended the constitution to award the president more power – including the power to dissolve parliament. A referendum in October 1998 made further reforming constitutional changes.

Parliamentary elections were held in early 2000 but, on this occasion, international observers were less impressed by the even-handedness of the proceedings and declared them invalid, as they also did with the presidential election later that same year. Akayev continued in power until spring 2005, when the so-called Tulip Revolution ousted him from power and Kurmanbek Bakiyev was appointed acting president at the head of an interim government. Bakiyev subsequently won a presidential election in July of that year with a landslide victory.

Revolution or not, the honeymoon period of the new administration did not last for long. In the brief period post-revolution there have been shootings of politicians (particularly those with alleged links to the criminal underworld), prison riots and further mass demonstrations. This has led to a renewed political crisis, with large-scale demonstrations in Bishkek in April and November 2006 calling for the president's resignation. The main accusation levelled at the president was his failing to live up to election promises to reform the country's constitution, and reneging on his promise to share power with parliament.

In April 2006, Bakiyev signed amendments to reduce his own power, but this was insufficient for many protesters who demanded his full resignation. As before in the Akayev period, there were wider criticisms of corruption and cronyism, along with what was perceived as increasing criminality in the country and a failure to alleviate poverty (a view fuelled by the frustrations of people who had seen no improvement in their lives since the new regime took over).

Bakiyev's fragile hold on power had not been helped by a rapid succession of incumbents in the role of prime minister. In the immediate period that followed the Tulip Revolution, Feliks Kulov, a former mayor of Bishkek who had been imprisoned in the period 2001–05 on trumped-up corruption charges, was appointed prime minister in September 2005, but was forced to resign just over a year later because of the worsening relations between the executive and legislative branches of government. Bakiyev attempted to renominate him in January 2007, but this move was opposed by parliament. The president then nominated Azim Isabekov, a close associate, as prime minister but he, too, was forced to resign in March 2007 when his move to dismiss a large number of ministers was rejected by Bakiyev. To replace Isabekov, Almazbek Atambayev, the former chairman of the opposition's Social Democratic Party, was appointed as acting prime minister. In April 2007, Atambayev attempted to address one of the mass demonstrations in Bishkek to demand President Bakiyev's resignation, but this was met with boos from the crowd.

Ex-prime minister Feliks Kulov went on to join the opposition in February 2007, an alliance that further weakened Bakiyev's authority. This split also served to highlight the traditional north–south rivalry that exists in Kyrgyzstan's clan-based politics, in which Bakiyev, with his many Jalal-Abad connections, represented the south of the country and Kulov, along with many other opposition leaders, served the interests of the north. Following the demonstrations and riots that ousted Bakiyev from power in April 2010, interim president Rosa Otunbayeva also appeared unable to unite the country's northern and southern Kyrgyz clans. The appalling inter-ethnic fighting between Kyrgyz and Uzbek factions that took place in June of that year is perhaps even more worrying in terms of a barrier against creating a politically united country in the future.

As a means of dealing with the failures of the past, the interim government held a referendum in June 2010 on a new constitution designed to increase the powers of the parliament and reduce those of the president. The referendum was approved by more than 90% of the vote. Parliamentary elections were held in October 2010 and a governing coalition was formed of the five parties that had more than the qualifying 5% threshold vote. Rosa Otunbayeva continued her role as head of the provisional government but was forbidden from running in the elections of October 2011, when the presidency was won by Almazbek Atambayev, who had previously been prime minister. With Atambayev now serving as president, Omurbek Babanov, who was previously deputy prime minister, was appointed prime minister, although he later resigned from the post in September 2012. As of 2014, Djoomart Otorbaev is the current serving prime minister.

ECONOMY

The 2013 CIA World Factbook estimates the GDP of Kyrgyzstan to be US$14.3 billion, making its position 145th in a world ranking of 227, just above Kosovo and Niger, but below Rwanda and Mali. This works out at US$2,500 per capita per year, at 185th place out of 228 – a similar figure to Cambodia and even lower than African countries such as Sudan.

Considering that Kyrgyzstan used to be an integral part of one the biggest economies in the world – the Soviet Union's – this is a very lowly position in economic terms. The catastrophic political and ethnic turmoil of 2010 depressed the economy even further from what was an already poor position. Nevertheless, an IMF report of February 2011 stated that the economy appeared to be recovering faster than might have been anticipated due to improved security, political stability and an upturn in agricultural performance. Economic growth was expected to be 4–5% in 2011, and gold production increased by around 10%. Because of inflation, which had been rising throughout the second half of 2010 to end the year at 19.2%, the IMF recommended that the Kyrgyz government implement protection programmes for low-income families and pledged a preferential US$100 million loan to help restore the flagging economy.

As is the case with the other central Asian republics, Kyrgyzstan was very badly affected by the collapse of the Soviet Union and its guaranteed trading market from the outset. In 1990, before independence, virtually all of the Kyrgyz SSR's exports went to Russia or other parts of the Soviet Union but, with the collapse of the USSR, these markets diminished, as did the subsidies that came from Moscow. In the early 1990s, immediately after independence, the weakness of Kyrgyzstan's economic performance was only surpassed by those former Soviet nations, such as Tajikistan, Armenia and Azerbaijan, which were embroiled in war at the time.

To overcome the initial economic difficulties brought about by the collapse of its markets, the new republic introduced major reforms, reducing expenditure, ending price subsidies and introducing VAT, which caused great economic hardships for its nationals but were seen as necessary measures in order to successfully make the transformation to a market economy and encourage long-term growth. These reforms were not echoed by Kyrgyzstan's immediate neighbours, Kazakhstan and Uzbekistan, which were on the whole better resourced, and even small-scale regional trade deteriorated as a result.

Such acts of economic reform ensured that, for a brief period at least, the newly independent republic became a darling of the World Bank and the IMF, and was lauded as a model of post-communist economic transformation. The downside was high unemployment due to privatisation, soaring food prices, fuel shortages and low wages. Fuel and energy shortages also meant that industrial production decreased significantly – a trend that was exacerbated by an exodus of skilled Russians from the new republic.

A slow recovery came about from around 1996 onward and, since accession to the World Trade Organisation in 1998, the economy has picked up to some extent. Nevertheless, many difficulties remain and these are felt most acutely by the poorest sector of society – the rural unskilled, the elderly and those who are dependent on pensions or state support.

Currently, nearly 21% of Kyrgyzstan's GDP is earned by agricultural production, 34% by industry and the rest by the service sector. Agriculture is the biggest employer, with the main crops being cotton, tobacco, hemp and vegetables, along with meat, wool and leather from livestock. Kyrgyzstan is rich in mineral wealth, with appreciable deposits of coal, uranium and gold, although it lacks oil and natural gas in any useful quantity and needs to import these – which is a major expense. There is seen to be much potential in developing Kyrgyzstan's mining base but the problem with this, even putting environmental considerations to one side, is the inaccessibility of most of its mineral resources. However, considerable investment has been made in extracting and processing gold with the establishment of joint ventures with Western companies, notably the Kumtor Gold Mine in the Barskoon Valley near Lake Issyk-Kul.

With a convoluted physical landscape that is 90% mountainous and an adequate water supply, mostly in the form of ice-melt, Kyrgyzstan has plentiful water resources and hydro-electrical power is one commodity that the country is able to successfully export to its immediate neighbours – although currently this is only exploited at a fraction of its true potential.

Apart from this, Kyrgyzstan's main exports are non-ferrous metals and minerals such as antimony, mercury and rare-earth metals, which by and large are exported to other CIS countries, while animal hides, fleeces and scrap metal are taken by lorry over the Tien Shan for sale in China. Goods like fuel, grain, medicine, machinery and agricultural equipment are all imported.

Beyond the major concerns about markets, investment and accessibility, one of the major stumbling blocks facing Kyrgyzstan's economic development is that of widespread corruption, which is widely acknowledged as being present at every level of bureaucracy from the top down. Despite this, in 2014 Kyrgyzstan was positioned 68th in the World Bank's Ease of Doing Business index, out of a total of 189 economies, with issues like 'getting electricity' and 'trading across borders' seen as being most problematic.

On a domestic level, Kyrgyzstan may be seen as having a 'kiosk economy', in which most local economic transactions take place at small local markets or at village kiosks. As a result, much local trade is unregulated. Many everyday consumer goods are unavailable outside the cities and this, coupled with low expectations that hark back to Soviet-era rationing and periodic shortages, has encouraged self-sufficiency in food products such as meat, dairy goods and fruit preserves.

Along with Armenia, Kyrgyzstan is set to join Russia's Customs Union in 2015. This move was predicted to temporarily increase inflation and unemployment because of a subsequent decline in the country's lucrative re-export trade with

China. To help adjust the Kyrgyz economy to the demands of the Customs Union, Russia has promised US$500 million in assistance.

PEOPLE

KYRGYZ It is easy enough to assume that, given its name, Kyrgyzstan is a country which is composed entirely of people of Kyrgyz ethnicity. While Kyrgyz form the majority in many parts of the republic, there are some areas of Kyrgyzstan where they constitute a minority or have hardly any presence at all. Overall, Kyrgyz form about 72% of the total population and are generally the most numerous ethnic group in northern and central Kyrgyzstan, especially away from the towns.

Although their precise origins are unclear, the Kyrgyz are a Turkic nomadic people who migrated to central Asia from the upper Yenisey Valley of Siberia from the 10th century onward. Recent genetic studies have demonstrated that they are closely related to the present-day indigenous population of the central Siberian region. Over the centuries, and in the course of numerous migrations, they have mixed and intermarried with local populations so that, in genetic terms, they are less homogenous than they were in the past. According to historic Chinese sources, the Kyrgyz had green eyes, fair skin and red hair but, on the whole, having mixed with Mongolian and other Turkic groups over the centuries, most contemporary Kyrgyz no longer exhibit these characteristics. Although they are of quite varied physical appearance, in general they are fairly short and dark skinned, with wide faces and almond eyes.

The name Kyrgyz comes from two Turkic words that either mean 'forty tribes' (*kyrk* – forty; *uz* – tribes) or, alternatively, 'forty girls' (*kyrk* – forty; *kyz* – girls). Both of these meanings correspond to the Manas epic; the first relates to the 40 small tribes that are said to have united against Chinese and Muslim expansion to the west; the second, to 40 servant girls who swam in a mountain lake and became pregnant, giving birth to the first Kyrgyz people. It is also represented on the national flag, which has 40 rays emanating from a central sun.

Another possible etymology is *kyrgys*, which means 'imperishable', 'inextinguishable' or 'undying' – a popular derivation that echoes the Kyrgyz propensity towards chivalry and bravery. Today the world's 4.5 million Kyrgyz are spread throughout the central Asian region, with the greatest population in the country which bears their name (around 3.8 million), alongside sizeable populations in northwest China (143,000), Tajikistan (60,000), Uzbekistan (250,000) and Kazakhstan (23,000). Many Kyrgyz also live in Russia as migrant workers, along with a permanent population there of around 103,000.

Kyrgyz are, for the most part, Sunni Muslims, although for some religious practice is little more than a veneer over an underlying core of shamanistic beliefs. Some Kyrgyz in China – and a very small number in Kyrgyzstan – practise Tibetan Buddhism.

UZBEKS Uzbeks are Kyrgyzstan's second most numerous group, with around 980,000 living in the country – about 14.5% of the total population – principally in the south in Osh, Jalal-Abad and Batken *oblasts*. With a population of around 24 million in neighbouring Uzbekistan, they are by far the most numerous ethnic group in central Asia.

Like the Kyrgyz, the Uzbek forefathers originally hailed from Siberia, although they settled down centuries earlier to become farmers, a practice that they keep to this day. The modern Uzbek population is composed of a heritage of Turkic,

Mongol and Iranian peoples and is generally considered to be descended from the tribes that arrived in the central Asian region with Shaybani Khan in the 16th century.

In contrast with the Kyrgyz population, Uzbeks are generally settled farmers who practise a more rigid form of Islam than their nomadic neighbours. They have a culture quite distinct from that of the nomadic Kyrgyz and are usually instantly recognisable by their dress: the older men in black, square skull caps called *doppi*; the women in brilliantly coloured long dresses with the *ikat* pattern that first became popular in Bokhara and Samarkand in the 19th century. Uzbek families usually live in houses surrounded by high walls, inside which is a private courtyard with individual rooms facing on to it. They dine at low tables with raised seating platforms, at which they sit cross-legged; restaurants with this seating arrangement can be found throughout southern Kyrgzstan.

RUSSIANS Russians, and to a lesser extent other Slavic groups such as Ukrainians, maintain a prominent, but decreasing, population in Kyrgyzstan. Many have left since independence, but currently they make up around 9% of Kyrgyzstan's population, with around 420,000 remaining in the country, mostly in the north in Bishkek, the Chui Valley and the north coast of Lake Issyk-Kul. Many Russians came as Cossacks and freed serfs to farm and trade in the region in the second half of the 19th century, lured by the offer of fertile land, tax breaks and other incentives

THE KYRGYZ CLAN SYSTEM

Traditional Kyrgyz society can be broken down into a hierarchy, of which the smallest component is the family unit called a *tutun* ('smoke'). Above this is the *uluu* (literally 'sons'), a group of families who are able to trace a common ancestor, then *uruk* or 'clan', which is comprised of several *uluu*. These clans of blood relatives, in turn, combine with other clans to form a tribe or *uruu*. Clan membership demands loyalty and any wrongs inflicted between clans need to be avenged or at least compensated for. To most Kyrgyz, clan ties are just as important as family ties and two Kyrgyz strangers meeting for the first time will be quick to establish their corresponding lineages.

According to the standard translation of their name, the Kyrgyz are a people made up of 40 separate tribes, although this number should not be taken too literally as the number 40 occurs frequently in Kyrgyz folklore and may have been chosen for its mystical quality rather than any precise anthropological meaning. Because the terms 'tribe' and 'clan' are rather vague, it is hard to be exact, but one current source suggests there may be a total of 38 tribes in Kyrgyz society.

Kyrgyz tribes may be roughly broken down into two separate groups: those of the north – the *Tagai* – where there are a small number of large tribes, and the southern group of tribes known as the *Ichkilik*, which has a large number of smaller tribes. The northern *Tagai* tribes, which belong geographically to the region north of the Naryn River, include the Bugun, the largest clan; the Solto, who are predominant in the Bishkek area; and the Sary-Bagysh, who prevail in the Karkara Valley and are the clan of former president Askar Akayev. In the south, the Adygene are the main clan found in the region around Osh, but other smaller clans include Boston, Kesek, Kydyrsha, Kypchak and others.

On the whole, given their greater degree of exposure to Russian culture, the northern clans tend to be more russified than those of the south, who tend to offered by the Russian government in its desire to populate the Chinese border regions. Later, during the communist period, and particularly at the height of Stalinist repression within the Soviet Union, other communities from further west, such as Ukrainians and Volga Germans, were moved here.

In the Soviet era, Russians tended to have the better paid and more skilled jobs in industry and collectivised agriculture, working more as technicians and managers than labourers. Since independence they have seen a considerable turnaround in their fortunes, particularly as there has been some resentment and prejudice against them by ethnic Kyrgyz, because of the more favourable positions they previously held. As a result, many, especially the young, have left for Russia, while those who remain tend to be the older and more vulnerable sector of the community.

DUNGANS Dungans are Muslims of Chinese origin who make up just over 1% of the population and mostly live in villages of the Chui Valley, in Karakol and, to a lesser extent, along the north shore of Lake Issyk-Kul. They arrived in central Asia in three separate waves of migration, following persecution in central China in the wake of the Hui Minorities War in the second half of the 19th century. Despite a shared religion and country of origin, they are not to be confused with Uyghurs, who are also Muslims from China but are of Turkic descent. Dungans are ethnically Chinese and, within China and their own communities, they refer to themselves as Hui. They speak a language closely related to the Shaanxi dialect of Mandarin Chinese, with

observe a slightly more orthodox version of Islam than their northern neighbours as a result of living for centuries side by side with the more conservative Uzbeks and Tajik of the region. Those tribes that live in the central part of the country in the mountains and valleys between Naryn, Lake Song-Köl, Suusamyr and Kazarman are probably those who are least affected by outside influences and hence have the 'purest' culture. One such clan from this region is the Sayak. The term Kara-Kyrgyz, which was used in early Soviet times to distinguish the mountain-living Kyrgyz from the steppe-living Kazakhs, is now sometimes used to refer to those clans that inhabit the border zones with China and Tajikistan.

Tribal conflicts were often the cause of bloodshed in the past and even today there are considerable rivalries between groups. Historically there has always been a struggle between northern Kyrgyz and the tribes of the south. At the time, just before the initial Russian migration into the region, there was a bloody civil war taking place between the Bugun and the Sary-Bagysh for supremacy in the region, and while most northern Kyrgyz tribes were keen to enlist the aid of the Russian Empire to help rid themselves of the Kokand khanate, many southern tribes, which had sometimes assisted the khanate in the past, were far less enthusiastic (see page 13).

Such divisions still exist today. In modern Kyrgyz politics, rather than straightforward clan loyalty, the struggle for influence is generally between the two tribal power blocks that represent the geographical regions of north and south. This polarised division carries far more weight than party or political ideology and goes some way to explaining why it is hard to completely eradicate bias and cronyism from Kyrgyzstan's political milieu, where the notion of democracy is a relatively new concept in comparison with tribal loyalties that have been firmly entrenched for centuries.

loan words from Arabic, Turkish and Persian, which is written in Cyrillic script. They work mostly as farmers and are well-known for their industriousness.

UYGHURS Like the Dungans, many of the Uyghur people found in the north of Kyrgyzstan arrived as refugees from oppression in China, where the vast majority of their kinsmen still live in the northwestern province of Xinjiang (East Turkestan). Uyghurs are Turkic Muslims who are closely related to Uzbeks in both culture and language, and who practise the same pursuits of farming and trading. Unlike those who live in the north, the Uyghurs in the south of the country, in the vicinity of Osh and Özgön, have been settled in the area for centuries. Altogether, Uyghurs make up around 1% of Kyrgyzstan's population.

TATARS Tatars – often spelled 'Tartars' in English – are a Muslim Turkic people descended from Volga Bulgars and the Mongol Golden Horde, who originally came from the Volga region of Russia and the Ukrainian Crimea. Some Tatars arrived in Kyrgyzstan along with the early waves of Slavic settlers at the end of the 19th century, while other groups, mostly from the Crimea, arrived during World War II as a consequence of expulsions by Stalin. In 1999 there were reported to have been around 45,000 Tatars living in Kyrgyzstan, but the number is undoubtedly lower now as many of those whose families arrived in the 1940s have since returned to the lands of their forefathers.

KAZAKHS Kazakhs are quite similar to the Kyrgyz in both linguistic and cultural terms, and during the early Soviet period were confusingly described as Kyrgyz in contrast to the Kara-Kyrgyz ('Black Kyrgyz') appellation that was given to the true Kyrgyz at the time. With a clan-based social structure and a traditionally nomadic lifestyle, Kazakhs are effectively a lowland or steppe counterpart of their highland cousins, the Kyrgyz. With about 33,000 Kazakhs living in Kyrgyzstan, mostly along Kyrgyzstan's northern border in the Chui Valley, the Karkara Valley and the Talas region of the northwest, they make up about 0.6% of the total population.

KOREANS Kyrgyzstan has a small population of Koreans, who arrived here during World War II as a result of mass deportation from the Vladivostok region in the Russian Far East by Stalin, who feared they might co-operate with the Japanese who had occupied Manchuria and Korea at the time. Like the Dungans, they tend to work mostly as farmers and market gardeners, and, despite some russification of their culture, manage to maintain a highly distinctive cuisine.

GERMANS Some of Kyrgyzstan's tiny ethnic German community arrived in the region during World War II as part of a mass deportation from the Volga region of southwest Russia where, from 1924 to 1941, they had their own Soviet territory – the Volga German ASSR. Others were already long established in Kyrgyzstan: Lutheran Mennonites who had joined the late 19th- and early 20th-century migrations of Russian colonists to the area. Many Germans have left for Germany since independence and the 2009 census recorded the number remaining at around 9,500 (see page 133).

TAJIKS Tajiks are an Indo-European people with Mediterranean features who are related to present-day Iranians and speak a Persian language. They are found in small numbers in the south, often close to the border with Tajikistan (although many more also live in Uzbekistan). There are also a couple of enclaves belonging to Tajikistan within Batken Province, as well as a Tajik majority in the large Uzbekistan exclave of Sokh in the same province (see page 287).

LANGUAGE

Kyrgyz is a Turkic language that has the usual characteristics of that language group, most notably vowel harmony, which is strictly adhered to (with the exception of Slavic and Persian loan words). As part of the Kyrgyz-Altay group of Turkic languages, it is most closely related to the Altay language and fairly similar to Kazakh.

Modern Kyrgyz did not have a standard written form until 1923, when an alphabet using Arabic characters, like Ottoman Turkish, was introduced (this is still used by the Kyrgyz population of Xinjiang, China). This was changed to a Latin-based alphabet in 1928, which in turn was replaced in 1940 by the modified Cyrillic alphabet that is still in use today. Following independence, there have been some suggestions of reverting back to the Latin alphabet, as has been the case in Uzbekistan, but this has not been followed through, probably because the Cyrillic suits the language well.

Modern-day Kyrgyz may be divided into two distinct groups of different dialects. Standard Kyrgyz was defined during the Soviet period as the northern variation of the language and has a large number of loan words from Mongolian languages, whereas the southern dialects contain far more words from the Uzbek, Persian and Tajik languages. Modern Kyrgyz naturally also has a large number of words of Russian derivation in its vocabulary.

When Kyrgyzstan was an autonomous republic within the Soviet Union, **Russian** was the official language of state but, immediately following independence in 1991, Kyrgyz was promoted as the official language, and in 1992 a law was passed that called for all public business to be converted fully to Kyrgyz by 1997. Kyrgyzstan's Russian-only speakers were strongly against this move and public opinion was so critical that it even caused an ethnic Russian member of President Akayev's staff to threaten resignation as a protest against what he saw as the 'Kyrgyzification' of the new republic's non-Kyrgyz population.

In response to this and other, more widespread, protests, a resolution was passed in 1996 to make Russian an official language of state alongside Kyrgyz. This move, which reversed the earlier commitment and bucked the trend of other central Asian states which had demoted Russian as the language of state, was meant to encourage ethnic Russians to remain in the new republic and not take their skills elsewhere, although by this stage many had left anyway.

It was a pragmatic reversal in many respects, considering that other minorities such as Uzbeks spoke in their own tongue, not Kyrgyz, in addition to Russian, and that for many northern, urban Kyrgyz, Russian was both their mother tongue and the preferred language of business and politics. Nevertheless, since independence, use of the Kyrgyz language has been encouraged to the extent that it is now the main language of parliament. The current constitution states that it is necessary for the president to be a fluent speaker of the language. For a guide to pronunciation, the Kyrgyz alphabet and a brief vocabulary see page 291.

Apart from Russian, of which almost all Kyrgyz citizens have some knowledge and in which many are fluent, the other widely spoken language in the country, though commonest in the south, is **Uzbek**, spoken by Kyrgyzstan's sizeable Uzbek minority. Like Kyrgyz, Uzbek is a Turkic language but, unlike Kyrgyz, it belongs to the Qarluq family of Turkic languages and is closely related to Uyghur. On the whole, Islam has had a greater effect on the Uzbek language than it has on Kyrgyz, and, as a result, Uzbek has a greater proportion of Persian and Arabic loan words. While in neighbouring Uzbekistan the language is now written using an adapted Latin script, in Kyrgyzstan a Cyrillic alphabet is still in use.

RELIGION

ISLAM After the 70-year interregnum of atheism under Soviet rule – at least officially – Kyrgyzstan has emerged from the post-Soviet meltdown as a secular, but predominantly Muslim, country in a region where Islam has held great sway for almost a millennium.

The relaxed version of Islam observed by most Kyrgyz, however, is in sharp contrast with that practised in more conservative parts of the region, and is best understood as a syncretic combination of Islam and earlier shamanistic practices. There is a saying that when the region was conquered by Muslim invaders the Kyrgyz took just enough Islam with them to suit their nomadic lifestyle, and there is some value in this as, on the whole, Islam forms a cultural background rather than a strict framework for religious devotion.

Technically, most Kyrgyz are Sunnis of the Hanafi School, but in practice many tend to mix and match their religion with animistic elements of pre-Islamic shamanism, along with other cultural practices that reflect Buddhist and even Zoroastrian influence. Most Kyrgyz today, if asked, would say they were Muslims, but few regularly attend Friday prayers at the mosque and many see no conflict in visiting a shaman healer or drinking vodka. In general terms, Kyrgyz tend not to attend mosque or pray unless led by a mullah. Ramadan also has little impact. Compared with much of the region, Islam came quite late to the Kyrgyz. Islam was first introduced to Kyrgyz tribes between the 9th and 12th centuries but it was not until the 17th century that it really took hold, when they were driven from the Tien Shan into the firmly Islamic Fergana Valley by invading Oyrat tribes of the Zhungarian khanate. Later, when their territory came under the control of the Kokand khanate in the 18th century, the Kyrgyz slowly converted to, or rather adopted, Islam, and by the end of the 19th century Islam was widely recognised as their chosen faith, even if on a rather superficial level.

In contrast to the nomadic Kyrgyz's light-hearted interpretation of Islam, Kyrgyzstan's long-settled Uzbek community tend to be stricter practitioners. They converted as early as the 8th century, when Arab armies invaded the region and defeated the Chinese at the Battle of Talas. Uzbeks are far more likely to attend mosque than their Kyrgyz counterparts and Ramadan is observed more consistently in predominantly Uzbek parts of the south, with cafés failing to open during daylight hours, and sometimes closing down for business completely, during the month of Ramadan.

Islam was tolerated by the Orthodox Church during the years of Russian colonisation that preceded the October Revolution, but during the Soviet period most religious practices were outlawed, and virtually all mosques and religious schools were closed down. Such intolerance was one of the factors that prompted the Basmachi rebellion in the conservative Fergana Valley (see page 15). Limited concessions were made later but only in cases where religious practice could be strictly controlled.

Since independence there has been a resurgence of interest in some quarters, particularly in the southern part of the country. One noticeable sign of this is the new mosques appearing throughout the country. Some of these are large and impressive, like those at Osh, Naryn and the capital itself, and these have been paid for by funding from Saudi Arabia or Turkey; elsewhere, even in small villages, modest brick mosques with stainless steel roofs are being erected, sometimes paid for by foreign beneficiaries, sometimes by local funding. In the south, there has been an even more enthusiastic revival with the Uzbek population, but as a people they have been practising Muslims for far longer than the Kyrgyz.

Unlike in neighbouring Uzbekistan, where President Islam Karimov's government heavily represses Islamic practice for fear of fundamentalism, Uzbeks in Kyrgyzstan's Fergana fringes are free to observe their religion. The Kyrgyz government, however, is keen to discourage radical Islamic and what it terms 'Wahhabi' elements, as these are seen to be a destabilising influence. Armed incursions into the mountains of Batken Province from Tajikistan in 1999 and 2000 by Islamic militants of the IMU did little to assuage these fears and, in 2008, in Nookat in Osh Province, 32 Islamist demonstrators were sent to prison by a Kyrgyz court. The turmoil that engulfed the Fergana Valley region of southern Kyrgyzstan in 2010 was predicted by some observers to further open the doors for radical Islamic groups in the region – in particular those linked with the Islamic Movement of Uzbekistan. In 2013–14 a small number of militants returning from fighting in Syria were arrested for planning to commit acts of terrorism in Kyrgyzstan. Some of these were members of IJU (Islamic Jihad Union). However, overall there is little evidence of a widespread jihadist trend in the country, which may be partly due to 2005 reforms that allowed for an open environment for Muslims to practise their religion, and also down to Kyrgyzstan's Islamic tradition being characterised by tolerance and moderation.

CHRISTIANITY Christianity first came to the central Asian region with Nestorians travelling the Silk Road in the 7th and 8th centuries, and traces of Nestorian churches have been found in the Chui Valley. It is thought that early Armenian Christian communities may have existed on the shores of Lake Issyk-Kul and there is even a popular and partly substantiated belief that St Matthew may have died at Svetly Mys on the lake's eastern shore (see page 163).

The Russian Orthodox Church came to the region with Slavic colonists who moved here in the mid to late 19th century. By 1914, Bishkek had two Orthodox churches, one of which still exists today, and Karakol had its wooden church, which was erected without the use of nails by the town's Orthodox community. As was the case with the region's Muslims, religious practice was discouraged during the Soviet period and churches were closed or, as in the case of Karakol's Holy Trinity Cathedral, which found a new function as a ballroom, put to more profane use.

Since independence there has been a renewed church attendance by the country's dwindling Slavic community. In addition, there have been a number of missionary and evangelical projects at work in the country, which includes Baptists, Seventh Day Adventists (who have six churches in Bishkek), Korean Presbyterians and Jehovah's Witnesses, who have had some success in converting small numbers of nominally Muslim Kyrgyz to their cause.

Bishkek has a small Catholic diocese that was officially registered in 1969, and a small church, which is attended mostly by ethnic Poles and Germans. Most of Kyrgyzstan's remaining ethnic Germans are, however, Lutheran Protestants and have their own modest churches in the villages in the Chui Valley. A further example of the sort of religious syncretism that is unabashedly practised in Kyrgyzstan is an ethnic Kyrgyz Baptist community in Naryn Province where Christian worship takes place using adapted Muslim modes of prayer.

SHAMANISM An earlier shamanistic practice of the Kyrgyz tribes had been a belief in totemism, in which they recognised a spiritual kinship with an animal, such as a bear or a snake, or a celestial body like the sun or moon. Traces of this survive in Kyrgyz religious practice today, a phenomenon that links to both their nomadic lifestyle and their Siberian origins. Traces of earlier shamanistic practices can also be seen in Kyrgyz cultural items like *shyrdaks* (Kyrgyz rugs), which bear many of the same designs seen on petroglyphs throughout the country.

Many shamanistic beliefs and practices have faded as a result of both Islamic influence and Sovietisation, but others persist as part of the everyday cultural backdrop of Kyrgyz daily life. One such practice is the hanging of an animal carcass or part of an animal (such as a tail) from a tree to render the place – a tree, stream or rock – of special spiritual significance. Another common practice, which extends right across the central Asian world as far west as the Caucasus, is the tradition of tying votive rags to chosen trees, usually close to a stream or a waterfall, or *en route* to a traditionally holy site such as the tomb of a Muslim saint. This common practice, which probably has little more significance to modern practitioners than mere good luck, is undoubtedly an echo of an ancient animistic tradition that worshipped the spirit of the earth rather than a single supreme deity. Also common is the burning of fragrant juniper branches – *archa* – to rid a house or a yurt of bad spirits.

Shamans still exist in Kyrgyz society, and there are both men and women – usually referred to as *bakshi* – who practise healing using herbs and chanted incantations. Even today, many Kyrgyz would consider using the services of a *bakshi* if they were ill, perhaps in tandem with Western medicine just to be on the safe side.

BUDDHISM There is a substantial amount of archaeological evidence to confirm that Buddhism was once quite widespread in the territory that is now Kyrgyzstan. The village of Tamga, on the southern shore of Lake Issyk-Kul, has a carved stone in a valley nearby that has the legend *Om Mani Padme Hum* inscribed in Tibetan script. There are more Tibetan inscriptions at Issyk-Ata near Bishkek (which also became the home of a well-known Uzbek female shaman in the 1950s and a place of pilgrimage) and the remains of a Buddhist temple at Ak-Beshim near Tokmok. Buddhist practices have little bearing on contemporary Kyrgyzstan but there are small numbers of Kyrgyz in China and the Central Tien Shan region of Kyrgyzstan who continue to observe a form of Tibetan Buddhism rather than Islam.

RELIGIOUS HOLIDAYS The Kyrgyzstan government recognises a number of religious events in its annual calendar. The Muslim feast of Orozo Ait is celebrated at the end of Ramadan, with Kurban Ait following nine weeks later. Orthodox Christmas on 7 January is also recognised. More important than both of these is Nooruz, which corresponds to the spring equinox and is a very important cultural event celebrated throughout central Asia, even in Iran, and which dates back to Zoroastrian times.

EDUCATION

Before the Russians came to the region almost all Kyrgyz were illiterate and the only educational facilities that existed were a few Koranic schools, attended by boys only, scattered throughout the territory. With the arrival of Russian colonists at the end of the 19th century, a few 'native' schools were opened for the children of the indigenous population, which taught Russian language and culture to mixed classes of Kyrgyz, Uzbeks, Tatars and Dungans.

After the revolution of 1917, a decree was passed that established the Commission on Enlightenment in the Turkestan Republic, which aimed to extend the educational system in the central Asian region. More schools opened and girls, for the first time, were also eligible to attend. The Soviet system was highly successful and raised education levels dramatically, so that a high degree of literacy was soon attained with levels as high as 97–100%, with 84% of the population completing a secondary level of education.

Despite problems of funding since independence, education continues to be a high government priority, with most five- to 17-year-olds attending school. The school year always begins with 'First Bell' (*Pyervi Zvonok*) on 1 September, regardless of whether or not this is a weekday. On this day, when children dress in their very best clothes and bring flowers to school, the streets of even the most isolated of villages are thronged with groups of excited girls with bows in their hair and boys smartly dressed in black suits and ties. The tradition of starting the school year on this day began during the Soviet era, when the first day of term was named the 'Day of Peace'. By convention, all lessons on this day were dedicated to the theme of peace, and this tradition has continued since independence. The school year officially ends on 25 May, a day known as *Posledniye Zvonok* ('Last Bell') in Russian, and summer examinations are taken after this.

As Kyrgyz has become an increasingly important language since independence there have inevitably been shortfalls with provision of adequately trained staff and textbooks for teaching the new language of state. Lack of funding has also meant many schools are currently in poor physical condition and an overall shortage of suitable buildings means 37% of students attend schools that operate a shift system. In recent years there has been a decline in educational achievement due to these shortfalls in funding, and some schools are pressing for subscriptions from parents to assist with costs. Part of the problem is down to a shortage of teachers, as an estimated 8,000 teachers left their posts in the immediate post-independence period due to poor salaries and the demands of being expected to work double shifts. Since then, more have emigrated to work abroad, mostly in Russia, but the situation is now beginning to stabilise. A trend of slightly decreasing enrolment has occurred since 2007 when school uniforms became mandatory for all students. Although there is no significant gender gap in education in Kyrgyzstan, a marked difference between town and country continues to exist, with 6% fewer children attending school in rural areas compared with their contemporaries in urban areas.

Higher education is a growing sector and there has been a considerable increase in student numbers since independence. On the whole, higher education tends to be more accessible for the urban, wealthier segments of the population. As well as Bishkek, there are universities scattered throughout the country to provide locally based higher education – in Osh, Talas, Jalal-Abad, Batken, Karakol and Naryn. The capital itself has the Bishkek Humanities University, the Turkish-Kyrgyz-Manas University, the Kyrgyz Russian Slavonic University and the American University of Central Asia, among others.

CULTURE

TRADITIONAL KYRGYZ CULTURE Kyrgyz nomadic society is traditionally organised into various **clans** and **tribes** (see box, pages 26–7), with clan leadership coming from a *bai* (or *manap*), a chief who makes decisions following consultation with a council

1

of *aksakals* who represent each village (or *ail* – collection of yurts) within the clan. An *aksakal*, quite literally, means a 'white beard', ie: an aged and presumably wise village elder. The *bai* is not elected but usually earns his position by being the most senior of the *aksakals*, a role in which respect has to be earned for the *bai's* decisions to carry any weight. Sometimes the position is hereditary but the son would always be required to earn the respect of the clan members, lest his position be usurped by a rival. Any petty tyranny by the *bai* would be to the chief's detriment as the various *ails* that constitute the clan are always free – as nomads not tied to a particular location – to join another tribal group with a less autocratic leader.

Although in traditional Kyrgyz society **women** have rarely held positions of power, there have been exceptions. The most notable of these was Kurmanjan Datka, who took on the leadership of the southern Kyrgyz tribes when her husband, Alymbek Datka, died – there is a statue of her in the centre of Osh. Kurmanjan Datka's place in Kyrgyz history is perhaps the exception that proves the rule, as women in patriarchal Kyrgyz society generally have little influence on decision-making other than within the home, and only a small percentage of the members of Kyrgyzstan's parliament are women. The exception to this pattern, of course, is Roza Otunbayeva, formerly ambassador to the UK and foreign minister, who took over as president of the transition government following the 2010 uprising. Her term, however, came to an end in December 2011.

In the pre-Soviet period, women had a subordinate status that depended exclusively on their fathers, until the time came for a potential husband to offer a **dowry** or *kalym* for them to become a wife. In some cases, the ritual of bride kidnapping took place and there are well-documented accounts that these incidents continue to occur quite frequently, even in recent times (see box, pages 38–9). The *kalym* was, and still is, usually paid in livestock and is viewed as promoting both financial and social ties between the would-be groom and the family of his prospective wife. On some occasions, in order to raise the necessary capital for the *kalym*, a young man will work for his prospective father-in-law for a specified period of time, thus cementing the social bond between the two families even further.

In standard *jailoo* (alpine grazing meadow) life, everyday tasks are shared between men and women, while domestic duties such as cooking, cleaning and milking are always performed by women. However, given the liberating nature of the nomadic Kyrgyz lifestyle, women are usually equal partners in practice, even if they are not in status in the eyes of Kyrgyz society.

The long period of Soviet rule brought about far more equality for Kyrgyz women, raising educational levels and life expectations enormously. While many women still have access to higher education and achieve important positions in society, economic pressures and a reversion in some quarters to pre-revolutionary chauvinistic values have meant there has been a slight reversal of this trend since independence.

The average age for **marriage** between Kyrgyz is around 25 for men and 22 for women. Providing he is not planning to commit *ala kachuu* (see box, pages 38–9), when a man decides to marry he goes with his family to visit the home of his prospective bride, where his intention is made known and negotiations begin regarding the *kalym* required to marry the girl.

Traditionally, once the *kalym* has been agreed between the groom and the bride's family, the groom gives a present of golden earrings to his future bride and they are considered to be engaged. The wedding takes place as soon as possible afterwards, although it is normally traditional for older brothers to marry before their younger siblings, and a younger brother may have to wait for his older brothers to marry before he can get wed himself.

On the day of the wedding, the bride's female relatives erect a white yurt from which the bride is collected by the groom's party. A ritual called *arkan tosuu* is frequently performed before the ceremony takes place, in which a rope is strung across the road and a ransom demanded for the bride, accompanied by wailing from the bride's female relatives and friends. The ceremony itself usually takes place at a register office or a wedding palace – a secular inheritance of Soviet times – after which the couple may go to the mosque for a blessing, although sometimes a mullah is invited to the wedding itself in order to bless the union. The ceremony is normally followed by a group promenade, in which frequent stops are made for photographs at scenic or historically important spots such as war memorials or sculpture parks. The party then proceeds to the reception where everyone present takes turns in expressing their good wishes to the newlywed couple.

After the ceremonial proceedings are completed the groom's family blesses the bride by placing a scarf over her head. The bride customarily spends three days with her new family, a period in which she receives visits from well-wishers. Following this, the married couple move to their own home, apart from occasions where it is a youngest son who has married, in which case they will stay with his parents because, as the most junior male offspring, it is his responsibility to care for his parents in old age. The bride herself is not permitted to visit her parents on her own until a preliminary visit has been made, in which she is accompanied by her new in-laws who offer a present to the bride's mother as recompense for the trouble she went to in raising the daughter. After marriage, a daughter-in-law is expected to be subservient to her new family and serve her new parents as dutifully as her husband.

YURT LIFE Before the Soviet period and the collectivisation of a nomadic lifestyle, the yurt – the round, felt-covered tent that has been the traditional dwelling throughout central Asia for centuries – was the centrepiece of Kyrgyz life. Since independence there has been a move back to a nomadic way of life or, as in many cases, a compromise lifestyle in which several months of the year are spent grazing livestock at an alpine *jailoo* and the rest settled in a village in the valleys. These days, Russian-made tractors and battered Zhigulis may have replaced the beasts of burden of earlier times, and some yurts may have the dubious benefit of battery-operated television sets, but to observe the gentle rhythm of the daily routine at a summer *jailoo* is to witness a way of life that has remained basically unchanged for millennia.

The daily routine starts early at a *jailoo*. Women start cooking breakfast at dawn and, once their menfolk have set off to lead their herds to pasture, they see to their other daily tasks such as cleaning, making *kumys* (fermented mare's milk) and *kajmak* (cream). Rarely do they move far from the yurt, unlike the men who often spend the whole day on horseback with their herds, only returning to the warmth and comfort of the yurt as dusk falls.

The yurt is a unique type of movable dwelling that can be found from Mongolia in the northeast to Turkish Anatolia in the southwest, but they are most numerous in the lands of the Kyrgyz, Kazakhs and Mongols. Yurts have been around for thousands of years; they were described by Marco Polo on his travels in central Asia, who was astonished to see nomads travelling the land with their homes disassembled in carts.

The structure of a yurt is simple but highly effective: a criss-cross framework of wooden laths, rather like a wall-trellis for climbing garden plants; a thick felt covering to keep the elements out; and a heavy wooden *tunduk* which is the centrepiece for the wooden struts that hold the roof in place and surround the smoke-hole. The basis behind the yurt's design is that of strength, warmth and portability; their design is such that they may be taken down and reassembled within a matter of hours, and the materials, although bulky and heavy, can be carried on the backs of a few horses, or more likely on a trailer tugged along by a Russian car.

Erecting a yurt Yurts, which in Kyrgyzstan are usually referred to as *bozoy* ('grey house') because of the grey sheep's wool that was used to make the poorer-quality felt of the past, are constructed entirely without the use of nails – instead, all of the wooden members are lashed together with leather straps. The setting-up procedure begins with the door frame (the *bosogo*), which is oriented to the southeast to catch the morning light. The round trellis wall (*kerege*) is attached to this, supported at intervals by long wooden poles, usually of birch or poplar, called *kanat*. Once the circular wall of *kerege* and *kanat* has been erected, the wooden struts that support the cupola are inserted into place and the *tunduk* raised and set in place. The *tunduk*

SETTING UP CAMP AT SONG-KÖL   *Hazel Adamson*

Sunset is fast approaching by the time we reach the mountain pass to take us down to Lake Song-Köl. First though, we must successfully navigate our vehicle through several feet of hard-packed snow and vast expanses of rutted ice. Tensions are high as we carefully steer our way across the tricky terrain. One wrong manoeuvre and we could tumble down the mountainside. Slowly, after dodging numerous marmots, we begin to poke through the top to catch our first glimpse of the magnificent blue waters of Song-Köl.

It has been hours since we last saw anybody roaming the countryside. Now in the distance we can make out a cluster of nomadic folk, although surprisingly there is no yurt in sight. We are arriving on the cusp of summer. As we get closer, we spot two horses laden with kitchenware and a truck, almost overturned, buckling from the weight of furniture and rugs piled inside. However, most of their home appears to be in flat-pack state with various wooden pieces scattered on the grass.

Moving house, for many people, ranks among life's most stressful events. However the nomadic family do not seem fazed as they instantly stop their activities to warmly greet us. They are as curious of us as we are of them, as foreigners driving around the country is still very much a novelty.

Having picked the location of their new home on the flattest ground that could be found, the nomads begin laying wooden foundations. Everybody pitches in to help with the hardest part of installing the door frame within a circular trellis wall. The component parts of a yurt are secured in place not by nails but with leather strips. We watch in awe as six Kyrgyz people steadily begin to raise a structure that is several feet high, comprising solely of poles, above the wall to form the roof.

The horses happily tuck into their new pastures while home insulation takes place. Reeds are strategically placed around the walls and the roof is covered with a thick grey-wool 'coat'. As darkness starts to creep in, the family neatly lay colourful woven carpets on the floor.

A bitterly cold wind now whips around the yurt and we are surprised at how warm and cosy it is inside. There are no actual walls but the kitchen and bedrooms rapidly take shape through the nature of the furniture being placed. With the yurt 'removals process' now complete the team invite us to share a celebratory shot of vodka with them.

is central to the entire structure and is without doubt the most valuable and least-easily replaced part of the yurt framework.

With all of the skeletal structure in place, the outer coverings of felt matting can be draped over the framework – successive layers that are called *chiy, kiyiz, tuurduk* and *jabuu*. The final layer is folded back from the *tunduk* in daytime, unless it is raining, to allow air to flow through the structure; in cold and inclement weather it is kept tightly shut. A final touch, if the yurt is new, is to toss a sheep's head through the *tunduk* as a gesture of good luck.

Yurt interior geography The yurt interior is laid out according to an age-old pattern. The fireplace goes directly below the *tunduk*, although many modern yurts have a flap at the side for the chimney of a stove that is set to the side. Behind the fireplace, opposite the entrance, is the stack of blankets, quilts and pillows known as the *juk*, which is piled high on top of chests and serves as an indicator of wealth. In front of the *juk* is the most prestigious position in the yurt, the *tyor*, which is reserved for the head of the family or guests of honour such as *aksakals* (see page 34) and, inevitably, curious Western visitors. The less favourable, draughtier area close to the entrance is the space designated for the women of the household. Right of the entrance is the female half of the yurt, the *eptchi zhak*, where tasks such as needlework and dishwashing take place, and where knitting, embroidery and decorative bric-a-brac are kept. The opposite side, the *erz zhak*, is the preserve of men, and is the area where manly possessions like whips, knives and harnesses are kept.

KYRGYZ TRADITIONAL DRESS The most visible feature of traditional Kyrgyz clothing, as worn by men, is the distinctive white felt hat, the *kalpak*, which tells, without any shadow of doubt, that the wearer is a Kyrgyz. This felt trilby, worn by many Kyrgyz men, young and old (but generally older), is made up of four panels of white felt, with a tassel dangling from the top. Traditional patterns in black are stitched to the panels in decoration, which are highly stylised and echo the sort of ancient designs seen in *shyrdaks* (traditional Kyrgyz rugs – see page 39).

In normal use, the brim is turned up all the way round, but there are great variations in the way *kalpaks* may be worn, which range from the rakish to the comical. Despite its awkward shape, Kyrgyz men who sport *kalpaks* tend to keep their headgear on without trouble, even in challenging circumstances, such as climbing into a small car or galloping at speed on a horse.

The traditional four-panel *kalpak*, which is said to resemble the shape of Khan Tengri peak in the Central Tien Shan, is by far the most widespread, but in recent years variations on the *kalpak* theme have emerged in which the same traditional designs have been adopted for brimless skullcaps (the traditional shape is quite hopeless for performing standard Muslim prayer rituals) and even baseball caps.

The traditional Kyrgyz headgear is certainly practical – it provides shade in hot weather and warmth in cold – and is such an icon of Kyrgyz culture that a number of traditions concerning the wearing of them have permeated Kyrgyz folklore. In fact, the hats are so iconic that in Kyrgyzstan even bus shelters are sometimes constructed in the shape of a *kalpak*. It is said you should never kill a man who is wearing a *kalpak* – certainly sound advice – and that, like bread, they should never be placed on the ground. At night they should be removed for sleep and placed beside the head, never next to the feet.

The traditional coat worn by the Kyrgyz – the *chapan* – is no longer as commonly worn as it used to be, having been replaced in the main by leather jackets and Russian-style sports gear for many younger Kyrgyz. It is, however, quite commonly worn by older men in rural areas. Designed for warmth and comfort while on horseback, the *chapan* is a type of three-quarter-length coat which is padded like a dressing gown. In some cases a felt cloak is worn over the top of it, while underneath an open, cotton shirt, called a *jegde*, is worn, with baggy trousers, which are sometimes fur-lined in winter (during which season the customary *kalpak* is replaced by a fur hat called a *tebetey* or a *telpek*). Light leather boots are worn on the feet, over which rubber slip-on overboots are pulled, to be removed whenever a dwelling is entered.

Women's dress tends to consist of long dresses in rich, dark colours, such as maroon, although the colour of preference varies from tribe to tribe. Most married women wear headscarves, which, in the summer at least, are tied at the back of the head to expose the neck. The traditional Kyrgyz women's costume of a tall headdress and white veil that surrounds the face and neck is now only worn on special occasions, such as horse sports and folklore events staged for tourists, and sometimes at weddings.

KYRGYZ CRAFTS Kyrgyzstan has a thriving craft tradition that mostly utilises raw materials produced by the livestock central to the Kyrgyz nomadic way of life – wool and leather. The handicrafts produced reflect the ancient traditions of the Kyrgyz nomadic way of life in both their design and the function that they serve. As a consequence, Kyrgyz handicrafts are essentially portable items produced without the need for complex tools or machinery. The best known of these handicrafts is undoubtedly the appliqué felt object known as a *shyrdak*.

BRIDE KIDNAPPING IN KYRGYZ SOCIETY

The tradition of bride theft in Kyrgyzstan is not as common as it was in pre-Soviet times but it has by no means died out. The practice, known as *ala kachuu* ('to take and flee'), dates back to times when the Kyrgyz were fully nomadic and similar customs are also found in other nomadic societies, like that of the Kazakhs. Today bride kidnapping is technically illegal – it was outlawed in Soviet times – and even in the past the tradition was usually frowned upon and often dealt with harshly by tribal councils. Notwithstanding this, the practice was relatively common in Kyrgyzstan's more isolated communities in the past and, with few victim families willing to bring charges against the kidnappers, the tradition of *ala kachuu* persists in the more remote regions of the country.

The kidnapping process is simplicity itself: a would-be Kyrgyz groom simply summons some accomplices to help him capture his chosen bride. He then carries her across the threshold of his family home, where the groom's female relatives attempt to persuade the kidnapped girl to accept the groom by tying on a bride's headscarf – a ritualised way of proclaiming the pair to be married.

In practice, the execution of the tradition can range from a purely ritualistic display in which a consenting couple put on an act simply for tradition's sake, to an almost caveman-like act of violent abduction. If the act is consensual between both families, it can hardly be considered a true kidnapping, even if the woman is supposed to put up some symbolic resistance, but on the other occasions, when the act is accompanied by physical violence, or even rape, the kidnapping is a terrifying ordeal for the victim.

The motivation behind the practice encompasses a spectrum of explanations that range from the mere observation of a time-honoured tradition to avoidance of, or inability to pay, the bride price, to evading the wishes of the bride's family who may not approve of the match. Kidnapping may even occur in circumstances

Shyrdaks The *shyrdak* is the Kyrgyz equivalent of a rug or a carpet – a thick, patterned piece of felt, which is usually rectangular in shape. They serve a wide range of purposes, from floor coverings and wall hangings to seat and table covers, and, more than any other domestic object, it is *shyrdaks* that characterise a typical Kyrgyz home, whether it is an isolated yurt on a lonely *jailoo* or a two-bedroom Soviet apartment in town.

Shyrdaks are made up of different pieces of coloured felt, which are arranged into patterns using a variety of traditional shapes representing stylised themes from nature. Many of the traditional motifs used – birds' claws, flying birds, mountain peaks, *kumys* containers – would formerly have had a symbolic meaning (ie: ram's horns would represent masculine power and wealth), but most of these are largely forgotten now.

Most modern *shyrdaks* are brightly coloured affairs made with chemical dyes, but this was not the case up until the 1960s, when most *shyrdaks* were produced in just two colours. To appeal to the sector of the tourist market that prefers 'natural', organically produced handicrafts, there has been a revival of the older, monochromatic tradition in recent years but, in catering for all tastes, these are produced alongside gaudily coloured pieces that would rarely have had a place in a traditional Kyrgyz home in the past. Kyrgyzstan produces a range of different patterns and styles of *shyrdak*, according to geographical region, but, as a rule, those made in the Naryn area are widely considered to be among the finest.

in which the groom's first choice of bride has already been kidnapped by another party. In the worst case scenario of an unfortunate woman being taken unwillingly by force, the victim may well find herself in the invidious position of being unable to return to her own family because of the disgrace her unplanned kidnapping has brought upon them. In such cases, she has little choice but to accept her fate. Similarly, would-be brides who do manage to return to their own families after abduction, often have to bear the brunt of malicious rumours spread by the family of the failed kidnapper who, equally, are incensed and shamed by an abduction that has been unsuccessful.

The number of such forced marriages appears to have increased in recent years, with some estimates suggesting as many as one-third of Kyrgyz women become married as a result of nonconsensual abduction by their husbands. The same statistics point to the practice being most common in the north and centre of the country, and in almost two-thirds of kidnapping cases the stolen brides were unwilling victims rather than consensual parties. Drunkenness on the part of the groom and his cohorts appears to play a significant part, too – hardly ideal conditions for the setting up of a successful marriage. Unsurprisingly, many such marriages end up in divorce; far more than in the case of those traditional marriages that have a negotiated *kalym* agreed between two families.

A documentary film on this practice, *Bride Kidnapping in Kyrgyzstan*, was made in 2005 by film-maker Petr Lom. The documentary met with a considerable degree of controversy, mainly because of ethical concerns about the filming of actual kidnappings. A Kyrgyz-made film of 2007, *Boz Salkyn (Pure Coolness)* also had the custom of *ala kachuu* as its central theme. For more information on this topic see *Non-consensual bride kidnapping and tradition in Kyrgyzstan* at http://faculty.philau.edu/kleinbachr/2007_study.htm.

The making of a *shyrdak* is extremely labour intensive – a slow, tiring process that requires both co-operation and considerable patience. Customarily, a group of women will work together to create a *shyrdak*, the production being a focused, but sociable, occasion which strengthens friendships and family bonds within the village or *ail*. First, the felt itself must be prepared. The wool is cleaned by laboriously beating it over a mesh. Once this has been done, the wool is spread out on a special mat made of reed (*chiy*) and hot water is poured over it. The wool is then rolled up tightly inside the mat and this is rolled and trodden for several hours to ensure the wool strands have fused into a single layer. The mat is unrolled, more boiling water is poured on to the wool, and the whole process is repeated, with the mat being rolled even more tightly, this time by the line of kneeling women working it. Once this is complete the felt is unrolled and allowed to dry in the sun.

When the felt is dry, the *shyrdak* is created by loosely stitching two square pieces of coloured felt together; an outline of a pattern is then made with chalk and this is pressed into the second piece of felt and outlined as a mirror reflection of the first. The process is repeated by further stitching and folding to replicate the design and create a symmetrical pattern. When the pattern is complete, the outline is cut out with a sharp knife and the pieces sewn together; larger *shyrdaks* are made by joining several smaller pieces together. Finally, a border is added – often of black and white triangles – and another piece of felt is used as a backing to give extra thickness.

Ala-kiyiz *Ala-kiyiz* are felt carpets that are produced in a similar way to *shyrdaks* but without the use of stitching. Instead of sewing appliqué motifs to a backing, *ala-kiyiz* are created by pressing different coloured wools together on a felt background and then wetting and rolling on a reed mat in the same way that the felt for *shyrdaks* is made. The wool that is used is not spun into threads but kept loose. One colour is chosen as the background and this is spread on to felt on a *chiy* mat. Clumps of other colours are then laid down to create a pattern. This is covered with a cloth and sprayed with hot water, before being rolled inside the mat as in the making of a *shyrdak*. Repetition of this process ensures that the wool fibres become firmly melded together and the multicoloured felt created remains whole after it is dried in the sun.

As no stitching is used to hold these carpets together, the end result tends not to be quite as strong as a *shyrdak*, but the advantage is they can be manufactured more quickly. Also, because of the inevitable imprecision of their design, *ala-kiyiz* tend, on the whole, to be more individual than most *shyrdaks*. Some contemporary *ala-kiyiz* designs, instead of having a symmetrical pattern, use the differing colours to create an image – typically a landscape scene – that can serve as a wall hanging.

Tush kiyiz *Tush kiyiz* are wall hangings made from embroidered cloth, in which chain stitching is used to create a montage of stylised natural shapes. Traditionally, *tush kiyiz* are sewn by grandmothers for young married couples and they often have the names of the couple sewn into the design. *Tush kiyiz* can sometimes be large enough to cover a wall, while most are smaller and are often used to decorate the headboard of a bed.

Kurak Another typical Kyrgyz embroidered handicraft is *kurak* or patchwork. This utilises scraps and oddments of material to create objects such as head coverings and other items of clothing, babies' blankets, crib covers and saddle bags. The patchworks follow two basic styles: either an assemblage of squares and triangles or one made up of a selection of long strips of material.

In Kyrgyzstan, *kurak* is associated with magical powers, and patchwork pieces are thought to bring luck and guard against evil. Sometimes special rituals are connected with patchwork pieces, such as the gown that newborn babies traditionally wear after 40 days, which is created from 40 pieces of material collected by the mother from the yurts of the *ail* – a sort of collective village blessing in the form of a garment. Dowries, too, usually contain items of *kurak*, which are made from scraps of material collected from the family and community, and are intended to pass on good fortune to the newly wedded couple.

Other crafts In the past, **weaving** was an important Kyrgyz craft but, with the ready availability of inexpensive factory-made goods, the tradition is far less common these days. Weaving used to be a summer, fair-weather activity that took place outdoors and involved only women. The wool was collected, cleaned and sorted before being spun into yarn. Natural dyes were used to colour the yarn before it was woven on a horizontal loom to produce a long, narrow strip of fabric. Sometimes, woven strips were sewn together to make rugs and coverings.

Carpet-making takes place mostly in the south of the country, in the Osh region. It usually uses woollen yarn (often from a camel), but sometimes cotton – in plentiful supply in the Fergana Valley – is used to weave the piles.

Leatherwork was a well-developed craft in the past and superb examples can be seen in some of Kyrgyzstan's cultural museums. The leather used would come either from the skins of nomads' livestock – cattle, goats, sheep, horses – or from animals caught on hunting expeditions, such as ibex and gazelle. Because of the Kyrgyz nomadic lifestyle, most of the objects produced would have a practical use, like harnesses, whips, footwear and clothing. In addition, everyday objects such as *kumys* containers, with their distinctive anchor form that has two upturned compartments at the base, would also be produced from leather. Unlike the majority of craft activities, leather-working was carried out by men and women alike.

Woodcarving was also important in the past, particularly in relation to *jailoo* life, in which the yurt would require a number of wooden chests for the storage of clothes and linen, as well as a *pishpek* (churn) for making *kumys* and wooden implements for cooking. Kyrgyz musical instruments, such as *komuz*, also require woodcarving skills in their manufacture.

KYRGYZ CUISINE The Kyrgyz are a nomadic people involved with raising livestock, mostly sheep, and so it is inevitable they have evolved a cuisine in which animal produce features heavily, and cultivated vegetables have little part to play.

Although there has been some influence from the cuisine of the settled people of the region – Uzbeks and Russians – and from cooking traditions that have been brought through the region by Turks, Persians, Chinese and Arabs on the old trade routes, on the whole Kyrgyz food tends to be robust, fat-laden and similar to that of the other upland parts of the central Asian region.

More than anything else, most Kyrgyz greatly enjoy animal fat, particularly that of fat-tailed sheep, and from the Kyrgyz perspective the more animal fat a dish contains, the better. Such a high-fat diet suits a tough, physical lifestyle in a region where winters are long, cold and harsh, although the same diet may not be at all appropriate for those of a more temperate or Mediterranean climate. Certainly, low-cholesterol cuisine is not a characteristic of Kyrgyz cooking. A typical Kyrgyz cookbook, if such a thing existed, would probably begin most recipes with 'First kill your sheep...'

In Kyrgyz culture there are a number of special dishes that are associated with special events and religious holidays, and this, coupled with a tradition of hospitality, means some dishes are produced with great ceremony given the occasion. Kyrgyz hospitality sets great store in providing food for honoured guests.

Meals are traditionally laid out on a large cloth on the ground called a *dostorkon*. Food is handled with the right hand only, in typical Muslim fashion, and legs and feet are tucked away from the food – to have feet pointing at the food is considered the height of rudeness. The end of the meal is signalled by the *omin* – a very

KUMYS – HORSE MILK FOR YOUR HEALTH

It may not seem the most obvious of alcoholic beverages, but fermented mare's milk is a Kyrgyz speciality and a much-loved tipple throughout the country. *Kumys* is made by storing mare's milk in a specially made and smoke-cleaned container, a *chinach*, for a day or two, before it is mixed with fresh milk and allowed to ferment in a warm spot. This is then churned in a special cylindrical wooden vessel called a *pishpek*, to produce a mildly alcoholic drink with a high lactic acid content. The finished product is traditionally stored in anchor-shaped leather bottles, called *kookor*, although in reality it often gets no further than a bucket from which it is decanted for use. *Kumys* keeps for just a few days before it goes off completely and so its manufacture only takes place at those times of year when mares are actively lactating.

As a by-product of horse rearing, *kumys* is very much a product of the Kyrgyz *jailoo* and in season it is widely sold from yurts at roadsides to willing customers who rate the drink far higher than modern upstarts such as imported Russian beer or Coca-Cola.

The health-promoting properties of *kumys* have long been established, both in Kyrgyz folklore and by 19th-century Russian scientists, who firmly believed in the drink's restorative properties and used it to treat a variety of diseases. Both Maxim Gorky and Lev Tolstoy took *kumys* rest cures at Russian sanatoriums in the late 19th century and Anton Chekov, who had long suffered from tuberculosis, attended a *kumys* cure resort for a period in 1901, although in his case he was not cured. News of the miracle cure spread far beyond Russia's shores, and in 1877 a treatise was published in the USA that extolled the health-giving virtues of the drink (*The Great Russian Remedy for Wasting, Debilitating and Nervous Diseases*), which dubbed the product 'milk champagne'.

Despite what some Kyrgyz might claim, *kumys* is found not only in Kyrgyzstan but also throughout the upland areas of the central Asian region. It has also been popular in Mongolia since time immemorial, where it no doubt accompanied the horseback armies of Genghis Khan on their plundering attacks throughout the region.

Indeed, it would appear the drinking of *kumys* has been around for as long as man has had an association with horses. Hippocrates is said to have declared it to be a drink 'of longevity, joy and mental agility' and Herodotus in his 5th-century BC chronicle, *Histories*, describes the Scythian processing of mare's milk. The Flemish Franciscan monk William of Rubruck, who travelled through the central Asian region in the 13th century, described the effect of *kumys* thus: 'It makes the inner man most joyful and also intoxicates weak heads, and greatly provokes urine.' In actual fact, *kumys* is not particularly intoxicating, having an average alcohol content of just 2%. Nevertheless, it is an acquired taste for most Westerners and drinking *kumys* can sometimes have a deleterious effect on the unprepared, making those unused to it become suddenly nauseous.

characteristic gesture used throughout Muslim central Asia in which the hands are drawn down the face as if washing and the word *omin* ('Amen!') is spoken.

Beshbarmak is perhaps the quintessential Kyrgyz dish. Its name means 'five fingers', an indication that it is meant to be eaten with the fingers rather than cutlery. A sheep is killed, butchered and boiled in a pot; the bones and meat are then presented to the guests. The best pieces are presented to the most honoured guests, with the head – and eyes – going to the lucky guest of honour. Traditionally, the *aksakals* are given pieces of the thigh bone, while female elders get the tail fat – the highly prized *kuirik* that delights all Kyrgyz but terrifies most Westerners. Leg and shoulder pieces go to the younger adults, while some of the remaining meat is separated from the bone and mixed with broth and a special sort of flat boiled noodles. *Beshbarmak* is very much a home-produced, special-occasion food, but sometimes the dish is offered in Kyrgyz restaurants, in which case it usually just means meat and noodles rather than a whole boiled sheep.

Other mutton dishes that are essentially Kyrgyz, with little Russian or outside influence, are **samsa** – meat dumplings, which are baked in an oven; **manti** – steamed or fried dough parcels filled with meat; and **kuirik boor** – fried sheep's tail fat and liver.

As well as mutton, **horse meat** is also highly prized, although it tends to be reserved for more special occasions. One popular dish is **chuchuk**, horse meat sausages, which are considered to be the ideal accompaniment for vodka-drinking sessions. Other meats, such as chicken and beef, are less popular and are rarely eaten by Kyrgyz (although they are easily found in restaurants). At animal markets, horses for horse meat are sold separately from those intended for riding, as different criteria are at play here.

Pork products are not eaten by Kyrgyzstan's mainly Muslim population, although these can be found in Russian, Chinese and Korean restaurants.

Meat aside, it is with some of its **dairy products** that the Kyrgyz diet really achieves its individuality, as there seems to be a strong preference for a sour, curdled milk flavour that is anathema to the average Western palate. **Korut** are one such example: small balls of sheep's milk cheese that taste rather like solidified – and very sour – yoghurt. *Korut* are extremely popular and are definitely the travel snack of preference for most Kyrgyz. Another sour milk product that is highly esteemed is the infamous **kumys**, a lightly alcoholic drink brewed from fermented horse milk, which has an inordinate number of health-promoting and life-affirming properties associated with it (see box, opposite). Other typical Kyrgyz drinks include *bozo*, another mildly alcoholic drink made from boiled, fermented millet and *maksym*, a wheat-based drink that is often referred to as *shoro* after the brand name of its commercially manufactured form.

Bread is central to Kyrgyz culture and is always afforded great respect. It should never be thrown away or tossed on the floor, and when it is offered to a guest it is imperative that they should at least take a small piece rather than refuse outright. At mealtimes bread is usually torn into pieces by the host once it is brought to the table (to indicate it is to share). Bread should never be placed face down on the table, ie: with the unpatterned side face up.

Homemade bread, *nan*, is invariably unleavened: the flat, round loaves found everywhere are often generically described by their Russian name – *lepyoshka*. Of these, *kalama* is the commonest, while another type of bread, *kattama*, is richer and made up of layers of rolled dough separated by butter. *Boorsok* are deep-fried pieces of dough that are often provided in large numbers at feasts and special occasions.

For a full account of food in Kyrgyzstan and what the visitor can expect to find, see page 75.

THE MANAS LEGEND Of all their legends and folk tales, nothing sums up the storytelling culture of the Kyrgyz people better than the thousand-year-old Manas epic, which in fact pre-dates the Kyrgyz as a unified people and offers a historical-mythological background to their genesis.

Manas is a 10th-century legendary hero of the Kyrgyz, and the Manas epic is a long, complex cycle of legends associated with the exploits of a heroic khan or *batyr*, who is deemed to have possessed all the valiant qualities associated with the Kyrgyz character. The complete cycle is estimated to be 20 times longer than Homer's *Odyssey* and *Iliad* combined, and about twice as long as the *Mahabharata*. Rather than being read as a text, the Manas legends are traditionally recited and embellished from memory by narrators called *manaschi*, who are highly revered as storytellers (*akyns*) in Kyrgyz society.

The *Epic of Manas* is made up of three parts that concern the legendary hero's life and legacy: that of Manas himself, his son Semetey and his grandson, Seitek. As an oral tradition the legend has survived for centuries without being written down and *manaschi* have always been valued as much for their improvisational skill as they have been for their powers of recall. Fragments of the legend were finally written down for the first time in Russian in 1858 but the epic was not recorded in its entirety until the 1920s.

Historically, Manas was a Kyrgyz chieftain, or khan, who came from the Talas region, where his mausoleum or *gumbez* still stands. The epic's narrative tells of his various heroic feats in fighting off Uyghur invaders and defending his homeland, as well as his marriage to Kanykei the daughter of a Samarkand khan, and the birth of their son, Semetey, and his subsequent exploits.

To sum up the thousand-year-old epic in one paragraph: Manas is said to have had tens of thousands of horsemen at his disposal and a personal guard of 40 warriors who represented the best of the various Kyrgyz tribes, and who would later become his personal friends and close companions. Manas was eventually killed by Kongurbai, a Chinese leader, and following his death the Kyrgyz tribes were led by his younger brothers, Abyke and Kobosh. The brothers wanted to marry Manas's widow Kanykei but she escaped with her son Semetey to Bokhara, where her father ruled as khan. When Semetey grew to become a man he returned to the land of his birth to avenge his father's death. Semetey managed to defeat his uncles in battle, but those of his father's original 40 companions who had survived would not serve him after being captured and so he had them beheaded.

The narrators of the legend – **manaschi** – are said to be born into their profession rather than made, chosen in dreams by visitations from Manas's spirit. As *akyns* dedicated to recounting the legends in time-honoured fashion, they have a vitally important role in keeping Kyrgyz culture alive. It is a calling that requires a great deal of devotion and responsibility as, apart from having to learn the world's longest epic by heart, they have a duty to pass it on to others and cannot refuse if asked to recount it.

The role of *manaschi* also calls for considerable dramatic, linguistic and people-handling skills in order to keep an audience fully engaged and stimulated. Expert *manaschi* are often revered by their audience as having considerable power, and a skilled practitioner is said to be able to make the story come alive for his audience, even for foreigners who cannot understand the language.

Some 20th-century *manaschi* who have become nationally famous include Sagymbay Orozbakov (1876–1930), who began reciting the Manas epic when he was 15 years old and was said to be able recount the classic version of nearly 200,000 lines; Seydene Moldoke-kyzy (born 1922), a rare female *manaschi*; and Toktogul Satylganov (1864–1933), Togolok Moldo (1860–1942) and Sayakbay Karalaev (1894–1971), the latter dubbed 'the Homer of the 20th century', who all appear on current Kyrgyzstan banknotes and often have streets named after them.

The *manaschi* tradition almost died out in the Soviet period, as much a result of vastly improved literacy as it was of state disapproval. Since independence there has been a renewed interest in the tradition, partly prompted by the considerable government expenditure that accompanied the Manas epic's 1,000th anniversary celebrations.

In recent years, the Manas tradition had been brought up to date with surprising ease, with books, films and even television serials making an appearance. Some contemporary *manaschi* have toured abroad and, although the tradition is no longer passed on orally, there are now *manaschi* schools and competitions in which young bards can compete for approval by a panel of experienced *manaschi*.

Despite uncertainties concerning the legend's true age, 1995 was declared the **1,000th anniversary of the Manas epic** by UNESCO and internationally recognised celebrations were held throughout Kyrgyzstan in that year. An architectural complex to commemorate the occasion was built in the Kyrgyz capital and a new museum dedicated to the Manas legend was opened next to the mausoleum, reported to have been built for Manas by his wife Kanykei, near the northwestern town of Talas.

For a translated selection of tales from the Manas epic look at: www.silk-road.com/folklore/manas/manasintro.html.

MODERN KYRGYZ LITERATURE The most celebrated Kyrgyz writer without a doubt is **Chingiz Aitmatov,** who was born in Sheker, near Talas, in December 1928. Aitmatov's parents were both civil servants, and his father was arrested and charged with 'bourgeois nationalism' in 1937 and secretly executed as part of the Chong-Tash massacre of that year.

While working as a journalist for the Moscow newspaper *Pravda*, he began writing fiction. His first work in the Kyrgyz language was *White Rain* in 1954, followed by the better-known novella *Djamila* in 1958 – a love story – which won him the Lenin Prize a few years later in 1963, the same year he published his collection of short stories, *Tales of the Mountains and Steppes*. These works were succeeded with further short novels – *Farewell, Gulsary* in 1966, for which he was awarded the State Prize for Literature in 1968, and *The White Steamship* in 1970 – and a play, *The Ascent of Mount Fuji*, in 1973. But it was not until 1980 that his best-known work, *The Day Lasts More Than a Hundred Years*, was published, having first been serialised in the controversial Russian literary magazine *Novy Mir*.

The book's action takes place over the course of a single day and involves a railwayman living at a remote station on the edge of the Kazakh desert, who is obliged to deal with the death of a colleague and bury him in the traditional Islamic fashion. The novel has an off-kilter science fiction subplot that involves two cosmonauts on a space station, an American and a Soviet, who make contact with intelligent life on another planet. The link between the two plots is the location of a Soviet space launch site close to the lonely railway station of the protagonist. The book is also peppered with strands of Turkic and central Asian mythology, in particular the phenomenon of a *mankurt*, the dreadful fate that befalls a man – or a people – if they forget their language, culture and history.

Another full-length novel, *The Place of the Skull*, was published in 1988, and tells the tale of a she-wolf and her cubs, and their interrelationship with human lives, along with a subplot that involves drug trafficking. The theme of animal–human interactions is a common one in Aitmatov's work: a deranged camel is a central theme in *The Day Lasts More Than a Hundred Years* and *Farewell, Gulsary* has a stallion as one of the two central characters.

Aitmatov also worked as Kyrgyz ambassador to the European Union, NATO, UNESCO and the Benelux countries before his death in 2008. His statue stands on Ala-Too Square in Bishkek.

KYRGYZ CINEMA Although Soviet film-makers produced films in other parts of central Asia as far back as the 1920s, the first feature film to come out of Kyrgyzstan itself was in 1955, when Vasili Pronin directed *Saltanat*, although this was essentially a Russian production featuring a local subject.

The first home-grown Kyrgyz film to appear was *My Mistake*, which appeared two years later in 1957. Larissa Shepitko and Andrei Konchalovsky adapted a work by Chingiz Aitmatov, *Shepitko Heat*, in 1963 and this and *The First Teacher*, by Andrei Konchalovsky (1965), paved the way for later Kyrgyzstan cinema by turning poor production values and a documentary tradition to aesthetic advantage.

Another film-maker to emerge during this period was Tolomush Okeyev who, like Aitmatov, told his stories through the landscapes they were set in, producing minimalist works with eco-political themes such as *The Fierce One* (1973), scripted by Andrei Konchalovsky, *There Are Horses* (1965), a beautiful, ten-minute documentary capturing the life-cycle of horses, and *The Snow Leopard's Descendant* (1984).

One of the best-known films to come out of Kyrgyzstan since independence is Aktan Abdykalykov's 1998 *Beshkempir* (Five Grandmothers), titled *The Adopted Son* in Anglophone countries, which depicts the life of a foundling adopted by five old women in a Kyrgyz village. It won the Silver Leopard Prize at the Locarno Film Festival of that year. The film was shot in black and white, with occasional short colour sequences, and documents several Kyrgyz customs such as funerals and engagement ceremonies.

Another contemporary Kyrgyz director is Marat Sarulu, whose 2001 debut, *My Brother Silk Road*, is an evocative modern-day journey through Kyrgyzstan that has two young boys and a girl boarding a train to cross the territory of the old Silk Road. It's a slow, bittersweet journey, which is tinged with nostalgia and longing as it examines both the future and past of the country of their birth.

The controversial theme of *ala kachuu* ('bride stealing' – see page 38) was explored in the 2007 film *Boz Salkyn* (*Pure Coolness*) by Kyrgyz director Ernest Abdyjaparov. It was nominated for Grand Prize at the Cottbus Film Festival of Young Eastern Europe Cinema in the same year and for a Nika Award for Best Film in Moscow in 2008.

Kurmanjan Datka: Queen of the Mountains, directed by Sadyk Sher-Niyaz and billed as the country's biggest ever blockbuster, was released in August 2014 and received its world premier at the Montreal World Film Festival that year. Based on the 19th-century true story of a southern Kyrgyz woman who fled an arranged marriage to lead Kyrgyz Alay tribes against Russian rule and become a national heroine, the film took three years to make and employed more than 10,000 people. Costing an estimated US$1.5 million this was the most expensive film in the history of Kyrgyz cinema, although in comparison with Hollywood it is a modest sum for a film of such high production values. The film, in Kyrgyz and Russian (and with English subtitles to attract foreign audiences), was made with the full backing of President Atambayev and Minister of Culture Sultan Rayev, although some critics have questioned the cost to taxpayers and the involvement of government in such projects.

KYRGYZ MUSIC Kyrgyz traditional music is mostly played on a three-stringed, guitar-like instrument called a *komuz*. The instrument, usually made of apricot or juniper wood, is strummed rhythmically and is either played alone or used as an accompaniment to singing or the narration of an *akyn*. An instrument that is often used in conjunction with the *komuz* is the *temir komuz*, a mouth harp that produces an evocative metallic drone. The *temir komuz* ('iron komuz') – or *ooz komuz* ('mouth komuz') – is usually played by women.

Another typical Kyrgyz instrument is the *kyl kyyak*, a two-string fiddle made from apricot wood. The bow is made from horsehair and the strings are not pressed to the fingerboard but touched delicately to produce a muted tone. Both the *komuz* and the *kyl kyyak* are pictured on the reverse of the Kyrgyzstan one som banknote.

Various flutes and drums are also occasionally used in traditional music, especially in larger ensembles. The *sybyzgy* is a side-blown flute and the *surnai* is a reed instrument, closely related to the *shenai* of the Middle East and Indian subcontinent, which is a little like a rudimentary clarinet. The *kerney* is a brass instrument, occasionally made out of goat's horns, which is a distant relative of the trumpet. Percussion instruments tend to be associated with the shamanistic practices of *bakshi* rather than storytelling *akyns*. The *dobulba* is a frame drum played with the hands, while the *asa-tayak* is a baton-shaped piece of wood that has bells attached to it.

Kyrgyz traditional music can be divided into two basic categories: *kyy*, which is purely instrumental music and *yr*, vocal music. The playing of instrumental music sometimes features Jimi Hendrix-style trickery, such as playing the instrument over the shoulder or between the knees. *Komuz* players, in particular, often demonstrate a degree of dexterity and instrumental virtuosity that is at odds with the rudimentary nature of the instrument itself. Rarely having a sound-hole, the *komuz* is perhaps a little too quiet to do itself justice in most circumstances unless amplification is used.

The vocal tradition, *yr*, which covers poetry and storytelling as well as singing, is performed by singer-composers (*akyns*) who are able to compose fairly spontaneously on any given topic, rather like calypso singers of the Caribbean region. Most *akyns* have a solid repertoire of well-known songs (as well as a supply of stories, folk tales and extracts from the Manas epic) but are able to extemporise as circumstances dictate.

Vocal performances in the Kyrgyz folk tradition are often characterised by the ability of the performer to hold a note for impressively long intervals. As elsewhere, unrequited love is a common theme; one much-loved standard is *Alymkan*, a ballad of the traditional repertoire that speaks of love for a village beauty who was married off to a village chief in the singer's absence.

KYRGYZ HORSE SPORTS Horses are central to the traditional Kyrgyz way of life and so it is natural that the most important sports activities all take place on horseback. Most of the activities mentioned below take place at tournaments held on special occasions throughout the year, particularly Nooruz on 21 March and Independence Day on the last day of August. Horse games also take place at the more informal *chabana* (cowboy) festivals that are not fixed events, but which are held place at a prearranged location at a time that largely depends on the harvest and the pressures of work of the participants.

In September 2014 the first World Nomad Games (*www.worldnomadgames. com*) were held at Cholpon-Ata on the shore of Lake Issyk-Kul. As well as Kyrgyz teams, competitors from all over central Asia, Mongolia and the Russian Federation participated in a variety of traditional horse games that included *ulak tartysh*, *oodarysh* and *at chabysh*.

At chabysh This is a long-distance race involving experienced riders and horses that are at least three years old. The race is generally held in connection with a public holiday or a festival, and the distance raced ranges between 4km and 50km, but is usually in the region of 20–30km. Although in the past participants included boys as young as ten, these days only those older than 13 are allowed to compete. The name *at chabysh* is now also given to an official annual cultural and sporting festival held in Bishkek and at Lake Issyk-Kul in the autumn.

Dzorgosalysh These are horse races that are run at a gallop over a short distance in which speed is the essential ingredient, rather than endurance, as in the case of *at chabysh*.

Jumby atmai This horseback sport involves shooting at a target while in motion, either with a bow and arrow or a rifle. Another variation that utilises similar equestrian skills is *tiyin enmei*, in which coins are picked up from the ground at a gallop.

Kyz-kumay *Kyz-kumay* ('kiss the girl') or bride-chasing has evolved from a practice that was once part of the traditional Kyrgyz wedding ritual. The object is for a male rider (the groom) to attempt to catch up with a young horsewoman who represents the bride so he can kiss her. The groom is put at a disadvantage by being given the slower horse and, in addition, the bride is allowed to use a whip to defend herself from her pursuer.

Kyz-dzharysh These are horse races in which only women and girls are allowed to participate.

Oodarysh This is essentially a horseback wrestling competition in which two riders do their utmost to pull their opponent off their horse and throw them to the ground.

Ulak tartysh Otherwise known as *kok boru* ('grey wolf'), this team game is the Kyrgyz version of the game of *buzkashi*, which is played in other parts of central Asia, particularly northern Afghanistan. The name is said to have come from wolf attacks on herds of cattle grazing in the mountain valleys of Kyrgyzstan. When they saw wolves attack their herds the *djigits* (horseriders) would chase them away and beat them with sticks when they fell. The game eventually evolved as *djigits* tried to snatch the wolf's body away from one another in good-natured competition.

The game is played with a goat or calf carcass, and loosely resembles a cross between polo and rugby. The object of the game is to grab the carcass from players of the opposing team and then pitch it into a target circle marked on the ground. *Ulak tartysh* is a rough, highly competitive game with players using more or less any tricks at their disposal to thwart their opponents. Because of this, participants usually wear heavy clothing and protective headgear (ex-Soviet tank helmets are a popular accessory) to cushion themselves from the whips and boots of the opposing team.

There are two principal forms of the game – *Tudabarai* and *Qarajai*. In the former, the simplest version, the goal is to grab the carcass and merely clear it of other players; in the more complex *Qarajai* version it is necessary to carry the carcass around a marker before depositing it in the scoring circle. Otherwise, the rules of the game are few. Teams must be of equal size – in formal competitions they are usually made up of four riders. Players may not tie the carcass to their saddles; horses are not permitted to rear up and you are not allowed to grab the reins of your opponent. The playing field is roughly 300m long by 150m wide and competition games are divided into three periods of 20 minutes each.

2

Practical Information

WHEN TO VISIT

With its tough, continental climate, Kyrgyzstan is very much a seasonal destination. Unless travelling to the country for purposes of business, most visitors tend to come between May and October. For those whose interest is primarily in outdoor pursuits, the peak trekking season is a little shorter – between early June and mid-September. The period from mid-July to late August is by far the busiest with overseas visitors, partly because of the climate and partly as a result of this being the main European summer holiday season.

Given complete freedom of choice in deciding when to come, it really depends on exactly what the visitor wishes to do and where they want to go. For **trekking**, the higher the altitude, the shorter the season, tends to be the general rule, and so those wishing to do high-altitude treks in the Central Tien Shan are realistically limited to July and August. Lower-level treks are usually possible between June and September, although snow is always a possibility at passes above 3,000m at virtually any time of year. If it is snow that the visitor is actively seeking, for **winter sports** like skiing or snowboarding, then January and February are generally the best months to come, although early January can get very busy with winter vacation visitors from Russia and Kazakhstan.

The south of the country has a warmer climate in general and the low-lying Fergana Valley can be very hot during the summer months. Even Bishkek can be unpleasantly muggy in August. If these are the prime destinations to be visited it makes sense to plan a trip for spring or autumn.

If no high-altitude hiking is to be attempted, coming slightly **out of season** has its benefits. The northern shore of Lake Issyk-Kul, particularly Cholpon-Ata, can become very crowded in August, mostly with Kazakhs rather than European visitors; however, a visit in late September or early October is a wholly different matter, with few tourists, blue skies, turning leaves and a light dusting of snow on the mountains. It is too cold to swim at this time, however. Early autumn is actually a very beautiful time to be in Kyrgyzstan, especially if visiting southern destinations of modest altitude, such as the Lake Sary-Chelek region and Arslanbob, which has its walnut harvest at this time of year. Nights may be quite cold but there are warm days with clear blue skies.

Spring is a little less certain, as it can take time for winter snow to thaw completely, and late snowfall can mean many passes and even parts of the main Bishkek–Osh highway are under snow until mid-May. The months of April, May and June have the highest amount of rainfall, and this, coupled with melting snow, can sometimes pose risks of landslides and avalanches. Because of this, trekking conditions at the end of the season are usually a little more reliable than those at the beginning.

Holidays and festivals may also have some bearing on the timing of a visit. Nooruz, the ancient, Zoroastrian-influenced festival celebrated throughout central Asia on 21 March, is well worth witnessing, although this is rather too early to see the country at its best. Horse games tend to take place during high summer, especially around Independence Day at the end of August, and special festivals that involve horse sports, Kyrgyz crafts and music are staged at upland *jailoos* (meadows) during July and August for the benefit of visitors and locals alike.

HIGHLIGHTS

Kyrgyzstan has few real manmade 'sights' but plenty of delightful locations. The first two listed below are the exceptions that prove the rule.

TASH RABAT An extraordinary Silk Road caravanserai high in a hidden valley close to the Chinese frontier (see page 236).

SAIMALUU-TASH An enormous gallery of 5,000-year-old petroglyphs spread across the top of a mountain in a particularly hard-to-reach location (see page 249).

LAKE ISSYK-KUL The world's second largest alpine lake, which has bathing beaches thousands of miles from the nearest ocean and great hiking in the valleys near Karakol (see page 145).

LAKE SONG-KÖL Quintessentially central Asia: a picture-perfect place to ride horses and stay in a yurt (see page 224).

LAKE SARY-CHELEK A jewel-like mountain lake surrounded by lush forest (see page 263).

ARSLANBOB Observe a traditional Uzbek community in a breathtaking setting amid the world's largest walnut forest (see page 251).

CENTRAL TIEN SHAN Serious hiking, enormous glaciers and disappearing lakes among 7,000m peaks (see page 189).

SUGGESTED ITINERARIES

Many visitors to Kyrgyzstan have just a couple of weeks to spare. Despite travel around the country being fairly slow, this allows a reasonable amount of the country, and a fairly wide variety of landscapes, to be visited. At the time of writing the British Foreign and Commonwealth Office (FCO) had no advice against travelling to Kyrgyzstan other than 'Take care if you travel to the *oblasts* (provinces) of Osh, Batken and Jalal-Abad'.

Starting in Bishkek, a **fortnight** would be enough time to travel along the north coast of Lake Issyk-Kul, stopping overnight in Tamchy or Cholpon-Ata before reaching Karakol. From here, a short two- or three-day trek could be made into the valleys south of the town. Return west along the south shore of the lake, possibly spending a night in Tamga or Barskoon *en route* to Kochkor. At Kochkor, arrange transport to Lake Song-Köl the next day, spending a night or two there in a yurt, horseriding or walking around the lake in the daytime. From Kochkor head south to Naryn and meet up with prearranged transport over the Torugart Pass to Kashgar in China, stopping at Tash Rabat along the way and perhaps spending an extra day here to hike up to the ridge above Lake Chatyr-Köl. An alternative route from Kochkor that returns to the Bishkek starting point might be to hike north to the Suusamyr Valley after visiting Song-Köl (or return to Kochkor to find transport here) and head west along the valley through the villages of Chaek and Kyzyl-Oi to loop around at the western end to reach the Chui Valley and Bishkek.

Another circular route through Kyrgyzstan that requires a little more time, say **three weeks**, is to follow the above itinerary as far as Naryn and then organise transport along the rough road west to Kazarman, perhaps visiting Saimaluu-Tash (late July to early September only). From Kazarman, arrange transport south to Jalal-Abad and spend a night here before continuing to Osh. Then spend a night or two in Osh, visiting sights in the city and around, before flying back to Bishkek or continuing east over the Irkeshtam Pass to Kashgar and China.

A further possibility is to miss out Lake Issyk-Kul altogether and travel due south from Bishkek towards Osh, making a detour west of the main trunk road towards Lake Sary-Chelek and/or on to the east to visit the Arslanbob region, before continuing south to Jalal-Abad and Osh.

There will be other visitors, passing through Kyrgyzstan as part of a longer overland route, who have a little more time at their disposal and can probably afford to be more flexible. Traversing Kyrgyzstan between Kazakhstan or Uzbekistan and China to the east, or Tajikistan to the south, allows much to be seen with a carefully planned route – although potential problems with closed border crossings should be checked thoroughly beforehand.

A **month** in the country should allow time to visit most of the places mentioned above. The best approach is to work out where you most want to go and, given the time available, try and plan the most obvious route connecting them. Kyrgyzstan does not have a very comprehensive or well-maintained road network, although it is slowly improving. Nor does it have a flawless public transport system, but with a spirit of adventure and a bit of luck you should get there eventually. Much time can be saved on circular tours by flying one-way; flights between Osh and Bishkek are inexpensive, regular and reasonably reliable.

TOUR OPERATORS

UK

Adventure Worldwide Long Barn South, Sutton Manor Farm, Bishops Sutton, Alresford, Hants SO24 0AA; ☎0845 304 8679 (for specialist consultant ☎01962 737630); www.adventureworldwide. co.uk. A specialist adventure travel company that offers 11-day tours & 14-day treks taking in Kyrgyzstan highlights.

Audley Travel New Mill, New Mill Lane, Witney, Oxfordshire OX29 9SX; ☎01993 838000 (for central Asia specialist ☎01993 838200); www.audleytravel. com. Audley organise tailor-made trips to central Asia that take in Kyrgyzstan & its neighbours & provide a bespoke itinerary according to the client's personal interests. Also offers escorted 19-day group tours through central Asia.

Cox & Kings 6th Floor, 30 Millbank, London SW1P 4EE; ☎020 7873 5000; e cox.kings@ coxandkings.co.uk; www.coxandkings.co.uk. Offers a 9-day escorted group tour or bespoke itineraries for individuals.

Dragoman Overland Adventure Travel Camp Green, Debenham, Stowmarket, Suffolk IP14 6LA; ☎01728 861133; e info@dragoman.co.uk; www. dragoman.com. This overland company has various overland tours passing through central Asia that include Kyrgyzstan in the itinerary.

Far Frontiers Ninestone, South Deal, Devon EX20 2PZ; ☎01837 840640; e fiona@farfrontiers. com; www.farfrontiers.com. Tailored itineraries, with programme suggestions including a 15-day Highlights of Uzbekistan, Kyrgyzstan & Kazakhstan tour & a 13-day Tien Shan ride that includes a 6-day horse trek.

Go Russia Boundary Hse Business Centre, Boston Rd, London W7 2QE; ☎020 3355 7717; e info@justgorussia.co.uk; www.justgorussia.co.uk. Offers a cultural 26-day Silk Road Odyssey tour that takes in Uzbekistan, Kyrgyzstan & China.

Intrepid UK regional head office – Cross & Pillory House, 1 Cross & Pillory Lane, Alton, Hants GU34 1HL; ☎0808 274 5111 (freephone enquiries); e enquiries.uk@intrepidtravel.com; www.intrepidtravel.com. A large Australian company with a UK base that offers a 16-day Mountain Kingdoms of Kyrgyzstan tour that also takes in Uzbekistan, plus a couple of tours that incorporate western China, & several lengthy pan-Silk Road trips.

KE Adventure Travel 32 Lake Rd, Keswick, Cumbria CA12 5DQ; ☎01768 73966; e info@keadventure.com; www.keadventure.com. KE has a 14-day Heart of the Tien Shan trek in the Tien Shan region of Kazakhstan & Kyrgyzstan.

Mountain Kingdoms 20 Long St, Wotton-under-Edge, Glos GL12 7BT; ☎01453 844400; e info@mountainkingdoms.com; www.mountainkingdoms.com. Trekking specialists, they offer a 5-day trek in the Tien Shan region, which includes a helicopter ride to North Inylchek base camp.

Oasis Overland ☎01963 363400; e info@oasisoverland.co.uk; www.oasisoverland.co.uk. Experienced adventure travel company specialising in overland tours. Several central Asia tour options pass through Kyrgyzstan & one 15-day tour is spent entirely within the country. See ad, page 84.

Outlook Expeditions 8–9 Chestnut Court, Ffordd y Parc, Parc Menai, Bangor LL57 4FH; ☎01248 672760; e info@outlookexpeditions.com; www.outlookexpeditions.com. Organises 23- & 24-day trekking expeditions for schools & groups of young people, either trekking in the Naryn region or climbing & hiking in the Jetim-Bel mountain range. They can also arrange bespoke itineraries.

Peregrine Adventures UK sales office, 76 Upper St, London N1 0NU; ☎0808 2745 438; e travel@peregrineadventures.com; www.peregrineadventures.com. Several tours on offer including a 14-day tour through Kyrgyzstan from Kashgar to Tashkent & longer central Asian itineraries.

Regent Holidays 6th floor, Colston Tower, Colston St, Bristol BS1 4XE; ☎020 7666 1244; e regent@regent-holidays.co.uk; www.regent-holidays.co.uk. Regent has a 13-day tour of Kyrgyzstan that takes in the Lake Issyk-Kul region, Lake Song-Köl & Tash-Rabat, plus a combined Kazakhstan & Kyrgyzstan 15-day tour, & several longer tours that include neighbouring central Asian countries.

Scotts Tours 141 Whitfield St, London W1T 5EW; ☎020 7383 5353; e enquiries@scottstours.co.uk; www.scottstours.co.uk. A company that specialises in Russia & the former states of the Soviet Union; they can organise flights, visas & accommodation for both business & leisure travellers.

Steppes Travel 51 Castle St, Cirencester GL7 1QD; ☎0843 6347 154; e enquiry@steppestravel.co.uk; www.steppestravel.co.uk. Tailor-made or small group escorted itineraries that cover Kyrgyzstan, central Asia & China.

Wild Frontiers 78 Glentham Rd, London SW13 9JJ; ☎020 7736 3968; www.wildfrontierstravel.com. Several adventure tours in Kyrgyzstan & surrounding countries, including Ride the Mountains of Heaven, a 15-day horse trek that includes Lake Song-Köl & Tash-Rabat.

Wild & Exotic Nunnington, York YO62 5XF; ☎01439 748401; e info@wildandexotic.co.uk; www.wildandexotic.co.uk. Bespoke tours in Kyrgyzstan.

USA

40 Tribes Backcountry Adventures PO Box 44, Jamestown, CO 80455; ☎+1 303 552 6034; e info@fortytribesbackcountry.com; www.fortytribesbackcountry.com. This pioneering adventure travel company offers packages & bespoke itineraries that combine traditional yurt living with guided & self-guided fly-fishing & winter skiing tours.

Boojum Expeditions 14543 Kelly Canyon Rd, Bozeman, MT 59715; ☎+1 406 587 0125; e info@boojum.com; www.boojum.com. Mongolia specialists who also sometimes organise Kyrgyzstan horse treks & visits to a Kyrgyz horse festival using Barskoon's Shepherd's Way company.

Distant Horizons 350 Elm Av, Long Beach, CA 90802; ☎+1 800 333 1240, +1 562 983 8828; e info@distant-horizons.com; www.distant-horizons.com. Offers customised cultural tours to central Asia & Kyrgyzstan.

East Site 3 Hadley Drive, Medford, NJ 08055; ☎+1 877 800 6287; e travel@east-site.com;

www.east-site.com. East Site has scheduled Silk Road tours of various durations that include Kyrgyzstan. They can also help with air tickets & visas.

GeoEx PO Box 29902,1008 General Kennedy Av, San Francisco, CA 94129-0902; ☏+1 415 922 0448, +1 888 570 7108; e info@geoex.com; www.geoex.com. Runs a Silk Road tour across the Torugart Pass to China & a 21-day tour including Turkmenistan, Uzbekistan & Kyrgyzstan.

MIR Corporation Suite 210, 85 South Washington St, Seattle, WA 98104; ☏+1 206 624 7289, +1 800 424 7289; e info@mircorp.com; www.mircorp.com. Offers various group tours along the Silk Road. They can also arrange tailored itineraries.

Red Star Travel Suite 102, 123 Queen Anne Av N, Seattle, WA 98109; ☏+1 206 522 5995, ☏+1 800 215 4378; e travel@travel2russia.com; www.travel2russia.com. Can arrange visas, flights, train tickets & tours to whole of the CIS region, including Kyrgyzstan.

Sokol Tours 27 Meetinghouse Lane, Bradfordwoods, PA 15015; ☏+1 724 935 5373; e sokol@sokoltours.com; www.sokoltours.com. An American Russia & CIS specialist offering tours of Lake Issyk-Kul coupled with Kazakhstan, as well as a multiple-country Silk Route tour.

CANADA

Bestway Tours & Safaris Suite 206, 8678 Greenall Av, Burnaby, British Columbia V5J 3M6; ☏+1 604 264 7378 (toll free ☏+1 800 663 0844); e bestway@bestway.com; www.bestway.com. Cultural tours to central Asia that include Kyrgyzstan.

Silk Road Tours 201–1571 Bellevue Av, West Vancouver, British Columbia V7V 1A6; ☏+1 604 925 3831; e Canadian32@gmail.com; www.silkroadtours.com. Iran specialists, though they also offer tailored programmes that include Kyrgyzstan & other central Asian republics.

AUSTRALIA

Gateway Travel 1a Bold St, Burwood, NSW 2134; ☏+61 2 9745 3333; e sales@russian-gateway.com.au; www.russian-gateway.com.au. Can assist with flights, accommodation & visas in Kyrgyzstan & throughout central Asia.

Intrepid Level 3/ 380 Lonsdale Rd, Melbourne, VIC 3000; ☏1300 364 512 (from outside Australia:

☏+61 3 9473 2626); e help@intrepidtravel.com; www.intrepidtravel.com. Intrepid has several multi-country tours through central Asia that take in Kyrgyzstan.

Peregrine Adventures 380 Lonsdale St, Melbourne, VIC 3000; ☏+61 3 8601 4444 (outside Australia); e websales@peregrineadventures.com; www.peregrineadventures.com. Several tours through Kyrgyzstan from Kashgar to Tashkent, as well as longer central Asian itineraries.

Sundowners Overland Level 1, 51 Queen St, Melbourne 3000; ☏+61 3 9672 5300; www.sundownersoverland.com. Offers several overland Silk Road & central Asia tours that include Kyrgyzstan.

KYRGYZSTAN The following are all based in Bishkek & between them offer a very wide range of tours & activities. To phone from abroad, add the country code, +996, plus the Bishkek code, 312, then the number below.

Advantour [102 B3] Kievskaya 131/2; ☏900 592; e bishkek@advantour.com; www.advantour.com. A travel agency with sister branches in Tashkent & Almaty, Advantour has a large number of Kyrgyzstan itineraries available of variable durations from 2 to 15 days. Advantour offers a Kyrgyz festivals tour, as well as rafting, horseriding, hiking & multiple-activity treks. Can also arrange transport to Torugart from Naryn via Tash Rabat.

Adventure's Seller [102 D3] Chui 125/1; ☏432 333; e saleman@saimanet.kg, seller-travel@mail.ru; www.seller-travel.biz. A small, relatively new company that offers tours in addition to services such as visa support & reservations.

Ak-Sai Travel [95 F7] Baytik Baatyr (formerly Sovetskaya) 65; ☏591 759; e info@ak-sai.com; www.ak-sai.com. Ak-Sai offers a wide range of cultural & adventure tours in addition to treks to the Inylchek Glacier, heli-skiing in the Tien Shan, mountain biking, horseriding & mountaineering to various peaks in Kyrgyzstan.

Asia Mountains [95 G6] Tugolbai Ata (formerly Lineinaja) 1a; ☏690 235; e office@asiamountains.net; www.asiamountains.net/en (English). Asia Mountains offers a full range of Silk Road tours, including travel to China via the Irkeshtam Pass; various trekking options that include Merzbacher Lake, mountaineering in the Pamir & Tien Shan ranges; & specialist programmes that investigate

2

the botany & geology of Kyrgyzstan. They can also organise heli-skiing, rafting & canoeing packages. The company runs the guesthouse of the same name in Bishkek.

Caravan Travel Agency [102 B3] Isanov 80/42; ✆311 811; e tourism@caravan.com.kg; www. caravan.com.kg. A Bishkek agency that can organise flights, hotels & Issyk-Kul tours.

Celestial Mountains Tour Company [102 B3] Kievskaya 131/2; ✆311 814; e celest@infotel.kg, tours@celestial.co.kg; www.celestial.kg, www. tours.kg. Celestial Mountains is a respected & reliable British-run company which can arrange local activities such as demonstrations of local crafts & traditional music concerts, as well as matters like transportation over the Torugart Pass to China. Director Ian Claytor is very knowledgeable regarding the logistics of travel in Kyrgyzstan & is happy to give advice. The same company has guesthouses in Bishkek & Naryn.

Central Asia Tourism (CAT) Corporation [102 D3] Chui 124; ✆663 664, 663 665; e cat@cat. kg, travel2@cat.kg; www.cat.kg.This is the Bishkek office of a Kazakh company which deals with all aspects of travel & tourism, visa support & flights, as well as tours & hotel bookings.

Dostuck Trekking [103 H1] Igemberdiev 42/1; ✆545 455, 503 082; e dostuck@saimanet.kg; www.dostuck.com.kg. Dostuck is a joint British-Kyrgyz venture founded in 1991, which organises trekking, climbing, heli-skiing, rafting & other adventure tours in Kyrgyzstan. Dostuck is a partner of the MIR Corporation in the USA & Steppes Travel in the UK.

EcoNomad [95 E7] 6/33, Microdistrict 3; m 0773 438 065, 0772 693 411; e info@eco-nomad.com; www.eco-nomad.com. Offers several Kyrgyzstan tours of cultural interest that include trekking & horseriding options. Also mountain-biking tours. French spoken.

Ecotour [102 C2] 46A Donskoy Pereulok; ✆460 803; m 0772 802 805 (English), 0555 913 245 (German); e info@ecotour.kg; www.ecotour.kg. Ecotour organises individually tailored or small group-themed (birdwatching, botanical, cultural) & soft active (trekking, cycling & mountain biking & horseriding) tours staying in yurts, homestays & guesthouses as appropriate. As well as yurt camps in the mountains, they own & are based at the Umai Hotel in Bishkek (see page 99). See ad, page 84.

Edelweiss [103 G4] Gastello 19; ✆542 045, 542 064; e edelweiss@elcat.kg; www.edelweisstravel. org. Edelweiss offers Silk Road tours between Almaty & the Torugart Pass, heli-skiing packages & a variety of trekking & horse tours. Also serious mountaineering to Khan Tengri & Pobedy. They can tailor services according to individual requirements.

Fantastic Asia [94 C5] Turusbekov 10/47; ✆456 749; e info@fantasticasia.net; www.fantasticasia. net. Tours include trekking & mountaineering in Tien Shan region, Silk Road tours through central Asia, heli-skiing, snowboarding & mountain biking. Can also provide transport & book accommodation.

Flagman Travel Company Dermontova 2; ✆937 979; m 0772 706 070; www.flagman-kg.com. Silk Road & historical tours; trekking, rafting & skiing.

Glavtour [102 B4] Toktogul 93; ✆663 232; e glavtour@infotel.kg; www.glavtour.kg. Also has office at Kievskaya 95 (✆662 295; e mon@ glavtour.kg) & at Moskovskaya 165 (✆318 500; e city-centre@glavtour.kg). A Russian-Kyrgyz joint venture that offers day trips to Ala-Archa, Alamedin & Kashka-Suu gorges, 1- & 2-week hiking tours, winter skiing & rafting trips, & services such as booking air tickets & hotels.

International Mountaineering Camp (IMC) Pamir [102 B3] Apartment 30, Kievskaya 133; ✆660 464, 660 469 e imcpamir@imfico.bishkek. su; http://home.tiscali.nl/imcpamir. Organises mountaineering expeditions to Peak Lenin, where it has a permanent base camp, & to the peaks of Central Tien Shan.

ITMC Tien Shan Travel [94 B1] Molodaya Gvardiya 1A; ✆651 404; e itmc@elcat.kg; www. itmc.centralasia.kg. ITMC has a wide range of programmes that include several Silk Road tours & trekking options in the Terskey Ala-Too & the Central Tien Shan ranges. Also offers horseback tours, heli-skiing, mountain biking, jeep safaris & mountaineering packages.

Kyrgyz Concept [102 D3] Isanov 42/1; ✆903 232, 906 262; e office@concept.kg; www.concept.kg/ eng. Several other offices in Bishkek including at Chui 126 (✆666 006; e chui@concept.kg), Kievskaya 69 (✆900 404; e lcc.bishkek@concept.kg) & Tynystanov 231 (✆900 886; e tynystanov@concept. kg). Kyrgyz Concept offers a range of services aimed at both business & leisure visitors that include visas, car hire, translation, flights & accommodation booking, in addition to a range of tours.

Muza Tours [103 E4] Erkindik 64; ✆901 295, 304 617; e booking@inspiro.kg; www.muzatravel.com. Muza offers a range of adventure & cultural tours around Kyrgyzstan, as well as trekking, horseriding, yurt stays & Silk Road tours to China. They can also organise business services like reservations & translations.

Nomad's Land [94 C7] Maldybaev 12/1, Microrayon 10; ✆564 743; e info@nomadsland. ch; www.nomadsland.ch. This is a Kyrgyz-Swiss ecotourism company which offers a variety of trekking, mountaineering, rafting & cycling tours, in addition to services such as camping equipment rental, bike hire & transportation.

NoviNomad [94 D2] Togolok Moldo 28, apt 10; ✆622 381; e info@novinomad.com; www. novinomad.com. NoviNomad has a wide range of cultural & Silk Road tours as well as treks, horseriding & mountain bike tours. They can arrange visas, OVIR registration & organise the documentation for the authorisation of exporting goods. They also offer city tours & can arrange overland travel to China & Tajikistan.

Tien Shan Travel [95 E1] Bakinsky 3/1; ✆466 034, 490 180; e travel@tien-shan.com; www.tien-shan.com. This is a well-established adventure company that specialises in mountaineering, high-altitude trekking, rafting & skiing. Tien Shan Travel has its own base camps at Maida-Adyr, South Inylchek & North Inylchek in the Central Tien Shan & at Achyk-Tash & the Lenin Glacier in the Pamirs.

Top Asia Shota Rustaveli 101; ✆664 583; m 0555 954 239; e topasia@mail.kg, info@ topasia.kg; www.topasia.kg. Top Asia offers a number of Silk Road tours, along with treks in the Central Tien Shan & Terskey Ala-Too, plus mountaineering trips to Lenin & Khan Tengri peaks, & horseback excursions. Also paragliding, kayaking & mountain-bike tours.

ELSEWHERE IN CENTRAL ASIA

Stantours ✆+49 3212 1039 960; e info@ stantours.com; www.stantours.com. Stantours is a pan-central Asian travel company run by German national David Berghof, with offices in Almaty & Ashgabat. As well as offering tours of the central Asian region, Stantours is excellent at sorting out red tape for groups or individual travellers. This is a good place to make enquiries if you plan to travel beyond Kyrgyzstan & require invitations or visa support for Uzbekistan or a Gorno-Badakhshan Autonomous Oblast (GBAO) permit for travel along the Pamir Highway into Tajikistan. Email enquiries are normally answered promptly. For matters relating to Kyrgyzstan travel, Stantours usually liaises with the Celestial Mountains Tour Company in Bishkek.

COMMUNITY BASED TOURISM The organisation Community Based Tourism (CBT) started life in 2000 as an initiative to organise local groups offering accommodation and tourist services to visitors. In 2003, a national umbrella association, the KCBTA (Kyrgyz Community Based Tourism Association), was created to unite the CBT and Shepherd's Life groups around the country (*KCBTA, Gorky 58, intersection with Matrosov, Bishkek;* ✆ *+996 312 540 069, 443 331;* e *reservation@cbtkyrgyzstan.kg, cbttours@mail.ru; www.cbtkyrgyzstan.kg*).

This was done with the support of partner Helvetas (*www.helvetas.kg*), the Swiss Association for International Co-operation, which had helped inspire the first Shepherd's Life groups in 1997 and has committed to a long-term alliance.

From a modest beginning, the organisation has quickly gained momentum, enabling foreign visitors to stay with families and utilise local services for adventure travel at a very reasonable price. In addition to offering a range of homestay accommodation at each of the organisation's 15 regional centres, the local CBT co-ordinator can arrange private transport and yurt stays at *jailoos*, organise guides and horses, advise on trekking and stage special demonstrations of folk craft, such as *shyrdak*-making, and Kyrgyz traditions such as eagle-hunting and horse games. The accommodation and services offered by CBT are of special value to backpackers and individual travellers who may not be able to afford, or wish to participate in, a fully organised tour of the country.

The national umbrella association KCBTA is able to advise and plan bespoke itineraries throughout Kyrgyzstan, either by phone, email or a personal visit to its Bishkek office. They can prearrange services throughout the country, or you can simply turn up at regional CBT centres and arrange it there ad hoc. Some, but by no means all, local co-ordinators speak English, but communication is rarely much of a problem. As well as the homes of local co-ordinators, CBT also has separate information offices in some towns throughout the country. At the time of writing these could be found in Karakol, Tamchy, Bokonbaevo, Kochkor, Naryn, Osh, Jalal-Abad and Arslanbob. The organisation is continually expanding its range of operations and in recent years new CBT networks have been set up in Alay and Sary-Mogol south of Osh. Details of local CBT groups are given as appropriate in the text.

Overall, CBT is a splendid organisation which offers excellent services for very affordable prices and has been a great boon to budget travel in Kyrgyzstan over the past few years. It is low impact, economically and socially sustainable, and it goes without saying that most of the income generated goes directly into the local community. Some critics point out that it is usually possible to do things slightly cheaper than CBT fixed rates, particularly in terms of hiring private transport, but at least with CBT there is the knowledge that the driver is approved, trustworthy and used to dealing with tourists. The CBT website (*www.cbtkyrgyzstan.kg*) has a great deal of information including a full list of available services, tours and events.

RED TAPE

Compared with most of its central Asian neighbours and Russia, Kyrgyzstan is a very straightforward place to visit with a minimum of paperwork for most visitors.

VISAS Since July 2012 visitors from the European Union (except Bulgaria and Romania), North America and Australasia no longer need a visa to visit Kyrgyzstan for a period of up to 60 days. The same waiver also applies to citizens of Bosnia and Herzegovina, Monaco, Iceland, Liechtenstein, Norway, Switzerland, Turkey, Cuba, Japan, South Korea, Singapore, Malaysia, Mongolia, Brunei, most Gulf Arab states – Bahrain, Kuwait, Qatar, UAE, Saudi Arabia – Russia and former countries of the Soviet Union. If planning to stay longer than 60 days a visa will be required, which should be obtained either in advance at a Kyrgyz embassy or on arrival at Manas airport.

For those passport-holders of countries that *do* require a visa – mostly African, Middle Eastern, South Asian countries and China – these can be obtained in advance at a Kyrgyzstan embassy. Most will be required to obtain a visa support letter from the Consular Department of the Ministry of Foreign Affairs if travelling for business purposes or, if travelling privately or for the purposes of tourism, an invitation letter (usually referred to as LOI – 'letter of invitation') issued by the Ministry of Internal Affairs. This additional paperwork can be issued, at a price and with some advance notice, by contacting one of the Bishkek travel agents listed on page 97. Visas are normally issued for 30 days.

Citizens of a small number of countries that require visas are able to obtain them *without* providing visa support or a LOI, and can obtain visas on arrival by air for US$50–100 depending on length of stay and whether single or double entry. The countries not requiring visa support are: Albania, Andorra, Argentina, Brazil, Bulgaria, Chile, Cyprus, Indonesia, Israel, Macedonia, Mexico, Montenegro, Oman, Philippines, Romania, San Marino, Serbia, South Africa, Thailand, Venezuela and Vietnam.

Applying for a visa If you are arriving overland or by air and you are *not* eligible for a visa on arrival, the best advice is to obtain a visa in advance in your own country. Visa applications usually involve the following: a valid passport with at least one blank page, a completed application form, one passport-sized photo, the appropriate fee and a stamped, addressed envelope if applying by post. An invitation letter and additional documents are required in some cases. Additional charges are made for an express service.

Countries that do not have a Kyrgyz diplomatic representation may usually apply at a Kazakh embassy or consulate instead.

Visas on arrival Tourist visas are issued on arrival of international flights at Manas Airport in Bishkek. The visa desk is opened for the arrival of international flights. Single-entry, one-month visas cost US$50 for 15 days, US$60 for one month; a double entry one-month visa costs US$70; business visas are US$70–100. Be sure to have the exact fee in crisp new banknotes. Visas are issued and stuck into passports before immigration; the whole process takes only about ten minutes once the issuing officer has turned up.

Visas in central Asia If possible, avoid collecting visas *en route* through central Asia as this can involve a lot of hanging around in capital cities, and may ultimately represent a false economy in terms of both time and money. For example, the Kyrgyzstan embassy in Dushanbe, Tajikistan, has erratic opening hours and then seems to take at least five working days to issue the visa. Similarly, the Uzbekistan embassy in Bishkek is infamously unhelpful and a bad place to apply for a visa to that country. Chinese visas are also hard, and sometimes impossible, to obtain in Bishkek. This said, applying for a Kyrgyz visa in Kazakhstan is usually straightforward and fairly swift.

Entry and exit stamps In legal terms, it is only possible to enter or leave Kyrgyzstan at an approved border post. The stamp proves that you have entered by such a post and any lack of one in your passport has the potential to cause problems with the authorities. The problem is that at some border posts, particularly those that are less frequently used, they may fail to stamp you in. This happens on leaving the country, too (although it is less problematic), with officials claiming they have no stamp, have run out of ink, or just cannot be bothered. Try and insist, but if they do not have a stamp there is not much you can do about it. If this is the case, make a note of the time and date that you crossed the border (and perhaps also get the officer's name and number) then go to the OVIR (Office of Visas and Registration) in the first big town you reach and explain the situation where they will, hopefully, stamp your passport. Any dated documentation like a ticket or hotel receipt would also be good to have.

Visa extensions Tourist visas of 30 days may be extended relatively easily in Kyrgyzstan at the Ministry of Foreign Affairs and OVIR offices in Bishkek or OVIR offices in Karakol, Naryn and Osh. Extensions are normally for one week, although some claim to have received a month's extension without any trouble. Bring a copy of your main passport page and one or two passport photos. Having a Russian-speaking accomplice is helpful if you do not speak the language as the forms are in Russian only.

Ministry of Foreign Affairs Togolok Moldo 10a;
📞 660 706, 663 270; www.dcsmfa.kg
OVIR Bishkek Kievskaya 58 (near junction with Shopokova); ⏰ 09.30–12.30 & 14.00–17.00 Mon–Fri

OVIR Karakol Kutmanaliev 146a, room 114;
⏰ 09.00–12.00 & 14.00–16.00 Tue–Fri
OVIR Naryn Togolok Moldo 11 (junction with Lenina)
OVIR Osh City Administration Building, Lenina 199 (junction with Sovetskaya)

KYRGYZ EMBASSIES ABROAD

Ⓔ Austria Invaliden 3/8, 1030 Vienna; ☏+431 5350 378, 5350 379: e kyremb@inode.at; www.kyremb.at

Ⓔ Belgium (also Netherlands, France & Luxembourg) 47 Rue de l'Abbaye, 1050 Brussels; ☏+322 6401 868; e kyrgyz.embassy@skynet.be; www.kyrgyz-embassy.be

Ⓔ Belarus Starovilenskaya 57, Minsk 220002; ☏+375 17 2349 117; e manas@nsys.by; www.kgembassy.by

Ⓔ China King's Villas 18, H 10/11, Xiaun Rd, Beijing 100016; ☏+86 10 6468 1297; e kyrgyz.embassy.china@gmail.com; www.kyrgyzstanembassy.net. Consulate in Urumqi: 58 Hetan Beilu, Urumqi, Xinjiang 830063; ☏+86 991 5189 980; e vs_kr@sina.ch

Ⓔ Germany Otto-Suhr-Allee 146, 10585 Berlin; ☏+49 30 3478 1338, 3641 1860 (consular section); e info@botschaft-kirgisien.de; www.botschaft-kirgisien.de. Consulate in Bonn (*Ännchenstr 61, 53177 Bonn;* ☏*+49 228 365 230;* e *bonn@botschaft-kirgisien.de*); consulate in Frankfurt (*Brönnerstr 20, 60313 Frankfurt am Main;* ☏*+49 69 9540 3926;* e *Frankfurt@botschaft-kirgisien.de*)

Ⓔ India Poorvi Marg 78, New Delhi 110057; ☏+91 11 2614 9582, 2614 8019; e delhi@kgzembind.in; www.kgzembind.com

Ⓔ Iran 5th Naranjestan Alley 12, Pasdaran St, Tehran 195 793 5611; ☏+98 21 2830 354; e krembiri.mydatak@gmail.com

Ⓔ Japan 6-16 5-chome Shimomeguro, Meguro-ku, Tokyo 153-0064; ☏+81 3 3179 0828; e office@kyrgyzemb.jp; www.kyrgyzembassy.jp

Ⓔ Kazakhstan Diplomatic City B-5, Astana 010000; ☏+7 3172 242 024; e kr@mail.online.kz. Consulate in Almaty: Lugansakaya 30A, Almaty 480012; ☏+7 3272 642 212; e almaty@consulkg.kgz; www.consul.kz

Ⓔ Malaysia 10th floor, Wisma Sin Heap Lee, Jalan Tun Razak 346, 504 00 Kuala Lumpur; ☏+60 3 2163 2012; e info@kgembassymy.com; www.kgembassymy.com

Ⓔ Pakistan 163, Str 36, F-10/1, Islamabad 44000; ☏+92 51 2212 196; e kyrgyzembassy@dsl.net.pk; www.kyrgyzembassy.com.pk

Ⓔ Russia Bolshaya Ordynka 64, Moscow 109017; ☏+7 499 9516 062; e info@kyrgyzembassy.ru; www.kyrgyzembassy.ru. Consulate in Ekaterinburg (*Bolshakova 105;* ☏*+7 343 2577 614;* e *genconkr@mail.ru*); consulate in Novisibirsk (*Krasniy prospect 220, section 2, apt 350;* ☏*+7 343 2106 624*)

Ⓔ Switzerland Rue de Lac 4, Geneva 1207; ☏+41 22 7079 220; e Kyrgyzstan.geneva@gmail.com; www.kyrgyzmission.net

Ⓔ Tajikistan Soid-Nosir 56A, Dushanbe; ☏+992 41 1000 056; e kg@kgembassy.tj; www.kgembassy.tj

Ⓔ Turkey Turan Gunes Bulvari 15, Caddesi No 25, Yildiz/Oran-Ankara 06450; ☏+90 312 4913 506, 4913 507; e info@kgembassy.org.tr; www.kgembassy.org.tr. Consulate in Istanbul: Lamartin Caddesi 7, Taksim, Istanbul; ☏+90 21 2356 767; e genkon@tr.net

Ⓔ Turkmenistan Garashsyzlyk 57, 744036 Ashkhabad; ☏+993 482 295; e kyrgtm@mail.ru; www.kgembassytm.com

Ⓔ Ukraine Pavlovskaya 26/41, Kiev 01901; ☏+380 44 500 5936; e embassy.kg.kiev@silvercom.net; www.kyrgyzembassy.com.ua

Ⓔ UK Ascot Hse, 119 Crawford St, London W1U 6BJ; ☏+44 20 7935 1462; e mail@kyrgyz-embassy.org.uk; www.kyrgyz-embassy.org.uk

Ⓔ USA (& Canada) 2360 Massachusetts Av NW, Washington, DC 20008; ☏+1 202 449 9822, 449 9823; e kgembassyusa@gmail.com; www.kgembassy.org. Consulate in New York at the UN: Suite 477, 866 UN Plaza, New York, NY 10017; ☏+1 212 486 5259; e kyrgyzstan@un.it; www.un.int/wcm/content/site/kyrgyzstan

Ⓔ Uzbekistan Niyazbek 30, 700000 Tashkent; ☏+998 71 2374 794; e kg.embassy.uz@gmail.com; www.kgembassy.uz

REGISTRATION Thankfully, this is a thing of the past for most foreign visitors now, as compulsory OVIR registration was abandoned in 2002 for the USA, Canada, Israel, Australia, New Zealand and most EU countries. Those passport holders who still need to register can report to one of the OVIR offices listed on page 113.

PERMITS Generally speaking, trekking permits are no longer required as these were abandoned, along with OVIR registration, in 2002. However, there is some uncertainty as to whether they are required in the Ak-Suu region of Batken Province. **Military border permits** are required for some areas, notably those zones within 50km of the Chinese border – the Central Tien Shan area around Khan Tengri peak, the Inylchek Glacier and Merzbacher Lake, and the Ak-Say Valley east of the Torugart Pass. A border permit (*propusk*) is *not* required for the straightforward overland journey to China by either the Torugart or Irkeshtam passes, as long as travellers are in possession of a Chinese visa and there is no deviation from the route in the border region itself. Tash Rabat caravanserai does not require a permit.

Border permits may be arranged by a travel agency or tour operator but should be applied for well in advance as they take at least a week to issue.

GETTING THERE AND AWAY

BY AIR Kyrgyzstan's main international airport is Bishkek's Manas Airport (*airport code: FRU;* ✆ *693 109;* e *info@airport.kg; www.airport.kg*) although a few flights from Russia also go direct to Osh. Manas Airport lies about 25km north of the capital, a 40-minute drive away. For details of how to reach the airport from the city see page 90.

From the UK There are no longer any direct flights between the UK and Bishkek. The nearest airport for flights originating in London is Almaty in Kazakhstan, a four-hour drive from Bishkek. **British Airways** (*www.britishairways.com*) flies three or four times a week to Almaty for around £550 return. **KLM** (*www.klm.com*) offers a similar service but this requires a change of planes at Amsterdam.

The best way to reach Kyrgyzstan by air from the UK or elsewhere in Europe is to fly to Moscow or Istanbul and then transfer to a direct Bishkek flight. Flying via Moscow, there are flights with **Aeroflot** (*www.aeroflot.com*) that change planes at Sheremetyevo Airport. These start at about £400 return and fly daily but there is sometimes a long wait at the transit airport. A little more expensive, but more comfortable and reliable, are the daily flights with **Turkish Airlines** (*www.turkishairlines.com*) via Istanbul's Atatürk Airport, which start around £420 return. Another, usually less expensive Turkish alternative is with the budget carrier **Pegasus Airlines** (*www.flypgs.com*) that flies daily to Bishkek from London Stansted via Istanbul's Sabiha Gökçen Airport. These flights can cost as little as £330 return and represent a real bargain, even if you do have to buy all your own drinks and meals on board.

From Europe Flights to Bishkek from western European countries also tend to connect with either Aeroflot in Moscow or Turkish Airlines or Pegasus in Istanbul. **Lufthansa** (*www.lufthansa.com*) and **KLM** (*www.klm.com*) do not fly to Bishkek but do regularly fly to Almaty in Kazakhstan (see page 60).

From Russia and CIS countries Kyrgyzstan has regular direct flights from Moscow with **Aeroflot** (*www.aeroflot.com*), **Ural Air** (*www.uralairlines.ru*), **Air Bishkek** (*www. airbishkek.kg*), **Air Kyrgyzstan** (*www.air.kg*), **Avia** (*www.avia.com*) and **Pegasus Asia** (*www.pegasus-asia.com*), as well as three times a week from St Petersburg, twice a week from Krasnoyarsk, three times a week from Yekaterinburg, and weekly from Novosibirsk and Omsk in Siberia. There are flights four times a week from Dushanbe in Tajikistan, with both Avia and **Tajik Air** (*http://booking. tajikairlines.com*), as well as regular flights to Tashkent in Uzbekistan and Almaty in Kazakhstan. **Air Astana** (*www.airastana.com*) also flies to Bishkek from Almaty and Astana. **Azerbaijan Airlines** (*www.azal.az*) has a weekly service from Baku.

Practical Information GETTING THERE AND AWAY

2

From elsewhere China Southern Airlines (*www.csair.com*) and **Air Kyrgyzstan** (*www.air.kg*) fly to Bishkek several times a week from Ürümqi in Xinjiang. There are three flights a week from Tehran in Iran and one flight weekly from Mashad. There are also flights from Ulaanbaatar in Mongolia with **Turkish Airlines** (*www.turkishairlines.com*) and Dubai with Air Kyrgyzstan and the budget carrier **Fly Dubai** (*www.flydubai.com*).

From the USA and Canada There are no direct flights. Flights from North America must go via Moscow (Aeroflot) or Istanbul (Turkish Airlines).

From Australia and New Zealand Probably the easiest way to reach Kyrgyzstan from Australasia or southeast Asia is to fly to Tashkent via Bangkok and then either take a connecting flight or, politics permitting, travel overland to Kyrgyzstan.

Flying to Almaty, Kazakhstan There are far more flights to Kazakhstan from Europe than flights to Bishkek. **British Airways**, **Lufthansa** and **KLM** all fly to Almaty from their respective hubs in the UK, Germany and the Netherlands. Air Astana also offers flights between London and Almaty, and Amsterdam and Almaty. However, return flights from London to Almaty cost only a little less than they do to Bishkek and so make little sense if Bishkek is the final destination. **Air Baltic** (*www.airbaltic.com*), based in Riga, also flies direct to Almaty in summer and sometimes has discounted flights.

Almaty is only three to four hours by road from Bishkek, and both KLM and Lufthansa provide their own shuttle service. The problem with this route is the need for a Kazakh transit visa and then for another if returning to Almaty for the flight home.

Note: In July 2014 it was announced that nationals of the US, UK, Germany, France, Netherlands, Italy, Malaysia, UAE, Korea and Japan would no longer need a visa to enter Kazakhstan for a period of up to 15 days. This visa waiver was to last for an experimental period of one year until July 2015. Whether or not this will be continued, and/or extended to a wider range of nationalities, remains to be seen.

International flights to Osh The airport at Osh in southern Kyrgyzstan may be small but it is international and might be worth considering as an entrance point to the country. Alternatively, it is possible to fly into Kyrgyzstan via Bishkek and leave via Osh – or vice versa. Osh has twice-weekly connections to Dubai with FlyDubai and services to Istanbul with Turkish Airlines three times a week. There are also flights to several Russian cities and to Ürümqi in Xinjiang, China.

BY TRAIN The great adventure of arriving in Bishkek by rail may not quite be as romantic as its sounds. It is a very long journey and there is an awful lot of dull Kazakh steppe to stare at before Kyrgyzstan is reached. In addition, many of the passengers travelling in *platskart* (third class) are smugglers, and many consider that it is not a safe journey for foreigners to take, at least in the lowest class.

In theory, at least, it is possible to reach Bishkek by train from anywhere in Europe by way of Moscow and the service from there. Naturally, having to travel through both Russia and Kazakhstan *en route*, there are going to be plenty of visa considerations. A transit visa for Kazakhstan will be required as well as a Russian visa.

Train numbers 18 or 28, the *Kyrgizia*, leave Moscow's Kazan station twice a week at 22.48, to arrive 74 hours later in the early hours of the fourth day. This currently costs about 7,000 roubles (US$180) in *platskart* (third class open carriage) and about 11,000 roubles (US$300) in *kupe* (four-berth sleeper) if tickets are bought at the station. Through an agency they will cost considerably more. Train 28 also has first-class, twin-berth compartments that are about twice the price of *kupe*.

An alternative to these services is to take the Moscow–Almaty service, train number 8, that leaves every other day on odd dates from Moscow to reach Almaty, 78 hours later. Rather than going all the way to Bishkek or Almaty it is possible to leave any of the trains at Taraz (Dzhambul) in Kazakhstan and then enter Kyrgyzstan's northwest Talas Province by minibus, saving six to eight hours.

Real rail enthusiasts might also wish to reach Moscow by train from the UK by taking the Eurostar to Cologne and then on to Moscow, or by changing trains in Berlin or Warsaw for overnight services to the Russian capital. For details of rail travel to Russia from the UK see www.seat61.com.

The Russian Railways website (*www.rzd.ru*) has details of all Russian services. Online booking and payment is possible (*http://pass.rzd.ru*) but it is Russian language only. Train tickets for travel in Russia and the CIS may be booked in advance using a Russian agency such as the following: Svezhy Veter (*www.svezhyveter.ru*), G&R International (*www.hostels.ru*) and Way to Russia (*www.waytorussia.net*).

Trains run three times a week between Bishkek and Tashkent but they are very slow (18+ hours), take a meandering route, and require a Kazakh transit visa.

BY ROAD
From Kazakhstan There are frequent services between Almaty and Bishkek by share taxi (2,500 Kazakh tenge) and *marshrutka* (1,200 Kazakh tenge) taking about four hours. From Taraz (Dzhambul) there are regular minibuses that connect with Talas in Kyrgyzstan's northwest. Having been closed for three years between 2010 and 2013, the Karkara Valley route between Kegen (Kazakhstan) and Ken-Suu/Tyup (Kyrgyzstan) is now open again between mid-May and mid-October. Public transport on the Kazakh side goes as far as Kegen (around 2,000 Kazakh tenge per person in a share taxi) from where taxis to the border can be caught (around 4,000 Kazakh tenge for the car).

From Uzbekistan The northern route between Tashkent and Bishkek passes through Taraz in Kazakhstan, where there is usually a change of transport. A Kazakh transit visa is vital on this route. To reach Bishkek from Tashkent it may well be quicker and cheaper, *if* the border is open, to go first to Osh via the Fergana Valley and then fly to Bishkek from there.

From Dostlyk, near Andijan in Uzbekistan's Fergana Valley, there are normally plenty of share taxis running to the Kyrgyz border close to Osh, from where a minibus (*9som*) may be taken into the city. Dostlyk may be reached either from Andijan or Tashkent by share taxi. There is another border crossing at Uch-Kurgan on the road between Karakol (not the Lake Issyk-Kul town) and Namangan. No public transport passes through here, so it is necessary to take a taxi both sides. There is also another Fergana Valley crossing from Uzbekistan at Khanabad, just to the south of Jalal-Abad, but this was closed at the time of writing. Although there are further crossing points between the two countries in the Fergana Valley, most of these will not allow foreign travellers through as they may be designated for locals only.

From Tajikistan There is no regular transport along the Pamir Highway between Murgab and Osh, although private 4x4 vehicles may be hired for this route in either direction. Travelling this route requires a Gorno-Badakhshan Autonomous Oblast (GBAO) permit in addition to a Tajik visa. There are share taxis between Isfara in the

Tajik section of the Fergana Valley and Batken in southwest Kyrgyzstan. The Kyrgyz-Tajik border between Garm and Daroot-Korgon has been mostly closed for foreign nationals for several years but it may become open at some stage in the future.

From China There are two overland routes to and from China. The **Torugart Pass** in the southern Naryn Province is technically closed to foreigners but permission to cross is granted if travellers have prearranged transport meeting them on the other side of the border and have documentation to prove this. The public bus that plies this route between Kashgar and Naryn cannot be used by foreign nationals. Further south, the **Irkeshtam border**, to the east of Sary-Tash in Osh Province, permits crossing in either direction without any special conditions or documentation. A public bus normally runs between Kashgar in China's Xinjiang Province and Osh twice a week in both directions and takes at least 18 hours overnight. It is available for all to use. For further details regarding these crossings see the appropriate chapters.

HEALTH *with Dr Felicity Nicholson*

Kyrgyzstan is a healthy place on the whole and although travellers should be prepared for any eventuality, you should not expect to fall ill here, excepting the odd bout of travellers' diarrhoea. Nevertheless, all visitors to Kyrgyzstan should be in possession of adequate **health insurance** as state health care in Kyrgyzstan is rudimentary at best. Insurance is particularly important if such activities as trekking, horseriding or mountaineering are planned, and ideally should cover emergency medical repatriation.

A list of doctors, dentists and health clinics is provided in the Bishkek chapter (see page 111).

Since 2014 a **yellow fever** vaccination certificate is required from all travellers one year and above arriving from countries with a risk of yellow fever disease including an airport transit of 12 hours or more. There is no risk of disease in Kyrgyzstan. Other vaccinations advised include tetanus, diphtheria, polio and hepatitis A. Vaccination against typhoid may be recommended for longer stays or in poorer areas. Hepatitis B vaccination should also be considered for longer trips and always for those working in medical settings or with children. Kyrgyzstan is considered to be a high-risk country for hepatitis B. Three injections are needed to give maximum protection and take a minimum of three weeks to complete for those aged 16 and over. Longer courses are required for younger travellers or when time allows.

Tuberculosis is all too common in Kyrgyzstan (the prevalence in 2012 was 217 per 100,000 of the population). Vaccination is recommended for tuberculin-naïve travellers aged 16 and under who will be staying for at least three months and living and/or working with local people. Vaccination may also be considered on a case-by-case basis for those under 35 years of age who are at high risk through their work, eg: working in hospitals or other healthcare settings. It is also wise to avoid any unpasteurised dairy products as this is also a route of transmission.

There is a low-grade risk of **malaria** which is mostly due to *Plasmodium vivax* carried by female Anopheles mosquitoes. The risk is more common from June to October, mainly in areas bordering Tajikistan and Uzbekistan (Jalal-Abad, Batken and Osh provinces). Up-to-date advice on this situation and the need for prophylaxis should be sought from a doctor or travel clinic. At the time of writing, the risk is considered low enough to not need to take tablets but prevention with a DEET-containing insect repellent both day and night is always advised. In rural areas, and especially if cycling, dogs may be a nuisance and present the potential threat of rabies. Kyrgyzstan is a considered to be high risk for rabies and there is not likely to be all the post-exposure treatment needed if the pre-exposure vaccine has not been taken (see page 64).

Although it is chlorinated, tap **water** is not of very good quality throughout the country and bottled or boiled water should be taken in preference. Thankfully freshly boiled tea is plentiful, abundant even, and perfectly safe to drink. Care should be taken with raw fruit and vegetables, particularly in the warmer months, and the standard recommendation to always peel or wash fresh fruit and vegetables is sound advice. Cooked food such as meat stews that have cooled and have been standing around for a while may be more problematic, as might some of Kyrgyzstan's dairy specialities such as *kumys* and *kurut* (dried yoghurt balls), which are sometimes plucked out of a horseman's grubby pocket to be popped in the mouth of the appreciative visitor. *Kumys* – fermented mare's milk – is generally not

LONG-HAUL FLIGHTS, CLOTS AND DVT

Any prolonged immobility, including travel by land or air, can result in deep vein thrombosis (DVT) with the risk of embolus to the lungs. Certain factors can increase the risk and these include:

* Previous clot or close relative with a history
* People over 40 but risk is reduced over 80 years
* Recent major operation or varicose veins surgery
* Cancer
* Stroke
* Heart disease
* Obesity
* Pregnancy
* Hormone therapy
* Heavy smokers
* Severe varicose veins
* People who are very tall (over 6ft/1.8m) or short (under 5ft/1.5m)

A deep vein thrombosis (DVT) causes painful swelling and redness of the calf or sometimes the thigh. It is only dangerous if a clot travels to the lungs (pulmonary embolus). Symptoms of a pulmonary embolus (PE) include chest pain, shortness of breath, and sometimes coughing up small amounts of blood, and commonly start three to ten days after a long flight. Anyone who thinks that they might have a DVT needs to see a doctor immediately.

PREVENTION OF DVT
* Keep mobile before and during the flight; move around every couple of hours
* Drink plenty of fluids during the flight
* Avoid taking sleeping pills and excessive tea, coffee and alcohol
* Consider wearing flight socks or support stockings (see www.legshealth. com)

If you think you are at increased risk of a clot, ask your doctor if it is safe to travel.

Practical Information   HEALTH

2

considered harmful (indeed many make claims to its health benefits), however, you should bear in mind that the fermentation process may not eliminate tuberculosis and it can upset the stomachs of those not used to its sour milk acidity and cause nausea and vomiting in the hapless visitor.

In the summer months, and particularly at altitude, some form of **sun protection** is essential in the form of a hat and/or sunscreen. Without this sunburn is likely, which causes not only discomfort but also dehydration and skin damage. The mountains may also bring problems of cold weather, too, and it is important to ensure that while trekking you have adequate food, clothing and warm sleeping bags.

Altitude sickness is an ever-present threat above an altitude of 2,500m. Usually a sudden increase in altitude just causes minor discomfort such as a shortness of breath, dizziness, a racing heartbeat, a mild headache and loss of appetite. These are normal symptoms that can be ameliorated to some extent by taking painkillers and drinking plenty of fluids. Alcohol should always be avoided at altitude, as should tobacco. If you have these symptoms then discuss them with your guide. It may be adequate just to rest for a while but if they persist beyond a day or rapidly worsen, then the only solution is to descend to a lower altitude. Altitude sickness is fairly indiscriminate in terms of who it affects; youth and fitness are no guarantees of avoidance – in fact, perhaps even the opposite, as it is often those in a hurry who come down with it. The best way to avoid altitude sickness is to ascend as slowly as possible, and if trekking over high passes observe the time-honoured maxim: 'walk high, sleep low'. There is an excellent PDF booklet that can be found on the internet by looking up 'Medex travel at high altitude'.

All warm-blooded mammals can potentially carry **rabies** so it is wise to consider any bite, scratch or saliva into an open wound as a risk, even if the animal appears well. It is not possible to look at an animal and know whether it has rabies, as they often look quite well. The first thing to do is to thoroughly wash the wound with soap and running water for about 15 minutes. Apply an antiseptic afterwards if you have one and then get straight to medical help. If you have not had any pre-exposure vaccine before travel then you will need a preformed antibody called rabies immunoglobulin (RIG) (ideally human, but horse will do) and five doses of cell-derived vaccine (HCDV/verorab/PCEP) over 28 days. RIG is expensive and is often hard to come by, which might mean that you need to evacuate to a country that has the supply. If you have had three doses of pre-exposure vaccine over a minimum of 21 days before travel then you no longer need RIG and just require two further doses of vaccine three days apart. Rabies vaccine is ideally advised for everyone, but certainly for those handling animals, for long-term travellers and for those who are more than 24 hours from medical help.

HIV/AIDS Be aware of the risks of sexually transmitted infection – whether you sleep with fellow travellers or locals. The prevalence of HIV in Kyrgyzstan is about 0.25% of the population aged 15–49. About 80% of HIV infections in British heterosexuals are acquired abroad through unprotected sex and other risky behaviours. If you must indulge, use condoms or femidoms, which help to reduce the risk of transmission. If you notice any genital ulcers or discharge, get treatment promptly since these increase the risk of acquiring HIV. If you do have unprotected sex, visit a clinic as soon as possible; this should be within 24 hours, or no later than 72 hours, for post-exposure prophylaxis.

TRAVEL CLINICS AND HEALTH INFORMATION A full list of current travel clinic websites worldwide is available on www.istm.org. For other journey preparation information, consult www.nathnac.org/ds/map_world.aspx (UK) or http://wwwnc.

cdc.gov/travel/ (US). Information about various medications may be found on www.netdoctor.co.uk/travel. All advice found online should be used in conjunction with expert advice received prior to or during travel.

SAFETY

Note: The information below should be augmented by checking with the current travel advisory of your own foreign office. At the time of writing the British Foreign and Commonwealth Office (*www.fco.gov.uk*) was not advising against travel to Kyrgyzstan, nor were the US Department of State (*http://travel.state.gov/travel*), Canadian Department of Foreign Affairs (*www.voyage.gc.ca*), Australian Department of Foreign Affairs (*www.smarttraveller.gov.au*) and New Zealand Ministry of Foreign Affairs & Trade (*www.safetravel.govt.nz*), other than expressing that visitors should exercise caution.

THEFT A few simple precautions will ensure that a visit to Kyrgyzstan is a safe and happy one. The countryside is mostly very safe in terms of human menace, although inebriated locals can sometimes be a nuisance. Larger towns, especially Bishkek, are more of a threat and caution should be taken after dark (see page 93).

At night the streets of all Kyrgyz towns and villages are generally pitch dark with little – or nothing – in the way of street lighting and, putting the very real threat of tripping up over something to one side, there is always a low risk of mugging by locals whose resentment and coveting of the foreigner's wealth is further fuelled by strong drink. It should never be forgotten that, compared with Europe and North America, Kyrgyzstan is a very poor country, and that most Western visitors walk around with more cash in their pockets than most Kyrgyz could possibly earn in a year.

Alcohol often has a part to play in both aggravating resentment and giving Dutch courage to would-be attackers. Bishkek is the most problematic in this regard and taxis should be used after dark as there have been some nasty violent attacks over the past few years. Karakol, Osh and Naryn have occasional incidents, too, although far less commonly than in the capital.

As well as the slight threat of robbery with violence, opportunistic theft is always a possibility – not especially common, but enough to ensure you should be on your guard. Bustling markets and crowded *marshrutki* are ideal environments for thieves to operate in. Special care should also be taken at ATMs and when leaving exchange offices. Cash and credit cards should be kept well out of sight, and preferably split up into a number of separate caches.

ALCOHOL Alcohol undoubtedly poses a serious social problem throughout the central Asian region; a problem that first came with Russian colonial rule, was ignored and partly contained during the Soviet period, and has been exacerbated by poverty and a general lack of hope since independence. Remarkably, vodka is available more or less everywhere at rock-bottom prices, even where there is little in the way of food to buy.

Heartfelt Kyrgyz hospitality is a wonderful thing but in all-male company it can sometimes quickly turn into little more than a kamikaze drinking session. It is crucial that moderate imbibers realise there is no such thing as 'a small one', 'a quick one', or 'just one for the road'. An invitation to drink can be effectively the laying down of a gauntlet. The guest will be expected to keep up with the other drinkers and will find it difficult to detach himself from proceedings once a session is under way. It is considered very bad form to turn down further drinks once engaged in a boozing session and refusal may be seen as a grave insult to the host.

The best policy for those lacking livers of steel is to politely refuse in the first place, perhaps making something up on health reasons. This will not be popular but it sets the tone and will be respected. If you start drinking, then you will be expected to continue to the dregs of the bottle ... and then maybe another.

ROAD SAFETY Probably the greatest danger facing visitors is the poor condition of the roads which, coupled with eccentric, macho driving techniques and badly serviced vehicles, make road accidents sadly all too common. The best advice is to be a little circumspect in choosing a driver, checking that they are not drunk or intending to become so during the trip (but do not worry about the odd bottle of *kumys*, this is standard issue and it is not very strong). Selecting an older driver is often a good idea as they tend to be calmer than tearaway youths, and also because if they have survived a driving career into middle age then they must be doing something right. Often, of course, you will have no choice, being squeezed into a minibus at the last minute before departure. Seat belts are rarely used, apart from in urban areas where opportunistic roadside police may stop and fine drivers not wearing them. Taxi drivers will sometimes laugh if you try to use them, or even be offended that you do not trust their skills. Overall, the best advice is to avoid travel at night where possible and shun drunken drivers and obvious speed merchants.

POLICE Crooked police officers are not exactly a safety issue but they can occasionally create problems in their attempts to extract money by subterfuge or intimidation (see page 96 for more details and for potential trouble spots). Happily, this sort of incident is much less of a problem than it used to be. The golden rules are to be polite, friendly even, stand your ground and try not to become separated from those around you. Police identification should always be shown and a note should be made of their name and number. Just doing this is usually enough to put off most would-be extortionists. It is important to remember that police do have the right to ask for passports, which you must carry at all times, but they are not permitted to stop and search in normal circumstances, or to count your money themselves. A missing high denomination note following a police money count appears to be by far the most commonly reported type of incident. If, for some reason, a *shtraf* (fine) needs to be paid, insist on paying it at a bank and not directly to the policeman in question, and also insist on a receipt.

TERRORISM Within Kyrgyzstan, **the region west and south of Osh** used to be considered dangerous by the British Foreign and Commonwealth Office (FCO) because of drug trafficking and incursions by Islamist fighters who took foreign hostages in 1999 and 2000. At the time of writing the FCO no longer advises avoiding this region other than taking care when travelling here. It also continues to warn about potential border tensions along the Kyrgyz/Uzbek and Kyrgyz/Tajik frontiers.

EMERGENCY TELEPHONE NUMBERS
Fire ☏101
Police ☏102
Urgent emergency medical assistance ☏103

WOMEN TRAVELLERS

The outward face of women in the country – both Kyrgyz and Russian – is one of self-confidence, independence and even feistiness. Even if this is not really an accurate picture, women travellers face no particular dangers in Kyrgyzstan. Sexual harassment is thankfully rare but, even though Kyrgyzstan is far from being a strictly Islamic regime, it is still unwise to dress scantily and in a provocative manner, despite the many young Russian women in the cities who do just that (see also page 93).

TRAVELLERS WITH A DISABILITY

Apart from a few concessions in the capital, Kyrgyzstan has almost nothing in the way of facilities for travellers with disabilities. Exploring even Bishkek in a wheelchair would prove to be a challenge given the lack of ramps and poor condition of the pavements. On a more positive note, the majority of restaurants are ground-floor based, which is a slight advantage, and Bishkek's top hotels at least have ramps and reliable lifts. However, outside of the capital it would be unwise to expect any facilities whatsoever. For those with disabilities planning to visit Kyrgyzstan, hiring private transport and a guide through one of the agencies listed here is a virtual necessity.

LGBT TRAVELLERS

Sexual acts between persons of the same sex have been legal in Kyrgyzstan since 1998 but same-sex unions have no legal standing. Kyrgyzstan, although more tolerant than neighbouring Uzbekistan and Tajikistan where homosexuality is illegal, remains a conservative country and, while gay relationships may be tolerated, open displays of affection between those of the same sex are frowned upon and may provoke hostility. Despite recent changes in the law, homophobia is still commonplace and there have been some reports of blackmail of homosexuals by corrupt policemen. The north is generally more easygoing than the south, and Bishkek, where a small gay scene has developed with a couple of gay bars/clubs, is the most tolerant. An organisation called Labrys (*http://labrys.kg*), established in 2004, is dedicated to improving the lot of lesbians, bisexuals, gay men and transgender people in Kyrgyzstan. The age of consent in Kyrgyzstan is 16.

TRAVELLING WITH A FAMILY

Like most people throughout the world, central Asians love children and travelling to Kyrgyzstan with a young family in tow will definitely win points in terms of popularity with the locals. Having said that, there may be some problems concerning hygiene with very young children, and the sometimes rather limited food available might prove problematic with those young travellers who are fussy about what they eat. The typical home cooking of homestays, with plentiful fruit, jams and baked goods, is likely to be more popular than standard restaurant fare.

Independent travel in Kyrgyzstan can be hard work at times, with long, uncomfortable journeys that have few rest breaks. This type of travel is probably too onerous for the average child; hiring a car with a driver would be a much better bet, allowing regular breaks and toilet stops (although probably not toilets) and the opportunity to stop whenever something of interest is seen. Most children will naturally love some aspects of the country like its horses, plentiful wildlife and colourful markets, and the beaches of Issyk-Kul are also likely to be popular with most young travellers. On the other hand, few children will patiently spend hours examining Silk Road monuments or archaeological sites, and even fewer will be willing to spend long hours energetically hiking in the hills.

Many visitors come to Kyrgyzstan to enjoy outdoor pursuits, and they should ensure they bring all the necessary clothing, such as walking boots, thermal gear and waterproofs with them. These are available in Kyrgyzstan, mostly in Bishkek, but the choice is poor and the quality generally not of a high standard.

A tent is essential for independent trekkers; these may be hired along with sleeping bags and other camping equipment from some trekking agencies or CBT groups but, again, the standard is usually not very good. Cooking stoves, if brought, should be of the multi-fuel type, such as MSR or Primus, that run on liquid fuel like white gas, or the gas type that run on Kovea cartridges, as Campingaz stoves and their canisters are virtually unknown. It goes without saying that any cooking stoves to be carried on aircraft should be packed carefully, completely drained of fuel and thoroughly dried out. Stove fuel of any sort is most definitely not allowed on flights and so must be bought after arrival.

Any prescription drugs should be brought along, as well as a spare pair of glasses for spectacle wearers, and their optical prescription. Sunglasses are essential, especially if walking at altitude, as is suncream, which is not easy to obtain in Kyrgyzstan. A torch (flashlight) is vital for those midnight forays to the outhouse at village homestays and is extremely useful even in Bishkek, where street lights are few and far between.

Photographers will find slide film very hard to obtain and should bring an adequate supply; similarly, digital photographers should bring sufficient memory cards to keep them going and also make sure they have the appropriate adaptor (standard two-pin European) for their camera battery charger.

Any specialist or unusually sized batteries should be brought along and, although standard AA and AAA batteries for electronic devices are widely available, these tend to be cheap Chinese ones that last a very short time, so a supply of these is a good idea, too.

Adequate reading matter is important for those who like to have their nose in a book at night (sometimes there may not be much else to do). Literature in languages other than Russian or Kyrgyz is very hard to come across, even in Bishkek. Bringing along something that you can swap with fellow travellers is always a good idea. A Russian dictionary and/or phrase book is invaluable.

As with any travel off the beaten track, a small collection of various-sized plastic bags can prove useful to keep equipment dust-free, store dirty clothes and prevent food items from merging with other luggage items.

Most important of all is to bring enough money along – more than you think you will need – as, although Kyrgyzstan is an inexpensive country for visitors, there may be incidental expenses that may not have been budgeted for, such as tours, car hire, souvenirs, visas and flights. As ATM machines, although far more plentiful than they were a few years ago, are still absent in some areas, and bank transfers of funds tend to be slow and problematic, an emergency fund of a few high-denomination dollar or euro banknotes is a wise precaution.

The **electricity** supply is standard for all of Russia and the CIS with 220V, 50Hz and European two-prong plugs. Despite supplying hydro-electric power to most of the region, power cuts are not unknown. Bring a good torch and perhaps buy some candles and a lighter.

MAPS Detailed Russian 1:200,000 topographical maps of Kyrgyzstan are available in Bishkek at the GeoID map shop (see page 109), as are a number of political and physical maps of the whole country. For planning purposes, and to give an overview of the whole central Asian region, it is also a good idea to buy a regional map before travelling to central Asia.

The *Nelles 1:1,750,000 Central Asia* map is reasonable and marks some of the historical sites of interest to travellers, but it uses an eccentric Turkish phonetic spelling system – ie: Biškek, Oš – which is unknown in Kyrgyzstan. The *Freytag & Berndt 1:1,750,000 Central Asia: Road Map* is a good alternative, as is the newly published *ITMB 1:1,135,000 Turkmenistan, Tajikistan & Kyrgyzstan* travel map.

MONEY AND BANKING

CURRENCY Following independence from the Soviet Union in 1991, Kyrgyzstan was the first central Asian country to introduce its own currency, the **Kyrgyz som**, which replaced the Soviet rouble on 10 May 1993. The Kyrgyz som is relatively stable and at the time of writing was trading at a rate of around £1 sterling = 88som, US$1 = 53som. It is further divided into 100 *tiyin*, but these are no longer used in transactions.

Kyrgyz banknotes come in denominations of one, five, ten, 20, 50, 100, 200, 500, 1,000 and 5,000som, although notes under 20som are rarely seen and coins of one, three, five and ten som have largely replaced these. All of the banknotes feature prominent Kyrgyz historical figures on the front, and a variety of images depicting Kyrgyzstan's buildings, sights and folklore on the reverse.

EXCHANGING MONEY Kyrgyzstan remains primarily a **cash economy**, although credit cards are catching up quickly, especially in the capital. **ATM machines** are quite numerous now, particularly in Bishkek and the larger towns, and they can even be found in some larger villages. Most will issue both Kyrgyz som or US dollars and work with Visa. Machines that accept MasterCard and Maestro are much harder to find, especially outside Bishkek.

Credit cards can rarely be used to pay for transactions, apart from in smarter hotels and restaurants or top-notch gift shops. It is possible to arrange cash advances against a credit card at some banks in Bishkek, Jalal-Abad and Osh. Cash transfers may also be organised through Western Union, which operates through several banks in Bishkek. Visa is the most widely accepted credit/debit card by both businesses and ATM machines.

Many banks will change cash, but it is usually simpler and quicker to visit an **exchange booth** or *obmyen valyoot* (обмен валюты). There are usually a handful of these in most large towns, often near the central bazaar. Take care in counting the notes given to you and also be sure to tuck the money away securely before leaving the booth or office. If there are no exchange booths, there will nearly always be someone who is willing to change money if enquiries are made, although, like the exchange booths, they will normally insist on pristine banknotes. Exchange booths do not charge commission but make their profit from the small difference between the buying and selling price (which is nothing like as extortionate as it is in travel agencies and banks on every high street in the UK). There is usually very little difference, if any, between the rates offered by individual offices and so it is hardly worth shopping around.

It goes without saying that it is sensible to take an adequate supply of Kyrgyz money when venturing into areas of the country that are off the beaten track, which could be almost everywhere. Outside of the major centres, 1,000som notes can be hard to change – 5,000som is almost impossible – so try to carry a stash of smaller bills. Generally speaking, US dollars are by far the most popular currency, but euros can also be exchanged, as can pounds sterling at a few places. The currency of surrounding countries – Kazakh tenge, Uzbek som, Russian roubles – may also be bought and sold at exchange booths. The bazaar in Osh is probably the best place to get hold of Tajik som and Chinese yuan.

For the time being at least, it is best to bring along a mixture of cash and debit and credit cards. **Travellers' cheques** are very much a thing of the past these days and it is difficult to find banks that will change them, especially outside the capital. Changing cash, large-denomination notes – US$50 or US$100 – are preferred and they must be in excellent, if not pristine, condition. Smaller-denomination bills – US$20 or less – will attract a lower exchange rate, as will any banknotes in a less than perfect state. Tatty, torn or scribbled-on notes will be rejected out of hand. US dollar bills should be of the post-1995 series, as forgeries of earlier series have created suspicion of these. If buying US dollars from a bank or exchange office before travelling to Kyrgyzstan, be sure to insist on brand new, high-denomination bills, as a tatty US$10 note is virtually worthless. Unfortunately, the dollar bills issued by ATM machines in Kyrgyzstan sometimes fail to live up to the same high standards that the money exchange industry insists upon itself.

BUDGETING

Travelling in Kyrgyzstan is generally inexpensive and it is an extremely good value destination. Costs are far lower than in Kazakhstan, and considerably less than in neighbouring Uzbekistan and Tajikistan. In Bishkek, staying in a five-star hotel, going to nightclubs and eating in the city's best restaurants, it is possible to spend almost as much as one would in a city in Europe; however, few come to Kyrgyzstan just to do this. Throughout much of Kyrgyzstan it is perfectly possible to get by on an equivalent of US$25–30 a day, as homestay accommodation with full board is usually little more than US$15–20 and public transport is cheap. Even prices in Bishkek are quite reasonable and a daily budget of US$20–30 should be sufficient once accommodation has been paid for, as long as you do not pursue the extravagant lifestyle of an oligarch.

What tends to dent modest budgets the most are incidental expenses like renting a car and driver, hiring a guide, paying for the services of a tour agency and obtaining visas and permits. Even including these in the equation, Kyrgyzstan is still a good value destination that offers adventurous travel at a budget price. By far the major expense will be getting to Kyrgyzstan in the first place. Having invested all that money in travelling there it seems churlish to scrimp and save mere pennies after arrival. Of course, if you are visiting Kyrgyzstan as part of a prepaid organised tour you will just need a little pocket money and some cash to buy souvenirs.

GETTING AROUND

Getting around Kyrgyzstan is reasonably straightforward between the major centres – Bishkek, Karakol, Naryn, Jalal-Abad and Osh. Public transport tends to be a little erratic at times and some of the roads are in poor condition. Hiring a taxi for a couple or small group for long distances is a relatively cheap and fast way of getting about. Self-drive car hire is in its infancy but slowly becoming more popular (see page 71). Given Kyrgyzstan's pot-holed roads, its eccentric driving habits and a police force keen to extort fines from their motorised victims, car hire is not for everyone but it undoubtedly affords a great deal more flexibility and spontaneity than is ever possible by public transport. Flying may be a viable option for some north–south travel as it is markedly quicker and may be only a little more expensive than travelling by road.

BY BUS AND MINIBUS Battered old Russian buses run between Bishkek, Karakol and other destinations. They are slow, reasonably comfortable and cheap. A conductor collects the fares along the way and they tend to make frequent stops. Smaller snub-nosed buses run along other routes, mainly to village destinations.

Many long-distance bus services have been largely superseded by minibuses (*marshrutki*) running the same routes, which are considerably quicker and charge about 1½ times the bus fare. Minibuses tend to congregate outside bus stations and leave when full, usually with about 12–18 passengers plus the driver. Some *marshrutki* that travel relatively short distances along fixed routes, such as those along the shores of Lake Issyk-Kul, operate rather like a local bus service and do not wait to fill up before leaving, as they constantly pick up and drop off all along their route.

Fares are fixed and are either collected before setting off or somewhere along the way. A common practice is to pass money forward to the driver who then passes the change back. Tickets are rarely issued and there are no formal

SELF-DRIVE CAR HIRE IN KYRGYZSTAN   *Eric Straw*

In the summer of 2014, my brothers and I hired a car in Bishkek. With that vehicle, the second edition of this guide, a good map and the echoing remarks of our worried mother, we embarked on an extraordinary ten-day tour. Though more expensive than the alternatives and not without risk, we found hiring a vehicle well worth the price and chances of mishap. We were able to explore, hike, photograph and eat through more of Kyrgyzstan than otherwise possible.

Most roads in the country are either unpaved or last tended to by the Soviets, so prospective drivers should be comfortable with poor conditions. City driving can be chaotic. In Bishkek, vehicles generally obey stop lights, but traffic flow between lanes is a free-for-all. Outside the capital, traffic tapers off and lanes generally only exist in spirit. In towns, police stand outside their parked cars, waiting to pull you over via the frantic waving of an orange wand. Though we probably looked like ideal candidates for extortion, police never stopped us for legitimate or illegitimate reasons. Sticking to speed limits and erring on the slow side is best.

The innumerable livestock peppering the countryside, while charming, add a degree of danger to driving. Cows, goats, sheep and horses roam unhindered by fences. On several occasions, we waited patiently as herds hundreds strong moseyed across the road. Always give animals the right of way and avoid driving at night. Drunk or aggressive drivers can also pose problems; one afternoon, we watched a man swerve from shoulder to shoulder, forcing others off the road. Although frightening, our greatest driving-related adversity was changing a flat tyre in the rain. With a little local help, we prevailed and found a garage to repair the tyre in Karakol.

After a few days of adjustment, driving in Kyrgyzstan became a worthy adventure unto itself. Even while remaining vigilant for police, pot-holes, pedestrians, reckless drivers and wandering livestock, you can't help but savour the spectacular scenery just beyond your windshield. So roll with the punches, drive safely and enjoy this gorgeous country at your own pace.

We hired from Evi Auto Centre in Bishkek (*Lev Tolstoy 19;* \ *+996 312 352 000;* e *auto@evi.kg; www.evi.kg*). A US$1,000 deposit was required, along with a photocopy of a valid passport and driver's licence. Drivers need to be over 25 years old. Vehicles come equipped with GPS and spares. Prices start at $60 per day. The paperwork and payment will take about 20–40 minutes in all.

Practical Information GETTING AROUND

2

timetables, but long-distance services more commonly leave for their destination in the mornings and early afternoons, avoiding travel at night. Minibuses tend to have almost no proper luggage storage space behind the rear seat, but baggage will always be squeezed in somewhere with the minimum of fuss. Typical minibus fares are Bishkek–Cholpon-Ata, 250som; Bishkek–Karakol, 300som; Bishkek–Naryn 350som.

BY TAXI Kyrgyzstan's taxis will go almost anywhere if you pay them: a road surface of little more than loose rocks and sheep holds little fear for the average Kyrgyz Lada or Zhiguli driver. Fares are loosely negotiable, but are usually about twice the bus fare multiplied by four, the number of passenger seats. In many instances there is no bus or minibus service and so a taxi is sometimes the only option.

CYCLING IN KYRGYZSTAN

This is the transport of choice for an increasing number of visitors to Kyrgyzstan and, for those with the appropriate spirit of adventure, it is an excellent way to see the country. Roads are often in a poor condition so the bicycle needs to be of robust construction, preferably a mountain bike or tough touring bike. As well as pot-holed road surfaces, road signs are extremely rare and drivers are sometimes drunk and/or too fast. Nevertheless, the general attitude towards cyclists is said to be respectful and most reports of cycling tours in Kyrgyzstan are favourable.

Away from the built-up Bishkek–Balykchy section, and the north side of Lake Issyk-Kul, roads are mostly quiet with light traffic. Cycling at night is obviously a very bad idea. Opportunities abound for trailblazers willing to get off the beaten track but it is vital that full repair kit, spares, food, stove and tent are carried to be fully self-supporting.

Popular routes include cycling around Lake Issyk-Kul, especially along the quieter southern shore, and common circular itineraries include Bishkek–Kochkor–Chaek–Suusamyr–Bishkek; Bishkek–Talas–Jalal-Abad–Naryn–Bishkek; Bishkek–Karakol–Kochkor–Bishkek; and Bishkek–Talas–Tash-Kömür–Bishkek. These range from 650km to 1,600km in length and sections of them may be combined to offer more varied itineraries. Even more adventurous, off-road possibilities exist along various routes that cross the Terskey Ala-Too range to reach the Kichi Naryn Valley and Naryn town, or up along the Barskoon Valley and east towards Ak-Shyrak, although this route probably requires a border permit and military permission.

Long-distance buses such as Bishkek–Karakol or Osh–Kashgar will generally take bicycles, but *marshrutki* and taxis usually will not have room unless they have a roof rack. The larger planes flying between Bishkek and Osh (ie: an Antonov AN-24, not a Yak-40) can also transport bicycles.

Nearly all of the spare parts found in Kyrgyzstan tend to be of Chinese manufacture but there is a specialist bike shop in Bishkek run by Oleg Yuganov: Bike Master (*Serova 14a;* \ *0312 670 974*). The Elite Sport bicycle shop (*Toktogul 170;* \ *0312 312 971;* e *giant-bicycles@mail.ru; www.giant-bicycles.in.kg*) also sells and repairs bicycles.

The best maps of the country for cyclists and hikers are the 1:200,000 Russian maps that are available at the GeoID map shop at Kievskaya 107 (\ *0312 212 296*) in Bishkek.

If there is a CBT network in the town or village they usually have drivers who are familiar with the funny ways of the tourist and knowledgeable about the sort of places that they wish to go. Taxis may be hired for less than the CBT rate in the bazaar, although this is very dependent on the language and negotiation skills of the client, as well as how desperate the driver is to find a fare.

More popular routes often have **share taxis** running the same routes as the minibuses and buses. They are effectively the same as ordinary taxis except they run the same route regularly and aim to fill the car with four passengers who all pay the same share. Like minibuses, they leave when full, but will leave earlier with less than a full complement of passengers if those present agree to pay for the empty seat(s) between them. Other than flying, share taxis are the best way to travel between Osh and Jalal-Abad and Bishkek. They tend to cost less heading south than they do returning to Bishkek. Typical share taxi fares are Bishkek–Osh, 800–1,000som; Osh–Bishkek, 1,200som.

BY TRAIN Kyrgyzstan's train system is very sparse and, apart from the possibility of arriving on the international service from Moscow via Kazakhstan, it is unlikely you will see a train, let alone use one. The only passenger service to speak of is the seasonal Bishkek–Balykchy service that takes up to seven hours to reach somewhere that most people do not wish to go. The equivalent bus or minibus takes just two hours.

BY AIR Bishkek has a regular service with Osh and there are usually several planes a day between the two cities. With promotional fares sometimes as low as US$35, this can be a worthwhile alternative to a long, tiring share taxi ride between the north and south of the country.

Other domestic services include a daily service to Jalal-Abad and flights two or three times a week to Batken. The domestic baggage weight limit is 15 kilos per passenger; anything over this will cost an additional US$0.20 per kilo.

ACCOMMODATION

Hotels in Kyrgyzstan range from luxurious to basic, although the majority fall into the mid-range category. For accommodation codes, see the inside front cover. As the capital and largest city, Bishkek has the largest number and the widest range of options, having the country's only five-star hotels, along with a handful of large, comfortable four-star hotels that have mostly been built with foreign funding. These cost more or less the same as would be paid in a Western city.

A few Soviet-era hotels from before independence have survived and these still tend to be run on much the same lines as they were during the heyday of the USSR, giving a taste of the Soviet period that is nostalgic for some. Most large towns have at least one example of this sort of place and, depending on the alternatives available, they are at least serviceable and can sometimes represent reasonable value for money. Typically, they cost anything between US$15 and US$30 for a double room.

In a few places a dual- or even triple-pricing policy applies in which foreigners pay twice as much as CIS passport holders, who in turn pay double that of a Kyrgyz citizen. It goes without saying that such places usually represent poor value. Some of the older state-run hotels have since been taken into private ownership and renovated, although sometimes the subsequent increase in room prices is not matched by an appreciable improvement in quality.

As well as Soviet-era hotels there are also health resorts and **sanatoriums** from the same period, particularly on the north shore of Lake Issyk-Kul, which offer residential packages that combine health treatments with full board and the option of a variety of vacation leisure pursuits. It is usually possible just to book a room and meals at these places but they are far more used to catering for the tastes of CIS clients than those of Westerners. A more basic version of these resorts are *turbaza*, simple vacation camps that house guests in basic wooden huts and that are usually found in mountain valleys such as Ala-Archa or resorts like Arslanbob.

In recent years a number of small, purpose-built **boutique-style hotels** have been built with foreign visitors in mind. These tend to be in the middle price range of US$60–90 for a double room and are found mostly in Bishkek, although there are examples of these in Karakol, Naryn, Osh and Jalal-Abad, too.

Organised **yurt camps** are another recent innovation, which are usually tucked away at beautiful, but reasonably accessible, *jailoos* and run by Bishkek tour companies who house their tour clients there as part of a trek. These are highly popular as they offer visitors the opportunity to stay in a traditional nomadic shelter without compromising comfort too much, as the best yurt camps provide a number of distinctly nontraditional features like hot showers, indoor toilets and Western food. Full board at a yurt camp usually costs in the order of US$20–25 a day.

More authentically, it is usually possible to stay in genuine **yurts** just by turning up at a *jailoo* in the summer months; indeed, some families erect an extra yurt for the use of guests. These usually lack any proper washing facilities and normally just have a pit toilet. The meals provided are often very good although, understandably, they tend to involve a high proportion of dairy produce. The price is usually negotiable but is in the region of 700som (US$14) per person including meals.

The most revolutionary trend in Kyrgyz tourism in recent years, especially as far as independent travellers are concerned, has been the setting up of a comprehensive **homestay** network through the **Community Based Tourism** (CBT) initiative. There are also homestays in Kyrgyzstan that are not affiliated to CBT or its sister network of Shepherd's Life, but those that do belong are vetted by local and national representatives for quality and their suitability for Western tourists.

Hotel bills are usually paid in Kyrgyz som cash in the more basic establishments. Many mid-range and all top-range hotels will also accept US dollars cash and credit or debit cards.

CBT homestays are found in many towns and villages throughout Kyrgyzstan, especially in those places of interest to tourists such as Kochkor, Karakol and Arslanbob. The only place they do not exist is in Bishkek, where there are plenty of other alternatives. Homestays are extremely variable and can range from a rural homestead with wandering cows and clucking chickens to a Soviet-era city apartment. Similarly, toilet facilities may be anything from a plush bathroom to an outhouse at the bottom of the garden. Food is normally available and the host usually makes use of home-grown ingredients to create delicious meals.

Prices are very reasonable and are set according to CBT criteria, which award a property a one-, two- or three-edelweiss rating based on facilities and quality. Most homestays fall into the one-edelweiss category. The beauty of staying in these, apart from their homeliness and quality food, is the experience of seeing everyday Kyrgyz (or Russian, or Uzbek) family life, and the knowledge that your money is going directly to the family and local community (once the co-ordinator's 10% commission has been taken off) rather than to a faceless multi-national hotel

THE KYRGYZ HOMESTAY EXPERIENCE

Lake Issyk-Kul in late summer: the crowds of holidaying Kazakhs at Cholpon-Ata on the north shore are starting to head back to Almaty; the Western travellers who have come to Karakol to trek in the valleys to the south are starting to thin out, too. This is a time of abundance, when apricots bend branches as they ripen and fall to the floor in every garden orchard. It is the jam-making season and nowhere does the jam taste better than in Kyrgyzstan's family-run homestays, especially those close to the shores of Lake Issyk-Kul.

Arriving at the homestay for the first time, hospitality dictates that refreshment is provided as you get to know your hosts and they try their best to make something of you. Tea is brewed and a large pot is placed centre stage on the table. Then saucers of boiled sweets and bowls of fruit are brought – apples, grapes, plums, apricots, pomegranates – whatever has been grown in the small orchard outside. Then bread is produced, perhaps more than one sort: crisp, usually fresh, often homemade, always delicious. Finally the *coup de grâce*, the jam ... or rather the jams: strawberry, apricot, plum and, best of all, wild blackcurrant. The flavour is intense, dark and delicious; you have arrived in jam heaven.

Full of tea, bread, jam and fruit, you are asked by your landlady what you would like to eat for dinner. The afternoon tea has just been the hors d'oeuvres, a ritual act of hospitality to welcome the foreign guest. You are shown to your accommodation, inevitably a room full of cushions, hand-embroidered throws and spare bedding, with carpets on the walls and Russian literature and children's school books in the bookcase. The room is cosy, homely and full of the dreams of the children who used to sleep in it. You lie down for a minute, close your eyes and, replete with fine bread and jam of an almost narcotic quality, nod off briefly and add your own reverie to the dream-pool.

company that really does not need it. Having said that, it is easy to forget that, even given the sometimes humble surroundings of a village homestay, the family that you are staying with is relatively well-to-do, at least in local terms.

CBT HOMESTAY ACCOMMODATION CHARGES Accommodation and meal prices vary between provinces, with the Naryn region being the cheapest and Jalal-Abad the most expensive.

B&B 1 edelweiss 400–500som
B&B 2 edelweiss 450–600som
B&B 3 edelweiss 550–700som

B&B in a yurt 500–600som
Lunch or dinner in a homestay 200–300som

EATING AND DRINKING

Food in Kyrgyzstan tends to fall into two main categories – Kyrgyz and Russian – although sometimes what is on offer is more of a hybrid of the two. For restaurant price codes, see the inside front cover. Staying in homestays, the food prepared by the hostess is always plentiful, usually very tasty and generally there is little point in looking to eat elsewhere. Away from the larger urban centres, the dining-out options are usually rather limited. Bishkek has a wide range of smart restaurants

2

that sell Turkish, Italian, American, Chinese, Indian, Korean and Japanese food, in addition to the standard fare. Outside of Bishkek, the larger towns have a few upmarket restaurants between them, but generally food is sold at simple cafés, traditional *chaikhanas* or Russian-style canteens, *stolovaya*.

Opening times are indicated in the text where known but generally places to eat in Kyrgyzstan tend to be open whenever you are likely to need them – from mid to late morning until at least mid-evening. As a rule they do not close at all in late afternoon as both lunch and dinner are quite fluid concepts and people tend to eat when they are hungry rather than at strict mealtimes.

Kyrgyz cooking is very meat-based and that meat is nearly always mutton, but sometimes beef is used, particularly for *shashlyk*. Chicken rarely finds its way into Kyrgyz cookery and when it does the quality is not usually very good. Horse meat is highly thought of and horse meat sausages, *chuchuk*, are a popular accompaniment to vodka sessions. As Muslims, Kyrgyz, Uzbeks and Dungans do not eat pork, but it can be found at some Chinese and Russian restaurants. Fish is uncommon, apart from the smoked fish that is sold by the roadside near Lake Issyk-Kul.

Kyrgyz dishes that can be found more or less everywhere are *shorpo*, a mutton stew that always comes with a big chunk of bone with fatty meat attached; *laghman*, noodles with mutton and a spicy sauce; and *manti*, steamed mutton dumplings. *Shashlyk*, the central Asian kebab of skewer-grilled mutton pieces, can be found almost anywhere; just look for the grill-man at the front of the café, as the cooking is always done outside. *Plov* is made from a simple mixture of rice, mutton, carrots and onions all cooked together in a big pot, which can be delicious when it is well made. It is actually an Uzbek dish but it can be found throughout the country, especially in the south.

The Kyrgyz national dish of *beshbarmak* is more of a home-cooked festival food than a restaurant item but some restaurants offer it. The ultimate Kyrgyz snack food is *samsa*, which are like Indian samosas but instead of containing spicy vegetables they are filled with mutton, onions and gravy. *Samsi* are generally sold directly from small bakeries, especially in the mornings and at lunchtime, and are a good takeaway snack or quick lunch. They can be very fatty and are best when hot and fresh. For more on traditional Kyrgyz food see page 41.

Popular **Russian dishes** include *pirogi*, fried ravioli-like pastry packets, and *pelmeni*, small ravioli served in a broth. *Blini* are pancakes, either sweet or savoury, that, if you are lucky, your homestay hostess might prepare for breakfast. Most Russian menus usually involve several different types of salad that utilise copious quantities of mayonnaise. One excellent and surprisingly delicious salad combination is grated beetroot and diced walnuts.

In addition to Kyrgyz and Russian food, **Dungan dishes** are also sometimes found in the north, especially in the Chui Valley, the Dungan stronghold. Dungan food is rather like Chinese food, but spicier. *Ganfan*, made of rice and meat, is probably the most popular Dungan dish and often sold at markets, as is *ashlyanfu*, a spicy, vinegary cold noodle dish that is especially popular in Karakol.

Vegetarians will have a little more luck finding something to eat in Russian restaurants than in their meat-centred Kyrgyz counterparts, but overall it is fairly difficult to find much in the way of purely vegetarian dishes. Fortunately, local markets always have a good selection of fruit, vegetables, cheeses and tinned goods. Some homestay hosts are able to rustle up vegetarian dishes, given adequate warning.

Bread, the staple carbohydrate in the area, is usually in the form of *lepyoshka*, a Russian flat unleavened loaf, or otherwise *nan*, the Kyrgyz equivalent. Both are delicious when fresh and far superior to the sliced, white variety found in supermarkets.

By far the most popular hot drink is **tea**, either green, which is preferred by most Kyrgyz, or black, the Russian favourite. Placing an order for food in a restaurant, it will more or less be assumed that you wish to order tea as well, even if you have already ordered beers or soft drinks. Kyrgyz going out to eat think nothing of ordering beer, vodka and tea all at the same time. Tea is invariably cheap at 10som or less for a pot, and drinking plenty of it is the best and safest way to ensure hydration where the water supply is questionable. Coffee, where it is found, is instant and quite horrible, the only exception being the handful of Bishkek cafés and restaurants that have espresso machines.

Beer is widely available and quite good, the commonest brand being Russian Baltika, which is numbered according to its strength – Baltika 0 is non-alcoholic (hard to find!), Baltika 3 is moderately low gravity, Baltika 5 is reasonably strong, Baltika 7 is very strong and Baltika 9 is like rocket fuel. Another Russian beer that is widely available is Sibirskaya Korona, and there are decent Kyrgyz brands such as Arpa and Akademiya that are served on draught. Kyrgyz bottled beers tend to be cheaper than Russian brands, although sometimes weaker and less reliable in flavour. The Steinbrau beers of Bishkek that are produced by an ethnic German brewery of the same name are excellent.

Other popular drinks are vodka (*arak*) and *kumys*, although the latter is not generally sold in cafés, as it is seen more as a homemade drink of the *jailoos*; it is, however, commonly sold at the roadside from yurts, especially in early summer. *Bozo* is a slightly alcoholic drink, made from fermented millet wheat, and Shoro is a well-known proprietary brand of *maksym*, a drink made from wheat. Kyrgyz wine is best avoided.

PUBLIC HOLIDAYS AND FESTIVALS

FIXED HOLIDAYS

1 January	New Year's Day
7 January	Orthodox Christmas Day
14 January	Orthodox New Year
23 February	Army Day
8 March	International Women's Day
21 March	Nooruz
24 March	Anniversary of the March 2004 Revolution Day
1 May	Labour Day
5 May	Constitution Day
9 May	Victory Day
31 August	Kyrgyz Independence Day
7 November	October Revolution Day

It is likely that October Revolution Day will be abandoned as an official public holiday in the near future. Other important days in the year that are not officially holidays are 1 September, **First Bell**, the first day of the new school year in which children dress up in their best clothes to go to school. **Teachers' Day** follows on the first Sunday in October.

Nooruz (Navrus), which takes place on 21 March, is probably the most important of the traditional holidays in Kyrgyzstan. The festival, which dates back to Zoroastrian times and is celebrated throughout central Asia, is a syncretic mix of Zoroastrian, Islamic and old shamanistic practices that celebrate the spring equinox. Although pagan in origin, Nooruz has been adopted by Islam in the region

2

and is even celebrated with great enthusiasm in religiously conservative Iran. Since independence, Kyrgyzstan and the other central Asian republics have reclaimed Nooruz as a national celebration after it had been officially discouraged, and even banned for a short while, during the Soviet period.

At Nooruz, a special meal that symbolises spring is prepared that includes seven items all beginning with a 'sh' sound: *sharob, shir, sheker, sharbat, shirinliklar, sham* and *shona* (wine, milk, sugar, sherbet, sweets, a candle and a fresh bud). In addition to this, *sumalak*, a special dish made from sprouted wheat, is served to women only, while men have their own special dish, *halim*, a sort of meaty porridge. *Archa* (juniper) twigs are burned for good luck, friends are visited, debts are traditionally paid off and the whole region celebrates with music, dancing and traditional games.

MOVEABLE MUSLIM RELIGIOUS HOLIDAYS
Kurban Ait (Feast of the Sacrifice) (*23 September 2015, 11 September 2016, 1 September 2017*) Known as Eid al-Ahda elsewhere, Kurban Ait takes place nine weeks after the end of Ramadan and is a signal for the beginning of the *hajj* season, the pilgrimage to Mecca (although few Kyrgyz actually do this). It is traditional to slaughter a sheep at this time if you can afford to.

Orozo Ait (End of Ramadan) (*17 July 2015, 5 July 2016, 25 June 2017*) Otherwise known as Eid al-Fitr in Arabic, Orozo Ait is the celebration that follows the end of Ramadan, in which a large meal is shared by families and friends, gifts of new clothes are given to family members and alms are given to the poor. Ramadan is not rigorously observed by the Kyrgyz but it is taken more seriously by Kyrgyzstan's more orthodox Uzbek population.

SHOPPING

Bishkek has markets, department stores, supermarkets, souvenir emporia and a range of specialist shops. These tend to follow office hours and are open between 09.00 and 18.00, often later, and some of them close for lunch between 13.00 and 14.00. Elsewhere in the country, particularly in the villages, there are few formal shops other than the odd village store; most goods are either bought at weekly or daily outdoor markets or at small kiosks that sell sweets, cigarettes, stationery and alcohol. Many people, especially old women, supplement their meagre incomes by selling a few things from a pavement pitch: pens, cigarettes, soft drinks, sunflower seeds and so on.

The bazaar is always the best place to purchase food items such as cheese, fruit and vegetables, as this is where the best produce will normally be found. Customers are often invited to taste the goods on offer and a little good-natured bartering is perfectly acceptable. Most town bazaars are open every day, although there is usually one day in the week when they are at their busiest. Smaller villages may have just a weekly market, although there may be a few stalls that are open every day.

SOUVENIRS Bishkek has by far the widest range of places selling souvenirs, although traditional crafts like *shyrdaks* may also be bought in the provinces in places like Naryn, Kochkor, Tamchy and Bokonbaevo, where there may be both better quality and lower prices on offer, because they are being sold direct from the manufacturer.

Shyrdaks are the most popular souvenirs bought by Western visitors, along with unstitched *ala-kiyiz*, but most souvenir shops usually have a range of other traditional goods on sale that include items like felt slippers, miniature yurts, ceramics, hand embroidery, *kurak* patchwork, wooden objects, leather items and musical instruments like *komuz* or *temir komuz* (see also page 46).

The exportation of antiques (which here means more than 30 years old) requires a special **export certificate** that can be time-consuming to obtain. Many of the Bishkek tour agencies are able to provide the necessary paperwork given reasonable notice. Some of the more upmarket souvenir showrooms will automatically provide the certificate and include the cost of it in the price.

TREKKING EQUIPMENT It is impossible to find Campingaz canisters in Kyrgyzstan and you will not be allowed to bring them with you on the plane. Korean-made Kovea screw-type gas canisters are available for US$5–6 and cost about 50som to refill. These may be found at the **Red Fox outdoor shop** (591 755; *www.redfox. ru*) in Bishkek, which is at Sovetskaya 65, near the junction with Kulatov, south of the railway station, in the same building as Ak-Sai Travel. Red Fox also stocks reasonable quality mountain bikes, a range of outdoor clothing, and trekking and climbing equipment. A safer bet for stoves is probably to take a multi-fuel type that runs on 'white gas', which will work using the lighter fuel (*benzin dlia zazhigalok*) sold in general stores in 0.5-litre plastic bottles.

Other outdoor shops in Bishkek include: **Mountain Project** (317 644; *www. mountainpro.kg*) at Toktogul 216/3, which has a good range of alpine, skiing and trekking equipment, mountain bikes and tents, and **Gergert Sport** (541 611) at Gorky 119, which has mountain bikes, skiing equipment and outdoor clothing.

ARTS AND ENTERTAINMENT

Bishkek has its nightclubs, cinemas, theatres and bars, but outside the capital there is little in the way of entertainment, apart from in larger towns that have cinemas showing films badly dubbed into Russian. Bishkek has at least one cinema that shows films in their original foreign language, although all theatrical performances are in either Russian or Kyrgyz. There are occasional classical music concerts and ballet performances in the city, especially in the winter months.

Throughout the more rural regions in summer, a number of traditional festivals are staged that celebrate typical Kyrgyz pursuits, such as horse games, eagle-hunting, dancing and Manas recitation. Although these may have the slightly artificial feel that comes from having been staged for the benefit of tourists, they are well worth attending for a first-hand experience of traditional games like *ulak tartysh* and *kyz-kumay*. The *chabana* 'cowboy' festivals held in late summer are an altogether more authentic experience if you manage to come across one, although they are harder to pin down in terms of time and place.

PHOTOGRAPHY

Kyrgyzstan is, as the cliché goes, a photographer's dream. With gorgeous scenery and striking-looking people, there is plenty to photograph throughout the country. Most people do not mind having their photograph taken but it is polite to ask first. Be a little cautious about snapping anything that might be considered to be of military importance – railway stations, industrial plants, border posts and airports – but generally speaking there are very few restrictions.

As well as sufficient batteries and memory cards, make sure you have an adaptor for the battery charger, a cleaning brush and a plastic bag to put the camera in when conditions get dusty. Some internet cafés may be able to write digital files on to disk but it is best to ensure you have sufficient flash cards or space on a portable memory device to cover your visit. Dedicated slide photographers should be aware that professional quality slide film is almost impossible to find, even in Bishkek.

MEDIA AND COMMUNICATIONS

MEDIA

Newspapers and magazines The main English-language newspaper in the country is the twice-weekly Bishkek-based *Times of Central Asia* (*www.times.kg*), which covers stories from all over the region and is available from newsstands in the capital. Another, more parochial, English-language weekly newspaper is the *Bishkek Observer*, which has both a local and international edition.

Spektator magazine (*www.thespektator.co.uk*) is a sporadically published online guide that started in 2008 and has plenty of Bishkek listings and features on the rest of the country.

Foreign English-language newspapers like *The Times* and *The Washington Post* can sometimes be found at newsstands and upmarket hotels in Bishkek but they tend to be at least two days old.

National newspapers include *Vecherniy Bishkek*, a privately owned Russian-language daily; *Slovo Kyrgyzstana*, a government-owned Russian-language paper that is published biweekly; *Kyrgyz Tuusu*, the oldest Kyrgyz-language newspaper, founded in 1924; *Agym*, a biweekly Kyrgyz-language newspaper, and *Respublika*, a privately owned Kyrgyz-language daily.

Television and radio The state-run Kyrgyz National TV and Radio Broadcasting Corporation (KTR) has two networks in Kyrgyz and Russian. There are a few private channels like Piramida and NTS in Bishkek, Ecological Youth in the Issyk-Kul region and Osh TV in Osh. Bishkek has cable TV, which offers packages that feature a large number of foreign stations like BBC World, Fox, CBS and Al Jazeera.

Internet news and resources

Akipress news agency www.akipress.com
Central Asia Caucasus Analyst www.cacianalyst.org
Eurasianet www.eurasianet.org
Internews http://internews.kg
Kabar news agency http://en.kabar.kg. Official news service.
News agency 24 www.24.kg

Institute for War & Peace Reporting www.iwpr.net
Radio Free Europe/Radio Liberty www.rferl.org
Registan News www.registan.net. News from across the central Asian region.
Times of Central Asia www.times.kg. The web version of the newspaper.

TELEPHONES Local calls within the city are free if made from a private phone, but hotels usually make a small charge for these and invariably charge way over the odds for long-distance or international calls.

To dial an international number the country code is preceded by 00; for an internal long-distance intercity call, 0 is dialled before the area code. Some phone booths survive in Bishkek that take tokens (*zhetoni*) bought from kiosks, although these may only be used for local calls (put in the token when the call is answered). More commonly public telephones use prepaid cards, which can also be bought from kiosks. Card phones can be used for both local and long-distance calls.

International calls are best made at Kyrgyz Telecom offices and the call prepaid at the counter before a booth is allocated. Change is given for time not used, or a complete refund if there is no answer. Some older exchanges require that you dial 3 when your call is answered in order to be able to talk.

Mobile phones Most people make use of mobile phones these days. The main providers are **Beeline** (m *(0775) 580 611*) and **MegaCom** (m *(0555) 500 000*). Both operate on the GSM system, so you may be able to use a roaming service and your own number.

See page 113 for details on buying a local SIM card.

POSTAL SERVICES The Kyrgyz postal service is slow but reasonably reliable. Postcards will usually get to their destination quicker if you post them once you have flown home. Letters and parcels home should have the destination country written at the top in Cyrillic *before* the rest of the address ie: АНГЛИЯ for the UK (*Anglia* = England = UK) or США for the USA. Parcels may be posted to international destinations from any main post office but will need to be left open to allow for customs inspection. For more certainty, and at correspondingly greater cost, important express mail may be sent from either Bishkek or Osh using the services of DHL or Federal Express.

INTERNET Most large towns have internet cafés. The quality of the service varies enormously from fast and efficient to painfully slow and erratic. Charges are usually around 40som per hour. Few internet cafés have facilities for writing CDs. Many mid-range hotels and the more upmarket cafés and restaurants offer free Wi-Fi, especially in Bishkek.

BUSINESS

In 2014, Kyrgyzstan ranked 68th in the World Bank's Ease of Doing Business index, just below Italy and Ghana but above Turkey, Greece and Romania. This was up two places from the previous year but still 18 places above its immediate neighbour Kazakhstan (in contrast, its other neighbour Uzbekistan languished at 146th place, just above Nigeria).

The country undoubtedly abounds with investment potential but for those used to doing business in the West things are done rather differently here. Kyrgyzstan is probably no worse than the rest of the CIS, perhaps a little better, but successful business ventures invariably involve a certain amount of palm-greasing that can range from the blatant to the virtually invisible. As elsewhere in the region, where newly founded republics are making the difficult transition from communism to capitalism, low-level corruption is a fact of life. It goes without saying that a trustworthy local business contact or contacts is vital in order to help smooth the way through the troubled waters of the local business world.

Whatever the pitfalls, the Kyrgyz government is keen to attract investors and overseas partners to modernise its industry and bring in new technology, and it is especially interested in investment in mining, industry, petroleum, hydro-electricity and agriculture. To encourage this, it has introduced a number of recent laws to encourage and protect foreign investors, in addition to some significant tax breaks.

To be eligible to invest in Kyrgyzstan, foreigners have to be registered with the Ministry of Economy and Finance. Applications to set up in Kyrgyzstan should be sent first to the State Technical Committee for Foreign Investments and Economic Assistance (contact details below).

State Committee for Foreign Investments &
Economic Assistance (GOSKOMINVEST) Room
210, Erkindik 58A, 720874 Bishkek; ☎ (312) 223
293; f (312) 220 363; ⊕ 09.00–17.00 Mon–Fri,
09.00–13.00 Sat

Kyrgyz Chamber of Commerce & Industry,
Foreign Affairs Department Kievskaya 107,
720001 Bishkek; ☎ (312) 210 565; e cci-kr@imfiko.
bishkek.su

CULTURAL ETIQUETTE

Kyrgyz are, for the most part, cheerful, highly hospitable people with a genuine interest in foreigners. In the villages and *jailoos* the tradition of hospitality is so strong that unexpected guests are still honoured and seen as a gift from God. An increase in the number of tourists over the past few years has taken the edge off this a little, as locals, understandably, are starting to view tourism as a viable way of supplementing their income; even so, foreign visitors are still courteously welcomed and are rarely seen as being little more than cash cows.

Having said this, it should not be forgotten that economic collapse and severe poverty since independence has engendered an atmosphere of resentment in some quarters, especially in Bishkek, where some foreign nationals are seen to be so patently overpaid and culturally insensitive that their lavish lifestyle and occasional boorish behaviour give some Kyrgyz the impression that all foreigners are of the same stripe. To try and counter this unfortunate image it is important to avoid flashing money about and to not act in a way that might be considered ostentatious, superior or immodest.

Kyrgyz society is relatively conservative, although far from hard-line Islam. Dress should be reasonably modest, with nothing too revealing, especially for women, and skimpy tops, shorts, miniskirts and skin-tight trousers should not be worn. Headscarves for foreign women are not necessary in purely cultural terms but they are useful on occasions, and provide a useful barrier against sun and dust.

If invited to a Kyrgyz home or a yurt, a small gift is appreciated. This does not have to be anything extravagant, just a little fruit or some sort of snack, or something for the children of the family. Family life is all-important and small gifts that say something of your own home life will be highly valued, such as family photographs or postcards of your home town.

As a foreign guest one is placed on a pedestal: honoured, but under close scrutiny at the same time. Therefore, it is important to acquit oneself well. A little of the language goes a long way, especially a few greetings and pleasantries in Kyrgyz, as does adopting the charming Kyrgyz gestures of putting the right hand on the heart after shaking hands and the *omin* face-washing gesture at the end of a meal.

Handshakes always take place between men, not between men and women, and it is considered unlucky to shake hands across a threshold. Shoes should always be removed on entry to a house or a yurt.

At any meal, bread is treated respectfully; it is never put on the floor, placed upside down or casually thrown away. If offered to a guest, bread should never be refused, even if it is just a matter of taking a little to eat. As elsewhere in the Muslim world, food is eaten and passed around with the right hand only, although there does not seem to be anything wrong with using the left hand for a bit of stabilisation when tearing bread into pieces.

Drinks – tea, vodka or anything else – do not have to be drained to the bottom of the glass; to do so is to invite a refill. It is quite acceptable to take just a sip, although with vodka there is usually much encouragement to drink it all down. To moderate intake, consider just drinking a third or half; this will, of course, be replenished, but at the end of the night it means a better outcome than having knocked back a dozen full glasses. As mentioned on page 65, once drinking has got under way it is usually impossible to make a polite withdrawal, so make an early decision on whether to participate or abstain.

TRAVELLING POSITIVELY

Kyrgyzstan is a poor country in transition, with a range of serious economic problems that are not going to improve overnight, despite a large number of NGOs working in the country. Much of the poverty is quite visible, particularly in the case of elderly Russians whose grown-up children have left for Russia, leaving them more or less abandoned on impossibly small state pensions. Many of these proud old people are forced into begging, hawking tissues and cigarettes or selling their few remaining possessions to make ends meet. Giving them a few notes, or buying something from them, is a drop in the ocean but at least it helps a little.

The elderly are not the only ones who suffer: wages are low, unemployment is high, and more than half the population lives below the poverty line.

The following NGOs are well established and highly regarded.

Helvetas House 65, 7 Liniya, Bishkek 720044; +996 312 214 572, 214 573, 214 574; e program@helvetas.kg; www.helvetas.kg. Helvetas is a Swiss NGO with long-established links in Kyrgyzstan, having supported agricultural & water resources programmes, the instigation of the CBT network & various co-operatives such as Altyn Kol. Donations may be made through their Swiss website at www.helvetas.ch. The contact details for information on their Kyrgyzstan projects are on the Helvetas Kyrgyzstan website at www.kyrgyzstan.helvetas.org.

Mercy Corps +44 131 662 5160; www.mercycorps.org.uk. A long-established NGO working in Kyrgyzstan, Mercy Corps is a Scottish-based charity that provides microloans & business advice for rural families to set up small businesses. Mercy Corps has worked in Kyrgyzstan since 1994 & was one of the first NGOs to work in the new republic. Donations can be sent to Mercy Corps, 40 Sciennes, Edinburgh EH9 1NJ, UK, or they can be made online at www.mercycorps.org.uk.

For those interested in sponsoring other good causes that are trying to improve people's lives in Kyrgyzstan, **Good Cause Kyrgyzstan** (*http://gk.kg/en*), administered by the Celestial Mountains Tour Company, lists a number of worthy projects and organisations on its website. These include two SOS Children's Villages in Bishkek and Cholpon-Ata (*www.soskyrgyzstan.kg*), the Children of the Tien Shan project that is helping to rehabilitate Balykchy's street children, and Health Prom (*www.healthprom.org*), a health support and social care programme focused on reducing maternal and infant mortality and disability. In addition to these worthy ventures, there are also projects that help people with disabilities as well as orphanages in Karakol and Krasnaya Rechka, and a boarding school for visually impaired children in Bishkek.

As well as supporting charities which work in Kyrgyzstan, another obvious way of 'giving something back' is to purchase hand-crafted souvenirs from a women's craft co-operative, such as Altyn Oymok (Golden Thimble) in Bokonbaevo or Altyn Kol (Golden Hands) in Kochkor, rather than from a souvenir shop. Similarly, using the services of Community Based Tourism guarantees that most of the money goes directly into the local economy.

Part Two

THE GUIDE

3

Bishkek

Telephone code: 0312

One story relates that Kyrgyzstan's capital, Bishkek (Бишкек), takes its name from the plunger of the wooden churn (*bishkek*) used to make *kumys*, the popular Kyrgyz tipple that is conjured from fermented mare's milk. This is far from certain, however, as there are several plausible alternatives: another possible derivation might be from *besh kek*, which translates literally as 'five chiefs', or even *besh bik*, which is Kazakh for 'five peaks'; or the name may even have a more ancient etymology and derive from *pishagakh*, an ancient Sogdian term meaning 'place beneath the mountains'.

Whatever the name's origin, all of these appellations are of central Asian derivation, a fact that is at odds with the reality that Bishkek is clearly a Soviet city with a Russian – or, at the very least, the ghost of a Russian – soul. Like a scaled-down version of its Kazakh rival, Almaty, Bishkek is a Russian city displaced several thousand kilometres to the east by the geography of empire: a purpose-built capital with buildings and monuments resonant of Europe west of the Urals.

Also, like the former Kazakh capital, Bishkek has a remarkable amount of green space, with swathes of parks and woodland dotted about the city to soften the traffic noise and freshen up the air (the city is said to have more trees per person than anywhere else in central Asia).

The streets – a textbook example of Soviet planning – are arranged on a grid system and, as in many provincial Russian or ex-Soviet cities, the boulevards and avenues that criss-cross the city are a tad wider than they realistically need to be to contain the traffic.

This is no urban jungle; in many aspects the city is almost village-like, with local communities focused around small markets and convenience stores. This village effect is heightened by the constant reminder of the alpine landscape that lies just beyond the city limits as, from virtually anywhere in Bishkek, the near-5,000m, snow-clad ridge of the Ala-Too is visible rising beguilingly to the south.

It is from the Ala-Too that the Ala-Archa, one of the range's main rivers, delivers much of the water needed to irrigate the city's impressive stock of greenery – the mountain melt-water channelled and distributed by means of a series of *aryk* canals. From the city, the mountains seem to be within a hand's grasp and, indeed, they almost are: to go hiking in any one of the valleys that sever the Ala-Too range is an easily manageable day trip from the capital.

North of Bishkek, the landscape is far less dramatic, with the gently undulating, fertile agricultural plain of the Chui Valley stretching modestly into neighbouring Kazakhstan. In such a vast geographical expanse as central Asia it might seem improbable that two large cities, one a capital, should lie so close together but they do: Almaty, Kazakhstan's largest city and former capital, lies just a few hours away by road.

In a country that is mostly characterised by mountainous terrain, Bishkek's modest altitude is unremarkable, almost an exception to the rule. The city stands at 700–900m above sea level, the land rising gently in the south to morph into the foothills of the Tien Shan. Bishkek lies on much the same degree of latitude as Chicago, Barcelona, Rome and Istanbul, although its extreme continental position ensures that it differs dramatically from these cities in climatic terms, with short, sometimes fiercely hot, summers and winters that are uncompromisingly subzero. Autumn is a brief blaze of cool nights, bright days and quickly turning leaves, while spring is generally the wettest time of year.

Bishkek's population has changed significantly since independence, when it was around 700,000 and predominantly Russian. Today population is estimated to be a little under 900,000, with many of those migrant labourers from Kyrgyzstan's rural areas. Russians are now the minority in the city and a large proportion of the city's graduates are permanently working abroad. Although the fabric of Bishkek still bears a largely Slavic appearance, the majority population these days is ethnic Kyrgyz. Nevertheless, Bishkek is still home to sizeable communities of Russians, Dungan Chinese, Tatars, Uyghurs, Uzbeks and Ukrainians, some of which – elderly Russians in particular – are suffering quite visibly under the new economic order.

Bishkek is not the sort of city you would travel halfway across the world to see for its own sake; it is not Samarkand, or Bukhara, or even Almaty. On the other hand, as a necessary stopover in most Kyrgyz itineraries, and with a good range of places to stay, a wide selection of restaurants and a few minor sights of its own, it is a pleasant enough place to relax and take stock while sorting out onward transport and visas.

HISTORY

Bishkek is the most recent appellation for a city that was known throughout much of the 20th century as Frunze, after the Bolshevik military campaigner and associate of Lenin who was born in the city. Before that it was known as Pishpek. Despite these two changes of name it is a relatively new city, barely a hundred years old, but built on the site of a much older Sogdian settlement that was a staging post on one of the lesser branches of the Silk Road. Even before this, there is evidence of habitation in the area, and stone hand tools that date back 7,000 years or so have been discovered close to the present-day city.

The Sogdian settlement, Jul, existed between the 6th and 12th centuries and, although many artefacts from this period have been found, all evidence on the ground has since been destroyed. Artefacts recovered from here suggest that it was a very diverse settlement, populated by a mix of Buddhists, Nestorians, Manicheans and Zoroastrians. However, like many other Silk Road towns, this was subsequently destroyed by Mongols under the fearsome leadership of Genghis Khan in the 13th century.

The Sogdian town was abandoned and languished in ruins for centuries until 1825, when the same site was fortified by the Khan of Khokand, who built mud-wall fortifications and settled it with Uzbek soldiers. This, too, was destroyed when Tsarist Russians annexed the region and, responding to the appeals of local chiefs desperate to rid themselves of Khokand domination, supported the Kyrgyz in their attack on the fortress in 1862. It fell after ten days of fighting and its administration was taken over by the Russians, who established an important Cossack base here, together with a relay point for mail travelling between St Petersburg and the far-flung reaches of the Russian Empire.

After the Russian headquarters in the region at Tokmok were flooded and damaged in 1877, the Russians subsequently built a more substantial fortress here the following year and named it Pishpek, although the etymology of this choice of name is now uncertain.

A slow migration of land-hungry Russians, many of whom were freed serfs, had started to settle here by now, attracted by the fertile soil of the Chui Valley as well as by tax breaks and a free supply of wood with which to build houses. By 1914 the city had grown to around 20,000, but these were almost entirely newly arrived Russians or Dungans who had migrated from China, as at this time the number of Kyrgyz settled here were very few.

Shortly after the 1917 October Revolution, a group of Bolsheviks attacked the garrison on New Year's Day 1918 and, within a few months, had gained control over the region. A counter-revolution broke out in December of the same year and anti-Bolsheviks based in the village of Belovodsk marched on the city. The counter-revolution failed, however, and was put down within a fortnight.

In response to Lenin's plea for international assistance, a group of Czech and Slovak socialist volunteers, members of the Interhelpa co-operative, arrived by train in 1925 and helped to rebuild and develop the city, constructing schools, hospitals and some of the civic buildings, which remain to this day. The city became the capital of the Kyrgyz ASSR in 1926 and was renamed Frunze; a decade later, it continued as the capital of the Kyrgyz SSR.

Despite its isolation far off in the central Asian steppe, many thousands of kilometres east of Moscow, the city was never beyond the iron grip of Stalinist repression. Many former members of Interhelpa were persecuted and executed, and another notorious incident in 1937 saw the whole of the republic's Supreme Soviet Central Committee, along with other important political figures, murdered by the NKVD secret police at the small village of Chong-Tash, just to the south of Bishkek – an event which did not come to light until 1991.

During World War II some of the Soviet war effort was moved here out of the reach of German attack, and it was at this time that much of the city's heavy industry became established. A number of clothing and pharmaceutical factories were created here, too. A great deal of this industrial base closed down following independence, to leave a capital that was noticeably less polluted but also undeniably poorer than before.

The city was renamed Bishkek on Kyrgyzstan's achieving independence in 1991: a new name for the new capital of a brand new country, and one that spoke more firmly of the country's Kyrgyz tradition than its previous appellation – a name taken from a European (Moldavian) hero of the communist revolution.

Some central parts of Bishkek, particularly around Ala-Too Square, were severely damaged during the violence that accompanied the country's 2010 regime change. The Ministry of Justice was torched on four separate occasions and, not surprisingly, the tax ministry also came under attack. Since then the city has fully recovered and, at the time of the most recent update (summer 2014), was thriving, with a large number of ambitious new building projects under way.

GETTING THERE AND AWAY

BY AIR Bishkek's Manas Airport [94 A4] (*airport code: FRU;* ✆ *693 109;* e *info@ airport.kg; www.airport.kg*) lies at some distance from the city – about 25km to the north. The airport receives a number of daily flights from various destinations in Russia, Asia and the former Soviet Union, most of which seem to arrive at an unsociable hour of the morning. Visas are no longer necessary for most Europeans and North Americans (see page 56).

There are several domestic flights each day between Bishkek and Osh, daily flights to Jalal-Abad, and thrice-weekly services to Batken in the southwest. Discounted flights to Osh can cost as little as US$35, which offers fierce competition to the alternative of a 12–14-hour, and only marginally cheaper, journey in a share taxi.

Once inside the terminal building there are a few facilities such as banks, shops, cafés and an information counter, which may or may not be open depending on the time of day. There are also ATMs in the arrivals hall.

To reach central Bishkek from the airport there are a number of options depending on the time of day. Cheapest is the **minibus** service, which takes about 40 minutes to reach the city. Minibus number 380 runs between the airport and the town centre (Molodaya Gvardiya, near junction of Chui) from 06.30 onward. It costs 40som each way.

Given the early hour at which many international flights arrive, a **taxi** may be the only option, although it is unwise to put yourself at the mercy of the taxi sharks who congregate in the car park outside and who may try to overcharge. A better option is to go into one of the taxi offices at arrivals and prepay the agreed fare for the trip into town. Manas Taxi (✆ 693 000) charge 400–500som to the centre. Another recommended firm is Super Taxi (✆ 152), which will charge 500–600som (US$10–12) for the journey (900–1,000som for a round trip), give a receipt and take you to the hotel of your choice. Taxis can also be booked in advance by some of the online hotel-booking services, and this is a good way of reducing the stress of an early morning – or late night – arrival after a tiring long-haul flight. You might, of course, do better than this on your own and find a driver who desperately wants to get back to the city centre and is willing to take you for 400som or less, but this is unlikely.

Some visitors to Kyrgyzstan take advantage of the more regular flights between Europe and Kazakhstan and fly into Almaty airport. From Almaty to Bishkek takes three to four hours by car, or five by bus. Currently, there are six flights a week between the two cities (see page 60).

Airline offices in Bishkek

✈ **Aeroflot** [103 E3] Erkindik 64; ✆ 620 071; www.aeroflot.ru; ⊕ 09.00–18.00 Mon–Fri. Airline desk also at Manas Airport (✆ 693 015)

✈ **Air Astana** Manas Airport ticket office; ✆ 900 886; e fru.airport@airastana.com; www.airastana.com

✈ **Air Bishkek** [102 A1] Manas 95; ✆ 298 213; e office@airways.kg; www.airbishkek.kg

✈ **China Southern Airlines** [102 D3] Chui 128/3; ✆ 664 668; www.csair.com; ⊕ 09.00–12.00 & 14.00–17.00 Mon–Fri

✈ **Air Kyrgyzstan** [102 A2] Manas 12; ✆ 316 500, 316 600; e airport@air.kg; www.air.kg

✈ **Avia Traffic Company** [94 D7] Panfilov 26; ✆ 544 788; www.aero.kg

✈ **Fly Dubai** [94 C6] Kerimbekov 13; ✆ 319 000; www.flydubai.com

✈ **Pegasus Asia (Air Manas)** [94 C7] Maldybaev 75; ✆ 564 040; www.pegasus-asia.com; ⊕ 09.00–18.00 Mon–Fri

✈ **Turkish Airlines** [95 F6] Abdrakhmanov 136; ✆ 301 600, 301 700; e info-kg@thy.com; www.thy.com; at airport: ✆ 313 561; e airport-kg@thy.com; ⊕ 09.00–18.00 Mon–Fri

✈ **Uzbekistan Airways** [102 D3] Kievskaya 107; ✆ 900 321; e fru@uzairways.com; www.uzairways.com

BY TRAIN There is a direct train link with Moscow via Kazakhstan and an indirect one to Tashkent in Uzbekistan that also passes through Kazakhstan. The journey between Moscow and Bishkek takes around 74 hours and costs in the order of 10,000som for *kupe* (four-berth sleeper) (see page 60). The only viable train link within Kyrgyzstan is between Bishkek and Balykchy on Lake Issyk-Kul, a journey of anything up to six hours that is probably for hardcore rail enthusiasts only, although it does pass through very attractive scenery along the way. It runs once a day in either direction in summertime and not at all out of season. Bishkek's railway station [95 E6] (Железнодорожная станция; ↘ *300 209*) lies south of the city centre at the junction of Erkindik Boulevard and Lineinaja.

BY BUS Buses rumble their way all over Kyrgyzstan from two main bus stations. Generally speaking, long-distance buses heading east to Issyk-Kul, south to Naryn, west to Talas and north to Almaty leave from the largest of the bus stations, the **West Bus Station** [94 A3] (Западный автовокзал – '*Zapadniy Avtovakzal*'; ↘ *344 696 for information*), on Jibek-Jolu at the junction with Kulijeva. Buses leave hourly for Karakol, in the morning at least, taking anything between six to eight hours and costing from 300som depending on how luxurious they are. To travel as far as Cholpon-Ata costs about two-thirds of the full fare.

Buses with destinations closer to home – Tokmok, Kant, Issyk-Ata, Kemin and Kegeti – tend to leave from the smaller and less confusing **East Bus Station** [95 H2] (Восточный автовокзал – '*Vostochni Avtovakzal*'; ↘ *482 004 for information*), which, again, is located on Jibek-Jolu, but this time further east on the junction with Osmonkula.

BY MINIBUS Minibuses run from the main bus stations, although the matter of which bus station serves which destination is not quite as clear-cut as it is in the case of buses.

Minibuses to Karakol and Issyk-Kul leave, when full, from in front of the West Bus Station and cost around 400som. Services to Talas and Naryn (via Kochkor) also leave from here. The East Bus Station is the place for minibus services to destinations east along the Chui Valley and also to Chong-Kemin and Issyk-Ata. Minibuses for other destinations like Kara Balta tend to leave from near Osh Bazaar (see page 110).

BY SHARE TAXI Share taxis running south to Osh and Jalal-Abad depart from **Osh Bazaar** [94 A4] at the western end of Chui. Share taxis to Cholpon-Ata and Karakol leave from in front of the West Bus Station. They generally fill up quicker than minibuses and cost something in the order of 600som to Karakol. Direct services to Almaty (Kazakhstan) and Tashkent (Uzbekistan) also leave from here or petrol stations nearby.

GETTING AROUND

The central part of Bishkek is relatively compact and one can get around here on foot quite well. The city is laid out in a grid pattern and, with the mountains usually visible to the south, it is hard to remain lost for long.

For longer journeys to the outskirts, or journeys across the centre at night, it is best to make use of a taxi or the city's public transport system. Bishkek has a complicated network of city **buses**, which are both very crowded and very cheap, costing just 8som. There are also a few remaining trolleybuses on some routes (enter the trolleybus at the rear door and pay the driver – also 8som – at the front on leaving).

Marginally better, and certainly more convenient, is the system of privately owned minibuses – *marshrutki* (singular *marshrutka*) – that travel everywhere in the city for a flat fare of 10som or 12som at night (pay the driver when you get on). The main difficulty with these is to know exactly when to get off, as much of the city is fairly devoid of recognisable landmarks and the minibuses tend to get so full that it is sometimes a problem to see out of the window.

A really useful website for public transport route planning is www.bus.kg. City bus and trolleybus maps can also be downloaded from the main CBT website (*www.cbtkyrgyzstan.kg*).

Whatever the time of day, *marshrutki* are invariably very crowded, with drivers who are under a lot of pressure to pick up the maximum number of fares from A to B, and who are not generally well disposed to having a chat or offering advice to a befuddled tourist. *Marshrutka* etiquette dictates that those who are travelling some distance should move to the back, and that young men and boys should give up their seats to the elderly.

In theory they will stop anywhere – just put your arm out – although they tend to have frequent fixed points where they pick up from; just look for groups of people waiting by the roadside scouring the numbers of the oncoming minibuses. *Marshrutki* generally display their destinations (in Cyrillic) along with their route number on a board in the front window but have usually whizzed past by the time you've read it. Many signs say TsUM (ЦУМ) or Osh Bazaar (Ош), which makes life a little easier. As a rule, it is best to know the number of the route you require (see box, below), otherwise, ask a local for advice. When you have reached, or are passing, your destination, ask the driver to let you off saying, '*Astanavitsya pazhalsta*.'

Both buses and minibuses run from early in the morning – 05.30–06.00 – until around 21.00 in the evening. After this time, taxis come into their own.

Taxis are everywhere in the city and, generally, are a good deal and the quickest way to get around. They can be easily flagged down at the roadside or phoned in advance. The latter are slightly more expensive but more reliable. Of course, as elsewhere in the country, the old adage remains from the former Soviet Union that 'every car is a taxi' and anything on four wheels may be flagged down to take you where you wish to go for an appropriate payment. However, in Bishkek there are so

USEFUL TRANSPORT ROUTES IN BISHKEK

(A = bus, T = trolleybus, number only = minibus)

A22 Between Osh Bazaar and Dordoi Bazaar via Chui
A35 Follows a circular route along Moskovskaya and between the railway station and the East and West bus stations
T4 Between Dordoi Bazaar and centre via Abdrakhmanov and Moskovskaya
T9 Runs along Kievskaya and Chui
110 From Osh Bazaar along Moskovskaya, then south
113 Circular route between East and West Bus Station along Jibek-Jolu then Osh Bazaar and railway station
166 Chui to and from Osh Bazaar
213 Circular route that takes in both bus stations, the railway station by way of long stretches of Jibek-Jolu and Moskovskaya
214 Similar to above but also passing close to Osh Bazaar

many official 'chequerboard' taxis plying the streets that it is best to stick to these as it is never a problem to find one.

Fares within the city centre tend to be around 100som per journey, sometimes a little more at night. For taxi trips to the outskirts, reckon on something more like 150som per trip. Fares are negotiable, of course, and should always be agreed upon before getting into the vehicle. If there is confusion, write down the price on a piece of paper. Generally speaking, Bishkek's taxi drivers are a cheerful lot and will conscientiously help you find your destination even if you are not too certain where it is.

Dial-up taxi services such as Super Taxi are more reliable but may cost a little more – about 120som per journey within the city centre. One problem for visitors is that, like the drivers, the operators tend to speak Russian only. If you are really unsure of where you are going, or uncertain as to how to pronounce it, then get a Russian speaker to write your destination on a piece of paper for you. Rather than knowing landmarks or details like the name of a restaurant, taxi drivers tend to base their knowledge on the city's grid of streets, so ask for a junction like Isa Akhunbaev and Sovetskaya rather than your precise destination, which they probably will not be familiar with.

Some recommended taxi firms are:

Ak Jol ☎182
Argo Taxi ☎178
City Taxi ☎166
Doka Taxi ☎695 555
Euro Taxi ☎150
Express Taxi ☎156

Narodnoye Taxi ☎333 333 or 1335
Salam Taxi ☎188
Smart Taxi ☎164
Super Taxi ☎152
Udacha Taxi ☎154

Super Taxi has a list of its tariffs online in English (*www.dos.kg/eng-152-tariffs-0-0. html*), although quite what '+10 catfish each km' actually means is anyone's guess.

SAFETY

Leafy, calm Bishkek does not feel dangerous at all, but after dark certain precautions should be taken, as violent attacks on foreigners do occasionally take place. The motivation for an attack is usually robbery, prompted by the obvious relative wealth of the traveller, who may well be carrying more on his person than a local might earn in a whole year. Other factors that might come into play are alcohol-fuelled resentment and dislike of Westerners (or Russians, for which Western visitors may be mistaken). Often it is a combination of these factors, coupled with the opportunity that a dark, quiet street offers to an impecunious drunk, or worse, a whole group of them. This is not to be alarmist, but forewarned is forearmed and late-night movements around the city, especially in the region of bars and nightclubs, are best done by taxi and preferably in a group. The red-light area around the Circus is said to be especially risky late at night.

Away from the centre Bishkek is a dark city at night, with street lights few and far between. To add to the danger, the pavements are in quite a dreadful state in places and it is easy to go careering down a pot-hole or trip on broken paving – many locals walk in the road itself. A precaution is to carry a torch (flashlight) but then, of course, this will clearly identify you as a foreigner.

The best advice is to not take too much money with you when you go out at night and hand it over without any heroics if you are unfortunate enough to be

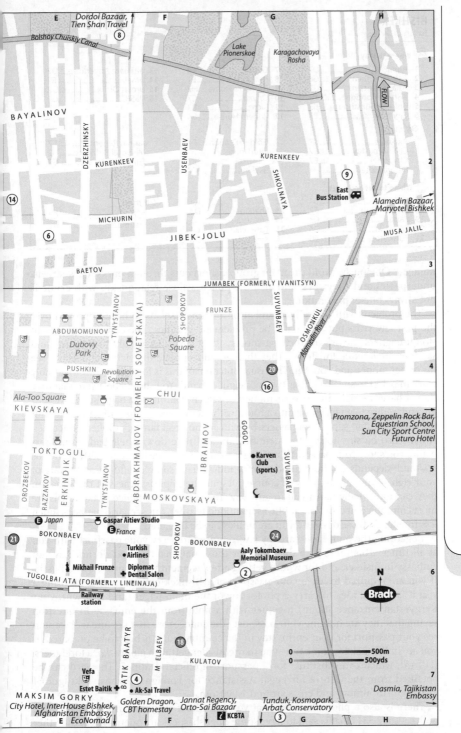

mugged. Obviously, avoid drunken groups, short cuts through parks, dark streets, underpasses and alleyways, and also the police, whose relationship with crime is not always one of prevention.

The problem with police harassment of foreigners seems to have improved over the past few years but it can still be problematic at times. The common ploy is to stop foreigners and ask for their passports – they have a legal right to do this – and say they are looking for drugs. They then go on to isolate the victim and ask to see his or her money and count it. The usual outcome of this is for them (they invariably work in pairs) to sneak a bill or two by sleight of hand. You should be aware that they *do not* have the right to see your money or search you or your bags, so stand your ground, refuse to go off alone into a room with them, make a fuss and try and recruit the assistance and support of passers-by who are no great fans of crooked policemen either. Also be sure to ask for identification and note down their badge numbers before you show your passports, making it clear that you are doing this. Their modus operandi depends on the intimidation of individuals, so be confident and aware of your rights – not always easy of course. Despite the unpleasantness of the situation they cannot actually harm you in any way. The place where police shakedowns are most common is at Osh Bazaar but, as mentioned earlier, this scenario happens much less frequently these days and you are unlikely to be bothered.

Regarding the police, you are, by law, required to carry your passport with you at all times. This presents a dilemma for those nationalities that do not have an embassy in Bishkek and for whom getting a replacement would prove a real hassle. If you are required to leave your passport at a Bishkek embassy while awaiting a visa it is a good idea to carry a photocopy of the main pages (and that with your Kyrgyzstan entrance stamp) together with a note from the embassy in question saying that they are holding your passport. The chances are that no-one will want to see your passport for your entire stay in the country, but it is best to be prepared. If you are in Bishkek for some time you may consider getting a *pamyatka*, a foreigners' ID card, which can substitute for a passport in official dealings. The card can be obtained from the Centre for Legal Assistance for Foreign Citizens, Toktogul 64 (Toktogul/Ibraimov) and costs around 1,000som.

There is also a phone number that you can dial if there are problems with the police (\ *662 331*) that is said to have some English-speaking operatives at the other end who deal with matters of police harassment. If you have a mobile phone with a local SIM card it is a good idea to key this in, as well as the number of your hotel and your embassy/honorary consul.

Emergency telephone numbers

Ambulance ☎103 (state service); ☎151 (private service)

Fire ☎101
Police ☎102

TOURIST INFORMATION

There is no national tourist board as such, nor a dedicated city tourist office, but there are a large number of travel agencies on hand to provide practical information. Bishkek is, of course, also the headquarters of the **Kyrgyz Community Based Tourism Association (KCBTA)** [94 G7] (*Maksim Gorky 58;* ☎ *443 331, 540 069, 443 331;* e *reservation@cbtkyrgyzstan.kg; www.cbtkyrgyzstan.kg*). This head branch of the national community tourism organisation can be found southeast of the city centre where Maksim Gorky intersects Matrosov.

Reputable Bishkek travel agencies such as CAT Corporation [102 D3] (*Chui 124;* ☎ *663 664;* e *cat@cat.kg; www.cat.kg*), Kyrgyz Concept [102 D3] (*Chui 126;* ☎ *666 006;* e *chui@concept.kg; www.concept.kg*), Celestial Mountains [102 B3] (*Kievskaya 131/2;* ☎ *311 814;* e *tours@celestial.com.kg; www.celestial.com.kg*) and NoviNomad [102 C3] (*28/10 Togolok Moldo;* ☎ *622 381;* e *info@novinomad.com; www.novinomad.com*) are all able to offer helpful travel information. The services offered by these and all other Bishkek-based tour operators are detailed on pages 94–5.

WHERE TO STAY   *Map, pages 94–5, unless otherwise noted.*

HOTELS

Hotels can be prebooked through a Bishkek agency such as Advantour (☎ *900 592;* e *bishkek@advantour.com; www.advantour.com*) or Muza Tours (☎ *304 617, 901 295;* e *booking@inspiro.kg; www.muzatravel.com*). The same agencies can also arrange airport transfers.

There are also several hotel booking websites that may be used, like Bishkek Hotels (*www.bishkek-hotels.net*), Kayak (*www.kayak.com*) &, especially useful for Bishkek, Booking.com (*www.booking.com*).

Top end

🏠 **Ak Keme****** (156 rooms, 12 suites, 4 presidential suites) Mira 93; ☎ *540 152, 541 790, 542 318;* e *reception@akkemehotel.com; www.akkemehotel.com*. Renovated to international standards a few years ago as a joint Kyrgyz-Malaysian venture, this 15-storey business hotel was known formerly as the Pinara. The hotel is some distance to the south of central Bishkek at the bottom end of Mira, close to Pobedy Park & the

US Embassy. All rooms have AC, minibar, satellite TV & soundproof windows to keep traffic noise from Prospekt Mira to a minimum. Some rooms have views over the mountains to the south. Health club, business centre, meeting rooms, casino, swimming pools & sports facilities, lobby bar, banquet hall in Italian style; also Star Sky terrace restaurant on upper floor with view over Tien Shan mountains. Airport pick-up costs US\$20 for a car & US\$50 for a minibus. **\$\$\$\$\$**

🏠 **Bishkek Boutique Hotel****** (25 rooms) Baitik Baatyr 67/1; ☎ *593 312;* e *reservations@bishkek-hotel.com; www.bishkek-hotel.com*. Price-wise at the bottom end of this category, this modern hotel south of the centre has clean, contemporary style, although some of the sgl rooms are on the small side. **\$\$\$\$\$**

🏠 **City Hotel****** (50 rooms) Baitik Baatyr 34; ☎ *976 262;* e *hotel@cityhotel.kg; www.cityhotel.kg*. A newly opened good-value business hotel south of the city centre. Facilities inc wellness centre, gym & sauna; soundproofed rooms have iPod docking stations, fast Wi-Fi, minibar, cable TV & well-equipped bathrooms. **$$$$$**

🏠 **Evropa***** [map, page 103] (18 rooms) Ibraimov 70; ☏ 979 070; e hotelevropa@ hotelevropa.kg; www.hotelevropa.kg. Fairly

central, modern hotel located a little way south of TsUM. Comfortable, classically decorated rooms, all with Wi-Fi, cable TV & minibar. **$$$$$**

🏠 **Golden Dragon***** (47 rooms, 5 suites) M Elebaev 60; ☏ 902 771; e gdhotel@gdhotel.kg;

BISHKEK STREET NAME CHANGES

Since independence many streets and avenues in Bishkek have been given new names. The problem for the visitor is that in many cases the old names are still in use and both old and new tend to be used interchangeably by locals and taxi drivers. Those given below are some of the more common changes that may cause confusion.

Old name	New name
16-th	Shoorukov
18-th	Igemberdiev
Almatinskaya	Kurmanjan Datka (north of Chui)/ Shabdan Baatyr (south of Chui)
Bakinskaya	Elebesov
Belinskya	Manas
Chapaev	Bakayev
Donetskaya	Suerkulov
Druzhby	Karasaev
Dushanbinskaya	Toktonaliev Aliarskaya
Dzerzhinsky	Erkindik
Engels	Chokmorov
Ivanitsyn	Jumabek
Kamskaya	Samanchin
Karasuiskaya	Kerimbekov Kulchoro
Karl Marx	Yunusaliev
Karpinsky	Suyumbaev
Kosmicheskaya	Borombay Sultan
Krasnaya Oktabarskaya	Tynystanov
Kremlevskaya	Abai
Krupskaya	Tabyshaliev
Leningradskaya	Bayalinov Kasymaly
Lineinaja	Tugolbai Ata
Molodaya Gvardiya	Mahatma Gandi
Nekrasov	Asanliev Uzengazy
Ordzhonikidze	Junusaliev
Pervomaiskaya	Razzakov
Pravda	Ibraimov
Remeslennaya	Altymyshev
Sovetskaya	Abdrakhmanov (N of Lev Tolstoy)/ Baytik Baatyr
Stroitelnaya	Maytyev
Sverdlov	Umetaliev Temirkul
Voroshilov	Kolbaev
Zhigulevskaya	Suvanberdiev

www.gdhotel.kg. All rooms with internet access, AC, minibar & cable TV. Restaurant with European, Indian, Chinese & Kyrgyz cuisine. Business centre, gym & sports facilities. Free airport pick-up. **$$$$$**

🏠 **Golden Tulip Bishkek****** [map, page 102] (64 rooms) Isanov 37; ☎ 610 707; e reservations@ goldentulipbishkek.com; www.goldentulip.com. This well-appointed 4-star chain hotel offers reasonable value for money in a city centre location. A variety of rooms & suites on offer, all come with Wi-Fi, HD TV & AC. Restaurant with French/Lebanese cuisine, bar & fitness club. **$$$$$**

🏠 **Holiday** [map, page 103] (50 rooms) Abdrakhmanov 204; ☎ 976 161; e hotel@holiday. kg; www.holiday.kg. Almost opposite the Hyatt, offering similar standards at much lower prices. All rooms with large HD TVs, cordless phones, minibar, well-equipped bathrooms & floor-to-ceiling windows. Complimentary iPads available & separate smoking & non-smoking floors. Good mountain views from top floor restaurant. **$$$$$**

🏠 **Hyatt Regency******* [map, page 103] (180 rooms, 5 suites) Abdrakhmanov 191; ☎ 661 234; e bishkek.regency@hyatt.com; www.bishkek. regency.hyatt.com. In the city centre, close to the Museum of Fine Arts & State Opera & Ballet Theatre, this remains the Kyrgyz capital's most prestigious & expensive hotel. With large, spacious rooms with cable TV, AC, internet access, separate work area & marble bath fittings, the Hyatt is clearly aimed at high-profile business visitors. Mediterranean-style Crostini restaurant & lobby bar; swimming pool, business centre & banqueting hall. Buffet b/fast is extra. **$$$$$**

🏠 **Jannat Regency******* (61 rooms, 11 suites) Aaly Tokombaev 21/2; ☎ 909 750; e jr.reception@ jannat.kg; www.regency.jannat.kg. A large, new hotel south of the city centre aimed squarely at business visitors & wedding parties. Comfortable rooms with modern Kyrgyz styling, satellite TV, internet & minibar. Outdoor swimming pool, business centre, conference halls & 5 restaurants. **$$$$$**

🏠 **Maryotel Bishkek******* (37 rooms, 4 suites, 1 apt) Pobedy Prospekt 351; ☎ 617 150; e info. maryotel@gmail.com; www.maryotel.kg. A long way from the centre, all rooms here have cable TV, Wi-Fi, minibar & safe. Large swimming pool, gym & free airport pick-up. **$$$$$**

🏠 **Park Hotel****** [map, page 103] (58 rooms, 9 suites) Orozbekov 87; ☎ 665 518, 622 495; e hotel@parkhotel.kg; www.parkhotel.kg. With a quiet, very central location, this has pleasant AC rooms that come complete with cable TV, minibar, work desk & free Wi-Fi. Conference facilities are available. **$$$$$**

🏠 **Silk Road Lodge****** [map, page 102] (10 suites, 18 rooms) Abdumomunov 229; ☎ 324 889; e reception@silkroad.com.kg; www.silkroad. com.kg. The Silk Road Lodge is a modern, centrally situated hotel, opened in 2000 under the same British ownership as the Celestial Mountains travel agency. All rooms have AC, bathroom with heated floor, tea/coffee-making facilities & cable TV. The hotel has a business centre & shop, conference room, bar & restaurant (with vegetarian options), sauna, heated pool & outdoor summer garden, as well as a well-stocked library of English-language books. The hotel has friendly English-speaking staff, & the tariff inc complimentary airport transfer. **$$$$$**

🏠 **Onyx****** (24 rooms) Gorky 141; ☎ 986 986; e onyx@onxhotel.kg; www.onyxhotel.kg. Close to the Botanical Gardens south of the centre, this modern hotel has friendly English-speaking staff. All rooms with cable TV, minibar, AC & free Wi-Fi. Sauna & fitness facilities & one-way airport shuttle service inc in rate. **$$$$–$$$$$**

🏠 **Urmat Ordo**** (18 rooms) Isanov 85; ☎ 312 003, 312 004; e hotel@urmatordo.kg; www. urmatordo.kg. A small, modern B&B-style hotel, opened in 2003, within walking distance of the city centre. All rooms have AC, minibar, satellite TV. Room rate inc b/fast & Wi-Fi. *Sgl/dbl* **$$$$**, *lux* **$$$$$**

🏠 **Umai** (8 rooms) Donskoy Pereulok 46A; ☎ 0700 584 245; m 0772 802 805 (English), m 0555 913 245 (German); e info@umai-hotel-kg.com; www.umai-hotel-kg.com. This family-run hotel is a 15–20min walk north of the city centre. It is part of the Ecotour travel organisation (see page 54). Clean, comfortable rooms with private shower & toilet, AC & satellite TV. Free Wi-Fi throughout. External bar. Garden. Special dietary requirements catered for. See ad, page 122. **$$$$**

Mid-range & budget

🏠 **Issyk-Kul***** (194 rooms) Mira 301; ☎ 550 746, 458 357; e bosteriyeva@exnet.kg. A large, ex-Soviet business hotel on the southern side of the city, close to the Flamingo Park & the American Embassy. The hotel was apparently constructed to represent the Soviet warship *Aurora* & it certainly does have something of the battleship in its design. Now part of the Best Eastern chain, facilities inc sauna, billiards hall, business centre, cable television & a conference hall for up to 200. Discounts are offered for longer stays & regular visitors. *Sgl/dbl* **$$$$**, *suite* **$$$$$**

⌂ **Alpinist*** (19 rooms) Panfilov 113; ✆699 621; e alpinist@elcat.kg. Centrally located between Lev Tostoy & Gorky, this is a small, comfortable place clearly aimed at climbing & trekking groups, hence the name. English & German spoken; all rooms with AC, cable TV & refrigerator. This is undoubtedly the only Bishkek hotel with its own climbing wall. *Sgls start from US$50.* **$$$–$$$$**

⌂ **Asia Mountains*** (12 rooms) Lineinaja 1a; ✆690 234; e hotel@asiamountains.net; http://asiamountains-hotels.com. This small, relatively new guesthouse, close to the railway station & central mosque, belongs to the tour company of the same name & is often used by their clients at the beginning & end of expeditions. All rooms have en-suite facilities, cable TV & AC. The reception staff speak English &/or German. Small bar & restaurant; email facilities. This place tends to fill quickly so it is best to book in advance. *Sgl* **$$$**, *dbl/suite* **$$$$**

⌂ **Asia Mountains 2*** (20 rooms) Gorky 156; ✆540 206; e hotel2@asiamountains.net; http://asiamountains-hotels.com. The sister hotel to the original Asia Mountains Hotel, built in 2009, this has equally high standards. All rooms with AC, cable TV & refrigerator. **$$$–$$$$**

⌂ **Dostuk*** [map, page 103] (124 rooms) Frunze 429b; ✆433 636; e dostukhotel@mail.ru; www.dostukhotel.kg/en. Soviet-style hotel of the Brutalist school built in 1983 & refurbished in 2001. Central location in the city centre, close to the Circus, in a slightly dodgy area known for its prostitutes. Most rooms have AC, satellite TV & refrigerator. Casino, disco, sauna, billiard parlour, gym, business centre & Arizona restaurant. The 5th floor of the building has been fully refurbished to become the slightly more expensive & upmarket **Club Hotel*** (✆ *433 888;* e *info@dostuk.kg; www.dostuk.kg;* **$$$$$**), which has better quality & more attractively decorated rooms. **$$$–$$$$**

⌂ **Futuro*** (20 rooms) Udmurtskaya 13; ✆986 868; e hotel@futuro.kg; www.futuro.kg. A friendly & comfortable modern hotel with just 2 disadvantages: it is some way from the centre (but with good transport connections along nearby Chui) & it is close to the city's main power station. Good value-for-money dbl rooms with stylish contemporary decor, AC, Wi-Fi & well-equipped bathrooms. **$$$–$$$$**

⌂ **Grand Hotel**** (27 rooms) Frunze 428; ✆340 000; e reception@grandhotel.kg; www.grandhotel.kg. Mostly geared towards locals & Russian speakers, this reasonably priced hotel has a convenient city-centre location. All rooms with Wi-Fi, AC & cable TV. **$$$–$$$$**

⌂ **Radison Guesthouse** [map, page 102] (7 rooms) Abdumomunov 259; ✆323 181; e radison@radisonhouse.com; www.radisonhouse.com. On the same street as the Silk Road Lodge & close to the centre, this is a small, friendly place run by a charming Tatar family. Comfortable, neat rooms face on to a courtyard & have AC, Wi-Fi, satellite TV & modern shower. There is no sign, but ring the bell at gate for admission. *Sgl* **$$$**, *dbl* **$$$$**

⌂ **Rich**** (22 rooms) Timiryazeva 111; ✆322 038; e reception@rich.kg; www.rich.kg. A good-value hotel with a reasonably central location that is mostly used to dealing with local guests. Fairly large, pleasant rooms with satellite TV, AC & internet access. Also gym, summer terrace with swimming pool, restaurant & 3D cinema. **$$$–$$$$**

⌂ **Ultimate Adventure** Kurienkeva 185; ✆671 183; e ultiadv@mail.kg; www.kirghizie.fr. A good-value, French-owned guesthouse located close to the Russian Orthodox church just north of the centre. Simple but pleasant sgl, dbl & trpl rooms & a shady garden terrace. **$$–$$$**

HOSTELS & HOMESTAYS
Most of the hostels listed below can be prebooked online using booking websites like www.hostelworld.com, www.hostels.com or www.booking.com.

⌂ **Rodem House** Umetalieva 109; ✆938 282; e rodemhouse@yahoo.com. Just off Chui close to the centre, this is really more like a small guesthouse & so quite expensive for dorm beds, which need to be prebooked through www.

hostelworld.com or similar. Helpful staff, good b/fasts, large common room & decent Wi-Fi. **$$$**

🏠 **InterHouse Bishkek** Topograficheskiy 9; ☎595 070; e interhouse.kg@gmail.com; www. interhouse.kg. Located some distance south of the centre but with good transport connections. With 3 small dorms (**$$**) & 1 dbl (**$$$**), shared kitchen, communal space & free Wi-Fi, this receives consistent good reports for its pleasant friendly atmosphere. There's also a sister hostel, InterHouse City Center [102 A4], closer to the centre just off Manas (*Toktogul 170, apt 1;* ☎*313 009*).

🏠 **Nomad's Home** Drevesnaya 10; m 0773 067 581; e nomadshome@gmail.com; http:// nomadshome.googlepages.com/home. Situated close to the East Bus Station this has been open for business since 2007. There is a dormitory & also sgl & dbl rooms, b/fast provided (*150som*). Dinners can be provided for 250som with advance notice. You can also stay in a yurt in the garden or set up your own tent. English, Japanese & Russian are spoken. *Dormitory* **$$**, *private rooms & yurt* **$$$**

🏠 **Nomad Hostel** [map, page 103] Usenbaev 44; ☎976 632; www.hostelinkg.com. Opened in summer 2013, this is already a very popular hostel with a convenient central location a little way east of the Turkish Embassy. English spoken, clean 12- & 14-bed dormitory, kitchen & common room. *Dormitory* **$$**, *private dbl room* **$$$**

🏠 **Bishkek Guesthouse** Molodaya Gvardiya apart-72, flat-26; ☎977 338; m 0555 152 207; e bishkekguesthouse@gmail.com; http:// bishkekhouse.ucoz.com/. A fairly centrally located apt with dormitories (**$** pp), private rooms (**$$** pp) & 'lux' rooms (**$$$** pp). English-speaking staff, meals on request & Wi-Fi.

🏠 **Hostel Inn Bishkek** [map, page 102] Chui 142; m 0703 144 445; e book@hostelinnbishkek. com; www.hostelinnbishkek.com. At the heart of things close to Beta Stores on Chui, this typical backpackers' hostel has a relaxed atmosphere & all the usual facilities. *Dormitory* **$–$$**, *dbl room* **$$$**

🏠 **Kyrgyz Host** Tynystanov 244; m 0552 772 168; e kyrgyz.host@gmail.com. Close to the canal, north of the centre, this has a homely atmosphere & spacious rooms in specific styles – Kyrgyz, Soviet & international. Free b/fasts, internet & parking. Dormitory **$–$$**, private dbl room **$$$**

🏠 **City Nest** Orozbekov 127/2; ☎626 058; m 0777 094 197, 0552 543 008; e citynest@ gmail.com; www.bishkekhostel.blogspot.co.uk. A small, cosy guesthouse with garden in a peaceful but reasonably central location between the bus stations just north of Jibek-Jolu. Shared kitchen & bathroom, with cooking & laundry facilities. **$$**

🏠 **Tunduk** Kubanski 46/1; m 0700 332 317; e tundukhostel@gmail.com. South of the centre, near the intersection of Ahunbaeva & Yunusalieva, this newish hostel has a choice of small dorms, private rooms & a yurt to sleep in. Aimed squarely at younger travellers, this also has a private garden with hammocks & swimming pool. Shared kitchen, washing facilities & bicycles available. **$$**

🏠 **USSR** Chui 127, apt 132. On Chui close to the centre, the decor here has a deliberate retro Soviet feel. Kitchen, free Wi-Fi, tea & coffee. Helpful, friendly staff & optional Russian lessons. *Dormitory* **$$**, *dbl* **$$**

🏠 **CBT Homestay** Ahunbaeva 58/4; ☎443 331; e reservation@cbtkyrgyzstan.kg. CBT's own homestay with 3 rooms & 6 beds, located 20mins' walk south of their office on Gorky. **$–$$**

✖ **WHERE TO EAT AND DRINK** *Map, pages 102–3, unless otherwise noted.*

Bishkek has a wide variety of food outlets to suit every taste and pocket. Within the city centre there is more or less everything available, from cheap takeaway *samsa* from a street stall to fancy international haute cuisine in a four-star restaurant.

Restaurants fall basically into two categories: simple *chaikhanas* which serve a fairly limited range of Kyrgyz and Russian dishes, and more elaborate, often foreign-owned, restaurants which serve international food at prices usually well beyond the budget of most nationals. By Western standards, however, even these seem quite reasonably priced, although in many cases it is the decor and atmosphere that you are paying for rather than the food. Foreign cuisines like Chinese, Middle Eastern and Italian, and even exotics like Japanese sushi and Tex-Mex quesadillas are relatively easy to find these days.

BISHKEK City Centre

For listings, see pages 97–107

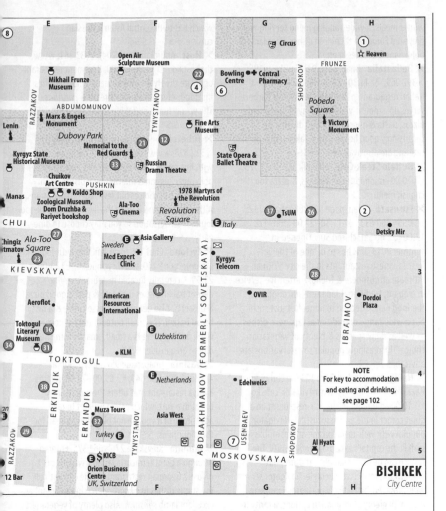

8

Circus 🎭

1 ☆ Heaven

Open Air Sculpture Museum

FRUNZE

Mikhail Frunze Museum

22

4

6

Bowling Centre ● ✚ Central Pharmacy

SHOPOKOV

Pobeda Square

ABDUMOMUNOV

RAZZAKOV

Lenin

Marx & Engels Monument

Dubovy Park

Fine Arts Museum

Victory Monument

TYNYSTANOV

Kyrgyz State Historical Museum

Memorial to the Red Guards

21

12

33

Russian Drama Theatre 🎭

State Opera & Ballet Theatre 🎭

Chuikov Art Centre

PUSHKIN

Koldo Shop

Manas

Zoological Museum, Dom Druzhba & Rariyet bookshop

Ala-Too Cinema 🎬

1978 Martyrs of the Revolution

Revolution Square

CHUI

37 ● TsUM 26

2

Detsky Mir

Chingiz Aitmatov

Ala-Too Square

27

23

Sweden ● ✚ Asia Gallery

Italy

KIEVSKAYA

Med Expert Clinic

Kyrgyz Telecom ✉

ABDRAKHMANOV (FORMERLY SOVETSKAYA)

28

Aeroflot

American Resources International

14

● OVIR

Dordoi Plaza

Toktogul Literary Museum

16

34

31

Uzbekistan

● KLM

TOKTOGUL

IBRAIMOV

NOTE
For key to accommodation and eating and drinking, see page 102

4

38

Netherlands

● Edelweiss

ERKINDIK

ERKINDIK

Muza Tours

32

Turkey

Asia West

TYNYSTANOV

USENBAEV

SHOPOKOV

Al Hyatt

29

RAZZAKOV

7

MOSKOVSKAYA

KICB

Orion Business Centre
UK, Switzerland

5

12 Bar

BISHKEK
City Centre

Bishkek WHERE TO EAT AND DRINK

3

For less formal dining there are numerous options for fast food in the city. There are snack stalls everywhere serving up *samsi*, *shwarma* and rather dangerous-looking *gamburgers* (hamburgers); one of the most popular spots for these is at the junction of Sovetskaya and Kievskaya near the university. There are stalls at the east side of Ala-Too Square, which sell a variety of breads, snacks and, of course, *samsi*, and there is the shady area just inside Panfilov Park, where in summer a clutch of simple outdoor restaurants offer cheap and tasty staples like *manti*, *shashlyk* and *laghman*.

RESTAURANTS
Top end

✕ **Crostini** Hyatt Regency Bishkek, Abdrakhmanov 191; ✆661 234; ⏲ 06.30– midnight. Expensive but beautifully prepared Mediterranean cuisine & monthly international food promotions. Good selection of imported wines & excellent range of teas. $$$$$

✕ **Four Seasons** Tynystanov 116a; ✆621 548; www.fourseasons.kg; ⏲ 10.00–midnight. On a leafy street next to Dubovy Park, this is one of the city's best known & most exclusive restaurants. There is outdoor dining on a cool terrace in summer & a warm, cosy interior for winter meals. A wide-ranging menu serving well-prepared European & Chinese dishes. Popular with politicians & businessmen. $$$$$

✕ Bella Italia [map, page 94] Kievskaya 195; ✆ 392 069; ◷ 11.30–22.00. Probably the best Italian restaurant in Bishkek. Chef Walter Barbaresi serves up a mouth-watering array of homemade pizzas, pasta & gnocchi, washed down with surprisingly good house wines. Takeaway & outside catering are also available. $$$$

✕ Buffalo Steak-Café Erkindik 36; ✆ 621 573; ◷ 10.00–midnight. Good steaks, & pizza too. English menu. $$$$

✕ Furusato [map, page 95] Bokonbaev 132; m 0554 400 633; ◷ 11.30–22.00 Mon–Fri, 17.00–22.00 Sat, closed Sun. Opened in summer 2013, this has to be one of the very best Japanese restaurants in the city. With an intimate atmosphere & friendly, attentive service in elegant, traditional Japanese surroundings, the food here is second to none. Not just sushi but a wide range of traditional Japanese dishes as well as daily specials & plenty of vegetarian choices. Increasingly popular so reservations are advisable. $$$$

✕ Navigator Moskovskaya 103 (on corner with Razzakov); ✆ 665 151; www.navigator-cafe.kg; ◷ 10.00–midnight. A chic bar-restaurant on a quiet corner in the embassy district. Navigator is popular with well-to-do businessmen, embassy staff & the capital's expatriate community. The service can be rather haughty at times, but perhaps this reflects its clientele. Navigator serves well-prepared, attractively presented European food with plenty of vegetarian options, a rarity in the city. Good, if expensive, coffee. There is a play area for children outside near the terrace. Equally popular as a place for an evening drink, there is live music at night. $$$$

✕ Prego Club Chui 219; ✆ 880 771 ◷ 12.00–midnight. One of Bishkek's best Italian restaurants, with good steaks, salads, pizzas & pasta dishes. $$$$

✕ Sushi Room Erkindik 30; ✆ 623 224; ◷ 09.00–02.00. One of several sushi places in the city, this is a modern, stylish bar-restaurant serving modern Japanese food… especially sushi. $$$$

Mid-range & budget

✕ Consul Frunze 477; ✆ 660 237. A large restaurant opposite Park Hotel (see page 99)

which has both central Asian & Russian cuisine. $$$–$$$$

✕ Host Abdrakhmanov 204; ✆ 933 361; www.thehost.kg; ◷ 11.00–23.00. Basement restaurant opposite the Hyatt with authentic Indian dishes inc good selection of *naan* breads & *parathas*. The w/day lunch buffet is particularly good value. $$$–$$$$

✕ Tubeteika [map, page 94] Turusbekov 31; ✆ 317 878; www.tubeteika.kg. A fairly smart place with live music & an imaginative & extensive menu of Kyrgyz, Russian & international dishes. Plenty of meat & fish choices but few vegetarian options. Although the food is good the live music can be too loud for conversation so you may choose to dine early. $$$–$$$$

✕ Cyclone Chui 136 (near junction with Togolok Moldo); ✆ 661 140; www.cyclone.kg; ◷ 11.00–23.00. A centrally located restaurant serving decent Italian dishes inc pesto & pasta, good pizzas & desserts. Also genuine espresso coffee & a tasty bread basket. The small outdoor terrace here is often full but there is a small, smartly furnished dining area inside. $$$

✕ Dasmia [map, page 95] Gorky 2 (Alma Atinskaya); ✆ 530 649; ◷ 09.00–23.00. A large Kyrgyz restaurant that offers the opportunity to eat in a yurt, which you may want to take advantage of if you are not planning to head for the mountains. $$$

✕ Mimino Kievskaya 27; ✆ 661 375. Entered through a giant terracotta jar doorway, this is 1 of just 2 Georgian restaurants in the city with all the staple dishes like *khachapuri* (cheese bread) & excellent lamb *shashlyk*. Also plenty of vegetarian dishes & a good selection of Georgian wines. Popular with groups. $$$

✕ New York Pizza Kievskaya 89; ✆ 662 544, 909 909; ◷ 10.00–23.00. As the name suggests, American-style pizza; also 24hr-delivery service. $$$

✕ Old Edgar (Stari Edgar) Panfilov 273 (in Dubovy Park, between Chui & Frunze, next to Russian Drama Theatre); ✆ 624 408; ◷ 12.00–midnight. The indoor dining room is rather like a Bavarian beer cellar, while the summer outdoor seating area has something of the *Arabian Nights* about it, with divans & plenty of cushions. There is an English menu & some English is spoken by the staff; good, friendly service; excellent lasagne & pizzas. Live music most nights. $$$

✕ **Parsi** Toktogul 103/Razzakov; ☎ 624 819; ⏰ 09.00–midnight daily. Near the Iranian Embassy at the junction with Razzakov, this is a restaurant with an Iranian flavour both in terms of food & decor. $$$

✕ **Shaolin** [map, page 94] Jibek-Jolu/Isanov junction; ⏰ 10.30–23.00. Chinese restaurant with authentic food. $$$

✕ **Yusa** [map, page 94] Logvinenko 14; ☎ 300 707. An old Bishkek favourite, renovated in summer 2005, Yusa is a Turkish restaurant with a range of medium-priced Turkish dishes & genuine Turkish coffee. With outdoor & indoor seating, it is popular with both expatriates & locals alike, especially at lunchtimes. There is a second fast-food branch at the Vefa Centre. $$$

✕ **Kent Café** Razzakov/Kievskaya junction; ☎ 624 456. Just behind Ala-Too Square, this 2-floor modern café-restaurant is a good choice for lunch, with a moderately priced international menu that, unusually for Kyrgyzstan, offers several vegetarian options as well as a good range of chicken, pork & fish dishes. Downstairs is a smart, modern café with window tables & a bar; upstairs is a little more formal. Menu in English & Russian. $$–$$$

✕ **Manty Bar** Shopokov 108b; ☎ 881 177; ⏰ 09.30–midnight. Opposite TsUM, the main dish in this cosy place is, of course, *manti* (steamed dumplings – 5 varieties to choose from), which are well above avg, but there are plenty of other typical central Asian dishes to choose from as well as excellent (& enormous) salads. $$–$$$

✕ **Ojak** Erkindik 27; 📱 0555 325 541; ⏰ 11.00–21.00. A popular Turkish/Azeri restaurant, on east side of Erkindik between Moskovskaya & Toktogul, with excellent kebab meals & Turkish-style *pide, ayran & chai*. Busy at lunchtimes. Non-smoking section. No alcohol. $$–$$$

✕ **Aroma** Tynystanov/Pushkin; ☎ 878 888; www. aroma.kg; ⏰ 24hrs daily. Fully renovated, this attractively decorated pizzeria is the most central branch of a city chain serving not just pizza but a wide range of dishes inc sushi. $$

✕ **Arzu Style** Togolok Moldo 194; ☎ 696 697; www.arzu.kg; ⏰ 08.00–23.30. One of several Arzu restaurants dotted around the city, this smart but sprawling restaurant is a cross between an upmarket beer hall and a stylish *chaikhana*. Good Kyrgyz food, especially *shashlyk & laghman*. Also

draught beer & live music. Popular with locals for its convivial atmosphere, well-priced food & airy outdoor seating area. $$

✕ **Astana** Kievskaya. An outdoor courtyard restaurant which offers a good range of Kyrgyz & Russian dishes, particularly *shashlyk*. Live music at night. $$

✕ **Beta Gourmet** Chui 150a; ☎ 611 076; ⏰ 09.00–21.00. This restaurant, on the 2nd floor of the Beta shopping centre on Chui, is a little canteen-like & lacking in character, but it does offer a wide range of Russian, Kyrgyz, Korean & particularly tasty Turkish fast food inc *pide* (Turkish pizza) & various kebabs. There is additional seating outside on a covered balcony overlooking Chui. A good place for b/fast or a quick lunch. $$

✕ **Derevyashka** Ryskulov 1; ☎ 323 574; ⏰ 24hrs daily. Opposite Gorky Park, this lively, expansive beer hall multitasks in providing good-value Kyrgyz & Russian dishes too. As you might expect, there is an excellent choice of beers inc draught. Outdoor terrace for warm weather. $$

✕ **Faiza** [map, page 94] Jibek-Jolu 555 (junction with Manas); ☎ 664 737; ⏰ 09.00–21.00 daily. A no-nonsense sort of place which is very popular with locals & family groups. It serves high-quality, good-value Kyrgyz staples like *manti, laghman & lepyoshka*, & what some consider to be the best *plov* in the city. Although it has a large dining area it can be hard to find a seat at lunchtimes. Fast, friendly service. No alcohol is served. $$

✕ **Fakir** [map, page 95] Suyumbaev 142; ☎ 438 825. Good-value restaurant, tucked behind Bishkek City shopping mall on Suyumbaev, which is popular with locals for its fresh *laghman* & other traditional dishes. Cuisine is a mixture of Chinese, Uyghur & European. The restaurant has a glass-fronted kitchen where you can watch your food being prepared. $$

✕ **Jalal-Abad** Corner of Kievskaya/Togolok Moldo; ☎ 362 619; ⏰ 08.00–midnight. This is a large sprawling Uzbek-style *chaikhana* with a vast, dimly lit dining hall inside & several separate dining pavilions on its terrace outside next to the road. The *shashlyk* grillers fan the flames in front of the entrance. There is a fairly limited menu but a decent choice of inexpensive grilled meats, *laghman* & salads. Very popular in summer at lunchtimes, when the outside tables are at a premium. No alcohol is served. $–$$

✘ **Sovetskaya Stolovaya** Next to TsUM, Chui. For a cheap city centre meal this is hard to beat, a Soviet-style *stolovaya* (self-service canteen). With a functional, but not unpleasant, interior & with a fairly wide choice of Russian-style food, you can have a full meal here for 150–200som. **$**

CAFÉS & BARS

Some of the places listed above also double as places to enjoy a leisurely drink, in particular Kent & Navigator. As well as many well-established café-bars, recent years have seen the rise of a number of places that specialise in that rare central Asian commodity, real barista-style coffee. Many cafés offer Wi-Fi as a perk. Most of the options below also serve food.

☕ **Adriano Coffee** Isanov 87; 615 417; 24hrs daily. Central coffee bar that many rate higher than the opposition. Other branches on Chui, Kievskaya & Mira. **$$$**

☕ **Coffee** Manas 9; 312 892; www.coffee. kg. Unambiguous given the name, this & 2 more branches at Toktogul 75/1 & Togolok Moldo 40/1 are fine places for a caffeine fix in pleasant surroundings. There's a huge choice of coffees, hot & cold, as well as teas, cakes & desserts. **$$$**

☕ **Masal** Erkindik 46; m 0700 221 010; 10.00–23.00. Ideally located on the corner of Erkindik & Chui, just a block from Ala-Too Square, this stylish coffee bar has a shady outdoor terrace with wicker furniture & serves a variety of light pasta dishes & ice creams as well as decent coffee & specialist teas. Free Wi-Fi. **$$$**

☕ **Sierra Coffee** Manas 57/1; 311 248; www.sierra.kg; 07.30–23.00. 'Life's too short to drink cheap coffee' is the motto on the door here. Very much a Bishkek expatriate institution, this is faithful to the American, Starbucks-style model & not only serves good coffee (they roast their own beans) but also b/fasts, light meals, snacks & juices. Other branches can be found on Razzakov [95 E5], at Vefa Center & Tash Rabat shopping mall. Outside seating, Wi-Fi & English-language books & magazines to peruse. **$$$**

☕ **Vanilla Sky** Moskovskaya 147; 976 768 08.00–01.00 Mon–Sat, 08.00–midnight Sun. Bright, airy café-restaurant with good salads, pasta dishes & cakes. **$$$**

♀ **Obama Bar & Grill** Toktogul 93/Erkindik; 624 902; 11.00–midnight. Gimmicky

American-themed bar covered with images of the US president. Steaks & Tex-Mex food. **$$$$**

♀ **Opera Lounge** Hyatt Regency Bishkek, Abdrakhmanov 191; 661 234; 06.30– midnight. Light & comfortable with pleasant piped music & occasional live pianist or string trio. Extensive range of organic teas, fresh coffee & homemade cakes & snacks. **$$$–$$$$**

♀ **Blonder Pub** [map, page 95] Ibraimov 24; 591 625; www.blonderpub.kg; 11.00–03.00. A German-style pub & beer garden with 9 types of home-brewed draught beer inc options like Irish Red, English Stout & pomegranate beer as well as more standard Czech Pilsner. There is also a wide choice of 'cocktails for dear ladies' & an extensive menu of beer snacks, meat dishes, pasta & salads. **$$$**

♀ **Buddha Bar** [map, page 94] Akhunbaev 97a; 510 359; 24hrs daily. This has a super-cool location in a log cabin south of the city centre. Popular with expatriates & Bishkek's bright young things. Pizza & Japanese dishes. **$$$**

♀ **Metro Bar** [map, page 94] (also known as the 'American Pub') Chui 168 (junction with Turusbekova); 310 710; 10.00–midnight. This is a long-established & popular expatriate hangout, especially for Americans. As well as a wide selection of drinks, the pub, in a converted puppet theatre, serves a variety of Mexican & American dishes like Tex-Mex burritos, nachos, hamburgers & pizzas. The Metro Bar attracts very few locals but is popular with Peace Corps volunteers & embassy officials. Mostly imported beers; live music some nights. Special foreign events like St Patrick's Day & Halloween are celebrated with some gusto here & there are large TV screens for sports events like World Cup football. The pub has a small bookshop area with English-language travel literature & regional guides & histories. **$$$**

♀ **Steinbrau** [map, page 95] Gertsena 5; 432 144. Incongruously situated close to Bishkek's main mosque, Steinbrau is a Munich-style beer hall run by an ethnic German family. The main hall is quite vast, with a high ceiling, enormous brass bar & large wooden tables. There is also an upstairs seating area & an outdoor courtyard. Busy waiting staff scurry about offering a choice of beers – Pilsner, amber, dark – bar snacks & a good choice of mostly German & Austrian meat & fish dishes that you can select from a multilingual picture menu. The excellent home-brewed beer can be seen bubbling away though the windows by the entrance. A resident pianist & violinist provide musical accompaniment. Steinbrau has an easy-going, convivial atmosphere & is popular with locals & visitors alike. $$$

♀**Johnny Pub** Toktogul 107 (Toktogul/Orozbekov junction); ☎891 111; ⏲ 14.00–02.00. A brewery & American restaurant popular with Bishkek's young set. $$–$$$

ENTERTAINMENT AND NIGHTLIFE

Bishkek's nightspots should be approached with some caution, as drunken violence and attacks on well-heeled foreigners are not uncommon. The cost of admission is usually in the order of 500–1,000som for men and 300–700som for women, and depends on both the club and the day of the week. According to some reports people are routinely robbed in front of some of them as muggers wait outside bars and nightclubs for inebriated foreigners to emerge. Reduce the risk of this by not walking from nightclub to nightclub, but taking a taxi instead (120–200som at night), even for a short distance (although waiting for a taxi outside a club you may also be vulnerable). Once inside avoid, if you can, any obviously dodgy Mafia-style characters and be careful whose drink you spill.

NIGHTCLUBS

☆ **12 Bar** [103 E5] Razzakov 32; ☎660 012; ⏲ 18.00–last customer. A rather exclusive rooftop club with 2 floors of lounges & dance floors with a panoramic view over Bishkek. Strict dress code.

☆ **Apple** [102 A4] Manas 28; ☎312 837; ⏲ 21.30–04.00 Tue–Sun. A popular city disco with a large dance floor, young crowd & special events on Sun.

☆ **Arbat** [95 G7] Yunusaliev 91; ☎512 087, 512 094; ⏲ 21.00–05.00, closed Mon & Tue. Club popular with Bishkek's elite, slightly older crowd, although the strip club in the back does lower the tone somewhat.

☆ **FM** [102 C2] Chui 209; ☎620 131; ⏲ 22.00–05.00. Next door to the White House. This popular, central nightclub, formerly known as the Golden Bull, has a lively crowd that usually inc a fair number of expatriates & foreign visitors.

☆ **Heaven** [103 H1] Frunze 429b; ☎439 923. Inside the Hotel Dostuk (see page 107).

☆ **Pharaoh** [102 A2] Chui 286; ☎614 677; ⏲ 21.00–04.00. On the east side of the State Philharmonic building. Small dance floor.

☆ **Promzona** [95 H4] Cholpon-Atinskaya 16; ☎900 244, 900 245; www.promzona.kg; ⏲ 20.00–04.00. Some way (a taxi ride) east of the centre, this has live music with rock, jazz & blues acts playing most nights.

☆ **Retro Metro** [94 C7] Mira 24; ☎210 202; ⏲ 14.00–02.00. 80s-themed popular venue for late-night dancing. The resident DJ spins discs from inside a section of a tube train engine.

☆ **Zeppelin Rock Bar** [95 H4] Chui 43; ☎365 849; ⏲ 14.00–02.00. A rock bar at the far eastern end of Chui with live music, a young local crowd & cheap beer.

THEATRES

Most performances follow the Russian tradition of starting and finishing early, often beginning around 17.00. Tickets are relatively easy to come by at the box office and good seats are very inexpensive by Western standards. Posters outside the venues themselves advertise what is coming up; occasionally there are adverts in the local press. Tickets can usually be bought from the box office on the night of the performance.

🎭 **Circus** [103 G1] Frunze; ☎661 808. Although run-down, this stages regular performances of local troupes & visiting performers from abroad (mostly CIS and China).

🎭 **Conservatory** [95 G7] Jantoshev 115; ☎570 225. Occasional student concerts take place here.

🎭 **Russian Drama Theatre** [103 F2] Tynystanov 122; ☎662 032. Puts on productions of national & international works in Russian.

🎭 **State Academic Drama Theatre** [102 D1] Panfilov 273; ☎665 802. Located next to Panfilov Park, behind the White House, this theatre stages mostly works in the Kyrgyz language, but also sometimes in Russian.

3

🎭 **State Opera & Ballet Theatre** [103 G2] Abdrakhmanov 167; ✆ 661 548. This elegant Neoclassical building opposite the State Museum for Fine Arts puts on both Kyrgyz & Western classical productions of ballet & opera. It has its own resident opera & ballet companies, although there are sometimes performances by visiting companies, too. Performances begin at 17.00 & tickets cost from 100som.

🎭 **State Philharmonic** [102 A2] (*'Filarmonia'*) Chui 210; ✆ 212 262, 212 235. On the junction with Manas, this Bishkek institution stages mostly Western classical concerts, with occasional dance, pop & Kyrgyz folklore events. Tickets are priced 300–500som depending on the programme.

CINEMAS

Entrance to most Bishkek cinemas is around 150–250som. Soft drinks, snacks and beer are usually available in the foyer. They rarely get crowded.

🎬 **Ala-Too** [103 F2] Chui/Erkindik; ✆ 661 957; ⏲ 10.00–midnight. Shows 2D & 3D films. Daytime showings are significantly cheaper.

🎬 **Bishkek Park** [102 A3] Kievskaya; ✆ 312 054. In the new Bishkek Park shopping mall on the 4th floor, this has 3 screens & the latest equipment.

🎬 **Dom Kino** [94 D6] ('House of Cinema') Logvinenko 13; ✆ 300 752; ⏲ 10.00–16.30. Sometimes hosts seasons of foreign films & shows foreign-language films in their original language as well as dubbed into Russian.

🎬 **Kosmopark** [95 G7] Yunusaliev (Karl Marx) at Donetskaya intersection; ✆ 299 494; www.cp.kg. 4 large floating screens equipped to show 3D movies.

🎬 **Manas** [94 B7] Mira 53, to the south of Isa Akhunbaev; ✆ 545 826. The largest cinema in central Asia, with 3 halls.

🎬 **Russia** [102 C2] Chui/Togolok Moldo; ✆ 660 960; www.cinema.kg; ⏲ 09.00–midnight. With 3 screens, 1 of the oldest & most attractive cinemas in the city. Bowling alley also on same site.

🎬 **Vefa** [95 E7] Gorky 27/1; ✆ 596 688. On 3rd floor of Vefa shopping centre, this has 2 modern comfortable halls with 3D screens showing the latest Hollywood blockbusters.

SHOPPING

Bishkek has a wide variety of shopping outlets where anything from stationery to souvenirs can be bought. As well as a handful of large, well-stocked **department stores**, there are numerous street stalls, especially around the pedestrian underpasses on Chui and, of course, bona fide **markets** like Osh and Dordoi bazaars. There are also **kiosks** everywhere selling stationery, magazines, phonecards, chocolate bars, and soft and alcoholic drinks. Whatever else they might lack, you can always be sure that they will have a comprehensive selection of vodka and beer available.

DEPARTMENT STORES & SHOPPING MALLS

Beta Stores [102 B3] Chui 150a (corner of Isanov); ✆ 661 080. With a similar range of goods to TsUM, perhaps a little more upmarket, this Turkish-owned concern has an excellent, well-stocked food hall on the ground floor & the handy Beta Gourmet restaurant on the 1st. Some souvenirs on the 1st floor, too, but these tend to be a little overpriced.

Bishkek Park [102 A3] Kievskaya; ✆ 691 111; www.bishkekpark.kg; ⏲ 10.00–22.00 daily. Bishkek's newest & swankiest mall with X-ray security on the door & a wide choice of upmarket designer goods. Also cafés, fast food, bowling, cinema & children's entertainment.

Caravan [102 B3] Kievskaya 128; ✆ 909 400; ⏲ 09.00–19.00 daily. An older mall selling mostly clothes & accessories.

Detsky Mir [103 H3] Chui 147/4; ✆ 621 313. With a name that translates as 'Baby's Land' in Russian, this has all kinds of goods for children ranging from games to clothes & school supplies.

Dordoi Plaza [103 H3] Ibraimov 115a (corner of Kievskaya); ✆ 690 040; ⏲ 09.00–20.00 daily. A large, modern shopping complex which contains over 100 individual shops.

Narodniy A good supermarket chain for everyday purchases with several branches around the city.

TsUM [103 G2] Chui 155; ✆ 909 808; ⏲ 09.00–20.00. Bishkek's main department store, established in 1956 & at this location since 1976, has several floors that sell a wide range of electronic goods, photographic supplies, mobile phones, CDs & other necessities of modern life. Also furniture, household goods & local crafts, & souvenirs on the 4th floor. Probably the best place in the city for a cheap 'I've been to Kyrgyzstan' T-shirt.

Vefa Centre [95 E7] 27/1 Baitik Baatyr/Gorky; ✆901 167; ⏰ 10.00–20.00 daily. Cinema & international food court on 3rd floor.

SOUVENIRS

In addition to the places listed below, both Beta Stores & TsUM have a good selection of souvenirs like *shyrdaks*, felt goods & pottery, as do the showrooms at Osh Bazaar, which is probably the cheapest place for souvenirs in the city. A concentration of small souvenir shops can be found along the south side of Chui Prospect between Manas & Logvinenko.

Anar Art Salon [102 B2] Chui 140; m 0556 977 726; ⏰ 10.00–20.00 daily. Clothes, bags & handmade felt goods.

Iman [102 C2] Chui 128;✆212 405; ⏰ 10.00–19.00 Mon–Sat. Opposite the Russian Cinema, this has Soviet-era antiques as well as the standard Kyrgyz craft souvenirs.

Kiyal [94 A4] Chui 202 (at Osh Bazaar);✆646 240; ⏰ 09.00–17.00 Mon–Thu. Carpets & Kyrgyz handicrafts.

Koldo Shop [103 E2] Pushkin 78a;✆793 993; ⏰ 10.00–20.00 Mon–Sat. Traditional handicrafts made & sold by people with disabilities & the socially disadvantaged.

Saima [102 B2] Chui 140; m 0555 487 700; www.embroidery.com.kg; ⏰ 10.00–19.00 Mon–Sat. A family-run shop with an emphasis on Kyrgyz embroidery, in particular antique *tush kiyiz* wedding cloths that are converted into decorative items like pillowcases, curtains & table runners. Also other souvenirs, felt goods & postcards.

Tumar [102 B3] Isanov 80;✆311 323; www. tumar.com; ⏰ 10.00–20.00 daily. Good range of high-quality Kyrgyz craft products designed to appeal to Western tastes. Products inc *shyrdaks*, pottery, felt goods & textiles, as well as charming decorations & toys.

ART

Al Hyatt [103 G5] Moskovskaya 49;✆438 974; ⏰ 11.00–19.00 Tue–Sat. Occasional exhibitions, with art for sale, are held here.

Asia Gallery [103 F3] Union of Kyrgyz Artists, Chui 108; ✆624 505; ⏰ 10.00–17.00 Mon–Fri, closed for lunch 13.00–14.00. This gallery on the 1st floor sells work by local artists. Let yourself in & hunt around for the elusive supervisor. There is a certain amount of flexibility on price, particularly if you are buying more than one painting, & it is possible to meet many of the artists whose work is represented.

Chuikov Art Centre [103 E2] Pushkin 78 (in Dubovy Park);✆662 343; ⏰ 10.00–18.00, closed Sun. Named after Semen Chuikov, the so-called father of Kyrgyz art, this has frequent exhibitions by local artists.

BOOKS

English-language reading material is hard to find in Bishkek, apart from English primers for language students. There is a small selection of English literature, local guides & history books on display inside the Metro Bar on Chui (see page 106) at slightly more than European prices. The Hyatt Regency Hotel (see page 99) keeps 2-day-old American newspapers & magazines. Otherwise, the following may have the odd English-language title among their mostly Russian stock.

Akademikniga [102 D5] Moskovskaya 141; ✆662 523

Odyssey [102 A2] Manas 40, between Chui & Kievskaya;✆613 673. Also has a good selection of stationery & greetings cards.

Rariyet [103 E2] Pushkin 78 (inside Dom Druzhba), east of Ala-Too Sq;✆664 524. There's a small selection of English-language books here, as well as a choice of maps & postcards. The shop entrance is down steps off Razzakov. There's another branch at Chui 271, just before Mahatma Gandhi.

MAPS

GeoID [102 B3] Kievskaya 107, room 4, 3rd floor; ✆613 821; ⏰ 08.00–17.00 Mon–Fri. This can be a little hard to find: take the entrance to the left of the DHL office; walk past the person at the corridor desk & take the stairs to the 3rd floor; the room is signposted. This is an excellent place to buy both Cyrillic & Latin script maps of Bishkek as well as maps for the whole of Kyrgyzstan. They also have various themed maps such as the Silk Road in Kyrgyzstan & 1:200,000 topological maps that cover the whole country, which are helpful for trekking (although not sufficiently detailed or accurate to completely depend on). Most maps cost 150–400som.

MARKETS

Bishkek has several markets, usually crowded and buzzing with customers and traders alike. Be very aware of your money & possessions amid the bustle & jostle, as pickpockets systematically work all of these markets, especially Osh. Weekends are usually the busiest days, particularly Sundays for Dordoi.

Alamedin Bazaar (Аламединский базар) [95 H2] Jibek-Jolu/Almatinskaya, just east of East Bus Station. The smallest of the 4 listed here but still pretty big. Most activity takes place within a covered main hall selling mostly food. Money-changers congregate opposite the main entrance.

Dordoi (also called Tolchok) Bazaar (Дордой базары) [95 F1] This enormous market is around 7km from the city centre to the north. Dordoi covers a large area filled with shipping containers double-stacked on top of each other, with narrow corridors for shoppers leading between them. There are said to be around 7,000 containers in total. At the edge of the site are outdoor stalls selling fruit & vegetables & cheap clothing. This is said by some to be the largest market in all central Asia (although also see Kara-Suu near Osh, page 277). This is easy to believe with what is said to be around 15,000 traders & an annual turnover of US$100 million. The goods on sale here range from food & cheap clothing

to household & electrical goods; a vast amount of it originates from China. There is also a section selling Turkish goods.

Kudai Bergen used car bazaar (Базар Кудайберген) [94 A4] This bazaar, 3km west of Osh Bazaar, is *the* place to pick up a bargain vehicle, with a huge range of secondhand cars, buses & minibuses on offer as well as spare parts. A Lada that has seen better days may be had for US$700 or less, while a German minibus will cost in the region of US$2,500. This is the obvious place to purchase that collectable 1970s Volga. The bazaar is open every day but is busiest at w/ends.

Orto-Sai Bazaar (Орто-сай базар) [95 F7] South of the centre, this is another open bazaar serving the needs of that part of the city. There's also an interesting flea market here.

Osh Bazaar (Ошский базар) [94 A4] Kievskaya/Beishenalieva, south of the West Bus Station. Osh Bazaar is the largest market within the city limits. This crowded market offers a genuine flavour (both literally & culturally) of the Kyrgyzstan countryside in the city. Selling mainly fruit & vegetables, but also meat, dairy & baked products, Osh Bazaar has both an open-air market & a covered area. It is liveliest at w/ends but is always busy with traders: bakers wandering the aisles with *lepyoshka* piled high on trays; Kyrgyz, Russian, Korean & Dungan vendors shouting out in their different languages to compete for business; & gypsies with smoking dishes of herbs wafting smoke over produce for luck. Right next to Osh Bazaar, across Kievskaya to the north, is Kyyal (Kyrgyz for 'fantasy'), a building full of souvenir stalls selling *shyrdaks* & other items with some of the lowest prices in the city.

SPORTS

GYMS

The city has a number of sports clubs & gymnasiums. Particularly popular are martial arts like jujitsu & taekwando.

Fitness Centre, Hyatt Regency Hotel [103 G1] Abdrakhmanov 196; ☎661 234; ⏰ 06.00–22.00. Immaculate facilities with English-speaking staff. Monthly passes available for use of the outdoor swimming pool, jacuzzi & gym.

Karven Club [95 G5] Gogol 77 (junction with Toktogul); ☎681 515; www.karven.kg;

⏰ 07.00–23.00. Tennis courts, fitness centre, sauna, solarium, badminton & swimming pool. Various membership tariffs available, discount for student-card holders.

Sports Palace [102 C2] Togolok Moldo 40; ☎625 169. Bishkek's largest indoor sporting venue, with a gym, open-air swimming pool & sauna.

Sun City Sport Centre [95 H4] Chui 2; ☎534 972; www.sun-city.kg. Sports complex with a range of activities inc martial arts & fitness training.

BOWLING

Bishkek Park [102 A3] Kievskaya 148; ☎691 111; ☺ 10.00–22.00. In the new shopping mall on Kievskaya, this also has a café & billiards room.
Bowling Center [103 G1] Frunze 338a; ☎681 700; ☺ 13.00–01.00. Behind the Hyatt Hotel. 170–230som per game.

HORSERIDING

Equestrian School [95 H4] Bakinskaya 204a; ☎279 698. Horseback riding lessons.

SWIMMING The Hyatt Regency & Golden Dragon hotels have outdoor pools; Ak Keme & Silk Road Lodge, indoor pools.

Delphin [94 A5] Molodaya Gvardiya 2; ☎254 607; ☺ 06.00–21.00. Swimming pool & sauna.
Karven Club [95 G5] Gogol 77; ☎681 515; www. karven.kg. Outdoor pool, ideal for warm weather. The day pass is much better value than paying by the hour.
Sports Palace [102 C2] Togolok Moldo 40; ☎625 169. Olympic-sized outdoor pool & a small sauna.

TENNIS

Tai Break [102 C1] Togolok Moldo 17; ☎217 842. This has a tennis school as well as courts to hire.

OTHER PRACTICALITIES

MEDICAL SERVICES AND PHARMACIES
Hospitals & clinics
Emergency health care is available free to foreign visitors. Although doctors are generally well trained, facilities & services will be well below normal European expectations, & so a visit to a private clinic is advised. This is where comprehensive travel insurance comes into its own. In an emergency a city ambulance may be summoned by dialling ☎103, but do not rely on it actually arriving. For a commercial ambulance, for which you have to pay, dial ☎151. Both are available 24 hours a day.

✚ **Med Expert Clinic** Tynystanov 219; m 0555 949 911. English-speaking private clinic for foreigners needing routine medical treatment. No emergency care. Prior appointment necessary.
✚ **NeoMed Diagnostic and Consultative Medical Clinic** [102 D5] Orozbekov 46; ☎906 090. A general clinic with a number of specialists, modern equipment inc CT scanner & hi-tech laboratory.
✚ **Trauma Clinic (Poliklinika stroitelei)** [102 A4] Manas 41 (junction with Toktogul); ☎216 875, 318 922. 24hr first aid for less serious accidents. No inpatient facilities.

✚ **VIP Clinic** [102 D3] Kievskaya 110; ☎621 575; ☺ 24hr medical service. Private ambulance.

Dental clinics
✚ **Diplomat Dental Salon** [103 G5] Abdrakhmanov 101; ☎386 606; www. stomdiplomat.kg; ☺ 08.00–19.00 Mon–Sat
✚ **Estet Baitik** [95 F7] Baatyr 51/Gorky; ☎543 884. Full range of treatments & high quality service but no English speakers.
✚ **Kairos Dental Clinic** [102 B1] Ryskulov 10; ☎612 302; www.dentist.kg. Modern, state-of-the-art clinic. English spoken.

Pharmacies
✚ **Central** [103 G1] Frunze 340; ☎681 005; ☺ 24hrs
✚ **Neman** All branches of the Neman Pharmacy network are ☺ 24hrs: Akhunbaev 31, ☎545 413; Chui 94, ☎342 021; Chui 113, ☎363 439; Kievskaya 38, ☎438 927; Manas 8, ☎315 634; Moskovskaya 139, ☎625 665; & Tokoluk Moldo 14, ☎663 350
✚ **Prestige** [102 B3] Kievskaya 95a; ☎621 462

MONEY EXCHANGE It is easy to change **cash** (US dollars, euros, Kazakh tenge, Russian roubles and to a much lesser extent, pounds sterling) at one of the numerous exchange booths, or *obmyen valyoot* (обмен валюты), that are scattered around the city; many hotels, too, have an exchange desk. There are many on Toktogul, on Sovetskaya north of Bokonbaev, inside (and beside) TsUM department store, and on Kievskaya near Osh Bazaar. Those at the top end of

Manas towards Chui are more likely to change pounds sterling, although places willing to deal with Uzbek som are much harder to find. They do not charge commission but make their profit from the differential between the buying and selling rate; exchange rates, however, seem to vary very little from place to place as long as you present them with pristine notes. Most are honest but be sure to count your money carefully. For more formal transactions, Bishkek is well provided with banks, although not all are of use for the general needs of overseas travellers. **Travellers' cheques** are accepted by few banks these days but they may be exchanged and **cash advances** organised with a little bit of paperwork, at the branches listed below.

$ **Bakai Bank** [102 B3] Isanov 75; ☎ 610 242; ⊕ 08.30–12.00 & 13.00–15.00 Mon–Fri. Will exchange Thomas Cook, American Express & CitiCorp travellers' cheques for 3% commission; Visa cash advances.

$ **Demir Kyrgyz International Bank** [102 A2] Chui 245; ☎ 610 610; ⊕ 09.00–12.00 & 13.00–16.00 Mon–Fri (closes 14.30 Fri). Will change Amex travellers' cheques for 3% commission & give advances on Visa & Maestro cards.

As with most large towns and cities in Kyrgyzstan, it is easy to withdraw cash from **ATM machines** in Bishkek, although be aware that some will work for locally issued cards only. Machines are ubiquitous in the city these days and can be found on every major street and inside the foyer of most supermarkets and department stores. Many will dispense both som and US dollars; a commission of 2% will be added to your bill, although this is not mentioned on the machine receipt. Most deal only with Visa but a number will also accept MasterCard. Cash dispensers of **Kazkommertsbank** at TsUM department store [103 G2], Dordoi Plaza at Ibraimov [95 H3], and at Abdrakhmanov 136, will accept Visa, MasterCard, Maestro and Cirrus credit and debit cards. Elsewhere in the country there are only a handful of ATMs that will deal with anything other than Visa and so it is worth bearing this in mind before leaving the city.

Money transfers from abroad may also be made by way of **Western Union** and **MoneyGram**, which operate through several Bishkek banks.

COMMUNICATIONS
Post Bishkek's **main post office** is at Chui 96, on the corner with Abdrakhmanov [103 G3] (☎ *915 293;* ⊕ *07.00–19.00 Mon–Sat, 08.00–18.00 Sun*). Large parcels may be posted from here but leave them open to allow for customs inspection. There is a separate room that deals with EPS (Express Postal Service).

DHL at Kievskaya 107 [102 B3] (☎ *611 111; e frucs@dhl.com*) and **Federal Express** at Moskovskaya 217 [102 B4] (☎ *353 111; e fedex@elcat.kg*) both provide courier services, while **American Resources International** [103 E3] (*ARI Cargo, Erkindik 35;* ☎ *660 070; e bishkek@aricargo.com; www.aricargo.com*) is able to ship larger items by air or overland.

Telephone The central **Kyrgyz Telecom** office is next door to the main post office [103 G3] (⊕ *07.00–22.00 daily*). The call boxes outside can be used for local calls, but national and international calls should be made from the booths inside. Calls are prepaid at the counter depending on the amount of time you want; change will be given after the call for any time not used, or a refund given if there is no answer. International dialling codes are preceded by 00 and you may need to dial 3 to talk when your call is picked up. The main office also has computer booths for Skype calls.

Most people make use of mobile phones in Bishkek these days, which are cheap and reliable, but a few phone booths survive that take tokens (*zhetoni*) bought from kiosks, although these may only be used for local calls (put in the token when the call is answered). Other phones use prepaid cards which, once again, can be bought from kiosks. They come in denominations of 50, 100, 200 and 400 units and the cost is clearly marked. Some kiosk vendors add a small mark-up to the indicated price.

Card phones can be used for both local and long-distance calls. Local calls within the city are free if made from a private phone, but hotels usually make a small charge for these and invariably charge way over the odds for long-distance or international calls.

Mobile phones The main providers are **Beeline** (m *(0775) 580 611*) and **MegaCom** (m *(0555) 500 000*). Both operate on the GSM system, so you may be able to use a roaming service and your own number.

Local **SIM cards** may be bought for very little from many outlets in the city, especially the ground floor of TsUM and the first floor of Beta Stores. Sometimes they are given away free as promotional offers. Both Beeline and MegaCom provide a service that does not entail setting up a local account. This works by purchasing a SIM card with a local number and a card with credits. When your credit is exhausted you will need to buy another card, dial the service provider and enter a serial number, which will add the new credits to your account.

Important telephone numbers All of the three-figure numbers below are free from both private and street call phones:

Ambulance ☏103	**Fire** ☏101
Directory enquiries ☏109	**Police** ☏102
Emergency medical service ☏151	**Police hotline** ☏662 331, 284 305

Internet With the advent of Wi-Fi there are now fewer internet cafés in Bishkek than there used to be. Charges are generally around 40–50som per hour, although some also charge for megabytes used. A concentration of these can be found in the area around the junction of Abdrakhmanov and Moskovskaya. It is also possible to buy a USB internet dongle in TsUM or elsewhere that allows Wi-Fi internet usage for laptops wherever there is a decent phone signal. Wi-Fi is now quite widespread in the city with many of the more upmarket cafés, restaurants and hotels offering it for free.

VISA REGISTRATION AND EXTENSION The **OVIR Office** [103 G3] (*Kievskaya 58/2;* ☏ *434 676;* ⊕ *09.00–17.00 Mon–Fri*) is the place to register your visa should it be necessary, although very few nationalities are still required to do this (see page 58). Visas can be extended at the Ministry of Foreign Affairs at Togolok Moldo 10a (☏ *663 270; www.dcsmfa.kg*).

Embassies Bishkek is not a bad place to while away time waiting for visas to be processed, although some are more straightforward than others. More often than not it makes more sense to arrange visas in advance before you leave home as obtaining visas for neighbouring countries like China and Uzbekistan can often be problematic.

❸ **Afghanistan** [95 E7] Jukeeva-Pudovkin 24a; ☏543 802; ⊕ 09.30–16.00 Mon–Thu, 09.30–12.00 Fri
❸ **Canada** Moskovskaya 189; ☏650 506; 650 101; e canada_honcon@akipress.org. This is an honorary consul only; for consular matters you should refer to the Canadian Embassy in Kazakhstan.

❸ **China** [94 C7] Mira 299/7; ☎597 483, 597 482, 597 484; e chinaemb_kg@mfa.gov.cn; http://kg.chineseembassy.org; ⏰ 09.15–12.00 Mon, Wed & Fri. It is definitely better to arrange Chinese visas before leaving home as it may not be possible here. At the time of the last update this embassy was no longer issuing visas to non-residents but this seems to change periodically.

❸ **France** [95 E6] Bokonbaev 113; ☎660 364; e france.kg@gmail.com

❸ **Germany** [103 E5] Razzakov 28; ☎666 624; e info@bischkek.diplo.de; www.bischkek.diplo.de

❸ **India** [94 B3] Mahatma Gandhi 100a; ☎979 256, 979 257; www.embassyofindia.kg; ⏰ 09.00–13.00 & 14.00–17.30 Mon–Fri

❸ **Iran** [103 E4] Razzakov 36; ☎621 281; e sefabish@amil.elcat.kg; ⏰ 09.00–17.00 Mon–Fri. Individuals who apply here are usually told to apply for a letter of invitation (LOI) through www.iranjasminco.com, which will take a matter of weeks. Expect problems & unexplained delays even if you have the LOI.

❸ **Italy** [103 G3] Abdrakhmanov 175 (honorary consul only); ☎666 463, 661 737; e italconsulkg@italpromo.org

❸ **Japan** [95 E5] Razzakov 16; ☎300 050, 300 051; www.kg.emb-japan.go.jp; ⏰ 09.00–17.00 Mon–Fri

❸ **Kazakhstan** [94 A6] Mira 95a; ☎692 098; e bishkek@mfa.kz; www.kaz-emb.kg; ⏰ 10.00–12.00 Mon–Thu. 5-day Kazakh transit visas can usually be obtained reasonably quickly without an LOI if you have evidence of tickets out of the country & a 3rd country visa.

❸ **Netherlands** [103 F4] Foundation Publishing Development Centre, Tynystanov 96, apartment 12 (honorary consul); ☎690 565; e ben@berwers.nl; ⏰ 09.30–12.30 Mon–Fri

❸ **Pakistan** [94 D2] Serova Bayalinova 37; ☎373 901, 373 902; e parepbishkek@aknet.kg; www.mofa.gov.pk/kyrgyzstan

❸ **Russia** [102 A3] Manas 55; ☎610 905, 610 891; e rusembkg@mid.ru; www.kyrgyz.mid.ru (consular department for visas: ☎612 614, 612 615, 612 617; e ruscons@saimanet.kg). You will need an invitation (try Kyrgyz Concept, Celestial Mountains or CAT), which will take a week to arrive. To apply you will need the original invitation voucher (2 stamped documents on an A4 sheet), passport (make a copy), completed application form, photo & the exact payment in US$, which will probably be in the order of US$70–100.

❸ **Sweden** [103 F3] (honorary consulate) c/o ABB Representation Office, Chui 114, room 407; ☎627 010; e abb@mail.kg

❸ **Switzerland** [103 E5] Erkindik 21, 11th floor; ☎301 036; e bik.visa@eda.admin.ch; www.swisscoop.kg; ⏰ 09.00–12.00 Mon–Fri

❸ **Tajikistan** [95 H7] Karadarinskaya 36, Kök-Jar Microdistrict; ☎511 637; e tjemb@ktenet.kg; www.tajikemb.kg. Visas usually issued within 24 hrs, with free GBAO permits on request.

❸ **Turkey** [103 F5] Moskovskaya 89; ☎905 900; www.bishkek.emb.mfa.gov.tr; ⏰ 09.00–12.00 Mon–Fri

❸ **UK** [103 E5] Erkindik 21 (Orion Business Centre, 4th floor, office 404); ☎303 637; e ukin.kyrgyzrepublic@fco.gov.uk; www.gov.uk/world/kyrgyzstan; ⏰ 09.00–13.00 &14.00–17.30 Mon–Fri. Consular assistance should be sought from the British Embassy in Astana (*Kosmonavtov 62, Renco Building, 6th Floor, Astana 010000, Kazakhstan;* ☎*+7 7172 556 200;* e *ukinkz@fco.gov.uk*).

❸ **USA** [94 C7] Mira 171; ☎551 241; http://bishkek.usembassy.gov; ⏰ 08.00–17.00 Mon–Fri

❸ **Uzbekistan** [103 F4] Tynystanov 213; ☎663 078, 662 065; e uzbembish@infotel.kg; ⏰ closed Mon. Kyrgyz-Uzbek relations continue to be strained & this has had an impact on visa applications. The embassy may require an LOI (but this keeps changing) & it sometimes insists that you produce an air ticket to/from Bishkek. The staff speak no English so you may need to make use of a Russian speaker & phone for an appointment in advance. You will need a copy of your passport & a photo. Visas take a minimum of 4–7 business days to issue.

WHAT TO SEE AND DO

Bishkek is a pleasant city but in terms of sightseeing there is little that might be described as a 'must see'. Nevertheless, there are a handful of worthwhile monuments, some pleasant parks and a few interesting museums and art galleries to seek out. All of the sights mentioned below are in the city centre, which might be defined as the area circumscribed by Jibek-Jolu to the north, Moskovskaya to the south, Molodaya Gvardiya to the west and Ibraimov to the east. Running east–west through this downtown area is the central avenue of Chui Prospect.

AROUND ALA-TOO SQUARE The heart of the city, such as it is, is centred upon **Ala-Too Square** [103 E3], which was previously known as Lenin Square up until independence in 1991. This large, rather anonymous, concrete expanse facing Chui Prospect is where most official celebrations tend to take place, and was also the setting for the violent protests and shootings that accompanied 2010's regime change. There is said to be an underground complex beneath the square that is connected to the White House by a secret passageway. The large subterranean assembly room here is purported to have portraits of the Soviet politburo still in place, but it has not seen much use since independence.

The square used to have a statue of the eponymous Soviet leader as its centrepiece, but the monument was shifted in 2003 to a less prominent location just behind the State Historical Museum. Lenin was replaced by something more symbolic of the nation's newly minted Kyrgyz character, the Erkindik (Freedom) Monument, but this in turn has since been replaced by an **equestrian statue of Manas** [103 E2] on top of a lofty plinth (see box, page 117). Just west of the monument stands the 45-metre high national flagpole, erected in 2009 to replace a shorter one installed in 1998. The flagpole with enormous national fluttering flag aloft is attended by an immaculately dressed guard of honour who changes every hour and devotedly packs away the flag for the night when dusk falls.

The relocated **Lenin statue** [103 E2], which captures the man in 'pointing to the future' mode, dates from 1984 and stands around 10m tall, presiding over the paved square to the north of the State Historical Museum, which was formerly home to the Monument to Labour Glory. This small square has since been designated as the replacement Lenin Square, although it is undeniably more low-key than its predecessor. In his former home, Lenin used to point south towards the Ala-Too peaks; now he has his back to the mountains and he gestures in the general direction of the American University, whether in righteous fury or in conciliation, no-one can be certain. Perhaps it says much about Kyrgyzstan that Lenin was merely demoted to a less prominent location (and a much lower plinth) rather than destroyed outright, as was the case in less-forgiving neighbouring countries like Uzbekistan. Bishkek is now the only remaining central Asian capital to have a Lenin statue.

On the south side of the square, above Kievskaya in front of the arches of Arabaev University, is a statue of the country's best-known modern writer **Chingiz Aitmatov** [103 E3] (1928–2008), looking rather casual with his tie undone and jacket slung over his shoulder. This, along with the equestrian statue of Manas across the square, was erected in 2011 to celebrate the 20th anniversary of Kyrgyzstan's independence.

Facing south on to Chui Prospect, just west of Ala-Too Square, is the **White House** [102 D2], a seven-storey Neoclassical marble edifice built in 1985, which is the seat of Kyrgyzstan's government and houses the president's office. The iron railings host monuments to those who died here in April 2010. Across the road, on the corner of the square between the State History Museum and the White House, is an impressive monument in black and white marble. Its symbolism of good triumphing over evil is clear to see, with three grim-faced men pushing the fractured black stone ('darkness', 'evil') away from the white ('light', 'goodness'). A Kyrgyz inscription dedicates the monument to the memory of those demonstrators killed by police fire at Aksy in Jalal-Abad Province in 2002 and also to those who died in the revolutionary events of April 2010.

Central to this square is the **Friendship Monument** [102 D2], a tall modernist study in concrete. The square here was inaugurated by Kosygin in 1974 to commemorate the centenary of the Kyrgyz peoples joining the Russian Empire. The trees around the monument were planted by key Soviet dignitaries such as Kosygin and Brezhnev.

PANFILOV PARK AND DUBOVY PARK Situated immediately behind the White House and its serious affairs of state is an altogether more fun-loving place – **Panfilov Park** [102 D1], one of Bishkek's most popular green spaces. Naturally enough, Panfilov Park boasts a statue of its namesake, Ivan Vasilyevich Panfilov, the Russian general and commander of the defenders of Moscow, who died heroically in battle against the Nazis in 1941.

These days most Bishkek citizens visit the park less to admire the greatcoated war hero than to avail themselves of the fairground rides, karaoke machines, ice cream stalls and *shashlyk* vendors who cluster near the eastern entrance. There is a Ferris wheel here, too, and for a mere 50som you can get a crow's-eye view across the concrete squares and tree-lined avenues of central Bishkek to the mountains beyond. The park started out as a municipal garden planted by horticultural students in 1879; later on it became known as Red Star Park, as its walkways trace the shape of the five-pointed communist star. There appears to be no campaign as yet to rename it 'Freedom Park'.

East of Ala-Too Square is **Dom Druzhba** (Friendship House) [103 E2], which now serves as a community centre and zoological museum, but which in Soviet times was the headquarters of the Kyrgyz ASSR Central Committee. Behind this is another popular green space, **Dubovy (Oak) Park** [103 E2], which began as a grove of oak saplings in 1890. Like Panfilov Park, this is another good location for a quiet drink or a cool stroll among trees and away from the traffic.

The park hosts the **Memorial to the Red Guards** [103 F2], a red granite obelisk erected in 1960 which marks the common grave of the Bolshevik casualties of the Belovodsk counter-revolutionary uprising of 6 December 1918. Dubovy Park also has a **monument to Marx and Engels** [103 E2], who are depicted sitting next to each other on a bench, deep in conversation. Their names have been removed from the plinth, which indicates some sort of compromise with the past, in which out-of-favour ideologues may be depicted as long as they are not named – the same sort of logic that does not dethrone Lenin entirely but simply demotes him. The park also has a 2004 monument to Kurmanjan Datka, the Queen of the Alia, whose plinth formerly supported a statue of Cheka-founder Felix Dzerzhinsky (see box, page 117), and an outdoor sculpture garden with representations of cities from all over the former Soviet Union. The park is also home to the Russian Drama Theatre and two of the city's best restaurants – Stari Edgar and the Four Seasons (see pages 103–4).

Tree-lined **Erkindik (Freedom) Boulevard** stretches due south of Dubovy Park all the way to the railway station, its twin avenues bisected by a shady pedestrian zone dotted with benches, ping-pong tables and an assortment of statuary depicting Kyrgyz poets and war heroes. A shorter section extends north of Dubovy Park, too, linking it with the frantic thoroughfare of Jibek-Jolu Prospect. The promenade dates back to 1883 when it was created by planting poplars along a filled-up stream bed.

In the summer there are always large numbers of people here taking advantage of the shade and welcome respite from the city traffic: cigarette vendors, office workers, students and exhausted Russian pensioners with carrier bags. The avenue had several names before its present-day appellation was settled upon: originally it was simply the Boulevard; in post-Revolutionary times, it became Komsomolskaya; and then later, Prospect Dzerzhinsky, after the founder of the Cheka secret police, the forerunner of the KGB.

With independence from the Soviet Union, and a political need for nation-building and a distancing from the past, 'freedom' must have seemed like an obvious choice for its new and, hopefully final, alias. Contrary to this new spirit of nationalism, and bolstering the city's former Russian identity, a monument to an existing Soviet hero has firmly remained in place. Right at the bottom of Erkindik, facing the railway station, and constructed in 1938, stands an **equestrian statue of Mikhail Frunze** [103 E6], the Bolshevik general who gave his name to the city in 1926 when it became the capital of the Kyrgyz ASSR.

MOVING STATUES

The Erkindik (Freedom) Monument, which was erected in 1999 to commemorate eight years of Kyrgyz independence, represents a winged female figure holding a flame-ringed *tunduk*, the traditional wooden centrepiece of a yurt and most familiar of all Kyrgyz symbols. The monument originally stood at Dubovy Park where it replaced a statue of Cheka secret police-founder Felix Dzerzhinsky that had been moved to a less prominent location next to the National Library on Tynystanov. The Dzerzhinsky statue had, in turn, replaced an obelisk with an image of V I Lenin, which was removed when a grander monument of the erstwhile Soviet leader was installed at Ala-Too Square in 1984. In 2003 the Erkindik Monument was relocated to be given pride of place in front of Bishkek's State Historical Museum when Lenin, who previously stood here, was discretely shifted to a lower plinth a block to the north. The void at Dubovy Park left by Dzerzhinsky, and then Erkindik, has since been replaced by southern Kyrgyz heroine Kurmanjan Datka.

Lenin remains in place, pointing north to Kazakhstan and Russia, his back to the mountains, but the winged woman representing freedom has since been airbrushed from monumental history to be replaced by a large equestrian statue of Manas, the 10th-century Kyrgyz hero. It is easy enough to understand why Lenin and his like have been demoted to lesser prominence in the city, but why was the Erkindik Monument dismantled and removed from its high-profile position? Seemingly, it was a matter of tradition: no Kyrgyz women would pick up a *tunduk* – that was a man's role – and to do so, according to legend, was an ill omen for the country. Some argued that the tragic events of 2010 bore this out and because of this the statue had to come down. Another factor may have been that the woman's face was said to bear a resemblance to that of the wife of former president Askar Akayev. The statue's removal In 2011 may even be linked to the effect of a protest song by influential Kyrgyz rapper Tata Ulan, a devotee of Manas and Kyrgyz nationalism, whose songs have made critical statements about the prevalence of non-Muslim female immodesty in Kyrgyzstan (Erkindik's *tunduk*-holding female body possessed a voluptuous figure and free-flowing hair).

Whether or not Bishkek's statuary continue to take part in an ongoing game of musical plinths remains to be seen. What is clear is that the Erkindik Monument has since found a new, and hopefully more permanent, home in Batken in the far southwest of the country.

REVOLUTION SQUARE AND VICTORY SQUARE A few blocks further east of Dubovy Park, continuing along Chui Prospect, stands **Revolution Square** [103 F2], with the 1978 **Martyrs of the Revolution Monument** as its centrepiece; it's the work of local sculptor Tinibek Sadykov, for which he won the All Union Lenin Prize. The central figure here is Urkuya Saliyeva (1910–34), a young socialist organiser from southern Kyrgyzstan who was murdered by reactionary locals. She is surrounded by figures who represent the 'awakening proletariat'.

Just north of here, along Abdrakhmanov (formerly Sovetskaya), stand two of the city's great cultural institutions almost face to face across the street. On the right is the elegant pink façade and classical columns of the **State Opera and Ballet Theatre** [103 G2] with its interesting friezes and hammer and sickle motifs on its pillars. A little further east, along Chui Prospect and immediately north of the TsUM department store, is the breezy plaza of **Pobeda (Victory) Square** [103 H1], which until 1985 was the site of the city's central bazaar. More Kyrgyz symbolism takes pride of place here, with three massive curved arches that represent a section of yurt towering above a statue of a Kyrgyz woman waiting for her husband or son to return from the front (or, as some local wags say, for them to emerge from one of the nightclubs that surround the square).

The bulky monument was erected in 1985 to commemorate the 40th anniversary of the end of World War II. An eternal flame burns here, a focus around which an assortment of the city's drinkers and nefarious characters sometimes gather like wayward moths. At other times the square is besieged by wedding parties seeking a suitable backdrop for souvenir photographs and video takes.

If this concrete symbolism of traditional *jailoo* life is not enough, then there are clear reminders of the alpine terrain that lies beyond the city: the square is broad and uncluttered enough to afford clear views to the south of the perpetually snow-clad Ala-Too range. The view in the opposite direction is altogether less romantic: the bland bulk of Hotel Dostuk faces the square to the northeast, while to the northwest stands the unmistakable lime green and pink form of the **Circus building** [103 G1], shaped rather like a 1950s flying saucer. Beyond lie some of the less savoury quarters of the capital, and after dark the streets around here become the home ground of prostitutes and their pimps.

Returning to Ala-Too Square and heading west along Chui Prospect past the White House, the Rossiya cinema is on your right at the corner with Togolok Moldo, which leads north to Jibek-Jolu past **Spartak Stadium** [102 C1] on the right and the humdrum Palace of Sports on the left. The sports palace has a **statue of Kojomkol** outside, a semi-legendary giant of a man who is depicted here lifting a horse – certainly a twist on the usual equestrian statue theme. Kojomkol, who hailed from the Suusamyr Valley and lived from 1899 to 1955, was reported to have been 2.3m tall and would lift enormous stones just for fun and, if the mood took him, even his own horse.

WEST ALONG CHUI PROSPECT Continuing right down Frunze and then north down Logvinenko brings you to the thoroughfare of Jibek-Jolu and the nearby **Russian Orthodox Cathedral** [94 D3] with its sky-blue onion domes. Back on Chui, two blocks further west is the intersection with Manas where the **State Philharmonic Concert Hall** [102 A2] stands set back from the road with a large area of paved walkways, fountains and flower-beds in front of it. This is a popular meeting spot and a favoured location for street photographers to set up their equipment to tempt passers-by. In front of the concert hall, surrounded by spurting fountains, is another **equestrian statue of Manas**. This one depicts him on his horse, Ak-Kula, killing a dragon, with his wife, Kanykei, and Bakai, his faithful friend and counsellor, represented at the base of the statue. Around the square itself are a scattering of smaller statues of well-known Kyrgyz *manaschi* (traditional storytellers).

The next road junction west along Chui, with Turesbekova, has a smaller but still grand building that was the original State Philharmonic building, which later became a puppet theatre and now serves as an American-style pub for homesick expatriates – the Metro Bar (see page 106). Continuing west leads past the National State Academy on the right.

This brings you to Molodaya Gvardiya, a tree-lined boulevard, which is now officially referred to as Mahatma Gandhi, although the new name does not seem to have caught on. The former name translates as the **Avenue of the Young Guards** and the section that lies immediately off Chui is referred to as 'Heroes' Lane'. Originally this was the course of a tributary of the Ala-Archa River, but it was filled and planted with trees to create the present-day boulevard. The busts that line it are Soviet-era military heroes, and there is a large Komsomol (young communist league) statue of Soviet soldiers bearing the legend: 'We went to war for Communism'.

MUSEUMS Most museums have a small entrance fee of 50som or less. Foreigners usually pay more than locals. Many are closed on Mondays and some close for an hour's lunch break in the middle of the day.

Fine Arts Museum (Музей Исскуств) [103 F2] (*Abdrakhmanov 196;* \661 544; ⊕ *09.00–17.00 Tue–Sun; admission 50som*) This museum, opposite the Opera and Ballet Theatre and sometimes referred to as the Gapar Aytiev Museum of Applied Art, is dedicated to displaying temporary exhibitions, along with a permanent collection of Kyrgyz folk and applied art, as well as Russian and Soviet fine art. The permanent collection was originally kept in St Nicholas's Russian Orthodox church in Dubovy Park (which now houses the Gallery of the Artist's Union) but the museum was built in 1974 to house the collection, and was renovated a few years ago.

Along with the obligatory yurt and a colourful display of *shyrdaks*, carpets and typical felt goods, there are several galleries of differing styles of Soviet-period art, including Soviet Realism and propaganda, and replicas of Egyptian, Roman and Greek statuary. Most captions are in Russian and Kyrgyz but some are in English. Sometimes Kyrgyz felt-ware craft markets are held in the courtyard facing the entrance.

Gaspar Aitiev Studio [95 E6] (*Tynstanova & Chokmorova;* \661 624) Aitiev was a sculptor and painter, and this museum of his work is housed in his former studio. The exhibits include landscapes, charcoal and pastel sketches, and driftwood sculptures.

Kyrgyz State Historical Museum (Кыргызский Государтсвенный Исорический Музей) [103 E2] (*formerly Lenin Museum, Ala-Too Square;* \626 090; ⊕ *10.00–17.00 Tue–Sun, but closed 13.00–14.00; admission 150som*) Despite its new name, much of this museum – all of the second floor and part of the third – remains dedicated to the life and works of Lenin. In a post-Soviet climate, yesterday's propaganda becomes today's history lesson, and so this unapologetic shrine to the man provides a fascinating window on the recent past.

There is a highly impressive mural on the ceiling of the third floor that depicts a wedding party attended by representatives of every Soviet nationality – Kyrgyz,

Uzbeks, Tartars, fair-haired Russians – all gathered in complete accord alongside the man making the speeches, Comrade Lenin himself; an idealised representation of the ethnic melting pot that was the Soviet Union (another superb mural shows reactionary religious types and Cossacks confronting revolutionary soldiers). In addition, there are various statues and paintings of Lenin addressing assembled revolutionary masses and doing a lot of pointing. Other Lenin memorabilia includes photos, texts and books associated with the leader. Unusually for this part of the world there are occasional labels in English, although the vast majority are in Russian and Kyrgyz.

Away from the Lenin exhibition are displays of Neolithic artefacts, including the Saimaluu-Tash petroglyphs, which are well worth seeing if you're planning to go there, or even if you are not, and examples of Turkic stone culture and Talas burial stones. Also: coins, Bronze Age objects and musical instruments; golden artefacts from the Chui Valley's Shushing tomb; beautiful blue pottery from the Talas Valley; models of the buildings of the Karakhanid period like those at Özgön; and a large ethnographic collection of Kyrgyz nomadic paraphernalia that includes traditional costumes and equestrian fittings such as saddles and harnesses. The old black and white photographs of pre-Soviet Kyrgyz life are particularly fascinating. The top floor has a large yurt *in situ*.

Mikhail Frunze Museum (Музей Михаила Фрунзе) [103 E1] (*Frunze 346;* ✎ *660 607;* ⊕ *10.00–17.00 Tue–Fri, 10.00–16.00 Sat–Sun; admission 50som*) This museum is built around the house where Frunze, the Bolshevik leader who led the advance into central Asia, is said to have been born, although it is far more likely that this merely represents the *type* of house he was born in rather than his actual domicile. The displays outline his life and achievements, and there is also an exhibition showing life in the city during the Soviet era. No photography.

Open Air Sculpture Museum (Музей скульптуры под открытым небом) [103 F1] (*Dubovy Park;* ⊕ *09.00–17.00 daily*) This was created in 1984 to commemorate the 60th anniversary of the Kyrgyz ASSR, and features work by sculptors from all over the Soviet Union on the theme of 'Peace and Labour'. Sadly, some of the bronze pieces have been stolen for their scrap value.

Ivan Panfilov Museum (Музей Ивана Панфилова) [103 C4] (*Toktogul*) Reconstructed in 2004 (see page 116).

Tinibek Sadykov Museum (Музей Тыныбека Садыкова) [102 C1] (*Togolok Moldo;* ⊕ *09.00–12.00, 13.00–16.00 Mon–Fri*) This houses a collection of work by the Kyrgyz sculptor Tinibek Sadykov, whose larger works include the Martyrs to the Revolution Monument as well as other works that stand in Victory Square and the grounds of the State Philharmonic.

Aaly Tokombaev Memorial Museum (Музей АалыТокомбаева) [95 G6] (*Chuikov 109;* ✎ *300 357;* ⊕ *09.00–17.00 Mon–Fri; admission 55som*) This is the house museum of the Kyrgyz poet, *akyn* (bard) and composer who made significant contributions towards the standardisation of the written (Cyrillic) Kyrgyz language and who translated many international works of literature into Kyrgyz for the first time. There is a statue of him outside the Fine Arts Museum. A further exhibition details the 1916 exodus of many Kyrgyz to China following widespread Russian repression after the uprising of that year.

Toktogul Literary Museum (Литературный музей имени Токтогула)
[103 E4] (*Toktogul 109;* ✆ *626 901;* ⊕ *09.00–12.30 & 13.30–17.30 Mon–Fri*)

Zoological Museum (Зоологический Музей) [103 E2] (*Pushkin 78, in Dom Druzhby, the 'Friendship House';* ✆ *392 068;* ⊕ *10.00–17.00 Mon–Fri; admission 40som*) Renovated in 2004, this has a collection of stuffed animals and birds from all over the country, along with portraits of scientists including Przhevalsky, who carried out a study of Kyrgyzstan's flora and fauna.

PARKS As already mentioned, Bishkek is a remarkably green city. As well as the central parks mentioned earlier, there are others, further away from the city centre, that may be worth visiting if you have time on your hands.

Atatürk Park [94 C7] South of the city on Akhunbaev between Mira and Baitik Baatyr (Sovetskaya), this park was formerly known as Druzhba (Friendship) Park but, post-independence, was renamed in honour of the founder of modern Turkey – Kemal Atatürk. The park is a popular place on summer weekends and attracts strollers, as well as buyers and sellers of collectables, such as stamps, coins and lapel badges. There is a statue of its eponymous Turkish founder near the entrance and a memorial to the fallen Soviet soldiers of the ill-fated Afghanistan campaign. In 2004, a memorial to the Batken heroes of 1999–2000 was erected in the park (see pages 18–19). Comprising three connected metal pylons 48m high, this is the tallest monument in the country and utilises a total of 60 tonnes of metal. The park also has a number of amusement rides and a large Ferris wheel, which some like to refer to as the 'Bishkek Eye'.

Botanical Gardens and Arboretum [94 C7] Sandwiched between Gorky and Lev Tolstoy, this extensive park is managed by the Academy of Sciences.

Fuchika Park [94 A4] West of the city centre, close to Osh Bazaar, this park was created by Czech socialist volunteers who came to help construct the city in 1936 and was named after the Czech socialist leader of the time.

Gorky Park [102 B2] On the corner of Isanov and Ryskulov, just west of the Palace of Sports, this is tiny compared with its Moscow namesake. Sometimes used as the location for protests and demonstrations, at other times as an impromptu sports training ground.

Karagachovaya Rosha (Elm Grove) [95 G1] This large park lies to the northeast of the city, north of Jibek-Jolu, with its southern boundary marked by the Bolshoy Chuisky ('Grand Chui') Canal and its northern by the Malyi Chuisky ('Little Chui') Canal. Originally swampland, there are two small lakes – Pionerskoe and Komsomolskoe – at its southern edge, and a road that bisects it north to south – Almykul Usenbaev. The northern part of the city around the park is a dusty Slavic suburb that has echoes of a rural Russia and Ukraine of yesteryear, with gingerbread houses, orchards and lovingly tended gardens – well worth a stroll in its own right.

Togolok Moldo Park [102 B5] A small, fairly central park south of Moskovskaya and just to the east of a 19th-century wooden house dating from the Tsarist period.

STATUES AND OTHER CURIOSITIES

Heroes of Batken [102 C3] This recent memorial on Kievskaya, at the junction with Logvinenko, has three Kyrgyz soldiers dressed in traditional costume. The monument commemorates those who fought against Islamist militants during the Batken incursions of 1999 and 2000. A much larger monument to the same cause stands in Atatürk Park.

MiG Fighter [102 C3] On Kievskaya, in front of the headquarters of the National Guard, stands an old silver MiG jet fighter on a pedestal. In Soviet times, Kyrgyzstan was an important pilot-training centre and President Assad of Syria trained here during the 1960s.

Lenin (another one) This can be found outside the Kyrgyz technical university on Mira Prospect. A crack developed on the pedestal in 2004 and the statue started to bend forwards – to remedy this it has been repositioned and turned 90° to face north. There's also a stone pillar with a plaque of Lenin to be seen on the central reservation of Jibek-Jolu heading east towards the East Bus Station.

Russian log house [102 B4] At Moskovskaya 145, this is a rare and well-preserved example of pre-Soviet architecture in the city.

4

Chui Province

Chui (Чуй), the name given to the valley and its river, is also the name of this most northerly province which extends well beyond the flat land of the valley itself to cover an area of 18,684km². North to south, the province stretches from the Kazakhstan border to the mountain valleys south of Bishkek, over the ridge of the Kyrgyz Ala-Too mountain range to the Suusamyr Valley beyond. Chui Province – or *oblast* (in Russian, Область) – is home to the capital and the towns of Kant, Tokmok and Kemin to the east of Bishkek, and Kara-Balta to the west. Following a brief period (2003–06) when Tokmok was designated as provincial capital, Bishkek has returned to being Chui's administrative centre once more.

VALLEYS SOUTH OF BISHKEK

Seen from almost anywhere in the city, the snow-flecked peaks of the Kyrgyz Ala-Too range to the south loom close, a physical barrier between the flat Chui Valley and the Kyrgyz hinterland. The Ala-Too range dominates the skyline, with peaks not far short of 5,000m, and stretches for almost 400km from east to west. Close to the city, and easily visited on day trips, lie a number of valleys that give an authentic taste of upland Kyrgyzstan and which can serve as suitable locations for anything from gentle picnics to strenuous trekking. The best in terms of accessibility and alpine landscape are probably Ala-Archa and Alamedin. It is between these two valleys that the highest peak of the range – Semyonov Tyan-Shansky (4,895m) – is found, its name given in memory of the 19th-century Russian explorer Pyotr Semyonov Tyan-Shansky. The information given below refers to the main valleys to the south that lie reasonably close to Bishkek.

ALA-ARCHA CANYON This rugged, yet accessible, valley and gorge lies immediately south of the capital. Most of it belongs to the 120,000ha Ala-Archa National Park, created in 1976, and is nominally protected to some extent. The park has everything that you might expect of an alpine zone – snow-capped peaks, fast-flowing streams, alpine meadows, pine forest and steep crags – and it can seem remarkable to find so much unadorned nature so close to a capital city. Having said this, there are less pleasant reminders that the metropolis is nearby, mostly in the form of litter, but this is only around the trail heads. It is this very accessibility that is actually the park's greatest draw, especially to foreign expatriates and Bishkek's middle classes who come here to picnic. As well as a convenient spot for picnicking weekenders, the park is also a magnet for hikers, skiers and mountain climbers.

The scenery of Ala-Archa Canyon is wild mountain nature writ large, with over 50 mountain peaks, more than ten glaciers and 30 mountain passes. It is rich in both flora and fauna, with over 800 plant species, 170 types of bird, including many

CHUI PROVINCE

KAZAKHSTAN

Almaty,
Kazakhstan

Taraz,
Kazakhstan

Chong-Kemin

Ozernly Pass
3,507m

Grigorievka

Bosteri

Cholpon-Ata

Chok-Tal
4,770m

Tamchy

Kaindy

Karakol

Kaji-Say

Bokonbaevo

Ak-Say

Kyzyl-Tuu

Lake Issyk-Kul

Issyk-Kul

Kara-Talaa

Terskey   Ala-Too

Ottuk

Toru Aygyr

Bälykchy

Karool-
Döbö

Shabdan

Orto-Tokoy
Reservoir

Kochkor

Köl-Ükök

Sary-Bulak

Naryn

Boom Gorge

Kemin

Shamshy
Valley

Burana
Tower

Komsomol

East Karakol

Nyzart Pass
2,664m

Kyzart

Lake
Song-Köl

Kegeti
Valley

Naryn

Krasnaya
Rechka

Ivanovka

Tokmok

Kant

BISHKEK

Alamedin

Issyk-Ata

Karakol Pass
3,452m

Jumgal

Tügöl-Say

Chaek

Sokuluk

Kashka-Suu

Ala-Archa

Ala-Archa
National
Park

West Karakol

Suusamyr

Kojomkul

Kyzyl-Oi

Chül

Great Chui Canal

Tash-
Bulak

Alplager

Sokuluk
4,446m

Betovodskoe

Ak-Suu

Kara-Balta

Kara-balta

Töö-Ashuu
Tunnel
3,130m

Suusamyr-Too   Range

Talas

Ötmök Pass
3,326m

Ala-Bel Pass
3,184m

Osh,
Toktogul

Chychkan State
Zoological
Reserve

Toktogul

N

50km

50 miles

Bradt

raptors, and roughly 170 other species of animal, with rarities like Marco Polo sheep as well as bears, marmots, deer, wolves, wild boar and even, it is said, the enigmatic snow leopard at high elevations. Spruce, birch and juniper woodland dominate most of the steep slopes of the park and diminutive alpine flowers cover the meadows in drifts of colour in the spring. The park's principal river is, of course, the Ala-Archa, but there are also two smaller rivers – the Adygene and Ak-Sai – that are fed by glacial melt-water.

Both river and park take their name from the *archa* tree, a brightly coloured juniper that is traditionally burned by Kyrgyz to chase away evil spirits.

The entrance to the park lies roughly 10km beyond the village of Kashka-Suu, around 20km south of the capital, at an elevation of about 1,500m. There is a road barrier and an entrance fee to pay here, both for visitors and their transport. Currently the levy is around US$2 per person and US$3 per car. Close to the park office by the barrier is a small nature museum filled with examples of the fauna found in the region. Beyond here, the road continues for another 12km or so, climbing gently up the valley beside the Ala-Archa River to reach the old Soviet mountaineering camp at 2,150m, known as the **Alplager**. This has a weather station, a small, slightly run-down settlement of wooden houses and a recently constructed A-frame hotel that looks like a ski lodge. This is as far as the road goes for standard motor vehicles, although confident 4x4 drivers are able to continue another 18km beyond the hotel to reach the mountain ski base along a poorly maintained jeep track.

Certain restrictions apply to the park itself, although these are all obeyed and ignored to differing extents. Fishing, hunting, and flower, plant and fruit picking are all prohibited, as are dogs and the catching of butterflies. For motorists, a speed limit of 40km/h is applied and parking is only permitted at designated locations. Fires and barbecues are only allowed at specially designated areas and smokers are requested not to carelessly drop cigarette butts because of the danger of fire. Litter is supposed to be bagged and dropped in the bins provided.

Getting there and away Any of the Bishkek **tour agencies** will be pleased to organise an excursion into the park. Travelling independently, there is little in the way of public transport that goes all the way to the park. In the summer, and particularly at weekends, there may be minibuses from the small bus station at the south end of Osh Bazaar running as far as the park gate (*vorota zapovednika*) and possibly even occasional services that travel as far as the Alplager. The trouble is the best chance of finding these services is at weekends, which is probably the worst time to visit if you want to experience peace and quiet rather than crowds from the city. It also means probably spending the best part of the day waiting for the minibus to fill up, before a slow drive and a long uphill walk of 12km to the Alplager.

Another, even less satisfactory, option is to take a *marshrutka* to Kashka-Suu and hitch or walk the remaining 7km to the park from there (there may or may not be a taxi in the village).

The best bet overall is to hire a **taxi**, which is really not prohibitively expensive if there is a group of you. You can either get the taxi to wait if you fancy a short hike, or pay for just one-way (*around 500som*) and take your chances getting back to Bishkek. Super Taxi will take you on the meter (*10som/km*), with a 100som surcharge, plus 200som per hour wait.

It is also possible to arrange for a taxi driver to pick up on another day, although it is best not to pay up front for this sort of arrangement. One way of saving money is to combine a taxi ride with a bus to the southern city limits. Take a number 11 or

26 bus from the city (catch it on Manas anywhere south of Moskovskaya) to the end of the line beyond the Alamedin Arch. From here, taxis will be much less expensive.

⌂ **Where to stay and eat** If coming for longer than a day trip, camping is the way to go unless you wish to stay in the Ala-Archa Lodge, an A-frame building like a small ski-lodge at the road-head, which has just eight rooms of different sizes and a restaurant where food must be ordered in advance – a double costs around US$60. There may also be basic rooms available at the Alplager itself, which also serves food when it decides to open. However, to fully enjoy what the park has to offer it is better to get away from the tawdry environs of the Alplager – and this requires being fully independent.

Hikes in Ala-Archa National Park
The hiking potential here is enormous, although most visitors choose one of three main options. Be aware that altitude sickness is a distinct possibility if immediately climbing up high having just arrived from relatively low-lying Bishkek. A 1:50,000 topographical map of the park (*Prirodniy Park Ala-Archa*) can be obtained from GeoID in Bishkek (see page 109).

A popular hike is to continue along the valley past the new hotel, following the dirt road all the way to **Upper Ala-Archa Mountain Ski Base**. Just a few kilometres along this track is a panoramic viewpoint with superb views of Ala-Archa peak and the Ak-Sai Valley. In the summer (July and August) a ski-lift operates from the base up to a high ridge where there is a ski chalet.

Another, altogether tougher, route is to head for the **Ak-Sai Canyon**, a hike that rewards the effort with excellent views of the Ak-Sai Glacier. Head up the dirt path beyond the hotel for about 30m, then take the trail that veers to the left – this should be signposted; after 100m the trail climbs steeply to the left. There are several paths that can be taken but they should all lead to the same place: a large rock on top of a hill. The trail is gentler from here on and angles right across an alpine meadow. Beyond the meadow is a waterfall, which may just be a trickle in late summer, and where the trail meets the river is a copse of trees that makes a good picnic spot.

From here, the steep, rocky path leads up to a run-down stone hut called the Ratsek at 3,350m. This is a popular place to camp in the summer although the hut itself has seen much better days. The hike from the Alplager takes around four hours to this point, so the stone hut is a good turnaround point for a strenuous day hike in the park.

Beyond this point, you really need mountain experience and the appropriate equipment. Just beyond the Ratsek is a large rock with memorial plates attached that commemorate perished climbers. A trail leads left from here towards Uchitel peak, a three-hour climb, and there is another trail a little further on that angles left towards the rock wall of Bachichiki and the north wall of Korona. At the end of this trail is another small metal hut, reached after about three hours' walking from the Ratsek.

Taking the trail past the rock with the plaques and then angling slightly right leads to the south side of Korona. The trail climbs steeply along the left side of the glacier before flattening out to reach a climbers' steel hut at 4,150m. From here, there are climbing routes to the peaks of Korona (4,860m) and Uchitel (4,572m).

For **climbers** there are numerous options in the valley, of varying degrees of difficulty, accessible from the Ratsek: the Bachichiki rock wall, Schwaba, Box, Tikitor, Free Korea and of course, Korona peak itself.

Another popular option, and ideal for a shorter excursion, is to head up the **Adygene Valley** that leads southwest from just north of the Alplager. This is reached by heading north back down the road for around 300m, then crossing the river by a rickety footbridge by a tree festooned with votive rags. Several paths lead up to both sides of the valley although they all eventually merge. The route on the left (south) side of the valley passes a cemetery for fallen climbers, which is hidden away in a larch grove. Most of the graves contain little more than fragments of clothing or scraps of climbing equipment, as the human remains of the victims were never found.

One mountaineer has a small monument positioned just outside the graveyard's boundary; this commemorates a climber who is reputed to have taken his own life, cutting himself free from his fellow climbers rather than dragging his comrades down with him. As such, this is regarded as an act of suicide and so he cannot be buried in consecrated ground. Elsewhere, a broken rotor blade commemorates helicopter pilots killed in the area.

The track from the climbers' cemetery continues for 7km or so through forest beneath the Adygene Glacier, ascending very gradually at first before becoming steeper as it approaches the magnificent glacial cirque of Stayanka Elektra. This route tends to be quieter than most and you are very likely to see birds of prey on the wing, particularly griffon vultures riding the thermals on the warm air radiated by bare rocky outcrops.

ALAMEDIN VALLEY Also south of Bishkek, running parallel to, and east of, the Ala-Archa Valley, is the Alamedin Valley, which follows the river of the same name, a tributary of the Chui River. Alamedin is reached by way of the village of Koy-Tash, which lies 30km south of Bishkek. Koy-Tash is a sprawling but pleasant enough place with many weekend *dachas* owned by wealthy Bishkek residents.

On the west side of the river, a road at the village's southern end climbs south over a ridge past the village of Tatyr and the Golubinyi (Pigeon) Falls, a well-known local beauty spot, before meandering west to reach the Ala-Archa Valley at Kashka-Suu.

South of Koy-Tash, the Alamedin Valley narrows and the road continues for another 10km south to reach the Tyoplye Klyuchi (Hot Springs) sanatorium at an altitude of about 1,800m. The sanatorium is run by the government's Ministry of Power and there is cheap and cheerful accommodation in chalets available as well as simple meals. The sanatorium has a swimming pool and offers warm baths with a massage service. The spring water here contains traces of radioactive radon and so ten-minute sessions are the order of the day unless you wish to emerge with a radioactive glow. The spa waters are extremely popular with Bishkek residents and the place can become very busy on hot summer weekends. The sanatorium complex is undoubtedly more run-down than it was when it was first set up in 1984, but for those desiring a taste of Soviet-era spa tourism this might be a good choice.

Most Western visitors tend to prefer the hiking opportunities the valley has to offer and the sanatorium serves as an excellent starting place for a day hike further up the valley. A trekking route continues south from the sanatorium, over the mountains through gorgeous alpine scenery, past waterfalls, meadows and birch, larch and juniper forest, to eventually skirt a glacier to reach the Alamedin Pass at 4,032m. Although this is certainly as beautiful a valley as Ala-Archa, it has not been granted national park status. Consequently, there are no facilities whatsoever other than those at the sanatorium.

To get here make an arrangement with a taxi driver, as for Ala-Archa – it should cost about the same as to the Alplager there. An alternative is to take a bus to Koy-Tash village from Alamedin Bazaar in Bishkek (near the East Bus Station) and hitch or try and find another taxi from there.

ISSYK-ATA VALLEY There is another extensive **spa complex** in the valley to the east, about 45km from Bishkek by way of Koy-Tash at the head of the Alamedin Valley. Another longer road reaches the spa via the Chui Valley towns of Kant and Ivanovka. The resort is nestled between meadows and orchards in the shadow of craggy mountains at an altitude of 1,775m. Minibuses run to the resort from Bishkek's East Bus Station, which tend to be more frequent (but more crowded) in high summer.

There is a 10th-century **Buddhist carving** of the Curing Buddha on a large boulder near the entrance to the complex, where 19th-century visitors used to smear sheep grease in gratitude. Now, there is an eagle sculpture on top of the rock and, sadly, plenty of contemporary graffiti. Not that surprisingly, given its Soviet origins, the overgrown grounds of the spa complex also boast a statue of Lenin in an 'addressing the masses' pose. Comfortable accommodation is available at the complex for around US$60 for a double. There is also a basic hostel with shared facilities. An outdoor bathing pool is available for public use.

Issyk-Ata (literally, 'Father Heat') has long been a place of pilgrimage for the healing properties of its waters. Both Turkic nomads and Russian colonists came here for the waters, and a female Uzbek shaman is said to have lived here as a hermit until the 1950s. Another legend tells of a local beauty who bathed every day in the river here and never grew old or wrinkled because of the magical power of the waters. Whether or not the river has such life-preserving properties is hard to ascertain but it certainly has plenty of trout and many come to fish here.

Trekking possibilities abound in the valley. The most ambitious route is to continue southwest to eventually reach the Issyk-Ata Pass at 3,929m. It would be possible here to either descend or turn around and climb over the Alamedin Pass (4,032m) from the south and return along the Alamedin Valley.

SOKULUK VALLEY This valley, southwest of Bishkek and to the west of Ala-Archa, is approached from the town of the same name, which lies 30km west of Bishkek on the main M39 to Kara-Balta and Kazakhstan. The main village here is **Tash-Bulak** ('Stone Spring'), which is sometimes also referred to as Belogorka, its Soviet-era name.

THE CHONG-TASH MASSACRE

Lying close to Kashka-Suu in the lower reaches of the Ala-Archa Valley is the tiny ski-resort village of Chong-Tash, a place which gained a sinister reputation in 1991 following the televised excavation of a mass grave of the victims of one of Stalin's purges. Of the 138 skeletons found here, it is thought many belonged to the political elite of the time, and that the entire Supreme Soviet Central Committee for the Kyrgyz ASSR, along with other dignitaries, were murdered here by the NKVD secret police over two nights in 1937.

A close associate of the victims was Torokul Aitmatov, father of the celebrated Kyrgyz author Chingiz Aitmatov (see page 45), who was arrested whilst visiting Moscow that same year. The crime finally came to light in the 1980s when a caretaker who had witnessed the slaughter, sworn to secrecy by the KGB and fearful of his life, told his daughter on his deathbed. When Kyrgyzstan became independent in 1991, the daughter felt able to inform the authorities of the deed. As a sign of respect for the victims and as a tribute to his own father, Chingiz Aitmatov financed the transfer of the victims' remains to the more hallowed ground of the Ata-Beyit Cemetery in the village.

The village is a sprawling settlement of attractively decorated wooden houses that cling to either side of the valley road. Formerly, when a large and successful collective farm operated from the village, it had a mixed Kyrgyz, Ukrainian and Russian population, but these days Tash-Bulak is almost entirely Kyrgyz and far less prosperous than it used to be. In Soviet times there were vast numbers of sheep in the valley, but now most of the villagers who remain squeeze a precarious living out of growing vegetables on private plots.

From Tash-Bulak, the road continues south up the valley for another 12km or so. With luck, you can arrange for a car in the village to bring you to the end of the road, from where a track leads through woodland to a waterfall, about an hour's walk away. You can continue from here further up the valley, following the river on your right. The valley narrows considerably after a couple of hours and a steep-sided valley with a waterfall veers off to the southwest.

In theory at least, it is possible to hike up this valley, crossing the river a few times, to reach the Suusamyr Valley over the 3,775m Sokuluk Pass – a guide, or at least first-hand local advice, is highly recommended. The river disappears just short of the pass but reappears on the south side after about 800m of descent. Following the river downhill for about 18km or so brings you to a rough road that runs parallel to the Karakol River. From here, it is a further 16km west to reach the small village of Karakol. In Soviet times this route was used to drive sheep to land in the Suusamyr Valley that was owned by the collective farm, but it has not been used as such for many years now. Because the snow now lies piled-up at the pass, undisturbed by livestock, any attempt at this route could only really be considered a viable option during high summer – July and August. Another possible trekking route leads from Tash-Bulak over the 3,900m Ozerniy Pass to the Ala-Archa Valley to the east.

Getting there and away To reach Tash-Bulak from Bishkek, there are buses that leave at least once, and possibly more, times a day from Osh Bazaar. It is best to go there in the morning. Buses and minibuses that pass through Sokuluk on the main road are far more frequent and it should be possible to find a local bus or a share taxi to the village from here. Taxis from Osh Bazaar are another possibility and should cost around 500som one-way.

Other practicalities There are limited **accommodation** options in Tash-Bulak village although it should be possible to find a homestay: try asking at the municipal administration office in the village, on Sovetskaya, or at the village shop. If you are planning to do much trekking from Tash-Bulak, bring supplies from Bishkek, as the village shop has a limited choice of goods on offer.

AK-SUU VALLEY This valley lies to the west of Sokuluk and is reached by turning south after the village of Belovodskoe before reaching Kara-Balta. The road passes the small village of Kyzyl Dyikan, which has one of the earliest Russian Orthodox churches in central Asia.

CHUI VALLEY (ЧУЙСКАЯ ДОЛИНА)

This wide valley, the largest in Kyrgyzstan, is one of the few big expanses of flat land in the country. Although, in many ways, it is atypical of mountainous Kyrgyzstan, this largely agricultural valley contains a number of sites that are intrinsic to the history of the region. It is also one of the most densely populated and fertile regions, with an adequate water supply, and fertile soils that produce sugar beet, potatoes, wheat, maize and fruit. Because of this, the Chui Valley is today one of the country's more well-to-do regions, with prosperity levels higher than most other parts of the country. The population of the valley is generally more mixed than in other parts of Kyrgyzstan, with ethnic Russians, Ukrainians, Dungans, Germans and Koreans in addition to native Kyrgyz. The Dungan presence is particularly noticeable in places, with white Muslim caps above Chinese faces, and houses that have roofs topped by small pagoda-like forms. None of the towns of the valley are of special interest, but there are a few key sites located nearby that are well worth seeking out.

KANT (КАНТ) This is the first town of importance heading east of Bishkek along the valley. Kant boasts a large cement factory, a Lenin statue and a war memorial – all pretty standard for a provincial Kyrgyz town. Many ethnic Germans used to live here and in the surrounding area (see box, page 133) and it might be assumed that the town takes its name from Immanuel Kant, the German moral philosopher. In fact, the name refers to the Kyrgyz for 'sugar cube', and there is a major sugar factory in the town which processes beet grown in the valley, a practice that dates back to Soviet times.

The town came into the news in October 2003 when it was announced that its airport would be used as a base for the Collective Rapid Deployment Force of the Russian Air Force. With the decline of Russian bases in Cuba and Vietnam, this was to become Russia's only new base abroad since Soviet times. Although the premise was one of 'joint security', the selection of Kant as a Russian base was undoubtedly viewed as a counterweight to the American military presence at the Peter J Ganci airbase at Manas Airport, which had been there to assist with Afghanistan operations since December 2001. As a result of this, Kyrgyzstan was, for a period of 12 years, the only country in the world to have both American and Russian bases. What is perhaps even more surprising is that the two bases were so close to each other: Manas was just five minutes' flying time away.

In 2005, Moscow proclaimed that it would double the number of personnel here and in 2006 it was announced that a ground force element would be added. This announcement came just before the statement that rent on the US Ganci airbase at Manas would be increased hundred-fold if the Americans wished to continue their presence. In 2009 the Kyrgyz government threatened to close the US base permanently, but the US was able to renegotiate the lease at a higher rent, angering the Russians. This is considered to be one of the contributory factors to the regime change in 2010.

President Atambayev called for the Kant base to be closed in 2012, but later that same year Russia obtained a prolongation of the agreement, allowing their military sites to remain for a further 15 years after the end of the current contract in 2017. The USAF base at Manas was vacated and handed back to the Kyrgyzstan military on 3 June 2014.

KRASNAYA RECHKA (КРАСНАЯ РЕЧКА) The village of Krasnaya Rechka ('Red River') lies 8km east of Kant on the main road to Balykchy and Lake Issyk-Kul. The village also gives its name to a nearby ruined Silk Road settlement that was known as **Navekat** ('New Town') in Sogdian times. Navekat was active between the 6th and 12th centuries and was the largest settlement in the valley at that time. The town was mentioned by the Chinese pilgrim Hsuan Tsang who visited the area in around AD620. The site was rediscovered in Soviet times when a tractor ploughing outside the village turned up a gold burial mask. Subsequent archaeological investigation has revealed a Buddhist temple containing the remains of an 8m-long reclining clay Buddha, originally painted red, and Bodhisattva forms that were discovered in another corridor and outside the sanctuary gates. These are all now in the Hermitage Museum in St Petersburg. Another 1.5m-high Buddha statue was discovered in 2011.

The settlement was probably established in the 6th century, although the temple itself dates from the 8th. As well as a Buddhist temple, Navekat also had a citadel, a large square, fortified walls and a Zoroastrian fire altar. There is also a necropolis which demonstrates burials in both the Buddhist and Nestorian Christian traditions. Other discoveries at the site have included fragments of wall paintings, a Chinese stela with inscriptions, and a birch-bark Brahmin manuscript in the Sanskrit language, along with deities of Sogdian and Indian origin.

The discovery of such a wide range of remains and artefacts demonstrates that Manicheans, Buddhists and Nestorians all coexisted here contemporaneously, and that Navekat was a true multi-confessional settlement. Indeed, the archaeological evidence of all of the Silk Road settlements in the Chui Valley – Navekat (Krasnaya Rechka), Suyab (Ak-Beshim) and Balasagun (Burana) – reveals that they were all centres where Chinese, Turkic, Sogdian and Indian traditions met and prospered in a symbiotic mélange of culture and religion: the typical, two-way exchange between East and West that characterised much of the Silk Road.

Although there is little to see on the ground here, the site is undoubtedly significant. It was excavated over 20 years ago and many of the remains were then backfilled to prevent further erosion. However, much degradation has taken place in the interim and the site is under threat. A UNESCO/Japanese Trust Fund project has begun to document and protect the most important structures here.

Visiting Krasnaya Rechka To reach the site from Bishkek, take a Tokmok *marshrutka* that passes through Krasnaya Rechka village from Bishkek's East Bus Station – this should cost about 50som. Get off at the end of the village by the Ala-Too petrol station on the left, where there is a sign pointing to the site along a dirt road on the left. The track leads around fields towards the site, which lies a couple of kilometres away; you should be able to see the low artificial-looking hill of the citadel from the main road.

At the site there is little evidence that this was an important Silk Road settlement other than a sign that says 'NECROPOLIS VII–IX AD' and another, in Russian, that prohibits the passage of farm traffic through the site. The citadel is a low, grassy penumbra with the remains of some chambers sunken into it. The necropolis just north of this is a sunken pit that has obvious traces of human remains in the form of bones and skulls creepily exposed in the cliff face. Fragments of pottery litter the site.

Krasnaya Rechka is the sort of archaeological site which is rewarding if your imagination is powerful enough to make its own interpretation from mere bumps and lines in the ground. Good views of the surrounding countryside can be had from the modest 30m elevation the citadel affords. The Kazakhstan frontier is very close – just a stone's throw north of the site. To return to Bishkek you could flag down a *marshrutka* heading west back at the garage, or you could continue eastward towards Tokmok to visit Burana Tower. The two sites combined make a good half-day trip.

TOKMOK The provincial town of Tokmok ('hammer' in Kyrgyz and sometimes spelled *Tokmak*) lies another 25km or so further east, beyond the smaller town of Ivanovka. Tokmok is situated right on the Kazakhstan frontier, which is marked by the Chui River flowing just to the north. Tokmok was the Kyrgyz regional administrative centre until 1878, when floods destroyed much of the town, necessitating the move of its bureaucrats west to what was then Pishpek, today's Bishkek. Before this, Tokmok was an important strategic centre for the 18th-century Kokand khanate, which had its forts strung along the Chui Valley to protect their trade interests. Just outside the town to the south lie the ruins of another Silk Road city, Ak-Beshim, but despite having unearthed a Buddhist temple and a Nestorian Christian church here, there is little to see on the ground of this once-important settlement. As well as Kyrgyz, Dungan and Russian residents, the town also has a small Chechen population descended from those who were deported here by Stalin in 1944. Others came as refugees fleeing Russian forces during the Chechen Wars of 1994–95 and 1999–2000 in their homeland. Most infamously, the suspects of the 2013 Boston Marathon bombing, Tamerlan and Dzhokhar Tsarnaev, of mixed Chechen and Avar parentage, spent part of their childhood here in the 1990s.

Tokmok became the administrative centre of Chui Province in 2003, but this role was returned to Bishkek in May 2006. The town's modern-day character is that of a quiet provincial town and farming centre. For those passing through, its most obvious feature is the MiG jet fighter mounted on a plinth in the middle of an intersection. Two roads pass by here from Bishkek: the new road that bypasses the town *en route* to Balykchy and an older road that reaches Tokmok via Kant and Krasnaya Rechka. The bus station lies on the main road near the entrance to the town, close to some large Soviet-era murals standing unashamedly on display outside housing blocks of the same period. There is a small museum at Tryasina 146 with examples of some of the archaeological finds in the Chui Valley region – petroglyphs, clay vessels, oil lamps and prehistoric tools – but most visitors push straight on to the Burana Tower, 15km to the south.

BURANA TOWER Burana Tower is probably the best-known monument in the north of Kyrgyzstan, although in a country where historic monuments are in short supply this is not so remarkable. Although the 'tower' cannot compare with any of the reconstructed architectural jewels that might be found elsewhere in the region, Burana is nonetheless worth a visit, both for its architectural merit and for the historical background of its location.

The tower is, in fact, a minaret: all that remains of the city of **Balasagun**, which was established by the Karakhanids at the end of the 10th century. Balasagun was the major Karakhanid settlement in the northern part of the territory that is today Kyrgyzstan, with southern counterparts at Mavarannahr, now Özgön, near Osh, and at Kashgar in Xinjiang, China. The city was extremely important in its day but, although it flourished for several centuries, it eventually declined and was virtually abandoned by the 15th century. The Uyghur poet, Yusuf (or Jusup) Balasagun, author of the epic poem *Katadgu Bilim* (*The Knowledge That Brings Happiness*) was born here in the early 11th century and gave the town its name. His image decorates the current Kyrgyz 1,000som banknote.

The minaret, when first built, would have been more than 46m tall, but the present-day version stands at just over half its original height, at only 24m. What you see today is the result of both destruction and reconstruction. A succession of earthquakes reduced the original building almost to rubble – the last was in 1900 – when the upper part collapsed and its bricks were utilised by recent Russian settlers in the area. The current building is very much the product of 1970s restoration.

The tower is constructed of banded honey-coloured brickwork in a gently tapering round structure with an octagonal base. Lacking its original cupola, the top of the tower is now a viewing platform that offers views over the Chui Valley north to Kazakhstan and to the mountains of the eastern Ala-Too range to the south. An external staircase has been bolted on to the tower's northern side, rather spoiling any sense of authenticity, and this leads inside to access a narrow, steep internal staircase that climbs to the viewing platform.

The name Burana is most probably a corruption of 'Monara', which means minaret. Originally the minaret and its accompanying mosque would have stood in the central part of the town. Major archaeological surveys in the 1920s, 1950s and 1970s discovered that the original town covered a total area of some 25–30km². There is a central fortress, dwellings, shops and baths, and a water main delivering water from a canyon nearby. The whole settlement was surrounded by two rings of walls.

Now very little else remains except for traces of three mausoleums, a large mound representing the ruins of a palace or temple, and around 80 Turkic *balbals*, stone grave markers dating from between the 6th and 10th centuries that have been gathered here having been collected from all over the country. There is a small **museum** (⊕ *09.00–18.00; admission 60som*) next to the tower, which has a display of artefacts found at the site including pottery and coins, as well as interesting black and white photographs that document the tower's reconstruction. The museum also has a small gift shop selling postcards and pamphlets.

Visiting the rather sterile reconstruction that is Burana Tower today, it is hard to get much sense of the grandeur that was Balasagun in its prime, especially if your visit coincides with noisy crocodiles of schoolchildren bussed in from Bishkek. Nonetheless, the Karakhanid city certainly impressed Genghis Khan sufficiently to persuade him to spare it and even rename it 'Gobilik' ('Good City'). Like the artefacts found at Krasnaya Rechka, there has been enough material evidence found here to indicate that Balasagun was an important Silk Road settlement where

A LONG WAY FROM HOME: GERMANS IN KYRGYZSTAN

When, in 1941, many ethnic Germans from Russia's Volga region were forcibly relocated by Stalin to central Asia, some ended up in the Kant region of Kyrgyzstan's Chui Valley, where there was already a sizeable German population established in the area. German settlers had started arriving in the area back in the late 19th and early 20th century as colonists of either the Russian Empire or the post-revolution Soviet Union. Most of these earlier settlers were Lutheran Mennonites who had been living in southern Russia and the Crimea, having emigrated from East Frisia 300 years earlier to avoid military service.

Some Chui Valley villages, such as Luxembourg and Bergtal (which was known as Rotfront – or 'Red Front' – from the time of its establishment in 1927 until independence in 1991), still carry their German names and have German-speaking minorities. Although many have migrated to Germany following independence – before 1991 there were around 100,000 Germans in what was then the Kirghiz SSR, nearly 3% of the total population – Bergtal is still probably the only village in central Asia with a substantial German minority. At the time of Kyrgyzstan's independence there were around 900 Germans in the village, but now the figure is down to something like 200. Most of these continue to eschew alcohol, tobacco, television and dancing in strict Mennonite tradition. According to a 1999 census there were 21,471 ethnic Germans remaining in the country as a whole, but by 2009 the figure was estimated to be down to 9,487.

culture, language and religion mixed easily in the tolerant atmosphere of commerce – Chinese coins, Nestorian crosses, magical charms and Indian cowries all bear testament to this.

A Kyrgyz legend tells quite a different story about the history of the tower. It tells of a witch's warning to a powerful local king that his new-born daughter would die on her coming of age. Alarmed by this presentiment, the king built a tower to protect his daughter and no-one was allowed to enter apart from the servant who brought her food. Despite this precaution, a poisonous spider hid in her food and bit her and the girl died in the tower, aged just 18 years old. The tower, of course, was Burana, and the girl's name was Monara. This is just one version; in another, the tower was built to protect the king's beautiful daughter from the advances of young men. In this case it was a scorpion that bit and killed her. On hearing of his daughter's death the king is said to have sobbed so hard that he brought the top part of the tower down.

Getting there and away To reach Burana Tower, take a *marshrutka* from Bishkek's East Bus Station to Tokmok (*50som*) and then get a taxi from there. Taxi drivers wait at Tokmok's bus station for independent visitors to Burana. A reasonable price for the return trip to and from the tower from Tokmok, including an hour or two wait at the site, should be 700som or so. There are also occasional buses from Tokmok's bus station.

KEGETI VALLEY The village of Kegeti, 14km southwest of Burana, lies at the head of another valley that penetrates southward into the Kyrgyz Ala-Too range. This is good hiking, mountain-biking and horseriding terrain, and the valley is used by some Bishkek adventure travel companies for their activities. Trekking routes lead up a side valley to the east to Köl-Tor ('Dead') Lake with numerous waterfalls. It is also possible to visit the **Bel-Saz** *jailoo* to the west, from where excursions can be made to the nearby Kushkonok Forest and Sharkeratma Waterfall. The road from Kegeti through to the Suusamyr–Kochkor road in the Karakol Valley that is shown on the GeoID 1:200,000 topological map is generally not passable, even in the summer. In Soviet times this was cleared regularly by snowploughs, but these days snow may lie until mid-August and this, coupled with frequent landslides, means even horses have difficulty here.

Getting there and away Kegeti can be reached by taxi from Ivanovka or Tokmok. Plenty of *marshrutki* pass through Ivanovka from Bishkek's East Bus Station and cost 50som. Heading for the Bel-Saz *jailoo*, it should be possible to organise a taxi in Ivanovka along the Kegeti Valley as far as the settlement of Leskhos, from where a horse and guide can be arranged for the one-hour ride to Bel-Saz. Another possibility is to go from Ivanovka by taxi to the village of Ak-Say, where a 4x4 may be hired to reach the *jailoo* by way of the German minority village of Rotfront (see page 133).

SHAMSHY VALLEY This valley southeast of Tokmok is considered by some to be one of the most beautiful in the province and is well known to archaeologists for its rich yield of Scythian treasure. A golden mask said to belong to a beautiful ruler, Queen Shamshy, was found in the valley and a former Shah of Iran chose it for the site of one of his hunting lodges.

As with all of the valleys of the Kyrgyz Ala-Too there are many hiking and horseriding opportunities to be had here. The **Shamshy** *jailoo* lies 36km south of Tokmok at an altitude of 1,800m. Here there is yurt accommodation available and horses for hire. Possible excursions from here include visits to alpine lakes or hikes up the Tuyuk Valley to the southeast. A side valley leading off to the west has another *jailoo* – Tura Kain – where it is possible to stay in a farmhouse. From the main valley, it is also possible in summer to hike over the 3,570m Shamshy Pass to the village of Shamshy and Kochkor beyond.

Getting there and away   Although there is no direct transport to the valley, it should be possible to arrange transport in Tokmok to reach both Shamshy and Tura Kain *jailoo*. The cost of a taxi should be in the order of 700som.

CHONG-KEMIN VALLEY (ЧОН-КЕМИН ДОЛИНА)

The Chong ('Big')-Kemin Valley is the long panhandle of Chui Province, extending eastward from the Chui Valley, which is circumscribed by the Kazakhstan frontier to the north and Issyk-Kul Province to the south. It starts at the town of Kemin, midway between Tokmok and Balykchy, and runs 80km west to east, parallel to the Kazakhstan frontier and sandwiched between the Kungey Ala-Too and Zailiysky mountain ranges.

Famously, the valley is the birthplace of erstwhile Kyrgyz president Askar Akayev, whose family hail from the village of Kyzyl Bairak. The Chong-Kemin Valley is a spectacular combination of both wild and pastoral landscapes, with a pleasing mix of lofty mountains, verdant pasture, coniferous woodland and alpine lakes. At its highest point, the valley reaches 2,800m in altitude and its upper reaches are shadowed by a number of peaks in excess of 4,000m – Kichi-Kemin (4,220m), Teke-Tor (4,190m), Alisher Novoi (4,170m) and Chok-Tal (4,770m), on the boundary with Issyk-Kul Province. Most of the people living in the valley are of Kyrgyz stock, as few Slavs, who commonly populate Lake Issyk-Kul's shores just to the south, have settled here.

The village of Kyzyl Bairak, still said to be the home of Askar Akayev's brother, has a mausoleum to Shabdan Baatyr, who was a powerful chieftain of the Sary Bagysh tribe who ruled the valley in the 19th century and remain the most populous clan here. The town of Kemin, formerly known as Bestrovka, at the head of the valley, also has an equestrian statue of the chieftain. Back in 1911, the town experienced one of the strongest earthquakes ever to be recorded in the region, measuring a massive 11 on the Richter scale.

In Soviet times, collective farms and mining in the town of Ak-Tyuz in the neighbouring Kichi-Kemin Valley provided employment for the valley; these days, the local economy, such as it is, is mostly based on cattle-raising and growing potatoes. The defunct mine at Ak-Tyuz which used to mine lead and other heavy metals, and which suffered a serious spillage in 1964, has apparently been bought by an Israeli businessman, although what he intends to do with it is yet to be seen. There is further uncertainty concerning the valley, as there is little doubt that Chong-Kemin's peaceful sanctity will be despoiled if a planned direct road between Almaty and Lake Issyk-Kul is ever completed in the future. Currently, many holidaying Kazakhs visit the lake in the summer by way of the long, circuitous route via Bishkek. A direct route constructed through the Chong-Kemin Valley would shorten the journey time considerably and encourage even more visitors to the lake; it would also shatter the valley's current isolation. Fortunately, this is looking increasingly unlikely.

For the time being at least, the Chong-Kemin Valley has abundant wildlife and a rich, varied flora. Its forests of Tien Shan fir, in particular, are held in high regard throughout Kyrgyzstan for the bounty of their medicinal herbs, mushrooms and edible berries. There are a number of burial mounds in the valley, most notably near the villages of Shabdan and Tegirmenty, which date from the 3rd and 4th centuries, and a 6–11th-century settlement has been discovered in the mouth of the valley. The Chong-Kemin Valley became a national park in 1997.

The valley offers several adventurous **trekking** possibilities. One very tough route starting from the village of Kaindy is to follow the Chong-Kemin River upstream, before climbing up and over the Kungey range to the 4,061m Ak-Suu Pass, from where a descent is made along the Grigorievka Valley to the village of the same name on Lake Issyk-Kul. Some knowledge of glacier walking is required here and this six-day route is only for the experienced, fit and determined.

There is a shorter (two- or three-day) easier route to Lake Issyk-Kul that also starts in Kaindy. This follows the Chong-Kemin River east, before climbing up to the 3,800m Kyzyl Bulak Pass and descending through arid mountains to the lakeside village of Toru Aygyr at the western end of Lake Issyk-Kul. A third route links the valley with the town of Balykchy at the lake's far western shore.

Rather than attempt to traverse high passes, another alternative would be to follow the valley eastward towards picturesque Lake Jassyk-Kul, 50km east of Kaindy. This could be shortened considerably by arranging transport in the village to reach the point along the valley where the Kashka-Suu River joins the Chong-Kemin. The Chong-Kemin Valley also serves as a start or end point for treks through to Kazakhstan (see page 168). Some travel companies also run white-water rafting expeditions in the valley, and kayaking is another popular pursuit here.

GETTING THERE AND AWAY Public transport runs as far as Kaindy village from Bishkek and two **minibuses** (*120som*) a day make the journey from Bishkek's East Bus Station. Alternatively, many **marshrutki** pass through Kemin at the head of the valley and you could take a **taxi** to Kaindy or other villages along the valley from here.

WHERE TO STAY AND EAT Kaindy, the last village in the valley, has several accommodation possibilities with local families, and the village makes an ideal base for trekking in the valley. Karool-Döbö, the village before this, a little way beyond Kalmak Ashu where the road crosses the Chong-Kemin River, also has accommodation at two **CBT homestays** (**$$**). The home of friendly co-ordinator Janybek Sariev (m *0772 832 065*) can be found at Bapakova 35 (follow the road that leads north downhill from the village shop then turn left at the junction by the school – it is at the next corner). Janybek can also help in arranging horse and foot treks along the valley. There is another comfortable CBT homestay at Bapakova 7 that can be reached by turning right at the school.

There is also very comfortable accommodation available at the **Ashu Travel Guesthouse** in Kalmak Ashu village at Boruev 22 (*23 rooms*; m *0552 700 552*; e *ashutravel@mail.ru*; *www.ashu.kg*; **$$$**), which includes Western toilets, traditional textiles and excellent meals.

Tört Köl village at the beginning of the Chong-Kemin Valley also has a good homestay, the first to be reached heading up the valley. The **Talant Guesthouse** (m *0771 907 183*; **$**), situated just outside the village close to the river, has an inside bathroom and serves delicious meals in a dining yurt. Foot and horse excursions are possible from here, as is fishing in the river that runs alongside the property.

BOOM GORGE (БООМСКОЕ УЩЕЛЬЕ)

This narrow, and slightly spooky, canyon ('Shoestring Gorge') lies at the eastern end of the Kyrgyz Ala-Too range, beginning about 20km south of Kemin. The gorge is the route by which the fast-flowing Chui River, the A365 main road and the railway all squeeze side by side to reach Balykchy and Lake Issyk-Kul. Before the coming of the road and the railway, the canyon would have been one of the major trade routes of the northern Silk Road, linking China with the West via Lake Issyk-Kul and the Chui Valley. The gorge is prone to fairly frequent landslides and so concrete barriers have been installed to protect the road and railway from falling rocks.

Just before entering the gorge is the Kyrgyz equivalent of a motorway service area, **Holodnaya Voda** ('Cold Water'), which takes its name from a local spring – a grand name for a collection of roadside restaurants, shops, kiosks and yurts. The restaurants serve up the usual staples – *manti*, *shashlyk* and *laghman* – while the yurts sell *kumys* and those ever-popular Kyrgyz snacks, *kurut* (yoghurt balls), in a variety of forms.

Close to the entrance of the gorge is a recently erected **monument** to the victims of the 1916 Urkun exodus, in which tens of thousands of Kyrgyz perished while fleeing over the mountains to China (see page 196). As the road climbs further into the gorge a number of other statues positioned above the roadside are passed. These date from the Soviet period but, rather than representing heroes of the revolution, they are in the form of animals, a sample of Kyrgyzstan's natural bounty – eagles, snow leopards and deer.

Approximately halfway down the gorge there is a small bridge (Krasniy Most – 'Red Bridge') crossing the river, and just beyond here to the west lies the rugged red sandstone terrain of the **Konorchok Canyon**, with its impressive wind-eroded rock formations. Konorchok is actually a network of canyons that includes Korgon-Terek, immediately west of the bridge.

The canyons were formed 1½–2 million years ago, and are generally much warmer than the surrounding region, with both rainfall and snow a rarity. Erosion by wind and rain has turned what was formerly a plateau into a forest of high stone pillars and curious landforms. As with many unusual geological formations, imagination has not been kept in check and the canyons which make up the network have been given names like Hiroshima, Bobsleigh, Sky Scraper, Fairy Tale and Aeolian Castle by those who have ventured here in the past. The whole canyon system is ripe for exploration. There is also an extinct volcano with lava flows and plentiful fossils on its surface.

Several Bishkek agencies organise treks and excursions here, or incorporate the Konorchok canyons into a longer Kyrgyzstan tour. With absolutely no habitation, and a location far away from any obvious cultural references, the area would serve as an ideal setting for a Western or even a science fiction movie. Comparisons with Arizona's Grand Canyon are ambitious but not entirely fanciful.

Boom Gorge itself is a popular location for outdoor pursuits, particularly whitewater rafting. The section of the river downstream from Krasniy Most to Kemin is said to offer some of the best and most challenging rafting in the country. The **Silk Road Water Center** in Bishkek (*Jibek-Jolu 285;* 0312 609 919; e *kyrgyzraft@mail.ru; www.rafting.kg*) includes Boom Gorge as the most adventurous of its various one-day itineraries. **Asian Tour** in Bishkek (*Turusbekova 82;* 0312 310 032, 310 041; e *info@ asiantour.org; www.asiantour.org*) also run one-day rafting trips in the gorge, as do **Turkestan Travel** (0312 511 560; e *psi61@mail.ru; www.turkestan.biz*).

Heading west from Bishkek, the M38 highway continues straight as a die towards the Kazakh border. This is the most direct road to Tashkent from the capital, although the necessity of a transit visa for Kazakhstan for many nationalities does not always make it the most practicable route. The same road splits at the town of Kara-Balta ('Black Axe') and heads south, skirting mountains and crossing passes on its way to Kyrgyzstan's second city of Osh and the southern part of the republic.

Kara-Balta is primarily a junction town and few visitors stop here on the way to more appealing mountain vistas further south. The town was founded in 1825 under the Kokand khanate and developed to attain city status under the Soviet regime in 1975. Formerly, the main industry here was the processing of uranium ore from mines in Kyrgyzstan and Kazakhstan, and because of this it was a closed city in Soviet times.

Following independence in 1991, the Kyrgyz mines closed down but Kara-Balta continued to process uranium imported from Kazakhstan. The uranium industry brought a certain amount of prosperity to the town and it is a reasonably attractive place, with leafy streets and Russian-style architecture. However, in environmental terms, the town has been left with an unenviable legacy in the form of unprocessed uranium tailings, and toxic residues of gold and molybdenum. In February 2007, the Russian government purchased the Kyrgyz government's majority stake in the Kara-Balta uranium production facility. Despite this, most Kyrgyz associate the town with jollier things: Kara-Balta is also the name of a best-selling brand of vodka.

SOUTH OF KARA-BALTA From Kara-Balta south, the road climbs steadily but steeply along the beautiful Kara-Balta Gorge to traverse the ridge of the Kyrgyz Ala-Too. Eventually it reaches the **Töo-Ashuu Tunnel** at 3,130m, which cuts through the mountain for 3km, considerably lower than the 3,586m pass itself, which the old road summits. The tunnel is said to have been built by the same Russian engineers who constructed the Moscow and Leningrad metro systems, although obviously they did not send in the same teams of artists to beautify it afterwards, as they had in the Russian metropolises.

The tunnel is a dank and stifling place; an exhaust-fume-laden plunge into a dimly lit underworld and is no place for the claustrophobic. Driving through it can seem to take much longer than it ought to and it is a tangible relief to emerge into daylight on the other side. The perceived horror is real enough: in 2001, several people died from the fumes when a car broke down in the tunnel and halted traffic.

The road up to the pass is kept open in both directions throughout the year by snowploughs and rock-clearing teams, but it is a cold, windswept spot, even in the summer, where slanting rain is the norm, and snow and ice might be expected at almost any time. On a clear day, though, the views in any direction are spectacular. Leaving the pass, the road descends steeply to continue west towards Ötmök, where a side road splits off to the west over the Ötmök Pass to Talas. Before this, close to the bottom of the pass, a lesser road turns off left to double back east along the Suusamyr Valley. Lining the road on the southern side of the pass in summer are numerous **yurts** selling *kumys*, the favourite tipple of the travelling Kyrgyz. The chances are that if you are travelling in a share taxi, you'll probably end up stopping at one of these for a spell while your driver and fellow passengers refresh themselves.

Less than an obvious valley, steppe plateau might a better description for the terrain of much of the Suusamyr region. Despite its position on the opposite side of the Kyrgyz Ala-Too from the Chui Valley this, perhaps surprisingly, is still part of Chui Province: a far-flung outpost that has many of the characteristics of Kyrgyzstan's more central provinces. The valley lies at an average altitude of around 2,200m and, in spite of its relative proximity to the capital, it remains a wild, bleak and generally little-visited part of the country.

Most of the population here are Kyrgyz who are still actively involved in herding and live a partially nomadic lifestyle. The population density is extremely low, a fact that is happily reflected in the zero casualty count that occurred when a spectacularly large earthquake, registering nine on the Richter scale, struck the valley in 1992.

In Soviet times, the Suusamyr Valley was an important centre for sheep grazing, and every year a large number were brought here from the collective farms of the Sokuluk Valley over high mountain passes to graze. The land use of the valley is a little more diverse these days, with potato and vegetable growing and honey production supplementing more traditional sheep raising. Adequate rainfall and not-too-high an altitude guarantees lush and nutritious grassland that provides excellent grazing for horses as well as sheep, and the lack of artificial fertilisers ensures the valley's meadows are a shock of colour, with drifts of herbs and wild flowers flourishing here in the early summer. Tourism, great potential though it might have, is still in its infancy here. The valley lacks through public transport, but with a decent enough road surface for the most part, together with conveniently spaced villages that offer places to stay, it makes an ideal cycle touring route and an interesting, back-road alternative between Kochkor and Bishkek.

This entry deals with the western Suusamyr Valley as far east as Kyzyl-Oi, which lies within Chui Province. The eastern end of the valley, which extends towards Kochkor in Naryn Province, is generally a little more geared up to providing services for travellers and hikers, and is covered in *Chapter 8, Naryn Province*. The GeoID 1:200,000 map *Suusamyrskaya dolina* covers the area around Suusamyr village and the western end of the valley.

SUUSAMYR VILLAGE AND SURROUNDINGS The turn-off to the valley lies some kilometres beyond the Töo-Ashuu Pass, where a minor road leads east off the main highway. Some 15km beyond the junction the small, eponymous village of **Suusamyr** appears – a series of single-storey houses strung nonchalantly along the roadside. This is said to be the coldest village in Kyrgyzstan, with winter temperatures falling as low as –53°C and six months of snow.

Getting there and away Public transport to Suusamyr is scarce. At least one share taxi (*200som*) operates between Kara-Balta and Suusamyr village daily. There may also sometimes be a minibus from Bishkek's Osh Bazaar that leaves in the afternoon and returns from Suusamyr very early in the morning. Taking a frequent *marshrutka* to Kara-Balta from Bishkek and then hiring a taxi to Suusamyr is probably the most straightforward option.

Where to stay and eat There is a simple but comfortable homestay at Nasirjan 7 (look for the battered 'Tourist Information' sign on the main road a little way beyond the mosque, coming from Bishkek). Bed and breakfast accommodation is available in a small cottage here for around 700som per person, including dinner. The family here can also help with seats in share taxis to Kara-Balta and help lay on transport to reach some of the nearby mountain *jailoos*, where further opportunities to stay exist.

Thirty kilometres east is the **Joo Jurak** *jailoo* where you can stay in a yurt belonging to the family of Negizbek Imankulov and rent horses for exploring the area. **Boirok** *jailoo* is a little nearer, 20km to the north of Suusamyr village, while closer still is **Sandyk** *jailoo*, just 13km southeast of Suusamyr. Both *jailoos* offer opportunities for a yurt stay. To return to Suusamyr after a *jailoo* visit, either make a prior arrangement to be picked up, or organise horses and a guide for the ride back to the village. A yurt camp is usually set up in the valley during the summer months.

What to see and do The village has a superbly ornate Kyrgyz **graveyard** on a hillside above the main road that can be reached by a path from near the mosque. Climbing up to the low plateau beyond the tombs affords a panoramic view over the valley, with mountains in every direction and the green swathe of the Suusamyr River just south of the village sprawl. The river itself is hard to reach from the village as numerous irrigation channels block the way.

The village of **Karakol**, 14km east of Suusamyr at the easternmost end of the West Karakol Valley, is tiny and in no way resembles its Lake Issyk-Kul namesake. Trekking south across the Kyrgyz Ala-Too from the Sokuluk or Ala-Archa valleys, this is the first village to be reached on the plateau. There is basic homestay accommodation available at a house in the middle of the village. Just ask around and someone should point you in the right direction.

KOJOMKUL (КОЖОМКУЛ) Continuing south along the main road, the next village reached is Kojomkul, about 20km from Suusamyr. The village takes its name from a man who lived here between 1889 and 1955 and who was reputed to be 2.3m tall and 164kg in weight (see box, opposite). This giant of a man lifted heavy rocks and even horses for fun (there is a statue of him in Bishkek, outside the Palace of Sports, performing this very act). A museum to his memory stands in the middle of the village with large stones outside its entrance. Photographs inside the museum reveal his truly impressive size, as do items from his wardrobe and examples of the objects he was fond of moving about. His grave stands in a white mausoleum in the centre of the village, next to a Soviet war memorial. On the road to Kyzyl-Oi stands another tribute to Kojomkul's strength, in the form of a massive stone that marks the yurt-shaped tomb of a local dignitary. The stone, which is said to weigh 700kg, is reputed to have been carried to the grave by Kojomkul himself, although there is undoubtedly some blurring of historical truth with legend here.

Accommodation in the village may be had at the comfortable home of Aybek and Gulnara Myrsakmatov. The whitewashed house is in the last (eastern) third of the village on the left. There are a couple of comfortable rooms available and meals can be provided on request.

KYZYL-OI (КЫЗЫЛ-ОЙ) This village lies in the gorge of the Kökömeren River, at an altitude of 1,800m, about 40km south of Suusamyr, at the Chui Province's most southerly limit. Here, the valley opens up to form a bowl surrounded by dry, red-coloured mountain slopes. In appearance, the village, which is 100% Kyrgyz, is more central Asian than most settlements in northern Kyrgyzstan, with a less-obvious Russian influence than most. The village's name is faithful to its geographical setting, as Kyzyl-Oi means 'Red Bowl', and the colouration of the local rock is also apparent in the houses and farm buildings here as many of the older ones are constructed from the red clay that characterises the area.

There is a Community Based Tourism project active in the village, with a good number of places to stay and this, coupled with the village's gorgeous natural setting, makes for an ideal stopover *en route* to Kochkor or Song-Köl or an excellent base for day hikes in the area. The only real drawback is the lack of public transport in either direction, as through traffic is quite rare and private arrangements will need to be made by those not cycling or willing to hitchhike. Given sufficient warning, Artyk Kulubaev (see page 142) should be able to help organise onward transport.

Getting there and away There is very limited **public transport** to and from Kyzyl-Oi, with minibuses or share taxis running to Suusamyr (and sometimes Kara-Balta) less than daily. Cars with drivers can be rented through CBT at the standard rate (currently 14som/km) to reach either Suusamyr or Chaek, from where occasional public services operate. A taxi to or from Kochkor will cost around 4,500som if booked through CBT, as you have to pay for both directions; a taxi from Kara-Balta will be about 4,000som.

Where to stay and eat Homestays tend to be allocated on a rotating basis – there are 14 in total. In addition to Artyk's house (see page 142), CBT homestays in the village include those of Ainagul Kulmurzaeva at the south (Chaek) end of the village by the river, and Murza Dubonaeva who has a comfortable homestay away from the main road – walk along the road opposite the shop, turn left, then right past an

---

KOJOMKUL – A KYRGYZ GIANT

Kojomkul was born in the Suusamyr Valley in 1889 and died in 1955 at the age of 66. As an adult he stood 2.3m tall (7ft 5in) and weighed 164kg (nearly 26 stone). Encouraged by his superhuman size and strength, he participated in many competitive bouts of strength in his youth. On one occasion, he took part in a wrestling competition in the Toktogul area where he beat many better-known wrestlers and won the prize of 50 sheep and several mares, which he is said to have distributed to the poor in his village. By the late 1920s there was no-one to rival him in Kyrgyzstan, and in the region as a whole the only challenge came from the Kazakh wrestler Cholok Balaban, who he eventually fought and beat in the 23rd minute of an inter-republic wrestling contest.

Following the revolution and the region's inclusion in the USSR, Kojomkul adapted well to Soviet ways and served as chairman of the Suusamyr Valley collective farm for more than 20 years. However, during this time he was forced to spend one year in prison as a result of his unwillingness to write a damning testimony against the chairman of a neighbouring collective farm. His 'gentle giant' reputation grew further in prison where he became widely respected by prisoners and guards alike. Later, during World War II, he is reputed to have provided many poor villagers with food thanks to his hunting skills.

His death in 1955 is surrounded by uncertainty, although one version, with echoes of the David and Goliath legend, suggests it was an insect which crept into his food that caused him to fall ill and die. His memory is still revered in the village and it is widely believed that it was Kojomkul's spirit that protected the village in 1992 when the earthquake hit, badly damaging property throughout the valley but claiming no lives.

attractive house; the homestay is at the next junction on the right. Other households include those of Tinatin Seydunova on the main road, and Gulmira Outbeava and Roza Abilgazieva on the main village street, a block west of the main road.

Other practicalities A good local contact is Artyk Kulubaev, who owns the Askar village shop on the main road and works as a guide and CBT co-ordinator in the village (m *0555 417 847*). There is a sign for **tourist information** just before the shop on the right-hand side coming from Suusamyr (the shop and homestay is on the left just after the new mosque). Artyk can arrange accommodation, advise on trekking routes and organise transport and horses.

Horses can be easily hired at any of the CBT homestays or through the co-ordinator. Only Kyrgyz and Russian is spoken as a rule. The village has three small **shops** but no bank or money-changing facilities. There is no internet access whatsoever and only MegaCom mobile phones work in the vicinity of the village. Kyzyl-Oi's electricity supply, which, like its water supply, is somewhat erratic, should be massively improved in the near future when the newly erected pylons running from Chaek come online.

Hiking routes There are numerous options for hikes and treks from the village, either on horseback or on foot. These vary in difficulty and length from pleasant two-hour circuits of the village to three-day treks. The Sary-Kamysh range to the south of the village has several peaks around 4,000m. Chychkan-Choku peak at 3,989m lies northwest of Kyzyl-Oi, and the best approach is along the Sandyk River on its northern slope. The highest peak in the area is Sary-Kamysh at 4,042m (also known as Ai-Soluu) and here the best approach is from the south by way of 3,701m Chukul-Tör Pass. Yr-Gailuu peak is lower at 2,664m and is situated to the east of the Kökömeren River.

One- or two-day treks can be made in either the Kobuk-Suu or Chong-Suu valleys, staying in yurts overnight. A three-day trek linking both valleys requires sleeping overnight in tents. The glacial lakes of Köl-Tör ('Four Lakes') lie to the southwest of the village along the Char Valley and over the Kum-Bel Pass, a four- or five-hour trip on horseback. One of the lakes contains plenty of fish. Easier options include a waterfall on the Borondu River to the north, 2km east of the Kökömeren River – a three-hour round trip from the village on foot or horseback – or hikes to flower-strewn summer *jailoos* above the village, such as Chet-Tör. The Choin-Tash *jailoo*, a mere 40-minute horse ride from the village, lies on the way to a glacier that can be visited via the Munkur Pass. Some mountain-biking groups pass through the village on tours between Bishkek and Kochkor, and a few Bishkek tour operators also offer late-summer rafting expeditions along the Kökömeren River.

The 1:200,000 *Vnutrenniy Tien Shan* map from GeoID has Kyzyl-Oi village in its far northwest corner. Hikes that range far from the village will require the surrounding maps.

A **shortish walk** that takes in excellent views of the village and surrounding area can be had by heading north along the main road as far as the *ulak tartysh* ground (look for the tyre-studded mounds at either end), then turn left and head up to the graveyard that stands overlooking the village on an isolated hill. From here it is possible to continue along tracks leading south before reaching one of the village streets that will bring you back to the main road. Another local walk, with even better views, is to go to the *ulak tartysh* ground and then turn right off the road to go down to the suspension footbridge that crosses the rushing Kökömeren River. After crossing the river, turn left and climb a little to follow a track that leads to the right up the Jamchukar Valley along the bank of a stream. This soon reaches two isolated buildings where it veers to the right away from the stream next to a ridge. From the top of the ridge are excellent 270° views of the Kyzyl-Oi basin and snow-capped peaks in the distance.

For a longer, **half-day hike**, follow the Chaek road south out of the village for about 45 minutes, going over a bridge where the tributary of the Chong-Suu River joins the Kökömeren, and past a track leading up to a cottage, to reach another bridge just before where the road starts bending to the left. Take the track to the right here, alongside the Kobuk-Suu River. This is shady to start with but soon becomes more open as it climbs away from the river. A short cut leads past a derelict building to reach a bend in the road where the path splits. Take the lower path and continue to where the road divides and then follow the footpath that leads along the valley parallel to the river below. The large pylons erected in 2014 to bring electricity to the valley from Chaek can be seen immediately above. The path becomes more indistinctive as it progresses along the valley, but continuing in this direction will lead eventually to a wide *jailoo* with seasonal yurts from where, given time and energy, it is possible to reach Chet-Tör, Köl-Tör and Mukur Köl lakes. For the half-day hike, simply return by the same route after two to three hours of walking.

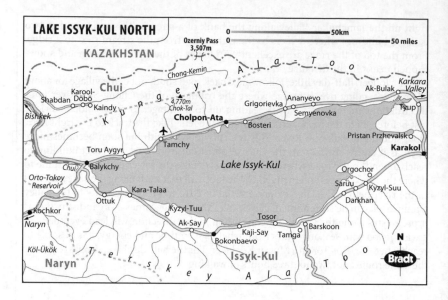

5

Lake Issyk-Kul
– North Shore

LAKE ISSYK-KUL (ОЗЕРО ИССЫК-КУЛЬ)

Lake Issyk-Kul, the second-largest alpine lake in the world (Lake Titicaca in Peru/ Bolivia is the largest), gives its name to the *oblast* that surrounds the lake's shoreline and extends across the high Tien Shan range south to the Chinese border. Issyk-Kul Province, which in area makes up around 20% of Kyrgyzstan's territory, has a population of less than 500,000, the vast majority of whom live around the lake's shores.

The lake's name, which is also spelled Ysyk Köl or Issyk-kol, means literally 'warm lake' in the Kyrgyz language, as does its Chinese equivalent, Ze-Hai. There is good reason for this: in a part of the world where winter temperatures can plummet to –25°C or worse, the shores of the lake have a microclimate that is relatively balmy and, even more aptly, its waters never freeze. This is all the more surprising considering the lake stands at considerable altitude – 1,606m above sea level. Scientists have long debated the precise mechanics of this, and it would seem it is down to a combination of deep-water physics, slight salinity and underground thermal activity. Most locals are less questioning and are merely grateful for the respite the lake offers, assuming it is because the water is warmed by heat wafting up from the earth's core.

GEOGRAPHY AND CLIMATE In geographical terms, the lake is one of two massive depressions that dent the Tien Shan range: in Issyk-Kul's case, the depression is ringed by mountains and filled with snow-melt to form a lake; the other depression, a lower and altogether hotter region, is the Fergana Valley.

Lake Issyk-Kul, 'the pearl of the Tien Shan', is in the shape of an eye, 182km long and up to 60km wide. The lake was created in the early Miocene period 20 million years ago, when tectonic activity created the depression that became filled with fresh water. During the Pliocene period it covered an area substantially larger than it does now. Today it covers an area of 6,236km². Over 100 rivers and streams flow into the lake, the largest being Jergalan and Tyup at its eastern end. The total distance around its shoreline is 688km. The lake's average depth is around 270m but it is as deep as 668m in places, making it the fifth-deepest lake in the world. Most of the water in Issyk-Kul comes from snow-melt or is provided by springs, some of which are thermal. In hydrographical terms, Issyk-Kul is an endorheic basin like the Caspian Sea, in that there is no outlet for its water either by river or underground and water can only leave it by evaporation or seepage through the soil.

The lake's slightly saline water, which had been dropping in level by around 5cm a year since the beginning of the 20th century, has been rising in level since 1998, and has risen by over 30cm since then, a remarkable increase for such a large body of water. Although this might be seen to be irrefutable evidence of the extent of global

5

warming and increased ice-melt, the rise in water level may be, for the most part, a result of a changing local climate in the region, in which there has been far more rain and snowfall in recent years and which is not necessarily connected with a global pattern. There are others who point the finger at industrial development, in particular the Kumtor gold mine south of the lake, and suggest that dust from the mine coats the glaciers to create a darker surface which absorbs more heat and melts quicker. Geological evidence suggests that the lake's water level has fluctuated considerably over millennia but the trend over the past 500 years has mainly been one of decrease.

Rainfall is generally low, but adequate, with an average of 248mm per annum in Cholpon-Ata and 475mm in Karakol. The eastern end of the lake around Karakol is considerably wetter than the western region close to Balykchy, due to the presence of air masses that collect moisture from the lake and release their payload as rain as they rise into the mountains.

The vegetation type here is one of steppe and meadows, with elm trees and, higher up, alpine meadows and forests of fir. The western part of the basin has rocky deserts and more sparse vegetation: the coastal plain and mountains in the southwest region between Bokonbaevo and Balykchy are particularly arid.

Temperatures, as already mentioned, are far milder than the Kyrgyzstan average, due to the moderating effect of the lake, with average summer temperatures rising to around 25°C at Cholpon-Ata and winter temperatures dropping to about –5°C. The area receives around 2,900 hours of sunshine a year, which is relatively high for the region.

Lake Issyk-Kul is flanked by two mountain ranges that run its full length from east to west: to the north is the Kungey ('Sunny') Ala-Too range, beyond which lies Kazakhstan; to the south is the Terskey ('Shady') Ala-Too. At the southeast end of the lake, close to Karakol, are a number of narrow valleys that run south from the Terskey range towards the lake – Altyn Arashan, Karakol and Jeti-Ögüz. Beyond the Terskey range to the south are the even loftier peaks of the Central Tien Shan chain, and the high glaciers that connect them. In the far southeast, nudged against the Chinese and Kazakhstan borders in a frozen wonderland of rock and ice, are the peaks of Khan Tengri (6,995m) and Pobedy, which, at 7,439m, is Kyrgyzstan's highest point. The extensive Inylchek Glacier stretches out beneath these peaks. This distant and inaccessible corner of the country is also home to the mysterious Merzbacher Lake, a geographical enigma *par excellence* (see page 192).

NATURAL HISTORY There are more than 20 types of fish in Lake Issyk-Kul, although human interference during the Soviet period has dramatically upset the lake's natural ecology (see box, page 153). The basic commercial fish used to be naked osman (*Dyptichus dybowslii*), Issyk-Kul chebak (*Leuciscus schmidti*), carp (*Cyprinus carpio*) and Issyk-Kul marinka (*Schizothorax pseudaksaiensis isskkuli*), but these have all diminished to a lesser or greater extent following the introduction of non-native species such as Sevan trout (*Salmo ischchan gegarkuni*).

Both eastern and western shores serve as wintering grounds for waterfowl – mostly pochard, mallards, bald coots and teal – with flocks that can be as big as 50,000. The lake was designated an official Ramsar Wetland Site in 2003. Altogether, around 200 species of bird can be seen around the lake and the nearby mountains, with many birds of prey such as saker falcon (*Falco cherrug*).

The mountains surrounding the lake also provide a habitat for scarce and endemic mammal species including lynx (*Flis unsia*), Marco Polo sheep (*Ovis ammon polii*), Siberian deer (*Servus eaphus*) and Siberian ibex (*Capra sibirica*). The highly elusive snow leopard (*Uncia uncia*) can also be found in small numbers.

In terms of vegetation, the foothill zone immediately next to the lake commonly has species such as artemisia, acanthus, ephedra and sea buckthorn, while tree species such as Turkestan juniper, and Tien Shan and Shrenk spruce, occur higher up, between 2,000m and 3,000m. Above this lie high meadows with specially adapted alpine flora.

Lake Issyk-Kul Biosphere Reserve This was established in 2001 with technical assistance from the German government. A draft plan was completed in 1998 and in September 2001, by decision of the co-ordinating committee of the UNESCO Man & Biosphere Programme (MAB), the Issyk-Kul Biosphere Reserve became No 411 on the list of the World Wide Network of Biosphere Reserves, with the dual goal of conserving its natural flora and fauna and supporting long-term economic and social development deemed to help restore natural resources.

The biosphere reserve is divided into four zones – core, buffer, transitional and rehabilitation – with each zone governed by rules about what sorts of activity are allowed or prohibited within it. Overall, the biosphere covers an area of 43,100km², which is about 22% of Kyrgyzstan's total area. It includes a number of previously protected territories of scientific value, like the Issyk-Kul State Reserve that was founded as the first protected territory of the Kyrgyz ASSR in 1948, to protect the lake's wintering waterfowl population.

The core area of the biosphere reserve incorporates a range of specially protected areas around the lake, the largest being the high-altitude, 72,000ha **Sarychat-Ertash National Preserve**, which lies deep in the Tien Shan mountains south of Karakol. Another important protected area is the **Karakol Natural Park**, founded in 1997, which has an area of 38,256ha and includes large stands of coniferous forest. In practical terms, one of the major challenges facing the integrity of the reserve is the activity of poachers and illegal loggers, along with the problems faced in containing polluting industrial development, especially the gold-mining operation at Kumtor, which is located just 20km from the Sarychat-Ertash preserve's western border.

HISTORY Much evidence of some of modern-day Kyrgyzstan's earliest settlers, the warrior tribes of the Saka – or Scythians – has been found in the Issyk-Kul region, and a variety of rich bronze and gold artefacts have been recovered from their circular burial mounds. The Scythians occupied the region between about the 6th century BC and the 5th century AD. Before them, Neolithic settlers left their mark on the region, most notably at Cholpon-Ata, where a large number of petroglyphs and settlement remains from around 1000BC to the 6th century AD, and later, can still be seen.

Although the general trend until recently has been a drop of the lake's surface level, it would appear that Issyk-Kul was some 8m lower than its present level in medieval times, as remains of settlements have been found beneath its surface at this level. The Russian explorer Pyotr Semyonov Tyan-Shansky believed that a 'Kyrgyz Atlantis' might be discovered beneath the lake's waters. In 1857, some locals showed him some ruins in the water at Kara-Bulun cape, where the Tyup and Jergalan rivers divide, and since then other underwater ruins have been found at various locations around the lake. The submerged city of Chigu in the Tyup gulf at the lake's eastern end has revealed artefacts that date back to the 2nd century BC. Chigu, referred to by the Chinese as 'the City of the Red Valley', was the capital of the state of Usun, and is presumed to have disappeared beneath the water in the 1st century AD.

Ancient legend points to St Matthew being buried close to the lake's shore at an Orthodox monastery, and some archaeologists believe this would have been at the northwest shore of the lake, near to the settlement of Toru Aygyr, where the present-day tourist settlement of Ulan is located. A medieval bath complex was excavated here 50 years ago by a Kyrgyz archaeologist, along with many pieces of ceramics.

Later theories concerning this shifted their attention further east: Vladimir Ploskikh, a Kyrgyz archaeologist, believes he has found remains of the monastery in which St Matthew was buried at Svetly Mys, on the northeast coast of the lake, although he admits his hypothesis remains unproven (see page 165).

Arabian chronicles make mention of many ancient settlements in the Issyk-Kul region, relating that the towns along the southern shore of the lake were celebrated for their riches and were populated by a large number of people. Of these towns, in the 8th century BC the major one was Barskhan, which roughly corresponds to present-day Barskoon, at the mouth of the river of the same name. This is mentioned in the works of the philosopher Biruni, who wrote that the residents of the town knew the secrets of iron alloys, which were only known to the Chinese at the time. All of these towns, it is believed, were later destroyed and inundated following an earthquake.

Because of its geographical position and obvious resources, Issyk-Kul became an important staging point along the more northern sections of the ancient **Silk Road**. Several routes used to ply its shores and one of the prime routes to the west led across the 4,284m Bedel Pass from China, before descending to the lake near present-day Barskoon. The lake was coveted by the Chinese for centuries, but they were never successful in conquering it and, despite its distance from St Petersburg, the Tsarist capital, it would be the Russians rather than the Chinese who would eventually colonise it.

Long before this, however, the lake's resources and mild climate were utilised by both Mongol and Turkic nomadic armies, who would often winter on its shores. Tamerlane is reputed to have banished captured Tartars to an island fortress that has long since vanished beneath the surface, probably as a result of earthquake activity. Whether or not this is true is uncertain, but whatever the precise history of the lake, washed-up fragments of pottery and brick bear witness to extensive periods of settlement here in the past.

Some historians believe the lake was the point of origin for the **Black Death** that devastated Asia and Europe during the 14th century. These same historians believe the plague began at a Nestorian Christian community at the northeast end of the lake in 1338 (while others say that it originated in the Gobi Desert). Archaeological excavations have revealed extraordinarily high death rates for 1338 and 1339, and memorial stones attribute these deaths to plague, which has led some scholars to conclude that the 14th-century pandemic may well have originated here. From its origin at the lake, the plague spread westward, as merchants unwittingly transmitted the disease by transporting infected vermin along with their goods.

Following the decline of the Silk Road, the lake languished in obscurity for centuries and remained virtually unknown to the Western world until the 19th century, when Russian explorers like Pyotr Semyonov Tyan-Shansky ventured into the area to send back reports. At that time it was thought that the Chui River was the outflow of the lake, but Semyonov Tyan-Shansky proved that, although it would have had an outflow to the river at earlier times, this was no longer the case, despite it flowing within 4km of the western end of the lake. Another Russian explorer following in Tyan-Shansky's footsteps, the scientist and geographer Nikolai Przhevalsky, died of typhoid in the town that then, as now, was known as Karakol but which, in the later Tsarist and Soviet era, was named after him.

Russian exploration arrived relatively late on the scene, but there had always been greater contact with the East: the Chinese traveller Jan Chan Tzan is reported to have reached the lake in around 128BC, while the first written account of the lake comes from another Chinese adventurer, Suan Zsan. The first written record of its name comes from an anonymous Tajik work from AD982, *The Boundaries of the World from East to West*, which also accurately estimated the size of the lake.

During the Soviet period, the eastern end of the lake was utilised as a base for testing submarine and torpedo technology for the Soviet navy. As the lake's waters were slightly salty and never froze, they were ideal for replicating the maritime conditions in which the Soviet fleet would normally be deployed. Even better was the lake's isolation, far from Europe and the prying eyes of the West. Throughout the late Soviet period, Lake Issyk-Kul was strictly off limits for non-Soviet citizens, although during this same period the lake was developed as a holiday destination for citizens of the USSR, and many sanatoriums were opened up along its shores, particularly in the north at resorts like Cholpon-Ata.

Because of its natural beauty, clean air and pleasant summer climate, the lake was considered to be one of the top leisure spots in the USSR. It was particularly popular with holidaying cosmonauts, and Yuri Gagarin journeyed here for well-earned rest and recuperation after his pioneering space mission in 1961 – there are monuments to him in the Barskoon Valley. The lake's popularity even extended to Soviet leaders: Leonid Brezhnev himself had a *dacha* built here at the lake's north shore.

Following Kyrgyzstan's independence in 1991, the holiday industry swiftly plummeted into decline as Russians stopped visiting, and many of the lake's sanatoriums were boarded up and abandoned. In recent times, there has been a turnaround of fortunes, with domestic tourists visiting the lake's shores in larger numbers, along with visitors from Kazakhstan, especially ethnic Russians, who make the trip over the mountains from Almaty to take advantage of the relatively low prices and visa-free entry.

As a result of this renewed interest, some of the former sanatoriums have been taken into private ownership and refurbished, and new hotels, especially small B&Bs, are being established. Since the late 1990s an increasing number of travellers from western Europe and North America have been arriving in the region. On the whole, these come mostly to hike in the valleys southeast of the lake, close to Karakol, or to visit the lake *en route* to the peaks of the Central Tien Shan. The administrative centre of Karakol has subsequently developed as the major centre for the outdoor pursuits and adventure tourism favoured by Western visitors, while Cholpon-Ata retains the crown for domestic tourism and the Kazakh beach set.

BALYKCHY (БАЛЫКЧИ) *Telephone code: 03944*

Balykchy (Kyrgyz for 'fisherman') is the largest settlement at the western end of Lake Issyk-Kul, and even a cursory glance tells that it is no longer the prosperous town that it once was. Originally named Kutmady, this town of around 40,000 was renamed Riybachye during the Soviet era, the Russian equivalent of its present-day name. The railway station still bears this name today, but it is not alone in echoing the name of a bygone age. Following independence in 1991, the town was known for a brief time as Issyk-Kul but, for obvious reasons, this caused considerable confusion, and so a couple of years later the Kyrgyz equivalent of its earlier name was settled upon.

Fishing was one of the first industries to develop here in the late 19th century, when Russian colonists settled here and started working the lake on their doorstep. Unfortunately for Balykchy, fishing has not played much of a role in the town's fortunes since independence, and over the past two decades the town has steadily declined to the sorry state it finds itself in today.

In Soviet times the town developed as an important transport and industrial centre, with shipping, fishing and shipbuilding all contributing to its economy; now, with the loss of the industrial base that the Soviet Union provided, all of these industries have virtually disappeared, and those who remain face unemployment and little promise for the future. Consequently, it is hardly surprising that depression, heavy vodka consumption and prostitution are pervasive in the town, given Balykchy's current unhappy lot. Even back in more prosperous Soviet times, the town had a reputation for crime and lawlessness, and the spectre of this remains.

The town's main function today is simply as the terminus of the seasonal railway line from Bishkek, and as a junction town on the road south to Naryn and China, and the roads to the east that skirt the north and south shores of the lake. For many locals, these roads are the best thing about the place, and many of those who are able to leave have done so, migrating to Russia, Ukraine and Germany. Those left behind – mostly the old – have to cope as best they can. As elsewhere in Kyrgyzstan, pensioners have been particularly vulnerable, as many are abandoned by their families in search of a better life elsewhere. Balykchy has more than its fair share of pensioners – perhaps 4,000 or more – all desperately trying to survive on the impossibly small pension of just a few dollars a month.

If you want a warts-and-all perspective of industrial decline in a post-Soviet transitional state, then Balykchy makes a good case study. Whatever your degree of interest, however, you probably do not want to stay here.

ISSYK-KUL LEGENDS

One legend relates the tale of a king who had ears like an ass. The king's barbers were ordered to hide his ears and then each was killed in order to protect his dark secret. Understandably, the king soon exhausted the kingdom's supply of barbers and so was obliged to spare the last one, swearing him to lifelong secrecy. The task proved too much for the barber, who fled to the mountains and asked a local hermit what he should do as he was tortured by the burden of his secret. The hermit suggested that he whispered the secret to a well, shutting the cover carefully after he did so. The barber did as he was told and announced his secret to a town well but he forgot to cover it afterwards. As a consequence of this, the water of the well rose up to flood the large-eared monarch's kingdom. Lake Issyk-Kul is said to be the result of this flood, its waters coming from the rising well of the legend.

Another story tells of a beautiful city that stood where the lake is today. One day, some young girls from the city went to the mountains to collect firewood. In their absence an enormous earthquake took place, flooding the city and killing all of its inhabitants. The girls came home to find a big lake where their city used to be. They were so grieved by the loss of their relatives and friends that they returned every day to the same place to mourn and weep. The salt of their tears slowly turned the lake's waters saline, which is why it does not freeze today.

A third tale tells of a cruel khan who once governed over a wonderful city. One day he saw a beautiful girl on a riverbank and immediately he wanted to marry her. The girl, however, was unimpressed and refused his proposal. Incensed by her refusal, the khan imprisoned the girl in a high tower until she changed her mind. Trapped in her prison tower she cried bitter tears and prayed to the

GETTING THERE AND AWAY There are daily **rail** connections with Bishkek in the summertime only but these are painfully slow, take up to six hours, and do not even deposit you in the town centre, as the passenger station lies some way out of town. Tickets are very cheap though and cost only 70som one-way. Overall, it is better to get there by **minibus** from Bishkek's West Bus Station (*200som*), a two-hour run. Balykchy's bus/minibus station is fairly conveniently situated, ten minutes' walk west of the town centre on Frunze. There are plenty of minibuses to Cholpon-Ata from Balykchy (*100som*), some of which continue to Karakol. Minibuses along the southern shore are less plentiful.

Local **buses** run these same routes several times a day, too. Most direct buses to Karakol from Bishkek bypass Balykchy, as does direct transport running south to Naryn, which takes a short cut via the west side of the Orto-Tokoy Reservoir. Travelling between Karakol and Naryn or Kochkor, it is usually faster and easier to go first to Balykchy (*200som from Karakol, 250som from Naryn*) and then change transport there.

WHERE TO STAY AND EAT There are no hotels should you wish to stay here, although if you are really desperate you could probably find some sort of accommodation by asking around at the bus station. It's better to continue to one of the nearby villages along the coast where there will be *komnaty* (rooms) to rent. Also, east of town on the way to Cholpon-Ata there is the **Ulan** *turbaza*, signposted just before you reach the village of Toru Aygyr. For food, there is the bazaar, or **Café Cholpan** (*Toktosunov 56*), and a few simple cafés along Frunze,

heavens to take pity on her. Her prayers were soon answered and the river that flowed through the town burst its banks to inundate the whole town. Everyone perished in the flood – the khan, the girl, the townspeople – and since that day the lake formed by the flood has been salty and changeable: sometimes it is calm and quiet, like the dead girl; at other times, it is threatening and violent, like the tragedy that created the lake.

This final legend has similarities to the story of the ass-eared king. Many years ago there was a big city where Lake Issyk-Kul is located today. The ruler of the city was Khan Iskender, a cruel and violent man who lived with the terrible secret that he had a pair of horns on his head. To keep the secret he routinely executed everyone who came to cut his hair or to shave him. One day it was the turn of the son of a poor old widow to clip the khan, and his mother was fully aware of the risk to her son. The widow cooked three round cakes made of her own milk and told her son to take them to the khan. On visiting the khan the son dropped the first two cakes as he had been told, but when he dropped the third cake the khan picked it up and tasted it, declaring it to be delicious. The khan asked what the cake was made of and, on being told, he realised he had inadvertently become a maternal brother of the son.

Because of this the son was spared, but made to promise to keep the khan's affliction secret. On the third day of visiting the khan the son was suffering from a stomach ache and an overwhelming desire to tell someone of the khan's secret. The khan ordered that a well in the middle of the town be opened up so that the boy could yell down it, 'Our Iskender Khan is two-horned!' On his third cry, water burst out of the well and flooded the city, thus creating Lake Issyk-Kul.

although all are equally uninspiring. The town centre has a couple of banks with ATMs that take Visa cards.

WHAT TO SEE AND DO Aficionados of Soviet-era statuary will find plenty to enthral them here: the town has at least three Lenin figures, along with a sad array of rusting communist totems. Also, on the outskirts of the town on the Bishkek side, set back from the road on a small hillock, stands a statue of Pyotr Semyonov Tyan-Shansky, in exploration mode leading a packhorse (see page 183).

Although it is undeniable that few towns in Kyrgyzstan have rejected their Soviet past outright, you get the feeling that in Balykchy they mourn the past more than most, and perhaps one indication of this has been a reluctance to dispose of the monuments and ciphers that point to more prosperous times. There again, much of the town has an abandoned look to it, and what remains is more likely a matter of indifference than any conscious effort to conserve. The street names here are largely unchanged from the communist period and Cyrillic signs still point you along the cracked tarmac of thoroughfares with heroic names like Gagarin, Frunze, Komsomol and Pioneer.

A change of minibuses here gives the opportunity to wander awhile through the town, which at the very least offers a very different perspective on the lake from Cholpon-Ata or Karakol; an important contrast worth seeing, even if you are not tempted to linger.

Leaving the bus station and heading east along Frunze, you go past a building that has a metal framework Lenin on its roof. After five minutes, you will reach a small, and rather threadbare, bazaar area, with lots of men in tracksuits hanging around waiting for something to happen – although they know it won't – and stalls selling cheap clothes and vodka, which never seems to be in short supply.

The road south at the crossroads by the bazaar leads past an Orthodox church to the lake's shore. A freight railway skirts the shore east to an area of docks with rusting hulls and idle cranes. The largest of the dock buildings has a hammer and sickle motif attached to its roof, along with what looks like a brace of torpedoes, a reminder of the days when Soviet torpedoes were tested on the lake.

There is nowhere in particular to go from here, just a meander back towards the bus station, which in a town like this seems to wield a strong gravitational pull. On the way back you might well pass another Lenin statue, this time in a weedy patch that fronts a closed-down cinema, which has had its windows filled in with breeze blocks to create a concrete cube rather like the space encapsulated by the artist Rachel Whitread's work, *House*. You will probably see a number of houses with 'for sale' notices outside; they're often wooden and attractive but with peeling paint, which just reinforces the impression that this is a town whose fortune has deserted it. Close to the bus station, huddles of local woman at the roadside hold up smoked fish on strings and wave them at passing vehicles. You may see these for sale all around the lake's shore, although only in Balykchy do the vendors seem so desperate to make a transaction. Apparently the demand for smoked fish is so great that these days the fish have to be imported for smoking from elsewhere in the region – a tragic irony given the town's fishing history.

TORU AYGYR (ТОРУ АЙГЫР) Leaving Balykchy along Lake Issyk-Kul's northern shore, this village is reached after about 20km. The remains of an ancient settlement have been found nearby, along with petroglyphs and stone statues. A medieval bathhouse was discovered here by archaeologists in the 1940s, which had ceramic pipes to channel the water, and glazed bricks on the floor. A potter's workshop has

Commercial fishing at Lake Issyk-Kul began in the 1890s with the arrival of Russian colonists who took advantage of the 22 native species the lake had to offer, many of which were good to eat. By the 1930s the populations of some of the more scarce species had declined, so commoner species such as *chebachok* or Issyk-Kul dace (*Leuciscus bergi*) were targeted, a fish with a population that was considered to be virtually inexhaustible.

In an attempt to increase the value of the lake's fish stocks, more valuable fish like trout were introduced around this time. The Sevan trout (*Salmo ischchan*), a species endemic to Armenia, was first introduced to the lake in the 1930s, partly to boost fish stocks in the lake and partly to conserve a species that was becoming rare in its native Armenia. The trout grew to a large size in their new home – some older fisherman claim they would catch 17kg specimens on occasion – but the project was not an unqualified success as the alien trout ravaged many of Issyk-Kul's native species like *chebachok*, and within a few decades catches of this once plentiful fish had declined dramatically.

Later, in the 1950s, a few other non-native species were introduced – bream, pike-perch and carp – and, in the early 1970s, efforts to restock the lake took a different turn when a plan was devised to gradually reduce the number of *chebachok* to a minimum and to turn the lake into a reservoir for valuable fish such as trout and whitefish. At this point, the Sevan whitefish (*Coregonus lavaretus*), another Armenian species, was introduced, along with *omul*, a fish from Lake Baikal in Siberia.

Like the Sevan trout, the introduction of whitefish turned out to be a misjudgement in ecological terms. Efforts were soon made to restrict their numbers but it was too late, as within a very short time the Sevan whitefish had established itself as the major component of the lake's fish stock. This has inevitably resulted in widespread changes in Lake Issyk-Kul's fish ecology. The number of most native species has diminished overall, while some species such as the naked osman have virtually disappeared altogether. The lake now produces relatively low fish yields.

It should not be forgotten that Lake Issyk-Kul is an oligotrophic lake (low in nutrients), with a low productivity, and that it could never realistically be expected to produce large sustainable fish stocks. Nowadays, with an increased population living around the lake, together with a large number of annual visitors, the demand for fish far outweighs supply. Due to Lake Issyk-Kul's growing importance for recreation, one management solution might be to concentrate on sport and recreational fishing in order to satisfy the demands of visitors and bring in income. The trouble with this is that the two most voracious feeders on the lake's endemic species – the Sevan trout and pike-perch – are those very species which are most in demand by recreational fishermen.

Poaching is a widespread problem, too, and has soared to massive levels in recent years. Bans on fishing during the spawning period have been introduced but, this being central Asia, corruption comes into play and many inspectors are said to be either involved in poaching themselves, or are intimidated by the threat of violence from poachers who gang together in groups.

also been unearthed. Trekking routes over the Kungey Ala-Too from the village lead into the Chong-Kemin Valley and Kazakhstan beyond. A two-day, 45km-route goes as far as Kaindy in the valley although, given the climb, Toru Aygyr is probably better used as the destination rather the starting point.

TAMCHY (ТАМЧЫ) *Telephone code: 03943*

Nestled on the northwest shore of Lake Issyk-Kul, this small village has become popular with domestic and Kazakh tourists in recent years as a quieter and less brash alternative to Cholpon-Ata. With a successfully established CBT project here, too, it is also becoming increasingly favoured by overseas visitors, either as an overnight stop while travelling along Lake Issyk-Kul's north shore, or as a place to relax after a stint of strenuous trekking. As a village it is a pleasant but fairly unremarkable place, but it does have something that most others do not have: a location right by the water and a long lakeside beach. For visitors circumnavigating Lake Issyk-Kul, Tamchy makes a good choice for a first night's stay.

GETTING THERE AND AWAY Perhaps surprisingly, Tamchy lies close to the largest airfield around the lake. The nearby airport, 3km east at Chok-Tal, was renovated in 2003 and mainly provides summer charter flights for holidaying Kazakhs and Russians from Almaty. In 2006 Moscow announced it would invest US$100 million dollars in the airport to upgrade it to international standards. This would involve lengthening the landing strip to make larger planes capable of landing there. There were also plans to build a hotel, casino and leisure complex, and to develop a large holiday resort in the area although nothing has come of this yet.

Frequent **minibuses** and **buses** pass by on the main road, heading west to Bishkek and east to Karakol. Both leave from Bishkek's West Bus Station (*Zapadniy Avtovakzal*) and most will be bound for either Cholpon-Ata or Karakol; the minibus fare is around 250som, the bus, 150som – the same as to Cholpon-Ata – and the journey takes three hours or so. Occasional **share taxis** also ply the same routes, although when returning to Bishkek most of these originate in larger towns like Cholpon-Ata, and are usually already full when they pass. Leaving Tamchy, there is a concrete bus shelter by the main road at the top of the park where transport can be flagged down. Coming from Bishkek, look out for the unassuming sign that announces the village – it is quite easy to miss, although from that direction it is probable that you have already caught sight of the Disney-esque tower of Villa Stariy Zamok on the approach to the village. The best place to get off is by the sign on the road opposite the CBT office, just before the mosque and graveyard on the left.

⌂ WHERE TO STAY *Map, page 155*

There is a small community tourism set-up in the village, although the CBT kiosk on the main road may not necessarily be open when you arrive. There are several good homestay choices in the village, all **$$**.

⌂ **Royal Beach Hotel** ☎536 76; e royalbeach@glavtour.kg; www.royalbeach.kg. A modern, comfortable hotel on the lakeshore which has both private rooms (*US$70–140*) & bungalows (*US$70–150*) with full 3-meal pension. Prices are much lower out of season.

Besides the beach, entertainment inc tennis, volleyball & horseriding, & catamarans can be hired on the lake. **$$$$–$$$$$**

⌂ **Homestay** On the main road at Manas 55, close to the CBT office; ☎212 72; m 0773 355 611. One of several good homestays in the village, run

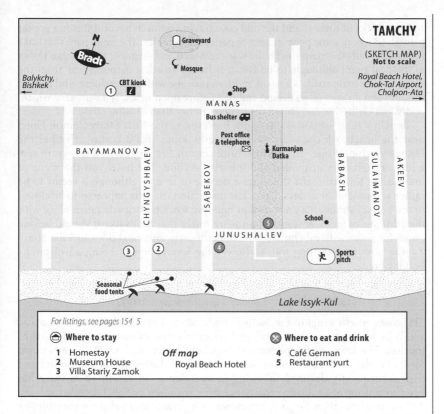

For listings, see pages 154–5

⌂ Where to stay
1 Homestay
2 Museum House
3 Villa Stariy Zamok

Off map
Royal Beach Hotel

✶ Where to eat and drink
4 Café German
5 Restaurant yurt

by Baktygul Asanlieva, who can also put you in touch with makers of good-quality *shyrdaks*, for which Tamchy is well known. **$$**

⌂ **Museum House** Chyngyshbaev 24. A homestay close to the lake with traditional Kyrgyz-style rooms. **$$**

⌂ **Villa Stariy Zamok ('Old Castle Villa')** This hotel in the village, with its mafioso connections, appeared to be closed at the time of writing, although the building had clearly been recently expanded & might be open for business again sometime in the future.

✘ **WHERE TO EAT AND DRINK** *Map, above*
Meals are best taken at the homestay, but there are seasonal tents along the beach which sell booze and snacks, and a couple of places along Chyngyshbaev and Isabekov like **Café German** that offer *shashlyk*, *manti* and *shorpo*. There is also a **restaurant yurt** in summer at the south end of the park. As Tamchy is popular with both Kazakh and Russian visitors, in the summer there is absolutely no problem in finding beer and vodka on sale.

WHAT TO SEE AND DO Tamchy's prime attraction is its natural setting: a beachfront location with the backdrop of the mountains of the Kungey Ala-Too range. There are pleasant walks to be had along the beach in either direction. In summer there will be plenty of Russians and Kyrgyz swimming in the lake, and families picnicking on the beach or eating in the tents which have been set up along it. Umbrella and pedalo hire are both available at the beach. Out of season, it is likely that the only company you will have on the beach is a few grazing cows or tethered horses. Immediately behind the beach is a wet grassy area with the improbable sight of flocks of turkeys and the odd cow grazing upon it; beyond this is a poplar plantation where some people camp or park their vehicles. The small park that links Junusaliev with the main road has a war memorial and statue of Kurmanjan Datka as its focal point although, to be fair, it is hardly worth a detour. Away from the shore, on the main road, is a small, modern mosque with a steel dome, and behind this, beyond an area of wasteland and just before open fields, is a cemetery which, oddly, has Orthodox and communist graves rather than Muslim ones.

Tamchy's most unmistakable sight, however, is the Villa Stariy Zamok Hotel near the beach, which, as its name suggests, looks like a castle, or rather the Disney version of one. This architectural conceit first appeared a few years ago, a blot on Tamchy's unspoiled and low-rise skyline. The hotel was the scene of internecine Kazakh mafia shootings a decade or so ago, although it seems to be rather somnolent these days. Upon last inspection the villa appeared to be closed to the public, although a great deal of building work had clearly taken place with the addition of an extension and a square tower that looks like it should belong on an English medieval church. The Moorish-style villa next door to Villa Stariy Zamok is rather startling too, and gives the impression of being an oligarch's holiday home.

CHOLPON-ATA (ЧОЛПОН АТА) *Telephone code: 03943*

This town marks roughly the halfway point along Lake Issyk-Kul's north shore and is by far the lake's most developed resort in terms of domestic (and Kazakh) tourism. The town, with a permanent population of around 8,000, is well known for its beaches and sanatoriums, which developed during the Soviet period and then subsequently declined following independence. In recent years there has been something of a tourism renaissance here, with new private hotels being built, and some of the older, larger sanatoriums being taken into private ownership for refurbishment.

The town stretches along the main road for some considerable distance, with new housing stretching north towards the mountains, while south of the main highway roads lead to hotels, a holiday complex, sanatorium, yacht club and the town's beaches. For visitors, the town's epicentre is the area along the main road just east of the bus station, where many of its shops, restaurants, services and accommodation options are located. Further east, beyond a park, is another area of activity with the El Nuur Bazaar, a bus stop and more bars and restaurants.

The resort was always popular with visitors from the former USSR, particularly Russians, who came here for sun, sea and sanatoriums. It used to be rather an elite sort of place, with intellectuals and writers coming from all over the Soviet Union to take to the waters here, and athletes coming to train and take advantage of its gentle summer climate and modest altitude.

Cholpon-Ata remains popular in the summer, and during July and August the town is full of both domestic tourists and visitors from Kazakhstan, particularly ethnic Russians. The town still has a large permanent Russian population and it is noticeably less Kyrgyz than many other settlements of its size around the lake – there is even a statue of Boris Yeltsin, who took regular vacations here in the past.

Because of its popularity the town can get rather crowded at the height of summer and it can be difficult to find a room. Unless you especially want to lie on the beach then a visit at either end of the main season is probably a better choice. Early autumn is an especially appealing time, with turning leaves, blue skies and the mountains with a dusting of snow. The problem here is that, as the resort is mostly

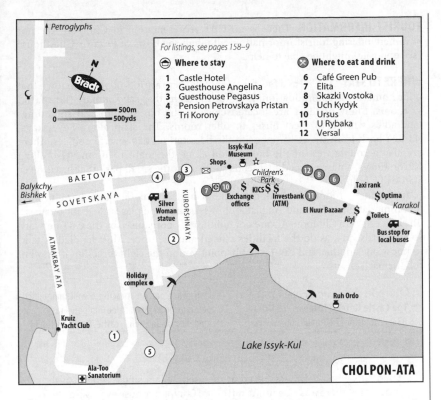

For listings, see pages 158–9

Where to stay
1 Castle Hotel
2 Guesthouse Angelina
3 Guesthouse Pegasus
4 Pension Petrovskaya Pristan
5 Tri Korony

Where to eat and drink
6 Café Green Pub
7 Elita
8 Skazki Vostoka
9 Uch Kydyk
10 Ursus
11 U Rybaka
12 Versal

CHOLPON-ATA

seasonal, many of the homestays may be closed, meaning that once again it might be hard to find somewhere to stay.

Beaches aside, there are other good reasons to come here: Cholpon-Ata has a good local museum, there is an excellent petroglyph site just outside the town, and it makes a good base for local walks or visits to other villages along the north shore that lack Cholpon-Ata's facilities.

GETTING THERE AND AWAY Regular **buses** (*250som*) run from Bishkek's West Bus Station and continue along the north coast to Karakol. However, during the summer months most buses arriving or leaving Cholpon-Ata's bus station seem to ply a route between the town and Almaty in Kazakhstan. Many of these travel overnight.

Minibuses also depart from Bishkek's West Bus Station, are generally faster and cost 250som. Minibuses from Balykchy are also regular and cost 50som, as do those caught in Tamchy. Share taxis charge 600som. In Cholpon-Ata, westbound minibuses and share taxis wait for passengers at the top end of the bus station by the road. Local minibuses to villages along the north shore are best caught at the bus shelter, at the eastern end of the town near the bazaar, as are through buses heading east to Karakol (*120som*).

GETTING AROUND Cholpon-Ata is not a large town, but it is quite spread out and you might wish to take a taxi. Taxis congregate on the main road by the entrance to the bus station and there is another small taxi rank at the El Nuur Bazaar. A short journey should cost 70–100som. A local taxi firm which can be called up is **Kul Taxi** (↘ 177).

TOURIST INFORMATION There is no CBT representation in Cholpon-Ata, nor anywhere offering tourist information, although the hosts of Pegasus Guesthouse (see opposite) might be able to help.

WHERE TO STAY As well as a few formal hotels there are lots of places in town that offer homestay accommodation; look for the signs that say *komnaty* (комнаты) – 'rooms'. Many of these are located close to the bus station, and sometimes landladies will go to meet buses to offer rooms. The strip along Sovetskaya, set just back from the road opposite the bus station, has several choices. There are also a couple west of the bus station along the main road, and also along Kurorshnaya, a narrow road that leads south after the small park that has a silver statue of Cholpon.

In summer, rooms tend to get full up and it can be quite hard to find accommodation in July and August; out of season, some places close for business. The homestays in Cholpon-Ata are not monitored or organised by the CBT network so standards vary, as do the facilities offered and the price. Most landladies tend to know one another and can probably point you in the right direction if they are full themselves.

In Cholpon-Ata   *Map, page 157*

The Castle Hotel (10 rooms) m 0700 668 833; e nbrowne174@gmail.com; www. kyrgyzstay.com. An attractive & well-maintained boutique hotel just outside Cholpon-Ata, modelled on an English castle. Owned & run by

---

HOW CHOLPON-ATA GOT ITS NAME

Long ago, when the Kyrgyz lived as one people in a single tribe near the mountains, there was a beautiful girl called Cholpon, whose eyes were bluer than the sky and brighter than the stars. Two brave *djigits* (young warrior horsemen), Ulan and Santash, fell in love with her, but Cholpon could not decide between them, so the men fought savagely for her attention. They wounded each other, drawing blood, and the fighting became so intense that their relatives joined in on each side. Cholpon was faced with an impossible choice as she knew she could not offend either of them with rejection, so she pulled out her own heart from her breast so that neither could possess it. The place where she fell dead on a hill facing the rising sun was named Cholpon-Ata in her honour. The Kyrgyz people wept bitter tears for a long time over the loss of their beautiful daughter. Their tears flooded the valley between the mountains and formed a lake – Lake Issyk-Kul – and the Kyrgyz became divided into two tribes who settled on the north and the south shores of the lake – Kungey and Terskey. Ulan and Santash live on as the winds that blow from east and west, and whenever they meet they fight to exhaustion, causing the storms that ravage the lake from time to time.

Another legend tells a similar story, except in this case it is a cruel khan who yearned for Cholpon's favours. The girl, who loved another, refused his advances and in the end hurled herself from the high tower in which she was imprisoned rather than submit to the khan.

It is said that if you stand at Cholpon-Ata's shore today you can see the face of Cholpon's father (*Cholpon-Ata*) in the mountains opposite, his tears flowing down the mountainside to add salt water to the lake.

British man Nigel Browne & his wife, who built the hotel in 2007 & have planted the garden with trees & roses. It is also possible to stay in a yurt in the hotel grounds. Rooms are US$50 (US$100 with en suite). **$$$$**

⌂ **Tri Korony ('Three Crowns')** (60 rooms); ☏ 433 84, 436 71; m 0558 085 002; e 3korony@ mail.ru; www.3korony.com. Secluded, spa-type hotel, close to the lake shore with its own beach. Modern facilities, sauna, swimming pool, satellite TV & internet access. Most rooms have lake-view balconies. Price inc FB meals. Lower prices out of season. **$$$$**

⌂ **Guesthouse Angelina** Kurorshnaya 21; ☏ 429 04. Run by a friendly Russian couple, Yuri & Angelina, this is a comfortable place to stay in a quiet location (apart from Cholpon-Ata's canine chorus at night). Angelina cooks up enormous meals. The house opposite also has rooms (**$$**). **$$**

⌂ **Pension Petrovskaya Pristan** Sovetskaya 87; ☏ 437 94. A comfortable place with a very central location. *Bed & 3 meals* **$$**

⌂ **Guesthouse Pegasus** Sovetskaya 81; ☏ 424 50; m 0779 094 047. A small place with just 2 rooms close to the post office. English is spoken & local excursions & horse-trekking tours can be arranged here. **$–$$**

Other hotel resorts near Cholpon-Ata

⌂ **Raduga** (58 cottages) Sary-Oy village (just before Cholpon-Ata, 243km from Bishkek); ☏ 580 31 (or in Bishkek ☏ (0312) 394 039); e rcraduga@ mail.ru; www.raduga.kg. Business centre, conference hall, swimming pools, tennis courts & disco. Price inc meals. **$$$$$**

⌂ **Rohat-NBU** (3 houses) Kara-Oy village; ☏ 450 25; m 0502 587 120. Built by the National Bank of Uzbekistan, this holiday complex with a variety of apts & 2/3/4-bed rooms is occupied mostly by Kyrgyz rather than Uzbek tourists these days. **$$$$**; *lux* **$$$$$**; *also cheaper family rooms* **$$$–$$$$**

⌂ **Karven Four Seasons** (32 rooms) Sary-Oy village; ☏ 577 79; e kfshotel@karven.kg; www. karven.kg. Swimming pool, Finnish & Turkish sauna, spa complex, tennis courts & aqua park. Price inc meals. **$$$$**

⌂ **Ak-Bermet** (350 beds in 3 hotel blocks & 6 cottages) Kara-Oy village. Bookable through Bishkek agencies like Asian Tour (*www.asiantour. org*) or Advantour (*www.advantour.com*). Swimming pool, sauna, massage room, internet café, tennis courts & children's playground. Price inc meals. **$$$**

✕ **WHERE TO EAT AND DRINK** *Map, page 157*

Most homestays offer full- or half-board but there is a good selection of cafés, bars and restaurants for lunch, snacks or an evening out.

Near the bazaar at the eastern end of town at Sovetska 11 is **Café Green Pub** (m *0555 007 780;* **$$**) with a variety of beers. Also close by are **Skazki Vostoka** and **Versal**, which has good *shashlyk* and Steinbrau beer from Bishkek. Opposite Versal at Sovetskaya 20 is the two-storey **U Rybaka** (m *0550 314 111;* **$$**) which has an open terrace on both floors and makes for a pleasant, breezy place to eat in warm weather. In the centre of town, on Sovetskaya opposite the post office, there are several places like **Elita** and **Ursus** (**$$**), which is clean and tidy and a good choice for lunch. **Uch Kydyk** (**$$**) on the corner of Sovetskaya next to the Pegasus Guesthouse has an outside terrace and Dungan cooking.

ENTERTAINMENT AND NIGHTLIFE The bars and cafés mentioned above are the obvious places which might lure you from tea and jam at your homestay. Otherwise, there is a **nightclub** resembling a mock fortress next door to the museum.

OTHER PRACTICALITIES There is a central row of shops close to the post office which stock the usual range of goods. For fresh fruit and vegetables, visit the **El Nuur Bazaar** at the eastern end of town. For internet access there is an **internet café** located between the Ursus and Elita restaurants on Sovetskaya. **Investbank** and **KCIS Bank** by the children's park both have ATM machines, as do the **Optima** and **Aiyl** banks to the east of the town close to El Nuur Bazaar and the Karakol bus stop. The Aiyl ATM is unusual in accepting both MasterCard and Visa cards. As well as the banks, cash can be easily exchanged at any of the numerous exchange booths on the strip along Sovetskaya opposite the museum.

WHAT TO SEE AND DO
Issyk-Kul Museum (*Sovetskaya 69;* \ *421 48.* ☉ *09.00–13.00, 14.00–18.00 daily; foreigners' admission 40som*) This museum is well worth a visit, giving as it does an overview of the culture and archaeology of the region, as well as having artefacts from further afield. Unusually for this part of the world, a lot of care has been taken over layout and lighting. Unfortunately, captions are only in Kyrgyz and Russian, but it is easy enough to get a reasonable impression of what is on offer.

Much of the museum is given over to local archaeological finds, which include items from Scythian burials, stones with Arabic inscriptions, pottery, underwater finds including jars from Lake Issyk-Kul, and some remarkable leather-ware pots. Black and white photographs show the excavations themselves.

There is an interesting display showing photographs of some of the more notable petroglyphs from Saimaluu-Tash, including an aerial shot giving a useful idea of the extent of the site, and some distinctly erotic petroglyphs which must be the closest thing to prehistoric porn. There are further petroglyphs from the Altai and Tuva regions of Russia that demonstrate many parallels to what has been discovered in Kyrgyzstan.

A room devoted to Kyrgyz history has photographs of everyday *jailoo* life that show women milking mares and sheep, singing and dancing, and erecting yurts. There are also some excellent *shyrdaks* and examples of weaving and embroidery.

Another room concentrates on the Manas legacy, with photographs of the thousand-year celebrations and performances of local *manaschi* storytellers. Further displays are given over to the work of writer Chingiz Aitmatov, who often used to summer at Cholpon-Ata (see page 45), and also the artist Yuristanbev Shigaev, whose work draws heavily on ritual and a Picasso influence.

Open-air petroglyph site This open site, sometimes referred to as the Stone Garden, covers an area of more than 40ha just outside the town to the northwest. Although petroglyphs can be found at a number of locations in Kyrgyzstan – most spectacularly at Saimaluu-Tash – the ones on display here are certainly the most easily accessible in the country. Unfortunately, there have been well-intentioned attempts to preserve the petroglyphs in recent years which may turn out to be more damaging than if they had merely been left alone. Only time will tell if the chemicals used to preserve the carvings have had any long-term deleterious effect.

The site is covered with stones and boulders of varying size, some of which have carvings dating from the period between about 1500BC and the 1st century AD. The majority date from the Saka–Scythian period (8th century BC to 1st century AD) and some from the Turkic period between the 5th and 10th centuries AD, but all pre-date the arrival of the Kyrgyz tribes in the region. It is thought the site may have represented a large open-air temple, where the heavenly bodies, in particular the sun, were venerated. In addition to the carvings there are some arrangements of rocks in circles, which may have served an astronomical or ritual function.

Most of the carved stones, which range from 30cm to 3m in size, are oriented to face southwest or southeast, and this would indicate some form of sun worship. Most of the petroglyphs represent hunting scenes, or rather the hunted – ibex and deer with antlers like Christmas trees – although there are also hunters, other animals and sun symbols. Images of deer commonly feature in prehistoric carvings worldwide, although there may be a connection with deer worship that was widespread in the Altai and Siberian region in the same period. One of the largest of the Kyrgyz tribes, the Bugu ('Red Deer'), also venerated deer but would have migrated to the region many years after these petroglyphs had been fashioned.

Walking to the site takes around 30–40 minutes from the town centre. To reach it on foot, head west along the main road past the bus station. Turn right along Akmatbay Ata, opposite the turn-off for the boatyard and by a sign that points to the mosque (Мечеть). Walk gently uphill past the mosque and a Muslim graveyard on your left, until you come to a blue house which has a line of poplars on its north side, and where the road twists to the west. Continue north along the road, which by now has become a dirt track with a pipe crossing it. Soon you will reach some large new houses and the site is just to the northwest behind these, in a partially enclosed area. Returning you can take a different route: head towards the concrete walled building then cross a field full of boulders to the south. This will lead to an electricity transformer and a small pond; continue south to reach a metalled road and then turn left, soon reaching the blue house on the corner and the road south to the mosque and town centre. Alternatively, if you have little time, take a taxi and get it to wait. One hour should be long enough.

The best time for a visit is in the late afternoon when the low sun hits the petroglyphs head on and makes them easier to see. It is also cooler and more atmospheric at this time of day, and the noise of water bubbling over rocks, which comes from the stream bisecting the site, can sound almost like distant thunder in the mountains. Many of the stones are numbered and some of the more interesting ones can be found at the top (northern) end of the site. There is an entrance fee to the site of 40som, although the caretaker who lives nearby may not always be present.

Beach and yacht club The **public beach** can be reached by heading down the dual carriageway that leads south from the bus station. At the bottom on the right is a modern holiday complex with lurid-coloured roofs. A road leads to the left past a small tree-lined lake to reach the beach just beyond a café. The **Kruiz Yacht Club** is reached by heading west out of town and turning left along Akmatbay-Ata, opposite the road to the mosque and petroglyphs. The club has yachts and motorboats that can be rented on an hourly basis. Short cruises on the lake are offered in summer for around 200som. There is another small beach just to the north.

Ruh Ordo (✆ 720 70, 720 73; e ruhordo@mail.ru; www.ruhordo.kg; ⊕ 09.00– 17.00; admission 300som) This outdoor museum complex, constructed in 2002, is effectively an open-air cultural theme park on an attractive lakeside two-hectare site. It celebrates the history and cultural heritage of the Kyrgyz people and has sections dedicated to iconic Kyrgyz and Kazakh figures like Kurmanjan Datka, Chingiz Aitmatov and the Kazakhstan president, Nursultan Nazarbaev. There are also chapels dedicated to all of the world's five great religions. The entrance fee includes a tour in Russian. An international festival of pop and folk was held at the complex in July 2014 with a view to it becoming an annual event.

EAST OF CHOLPON-ATA

BOSTERI (БОСТЕРИ) The resort village of Bosteri lies 10km east of Cholpon-Ata and is given over entirely to mass tourism. There are several sanatoriums and large hotel complexes here which hark back to Soviet times, albeit at the more luxurious end of the market. A stay here certainly gives an insight into Russian and Kyrgyz domestic tourism if that is what interests you.

Where to stay

⌂ Kyrgyz Vzmorye ☎456 48; e ksr_bostery@ mail.ru; www.ksr.in.kg. Also known as the 'Kyrgyz Seaside Resort', this sanatorium has extensive leafy grounds & beach access, & has been used for presidential conferences in the past. **$$$$$**

⌂ Hotel Alma-Ata ☎451 44. This Kazakh-owned hotel has 2 swimming pools, tennis courts, discothèques & private beach. **$$$$–$$$$$**

⌂ Issyk-Kul Resort (147 rooms, 7 luxury apts) ☎465 566 (or in Bishkek ☎ (0312) 313 187); e aurora.kg@gmail.ru; www.aurora.kg. In the village of Bulan Sogottu, formerly known as Komsomol, about 10km from an impressive Kyrgyz graveyard in the east of Bosteri, the most impressive of all the north shore sanatoriums is reached. The Issyk-Kul Sanatorium is known as the Avrora for fairly obvious reasons: it resembles a beached ship, specifically the cruiser *Avrora* of revolutionary fame – the warship which fired the shot that prompted the storming of St Petersburg's winter palace in 1917. This battleship of a hotel complex has just about

every facility you could wish for – swimming pool, tennis courts, exercise rooms, conference & banquet rooms &, of course, its own private beach. Its guests are not solely from Kyrgyzstan, but from all over the central Asian region & beyond, & at w/ends in the summer many come from Bishkek to live it up at the hotel's nightclub. The sanatorium treats a wide range of conditions inc diseases of the blood system, digestive problems, bone & muscle illnesses, & urological problems, among others. Treatments may inc dousing with spring water from hosepipes, beating with birch twigs and time spent in the salt rooms. *Sgl* **$$$$**, *dbl, suites, apts* **$$$$$**; *winter prices about half summer tariff.*

⌂ Talisman Village (34 rooms) ☎465 28; m 0707 906 268; e info@talisman.kg; www. talisman.kg. Smaller but equally upmarket than those mentioned above, this has 1- & 2-room cottages available. *All* **$$$$–$$$$$**, *depending on the class of room & the time of year.*

GRIGORIEVKA (ГРИГОРЬЕВКА) This pretty village 40km east of Cholpon-Ata is the starting point for treks up the Chon Ak-Suu Canyon to a clutch of glacial lakes. The canyon is some 32km long, its slopes carpeted by dense stands of fir. From the lakes a trail leads onward to the Chong-Kemin Valley, as well as over the mountains to Kazakhstan (see page 168).

SEMYENOVKA (СЕМЕНОВКА) Just to the east of Grigorievka, along the main road, this smaller village is the starting point for an asphalt road that leads into the mountains up the Chon Ak-Suu Valley, past a defunct *turbaza*, to reach a *jailoo* at 2,010m which has a yurt village in the summer. A new ski base was constructed in the valley in 2002 and opened by the then president Askar Akayev. Just outside Semyenovka to the northeast are Scythian burial mounds that date from the 5th–3rd century BC. By the lakeshore close to the village is the *dacha* that was built in the 1960s for the use of Leonid Brezhnev. It was used just once by the former Soviet leader and now lies in a state of disrepair.

⌂ Where to stay and eat There is a good **homestay** in the village at the house of Svetlana and Gennadi (m 0543 883 012; **$–$$**), who also run a children's home. The homestay has excellent home cooking and its own *banya* (Russian steam bath) for the use of guests, and the hosts can provide transport to the mountains, suggest hikes and even provide a guide service. They also have their own bus and drive to a beautiful, remote beach every afternoon with the children from their home – guests are welcome to accompany them.

ANANYEVO (АНАНЬЕВО) This is the next sizeable village heading east, 52km from Cholpon-Ata. The village's name derives from that of a Soviet hero who was born there, Nikolai Ananyev, one of the 'Panfilov Heroes' who died defending the small village of Panfilov outside Moscow during World War II. There is a memorial to him in the village, in a small park just off the main street (the next village east along the road, Zharkinbaevo, is similarly named after a local World War II hero).

Ananyevo was founded as a Cossack settlement in the 1890s and still retains much of this identity, with its quaint Orthodox church, and plenty of Slavic faces and blond hair on the streets. Slavs – Russians and Ukrainians – still constitute more than half of the population here, with Kyrgyz and a few Dungans making up the rest.

The Orthodox church, with its blue and yellow spire, is just off to the left at the start of the village coming from Cholpon-Ata. There is also a newly built mosque with a pepper-pot minaret along this stretch of road. The village is typical of the region, but more attractive and better preserved than most, with low houses which have tidy gardens and blue window frames. Heading east, there is a road (Lenina) that leads off to the right to a small bazaar and a threadbare Univermag store. Taxis congregate on the corner here and *marshrutki* stop at the junction, too – a regular service to Cholpon-Ata costs just 40som.

One of the monks, Irakily, survived the ransacking of the monastery at Svetly Mys and escaped here in 1916. After the revolution some Ananyevo villagers are said to have built a secret cell for him, in which he died in 1937. It was discovered 38 years later, in 1975, when another villager was being buried, that the monk's remains had not decayed at all. He was canonised by the Russian Orthodox Church in Moscow in 2000 and his body was exhumed and transferred to Bishkek's Orthodox cathedral.

SVETLY MYS This tiny hamlet, which translates as 'Bright Cape' in Russian, is 48km from Karakol, just south of the village of Ak-Bulung (formerly Belovodsk), on the Zayachy Peninsula at Lake Issyk-Kul's northeast corner. It is the site of up to eight monasteries which were founded here over a period of 2,000 years and, more controversially, as the supposed burial place of the apostle Matthew. The macabre truth is that it is also perfectly possible that it was at this same Armenian monastery that the late 14th-century plague pandemic – the 'Black Death' – broke out before travelling west and east to devastate both China and Europe.

A Russian Orthodox monastery stood here in the late 19th and early 20th century, founded by the Tsar in 1888. The monastery was attacked by rebels in 1916 who killed all but two of its 26 monks. The surviving pair escaped to Almaty and Ananyevo, and both have since been canonised. Today there is little to see, as the remains of the church, which was burnt down in the 1930s, have since become a craft workshop, and the monks' storehouse is now a mill. The 19th-century almshouse and refectory have been renovated under the directorship of Gulnara Degenbaycva, who uses the buildings as the Meerim Bulagy ('Spring Grace') children's home for 25 or so adopted children.

Svetly Mys certainly abounds in mystery. As well as the St Matthew claims, the monastery church was also once the home of an icon of the Virgin Mary that was said to cry blood, repel bullets and glow with an ethereal light when it came under attack by the rebels in 1916. The icon can now be found in the Orthodox cathedral at Karakol.

A network of ancient catacombs and underground cells said to belong to a 4th- or 5th-century Armenian monastery have been discovered nearby on small lakeside peninsulas. Most of these are overgrown and filled with silt, but it is possible to explore some of them with a torch and little local expertise. **Turkestan Travel** based in Karakol (see page 174) is able to organise excursions to the catacombs of Svetly Mys.

In addition to the archaeological interest at Svetly Mys itself, nearby Ak-Bulung also has several unexcavated Scythian *kurgani* (tumuli), which can be seen just to the west of the village.

TYUP (ТЮП) Tyup (or Tüp) lies at the far eastern end of the lake and is at the junction of the main road connecting Karakol with Bishkek, and another that follows the Tyup River east before stretching round the eastern limit of the Kungey Ala-Too mountains to enter Kazakhstan after Karkara. The town suffered a crushing defeat during the 1916 Kyrgyz uprising.

Today, there is little of interest in the town other than it serving as a gateway to the Karkara Valley, but just to the west archaeologists have discovered the ruins of what is believed to have been the 2nd-century BC settlement of Chigu ('Red Valley') on a nearby lake peninsula. This would have been the capital of the Usun people, who were the prominent tribe in the Issyk-Kul basin at this time.

The large statue of a man in traditional Kyrgyz dress and a turban that stands by the main road in the town might seem to resemble an ancient central Asian warrior or *manaschi*, but it actually commemorates the father of a modern-day Kyrgyz petrol magnate who was born in the town.

KARKARA VALLEY (КАРКАРАНСКАЯ ДОЛИНА)

This long, wide fertile valley, at the far eastern end of northern Issyk-Kul, has lush summer grazing that attracts herders from both sides of the Kyrgyz-Kazakh border. The valley extends west to east, from the vicinity of Tyup to the Kazakh border and beyond, squeezed at its eastern end by the parallel ranges of the Kungey Ala-Too and the Central Tien Shan. Here, the Kazakhstan border is mostly undefined, and not delimited by a physical barrier such as a mountain range or a river as elsewhere in northern Kyrgyzstan. As a consequence, herders from both sides of the border move along the valley with impunity, unhindered by artificial barriers, such as political divides, and the yurts of both Kyrgyz and Kazakhs pepper the lush valley floor like odd clusters of mushrooms in summer.

The name Karkara translates as 'black crane' and comes from the delightful birds which are said to visit the valley twice annually, touching down in June *en route* to

SCYTHIAN BURIAL MOUNDS

Scattered throughout the terrain of the Chui Valley, the shores of Lake Issyk-Kul and southeast Kazakhstan are enigmatic tumuli which represent the graves of the Saka warriors, otherwise known as the Scythians, who lived in the region over 2,000 years ago. Some of the mounds, known here as *kurgani*, excavated in Kazakhstan have revealed considerable treasures such as intricate jewellery, bronze drinking vessels, weapons and armour. The most lavish find so far has been the so-called 'golden man' from Esik, just outside Almaty in Kazakhstan, in which the interred had a costume made up of 4,000 beautifully worked gold pieces. In 2001 it was rumoured that a second gold man had been discovered, and it begs the question as to what might be found if the Scythian mounds at Ak-Bulung or elsewhere were excavated.

Several sources hint that the remains of St Matthew are buried somewhere in the Lake Issyk-Kul area. It is thought the apostle was on his way to India after having written the Gospel of St Matthew in Palestine, and left his homeland in AD42 to escape persecution. Other sources suggest he may have travelled elsewhere, to Persia or even Africa. Whatever the reality, it is perfectly possible that he made it into central Asia and Kyrgyzstan before dying here.

One Kyrgyz archaeologist, Vladimir Ploskikh, believes he has found remains of the monastery in which St Matthew was buried. According to legend, St Matthew died while *en route* to India and established a number of Christian communities on his way there. A 14th-century map, which is kept in Venice and is referred to as the 'Catalan map', mentions a place called 'Issicol' where it says there is a 'cloister of the Armenian Brothers where the body of the Apostle and Evangelist Saint Matthew is kept'. It marks a sign, shaped like a temple and decorated with a cross, on the lake's northeastern bank with a note that says 'The Monastery of the Armenian brothers and the place where relics of St Matthew are kept'.

Aware perhaps of the risk of striking out prematurely into Dan Brown territory, Ploskikh insisted that further investigation was necessary before the theory could be proven. In September 2006, Ploskikh reported that he had discovered a medieval settlement with catacombs in the Zayachy Peninsula on the northeast coast of the lake, although he admitted that the hypothesis about the discovery of the monastery 'still needed to be confirmed'. In a less cautious frame of mind, the claim to have found St Matthew's grave had already been announced four years earlier by Russian-born US photographer Sergei Melnikoff, a claim that was subsequently rejected by the Kyrgyz Academy of Sciences.

Whatever the truth of the matter, it is indisputable that Svetly Mys has had religious institutions based here for almost two millennia, and has served as a place of pilgrimage throughout this period.

their Siberian breeding grounds, and again in September when returning to their winter quarters in southern Africa. In summer there is usually a well-attended **horse festival** held in the valley, frequented by both Kyrgyz and Kazakh *chabana* (cowboys), in which a variety of horseback games and competitions take place, accompanied by much drinking, eating, singing and Manas-reciting. There is no fixed date for the event and it tends to be arranged fairly spontaneously by local word of mouth, so it is important to keep your ear to the ground if you wish to attend. Horse festival or not, the valley is alive with the beasts in early summer, with numerous horse camps dotted along its length. The valley is also where some of the country's most prized *kumys* originates and many come from far and wide in June and July to buy it by the trailer load. Yurts and railway carriages stretch intermittently along the roadside as far as the Kazakhstan border, many with hand-painted 'КЫМЫС' ('*kumys*') signs to advertise their wares. Most of the horses, sadly, are destined to be sold for meat rather than for riding.

GETTING THERE AND AWAY Public transport in the valley is limited, most of it going only as far as Tyup, which has regular buses from Bishkek and Karakol. A couple of **minibuses** run to San-Tash village daily from Karakol's bus station, via Tyup, and

There are around 20 locations around Lake Issyk-Kul where traces of old townships have been discovered. Some date back two millennia or so, while other settlements evolved during the peak years of the Silk Road trade from the 7th century AD onward. Legends relate that four flooded cities lie beneath the present-day waters of the lake. In support of this, archaeological discoveries have been made which reveal dwellings and foundations beneath the lake's surface.

The sunken village of Chigu, which was the capital of the ancient Usun state in the 2nd century BC, has been discovered offshore near Sary-Bulan and the present-day town of Tyup at the eastern end of the lake. In 1956 divers exploring the underwater site discovered a range of artefacts including fragments of pottery, a ceramic pipe, arrowheads, ironwork, and human and animal remains. In addition, just offshore, near the villages of Korumdy and Temirovka and close to Grigorievka harbour, fragments of Bronze Age pots and various artefacts, such as knife handles carved with figures of horses, have been unearthed. Another major find was what was thought to be a square sacrificial table with legs like a woman's body, with slanted eyes, oval chin and wide nose. Another discovery has been a large round pot with twin handles whose purpose is believed to have been sacrificial. More than ten similar pots have been found in the Issyk-Kul region and they appear to date to the second half of the first millennium.

Various historic sources point towards the existence of sunken cities in the lake. Medieval Muslim recluses mention old fortresses being flooded and the existence of an island where Tamerlane is said to have imprisoned enemies in the late 14th century. A Russian merchant, Isaev, writing in the early 19th century, mentions underwater buildings being visible in the Tyup region, and around the same time the explorer Pyotr Semyonov Tyan-Shansky discovered bricks that had been carried ashore between the estuaries of the Tyup and Jergalan rivers.

Up until now, only a fraction of the underwater sites have been thoroughly investigated and the potential for future treasures to be discovered in the region is enormous.

there are also services to the mining town of Jergalan to the south. If visiting the San-Tash stones by taxi it is important to stress that you mean the stones themselves and not the village of San-Tash that lies about 30km closer to Karakol. No **buses** cross the border through to Kegen in Kazakhstan, so if you wish to enter Kazakhstan this way – only possible in summer – you will need to arrange a taxi along the valley (best arranged in Karakol) from where public transport continues onward to Almaty. A **taxi** organised in Karakol to take you as far as Kegen via San-Tash should cost in the region of 2,500–3,000som. If **hiring a vehicle and driver** it is probably best to approach San-Tash and the eastern Karkara Valley by way of the minor road that goes via Novovoznesenovka, rather than the longer route through Tyup, although the latter has better roads. Those taking a **helicopter flight** to access Khan Tengri, Pik Pobedy or the Inylchek Glacier will need to visit the valley to reach the helipad.

ORGANISED TOURS The crossing between Kyrgyzstan and Kazakhstan via the Karkara Valley was closed for several years and, as a result, tour companies that previously had itineraries that encompassed the Karkara Valley as part of a long-distance trek to or from Kazakhstan stopped offering this option. The cross-border route reopened in summer 2013, and again in May 2014, for the duration of the summer. Currently, the following companies offer tours that take in the Karkara Valley as part of the itinerary.

Ak-Sai Travel Sovetskaya 65, Bishkek; \0312 591 759; e adventure@ak-sai.com; www.ak-sai. com. Offers a Tien-Shan trekking itinerary that uses Karkara base camp & transits Karkara Valley.
Edelweiss Travel Gastello 19, Bishkek; \0312 542 045; e edelweiss@elcat.kg; www. edelweisstravel.org. Nature tours in Kyrgyzstan & Kazakhstan that incorporate Karkara Valley.
Kan Tengri www.kantengri.kz. An Almaty-based tour company offering trekking, mountain biking & horseriding options.
Spice Roads Cycle Tours www.spiceroads. com. Mountain biking in Kazakhstan & Kyrgyzstan involving circuits around Karkara Valley.

Turkestan Travel Toktogul 273, Karakol; \(0543) 911 452; e psi61@mail.ru; www.karakol. kg. Runs hiking tours that cover both Kazakhstan & Kyrgyzstan & incorporate the Karkara Valley *en route* from Almaty. They can also organise day trips with return helicopter flights between the Karkara base camp helipad & South Inylchek base camp.
Wild Frontiers www.wildfrontiers.co.uk. 15-day tours which trek through the valley before flying by helicopter to the Inylchek Glacier.
World Expeditions www.worldexpeditions. com. 15-day cycling tours starting & ending in Almaty inc Karkara Valley & heli-biking from Karkara base camp.

WHERE TO STAY There are a few **yurt camps** set up in the Karkara Valley where it is possible to stay. Get in touch with the Karakol Tourist Information Centre for contact details. Just over the border in Kazakhstan, **Kan Tengri** (see above), an Almaty-based adventure travel company, has a base camp with yurts, showers and most mod cons.

WHAT TO SEE AND DO
Ken-Suu Halfway along the Kyrgyz section of the Karkara Valley, 38km beyond Tyup, this village has Saka burial mounds to the north and west which date from between the 3rd century BC and the 3rd century AD; other mounds may be found close to the village of Chon-Tash further west along the valley. Further east, just 3km short of the border, are more burial mounds from between the 7th and 1st centuries BC, and the remains of a medieval castle that would have guarded this section of the Silk Road.

San-Tash stones It is widely believed that Tamerlane used the Karkara Valley as an occasional summer base for his campaigns and at San-Tash ('Counting Stones') at the eastern end of the valley, just 20km short of the Kazakh frontier, there is a large, flat cairn of stones said to be composed of stones deposited by his troops. The stones were written about by the Russian explorer Pyotr Semyonov Tyan-Shansky during his 1857 expedition. The legend goes that in the late 15th century Tamerlane led a campaign into China's Ili Province from his base at Lake Issyk-Kul. The most convenient pass into Chinese territory was by way of an as yet unnamed pass to the northeast of the lake along the Karkara Valley. Tamerlane ordered that each of his soldiers collect a stone from the shore of Lake Issyk-Kul and, close to the pass, they were required to deposit it on a pile before going off to battle in China. Returning to the lake later, after a long and successful campaign, the battle-weary soldiers were ordered to remove a stone from the heap, so that their leader was able to estimate overall troop losses. The fact that the pile contains such a large number of individual rocks would indicate that many of his troops must have perished in battle during the campaign. In their failure to return, the fallen had already contributed to building a monument to their own death. Although this is a highly appealing story, it is more likely that the low cairn was created from stones that were piled up when a stone-lined burial chamber adjacent to the site was exposed.

The San-Tash stones stand in the middle of a wide, wild flower-rich plain close to a small village. A sign on the main road says 'San-Tash Caravansary – 2km', although it is not really a caravanserai and it is not 2km either, more like 500m. There's a border checkpoint on the main road just before here, which may or may not drop the barrier to check your passport. On the main road beyond the stones, after the left turn-off for Kazakhstan, there is another checkpoint beyond which border permits are supposedly required for foreigners. The road continues along the frontier next to the Karkara River to reach the Karkara base camp helipad just across the river on the Kazakhstan side of the border. Turning right at the stones and following the rough track along the parallel valley will bring you to a very rough (4x4 transport essential) track that leads left up the ridge towards the wide plateau of Dongolok Saz, from where there are excellent views of the upper Karkara Valley. This track eventually returns to the Karkara River road some way beyond the second checkpoint. Foreigners are not supposed to be here without a border permit, however, and you might have difficulty returning along the main road when you reach the checkpoint. Better to return the same way, although it is hard going.

An alternative route back to Karakol from the San-Tash stones is to take the track to the left just after the first checkpoint. This leads up to Kyzyl-Kiya Pass and eventually to the village of Novovoznesenovka before joining the Jergalansky Valley road at Teploklyuchenka (Ak-Suu). The valley is part of the Tyup State Zoological Reserve and is best known for the Jergalansky Gorge, with its dramatically layered rocks, that lies further east.

Trekking routes to and from Kazakhstan In theory, there are a number of possibilities in addition to following the straightforward and drivable route along the Karkara Valley, where the border is open approximately mid-May to mid-October between 09.00 and 18.00. These routes were popular with long-distance hikers in the Soviet era, but have become fairly neglected following independence. In recent years they have been **closed to hikers** but, like the reopening of the Karkara Valley route in 2013, they might become viable again sometime in the future and so the information below is included in the light of this.

One route that ends in **Grigorievka** begins at **Bolshoe Almatynskoe Lake** south of Almaty. It climbs south along the Ozerniy River to reach the Ozerniy Pass (3,507m) into Kyrgyzstan and descends to the Chong-Kemin Valley. Here it briefly strikes east before climbing south past Jassyk-Kul Lake to the Ak-Suu Pass at 4,061m on the Kungey Ala-Too range, where there is a short stretch of glacier to traverse on the northern side. From here it follows the Chon Ak-Suu Valley eastward and then south to Grigorievka near Lake Issyk-Kul.

A longer and harder alternative route begins at **Medeu** outside Almaty and crosses the Bolshoe Talgarsky Pass (3,160m), before heading south along Levy Talgar River and west over the Turistov Pass (3,930m). It then continues along the valley of the Kyzylsai River to reach the Ozerniy Pass and Kyrgyzstan. The route generally takes between four and six days – add on another two or three days if the Turistov Pass alternative route is taken.

A more westerly route begins in the village of **Kokshoky**, south of Almaty, and climbs up alongside the Prokhodnaya River to the 3,699m Prokhodnaya (or Almaty) Pass that marks the border with Kyrgyzstan. The route descends south past

Primul Lake to the Chong-Kemin Valley, from where it follows the Chong-Kemin west for a short distance before continuing south to climb up to the ridge of the Kungey Ala-Too to the Kök-Aryk Pass (3,890m). From here it descends along the Yuzhnaya Orto-Koy-Suu River to **Chong Sary-Oi** on Lake Issyk-Kul, 12km to the west of Cholpon-Ata. This route also takes around six days in total.

A five- to six-day route, which combines elements of both of the above, links **Grigorievka** with **Kokshoky** in Kazakhstan by following the Chong-Kemin Valley to the Ak-Suu Pass and Jassyk-Kul Lake, before climbing to the Ozerniy Pass at the frontier and down to the Bolshoe Almatynskoe Lake and Kokshoky.

A shorter, more easterly, route begins or ends in the village of **Sary-Bulak** (Balbay) at the northeast end of Lake Issyk-Kul. The route leads over the 3,274m Sary-Bulak Pass to Kazakhstan's three Kolsai lakes, near the village of Saty, 110km east of Almaty. This relatively easy route could be done on horseback as well as on foot, in either direction.

LAKE ISSYK-KUL SOUTH AND THE CENTRAL TIEN SHAN

Lake Issyk-Kul
South and the Central Tien Shan

KARAKOL (КАРАКОЛ)   *Telephone code: 03922*

Of all the towns in Kyrgyzstan, Karakol tends to be the one in which the majority of foreign visitors spend the most time. This is down to the fact that as well as possessing a number of sights and monuments worth seeing, Karakol is also ideally situated for forays into the mountains to the south that beckon so tantalisingly from the town. Because of this, Karakol represents one of the focal points, perhaps *the* focal point, of Kyrgyzstan's fledgling tourist industry and has, more than anywhere else in the country, including even Bishkek, a well-developed tourist infrastructure concerned with outdoor and adventure pursuits.

Knowing this, and seeing the relatively large number of European and North American travellers that congregate here in high summer, it comes as a surprise to learn that the town is actually at its busiest during the midwinter period. It is in December, and especially around Orthodox Christmas in early January, that the town's tourist infrastructure really comes under strain accommodating the large number of Russians and Kazakhs that flock here for inexpensive skiing holidays.

Having said that, Karakol remains low-key in the extreme; as yet, there are no brash hotels, fancy restaurants or lurid nightclubs. It is a delightfully serene sort of place, still resonant with the ghosts of 19th-century rural Russian life (along with the odd phantom from the Soviet period) and with an ambience that, paradoxically, feels both homely and comfortable *and* frontier-like.

Karakol can seem like a big village at times; apart from a park, a small bazaar, a cluster of shops and, of course, the ubiquitous Lenin statue, there is not really much of a centre. The town streets, set in a typical Russian grid plan, are long, straight and lined with poplars. Most of the houses are old, wooden 'gingerbread' houses, with neat florid gardens, picket fences and fruit-laden orchards – it might even be a Siberian village, or at least an idealised version of one.

The town has a pleasant climate, with warm summers and winters much milder than elsewhere in the region, a phenomenon that owes much to Karakol's modest altitude of 1,770m and the moderating effect of Lake Issyk-Kul. Despite having something of a frontier feel about it – perfectly justifiable considering Karakol was in a forbidden zone during the Soviet period – the town serves as the administrative centre for Issyk-Kul Province.

There is not a lot to do here; rather, it is a town to savour and absorb the atmosphere while preparing for, or recovering from, strenuous hikes in the nearby valleys. Beyond relishing the relaxed pace of the town, there is a handful of genuinely interesting sights that can be enjoyed at leisure, as well as an excellent animal market on Sundays. There are few facilities for tourists with a taste for

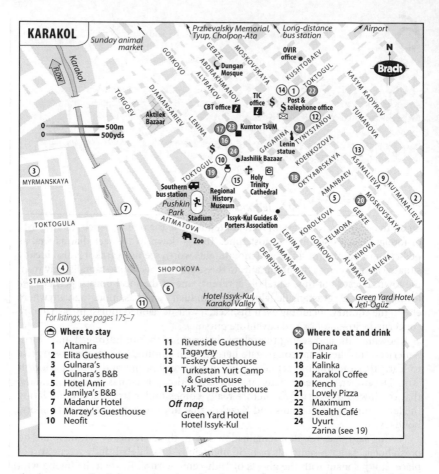

KARAKOL

For listings, see pages 175–7

🛏 **Where to stay**

1 Altamira	11 Riverside Guesthouse
2 Elita Guesthouse	12 Tagaytay
3 Gulnara's	13 Teskey Guesthouse
4 Gulnara's B&B	14 Turkestan Yurt Camp & Guesthouse
5 Hotel Amir	15 Yak Tours Guesthouse
6 Jamilya's B&B	
7 Madanur Hotel	*Off map*
9 Marzey's Guesthouse	Green Yard Hotel
10 Neofit	Hotel Issyk-Kul

✴ **Where to eat and drink**

16 Dinara
17 Fakir
18 Kalinka
19 Karakol Coffee
20 Kench
21 Lovely Pizza
22 Maximum
23 Stealth Café
24 Uyurt
Zarina (see 19)

the luxury end of the market, but for those seeking a pleasant base for hiking and adventure travel Karakol is unparalleled.

HISTORY Karakol ('black wrist' in Kyrgyz) developed as a Russian settlement in the latter part of the 19th century, having been founded as a Russian military outpost and administrative centre of the *uyezd* (administrative unit) in 1869. The town's population, mostly Cossacks from western Siberia, swelled considerably in the 1880s when an influx of Dungans – Chinese Muslims fleeing persecution in their home country – came to live in the town. Later influxes brought Tatars, Uyghurs, Ukrainians and more Russians to engage in agriculture and cattle-breeding. By the beginning of the 20th century the town had three breweries, seven soap factories, two saw mills, 12 flour mills, two churches, nine mosques, seven schools, a military hospital and more than a thousand houses.

The Russian explorer Nikolai Przhevalsky first came here in the 1860s and returned again in 1888 suffering from typhoid – or possibly TB – from which he died. Today there is a museum to his memory on the spot where his house once stood – 10km from the town centre, close to the lake at Pristan Przhevalsk. To honour the explorer, the town was renamed Przhevalsk by the Tsar, but under instructions from Lenin it reverted to its original name in 1921. It returned to being called Przhevalsk once more in 1939, this time at the command of Stalin, who was generally less sensitive than Lenin to local mores. This time the name stuck and the town continued to be known as Przhevalsk until Kyrgyzstan became independent of the Soviet Union in 1991.

During the Soviet period the town became home to a considerable number of scientists and military experts, as Lake Issyk-Kul and the secret submarine and torpedo-testing base at the lake's Mikhailovka inlet were just a few kilometres away. Since independence the town's population has, as elsewhere in the country, seen hard times, although the Russian population is, on the whole, a little less desperate to leave than it is in the rest of Kyrgyzstan.

GETTING THERE AND AROUND Regular **buses** run to and from Bishkek's West Bus Station between early morning and mid-afternoon, taking between five and seven hours. Night buses also run to Bishkek and depart in the evening between 20.00 and 23.00. Most of these travel along the north shore via Cholpon-Ata and Balykchy. There are more limited services along the southern route to Balykchy and Bishkek via Bokonbaevo, which is a slower route to the capital. The bus fare to Bishkek is around 300som. Heading south to Kochkor or Naryn requires a change at Balykchy as there are no direct services. There are no buses to Almaty by way of the Karkara Valley, although there may be occasional services that reach the Kazakhstan city via Bishkek.

The **long-distance bus station** is at the northern end of town, a 20-minute walk or 70som taxi ride from the centre. There are also minibuses that ply between the bus station and the central Jakshilik Bazaar. Other limited bus services from this station run along the southern shore as far as Bokonbaevo, via Tamga and Barskoon.

Minibuses leave from in front of the long-distance bus station and run along the same routes as the buses. They leave when full and are a little faster than buses, typically costing around 350som to Bishkek. **Share taxis** to Cholpon-Ata, Balykchy and Bishkek leave from the same place and charge about twice the bus fare.

For most destinations along the southern shore there is the small **southern bus station** next to the municipal stadium, a five-minute walk southwest of the central Jakshilik Bazaar. This has regular bus and minibus services to Kyzyl-Suu, Barskoon, Tamga and Bokonbaevo.

Local minibus services to destinations such as Pristan Przhevalsk and the Przhevalsky Museum leave from a stand just northeast of Jakshilik Bazaar on Alibakov. Minibuses to Jeti-Ögüz (*20som*) leave from the southwest corner of Aktilek Bazaar, while regular minibuses to Ak-Suu (*20som*) leave from a little further northeast along Aldashev (Karla Marksa). Occasional share taxis to the same destinations also leave from here.

Taxis can be found outside Jakshilik Bazaar or at the bus stands. Trips around the town cost anything between 70som and 100som and whole- or half-day hire can be negotiated for excursions beyond the town limits. As always, establish a price before getting in. The old saying that, in the former Soviet Union, every car is a taxi certainly applies here, and you can basically flag anything down at the roadside, state your destination and negotiate a price. If you want to telephone a taxi, **Salam** (✆ *222 22*), **Tulpar** (✆ *500 00*) or **Issyk-Kul** (✆ *161*) are all reliable choices.

Karakol has a small **airport** but this currently has no flights. It would appear that the main airport to serve Lake Issyk-Kul in the future will be the one earmarked for development at Tamchy on the north shore.

Bicycle hire can be arranged at **Karakol Bikes** (✆ *269 39*) where mountain bikes, helmets and cycling gear can be rented. They can also organise the transport of bikes to passes for downhill rides. All profits go to support the training needs of students at the guide school. Contact them through the Tourist Information Centre or CBT. The Teskey Guesthouse (see page 176) also has a few mountain bikes for the use of its guests.

TOURIST INFORMATION

ℤ Tourist Information Centre

(TIC) Abdrakhmanov 130; ☎ 523 41; e tourinfocentre@gmail.ru; ⏱ 09.00–17.00 Mon–Fri, 09.00–15.00 Sat. Karakol is privileged in having what must be the only official tourist information centre in the country (apart, of course, from what the CBT organisation has to offer). The office here, which opened in 2003 with EU development funding, has lots of information, brochures & listings, plus books, postcards & maps for sale. The volunteers here can give advice on trekking in the region & help organise accommodation in yurt camps & homestays. As tourism is in its infancy in the country, even here in Karakol, it helps if you have specific requests & questions to ask rather than just coming in for a general chat. Very usefully, they stock the 1:200,000 topographic maps of the region that otherwise are only available in Bishkek at GeoID.

ℤ Community Based Tourism (CBT)

Abdrakhmanov 123; ☎ 550 00; m 0555 150 795; e cbtkarakol@rambler.ru; ⏱ 09.00–16.00 Mon–Fri, 10.00–14.00 Sat–Sun. Just down from the Tourist Information Centre on the other side of the road, this is another excellent source of information about the region. Often staffed by working guides at w/ends, & the local co-ordinator Azamat Asanov, who give good insight into the various hiking options in the Karakol region & beyond. CBT Karakol offers a wide variety of tours ranging from a 4hr city tour by car to 6-day guided treks through the Terskey Ala-Too, from Jeti-Ögüz to Altyn Arashan. They are happy to book accommodation & offer advice on trekking without any pressure to use their own services. Naturally, they will arrange everything from guides, porters & equipment should you require it, & can arrange border permits for the Inylchek region within a week.

TOUR AND TREKKING OPERATORS

Ala Too Travel Kravkova 170; ☎ 727 60; m 0550 660 352 (English), 0556 410 566 (German); e info@alatoo.nl; www.alatoo.nl. A small tour company run by a Dutch-Kyrgyz couple based at the Riverside Guesthouse, Ala Too offer a variety of cultural tours in the Issyk-Kul region inc yurt stays & felt-making demonstrations; also hiking & horseriding.

Alp-Tour Issyk-Kul Ltd elmona 154–8; ☎ 594 86; e khanin@infotel.ru, alp-tur@yandex.ru. Run by a Russian called Igor Khanin, this small yet professional company mostly deals with visiting Russians. They have a tent camp in the Karakol park at the base of some excellent mountain hikes. They also offer treks to Khan Tengri base camp & climbing expeditions to the Central Tien Shan peaks.

Ecotrek Trekking Workers Association Koyonkozov 48; ☎ 511 15; e karakol@rambler.ru; www.ecotrek.kg; ⏱ 08.00–17.00 daily. This collective of guides, porters, cooks & horsemen can provide a range of services to trekkers inc guiding, yurt accommodation, horse hire & transport. Their stated aims are to increase the standard of living & level of qualification of trekking workers, develop

sustainable tourism & promote ecotourism. They can organise anything from day treks in the Altyn Arashan Valley to 2-week helicopter-supported expeditions to the Inylchek Glacier.

Issyk-Kul Guides & Porters Association (IGPA) Lenina 130/1; ☎ 52 529; e karakolguides@hotmail.com; www.kyrgyz-tours.info. The IGPA is a co-operative of young guides overseen by a Russian mountaineer with 30 years of experience. English-, French- & German-speaking guides are available, & the association can organise mountain-biking trips as well as hikes. They also offer accommodation in their guesthouse & camping in its garden.

Neofit Jamansariev 166; ☎ 558 50; e neofittravel@gmail.com; www.neofit.kg. Neofit is a Karakol company which has worked in the tourist industry since 1996 & is able to organise trekking, cycling & mountaineering expeditions anywhere in the Issyk-Kul region & beyond. It can also arrange city tours & cultural excursions. Neofit also runs a guesthouse in the town that is popular with trekkers (see page 176).

Turkestan Travel Toktogul 273; m 0543 911 452; e psi61@mail.ru; www.turkestan.biz. A highly regarded & well-established travel company based in Karakol, Turkestan has a wide range of tours & treks on offer, inc treks to Merzbacher Lake, the Inylchek Glacier & Khan Tengri base camp. They can organise climbing expeditions to Khan Tengri & Pobedy peaks, cycling tours, winter ski programmes in the Karakol Valley & even helicopter flights over the Inylchek Glacier. They also share a yurt camp in the Kazakh part of the Karkara Valley with the Kazakh operator Kan Tengri. Cultural tours can be arranged too, such as trips to see eagle-hunting displays or Kyrgyz musical events. Prices are not cheap but the service is certainly highly professional. Turkestan also has a yurt camp in the centre of Karakol which is open to all-comers, whether booking a service or not (see page 176).

Yak Tours Gagarina 10; 569 01, 505 39; e yaktours@infotel.kg. Yak Tours is run by Valentin Derevanko, an ethnic Ukrainian who, in a former life, worked as a motorcycle instructor in the Soviet army. Valentin also has a lifetime of trekking experience & is an institution in Karakol trekking circles. He runs a couple of standard trips in the Altyn Arashan Valley, which are firmly at the cheap & cheerful end of the market, & you tend to get what you pay for. Valentin is happy to deal with impecunious hikers on a tight budget & can rent hiking equipment & provide transport to & from trail heads. As well as running the town's oldest backpacker hostel (see page 176) he also has a basic trekker's lodge in the Altyn Arashan Valley, from where he runs a couple of standard treks. He can provide inexpensive transport to & from the lodge in his jeep most days. Valentin is very fond of engines & old vehicles like UAZ jeeps & Russian motorcycles, & can probably help if you are having problems with your own vehicle.

🏠 WHERE TO STAY *Map, page 172*

Several years ago there were few options in town, apart from the Hotel Issyk-Kul just outside the town (see below) and the tawdry, state-run pile of the Hotel Karakol on Gebze, close to the university, which was well known for having alcohol and prostitution problems and which has since closed down. These days, partly because of the town's importance as a winter skiing centre, there is a far wider choice of places to stay, with a good selection of hotels and more than 40 homestays, five of which belong to the local CBT network. A full list can be provided by either the CBT office or the TIC. Standards are generally high, although location may be a factor in deciding which to choose as some homestays are a considerable distance from the centre (*all* **$–$$**).

Hotels

🏠 **Green Yard Hotel** (16 rooms) Novostroika 14; 432 28; m 0555 451 515; e green_yard@ rambler.ru; www.greenyard.kg. Family-run mini-hotel some way southeast of the town centre. Rooms are clean & light, & meals are available on request. Friendly staff & excellent b/fasts. **$$$$**

🏠 **Hotel Amir** (18 rooms) Amanbaev 78; 513 15; m 0556 100 952; e info@hotelamir.kg; www. hotelamir.kg. This colourfully painted, fairly new hotel in the town centre has good facilities & clean, nicely furnished rooms. Facilities inc conference room, a sun terrace & a restaurant that serves Kyrgyz & European dishes. The location is quiet & the hotel is proving to be a popular choice for visiting tour groups. **$$$$**

🏠 **Altamira** (11 rooms) Toktogul 277; m 0559 998 388; e gdaltamira@rambler.ru; www.altamira.kg. A sparkling new mini-hotel close to the centre with welcoming staff, comfortable rooms, satellite TV & Wi-Fi. **$$$**

🏠 **Hotel Issyk-Kul**** (11 dbls, 6 'lux' rooms) Fuchika 38; 404 76, 407 73. This old Soviet hotel is set in wooded grounds, 3km from the town centre to the southeast, near the hippodrome. One of the hotel's 2 blocks has been requisitioned & refurbished by the government, while the other is in private ownership. Price inc HB. **$$$**

🏠 **Madanur Hotel** (13 rooms) Toktogul 201; 715 38; m 0777 757 757; www.madanur-karakol.kg. Next door to a supermarket, west of the centre, close to the river & Pushkin Park, this modern hotel offers decent, good-value rooms, satellite TV, free Wi-Fi & good b/fasts. **$$$**

🏠 **Tagaytay** (16 rooms) Tynstanov 29a; 521 61; m 0550 454 034. Another newish central hotel with helpful staff & spotless, good-value rooms. **$$$**

Guesthouses & homestays

🏠 **Elita Guesthouse** Kutmanaliev 56; ✆501 50. Medium-sized guesthouse in pleasant surroundings. B/fast is inc & a kitchen available if you want to cook your own food.

🏠 **Gulnara's** Myrmanskaya 114; ✆701 71. Gulnara's is also sometimes known as the Artisans' B&B & has just 3 very comfortable rooms, modern bathroom, plenty of interesting art on the walls & excellent veg & non-veg cooking.

🏠 **Gulnara's B&B** Stakhanova 67; ✆555 44. Another Gulnara's, this time at the comfortable home of Gulnara Mamyralieva, who is also an excellent cook.

🏠 **Jamilya's B&B** (2 dbls & 1 sgl) Shopokova 34b; ✆430 19. A popular homestay about 20mins' walk from the centre; close to the river.

🏠 **Marzey's Guesthouse** (4 rooms) Korolkova 86; m 0772 545 620; e marzy@ nomansland.ch. A guesthouse run by Marzey, an English-speaking Iranian woman married to a Swiss. Has a lovely flower garden & is in a fairly central location.

🏠 **Neofit** (14 rooms) Jamansariev 166; ✆558 50; e neofit@issyk-kul.kg; www.neofit.kg. A centrally located guesthouse, run by the trekking company of the same name, with clean, simple rooms – mostly with private toilets & TV. Use of kitchen.

🏠 **Riverside Guesthouse** (6 rooms) Kravkova 170; ✆727 60; m 0550 660 352; www. guesthouse-karakol.com. A stylish, modern guesthouse run by a Dutch-Kyrgyz couple who also run the travel company Ala Too Travel (see page 174). As its name suggests, the guesthouse is located next to the river south of the centre. Spacious rooms, comfortable beds, good food & helpful owners; Wi-Fi available.

🏠 **Teskey Guesthouse** (6 rooms) Asanalieva 44; ✆577 26; m 0772 801 411; www.teskey. narod.ru. This guesthouse is very popular because of its reasonably central location & also because of word-of-mouth recommendations (there's no sign). This place gets filled quickly in season & its reputation is certainly justified, having spotless facilities, a flowery garden & a charming host family. Taalai Janybekov speaks excellent English & is a considerate host, full of good advice. As well as the well-established CBT homestay there is also a pristine, newly built private guesthouse (16 rooms) on the same site. This is only fractionally more expensive (**$$**) & has bright dbl rooms & shared facilities; also underfloor heating in winter & a communal computer, map & reading room.

🏠 **Turkestan Yurt Camp & Guesthouse** (8 yurts, 5 rooms) Toktogul 273; ✆598 96; e psi61@mail.ru; www.turkestan.biz. As well as the yurt camp which shares 6 toilets & 2 showers, this camp run by Turkestan Travel (see page 174) also has a small guesthouse. There are 2 yurts selling handicrafts. With internet access, car park, climbing wall, garden & a place for campfires to recreate that genuine *jailoo* ambience. Its very central location is also a bonus. Sometimes folklore concerts & *manaschi* recitals are staged here.
Prices: **$$** *without b/fast, whole yurt* **$$$** *(max number 5), bed in a shared yurt without bedding* **$** *(they claim to distribute guests between empty yurts before asking them to share). Camping is also possible* **$**

🏠 **Yak Tours Guesthouse** (10 rooms) Gagarina 10; ✆505 39; e yaktours@rambler.ru. This place, run by Valentin Derevanko & his wife, is the closest thing Karakol has to a backpackers' hostel. There are various colourful & eccentrically decorated rooms of different sizes scattered throughout the house & comfort is partly determined by how many people are staying there. A little chaotic & crowded at times – there is just 1 bathroom for the use of guests. The food here is claimed to be the best in town, which is perhaps an exaggeration, but it is certainly good. Tents can be pitched in the garden. **$**; *with meals* **$$**

✗ WHERE TO EAT AND DRINK *Map, page 172*

Most of the guesthouses provide evening meals on request, and this is often the cheapest, most convenient and tastiest option, especially if staying in a far-flung homestay. For daytime snacks there are several places near Jakshilik Bazaar which produce freshly baked *samsi* to take away, and there are a number of decent cafés and restaurants in this part of the town. There is also a modern Turkish bakery on Toktogul facing the bazaar. Both Jakshilik and Aktilek bazaars have a good choice of fresh vegetables and fruit, especially in the late summer, and a few food stalls selling Kyrgyz staples and some Dungan dishes – *ashlyanfu* (cold noodles in a spicy, vinegary sauce) is a tasty local favourite that costs next to nothing for a bowl. For Dungan food in more formal surroundings, Valentin of Yak Tours can arrange a feast in a Dungan house for around US$12 per head.

✗ **Karakol Coffee** Toktogul 112a; m 0557 779 663; ⊕ 08.00–22.00. Undoubtedly serving the best coffee in Karakol (& probably in the country outside Bishkek), this has all manner of snacks, pizzas & sandwiches too, as well as fruit juices & bottled beers. A popular expatriate hangout, with Wi-Fi, English-language magazines & slightly higher than avg prices. $$$

✗ **Kench** Telmona, just east of junction with Gebze; ☏ 207 07; ⊕ 11.00–midnight. In the southeast part of town near Victory Park & not too far from the Teskey & Marzey guesthouses, this is considered to be 1 of the best restaurants in town. Indoor dining room & partially covered outdoor patio with fluorescent lights, English menu with a wide range of beef, chicken & continental dishes. The service is efficient & the food imaginative & reasonably priced for the quality. $$$

✗ **Kalinka** Abdrakhmanov/Koenkozova; ☏ 277 77; ⊕ 10.00–22.00. Good food served in a fancy Siberian-style log cabin, near the university. Serves a wide variety of Russian dishes, inc salads, borsch & *blini* as well as cold draught beer. Service can be slow though. $$–$$$

✗ **Lovely Pizza** Tynystanov 125; ☏ 576 40; ⊕ 09.00–23.00. No prizes for guessing what the speciality here is. Surprisingly, there's also sushi on the menu… and water pipes! Outdoor terrace. $$–$$$

✗ **Dinara** Lenina 160; ☏ 546 67; ⊕ 10.00–22.00. Big purple arches lead into a courtyard with dining booths separated by purple curtains. Kyrgyz, Russian & a few Dungan dishes are served. $$

✗ **Zarina** Toktogul/Lenin; ☏ 599 39; ⊕ 11.00–midnight. A central café-restaurant close to the bazaar, with an English menu & a reasonable range of Russian & continental dishes. Also a few Chinese dishes & real espresso coffee. The main dining room is non-smoking & has wooden, garden-terrace-like furniture & private VIP booths that resemble garden sheds. Music & dancing after 21.00. $$

✗ **Maximum** Toktogul 126; ☏ 519 51; ⊕ 10.00–midnight. A large restaurant on Toktogul close to Altamira Hotel, this serves large portions of typical Kyrgyz food at competitive prices. There's often music & dancing later in the evening. $–$$

✗ **Stealth Café** Gorkovo; ⊕ 10.00–22.00. Almost opposite Fakir, this friendly place comes highly recommended by locals & has a varied menu inc salads, fish dishes & excellent *laghman*. $–$$

✗ **Fakir** Gorkovo/Kushtobaev, 1 block from Toktogul; ☏ 206 56; ⊕ 10.00–22.00. Large, but dark & slightly soulless, centrally located café with a varied menu & good food. Portions are large & menus are available in English. Handy ATM inside. $

✗ **Uyurt** Jakshilik Bazaar; ☏ 532 96; ⊕ 09.00–21.00. A bright green, 2-storey building at the northeast corner of the bazaar serving standard Kyrgyz dishes. $

ENTERTAINMENT AND NIGHTLIFE Karakol is not known for its nightlife. After dark the town's streets are unnervingly quiet, as if most people have gone to bed – most probably have. Like Bishkek, the streets are poorly lit at night, with the trees blocking any light from the moon or the odd streetlamp. In fact, Karakol is actually darker than Bishkek so be careful at night as, although muggings and attacks may be uncommon, they are not unknown.

For those hedonists for whom a pot of tea and a chat at their homestay is not enough, there are a few disco and karaoke places scattered about, like the Manhattan Karaoke Disco Bar on the corner of Toktogul and Derbishev near the southern bus station. Some of the restaurants like Maximum and Zarina also turn up the volume to encourage customers on to the dance floor around 21.00.

SHOPPING The small **Jakshilik Bazaar** in the town centre has meat, fruit and vegetable stalls, as well as stationery, clothes and household appliances. Facing the bazaar on Toktogul is the **Karavan** supermarket, with an enormous selection of loose biscuits and other trekking staples. **Kumtor TsUM**, just north of the bazaar on Toktogul, is Karakol's main department store and stocks more or less everything that you might reasonably wish to find, such as household goods, camera accessories and electrical appliances. For souvenirs and Kyrgyz handicrafts there is the art gallery at the southeast corner of Jakshilik Bazaar. Aktilek Bazaar also has a small selection of souvenirs on sale. Another place worth checking close to the bazaar is the **OVOP** (One Village One Product) shop on Toktogul (m *0552 430 307*), the outlet of a Japanese-funded community development organisation, which has a range of local products like natural soaps and honey as well as unusual felt products. The Tourist Information Centre has good quality postcards and a small selection of handicrafts.

OTHER PRACTICALITIES
Communications The main **post office** is at Gebze, opposite the park (⊕ *08.00–17.00 Mon–Fri, 12.00–13.00 Sat, closed Sun*). The **Kyrgyz Telecom** office is next door to the post office at Gebze 126. Book international calls at the counter and say how long you want. The cost of calls to Europe depends on the time of day. Dial the international code plus the number, then 3 when the call is answered.

Internet Internet cafés tend to come and go. The best place to look for them is on the streets close to the university. At the time of research the two options were **Delta** (*Tynystanov/Gorkovo*; m *0553 262 261*) and **Issyk-Kul Guides & Porters Association** (*Lenina 130/1*; m *0552 552 529*), which is also a computer shop.

Money Karakol has branches of both **RSK** and **Optima Banks** more or less facing each other on Toktogul between Gebze and Moskovskaya. There's also a branch of Optima Bank right in the centre, just off Toktogul close to Jakshilik Bazaar. All of these have ATMs (Visa only) and they will also change dollars and euros over the counter. In addition, there are several kiosks that will change dollars, euros (and possibly even pounds sterling) along Toktogul.

Red tape For **visa extensions** visit the office of **OVIR** (*Kutmanaliev 146a, room 114*; ⊕ *09.00–16.00 Tue–Fri*) where an extension should be relatively simple to arrange. You'll need two photos, passport, a photocopy of the relevant pages and will be instructed to make a payment at a local bank.

Border zone permits, necessary for anywhere within 50km of the Chinese border, ie: for the Inylchek Glacier or the peaks of the Central Tien Shan, are trickier to arrange and are best done through a travel agency in advance. Locally, they may take at least a week to arrange, probably longer. CBT claims it can organise them within seven days, whereas a company like Turkestan can usually do this more quickly, within a few days, although this will cost more.

WHAT TO SEE AND DO Karakol is a spread-out sort of place without much of an obvious focus for a centre. Such as it is, the town centre is the area immediately around Jakshilik Bazaar and the central square south of the university, which has stands of pine trees, some broken benches, a scattering of memorials and a statue of Soviet hero, Yusup Abdrakhmanov (1901–38), who was the first secretary of the Kyrgyz Communist Party from 1924 to 1925. Another Soviet hero, Lenin, stands nearby at the junction of Gebze and Tynystanov.

Other than the obvious sights below, much of Karakol is pleasant enough to wander at will and enjoy the wooden Russian domestic architecture which characterises much of the town. In particular, the area along Lenina and Gorkovo, southeast of the Holy Trinity Cathedral, is a rewarding quarter to explore.

Holy Trinity Cathedral

Holy Trinity Cathedral (⊕ *normally until about 17.00; after this time you may have to pay a small fee to enter*) This wooden Russian Orthodox church dates back to 1895 when it was constructed to serve the spiritual needs of the new influx of Russian settlers in the town. It replaced an earlier stone structure that was destroyed in an earthquake in 1890 (this, in turn, had replaced a yurt, which had been the first place of Orthodox worship in the town).

Made almost entirely of wood on a stone foundation, the church was stripped of its five green domes during the Soviet period, when it also suffered the ignominy of being used as a dance club in the 1930s. Reconstruction began in the 1960s and it was reconsecrated as a place of worship in 1991, and again in 1997.

Today the church, under the auspices of Father Vladimir, oversees the entire Issyk-Kul Russian Orthodox diocese. The church's greatest treasure is an icon of the Virgin that came from the monastery of Svetly Mys near Tyup, where the monks were savagely murdered in 1916 on the eve of the revolution. The icon is said to have wept tears and blood and repelled the bullets of rebel soldiers (see page 163). For true Old Russian atmosphere, the best time for a visit is Sunday mornings before 10.00, when the choir will be singing and the air is redolent with incense and candle wax.

Dungan (Chinese) Mosque

Dungan (Chinese) Mosque Like the Holy Trinity Cathedral, this place of worship is also built of wood and, at first glance, this brightly painted, red, green and yellow building resembles a pagoda or a Mongolian Buddhist temple more than it does a typical Islamic building. The similarity with Buddhist structures is no accident as the Dungans who built it – ethnically Chinese but with a Buddhist past before conversion to Islam – unconsciously incorporated a great amount of Buddhist symbolism into its design, adding details such as conch shells and the Buddhist wheel of life, as well as representations of dragons and phoenixes to reflect the unmistakable influence of Chinese mythology.

The mosque was built by the Dungan community in the years 1907–10, using a Chinese architect working with a team of 20 artisans. It was constructed entirely without nails. There is a low powder-blue minaret and, similar to many mosques in Xinjiang and Muslim China, there is a veranda either side of the entrance.

The mosque was closed down by the Soviet authorities in 1933 but then reopened for worship in 1943. These days the mosque no longer serves the Dungan community exclusively and is attended as much by Kyrgyz as it is by Chinese Muslims. It is usually filled to overspill during Friday morning prayers.

Regional History Museum

Regional History Museum (*Jamansariev 164;* \ *218 68;* ⊕ *09.00–17.00 daily; admission 70som*) This museum houses a collection spread throughout seven rooms that has a number of Scythian artefacts, including some large bronze pots, artefacts of traditional Kyrgyz culture, such as leather *kumys* containers and musical instruments, and a display of Kyrgyz felt art and *shyrdaks*. There are also black and white photographs of old-time Karakol detailing the colonial Russian and Soviet history of the region, and a section on the petroglyphs found in the Issyk-Kul region. There is also the requisite display of stuffed indigenous wildlife.

Sunday animal market

Sunday animal market This is well worth attending if you are in Karakol on a Sunday, and is a weekly event deserving of planning your trip around to some extent. The livestock market (*skotniy bazaar* in Russian) takes place at the northern edge of town each Sunday. Take a taxi or flag down a car to reach it (*70som*) and get there reasonably early, as it tends to start at around dawn and is all over by 10.00. City minibus 102 also runs to and from the bazaar from the centre but does not start running until 07.00.

The market is a vast concentration of horse, sheep and cattle, but mostly the first two, which are traded in two separate enclosures. Pigs are sold here as well, but these are kept separate from the main market animals because of their proscription by Islam. Kyrgyz come from all over the region to visit the market, and to buy, sell and socialise, sometimes travelling for days with their livestock to reach it.

Whether you're interested in the animals or not, the weekly bazaar gives a good insight into the culture and the livelihood of the people here. Scattered among stands of tightly tethered, complaining livestock are Kyrgyz who have come to examine and bargain for the goods on offer, trying out horses with a short test trot or assessing the weight of the fat on the behind of a fat-tailed sheep with their palms. This is Kyrgyz rural life in its unadorned form and here, as much as anywhere in the region, will you see wizened Methuselahs with straggly beards and white *kalpaks* going about their everyday business.

The market, which is remarkably calm and dignified given all the activity going on, is as much a country fair as it is a place of commerce. It is a great place to wander, take photographs and watch the morning unfold; it is also a good place to buy a horse or a sheep if you know what you are doing (take a sympathetic local along for advice). Sheep usually cost around US$120 and horses start from US$300.

Those who have visited the Sunday market in Kashgar, across the border in Xinjiang, may find the scale of the Karakol market a little disappointing, but there is certainly nowhere else in Kyrgyzstan where such old-style commerce can be witnessed in such a hassle-free, tourist-friendly manner.

Pushkin Park Karakol's largest park lies in the southeast sector of the town next to the stadium. It's a leafy expanse of grass and woodland that is a pleasant place to stroll or sit and read. The park has a monument of a border guard with a dog, which is dedicated to 11 border guards who were killed during a cross-border clash with illegal immigrants in 1926. The park also has a stone memorial to Red Army soldiers who died in battle against White Russians in 1919.

Zoo (*Aitmatova;* ⊕ *09.00–18.00, closed Sun; admission 50som*) Near the stadium, just south of Pushkin Park, this is Kyrgyzstan's only zoo. The regional fauna is well represented here, with wolves, bears and even native Przhevalsky horses on show. As far as zoos go it is relatively humane, although the cages and enclosures tend to be quite small and bare.

AROUND KARAKOL

PRZHEVALSKY MEMORIAL This memorial park and museum to the Russian explorer who gave the town its earlier name lies just outside Karakol near the village of Pristan Przhevalsk, 9km to the north on the shores of Lake Issyk-Kul. The museum stands on the same site as the house he had built for himself close to the lake. The monument and small chapel which stand here were built on the site of his grave in 1894, just six years after his death. In 1957, the Soviet authorities constructed the museum and gardens which stand here today, removing and desecrating the best part of a village graveyard to do so. Quite fittingly, this considerable slight to local sensibilities was carried out to commemorate a man who could hardly be described as a loyal friend of the Kyrgyz people (see box, page 182).

The **grave** and **monument** stand at the north end of the park overlooking the waters of the Mikhailovka inlet. The park is landscaped with bright flower-beds and planted with a variety of trees native to the region, such as Tien Shan spruce. The monument itself, comprising 21 pieces of stone sculpted to form a precipitous mountain peak with a spread-winged eagle on top, is a popular spot for wedding parties to congregate for photo shoots. The inlet that lies beyond, of which you get teasing glimpses through the railings, is one of the few zones of modern-day Kyrgyzstan that remains firmly off-limits to visitors – it was once part of the old Soviet top-secret military zone which included the nearby villages of Mikhailovka and Lipenka. Now that the Soviet navy's torpedo-testing facility has closed down for good, it would seem there is little that requires military secrecy here any more. The view along the inlet just offers up a glimpse of cranes and warehouses, a boat or two, and a few wooden *dachas*.

The **museum** (⊕ *09.00–17.00 daily; admission 100som inc guided tour*), near the park entrance in a Neoclassical building topped by another sculpted eagle, has a large globe and an enormous 3D map of central Asia showing the routes of Przhevalsky's various journeys. The accompanying displays detail the ways in which his passion for exploration was aroused, and how he managed to organise his trips to central Asia and beyond (by doing a bit of spying on the side). There are lots of his letters, photos and books, and also some excellent line drawings of the scenery and sights encountered during his explorations by his second-in-command. Labels are mostly in Russian and Kyrgyz but there are some that are in English. A curiosity of the museum, which should be pointed out to you by your guide, is the wall mural which changes perspective according to the viewer's position.

This would not be a proper museum, of course, without a few stuffed animals, and there are a few dioramas with representations of the region's birdlife, including griffon vultures and a golden eagle. There is also a rather moth-eaten specimen of the native Mongolian horse named after the explorer himself: the short-legged Przhevalsky horse.

The cost of admission includes a guided tour, which may be in Russian, English or, more likely, a combination of the two. Guides are friendly and will gladly answer questions, although they might not appreciate being diverted too much away from their rehearsed spiel. To reach the Przhevalsky museum and memorial from Karakol either take a minibus marked 'Дачи' ('*dachi*') from the bus stand near the central bazaar or negotiate a taxi. A taxi there and back, with an hour or so of waiting time, should cost no more than 500som.

KARAKOL VALLEY This stunning valley lies immediately south of Karakol along the river of the same name that passes through the town. The valley has a ski base, which is visited by local and Russian skiers in winter, while in the summer it is a popular area for trekkers and campers. There are no villages anywhere along the valley, nor any facilities for tourism other than a summer tent camp, but this makes it all the more desirable as an ideal location for independent campers who bring all they need with them.

The Karakol Valley has been awarded national park status and there is an entrance fee to pay (*250som for foreigners*). Beyond the entrance, a track leads up to the left along the course of the Kashka-Suu tributary to reach the ski base. The dirt road continues along the river to reach a wooden bridge across the river, where the track continues along the valley with the river to the left. The steep slopes here are covered with stands of spruce and the distinctively pyramid-shaped Tien Shan fir, while the grassy fringe beside the track is carpeted with herbs and wild flowers.

After a gradual climb along the valley for 8–9km from the first bridge, a path leads east through woodland across the river towards Lake Ala-Köl, while the Karakol Valley itself continues south for a few more kilometres, before dividing into the valleys of the Köl-Tör and On-Tör rivers which run down from the high glaciers of the Terskey Ala-Too.

A tent camp run by the Alp-Tur Issyk-Kul trekking company (see page 174), with basic washing and cooking facilities, stands close to the confluence. Park permits

NIKOLAI PRZHEVALSKY 1839–88

Nikolai Mikhailovich Przhevalsky was born in Smolensk, Russia, in 1839 to a noble Belarusian family. He studied both in Smolensk and at the military academy in St Petersburg before spending a period as a geography teacher at the Warsaw Military School in 1864.

As well as a taste for military life, Przhevalsky also had a fascination with Asia and exploration; an interest that had been with him since childhood, inspired by contemporary European explorers like David Livingstone. His first exploratory trip to Asia was sponsored by the Russian Geographical Society in 1867, when he was sent to Irkutsk in Siberia to investigate the highlands of the Ussuri River. This expedition opened the door for four subsequent trips to inner Asia, heralding a new era in the geographical exploration of a region that, until then, was virtually unknown to the West.

In exploration terms, Przhevalsky's main obsession lay in reaching Lhasa, the mysterious and forbidden capital of Tibet. Between 1870 and 1873 he traversed the Gobi Desert to Peking, before exploring the Yangtze and crossing into Tibet itself. In his third expedition of 1876–77 he travelled through the region of Chinese Turkestan, rediscovering Lake Lop Nor, which had not been seen by another European since Marco Polo's visit in the 13th century. On his fourth journey in 1879–80 Przhevalsky visited China's Qaidam basin before traversing the Tien Shan range to Tibet once more. Finally, between 1883 and 1885, he crossed the Gobi once more to reach the eastern Tien Shan, before journeying back to Koko Nor and west to Lake Issyk-Kul.

Despite such extensive explorations, Przhevalsky's interests lay beyond that of mere geography, and he was as much obsessed with military and strategic matters as he was with scientific exploration. For Przhevalsky, as well as his sponsors, the explorer's responsibility was political as much as it was scientific and he relished his military role, viewing himself as a servant of the Russian state rather than as any sort of independent spirit.

While he was undoubtedly a dedicated geographer and biologist with a genuine scientific interest in the terrain he crossed, he chose his destinations primarily for the sake of military reconnaissance: the three areas he explored most thoroughly – Chinese Turkestan, Mongolia and northern Tibet – were all strategically important to the Russian crown. This was at a time of imperial expansion, when the Great Game was being played to the full, and when Britain and Russia competed for dominance of the central Asian world which lay between their two respective empires.

Despite his military brief, Przhevalsky made many zoological discoveries during these journeys, discovering native species of horse and gazelle, which were are usually checked here. Just beyond, a trekking route leads west towards the Teleti Pass and descends along the Teleti River to the valley of Jeti-Ögüz.

Getting there and away   Minibus 101, which runs past Aktilek Bazaar, along Toktogul and down Gorkovo, goes almost as far as the park entrance. There is also the option of a taxi to the park entrance; a more robust vehicle will be able to take you as far as the wooden bridge – a good place to begin a trek.

Where to stay and eat   Apart from wild camping, the only possibility is the Alp-Tur Issyk-Kul tent camp, mentioned on page 182, where a camping fee of 100som will be charged.

subsequently named after him – Przhevalsky's horse (*Equus caballus przewalski*) and Przhevalsky's gazelle (*Procapra przewalski*) – as well as stumbling upon a wild population of Bactrian camels. He was equally industrious in his botanical work, bringing back a total of 16,000 specimens of 1,700 species to St Petersburg over the 21-year period of his five expeditions.

His fifth journey to central Asia brought about his downfall. After drinking infected water from the Chui River on a hunting trip he fell ill with typhus. Worsening in health, he elected to return to the shores of Lake Issyk-Kul to die. He passed away in a military hospital at Karakol without ever having achieved his greatest dream – to enter Lhasa. He had come close but his efforts to reach the Tibetan capital had always been thwarted: by bad weather, by hostile rumour and now by death itself.

During the Soviet period Przhevalsky was lauded as a tolerant explorer who had nothing but respect for the people of the region, but a closer reading suggests that this was hardly the truth of the matter. Przhevalsky may have been a brilliant geographer, naturalist and explorer but as a 'man of his time' he was sadly lacking in some of the human qualities we take for granted in the modern age. Despite spending many years in their presence, he held a low opinion of many of the people whom he travelled among, despising the indigenous people of the region – Kyrgyz, Mongolians, Chinese, Tibetans and Uyghur – as lowly beings who required the enlightenment of Russian colonialism to render them half-decent. It was his dislike and distrust of the Chinese, in particular, which led him to try and persuade the Russian Tsar to go to war with China, as he sincerely believed that only Russian colonisation could redeem them as a race.

It should not be forgotten that his journeys took place at a time when a belief in social Darwinism was prevalent, and when most Europeans considered themselves to be morally and intellectually superior to other races. He was not alone in this: Pyotr Semyonov Tyan-Shansky himself, president of the Russian Geographical Society and an enthusiastic sponsor of Przhevalsky's expeditions, claimed that 'scientific material is necessary for the definitive conquest of these (inner Asian) lands for culture and civilisation'.

In his last book, *Ot Kyakhty*, Przhevalsky maintains that he had been kind to the local population at first, but that it was their unending trickery and stupidity that drove him to cruelty. Regarding this, he claims: 'Only the experience of later expeditions convinced me that three things are necessary for the success of long and dangerous journeys in central Asia – money, a gun and a whip.'

KARAKOL SKI RESORT Aside from hiking and camping, the big draw in the valley is winter skiing (and snowboarding) between late November and mid-March. The Karakol Valley has one of the best and most popular ski resorts in central Asia and has been mentioned by *Forbes* magazine as one of the top ten places to ski in the world. In Soviet times the ski resort, at 2,300m, was used for Olympic winter sports training. The resort has a total of four chair-lifts and over 20km of trails and runs, and equipment including snowboards can be hired from the lift base (m *0772 534 081; www.karakol-ski.kg*).

Getting there and away Taxis from central Karakol cost in the order of 500som. *Marshrutki* go only as far as the national park gate, several kilometres short of the ski base.

Where to stay and eat Accommodation is available at either a three-storey ski lodge, in apartments or in chalets (*all* **$$$$**). Another option is the **Hotel Kapriz** (\ *905 170;* m *0551 905 175;* e *reservation@skd.kg; www.kapriz.kg*), a large A-framed ski lodge with comfortable rooms that is open in summer (**$$$**) as well as during the ski season (**$$$$**). The hotel also has ski gear to hire at reasonable prices.

ALTYN ARASHAN VALLEY Running parallel to the Karakol Valley to the east, but separated from it by the ranges of Kara-Beltek, Aylanysh and the high 4,000m-plus peaks of the Terim-Tör, is the Altyn Arashan ('Golden Spa') Valley. Of all the valleys that lie close to Karakol, this is probably the most popular overall, and with good reason. Even by Kyrgyzstan's high standards the valley is extraordinarily lovely, with silver threads of streams trickling down to join the Arashan River, lush meadows sparkling with wild flowers, and smooth green slopes cloaked by dense stands of conifer higher up.

Getting there and away Valentin of Yak Tours in Karakol makes regular trips in a decommissioned Russian army 6x6 between Karakol and his valley guesthouse which lies just short of the hot springs. He charges 300som one-way but will only make the trip when there are enough passengers to make it worthwhile. Yak Tours also offers a US$40 package that includes transport, meals and lodging, and a guided day trek. Several **minibuses** run each day from Karakol's Aktilek Bazaar to Ak-Suu Sanatorium. To make use of this service, get off at the Altyn Arashan turn-off just before reaching the sanatorium, from where it is a four- to five-hour hike that climbs 1,000m uphill to the hot springs complex. Walking downhill along the same route will take three to four hours. Alternatively, a Karakol **taxi** will drive to the beginning of the dirt road up to Altyn Arashan, just south of Teploklyuchenka village, for around 250som.

Where to stay and eat The **Kolkhoz Hostel** (*dormitory* **$**) has concrete hot pools where you can bathe (*100som*), dormitory beds, a kitchen and dining room, and outside toilets. It is also possible to camp outside and use the facilities here for 100som. There is a very basic shop that sells a few essentials such as biscuits and beer.

The **Yak Tours** guesthouse is a rather run-down wooden cabin a little further down the valley with its own hot spring (**$**, *or* **$$** *with three meals*).

Camping is possible almost anywhere, with the best sites further south up the valley beyond the hot springs.

What to see and do Heading up the valley, the picture-perfect **view** is dominated by the snow-topped 4,260m Palatka ('Tent') peak that lies far to the south beyond the Altyn Arashan hot springs that give the valley its name. Bears are said to inhabit the area, although there does not seem to be any record of attacks on humans in the region. The area includes the Arashan State Reserve, a botanical research preserve.

The valley begins close to the village of Teploklyuchenka, to the east of Karakol town. Just south of the village the road splits, veering left to reach the spartan Ak-Suu Sanatorium and continuing straight on for the Altyn Arashan springs, along a steep, and extremely rough, 12km track through pine woodland close to the Arashan River. The road is only suitable for a really tough 4x4 vehicle and is such a slow, uncomfortable drive that walking may be the longer but more appealing option.

Along the road up to the hot springs complex are a number of hidden **cold and hot springs**, and there is a small cave 500m downstream from the Yak Tours guesthouse that has hot sulphurous water piped from a nearby spring. There are free hot springs for bathing between the jeep track and the river, about 15 minutes' walk downhill, although these may be hard to find. The hot springs 'complex' at the end of the track is fairly rudimentary, but a wonderful place for a hot bath after trekking (*200som*), or as a place to stay and use as a base for hikes further up the valley. Day treks may be made to nearby 3,800m peaks – around seven hours' round trip from the hot springs complex.

AK-SUU VALLEY Beginning at the village of Ak-Suu on the main Karakol to Novovoznesenovka road, and following the river of the same name as it climbs southeast into the Terskey Ala-Too range, the Ak-Suu Valley is another valley with great trekking potential. The Ak-Suu Sanatorium at the lower end of the valley can easily be reached from Karakol by *marshrutka* (*minibus 350 from Aktilek Bazaar, frequent in summer*) and day treks further along the valley can be made from here. Alternatively, the valley can be used as a starting point for treks that cross the Adyr-Tör Pass to reach Altyn Arashan. The sanatorium is actually several separate places, the newest and best of which is the first one to be reached, 'Res', which charges 50som for a bathing session. The others charge 25som. Understandably, the hot springs are at their busiest at weekends in summer.

Ak-Suu village on the main road is the place to come for **paragliding** as enthusiasts use the hills near the village as a launch pad. Flights last between five and 20 minutes and land (with luck!) in the flat arable fields around the village. For information on tandem flights contact Sky Trial (m *0555 434 753*; e *troff-kgz@rambler.ru*).

FROM KARAKOL TO JETI-ÖGÜZ Halfway between Jeti-Ögüz and Karakol, just off the main road, is the village of **Yrdyk**, which has a large Dungan population and a mosque, medical centre and a number of houses all built in typical Dungan style. The central mosque is a replacement of an earlier one which dates from 1916.

JETI-ÖGÜZ (ДЖЕТИ-ОГУЗ) Southwest of Karakol town, parallel to the Karakol Valley, the valley of Jeti-Ögüz begins at the village of the same name and climbs south along the Jeti-Ögüz River, past a well-developed health resort, towards the Terskey Ala-Too range. The valley gets its name from a rock formation called Jeti-Ögüz ('Seven Bulls') that lies a few kilometres south of the village on the main road. The rocks in question form a ridge of distinct red sandstone bluffs, which number seven or possibly eight depending how you count them. Remarkable though they are, the rocks do not resemble bulls in any discernible way, but Kyrgyz folklore provides the legend to explain this appellation.

The legend tells of a Kyrgyz khan, who had stolen the wife of another khan who sought revenge for the deed. A wise man reluctantly offered counsel and suggested the aggrieved khan should seek out and kill his stolen wife so that the khan might own a dead wife rather a living one. A scheme was hatched that enabled him to sit next to his stolen wife at a funeral feast, and as the last of seven bulls were being slaughtered he stabbed and killed her. Her heart gushed blood down into the valley below, taking the carcasses of the seven sacrificial bulls with it to become the seven large red rocks which can be seen today. Another legend tells of seven rampaging wild bulls which were turned to stone by the gods in order to protect the local population.

Just before the ridge of Jeti-Ögüz stands another large red rock that also comes with legends attached. This is the fractured mass of Razbitoye Serdtse – **Broken Heart** – which resembles a heart that has splintered down the middle. The legend tells of a rich but cruel khan who spotted a beautiful girl while out hunting. Although he already had many wives the khan insisted on marrying the girl, who came from a poor family. The girl was already engaged to be married and when she heard of the khan's intentions she fled from the area with her lover. The couple were caught by the khan's servants, and the girl was taken by force while her betrothed was killed immediately. The death of her lover made her so distraught that she died on the way to the khan's residence, leaving the mark of her broken heart on the landscape. This is the 'cruel khan' variant of the legend; a similar version exists in which it was the quarrelling of two competing suitors that broke her heart.

More or less opposite the Broken Heart rock is a low ridge that you can climb to get a good view of the valley. In summer it has a photogenic collection of yurts that sell honey and other food items in front of it. A little further south, on the other side of the ridge and largely hidden from view, is **Dragon Gorge**, which has attractive wind-cut red sandstone cliffs and an impressive bird population of alpine swifts, choughs and peregrine falcons. Like Broken Heart and Seven Bulls, the deep red colouration is even more impressive after rain.

Just south of the Seven Bulls rocks is the **Jeti-Ögüz Sanatorium** (Jeti-Ögüz Kurort) built in 1932. This was the setting for the historic meeting between Boris Yeltsin and Kyrgyzstan's first president Askar Akayev in 1991, after the abortive Moscow coup. The concrete complex has seen better days, but it is an option in summer for those who want to stop in the valley but do not wish to camp or stay in a yurt. A good overview of this part of the valley can be had by walking a little way up the dirt road that leads off from the café opposite the sanatorium entrance. From here, there are excellent views over the Seven Bulls and the Broken Heart formations, and glimpses of the small canyon that lies to the east.

Continuing south along the valley for another 6km or so, and crossing the river a total of five times over rustic tree-trunk bridges, leads through a narrow canyon to an area where the valley suddenly widens out at a sloping *jailoo*. This is the **Valley of Flowers**, which is known as Tsvetov Dolina in Russian and Kök-Jayik in Kyrgyz, although the Kyrgyz also tend to refer to it as the 'Blue Valley' for similar reasons. The name is highly appropriate, and the best time to witness the bounty of its meadows is in the early summer when edelweiss, crocuses, tulips and poppies all put on a colourful show. The colourfulness of the flower show is said to depend on how harsh the previous winter has been. The valley is equally famous for its edible wild mushrooms, which are harvested in the summer for the Chinese and

Kazakhstan markets. The Valley of Flowers gets quite busy on summer weekends when many locals visit for family picnics and the dirt road that leads to it may become less than pleasant for walking because of traffic kicking up dust. Otherwise, it is a delightful hike. The *jailoo* has a large birch plantation established during Soviet times and following the path that leads right here should bring you to a waterfall after about 45 minutes walking. A horse is not necessary to reach this, despite what some insistent local horse owners might tell you. There are also said to be petroglyphs in the area.

Getting there and away Buses and minibuses from Karakol's southern shore bus station pass by the turn-off for Jeti-Ögüz on the main road, where there is a petrol station and a bus shelter in the form of a yurt. From the main road it is 5km to Jeti-Ögüz village and a further 12km walk up to the sanatorium. It is relatively easy to flag down a vehicle on this stretch, paying 30som or so for a ride. Fairly frequent direct minibuses run between Aktilek Bazaar in Karakol and Jeti-Ögüz village, where there are share taxis to the sanatorium, and there is usually one service a day that runs all the way in both directions between Karakol and the sanatorium. A taxi from Karakol to the sanatorium should cost around 600–700som, plus another 200som to Tsvetov Dolina and the yurt camps.

Where to stay and eat The Soviet-era **Jeti-Ögüz Sanatorium** consists of a number of fairly basic hotel buildings, along with a hot pool, a treatment centre and restaurant (*summer only; FB $$ pp*). A stay in any of the **yurt camps** in the Valley of Flowers is best prearranged through the Karakol Tourist Information Centre (✆ 523 41) rather than just turning up. Two companies that have yurt camps here are the Bishkek-based tour operators **Ecotour** (*www.ecotour.kg*) and **Muza Travel** (*www.muzatravel.com*).

There are a couple of restaurants and shops outside the grounds of the sanatorium. The **Kök-Jayik café** opposite the entrance has the usual Kyrgyz menu and a few seats outside ($). A little further down the valley, along the roadside, at the base of the Jeti-Ögüz and Broken Heart rocks, are a number of summer **food yurts** dishing up *shorpo* and *shashlyk*.

TREKKING SOUTH OF KARAKOL

Although the possibilities are almost infinite, the most popular routes tend to be those listed below. All of these can be done without support, by anyone who is reasonably experienced and fit enough to both hike and carry the tent, food and equipment needed. Alternatively, a trek can be arranged using the services of a local tour agency or through CBT.

The trekking season is fairly short, from the end of June until early October, and the majority of visitors trek between late July and early September; August is the peak month. Beyond this season, nights are very cold and snow is possible. Bad weather can, of course, occur at any time and rainstorms are something that should be prepared for.

A useful map for the region that shows trekking routes (available from the Tourist Information Centre in Karakol or GeoID in Bishkek), is the 1:100,000 *South-East Issyk-Kul Lake Coast* map published by Goskartografia. The 1:100,000 topological map of the area from GeoID is also invaluable.

Details on reaching the trail heads are given in the individual entries for each valley above. If starting in Kyzyl-Suu (Pokrovka) there are plenty of minibuses passing on the main road to and from Karakol.

KARAKOL VALLEY TO ALTYN ARASHAN AND AK-SUU This route takes a minimum of three days and two nights, although an extra day would be a bonus. The trek begins in the Karakol Valley at either the park entrance or at the wooden bridge a few kilometres further upstream.

The route follows the **Karakol River** upstream for three hours or so, gently climbing all the time. Here, the river is crossed by a footbridge and the route climbs steeply to the east, along the course of the **Kurgak-Tör stream** flowing down from Lake Ala-Köl. After about a three-hour climb from the Karakol River through woodland and juniper scrub and over rockfall, the **Sirota campsite** is reached, which is where most trekkers spend their first night. The campsite, which is in a rocky patch of pine woodland and has a very rudimentary log cabin shelter, tends to be rather cramped in the peak season, and there is generally quite a lot of litter lying about. There is an alternative place to camp beneath a waterfall 1–1½ hours further on – a beautifully scenic spot – although there is only room for about three small tents here and late in the day you take the risk of it already being occupied.

From the Sirota campsite, the path climbs up over rocks to beyond the treeline and a small rocky plateau by a waterfall, mentioned above, is reached. From here, fantastic views back along the valley to the west may be had. The route continues to the left of the waterfall until eventually a plateau with rocky outcrops is reached, from where there are dramatic views over the brilliant blue-green waters of **Lake Ala-Köl** that lies immediately below.

Some hikers descend to the lake to camp for the night; the alternative – or imperative, if you are doing the trek in just three days – is to continue east above the lake before striking northeast up to the high ridge that is the 3,860m **Ala-Köl Pass**. The scree on this section can be treacherously difficult to negotiate. From the top of the pass, you can enjoy views over the lake to the **Takyr-Tör Glacier** glistening to the southeast and the meandering stream snaking across the floodplain beneath it.

From the pass the path descends steeply down another difficult scree-slope to a wide open meadow, and then follows the course of the **Köl Dike stream** on its northern side. The landscape here is notably different from the other side of the pass and the Karakol Valley before it. Whereas the Karakol Valley might have been the Canadian Rockies or the Alps, the landscape here, with open, undulating meadows, massive walls of scree and jagged peaks to the south, seems to uncannily resemble parts of the Scottish Highlands.

Unless the option of an overnight pitch next to Lake Ala-Köl has been chosen, an overnight camp is usually made somewhere in this vicinity. A good spot to camp is in the pine woodland that lies close to the stream's southern side, having first descended through meadows from a *jailoo* that has horses and a wooden shelter. From here it is only 1½ hours down to the **Arashan Valley** and the **Altyn Arashan hostels**, where a hot bath may be enjoyed. It is possible to spend the night here instead, camping next to one of the hostels or a little further up the valley. From Altyn Arashan it is an easy descent of about three hours along the valley to the Ak-Suu Sanatorium turn-off, following a rock-strewn dirt track which is murder to drive on but a pleasure to walk along. Transport can be prearranged for a pick-up at the bridge at Ak-Suu, or you could catch a passing Karakol-bound *marshrutka* from the sanatorium or continue on a little further to the village of Teploklyuchenka, from where there is plentiful public transport to Karakol.

For the really intrepid, the route above could be extended by at least one more night by continuing east from Altyn Arashan across the 3,600m **Adyr-Tör Pass** and then descending along the Ak-Suu Valley to the sanatorium or Ak-Suu village, from where public transport is available.

JETI-ÖGÜZ TO ALTYN ARASHAN This trek extends the itinerary above by adding on a leg between Jeti-Ögüz and the Karakol Valley. Beginning at the **Jeti-Ögüz Sanatorium** the route continues south along the valley through the **Valley of Flowers** (Tsvetov Dolina), which is a good place to camp. About 5km further on the gorge of the **Teleti River** leads off to the east. The route follows the river as far as a small confluence a couple of hours upstream. The valley bottom here is another suitable place to erect a tent for the night.

From here, the route climbs sharply to the northeast towards the 3,759m **Teleti Pass**, from where it descends to join the Karakol Valley, a five- to six-hour trek in all. Reaching the Karakol Valley, the river is followed north for two hours as far as the footbridge, where the route to the **Ala-Köl Pass** alongside the **Kurgak-Tör**, detailed above, is followed. Following this route would take a bare minimum of five days and four nights.

KYZYL-SUU TO ALTYN ARASHAN This is as mentioned above but also incorporates a trek up the Chong Kyzyl-Suu Valley, west of Jeti-Ögüz, lengthening the trek by two more days, or three if the trek is started in Kyzyl-Suu village (also known by its Russian name, Pokrovka). West of the Chong Kyzyl-Suu Valley is the **Juukuchak Valley**, which has hot springs, and west of this is the **Juuku Valley**, which follows the course of one of the old Silk Routes south, over the 3,633m Juukuchak Pass to the 4,284m Bedel Pass into China. Apparently it has bones lying around that date from Silk Road times, as well as hot springs and Buddhist rock paintings. It is likely that at least some of the bones date to the Urkun incident of 1916 when many Kyrgyz attempted to flee over the mountains to China (see page 196).

Beginning at the **Jyluu-Suu hot springs**, 20km up the valley from Kyzyl-Suu village, the route follows the **Chong Kyzyl-Suu River** southeast until an old meteorological station is reached where the river splits in two. There is a rustic hot spring pool along the way, 4km short of the weather station. The route follows the course of the left-hand river, the **Kara-Batak**, which is followed until a suitable camping area is reached. From here a steep path climbs to the east alongside a stream and up to the 3,800m **Archa-Tör Pass**. From the pass the route descends along the **Asan-Tukum Gorge** to reach the Jeti-Ögüz Valley after a total of about six hours' hiking from the campsite. At the Jeti-Ögüz Valley, the route heads north and downstream for a few hours before reaching the track along the **Teleti Gorge** and up to the Teleti Pass and the route outlined above.

THE CENTRAL TIEN SHAN (ЦЕНТРАЛЬНЫЙ ТЯНЬ-ШАНЬ)

The corner of the Kyrgyz Republic that wedges itself between Kazakh and Chinese territory to the east of Karakol is indisputably the country's wildest and least accessible region. It is in this region that superlatives abound: the highest mountains, the coldest temperatures, the longest glaciers, the grizzliest mountaineers and the strangest natural phenomena. This is a region of ice, snow and unexplored peaks – too high and inhospitable even for most hardy Kyrgyz nomads. It is home to Kyrgyzstan's highest peak (the second highest in the former USSR), the world's fourth longest glacier, an amazing disappearing lake and, if you believe in that sort of thing, the remote location for the crash landing of a giant UFO.

Unlike the valleys closer to Karakol this is no place for gentle mountain hikes and is really only for committed, experienced mountaineers and those who avail themselves of the support services of guides and porters. Whatever the degree of tactical support enlisted, fitness and stamina are essential. Visiting the area requires a considerable commitment of time, energy and money, but those returning from time spent trekking in the region invariably insist that it is well worth it.

GEOGRAPHY The Central Tien Shan (sometimes spelt Tian Shan) forms the pinnacle of the Tien Shan mountain range, a name that translates from Chinese as 'Celestial Mountains' and which seems highly appropriate. This citadel of high, snow-ravaged mountain peaks is known collectively as Muztag, the 'Ice Mountain', and it is this range of twisted valleys and towering peaks, connected by rivers of ice that is home to Kyrgyzstan's highest mountain, **Pik Pobedy** ('Victory Peak'). At 7,439m, it is a fraction lower than the CIS's highest, Peak Ismoil Somoni (formerly Communism Peak) in Tajikistan that stands at 7,495m.

The bulky peak of Pik Pobedy stands like an enormous rock sentinel watching over the Kyrgyz-Chinese border, but it is the slightly lower guardian of the Kyrgyz-Kazakh border, **Khan Tengri** (7,010m), which is the greater beauty by far. Khan Tengri is a perfect pyramidal icon of a peak that is known locally as Kan-Too ('Blood Mountain'), thanks to the roseate glow its marble upper reaches emit at sunset, almost as if the light comes from within. Khan Tengri, which translates as either 'Lord of the Spirits' or 'Ruler of the Skies', is a slightly controversial member of the 7,000m-plus club, as its geological height is measured as 6,995m and it is only its glacial cap that elevates it to 7,010m. Nevertheless, Khan Tengri has been accepted as one of the former USSR's five peaks above 7,000m, and in Soviet times mountaineers who climbed this, along with the remaining four peaks, were eligible for the state's Snow Leopard Award. Of the five peaks – two in the Kyrgyz Tien Shan, three in the Tajik Pamirs – Pik Pobedy was considered to be the most difficult by far, followed by Khan Tengri.

Pik Pobedy is now officially known as Jengish Chokusu, a Kyrgyz translation of the mountain's Russian name that was given to it at the end of World War II. Rather than a single peak, Pik Pobedy is a massif with several summits along its ridge but only the main summit rises above the 7,000m mark. It is also the most northerly 7,000m rock peak in the world if Khan Tengri, just 16km northeast, is excluded from the equation because of its icy summit.

It is also one of the most deadly, with a very high death toll for climbers. The standard approach to the summit involves a 4km traverse along the mountain's west ridge at an altitude above 7,000m, where many climbers become trapped by storms. The route via the north face is even more treacherous.

Lying beneath both mountains is the 62km-long, 3.5km-wide **South Inylchek Glacier**, which is considered to be the fourth longest glacier in the world. Together with its northern arm, which wraps around the ridge of Khan Tengri like an icy tuning fork, the glacier locks up a vast volume of water that is released as melt-water to supply the Inylchek River and the Sary-Jaz, which flows southward into China's Tarim Valley.

The glacier covers a total area of 583km² and the ice in places is as much as 540m thick. Located close to where the glacier's northern arm, the **North Inylchek Glacier**, joins its southern partner, a remarkable blue, iceberg-filled lake called **Lake Merzbacher** forms every summer as the glaciers melt. Every year, usually around mid-August, the lake bursts its ice banks and water and icebergs dramatically explode from the lake, draining it to suddenly swell the waters of the Inylchek River below. In some years the phenomenon occurs twice.

HISTORY The Chinese were the first to explore this foreboding mountain zone, but it was not until the middle of the 19th century that European explorers penetrated the region. The Russian Pyotr Semyonov Tyan-Shansky was the first, for which he was given his honorary epithet 'Tyan-Shansky' by the Tsar.

In 1857, Semyonov Tyan-Shansky followed the course of the Inylchek River upstream to discover the glacier. His pioneering journey was succeeded in the 1870s by expeditions by the geographer and biologist Nikolai Przhevalsky and then, just after the turn of the 20th century, by the German geographer, Gottfried Merzbacher. Merzbacher failed in his attempt to climb Khan Tengri but he did succeed in discovering a highly unusual lake that would become named after him, in addition to proving that Khan Tengri did not lie on the main watershed of the Tien Shan, as had been previously thought.

The area was completely closed to outsiders during the Soviet era, although some climbers from within the Soviet Union were able to come here, with permission from the military authorities, to experience the ultimate mountaineering challenge the USSR had to offer. Khan Tengri was first climbed from the south in 1931 by a Ukrainian team, and from the north for the first time in 1964. Pik Pobedy-Jengish Chokusu was not climbed officially until 1956, although alternative accounts claim that the peak had previously been climbed in 1939, when the climbers had believed it to be less than 7,000m.

TREKKING IN THE CENTRAL TIEN SHAN
The only viable time for non-winter alpinists is high summer – July to August. Border permits will be needed for any sort of visit (see page 59) and should be organised well in advance. Mountaineering permits are necessary for all climbing expeditions.

Several tour companies arrange expeditions to the area for both trekkers and climbers and all of these operate base camps in the Inylchek Valley. The usual overland route into the region is via the depressed and almost deserted tin-mining town of **Inylchek**. Until the 1990s, Inylchek was a small town of around 5,000 citizens who worked in the mines and factories of the town. Now fewer than 20 families remain, determinedly staying on by adapting to a far more rural mode of life.

Consequently, Inylchek is rather like a ghost town: an eerie sort of place with empty streets and abandoned *khrushchevki* apartment blocks. Beyond Inylchek, a dirt road continues to **Maida Adyr**, a five-hour drive from Karakol, from where it is a four- to six-day trek to the base camps. Maida Adyr itself is little more than a helicopter landing pad, a tent camp which provides basic food and accommodation needs, and a clutch of the ubiquitous recycled freight wagons seen all over the country. There is another, rather nicer, base camp run by Tour Khan Tengri at **At-Jailoo** further up the valley, which has both yurts and wooden huts to stay in, in addition to space for tents (*a bed in a hut costs about US$30, in a yurt US$18, in a tent $9, 3 meals US$20*).

Helicopters are used to provide fast and expensive transport in the region, linking Maida Adyr with the base camps, and spectacular pleasure flights over the glaciers can also be arranged. The helicopters are chartered by the tour companies but it may be possible to pay for a ride to the base camps if they have room and you are travelling independently. They are not cheap: fares start at around US$100 per person per flight or US$2,000–2,500 to hire the whole helicopter.

Trekking from Maida Adyr to the base camps at the Inylchek Glacier takes four to six days. It is important to have some knowledge of glacier walking and an experienced guide who knows the terrain. The route follows a dirt road along the Inylchek River for 15km before arriving at a confluence with another river where there is a good campsite. From here, it is another day's hike to Chong-Tash, which

This unique lake, 3,500m above sea level, was first discovered by the German mountaineer and geographer Gottfried Merzbacher in 1902. While on an expedition for the Russian Geographical Association, attempting to reach Khan Tengri peak by way of the South Inylchek Glacier, Merzbacher observed the unique phenomenon of a glacial lake that lost all of its water in the space of just three days.

Making another journey to the same region the following year he was able to observe that the lake had fully replenished its waters and that the filling and rapid draining were actually part of an annual cycle. How this process takes place is unclear. The lake first starts to appear when an ice dam blocks the gorge and melt-water starts to accumulate from the glacier. There is a higher basin 400m above the lower one and it is icebergs that have plunged down from this which combine to form the ice dam. The lower lake grows to around 3.5km in length and 1.2km wide until a point is reached, usually in mid-August, when the lake's waters have risen to such a point that the ice dam is lifted and the accumulated water suddenly breaks free underneath the floating ice creating a great deal of noise and vibration, which causes local landslides.

This is one theory; another suggests that the pressure of the water causes the ice wall to deform, opening cracks that allow the water to escape. A third theory links the drainage of the lake with a canyon in the South Inylchek Glacier, which when it fills with water and subsequently drains away, it is suggested, creates a suction effect that draws the water away from the glacial lake. Whatever the true science of the matter, the rapid drainage causes floods in the valleys of the Inylchek and Sary-Jaz rivers for about a week afterwards. The lake is then left completely empty until it starts to fill the next spring, repeating the annual cycle.

Although the emptying of the lake might appear to be a unique occurrence, there are a handful of similar events that take place elsewhere in the world – in Iceland, Greenland and Switzerland – but it is at Kyrgyzstan's Merzbacher Lake that the phenomenon is so regular and relatively reliable. The timing of the August event is not written in stone, however – in 2003, it took place in July and in other years it has been as late as September. In some years an additional flood has occurred in either the spring or late summer.

is marked by a 9m-high boulder on the left bank (hence Chong-Tash, which means 'Big Stone'). This has a freshwater spring and is another good place to camp.

From Chong-Tash, the standard route soon reaches the glacier, which it crosses diagonally, climbing all the time. Then the right-hand moraine is followed, sometimes on the glacier itself, sometimes beside it. **Merzbacher's Glade** is reached after a long day's (eight to ten hours) hike from Chong-Tash, at the point just below where the northern arm of the glacier joins the main southern one. From Merzbacher Glade, a side trip directly to the north leads to Merzbacher Lake after a few hours' ice walking. The main trek continues past several other glaciers flowing into it to reach **Red Moraine**, another campsite. Beyond Red Moraine it is another five- to seven-hour glacier hike to the South Inylchek Glacier base camps.

Another tough, and even wilder, approach is to make a four- to six-day trek from the town of **Jergalan** along the Jergalan Valley and across the Sary-Jaz mountains to

Chong-Tash, near the foot of the South Inylchek Glacier. It is a two-day trek from **Maida Adyr**, or another four days along the glacier, to reach the base camps. This route can be shortened by arranging 4x4 transportation in Karakol to drive as far as Echkili-Tash, from where it takes two or three days to trek to Chong-Tash.

There is no public transport into the area apart from a single daily bus to Jergalan from Karakol. It should also be possible to hire transport to go as far as Inylchek town from Karakol but a 4x4 is necessary.

TOUR OPERATORS Be sure to ask all the questions that you think you need to before committing to a tour in this region, and check carefully on things like food and equipment, and *exactly* what services they offer. It is also wise to check how much walking you will be expected to do each day, and what level of fitness is expected. As well as treks to the Inylchek Glacier, Merzbacher Lake and the base camps, some companies offer the option of an ascent of 4,832m Pik Diki, which is considered to be a 'trekking peak'; it's an eight- to ten-hour round trip from the base camp.

Several **Bishkek**-based companies, plus one in Karakol, offer itineraries of different lengths to the Central Tien Shan region. In **Karakol**, many of the tour and trekking agencies are able to offer tours and support services (see page 174).

Dostuck Trekking Igemberdieva 42/1, Bishkek; \(0312) 545 455, 503 082; e dostuck@saimanet. kg; www.dostuck.com.kg
ITMC Tien Shan Molodaya Gvardiya 1a, Bishkek; \(0312) 651 404; e itmc@elcat.kg; www.itmc. centralasia.kg

Kan Tengri Expeditions Kasteyev 10, Almaty, Kazakhstan; \+7 7272 910 200, \910 880; e info@kantengri.kz; www.kantengri.kz

RED TAPE Trekking anywhere beyond Inylchek requires a **border zone permit**. These can be obtained through tour operators in Karakol, but are best arranged well in advance as they usually take several days to organise. **Climbing permits** are required for actual attempts on the peaks themselves and, similarly, these should be arranged with a local operator well in advance of your trip.

LAKE ISSYK-KUL'S SOUTHERN SHORE

The southern shore of Lake Issyk-Kul is quite markedly different from the northern shore. It lacks the Soviet-era sanatoriums of the north coast and, as a whole, it is a poorer, drier region, with a more remote feel. There are fewer opportunities for organised bathing than on the north shore, although for the more adventurous there are plenty of options for wild camping close to the lake. There is scope for adventure away from the water, too: many of the valleys which run down to the lake from the Terskey Ala-Too range to the south are rarely visited by foreign visitors and are ripe for exploration.

Heading west along the southern shore from Karakol, the first places of any real significance for visitors are the twin villages of Barskoon and Tamga, but before these there are one or two places that may warrant a brief look.

Orgochor is a small Kyrgyz village just east of Kyzyl-Suu, which is said to have had an internment camp for Japanese prisoners of war during World War II. The village is now home to the **Historical Museum of Jeti-Ögüz**, a museum which was set up in 1998 to document local history from a Kyrgyz (rather than Russian or Soviet) viewpoint – all labelling is in Kyrgyz only. The village is the birthplace of Sartikiev Telekmat (1799–1863), who served as ambassador to the Kokand khanate

6

and both China and Russia during the mid-19th century. The village has a monument to Telekmat, who was also a talented singer and orator, opposite the museum, a gift from the Kumtor mining company. On the edge of the village, just before Kyzyl-Suu, there are four Scythian *kurgani* that date from between the 6th and 4th centuries BC. Between the village and the lake is a scrubby isolated hill where a winding road leads past the village graveyard up to the radio transmission station at the top. From here, there are panoramic views of the whole eastern end of Lake Issyk-Kul.

The village of **Saruu**, which is reached after passing through the roadside sprawl of Kyzyl-Suu at the head of the Chong Kyzyl-Suu Valley (see page 189), also has a number of Scythian burial mounds in its vicinity, which date from the 7th–6th centuries BC and measure 20–70m in diameter and 3–8m in height. There are yet more *kurgani* west of the village: 20 or so that stretch in a line along the east bank of the Juuku River.

The route up the Juuku Valley is, like the Barskoon Valley below, an old Silk Road route, and evidence of this may be seen in Buddhist rock paintings and the bones of those who failed to make it. There is also a 19th-century mausoleum in the valley, Gumbez Balchak, 5km south of Saruu, which is built of brick and wood and is the work of artisans from Kashgar in Xinjiang.

Darkhan is the next village to the west and this has another burial mound that dates from between the 6th and 4th centuries BC, which, measuring some

THE STRANGE TALE OF THE SHAITAN MAZAR UFO

In the early morning of 28 August 1991, an extremely large flying object, described as being 600m long and 100m in diameter, showed up over the Caspian Sea, tracked by the Soviet radar station on the Mangyshlak Peninsula. The radar showed the object to be travelling at a speed of around 960km/h and at an altitude of 6,600m.

Alarmed by this unexpected manifestation, the Soviet authorities immediately broadcast a 'friend or foe' radio signal but it received no answer. Knowing that no test flights were taking place in the vicinity, the operators at Mangyshlak issued a military alert. Two MiG-29 fighters were diverted from a routine mission to intervene over the Aral Sea and their pilots were shocked to see a gigantic zeppelin-shaped object when the vessel came within range. The UFO was described as being metallic grey, with two portholes towards its front and strange green symbols at the rear. There was still no response from the craft so it was decided that the pilots should fire warning shots across its flight path, forcing it to follow the MIGs to land. However, the pilots could not fire, as when they drew close there was no response from their flight controls, so they had to abandon their mission. As they withdrew, the pilots regained control over their planes and were able to make a safe landing.

Ground radar continued to track the vessel, which made a zigzag course back over the Aral Sea at an astonishing speed estimated at 6,800km/h. After a total of 45 minutes of radar tracking, the craft vanished from the radar screen somewhere in the region of Lake Issyk-Kul in Kyrgyzstan.

By the end of September, rumours started to emerge that a large object had crashed in the Shaitan Mazar Gorge near the source of the Sary-Jak River in the Central Tien Shan mountains of eastern Kyrgyzstan. Witnesses from the region claimed they had seen an immense object crash deep into the mountains of the east. At the same time, rumours spread that some locals had found the crash

100m in diameter and 12m in height, is the largest *kurgan* in Kyrgyzstan. This can be reached by taking the road that heads towards the lake at the western end of the village, leading past a cemetery. After a couple of kilometres the mound can be seen, impressively set among arable fields to the right. A dirt track leads right up to it.

Just before Barskoon is reached, the road passes through the lakeside village of **Ak-Terek** which has no facilities for visitors, but which is a good place to experience traditional village life unaltered by even the low-impact version of tourism that is characteristic of Kyrgyzstan.

BARSKOON (БАРСКООН) *Telephone code: 03946*

Across the river from its immediate neighbour, Tamga, and the first of the two to be reached from Karakol, this predominantly Kyrgyz village is set back a little from the main road, just inland from the shoreline. Barskoon stands at the head of the Barskoon Valley – an interesting diversion that is a fragment of one of the strands of the old Silk Road. There is an impressive waterfall, popular with domestic tourists, 20km along the valley road, but this same well-maintained road is also the approach to the controversial Kumtor gold mine, a Kyrgyz-Canadian venture with a less than pristine environmental record.

site but had received radiation burns when they approached the wreckage. An expedition was set up to investigate. A UFO group travelled into the mountains for two weeks but could not find any evidence of a crash and eventually had to leave, suffering from frostbite and exposure.

A report came to the attention of the same Russian UFO group in November 1991 that the Russian Air Force had found the crash site, but while attempting to hoist part of the wreckage from the snow a helicopter had crashed, killing all on board. As it was winter there was no opportunity to explore the crash site further until the following year. The group prepared to make a journey to the site in June 1992. This time they found the crash site, but as they approached to within 1,000m of the craft they suffered from an overwhelming sense of dread and fatigue. In addition, the group's instruments started to fail spectacularly, as if they were being affected by a powerful electro-magnetic field emanating from the wreckage. They were not able to approach closer than 800m as some of the team were experiencing radiation burns. Photographs were taken but these turned out to be hopelessly overexposed and useless, as did the video tapes they tried to record.

A third journey was planned a few months later but this was ill-fated and ended up being delayed for six years. By the time they returned the UFO was gone, as was the Russian helicopter.

Whether the name or location of Shaitan Mazar ('Devil's Grave') has any real bearing on the story – or is merely there for dramatic effect – is unclear. The district of Shaitan Mazar, close to the source of the Sary-Jak River, already holds some mystical intrigue for the local population as there is said to be a sacred stream here which is gifted with mysterious healing properties. Today, the name Shaitan Mazar will forever be linked with the strange, and perhaps apocryphal, incident that is claimed to have taken place on the eve of the birth of the Kyrgyz Republic. It is also the name adopted by an American heavy metal band.

6

Barskoon village grew up around a military post, while its neighbour Tamga, across the river, developed as the location for a military hospital. Mahmud al-Kashgari, an 11th-century scholar, came from the Barskoon area, from the Silk Road settlement of Barskhan which lay somewhere near the present-day village. The scholar, who was also known as Barskhani, travelled a great deal during his lifetime: he compiled the first comparative Turkic language dictionary while resident in Baghdad but ended his days in Kashgar in Xinjiang where his tomb still stands.

If you wish to buy a yurt, and are prepared to deal with the bureaucracy of shipping the thing home, then this is a good place to do it. The **Ak-Örgö yurt workshop** (*Lenin 93;* \ *267 54;* e *mekenbek_1958@mail.ru*) run by Mekenbek Osmonaliev manufactures yurts that sell for around US$6,000 for a full-sized model. The workshop is also open to visitors and Mekenbek or one of his assistants (no English spoken) will be happy to show you all the stages of the construction process. Mekenbek also plays a mean *komuz*. There are plans to create a yurt camp here in the future from where guided trips up the Barskoon Valley will be offered.

GETTING THERE AND AWAY Buses and minibuses running along the southern shore of Lake Issyk-Kul between Karakol and Balykchy will drop off and pick up at the junction on the main road. There are several minibuses each day to and from Barskoon from Karakol's southern bus station by the stadium; check for precise times. The fare is 80som each way.

TOUR OPERATOR Based in Barskoon, **Shepherd's Way Trekking** (♠ *961 33;* e *shepherd@elcat.kg; www.kyrgyztrek.com; in Bishkek, PO Box 2032;* \ *(0312) 434 532,* \ *661 392;* m *(0772) 518 315;* e *shepherd@elcat.kg*) is a family company run by brothers Ishen and Rash Obolbekov, and Ishen's wife Gulmira. They specialise in horse treks in the surrounding region, offering a total of 20 itineraries for riders of varying abilities. They can also organise visits to traditional eagle hunters in the area. The Obolbekovs have a genuine interest in local culture and are enthusiastic in sharing their love of horses and the Kyrgyz landscape. They speak excellent English (they worked as English teachers back in Soviet times) and are very professional and experienced, having been in business for the best part of 20 years. They have many clients who return year after year.

WHERE TO STAY AND EAT Most of the accommodation options are over the river in Tamga, although Shepherd's Way may be able to help find beds in the village.

THE BARSKOON VALLEY The road that leads up the Barskoon Valley to the waterfall and Kumtor mine is reached 1km west of Barskoon village, turning left off the main road. The route up the Barskoon Valley from the village was formerly one of the strands of the Silk Road that led the way to the 4,284m Bedel Pass into China, a route that is no longer open. There are said to be human and animal bones still lining the route to the pass in places, which rather than being the ancient remains of Silk Road travellers are the bones of Kyrgyz herders and their livestock who perished from exposure during the mass exodus which followed the Urkun incident in 1916. A minimum estimate of 100,000 Kyrgyz are said to have died in their attempt to flee persecution from the Russian Tsarist forces.

The valley road, the A364, serves as the main thoroughfare for traffic travelling to and from the Kumtor gold mine, hence its well-maintained condition (see box, page 199). The road is wetted with water twice a day to keep the dust down and help prevent glacial melting. Transport to the mine tends to travel in large convoys on specified days that are best avoided if at all possible.

There are **waterfalls** above the road approximately 20km from Barskoon village, and the grassy meadow at the start of the trail to reach these is a favourite place for picnics, with temporary summer yurts selling *shashlyk* and *kumys*. The lower waterfall is quite close to the road and an easy walk, although the upper falls, glimpsed through the trees above, are more difficult to reach. On the roadside here is a bust of Soviet cosmonaut Yuri Gagarin (he holidayed at the nearby Tamga sanatorium after his pioneering spin in space in 1961); there is also another bust of Gagarin with a cosmonaut helmet on a plinth on the picnic meadow opposite. A couple of kilometres before reaching the waterfalls and the Gagarin monuments, there is a strange monument of a lorry mounted on a plinth above the roadside – a warning to Kumtor mine traffic that they should drive carefully, perhaps?

Beyond the waterfall the road continues towards the mine and the **Barskoon Pass** at 3,754m amid wild, treeless scenery, although permits are required to get anywhere near the mine. From the top of the pass, the road drops down slightly past a small lake to the wide Ara-Bel Valley, before rising again to the higher (4,021m) **Söök Pass**, which leads down to the Naryn River and the military post of Kara-Sai. To continue east from here along the track to Ak-Shyrak, another military post and the end of the road, requires a border permit. It should be borne in mind that although this road is shown on some maps as continuing on to Inylchek, this is no longer possible, as many of the bridges maintained in Soviet times are now permanently down.

Trekking from the Barskoon Valley

There are a number of **trekking routes** that lead off the Barskoon Valley, both east and west. One recommended route follows the Burkan Valley west to eventually reach the Balgart Valley and Kichi-Naryn River to Naryn beyond, a spectacularly wild tract of true wilderness, with the narrow valley hemmed in by snow-capped peaks on both north and south sides. Although this route is just about possible on both **mountain bikes** and **horseback**, it passes through large tracts of difficult, unpopulated terrain and to attempt it unsupported requires adequate preparation. It also requires the occasional crossing of shallow but freezing cold rivers. The Burkan Valley is reached by following faint and unclear tracks, which lead to the west after the big lake at about 3,600m along the main road. This track climbs gradually past some smaller lakes, before passing through a ravine to reach the Burkan Valley.

North of, and parallel to, the Burkan Valley, leading west off the Barskoon Valley before the Barskoon Pass is reached, is the valley of Kerege-Tash, which offers further possibilities leading west towards the Jyluu-Suu, Balgart and Kichi-Naryn valleys. Sometimes this route is impassable because of swollen rivers, so seek local advice. Alternatively, a more circular trek could be made by turning north from the valleys of Kerege-Tash or Jyluu-Suu, to return to Lake Issyk-Kul over high passes by way of the Ton, Tosor or Tamga valleys. With the right documentation, long treks east beyond Ak-Shyrak are also a possibility, even as far as the Sary-Jaz River in the Central Tien Shan massif.

A number of trekking companies offer combination 4x4, foot and horse treks in this region. They include Kyrgyz Travel, Alltournative, Ecotour and Shepherd's Way, among others (see pages 53–5).

Lying just west of Barskoon, across the Barskoon River, along an approach road marked by a MiG jet fighter on a plinth, Tamga is a smallish village which has a predominantly Russian character and population, in contrast to its larger, more Kyrgyz, neighbour, Barskoon. Tamga means 'Seal' or 'Letter' in Kyrgyz and the village takes its name from a Tibetan Buddhist-inscribed rock, **Tamga Tash**, which lies along the Tamga River gorge at some distance from the village. Tamga is a quiet, pretty place, with a sanatorium, lush orchards dripping with apricots in summer, and a few streets lined with traditional Russian wooden houses. It also has the benefit of a beach and an area for camping near the lakeshore. Because it has a number of accommodation options, it is a good choice for a relaxing stopover on the southern shore.

Yuri Gagarin famously holidayed here after taking part in the world's first manned space flight in 1961. The **sanatorium** where he stayed is still open for business, although it has certainly experienced leaner times since Kyrgyz independence. It was purportedly built at the end of World War II by Japanese prisoners of war and the grounds of the complex, which incorporate pavilions, parkland walkways and gardens, as well as accommodation, cover a considerable area, stretching from its entrance near the town bazaar down to the lakeshore.

The village's **beach** beside the main road is a 15-minute walk from the centre of the village. The coarse sandy beach lies in front of a marshy tree-covered area which is home to a considerable mosquito population, so insect repellent is a good idea for those choosing to bathe in the lake here. Although this a popular place for swimming, picnicking and camping, the beach at Tosor, 6km to the west, is said to be better.

The village itself has just two principal streets: the one that leads to the coast road and the beach, past orchards and a silver statue of a grim-faced soldier with a machine gun, and the main street, Issyk-Kulskaya, which has the village's shops (mostly in recycled railway wagons), and the sanatorium and bazaar at its western end.

GETTING THERE AND AWAY As with Barskoon, it is possible to pick up a bus or a minibus heading along the southern shore road; the bus stop is by the beach and vehicles can be flagged down here in either direction. There are also direct minibuses (*90som*) to Tamga from Karakol's southern bus station. These leave during the morning and afternoon, take two hours, and terminate at Tamga's small bazaar, near the entrance to the sanatorium.

WHERE TO STAY AND EAT There are a few **guesthouses** in the village itself. **Camping** can be had for free next to the village beach, although insects (ants and mosquitoes after dusk) might be a problem, as might the night-time noise from the radios and karaoke machines of some fellow campers.

The village of **Tosor**, just to the west, also has a beach for camping, as well as a **yurt camp** overlooking the lake from June to September which is run by Dostuck Trekking (*www.dostuck.com.kg; FB $$$*).

🏠 **Askar & Tamara Guesthouse** (12 rooms) Issyk-Kulskaya 3; \ 253 61; m 0773 988 449, 0550 326 914; e timnyc@mail.ru. This welcoming guesthouse is in a pink-washed building next door to the bazaar & sanatorium, close to where the bus stops. It has very good food, pleasantly decorated rooms, indoor toilet facilities & hot showers. There's also an orchard garden & outside terrace. Tamara speaks excellent English & can provide advice & help organise local sightseeing trips to the Barskoon Valley & Tamga Tash; her cheerful husband Askar can provide a taxi service on request. **$$**

🏠 **Tamga Guesthouse** (7 rooms) Ozyornaya 3; ☏ 953 33. This popular guesthouse, close to the beach & identified by a hand-painted sign outside, is an attractive, 2-storey Russian house with a pleasant garden. The toilet & bathing facilities are shared & there is a sauna. Good views of the lake & the Terskey Ala-Too range can be had from the windows of the upstairs rooms & there is a rooftop observation deck. As the guesthouse for the Bishkek-based Kyrgyz Travel it tends to fill quickly in season & so it is best to call ahead. The guesthouse can organise horse tours in the region & the proprietor, Zhenya Nikoforov, can advise on directions to, or provide a guide to visit, Tamga Tash. B&B **$$**

🏠 **Flora Guesthouse** Issyk-Kulskaya 18; 📱 0543 700 179. A few doors up from Askar & Tamara, next to the telephone office, this friendly place has 5 rooms with good beds; toilet in the garden. **$**

OTHER PRACTICALITIES There is a **general store** at either end of Issyk-Kulskaya, together with a few railway carriages along its length which sell vegetables and

---

THE KUMTOR GOLD MINE

The Kumtor open-pit gold mine has been in operation since 1997 as a joint Canadian-Kyrgyz venture. The gold deposits here, in an area 4,000m above sea level, are so rich – an estimated 700 tonnes – that the opening of the Kumtor mine has made Kyrgyzstan the third most important gold-mining state in the CIS, and the income from the mine accounts for one-tenth of Kyrgyzstan's GDP. However, the mine and its operating company KOC, a subsidiary of the Canadian firm Cameco, have come under a great deal of criticism for both the mine safety record for its workers and for its environmental record.

The worst environmental damage took place in May 1998 when a drunken lorry driver crashed *en route* to the mine, spilling almost two tonnes of sodium cyanide into the Barskoon River. As well as obvious environmental repercussions, the spill had a deleterious effect on the region's tourist industry and more than half the holiday reservations made by would-be visitors from fellow CIS countries were cancelled.

More seriously, several local people died of poisoning and dozens underwent hospitalisation, despite the announcement that there was 'no need to panic' and 'no ecological damage is expected'. Since then there have been additional environmental and human disasters connected with the mine: 70 litres of nitric acid were spilled in the same year as the cyanide incident and in 2000, 1.65 tonnes of ammonium nitrate were leaked while being transported. In 2002, a Kyrgyz worker died as a result of the collapse of a pit wall. Sickness and mortality rates in the region continue to be higher than average.

Following this sorry track record, there has been some local pressure to close down the mine, and the road to the mine was blocked for ten days during political protests in late 2005 and again in 2007. Protesters blocked the road once more in May 2013, demanding that the mine be nationalised. Since 2012 Kyrgyzstan has had a 33% stake in the mining company, although the mine itself is 100% owned by the Canadian company, Centerra Gold. In recent years the company has been keen to improve its image and has invested in numerous local development projects as well as attempting to combat environmental issues like glacial melting due to dust.

staple items. A larger **supermarket** stands at the crossroads of Issyk-Kulskaya and Dokombaev, the street that leads down to the lake shore. Next to the sanatorium is a small green market. The only café in the village is a basic place inside the sanatorium, just beyond the gates to the left. The **post and telephone office** lies about halfway along Issyk-Kulskaya.

WHAT TO SEE AND DO

Tamga Tash Tamga Tash is a large stone carved with a worn Buddhist inscription that spells out the incantation *Om Mani Padme Hum* ('Hail the jewel in the lotus') in Tibetan script, providing evidence of just how far the sphere of Tibetan Buddhism extended in pre-Islamic times. The stone, which dates from sometime between the 2nd and 8th centuries AD, is located high above the Tamga River, about 6km from the centre of the village, and is difficult to find without local assistance. The stone is partially split into two, which local legend relates as being the result of a strike from the sword of Manas (see page 44). The trees close to the stone are festooned with votive rags, in the same way they would be at any Muslim shrine in the region, but there are also a surprising number of genuine Tibetan prayer flags and Buddhist silk scarves here too. The correct Buddhist thing to do here is to light sprigs of dried juniper and circumambulate the stone three times anticlockwise – your guide will probably instruct you how to do this. Dried juniper burns like a petrol-soaked rag, so watch your fingers. There are said to be more Buddhist stones nearby in the gorge.

The road that reaches Tamga Tash is in poor condition and requires a 4x4 for part of the way, the remainder is done on foot or horseback. The Tamga River gorge lies just west of the village and is reached by heading west from the sanatorium along a dirt road that passes an impressive Kyrgyz graveyard standing on a ridge opposite an electricity transmission station.

Graveyard Just southwest of the village, this is well worth a look, and has two parts to it – one Orthodox Russian and the other Muslim Kyrgyz. As elsewhere in Kyrgyzstan, there are many graves which are surrounded by the wrought iron framework of a skeletal yurt, while others have low adobe walls and arched entrances. Most sport an engraved image of the deceased that has been etched from a photograph.

Sanatorium This is a strange sort of place – a piece of old Soviet culture preserved in aspic. Perhaps it was livelier in Soviet times, but now it seems rather staid, and it is hard to imagine the anticlimax Yuri Gagarin must have felt being confined here for R&R after the unique and very solitary experience of being the first man in space. Outside the peak season in July and August things are very quiet here.

There are a considerable number of both residential and administrative buildings within the complex, and amid the leafy grounds that stretch down towards the lake are sports courts, gardens and a central fountain around which old women gather to sell apricots from buckets in high summer. There are also a few shops selling biscuits, vodka and cigarettes, and a café. The shady gardens of the sanatorium also contain a number of interesting Soviet-era statues and murals, and there is a promenade that leads directly down to the beach from the lower part of the gardens – a more attractive alternative to reaching the beach by road.

BOKONBAEVO (БОКОНБАЕВО) *Telephone code: 03422*

The stretch of road heading west between Tamga and Kaji-Say has some of the most striking scenery along the lake's southern shore. Here, the bare, dry foothills above   *Balbal* stone sculptures are Turkic grave markers that date from between the 6th and 10th centuries (P/S) page 133

right   Tash Rabat, a 15th-century caravanserai located 3,530m above sea level, is one of Kyrgyzstan's most remarkable Silk Road monuments (PH/AWL) pages 236–7

below   The open air petroglyph site near Cholpon-Ata, with animal carvings that date from between around 1500BC and the 1st century AD (PS/S) pages 160–1

bottom   A typically impressive Kyrgyz cemetery at Suusamyr in Chui Province (LM) page 140 *above* Herding sheep along the main road in the Karkara Valley in early summer (LM) pages 164–9

left Traditional Kyrgyz music is usually played on a *komuz*, a three-stringed, guitar-like instrument made of apricot or juniper wood (TT/S) page 46

below *Kumys* (fermented mare's milk) and *korut* (yoghurt balls) for sale at roadside yurts near Ötmök Pass on the main Bishkek–Osh road (LM) pages 63–4

bottom Traditional Central Asian horse games – like *ulak tartysh*, played with a headless goat carcass – are an important part of sporting life in Kyrgyzstan (TT/S) page 48 *above* A variety of loaves on sale at Bosteri market, including flat, round *lepyoshka* and dark Russian rye bread (ELM/S) page 76

right A Kyrgyz family making *ala-kiyiz* out of felt in Bokonbaevo, close to the southern shore of Lake Issyk-Kul (LM) page 40

below Traditional Kyrgyz textiles at the Altyn Kol women's cooperative showroom in Kochkor (TT/S) page 218

bottom Eagle-hunting is a long-established Kyrgyz tradition that probably dates back to the Mongol conquest in the 12th and 13th centuries (TT/S) page 204 left   A congregation leaving the Russian Orthodox Cathedral in Bishkek (LM) page 118

below   The colourful New Mosque in Naryn, built with Saudi financial support in 1993 (R/S) page 231

above left Head to the mountains for white-winged crossbill (*Loxia leucoptera*) (PRP/S) page 6

above right Lake Issyk-Kul is good for breeding birds such as Kentish plover (*Charadrius alexandrines*) (FC/S) page 6

left & below Raptors are particularly well represented in Kyrgyzstan, such as the saker falcon (left; *Falco cherrug*) and golden eagle (below; *Aquila chrysaetos*) (SS) and (TT/S) page 6 *above* Horses at Boz-Salkyn *jailoo* near Bokonbaevo (LM) page 202

right Wild orchid growing in a *jailoo*, Suusamyr Valley, Chui Province (LM)

below The mountains surrounding Lake Issyk-Kul are home to endemic mammal species such as Siberian ibex (*Capra sibirica*) (DG/S) page 7

bottom Wildflower alpine meadow above Arslanbob (PH/AWL) pages 5–6 above   Round, felt-covered yurts have been a centrepiece of Kyrgyz culture for centuries and are a familiar sight throughout the country (TT/S) pages 35–7

left   Constructing a yurt frame at a workshop in Barskoon — yurts are erected entirely without the use of nails (LM) pages 36–7

below   The inside of a yurt with typical brightly coloured decoration and carpeting of felt *shyrdaks* (EP/H/A) pages 39–40

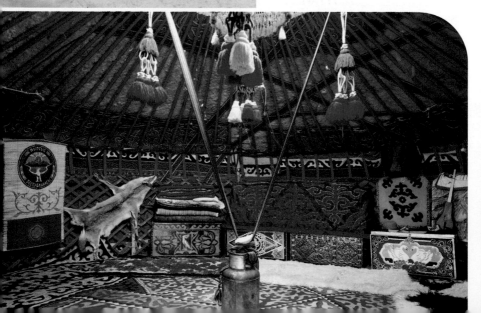

come almost all the way down to the lakeshore, to contrast appealingly with the high snow-topped peaks of the Terskey Ala-Too which lie beyond. Just inland from the lakeside village of Tosor is the **Skazka Valley**, an impressive canyon of red sandstone cliffs and outcrops that have been weathered by the elements to create fantastic shapes that resemble castles and anthropomorphic forms – a popular port of call on many organised group trek itineraries. There are several sandy beaches too: at **Tosor**, where there is a seasonal yurt camp, and then again at the village of **Kaji-Say**, where you will find a concentration of cafés and an information centre which should be able to point you towards any local accommodation possibilities.

Kaji-Say, a former uranium-mining centre and a bit of a post-industrial disaster zone, was the scene of several archaeological digs back in Soviet times, when the remains of a caravanserai dating back to the 10th–12th centuries were discovered. From Kaji-Say, the road continues to hug the shoreline as far as Ton, where there are radon mineral water springs. Here, the road turns inland to shortly arrive at Bokonbaevo, a small town just out of sight of the lake.

Bokonbaevo, which takes its name from a Kyrgyz poet, is the largest settlement along the southern shore between Karakol and Balykchy, and has a mostly Kyrgyz population of around 12,000. Formerly, it was a fairly prosperous town but, as elsewhere in the more industrial zones of the country, it has seen a considerable downturn in its fortunes since independence, and now unemployment, along with its faithful attendants, poverty and alcoholism, is prevalent. Despite its dusty, unprepossessing appearance, Bokonbaevo is not a bad place to stay over for a night and some reasonable homestays have sprung up to accommodate tourists heading into the hills. It has some comfortable places to stay and the town serves as a suitable base for hikes into the largely unexplored hinterland of peaks and valleys which lie to the south. There is also a *shyrdak*-manufacturing collective based in the town, and a visit to a traditional eagle hunter can easily be arranged through the town's CBT representatives.

GETTING THERE AND AWAY Bokonbaevo has four direct buses a day (*around 300som*) that link with Bishkek's West Bus Station, a four-hour drive away; three of these originate or end in Karakol. There are also direct bus services to Karakol (*100som*) and Balykchy (*100som*) with several buses a day. Minibuses and share taxis also stop in the town to provide transport to Balykchy to the west and Karakol, Tamga and the lakeside villages to the east. Most buses leave in the morning or early afternoon.

TOURIST INFORMATION The office of **Community Based Tourism** (*Café Argymak, 2nd floor, Bolot Mambetova;* m *0779 455 045;* e *cbt.kyrgyzstan.bokonbaevo@gmail. com;* ⊕ *10.00–19.00 daily*) is located in the terrace of a café near the bus stand. There's even an indoor yurt here that serves as a display area for information on tours and local homestays. If there's no-one around when you call in then just stand around for a bit and someone should turn up to summon the CBT representative. As well as arranging **accommodation**, CBT's co-ordinator Saltanat Kadyrkulova can organise **treks** in the region and set up **eagle-hunting** demonstrations given a little notice. Tour manager and guide Mir Bazarov (m *0779 182 834*), who speaks English, may also be able to help. Some of the standard treks on offer range from two to seven days and include visits to Skazka Valley, overnight stays in yurt camps at Bel-Tam and Jaychy, visits to Shor-Köl Lake and the sacred mountain of Tash-Tar-Ata, and treks over the Ton Pass to the Jyluu-Suu Valley and Tosor Pass. The

For listings, see pages 202–3

Where to stay
1 Hotel Rahat
2 Musabek Baisetov

Off map
Bel-Tam yurt camp
Boz-Salkyn yurt camp
Guljan
Jaichy yurt camp

Where to eat and drink
3 Café Argymak
4 Café Aydyn-Köl
5 Café Gulzar

Bel-Tam yurt camp,
Jaichy yurt camp,
Balykchy, Bishkek

War
memorial
Town Museum

BOLOT MAMBETOVA
TURUSBEKOVA
KYRGYZSKAYA
TOICHUBEKOVA
SHAKIR USTA
KOLKANOVA

LENINA
TOIGONOV MUKANBET
LENINA

SAKE AIY
Bazaar
CBT
office
Altyn Olmok
('Golden Thimble')

Concrete
town sign

ATAKAN
MUKANBET
Kirchin
store
ATAKAN
Karakol

1
Post &
telephone
office

2

(SKETCH MAP)
Not to scale

BOKONBAEVO

Guljan,
Boz-Salkyn yurt camp,
Kongur-Olön Valley

most ambitious of the treks available is probably a seven- to nine-day horse trek between Bokonbaevo and Naryn via the 3.6km Kongur Ulun Pass and Eki Naryn. Single-day car excursions to Shor-Köl, a small salty lake, and to Kyzyl-Tuu village for felt-making demonstrations, can also be arranged.

WHERE TO STAY Map, above

There is the basic **Hotel Rahat** (m *0777 465 783*, **$$**) on Atakan but you are better off staying at one of the local **CBT guesthouses**. There are also several **yurt camps** in the vicinity, which are an even better bet if you have a couple of days at your disposal. The Bel-Tam yurt camp is close enough to Bokonbaevo to use for an overnight stay rather than staying in the town itself (*taxi, 250som*). All those listed below come recommended and can be booked via CBT.

Guljan Seitek 28; m 0777 406 108. On the edge of Bokonbaevo, this attractively decorated home has Kyrgyz-style rooms & Wi-Fi. Visitors can do hands-on *shyrdak* & felt-making with the women of the house here. English spoken. **$–$$**

Musabek Baisetov Kolkanova 34; 911 15. A very comfortable family home a little out of the town centre with modern bathroom & excellent food. **$**

Bel-Tam yurt camp m 0773 881 129, 0709 881 129; e beltamcamp@mail.ru. A yurt camp 8km north of the town by the lake close to a former Soviet pioneer camp. This has a very peaceful setting & good facilities inc hot showers & flush toilets. Tasty meals served in kitchen yurt or at outside tables. *B&B* **$**, *meals 200som*.

Boz-Salkyn yurt camp (bookable through CBT Bokonbaevo, see page 201) High on a *jailoo* at 2,800m, with views of Lake Issyk-Kul far below, this is reached along a rough road, 18km southeast of Bokonbaevo. With 5 yurts, guests can go horseriding & participate in *kajmak*-making. Various hikes & horse treks available. *B&B* **$**, *meals 200som*.

Jaichy yurt camp m 0773 622 962 (also bookable through CBT Bokonbaevo, see page 201). Situated next to an old Soviet collective farm, 25km from Bokonbaevo, this has 2 comfortable yurts & tasty meals inc *beshbarmak* & *plov*. Horse treks can be made to Shor-Köl salt lake from here. *B&B* **$**, *meals 200som*.

WHERE TO EAT AND DRINK *Map, opposite*

In addition to the homestays (see page 202) there are a few rudimentary cafés in the town centre such as **Café Gulzar** and **Café Aydyn-Köl**, and also the **Café Argymak** behind the CBT office (*all $*).

OTHER PRACTICALITIES
The town has a number of banks with ATMs, like RSK Bank and Optima Bank, both on Bolot Mambetova. There's also an internet club on the same street opposite Café Gulzar.

For everyday shopping there is the unselfconsciously retro **Kirchin** store opposite the bus stand, as well as several more up-to-date shops around the town centre. For souvenirs, **Altyn Oymok** ('Golden Thimble') (*Kyrgyzskaya 73*) is the outlet of a local women's craft collective, set up as a community development project in 1996 to generate income for local women and to encourage innovation in *shyrdak* design. There is a range of *shyrdaks*, hats and other felt goods on sale at reasonable prices.

WHAT TO SEE AND DO
There are few specific sites in the town itself, apart from a museum and a few reminders of the recent Soviet past – a Lenin bust with a hammer and sickle, and an abstract concrete war memorial. In contrast to these Soviet-era reminders, there is a recently built mosque at the corner of Atakan and Turusbekova.

The **Town Museum**, next to the war memorial (*Lenina;* ⊕ *09.00–16.00 Mon–Fri*), has a collection of work by local artists depicting Kyrgyz folk themes. Particularly interesting is the work of Karypbek Ryskeldiyev, a graduate of the Bishkek School of Art, who manipulates the abstract patterns on small stones to represent scenes from everyday Kyrgyz life.

Festivals
CBT organises a folk festival in the area each year in late August. Attractions include hunting with eagles and falcons, exhibitions of traditional crafts, and the opportunity to try national dishes. Advance information about festival dates and designated locations is available from the CBT's main office in Bishkek (✆ *0312 540 069;* e *reservation@cbtkyrgyzstan.kg; www.cbtkyrgyzstan.kg*).

AROUND BOKONBAEVO
This is a fairly unexplored region of the lake's hinterland. The Terskey Ala-Too to the south forms an almost an unbroken ridge of 4,000m-plus peaks, there for the taking for enterprising mountaineers, many of which remain both unclimbed and unnamed.

The pickings are good for trekkers, too: just southwest of the town lies the **Kongur-Olön Valley**, a beautiful and surprisingly populated valley at around 2,200m. This wide, 40km-long swathe of meadows, marshes and gentle slopes offers excellent, uncomplicated trekking opportunities. There is a road running the whole length of the valley from east to west. The valley's eastern end is reached by taking the road south from Bokonbaevo, which loops around to the west at the valley's start. The main village at the eastern end is Temir-Kanat.

To reach the slightly lower, western end of the valley, there is a road that leads south from the main coast road at Kara-Koo to climb to the village of Dön-Talaa. The road south of here turns east towards Kongur-Olön, the village at the western end of the valley, where there are two *gumbez* (mausoleums) just west of the village. There are said to have been 40 of these in the valley originally: one for each warrior who fought alongside a local leader to secure the valley in the 18th century.

A complex of **ancient ruins** which date from the 10–12th centuries has been found at the valley's western end at Bar-Bulak. About 10km east of Kongur-Olön is Toguz-Bulak, the principal village of the valley's western end. A single daily bus

EAGLE-HUNTING IN KYRGYZSTAN

The tradition of hunting with large birds of prey, mainly golden eagles, goes back hundreds of years in Kyrgyzstan, and probably dates back to the Mongol conquest around the 12th and 13th centuries. These days, the art is slowly dying out, and it is only practised by a handful of Kyrgyz and Kazakhs in the region.

Before the collectivisation that took place during the Soviet era, the practice was an integral part of normal *jailoo* life rather than the tourist spectacle it has mostly become today. *Bürkütchülük*, as the practice of hunting with eagles is known in Kyrgyz, is now mostly put on as a demonstration for tourists, but it was not so in the old days, when a whole family, or even a small village, might depend on the eagle hunter's skill to provide a reliable supply of animal protein and fur.

The hunters who practise *bürkütchülük* are obliged to forge an intimate relationship with their birds. The birds are captured as chicks from their nest in the wild, a hazardous and, it must be said, environmentally unsound pursuit that requires scaling precipitous cliffs and avoiding the murderous talons of an enraged and powerful parent. The training process is a highly ritualised procedure that takes three or four years. It has to be done by just one person so that the necessary bond can develop between master and eagle. The birds generally have a life expectancy of up to 40 years and so it often becomes a lifelong relationship. After capture, the eaglets are hooded and placed in a cage with a perch that sways as the hunter sings to the bird to imprint the sound of his voice. When it is almost fully fledged the trainer starts to show the bird the hides and furs of the animals it will hunt, and training continues with the eagle learning to pursue a fox fur tied to a galloping horse.

Some birds fail and cannot be trained, but those that succeed repay all of their master's effort with intense loyalty: the hunter has effectively become the bird's parent. The relationship between hunter and bird is so close that Talgarbek, one of Bokonbaevo's established *münüshkör* ('trainers'), jokes that his relationship with his golden eagle Tamara is closer than the one he has with his wife!

To carry the eagle on hunting forays, a special device, a *baldak*, is fitted to the saddle to support the rider's arm. The bird hunts mostly foxes, fawns and other small animals, although they are capable of killing young wolves on occasion. A skilled combination of hunter and eagle is said to be capable of catching 50–60 foxes, a dozen badgers, a couple of lynx and four wolves in a normal four-month hunting season, which begins in late autumn. The displays staged for visitors usually take place outside of this season, and with no snow on the ground prey is harder to find, and so a semi-tame hare or rabbit is released from a sack for demonstration purposes.

Whatever the realities of Kyrgyz life over the past century, the tradition of eagle-hunting is hanging on mainly due to the interest in nomadic culture that the foreign visitors bring. *Bürkütchülük* is often a hereditary calling that is passed from father to son but, as young people move the towns and pursue other jobs, the art is going slowly into decline. Fortunately there are still many eagle hunters in Bokonbaevo, and men like Talgarbek have several apprentices eager to continue the tradition.

leaves Bokonbaevo for the valley each afternoon; otherwise, a taxi can be hired for around 500–700som.

The Bishkek-based trekking company Ecotour (*www.ecotour.kg*) has a well-equipped **yurt camp** in the valley at Temir-Kanat, in the east, and also at Tuura-Suu, south of Bokonbaevo, just beyond the eastern limit of the valley. The yurt camps come complete with solar-heated water for washing, guided horse-hire and options for demonstrations of Kyrgyz folklore that include music and eagle-hunting.

Immediately south of Bokonbaevo, close to the village of Tuura-Suu, are the remains of an 8th-century settlement, **Khan Dëbë**. Although there is little to see other than a gateway and a 1km stretch of fortifications, a large amount of pottery has been found at the site that dates from between the 8th and 12th centuries. A taxi from Bokonbaevo should cost around 350som for the round trip, including waiting time.

East of Tuura-Suu, about 20km from Bokonbaevo, is the 3,847m peak of **Tash-Tar-Ata**, which is considered sacred by many locals. The top of the mountain has a small flat area where Manas is said to have lived while protecting the Kyrgyz from their enemies (see page 44). There is a stone pot in the ground here and it is believed that in order for young men to be strong they have to climb the mountain and drink from the vessel, asking for Manas's blessing. Surrounding the area are stone pillars known as the Forty Soldiers of Manas. The best way to reach the top is to walk up the grassy slopes on the mountain's southern side rather than approach from the north, which is densely forested. CBT Bokonbaevo can organise one-day car and hiking excursions here.

THE SOUTHWEST SHORE

The route to Balykchy, west of Bokonbaevo, passes through a dry, scrubby, 'badlands' landscape which is almost like semi-desert. The road veers well away from the lake here, but those determined enough to find a way down to the shoreline will find some excellent, isolated campsites by the water. This is probably the most unspoiled and least visited sector of the lake's shoreline and is an area ripe for exploration. The beautiful stretch of shoreline around the villages of Kara-Talaa and Ottuk is part of the Issyk-Kul Nature Park and is an excellent region for birdwatchers. The award-winning Kyrgyz film *Beshkempir* was shot around here, in the village of Bar-Bulak, near Kara-Koo.

South of the main road, between the villages of Ak-Say and Kyzyl-Tuu, is the **Kök-Say Gorge**, where there is the Jaichy yurt camp (book through CBT in Bokonbaevo; see page 201). Ecotour (*www.ecotour.kg*) has yurt camps near **Ak-Say**, where there is the opportunity to ride camels, and at **Kara-Talaa** further west, where a *shyrdak*-making workshop may be visited. There are several Scythian burial mounds in the area. Close to the lakeshore near the village of Kyzyl-Tuu is the small, very salty **Tüz-Köl Lake**, where it is possible to float without sinking, rather like a miniature Dead Sea. The lake is often simply referred to as Shor-Köl – 'Salty Lake'. Further west at **Ottuk** village, where the road rejoins the shoreline, there is a Lenin bust with 15 flagpoles (one for each republic of the former USSR) and a yurt camp belonging to the Neman tour company.

7

Talas Province

Talas Province (Таласская область), in Kyrgyzstan's little-visited northwestern corner, stands apart from much of the rest of the country for reasons of geography. The main road that leads here comes not from Bishkek but from Taraz in Kazakhstan and, almost cut off from the rest of eastern and central Kyrgyzstan by the high peaks of the Ala-Too range, it is easy to imagine that the province looks as much to its giant neighbour as it does to Bishkek. In reality, this is not the case at all, and for those who take the trouble to reach here, Talas shows a face that could hardly be any more typically Kyrgyz. After all, it is here that the Manas legend has its epicentre, at the museum and *gumbez* of the Manas complex outside the provincial capital (see page 210).

The smallest of Kyrgyzstan's *oblasts* with an area of just 11,440km², this province has the regional capital of Talas Valley as its dead centre, midway along the valley of the same name that runs east to west. North of the valley, the Kyrgyz range defines the frontier with Kazakhstan; to the south the loftier peaks of the Talas Ala-Too separate the province from Jalal-Abad Province and the Chatkal Valley across the 3,302m Kara-Buura Pass. Just west of here, Uzbekistan's far northern Piskom mountain range prods Talas Province with a finger of convoluted political geography. On the frontier here, at 4,484m, stands the province's highest point which, appropriately enough, is called Manas Peak.

The Talas Valley itself has witnessed some pivotal events in central Asian history. It was here, after all, just over the border in present-day Kazakhstan somewhere near Taraz, that the Battle of Talas River was fought against the Tang Chinese in AD751; Sogdians and Turks gritted their teeth to reluctantly join forces with invading Arabs in order to defeat what they perceived to be the greater enemy, thus ending Chinese hegemony in the region and ushering in Islam, still the major faith across central Asia (see page 10). The conflict was also central to the spread of the paper-making process to the West, which hitherto had been a well-kept Chinese secret. Whatever the historical chronicles tell of earth-shaking battles in the 8th century, petroglyphs and traces of Stone Age settlements indicate that the valley has a far older pedigree.

More recently, a thousand protesters took to the streets in Talas on 6 April 2010, railing against government corruption and rising living costs. They stormed government buildings and briefly took civil servants hostage before being pushed back by security forces. Violence in Talas spread swiftly to Bishkek and was a significant step in the overthrowing of President Bakiyev. A number of buildings were damaged in the rioting, and a few still bear their battle scars.

TALAS (ТАЛАС)   *Telephone code: 03422*

HISTORY The area around Talas has been settled for more than a thousand years, but the town did not develop until the Russians came in the mid to late 19th century.

TALAS

Bus station

FLOW

Talas

0 ———— 500m
0 ———— 500yds

N

Bradt

CHINGIZ AITMATOV

Manas Ordu
Complex (15km),
Bishkek

World War II
memorial & mosque

Central
park

City administrative
building

Kyrgyz Telecom
office

BERDIKE BAATYR

(FRUNZE)

TOKTOGUL

CHALAEVA

PUSHKINA

MAYAKOVSKAYA

PANFILOV

NEKRASOVA

LOMONSOVA

O TURDALIEV

SARYGULOVA

MARKSA

SATAEVA

SHAMETOVA

TELMANA

KIROVA

For listings, see page 209

🏠 **Where to stay**

1 Hotel Erlan
2 Hotel Talant

Off map
    CBT homestay

❌ **Where to eat and drink**

3 Chaikhana
4 Komtom

OTORBAEVA

MANAS

Shopping
centre
Bazaar

Energo

Exchange
offices

Minibus
stand

Taxis &
share taxis

A OGOMBAEV

CBT
homestay

The town which exists today was founded in 1877 by Slavic settlers who came to farm the fertile soil of the Talas Valley. A Russian Orthodox church was built in the 1920s to provide for their spiritual welfare and this remains today, along with a fair number of the town's Slavic population.

Before independence, Talas's economic links were closely connected with the larger city of Taraz (formerly Dzhambul), further west up the valley, which now belongs to Kazakhstan. When the state frontier became an international one in 1991, and Kazakhstan started to impose rigid border controls, the town was obliged to forge stronger links with Bishkek, although the only road that links Talas with the Kyrgyz capital that does not pass through Kazakhstan has to climb laboriously to 3,326m to summit the Ötmök Pass, before descending to the Chui Valley. Today, Talas is a quiet market town with a population of around 30,000, and is the administrative centre of Talas Province.

Manas, the Kyrgyz national hero and eponymous central figure of the epic cycle, is believed to have been born in the Talas Valley nearby. His mausoleum lies a few kilometres outside the town to the east.

GETTING THERE AND AWAY Most transport from Bishkek takes the direct route over the Ötmök Pass rather than the longer route through Kazakhstan, which heads west from Kara-Balta, through Kazakh territory, to Taraz at the head of the Talas Valley, from where the road heads south then west to Talas town. This is just as well, as the Kazakhstan route requires a transit visa. **Minibuses** to Talas leave, when full, from Bishkek's West Bus Station and are more frequent in the morning. To be on the safe side check on the route the driver is taking before committing yourself. The journey takes about five hours, with brief breaks, and costs 300som. Share taxis do the same journey in a little less time for around 500som. The road that turns off the main Bishkek–Osh highway to lead up to the 3,326m Ötmök Pass is quite rough in places, but improves considerably after the top of the pass is reached. Because of snow on the pass they do not run in winter, and the Kazakhstan route provides the only possibility at this time of year.

Coming from Kazakhstan, there is plenty of transport from Taraz. This would be a good way to enter Kyrgyzstan if coming by train from Russia, as it would save the considerable time taken in continuing the rail journey to Almaty or Bishkek.

The **bus station** is some way west of the town centre, a couple of kilometres out on Chingiz Aitmatov. Both buses and minibuses arrive and depart from here, although most minibuses also drop off in the town centre opposite the bazaar, from where most local *marshrutka* services also operate. Buses, via Taraz, take around nine hours to reach Bishkek; minibuses, five to six hours. The cost is 400som. Occasional local buses run west to Sheker and east to Aral and Köpürö-Bazar, although no services run south over the Kara-Buura Pass to the Chatkal Valley.

Taxis for local or longer trips congregate on a corner near the bazaar. The journey from Bishkek costs around 500–600som each way for a seat in a share taxi.

WHERE TO STAY   *Map, page 208*
As well as the one listed below, there are a few more **homestays** in the town that may be arranged through the CBT co-ordinator. English is spoken at the home of Aisuluu Madieva and Muhaya Murzahmedova, and German at the home of Kishiman Tashtekeeva.

CBT homestay Turdubek Ayilchiev, 76 Kasym Kaimov; 529 19; m 0772 643 466; e cbt_talas@list.ru. Turdubek Ayilchiev runs an excellent homestay on the edge of the town. It is quite a long way out & a little hard to find, so it may be best to get a taxi (*50som*) to take you there the first time. There is a yurt in the garden where meals may be taken in traditional Kyrgyz style. Turdubek's wife is a German teacher in a local school & speaks that language, although no English is spoken. As local CBT co-ordinator, Turdubek can help arrange local excursions, longer tours & onward transport. The homestay is a '3 edelweiss' establishment & so is a little more expensive than most, but the standards are high & the food excellent. B&B **$$**

Hotel Erlan (5 rooms) Sarygulova, near junction with Berdike Baatyr (Frunze). A basic, but clean-enough, place which has just 5 dbl rooms & a shared toilet. **$**

Hotel Talant 1 Berdike Baatyr (Frunze); 563 01. Another basic *gostinitsa* like Erlan. **$**

WHERE TO EAT AND DRINK   *Map, page 208*
There are several simple cafés and restaurants serving the usual staples close to the bazaar (*all* **$–$$**). There is also a large, traditional **chaikhana** on Joldoshali, parallel to and west of Sarygulova at the corner with Frunze. **Komtom** (52 890; **$$–$$$**) is on the second floor of a building on Berdike Baatyr (Frunze), opposite the large Talas provincial administrative building, above a mini-market and pharmacy. It is a neat little place with a good range of mostly Russian dishes at reasonable prices.

OTHER PRACTICALITIES For shopping, the **bazaar** has a good range of foodstuffs and household items, while just along Sarygulova is a small, modern shopping centre with its own restaurant, **Café Altyn Kazyk**. The **post office** is on Sarygulova, as is the Energo **bank**. There is a branch of RSK Bank at 198 Berdike Baatyr (Frunze) and Optima Bank at Sarygulova 59, both with ATMs. The Kyrgyz Telecom office is further north on the corner at Frunze 202.

Money **exchange offices** may be found at the south end of Sarygulova, near the bazaar, and there is an **internet café** along the same stretch. The post office and telephone office can also both provide internet access.

WHAT TO SEE AND DO Talas, like almost any medium-sized town in Kyrgyzstan, sprawls in a grid pattern away from the centre, where there are the usual trappings of civilisation: a bazaar, a park or two, a few large civic buildings and a taxi rank. The Soviet-era *khrushchevki* apartment blocks are concentrated mostly in the centre, too – a few blocks of grey concrete, broken paving and flapping laundry that might be Omsk, Saratov or any of the less aesthetically appealing neighbourhoods of any Russian provincial town.

A little further away from the centre in any direction lie quiet, leafy neighbourhoods of attractive Russian-style wooden houses, the legacy of the town's Slavic past. The town's **Orthodox church**, built for the Russian community in the 1920s, is worth a look. The central park behind the administrative headquarters on Frunze has a World War II **memorial obelisk**, complete with red star and hammer and sickle, which is surrounded by fencing with a Soviet-era red star motif. This sits in odd juxtaposition to the new building that stands just beyond it – a relatively new **mosque**.

Manas Ordu Complex (*To reach the Manas Ordu Complex from Talas, continue in the direction of Bishkek for about 10km, then turn north at the junction with the eagle on a large plinth for another 4–5km. A return taxi from Talas costs around 500som with waiting time.* ⊕ *09.00–19.00 daily; admission for a foreign adult/child is 40/10som, guided tour 300som*) The Manas complex of museum, parkland and mausoleum stands 15km outside Talas, just off the main road towards Bishkek at the village of Tash Aryk. Because of the Manas connection the complex is an important place for Kyrgyz, who come here as pilgrims to catch a glimpse of their nation's historic soul. Certainly, it is clear from the hushed voices and the devout, serious faces that this is as close to a religious experience as many Kyrgyz get.

For foreign visitors, a visit to the complex is an interesting outing but somehow an experience that fails to satisfy completely. Perhaps it is because there is the hint of the theme park about the place: the atmosphere is quiet and reverent, the parks and gardens tranquil, but somehow the authenticity of the historical background seems to be a little doubtful. There is nothing intrinsically wrong with this: after only a little more than two decades of having a country to call their own, many Kyrgyz are still in the process of defining themselves as a nation, so it may be that a theme park is exactly what is required.

The car park has a few stalls and yurts selling souvenirs, cold drinks and, inevitably for this bastion of all things Kyrgyz, *kumys*. Just inside the grounds of the complex is a statue of Manas on a plinth, amid well-tended flower-beds. The lovingly maintained grounds and remarkable cleanliness of the complex may come as something of a culture shock after weeks travelling in the scruffier regions of central Asia – there are even waste-paper bins.

The Manas gumbez The mausoleum is a few minutes' walk from the car park, along well-tended pathways lined with rose bushes, trees and shrubs. There is a shaded seating area opposite the entrance, where pilgrims gather as a mullah says prayers and recites from the Koran. A couple of large boulders stand nearby that some believe to be meteorites.

The *gumbez* was discovered in 1898 and has been dated to having originated in 1334, although there is some evidence of later rebuilds. The single-chambered tomb is relatively small and built of pale red bricks, with a richly decorated façade at the entrance that bears an inscription in Qufic script that repeats the Arabic word *al-mulk*, which means 'power' or 'rule'. Another, partly obliterated, inscription tells of a woman, Kanizyak-Khatun, who was the daughter of a local ruler. The 16-sided dome roof is a recent addition, but has been executed in a style that is thought to be appropriate to the period and building style of the original, which has not survived.

Two different stories relate the origin of the *gumbez*. The first suggests that Manas's son, Semetey, carried his body here and built the mausoleum for him. The other, generally more accepted, version says that it was his wife, Kanykei, and his friend and counsellor, Bakai, who built it and, in order to avoid desecration by his enemies, they put an inscription over the door that declared it was the mausoleum of a young girl. This version corresponds better with the inscription relating to the emir's daughter, although the dates are quite wrong if we are to believe that Manas perished in the 10th century.

The archaeologists who excavated the tomb during its renovation in 1969 are said to have found the bones of a very tall man within and many insist that these were the remains of Manas himself. The exact whereabouts of Manas's remains will never be known with certainty – there are those who believe his body lies in the Kara-Too district of Batken Province – but what is more important in the hazy territory where history and legend overlap is that a symbolic resting place be found. This is certainly that.

Manas museum The marble museum has a ground floor that is mostly dedicated to the lives of some of Kyrgyzstan's most well-known *manaschi*, with black and white photographs and text in Kyrgyz. There are also photographs showing the *gumbez* before reconstruction, and some very elaborate wooden carvings of horsemen fighting and mythological scenes with dragons, snakes and eagles. There is a large, dream-like mural on the wall of the staircase leading up to the second floor, the walls of which are also completely covered in murals. There are dioramas of scenes from the Manas epic, and displays of the accoutrements of the Kyrgyz chivalric and nomadic tradition: saddles, leather goods, weaponry

STREET NAMES

Note that in recent years Talas has changed almost all of its street names, rejecting its Soviet heritage for a slightly erratic alternative. Needless to say, most of the taxi drivers and local population have ignored the changes and still use the old names. The new street names are used here, but the following list of old and new roads may help you get around.

Old name	New name
1st May	O Turdaliev
Dzerzhinskiy	Sarygulova
Frunze	Berdike Batyr
Gorkiy	A Aldashukurov
Kyrgyz	B Sarnogoev
Lenina	Chingiz Aitmatov
South	Kasym Kaimov
Sovetskaya	A Ogombaev

and an enormous suit of armour that is said to have been the type that Manas wore. Many of these, like the suit of armour, are quite clearly reproductions but, as elsewhere in the complex where a vague, murky territory exists between historical fact and legend, the same blurring exists here between genuine historical artefact and replica.

Above the museum is a large manmade mound that offers good views from its summit. Pathways lead up it from both the *gumbez* and the museum. The hill has a stone carved with a 13th-century Arabic inscription, which relates to a fortress that used to stand nearby. A little further afield, there are also said to be 2,000-year-old **petroglyphs** in nearby Ken-Köl Gorge, a few kilometres north of Tash Artyk village. A guide from the Manas complex should be able to locate them.

SOUTH OF TALAS

BESH-TASH VALLEY This beautiful valley to the southeast of Talas is home to the **Besh-Tash National Park**, which begins 13km from Talas (*no entrance fee*) and covers 32,411ha in total. The national park was set up in 1996 and contains more than 800 plant species, along with threatened brown bear, snow leopard, Turkestan lynx, eagles and falcons.

Besh-Tash means 'Five Stones', a name which comes from five tall standing stones that are found in the upper part of the park. As with many isolated groups of standing stones, there is a legend connected with them. This one tells of five bandits who lived in the valley and robbed everyone who travelled this way. One day they carelessly robbed a holy woman who cursed them and turned the robbers into stone.

From the entrance to the canyon, where there are hot springs, the road from Talas follows the Besh-Tash River to a height of around 3,000m in the Talas Ala-Too range, before it strikes off to the 3,573m Terek Pass. Here, there are two crystal-clear lakes, a small and a large one, the larger of which offers superb views over the surrounding mountains.

The mountain scenery here is quite spectacular and the area makes for an excellent day trip from Talas or as a base for hiking trips. There are many idyllic camping places along the valley and it may be possible to stay in yurts in summer – check with the CBT co-ordinator in Talas (see page 209). With adequate provisions and experience it is also possible to trek from the lakes over the Terek Pass to Toktogul in two days.

URMARAL VALLEY Southwest of Talas, and south of the village of Leninopol, is the valley of the Urmaral River, which has many petroglyphs from the 7th to the 6th century BC, although it requires the services of a guide to locate them. Leninopol itself, on the main Talas–Taraz road, has several interesting Muslim mausoleums from the 18th and 19th centuries, just to the east of the village. The Urmaral Valley climbs up to the 3,601m Chimin-Tash Pass, which forms the boundary with Jalal-Abad Province. Close to the pass are more petroglyphs which date from the 6th to 8th centuries.

It is possible to hike, or ride, over the pass to descend to a jeep track that leads east upstream, alongside the Chatkal River, before striking north and climbing over the Kara-Kulja Pass to eventually reach Lake Sary-Chelek and the village of Arkyt – a tough six- to eight-day trek. CBT Talas can organise guided excursions into the valley and, with adequate notice, arrange the trek to Sary-Chelek, although it is probably wiser to prearrange this with KCBTA headquarters in Bishkek.

The main road to Taraz in Kazakhstan passes through the small town of Kyzyl-Adyr (previously known as Kirovka), before turning north to reach the frontier. Just north of Kyzyl-Adyr is the Kirov Reservoir, which has a giant head of Lenin carved into the side of the dam. Under the reservoir's waters lies a ruined town, Sheldy, which for the millennium up until the 16th century was an important producer of silver goods for the whole region. When the reservoir's waters are low, particularly in the autumn, it is said to be sometimes possible to see fragments of the ruined town standing proud of the water.

There are two routes to the border from Kyzyl-Adyr but only the main route through the village of Kyzyl-Jylduz allows non-CIS passport-holders to pass through. Just inside the border at Ak-Dëbë (also called Joon-Dëbë), due south of Taraz, there is the site of a settlement that existed between the 6th and 7th centuries.

SHEKER (ШЕКЕР) This village in the far west of Talas Province, snuggled up against the Kazakhstan border and within sight of the province's highest peak, Manas (4,484m), is famous for just one thing: its well-known son, Chingiz Aitmatov, Kyrgyzstan's most famous writer, who was born here (see page 45). The village has a small, three-room museum dedicated to the life of the novelist, which was opened in 1978 to mark his 50th birthday. The museum has a range of newspaper articles, photographs, manuscripts and books, as well as a section on his family history.

EAST OF TALAS

The road to Bishkek heads west towards the Ötmök Pass to the village of Chat-Bazar, where another road heads off into the hills to loop through the villages of Aral and Köpürö-Bazar, before rejoining the main road at the sprawling village of **Taldy-Bulak**. Close to Taldy-Bulak, but difficult to reach, is a high 3,000m plateau that has flower-decked meadows and a stone with a central hollow, known as the 'cup of immortality', as it fills with rainwater and is said never to evaporate. Water drunk from the hollow is considered to be holy and to have magical healing properties.

ARAL (АРАЛ) Both Aral and Köpürö-Bazar lie close to the Kazakhstan border in the valley of the Talas River, which nestles between the Kyrgyz Ala-Too and the slender Erchilik-Too range to the south. There are some who maintain that the Erchilik-Too mountains are where Manas's true burial place may be found, suggesting that the revered mausoleum near Talas was built just as a ruse to detract his enemies. The valley near Aral has a number of waterfalls and unusual rock formations that may be visited.

KÖPÜRÖ-BAZAR (КОПОРО-БАЗАР) This village lies another 30km east of Aral along the Talas Valley. It stands near the mouth of a gorge and is almost entirely surrounded by mountains. Its environs are surprisingly lush and productive: there is a 12km-long expanse of birch woodland, Ak-Kaiyn, close to the village, which is full of edible wild mushrooms in season, and the Talas River itself is heaving with trout. The area around the village is also imbued with history: there are prehistoric petroglyphs nearby at Tuyup-Tor and Kiddik-Tash; Genghis Khan is said to have rampaged through the area with his hordes (one of his wives is thought to be buried in the vicinity), and Kyrgyz tribes fought against Kalmyk invaders in the valley in the 4th century.

7

Köpürö-Bazar happens to be where former president Askar Akayev's wife, Mairam, hails from. Consequently, the village has received more than average state funding in the past, despite what may seem like an archaic, unchanged exterior. The village has facilities for homestays and services such as guided treks and horse hire (arrange via CBT co-ordinator in Talas, see page 209), the development of which has been supported by the Sustainable Livelihoods for Livestock Producing Communities Project (SLLPCP).

Visits to local petroglyph sites, caves, a strange local rock shaped like a skull and waterfalls may all be arranged in the village. A small mountain lake, Köl-Tör, at 3,305m, can be reached on horseback from the village. The lake is considered to be sacred by the local population and the custom is to construct a pile of seven stones and make a wish, which is then supposed to come true. There is an abandoned gold mine close to the village. The village is also the starting point for a spectacular four-day horse trek via Köl-Tör Lake and over the Korumdu Pass to the main Bishkek–Osh highway.

Several minibuses run each day to Köpürö-Bazar from Talas via Aral.

CHYCHKAN VALLEY Kyrgyzstan's main north–south trunk road between Bishkek and Osh loops through the far southeast corner of Talas Province, between the 3,184m-high Ala-Bel Pass and the border of the Jalal-Abad Province. Much of the valley west of the pass is given over to the Chychkan State Zoological Reserve. Stalls along the stretch of the road below the pass sell birch sap and locally made honey to passing motorists; look for the signs, 'МЕД' ('*myod*'). Other than this, there is almost no habitation along the way, just open *jailoo* with occasional herders with their flocks. For those wishing to stay over in the region there is a roadside tourist complex with hotel and restaurant, **Ak-Ilbirs ($$$)**, 30km from the pass. From here, the road follows the Chychkan River gorge, with its red sandstone walls, south to descend towards Toktogul and Jalal-Abad Province.

8

Naryn Province

Naryn Province (Нарынская Область), the large central province that links north and south Kyrgyzstan, is, in many ways, the most typically Kyrgyz *oblast* in the entire country. At around 45,000km² (slightly larger in area than Issyk-Kul Province), it is the largest province in the republic. At an average of just six persons per km², the population density is the lowest in the country and the total population of the entire province is only around 270,000.

In terms of physical geography, the province is far more homogenous than Chui or Issyk-Kul, being almost entirely made up of mountainous terrain, interspersed with valleys and upland grasslands. The lowest point is at around 1,400m above sea level; the highest, almost 5,000m.

The population of the *oblast* is more uniform, too, with 98% being Kyrgyz. The region is one of the poorest in the country, with a local economy that is dominated by animal herding – mostly sheep but also horses, cattle and yaks. In Soviet times, mining was well established in the province but, since independence, most mines have ceased production, having been pronounced uneconomical. This removal of employment that was formerly guaranteed has further contributed to the poverty of the region.

Like most of Kyrgyzstan, the province is an area of high seismic activity. On 26 December 2006 the Kochkor region was hit by an earthquake that measured 5.5 on the Richter scale and damaged an estimated 5,500 buildings, including nine schools, a kindergarten and five administrative buildings; ten houses were destroyed completely. The epicentre was just 30km from Kochkor, in the Terskey Ala-Too range, on the borders of Issyk-Kul and Naryn provinces. Fortunately there was no loss of life.

The administrative capital of the province is Naryn, and this town is often visited by travellers *en route* to China via the Torugart Pass. The other key town in the *oblast*, certainly as far as foreign visitors are concerned, is Kochkor, a small market town that locally is best known for its potatoes, but which serves as a departure point for visits to Lake Song-Köl and other destinations in the immediate area.

KOCHKOR (КОЧКОР) *Telephone code: 03535*

This small market town, at 1,800m above sea level in the northern part of the province, stands at the crossroads of many foreign visitors' journeys around the country. The town, which with just 14,000 inhabitants is really more of a big village, is considered to be the site of the first settlement in the valley. It was given the name Stolypin in 1909 in honour of the Russian prime minister who advocated colonisation of central Asia. Stolypin fell out of favour with the Bolsheviks after the October Revolution and so the town was renamed Kochkorka (Russian: Кочкорка), its name possibly deriving from the Kyrgyz *kach kar*, which means 'go away snow' (apparently it rarely snows in Kochkor). Since independence the

NARYN PROVINCE

CHINA

CHINA

Lake Issyk-Kul

Issyk-Kul

Terskey Ala-Too

Chui

Jalal-Abad

Osh

Fergana Range

Moldo-Too Range

Baybiche-Too Range

At-Bashy Range

Suusamyr-Too Range

Jeti-Ögüz
Kyzyl-Suu
Sandu
Darkhan
Barskoon
Tosor
Okaji-Say Tamga
Tamga
Bokonbaevo
Kara-Talaa
Kyzyl-Tuu
Ak-Say
Ottuk
Balykchy
Kara-Say
Burkan
Naryn
Eki-Naryn
Ichi-Naryn
Tash-Bashat
Ak-Say
Ak-Bashy
Kochkor
Köl-Ükök
Sary-Bulak
Dolon Pass
3,028m
Dostuk
At-Bashy
At-Bashy
Naryn
Orto-Tokoy
Reservoir
Kyzart Pass
2,664m
Kyzart
Lake Song-Köl
Komsomol
Jumgal
East Karakol
Karakol Pass
3,452m
Tügöl-Say
Kurtka
Ak-Tal
Baetov
Kara-Suu
Koshoy
Korgon
Tash Rabat
caravanserai
Tash Rabat Pass
3,968m
Lake
Chatyr-Köl
Torugart Pass
3,752m
Kashgar
Torugart
Tüz-Bel Pass
3,574m
Kök-Jar
Ügyut
Kosh-Döbö
Chaek
Min-Kush
Kazarman
Ak-Moinok Pass
2,932m
Saimaluu-Tash
Suusamyr
Kyzyl-Oi
Töo-Ashuu
Tunnel
3,130m
Bishkek
Chui
Bishkek
Talas
Ala-Bel Pass
3,184m
Chychkan State
Zoological
Reserve
Toktogul
Reservoir
Kaldama Pass
3,062m
Kyzyl-Ünkür
Ortok
Mihailovka
Kok-Yangak
Jalal-Abad
Kara-Kulja
Özgön
Osh

N
Bradt

50km
0

50 miles
0

216

town has been better known by its Kyrgyz equivalent, Kochkor. It used to have a more mixed population of Kyrgyz, Russians and Dungans, with even a few German families, but these days it is at least 95% Kyrgyz.

Kochkor lies in a position where the roads from Lake Issyk-Kul, Bishkek and the Suusamyr Valley meet, and because of this, and in particular because of the town's convenience as a jumping-off spot for excursions to the surrounding countryside, almost all first-time visitors to Kyrgyzstan end up spending a day or two here. They could do far worse: Kochkor may be the sleepy sort of place where cattle can lie down in the road with impunity but, as far as visitors are concerned, the town has everything they need – good accommodation and food, adequate shopping facilities and a well-run information centre. Both CBT and Shepherd's Life have homestay projects here and it is by far the best place in the area to organise trips to Lake Song-Köl or yurt stays in *jailoos* to the north.

GETTING THERE AND AWAY Regular **share taxis** (*300som*) and **minibuses** (*170som*) run from Bishkek's West Bus Station to Kochkor. These, along with share taxis to Naryn (*250som*) and Balykchy (*100som*), arrive and leave from outside the bazaar on the main street. Infrequent buses and minibuses running along the Jumgal Valley to Chaek, Jumgal and Min-Kush leave from the same location.

TOURIST INFORMATION AND SERVICES

CBT Kochkor Pionirskaya 22a; 511 14; m 0777 265 559; e cbt_kochkor@rambler.ru, cbtinfokochkor@gmail.com; www.cbtkyrgyzstan. kg; ⊕ Jun–Sep 09.00–19.00 daily. CBT Kochkor runs a very well-organised operation under the auspices of co-ordinator Bekbolot Builashov, which provides invaluable local advice as well as offering accommodation & tour-booking services. The office has several English-speaking staff who can advise on local destinations & the best way to arrange a trip there. The CBT office, which has a shop selling *shyrdaks* & felt goods next door, is also a useful meeting point for travellers who want to join up with others to form groups. There is also limited Wi-Fi available here.

Shepherd's Life Pionirskaya/Orozbekova; m 0777 013 747; e shepherdslifekochkor@mail.ru;

⊕ Jun–Sep 10.00–19.00 daily. Working from a booth on the junction with the main road close to the CBT office, this is run by capable former CBT co-ordinator Ainura Japarova & offers much the same sort of services at slightly lower prices – Song-Köl yurt stays, transport, horseriding tours & Kochkor homestays.

Jailoo Tourism Community Orozbekova 125/3; m 0555 494 203. Sharing office space with a gift shop and open for business sporadically, this local tour company has a mixed reputation although it does offer prices a little lower than CBT.

CBT Plus Eco (EJT) Orozbekova; 502 99; m 0772 510 628; e cbtpluseco07@rambler.ru; www.cbtpluseco.kg. Another CBT spin-off operating from a kiosk opposite Shepherd's Life, this offers CBT-type services with more of an ecology bent.

WHERE TO STAY   *Map, page 218*

There are nearly 20 **CBT homestays** in the town, all of a good standard. Some are quite far from the centre so you should specify if you do not wish to be a long way out. The guesthouse (#14) at Shamen 14 near the bazaar is very close to the centre, as is guesthouse #12 (Asyl Kubatbekova) near the park. Guesthouse #10 (Kuban Karymshakov) on Komsomol is further from the centre but has superb food (*all B&B $–$$; lunch or dinner 200som*). Shepherd's Life (see above) also has seven homestays (*$*) in the town, which are a little less expensive and a little more 'traditionally Kyrgyz'.

There are also two **hotels** in the town: an extremely basic one on Ömurov, the street north of the post office, and the better, newly opened Hotel Adamkaliy (*m 0773 313 537; $ –$$*) on Orozbekova, next to the police station.

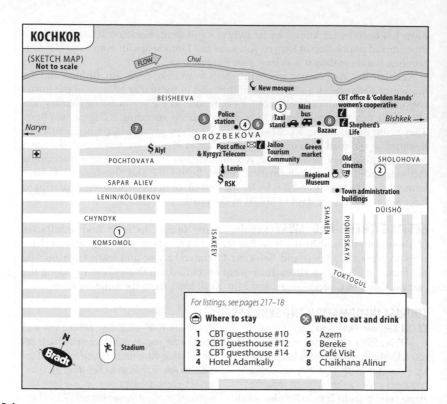

KOCHKOR

(SKETCH MAP)
Not to scale

FLOW — Chui

New mosque

BEISHEEVA

CBT office & 'Golden Hands'
women's cooperative

Naryn ←

③ Mini bus

⑤ Police station ④ ⑥ Taxi stand ⑧ Bazaar

Shepherd's Life

Bishkek →

⑦

OROZBEKOVA

$ Aiyl

Post office & Kyrgyz Telecom

Jailoo Tourism Community

Green market

Old cinema

SHOLOHOVA

POCHTOVAYA

Lenin

②

Regional Museum

SAPAR ALIEV

$ RSK

LENIN/KÖLÜBEKOV

Town administration buildings

DÜISHÖ

CHYNDYK

①

KOMSOMOL

ISAKEEV

SHAMEN

PIONIRSKAYA

TOKTOGUL

N

Bradt

Stadium

For listings, see pages 217–18

🛏 **Where to stay**
1 CBT guesthouse #10
2 CBT guesthouse #12
3 CBT guesthouse #14
4 Hotel Adamkaliy

✗ **Where to eat and drink**
5 Azem
6 Bereke
7 Café Visit
8 Chaikhana Alinur

✗ WHERE TO EAT AND DRINK *Map, above*

Beyond the homestays, where inevitably the best food is served, there are a few places in the centre of town near the bazaar, such as the **Bereke** ($) café or **Chaikhana Alinur** ($) which offer basic meals or snacks. The **Café Visit** ($$) on the main street, Orozbekova, west of the bazaar, probably has the most pleasant situation in town, having some outdoor tables. The choice of food here is better than most too, and there's draught beer. Alternatively, there's also **Azem** ($$) just off Orozbekova, a large dining hall more geared towards wedding parties and special celebrations, and in summer, a few yurts which sell meals and *kumys* along Orozbekova, between the CBT office and the bazaar.

SHOPPING The green **market** on the corner of Shamen and Orozbekova has a good range of fresh fruit and vegetables. There are plenty of small shops and stalls along the main road where most types of standard household goods can be obtained, within reason.

For *shyrdaks* and other felt handicrafts, the showroom of the **Altyn Kol ('Golden Hands')** women's co-operative (\ 225 34; e *altynkol@gmail.com; www.altyn-kol. com*), right next door to the CBT office, offers an outlet for crafts manufactured by local women, with a good selection of well-made handicrafts on display. The co-operative, formed in 1996, has more than 800 active female members from around the region and, like the Shepherd's Life programme, has benefited from backing by the Swiss Helvetas organisation (see page 83).

Because of the fine wool produced by sheep on nearby *jailoos*, Kochkor has gained a reputation for high-quality *shyrdaks*, and this is evident in the goods on sale. As well as *shyrdaks* there are also cushions, slippers and cuddly toys all made from high-quality felt. A *shyrdak* will cost anything from US$25 upwards if bought here, depending on size and the intricacy of the design. The quality tends to be better than many of those found in souvenir shops in Bishkek or elsewhere, and the prices are generally a little lower. It is also good to know that money goes directly to the maker of the *shyrdak* rather than into the pocket of a middleman.

There are also handicrafts on sale in the shop at the Jailoo Tourism Community travel agency (see page 217).

OTHER PRACTICALITIES The **Aiyl Bank** on Orozbekova and **RSK Bank** on Isakeev both have ATMs and can change US dollars in cash. Telephone calls can be made from the **Kyrgyz Telecom** office, also on Orozbekova, where *very* slow **internet access** may also be had. Jailoo Tourism (see page 217) also has internet access and the CBT office has Wi-Fi on request.

WHAT TO SEE AND DO Kochkor is mainly useful as a base for arranging excursions into the hinterland and, while the town is pleasant enough, there is little to see here. There is a silver statue of Lenin standing on Isakeev just off the main road, and another bust of the man along Orozbekova, outside a bus depot west of the Café Visit (for completists there is yet another Lenin bust to be seen on the right on the run into town from the Bishkek direction). The same main street has curious metal cut-outs decorating its lamp posts – hammer and sickles, space rockets, masonic instruments, atoms and gear wheels – which serve as reminders of the recent Soviet past. The decrepit cinema between the town park and the museum has clearly seen better days, and is now boarded up and its grounds overgrown with weeds. What was once an important civic institution has no doubt since been replaced by TV screens showing pirated DVDs in anonymous back rooms around the town.

There is a new steel-roofed mosque near the river to the north of the post office, and another one in the south of the town along Isakeev. For fans of quirky vernacular architecture there is a building constructed entirely of recycled shipping containers on the corner of Pochtovaya and Isakeev. On Saturday mornings, there's an animal bazaar at the western end of the town.

Regional Museum This small museum (*Sapar Aliev 8; ⊕ 09.00–17.00 Mon–Fri, closed for lunch 12.00–13.00 approx; admission 50som*) has a few rooms dedicated to showing the traditional Kyrgyz way of life, with plenty of photographs of yurts, herdsmen and windswept *jailoos*, alongside displays that illustrate the changes brought by the Soviet period – education, health and military service. There are numerous portraits of local Kyrgyz weighed down by their war medals. There are also paintings of Kyrgyz life, a large stuffed sheep, a diorama of stuffed animals and best of all, a splendid yurt that entirely fills a room. The floorboards are quite badly damaged in places and there is a general air of neglect. It is unlikely that any of the displays have changed significantly since the early 1980s.

EXCURSIONS FROM KOCHKOR

SARALA-SAZ (САРАЛА-САЗ) Sarala-Saz is a large *jailoo* 54km north of Kochkor that lies *en route* to the 3,573m Shamshy Pass, which leads over the Kyrgyz Ala-Too into the Chui Valley. As with many similarly romantic locations in Kyrgyzstan, the country's legendary hero, Manas, is reputed to have frequently visited the region and played the game *ordo* here with his warriors (see page 44). The legend goes that one day, noticing that his horses were wandering away, he threw boulders in front of them to prevent their escape. The stones are said to remain there to this day as testament to his superhuman strength.

The drive up to the *jailoo* passes a number of large *kurgan* burial mounds that date from the 1st–5th centuries AD, as well as an interesting Kyrgyz cemetery just beyond the village of Shamshy. At the *jailoo* itself, which lies at around 3,300m, there is plenty of scope for walking or riding in the vicinity, with wide open vistas in all directions that have a stark, desolate beauty. With little to spoil the natural landscape other than sheep, cattle, a few yurts and the ubiquitous recycled railway carriages, this is a marvellously accessible location for an overnight stay. What is so noticeable here is the absolute quiet that permeates the place. Distant human voices and animal sounds carry so far here that it is possible to hear the movement of a crow's wings as it flies past.

With a horse and a guide it is possible to visit nearby petroglyphs, or a waterfall which is half-hidden among the rocks of a small canyon, known locally as 'Look for me'. Upstream from the waterfall are extensive patches of wild onions, the plants that the Chinese used to think caused altitude sickness. Higher still is a permanent glacier.

Rather than hike with a specific destination in mind, it is equally pleasurable to just wander at will close to the *jailoo* and observe the Kyrgyz herders going about their everyday tasks. More adventurous spirits may wish to make a horse trek over the pass to Kalinovka and Tokmok in the Chui Valley (*two to three days*). A horse games festival is staged at the *jailoo* by CBT Kochkor each year in August.

Two other *jailoos* that may be visited in the Kochkor vicinity are **Korumdu**, a high *jailoo* 60km to the west in the Kyzart range, and **Tündük**, 40km northwest of the town. Both have CBT projects in place which include yurt stays and horse hire, and day tours that include horseriding can be arranged by CBT Kochkor. Another possibility is **Kapa** *jailoo*, 35km from Kochkor, from where it is possible to get a view of Lake Issyk-Kul from the peak of one of the surrounding mountains.

Other practicalities CBT Kochkor can organise yurt stays at Sarala-Saz, as well as transportation there and back (there is no public transport). The road to Sarala-Saz is quite rough in places beyond Shamshy village, but it is not difficult and any robust car (ie: a Zhiguli) is perfectly capable of making the journey. Unless you arrange for the driver to return for a pick-up on another day you will need to pay for the driver's meals. CBT charges around 3,000som for transport there and back, together with a night's sleepover for the driver (*yurt accommodation, with meals $–$$*).

CHON-TUZ SALT CAVES This is actually a sanatorium, 30km from Kochkor, where, in Soviet times, caves were mined for the extraction of rock salt. The salt is still mined and is mostly used as a food supplement for farm animals. The sanatorium was formerly popular as a treatment centre for allergies and asthma, as it was thought the dry air of the salt caves was beneficial for these ailments. The sanatorium is still in use and visitors may stay whatever their state of health. There is also a *jailoo* that may be visited, a three-hour trek above the sanatorium.

KÖL ÜKÖK (КОЛ УКОК) Köl Ükök is a mountain lake in a gorgeous natural setting above a *jailoo* known as Tez-Tör, which lies around 17km southeast of Kochkor. Köl Ükök means 'Lake in a Chest' and some of those who visit it rate the lake's tranquillity and natural beauty above even that of Song-Köl (see page 224). In fairness, it has to be seen as a different sort of experience: Song-Köl is certainly more commercialised than Köl Ükök but at the same time it is also far bigger and better equipped to deal with visitors. In contrast to Song-Köl's wide, glimmering waters, Köl Ükök is small and jewel-like. Just like Lake Issyk-Kul, the lake has a good stock of Sevan trout in its waters, and several rivers which flow into it, but none that drain out, meaning water can only leave the lake by evaporation or seepage. The comparisons end here, however, as Köl Ükök has a maximum depth of only 17m.

From Köl Ükök it is possible to hike for a couple of hours up to another spectacular glacial lake, Köl-Tör.

Other practicalities Köl Ükök can be reached by way of the village of Isakeev, just 6km southeast of Kochkor, or from Kara-Suu, 7km to the east of the town. From either of these it is a five- to six-hour horse trek to the lake, or three to four hours to Tez-Tör *jailoo*. CBT Kochkor can organise transport, horse hire and accommodation at the standard rates.

SOUTH OF KOCHKOR The Bishkek–Naryn road leads south from Kochkor through Sary-Bulak and the turn-off for Lake Song-Köl over the 3,028m **Dolon Pass**. This is the highest point along the way and here the roadside is lined with the railway carriage dormitories of workers who maintain the road, which is kept open throughout the winter despite deep snow. In the summer months, the yurts and tents of Kyrgyz herders join the roadside carriages to sell *shorpo*, *manti* and *kumys* to passing motorists.

From the summit of the pass, the road plunges into a rocky gorge before reaching **Ottuk**, a small village, where the road emerges into an open valley. A little further on towards Naryn, 25km short of the provincial capital, stands a large **memorial** on a hillside dedicated to the Kyrgyz writer and poet Arstanbek Bunlash Uluu (1824–78), who was known to his admirers as 'The Nightingale'. His poems were banned during the Soviet period because of his calls for the preservation of Kyrgyz culture and independence of spirit, and warnings of 'dark times' to come – clearly references to the influence of early Russian colonists. The few of his works that survive today were published as an anthology in 1994.

WEST TO THE SUUSAMYR VALLEY

For the northwestern end of the Suusamyr Valley, see page 139. Just after Kyzyl-Oi in Chui Province the road crosses into Naryn Province and leads east towards Kochkor, along the Jumgal Valley via the villages of Chaek, Tügöl-Say, Kyzart, Jumgal and Uzunbulak. The eastern end of the valley beyond Kyzart is rich pasture and there are many yurts here in the summer. This road is quite decent and there are plans to upgrade it in the future. Between Chaek and Kyzyl-Oi there is absolutely no public transport and little through traffic, although hitching should be possible given sufficient time. CBT Kochkor can organise taxis between Kyzyl-Oi and Kochkor, although these work out quite expensive because you have to pay for the return journey. It may be possible to find a taxi in Chaek that will take you through to Kyzyl-Oi for a much lower price than the journey from Kochkor, but it is best not to depend on this. At the time of the last update there was a great deal of construction near the Min-Kush turn-off at Aral where Chinese road builders were working on the new Balykchy–Kazarman–Jalal-Abad link road.

Another more northerly route to the Suusamyr Valley runs from Kochkor through the village of Komsomol to the Karakol Pass at 3,452m, then descends along the

8

Karakol Valley in Chui Province to Suusamyr village. This northern route, however, is all but deserted, having almost no villages, bad roads and very little traffic.

There are some good trekking routes to the villages of the southern route from Lake Song-Köl, which are outlined under that entry, and there is homestay accommodation available in some of the villages like Jumgal and Kyzart through the Shepherd's Life programme.

CHAEK (ЧАЕК) Chaek is the largest of the villages in this wide, arid valley. The flat landscape that surrounds the village is agricultural, with fields of vegetables and livestock, but further west towards Kyzyl-Oi the scenery becomes increasingly more dramatic, with colourful rock formations and rugged cliffs.

KYRGYZ CITIES OF THE DEAD

You see them all over Kyrgyzstan: what appear from afar to be villages of tightly packed mud-brick dwellings but which, upon closer inspection, turn out to be cemeteries. These evocative, although usually crumbling, villages of the dead are a unique feature of the Kyrgyzstan countryside. Often standing a little way outside the village, sometimes on top of a low hill, they are frequently more impressive visually than the villages they serve. A slightly chaotic mixture of mud-brick, shrine-like tombs, gravestones with etched images of the deceased in their serious Sunday-best pose, and Islamic crescent moons intermixed with communist five-pointed stars, they represent an odd amalgam of styles in their tribute to those who have died. What makes them unmistakably Kyrgyz, though, is the presence of large, wrought-iron, birdcage-like structures in the form of a yurt.

The Kyrgyz were a nomadic people until well into the 20th century and because of their peripatetic existence they were normally buried without fuss wherever they died. Prominent nobles and warriors were sometimes honoured with showy mausoleums but, generally, Kyrgyz graves were simple and quickly forgotten. During the Soviet period, nomadism was forcibly abandoned and the erection of large memorials to the dead became more fashionable with the newly sedentary Kyrgyz, although the size of the monument depended largely on wealth and status. Although it might seem ironic that a nomadic people should choose such a fixed, earth-bound dwelling after death, a tradition began in the 1930s of erecting monuments that recalled the Kyrgyz people's previous nomadic lifestyle. Along with the old – the wrought-iron yurt frames that reflected nostalgia for the old nomadic life – came the new, and etched portraits, a Russian custom, also started to feature on gravestones. Reminders of pre-Islamic shamanic traditions are also clearly visible, with antlers, animal skulls, clay animals and horses' tails all utilised to decorate tombs.

What makes these graveyards most noteworthy is the way that disparate traditions, seemingly at odds with each other, intermingle freely. Shamanic, Islamic, communist – it is perfectly possible to find yurt tombs that have been decorated with an (un)holy mix of goat horns, Islamic moons and Soviet stars. These days, most tombs are less elaborate, largely due to economic decline, but the old ones remain on hillsides around the country, gently crumbling as they slowly decay back into the earth. Such cemeteries are visible everywhere in the country, but perhaps the finest are those that can be seen gracing the hillsides along the Suusamyr Valley.

Getting there and away A daily morning **bus service** runs between Chaek and Kochkor along the valley, stopping at all the villages on the way. Faster **share taxis** also run to and from Kochkor for 250som. There is no public transport running west but a private car can be organised through Shepherd's Life or CBT.

Other practicalities Chaek stretches east to west along the main road. The main **bazaar** area is at the eastern end of the village and continuing west from here you'll come to a statue of Lenin, a drama theatre, two **banks** with ATMs side by side – RSK and Aiyl – and a war memorial. There's also a handful of simple **restaurants** like U-Man Gril and U-Man+ café (*both* $$), and a friendly place to stay at the western end of town that advertises itself as 'Hotel of Tourists' (☏ *03535 238 79*; $), although it is really more of a homestay.

KYZART (КЫЗАРТ) This long, rambling village, also known as Jang-Arakh, lies just a couple of kilometres south of the main road that links Kochkor and Suusamyr. It is a useful start point for a trek over the mountains to Lake Song-Köl, which involves a climb of around 1,000m and a descent of around 400m. An easier option would be to do it in reverse, starting at the lake.

Getting there and away There is a CBT project established in the village, which can provide accommodation, horses, guides and transport out of the valley. The co-ordinator's house can be found at the far eastern end of the village. A CBT **car** to Kyzart from Kochkor will cost around 2,500som, although you should be able to find a taxi that will charge less than this. There is also reputedly a 06.00 daily **bus** that leaves for Kochkor from the village. Alternatively, Chaek-bound minibuses and share taxis can drop you off at the junction.

Kilemche *jailoo* can be reached in a few hours on **horseback** from Kyzart village. The Shepherd's Life co-ordinator in the village can provide horses and organise an overnight yurt stay at the *jailoo*. From here it is possible to reach Lake Song-Köl in five hours by horse. Another *jailoo* in the area that also has yurts to stay in is at Chaar Archa, 10km from Kilemche.

MIN-KUSH (МИН-КУШ) Very much the end of the road in every sense, Min-Kush ('A Thousand Birds') lies in a valley south of Chaek surrounded by the peaks of the Moldo-Too range. Like Kazarman further to the south, it was once a prosperous mining town of 20,000, but now it has a deserted feel to it and many of its Soviet-period apartments are partially empty. Since the uranium ore mine and the felt-tip pen factory has closed down there is hardly any work here.

Even more worryingly, there are four uranium ore waste dumps in the vicinity of the town that have stood here since the uranium mines were closed down in 1969 and have yet to be sealed adequately. There is great concern that the threat of landslides caused by earthquakes could destabilise the dumps and cause river dams to fracture, which would result in the River Naryn (and subsequently the Syr Darya, one of the major water sources in the central Asian region) becoming heavily polluted with radioactivity. As it is, local cancer levels are already said to be high. A joint US-Russian project to clean up radioactive storage facilities in Kyrgyzstan was launched in 2003 and various interministerial and international assessments of the potential hazard have been made since, although it would appear that the matter has yet to be adequately dealt with and the risk remains.

In many ways, Lake Song-Köl (sometimes written Son-Kul) is Kyrgyzstan's poster girl. The lake is an almost archetypal destination of the wilderness variety, having all of the necessary ingredients to create a picture-perfect vignette of the Kyrgyz nomadic way of life: a wide alpine lake, nomads on horseback, yurts, lush green pasture, bare snow-capped mountains and contented herds of livestock. With the right conditions – a golden sun setting over still waters; the ring of surrounding mountains transformed into a purple velvet backdrop; unseen cattle lowing as dusk falls – it is almost too perfect to be true. Even in less than optimal circumstances – sloping rain, wind-driven sleet, an electrical storm crackling around the shore – it is still wholly exhilarating. Lake Song-Köl certainly lives up to its reputation: a heart-wrenchingly beautiful place where only the most begrudging of critics would make much of a fuss about the way that low-level tourism has crept in to mildly affect its character in recent years.

Kyrgyzstan's second-largest lake stands at 3,016m, at almost the dead centre of the country. One meaning of its name may be translated as 'The Last Lake' and this seems wholly appropriate for such a large, pristine isolated lake that can seem like it is at the end of the world. The lake is 18km wide and 29km long, but only 13m deep. Altitude keeps its temperatures low, with a year-round average of around –3.5°C, a summer temperature average of about 11°C and winter down to –20°C. The lake freezes over in the winter and, with over 200 days of annual snow cover, access is very difficult at this time of year. The lake comes into its own during the short summer (June–September) when the extensive *jailoos* that surround it are utilised for grazing by herdsmen from across Naryn Province. At this time of year there are a considerable number of yurts clustered in small family groups around its shores.

There are no trees at the lake, nor in the surrounding hills, but in season there is an abundance of alpine flowers, most notably gentians, wild tulips and edelweiss, and herbs such as sage and chamomile. The lake is rich in waterfowl and waders, with a total of 66 species recorded that include several species of gull and duck, bald coots and the rare Indian mountain goose. Raptors are also well represented with golden eagles and various falcons present in the summer.

Migratory birds, such as storks and cranes, stop here on passage. Animals recorded in the vicinity of the lake include foxes, deer, lynx, wolves and, of course, marmots, which are plentiful in the surrounding hills. The lake was devoid of fish until 1959 when it was stocked for the first time. A two-year moratorium on fishing for some species was announced in 2004 because of depleted stocks. The lake and its immediate shoreline is part of the Karatal-Japyryk State Reserve.

The **best time to visit** Lake Song-Köl is between June and September, although the beginning and end of the season can be very cold at night – even in August it is barely above freezing. Outside this period, there will be nowhere to stay at the lake as all of the yurts will be dismantled and the herders returned to the valleys. A visit outside the summer months is ill-advised, not simply because of a lack of accommodation or cold temperatures: part of the Song-Köl experience is an appreciation of how Kyrgyz nomads live in tune with their environment and to experience the lake without people would not do it full justice.

GETTING THERE AND AWAY
By private transport There are four routes that approach the lake, more or less from the cardinal points of the compass. These vary in terms of difficulty, time taken

and convenience. There is no public transport to the lake, and so transport to and from it needs to be arranged, either privately through CBT, or with a travel agency. Probably the commonest approach is from the **east** via the village of Sary-Bulak, which lies 45km south on the main Kochkor to Naryn road. Sary-Bulak is little more than a truck-stop, with yurts and cafés selling food, with usually a line of Chinese lorries parked up for a meal *en route* to China via the Torugart Pass. The road climbs up from the main road through Köng-Suu village (sometimes called Tölök) and twists along the Tölök River past pasture full of sheep, cattle and horses, and higher up, yaks. This route is 85km long and takes about 1½ hours to drive. The road is quite reasonable most of the way, although the last section can be a little rough, and this route is perfectly possible in a solid Russian car such as a Zhiguli. For the other routes listed below, or for driving any distance around the lake's muddy perimeter, a 4x4 such as a Niva is necessary. In high season it is sometimes possible to hitchhike with other foreigners from outside the CBT office.

Another approach that is often used if the lake is to be reached from the direction of Naryn is the route from the **southeast**, a dirt track that leads off the Kochkor–Naryn road, near the village of Kara-Ünkür south of Sary-Bulak, and follows a dramatic series of hairpin bends to reach the lake at its southeast corner. This route to the lake is 90km long from Naryn and takes about 2½ hours.

The **western** side of Lake Song-Köl may be reached from Chaek, turning off the road south at Bajzak to lead past the coal mines of Kara-Kichi, from where a track climbs up through hairpin bends to a 3,300m pass, before it gently descends to the lake. The fourth route is from the **south**, over the Moldo Pass from the village of Kurtka (also known as Jangy-Talap), across the Naryn River from Ak-Tal on the Naryn to Kazarman road.

Outside the summer months some of these routes will be periodically blocked by snow. It is also possible to arrange a vehicle to take you in by one route and leave by another, which is an advantage if you want to fit in a visit to the lake between Kochkor and Naryn without retracing any steps. Taxis from Kochkor that take up to three people charge around 3,000som to reach the lake. CBT and the other agencies charge a little more for up to four passengers, plus 200som per night for the driver if you want them to stay. To continue to Naryn from the lake would cost more. A CBT car from Naryn charges around 4,500som. If you are planning on hiking out of Song-Köl, say, to Kyzart, be aware that a one-way trip will prove expensive because you are obliged to pay for the return journey to base.

On foot or horseback There are two principal trekking routes to the lake. The first is from the north, starting at the village of Kyzart. The other main approach is from the south from the village of Kurtka, 4km north of Ak-Tal on the Naryn–Kazarman road. CBT Kochkor can help organise the Kyzart approach and CBT Naryn the Kurtka route. Other routes are also possible with proper planning, such as a three-day horse trek from the Chon-Tuz salt caves. For those wishing to walk around the lake – an excellent idea – allow four or five days for a leisurely circumnavigation. A two-day, one-night horse trek to the lake from Kochkor booked through one of the agencies costs around 5,000som per person.

WHERE TO STAY AND EAT There are **yurts** dotted all the way around the lake, many affiliated to the CBT organisation, some dedicated for the use of particular tour companies, and some belonging to families of no affiliation who will, nonetheless, also take in paying guests. You can, of course, **camp** almost anywhere, but bring all the food you need, warm clothes and some means of water purification.

Most of the CBT yurts are located to the south, southeast and east of the lake. There are also some in the northwest, close to the track over the mountains that leads to Kyzart. The biggest group of all is on the east side close to the lagoon, where the road from Kochkor terminates. This is where most visitors arrive at the lake and the yurt 'village' here is where the bulk of group-tour cultural activities, such as folk music recitals, tend to take place.

As well as accommodation, hot meals can be organised for around 200som if you are starting or ending a walk around the lake, although you may have to wait an hour or two for it to be cooked if it is an ad hoc request. The strip of land that divides the lagoon from the lake is a pleasant place for a stroll while waiting. Horses may be hired here too, and it is perhaps a good idea to rent horses and ride some distance north or south for a little more tranquillity away from the yurt 'village'. Having said that, even here the commercialisation is at quite a low level, all things considered.

A three-hour hike north of here along the shore (less on horseback) brings you to an area on the northeastern shore where there is a shallow river outlet and low hills that almost come down to the lake. There are a few CBT yurts here as well as others, across the river, which are used by the NoviNomad tour company. This is a wonderful spot for an overnight stay. Others recommend the western shore – it is all marvellous really.

Standard CBT rates apply for B&B, although private yurts may charge a little less. Yurt accommodation is 1,000som per person with meals; horse hire is around 200som per hour or 700som per day. If a horse guide is required it is also necessary to pay for him and his horse (*1,400som per day*). There are absolutely no shops at Song-Köl, although some yurts may sell *kumys* and other dairy products.

NARYN (НАРЫН) *Telephone code: 03522*

Naryn is rarely cited as one of Kyrgyzstan's 'must see' attractions and, although there are few who can be bothered to write about the town, it still tends to get a bad press. Certainly, it is not the most attractive of places, and there is little to see in the town, but given the harsh reality that most visitors need to stop for at least a night here on their way to the Torugart Pass, Tash Rabat or elsewhere, it seems disingenuous to run it down as it really could be far worse. Naryn may be a rough, tough sprawl that lacks much genuine charm, but it is an interesting place in a warts-and-all sort of way, and probably more typical of post-independence Kyrgyzstan than either Bishkek or Karakol. It also has an efficiently run local CBT group and some reasonable places to stay and eat.

Naryn started life as a Russian garrison in 1868 and there is still an army base in the town today, but it was in the post-World War II period that most of the current town was constructed, and this is characterised by the large number of *khrushchevki* apartment blocks found throughout.

In 1920 the town was the scene of a battle between Bolshevik soldiers and White Russian forces, led by *kulaks* from Tokmok and Naryn, who succeeded in killing the local party chairman, Orozbekov, and capturing the communist commander. The counter-revolutionaries were later defeated at battles at the Shamshy and Dolon passes.

Since 1927, the town has served as the provincial administrative centre for Naryn Province and has a population of around 45,000. The town will ultimately host one of three campuses of the University of Central Asia, an international university founded in 2000 by the governments of Kazakhstan, Kyrgyzstan and Tajikistan with backing from the Aga Khan. The first phase of construction of the campus started in September 2013 and the university plans to open its doors to its first classes in September 2016.

The town is long and thin, following the course of the Naryn River for several kilometres east to west. Sandstone cliffs fringe the town just beyond the river to the north, while south of the town a wide, flat plain gives way to arid pale mountains. The town's linear form is one possible etymology for its name, which may come from the Chinese for 'narrow'. Another potential derivation is from the Mongolian word for 'sunny', which is not without irony: the town is undoubtedly sunny in the summer – and also hot and dusty – but the winter climate here, at an altitude of 2,040m above sea level, is extremely harsh, with temperatures that plunge, on occasion, to as low as –40°C. Such an unforgiving climate, coupled with the relative poverty of the place, may well have some bearing on the tough character of the town's inhabitants. Naryn's population, which is almost entirely Kyrgyz, has something of a reputation for confrontation and drunkenness, although in fairness this does not seem to be any worse than elsewhere in the country.

GETTING THERE AND AROUND There are several direct **minibuses** daily from Bishkek's West Bus Station, which run in the mornings and take at least six hours to reach Naryn by way of Tokmok and the Chui Valley, and Kochkor and the Dolon Pass. Most minibuses bypass Balykchy and take a short cut via the Orto-Tokoy Reservoir. A similar number leave in the reverse direction from Naryn's **main bus station** on Lenina, mostly in the morning. The cost is in the order of 300som.

The twice-weekly service to Kazarman no longer runs. Buses for At-Bashy leave three times daily in the afternoons and take one hour, costing 150som. There is also a daily bus to the villages of Kara-Suu, Kara-Bulun and Kyzyl-Tuu that lie beyond At-Bashy on the road to Torugart. A daily bus for Baetov along the Naryn Valley west leaves at 08.00, costing 150som, and several buses leave for Tash-Bashat on the road to Eki-Naryn between 08.00 and 16.00 (*50som*). To Eki-Naryn itself, there is a bus three times a week that leaves on Monday, Wednesday and Friday mornings (*75som*). Other daily services include Tokmok (*215som*), Balykchy (*135som*), Karakol (*400som*) and Kochkor (*100som*), although any Bishbek-bound bus or minibus will drop you in Kochkor.

The **central bazaar** also has a small bus station which has daily departures in very crowded dilapidated buses to villages west along the Kazarman road, such as Dostuk and Kurtka (Jangy-Talap). Foreigners are still not permitted to use the occasional public buses that run over the Torugart Pass to Artysh and Kashgar in China.

Hiring a **taxi** in Naryn can pose a problem as there appears to be something of a taxi mafia in which no-one will negotiate a reasonable price to a destination. Any attempt at sensible negotiation with an individual driver is met by other drivers coming up to argue, effectively intimidating their colleague into not dropping the price. This is perversely counterproductive as they end up getting no fare at all. In many Kyrgyz towns it is quite possible, with a bit of leg work and bartering, to find a taxi at considerably less than the CBT price; this does not seem to be the case in Naryn. The irony is that Naryn seems to have more than its fair share of would-be taxi drivers; they congregate on Lenina opposite the bazaar, in the bazaar itself and at the main bus station.

Share taxis congregate at the bus station, poaching customers from buses that are due to leave. To Kochkor, it costs 250–300som per place; to Bishkek, 600–800som.

Naryn has a small **airport** to the east of the town, but it is currently closed and is not likely to reopen for commercial flights.

NARYN

For listings, see pages 229–30

Where to stay
1 Celestial Mountains Guest House
2 Hotel Ala-Too
3 Hotel Khan Tengri

Where to eat and drink
4 Adek
5 Anarkul Apa
6 Korona

Most of Naryn lies within reasonable walking distance, but consider taking a taxi for longer distances (*60–100som, but haggle*), or take one of the rickety trolleybuses that ply up and down Lenina.

TOURIST INFORMATION

CBT Naryn Apartment 8, Lenina 33; 508 65, 508 85; m 0559 567 685; e naryn_tourism@ rambler.ru. This CBT branch, in the very capable hands of co-ordinator, Gulira Kenjekaraeva, has an information office where homestay accommodation can be booked & advice given on travel in the region. The office staff are very knowledgeable about the region & are very helpful whether you take their tours or not. Private transport can be booked using their pool of drivers at the standard rate. As it is hard to get a good deal from local taxi drivers in Naryn, this is not a bad option. Standard 2-day tours may be arranged to At-Bashy, Tash Rabat & Lake Chatyr-Köl, along with various local tours to places such as the deer nursery at Iiri-Suu.

They can also organise longer horseback tours from Ak-Tam, west of Naryn, to Lake Song-Köl or Lake Issyk-Kul. Horseback tours to Lake Song-Köl from Kurtka village to the south, or Kyzart to the north, may also be arranged here, as can transfers to China over the Torugart Pass. The office also has internet access, 2 computers & a good store of maps, brochures & guidebooks.

Kubat Tour Apartment 51, Lenina 6; m 0772 689 262; e kubat-tour@mail.ru. Close to the CBT office on Lenin, this is a spin-off company run by former CBT co-ordinator Kubat Abdyldaev that offers similar services to CBT, inc homestays in Naryn & Torugart Pass transfers. Prices tend to be a bit lower than those of CBT.

WHERE TO STAY *Map, opposite*

As well as the hotels listed below, Naryn's Community Based Tourism network (see above) has a total of 15 homestays (**$$**) around the town, most of which are in Soviet-era apartments off Razzakova in the east end of town over the bridge. Kubat Tour also have a handful of homestays (**$**) at slightly lower prices.

Celestial Mountains Guest House (12 rooms) Razzakova 42; 504 12; e naryn@ celestial.com.kg; www.cmgh.kg. Also known & advertised as The English Guest House, this small hotel, tucked away from the town centre in a quiet neighbourhood next to a park, is the most comfortable place to stay in Naryn. The guesthouse has helpful, English-speaking staff & facilities inc hot showers, emergency generator, internet access, video room with library & a menu that has both national & Western dishes. Prices inc evening meal & b/fast. *Rooms* **$$$–$$$$**, *yurt accommodation* **$$** *pp.*

Hotel Khan Tengri (10 rooms) Jusupova 2a; 549 46; m 0556 035 063; e khantengri.hotel@ gmail.com; www.khantengrihotel.kg. A newish hotel in a peaceful setting at the far eastern end of town, this has good-value, spacious, comfortable rooms & English-speaking staff. Computer available for guest use. **$$$**

Hotel Ala-Too (100 rooms) Lenina; 521 89. The Ala-Too is a large, central hotel which has seen few changes since the break-up of the Soviet Union. The cheaper rooms are quite poor but the 'lux' rooms are perfectly reasonable & it is worth paying the extra if you stay here. There is a small café but the restaurant is a long-abandoned ruin. *Standard room* **$**, *lux* **$$**

WHERE TO EAT AND DRINK *Map, opposite*

Homestays aside, Naryn has disappointingly few pleasant places to eat, and those restaurants that are open are poorly marked. The bazaar has a wide range of Kyrgyz dairy products and a good selection of fruit in season.

Anarkul Apa Orozbekova 21; 513 17; ⏰ 10.00–21.00 Mon–Sat. Near the junction with

Kyrgyzskaya, this large, multiroomed restaurant is popular with locals at lunchtime & gets very busy with policemen & officials from the Hakimyat. It has a well-stocked bar with a variety of beers & that Kyrgyzstan rarity, an English-language menu. Be aware that not everything listed will be available though. $$

✕ **Korona** Kulumbaeva/Lenina; ☎ 502 94; ☺ until 23.00. This large, purpose-built restaurant is probably the smartest place in town. Korona has a cavernous interior almost like a hotel lobby, with a high roof & discrete sunken lighting. The menu (in Russian) has a wide range of Russian, Chinese & Kyrgyz dishes at prices little more than anywhere else in town. Popular with large, celebrating parties on special occasions, at other times it is almost completely deserted. $$

✕ **Adek** Kulumbaeva 41; ☎ 524 92. Pleasant café-restaurant with reasonable prices. No English menu. $

SHOPPING The **central bazaar** has a wide range of foodstuffs and everyday items that are central to livestock rearing. There are more fruit and vegetable stalls at the eastern end of Lenina before the bridge. The Univermag **department store** stands on the corner of Lenina and Kyrgyzskaya and there a couple of **pharmacies** on Kyrgyzskaya nearby. Both the CBT office and nearby Kubat Tour have a small range of souvenirs for sale – felt products, *shyrdaks* and the like. Körköm Galerija next door to the CBT office also has a selection.

OTHER PRACTICALITIES Naryn has plenty of **banks** like RSK and Akai along Lenina that have ATMs, although there is nowhere that accepts MasterCard. Cash (US dollars and euros) can be changed at most of these banks and also on the first floor of the AKB Bank on Kulumbaeva, south of Lenina. It is also probably possible to change money in the bazaar and at the Celestial Mountains Guest House, providing they have sufficient cash.

The town's large **post and telephone office** is on the corner of Lenina and Kyrgyzskaya, and international telephone calls may be made from here. **Internet access** is also available here round the clock. There is another internet café downstairs at the art gallery in the main square, and the CBT office also has reliable internet access.

The **OVIR** office, where visas may be extended, is at the Ministry of Foreign Affairs office on Togolok Moldo.

WHAT TO SEE AND DO Naryn is a long, sprawling town with few opportunities for sightseeing. The centre of the town revolves around the main square that faces the municipal administrative building, the Hakimyat, where there is a tall, modern statue of a Kyrgyz couple holding an eagle aloft, which is meant to represent Kyrgyz youth. This area was redeveloped in 1999 and the **statue of Lenin** which used to stand here has been moved a couple of blocks west to the leafier surroundings of a park.

The square is also home to a new, purpose-built **art gallery**, which is worth a visit (☎ 507 79; admission 50som). The gallery has the work of several Kyrgyz artists on display, like Torobekov Kojogulov, who paints scenes from Kyrgyz life and semiabstract landscapes and still lifes. There are also some evocative charcoal drawings, attractive ceramics with Saimaluu-Tash petroglyph designs and, naturally, a plushly decorated yurt. The main building of the recently established University of Central Asia stands opposite the art gallery. A little further west stands the Naryn Drama Theatre, with a small plaza in front of it that serves as a location for meeting friends and eating ice creams in summer. The central bazaar lies immediately north of this.

Victory Park At the far eastern end of the town, close to the Celestial Mountains Guest House and the regional museum, this pleasant, wooded park has a Soviet tank as its centrepiece, which faces a line of seven arches that frame the arid mountains beyond. The park is pretty much deserted most of the time, but on summer nights it is sometimes used as the venue for drunken outdoor discos.

Regional Museum The museum (*Razzakova 4;* ⊕ *09.00–17.00 Mon–Fri; admission 60som*) is located just across the bridge over the Naryn River, at the eastern end of town close to the Celestial Mountains Guest House. The different rooms here include ethnological displays on the Kyrgyz nomadic way of life, a dissected yurt, traditional costumes (which include some interesting headgear), a room devoted to the life of local revolutionary hero Jukeev Tubaldy Pudovkin, and the obligatory display of stuffed animals. There is also artwork by local artists and a few of the excellent *shyrdaks* for which the province is famous.

New Mosque The new mosque at the western end of town, a couple of kilometres from the centre, is both a dazzling and incongruous sight: a rare splash of colour – blue, turquoise and white – against the khaki-brown hills that form its backdrop. The mosque was built with the help of Saudi money in 1993 and has a number of different architectural elements in its design that combine together in a postmodernist sort of way. There is, without doubt, a definite Arabian element in its design, and the irregular, patterned frieze that frames the doorway resembles a Kyrgyz traditional *shyrdak* pattern to some extent. In contrast, the wooden cupola that tops the pepper-pot minaret seems to be at odds with the rest of the building, and devalues the integrity of the design with its *Arabian Nights* appearance.

EAST OF NARYN

The Naryn River, passing through the regional capital, leads east past the airport to Salkyn-Tör, an attractive canyon which is popular as a picnic spot for Naryn's citizens. The area is partially protected as being part of the Salkyn-Tör State Park, which covers a considerable area along the Naryn River immediately to the east of Naryn. The road continues east to reach the quiet village of Tash-Bashat. East of here, further along the Naryn River and close to the border with Issyk-Kul Province, lies the Naryn State Reserve, one of Kyrgyzstan's six state reserves, which was established in 1983 to preserve coniferous forest and alpine meadows.

Tash-Bashat (formerly Kalinin) is famous for one thing and one thing only: close to the village on a hillside in the Naryn-Too range is an area of forest that has clearly been planted in the shape of a swastika, a tangible reminder of the horrors of Nazism in World War II (see box, page 232). The forest can be best seen from the roadside just north of the river crossing, on the road that leads past the village's small mosque.

A very rough unmade road leads east from Tash-Bashat's village mosque, up and over a steep hill, to reach the **Iiri-Suu deer nursery**. The road really needs a 4x4 to be on the safe side, although I managed to reach it in a Volkswagen Golf with a feisty driver – an object lesson as to what Kyrgyz drivers will put their cars through for a fistful of som. The deer nursery, which covers 50ha, was established in 2002 for the protection of orphaned, sick and injured maral deer, which are often poached in the surrounding region for their antlers and are then sold in China. Once recovered, the deer are released back into the wild.

The reserve, which has up to 250 deer, consists of a fenced-off portion of a gorge, as well as small enclosures where younger deer are kept. While the cause is no doubt praiseworthy, a visit to the nursery is rather like a trip to a zoo at feeding time, although it makes for an enjoyable experience for children.

Returning to Tash-Bashat, the road continues north along the east bank of the Kichi-Naryn River to the village of Eki-Naryn, crossing a bridge just before the village.

EKI-NARYN (ЕКИ-НАРЫН) The village of Eki-Naryn ('Two Naryns', ie: the confluence of the two rivers) is spread out on a flat area above the gorge of the Kichi-Naryn River, just beyond the point where the river divides into the Naryn and its equally impressive tributary, the Kichi-Naryn. The road crosses the Naryn River to follow the east bank of the Kichi-Naryn for a short distance to reach the village.

Eki-Naryn is a pretty village and its setting, even by Kyrgyzstan's high standards, is glorious, with red sandstone cliffs along the river and the high peaks of the Jetim and Naryn-Too ranges looming to the north and south. The valley is so gorgeous here that it begs to be followed north and east deep into the Terskey Ala-Too. It is certainly possible to cycle, hike or ride the route that leads along the Kichi-Naryn and Burkan or Jyluu-Suu valleys to Lake Issyk-Kul over the Tosor Pass, although this would require total independence in terms of food and shelter, and would make more sense done in the opposite direction.

THE SWASTIKA FOREST OF NARYN PROVINCE

The 200m-wide swastika, which can be clearly seen in a fir plantation on a hillside near the small village of Tash-Bashat in Naryn Province, is an enigma that is clouded by legend and conflicting memories. The so-called Eki-Naryn swastika is actually a reverse, left-handed swastika, with the top and bottom arms incomplete. Nevertheless, it is still an unmistakable symbol, with all the chilling resonances that are normally associated with it.

The swastika is said to be at least 60 years old, and common legend tells of stranded German prisoners of war, forced into forestry after the end of World War II, planting rows of seedlings in this shape. This legend is probably not the exact truth. There are others who say that it was planted in the 1940s by Kyrgyz labourers from a local collective farm that was managed by a German Nazi sympathiser who, like many ethnic Germans in the Soviet Union, had been exiled to central Asia by Stalin during the war. Another theory suggests that the trees were planted just after Stalin's death in 1953 under the supervision of a female German forester. Another, unlikely, suggestion is that the trees were planted in the late 1930s at the time that Stalin and Hitler were signing a peace pact together, as a symbol of Soviet-German friendship.

Whatever the exact truth, it is unlikely that German prison gangs ever worked in the area. There were labour camps near Bishkek and Osh, and some prisoners were forced to dig uranium mines at Mailuu-Suu, but no-one in the area remembers Germans being used as labourers, although there do seem to be several recollections of a German woman supervising the planting using local Kyrgyz labour.

There are those of New-Age persuasion who decry the Nazi connotations entirely, saying that as a reverse swastika it is actually a representation of the sacred symbol frequently used in the Hindu and Buddhist religions, even suggesting that the name Eki-Naryn is a distortion of *Eki Narayan*, 'one God'. However, such a theory does not really correspond with the certainty that the trees were planted in the mid-20th century.

Returning to Naryn, rather than retracing previous steps, a 4x4 could continue northeast from Eki-Naryn along the valley to reach the tiny village of Oryook-Tam. From there it could then leave the river to loop north along the Kara-Saz stream, before heading west along a track that climbs over a couple of passes to follow the Kara-Kujur River back to the main Kochkor–Naryn road at Sary-Bulak. There is plenty of scope for wild camping close to the village. Public buses from Naryn run three times a week on Monday, Wednesday and Friday mornings. More conveniently, a taxi costs about 700som for the return trip, including a two-hour wait.

NARYN TO THE TORUGART PASS

The road south to China from Naryn caused some consternation when its presence was first discovered by the British in the early 20th century. This was in the latter days of the Great Game era, when British and Russian diplomats in the region kept a close eye on each other's activities, wary that their colonial competitors might gain the upper hand. In 1905, the British Consul to Kashgar, Sir George McCartney, made the unsettling discovery that the Russians had constructed a road from At-Bashy, near the Russian garrison at Naryn, to the Torugart Pass on the Chinese border, a road which extended a little way into China itself. The main concern at the time was the possibility of the Russians annexing China's Xinjiang Province by means of the new road.

As it transpired, the foremost motive was actually that of international trade. The Chinese side of the road that led to Kashgar was completed in the following year by means of a Russian loan to the Chinese government, which was to be repaid by imposing a toll to use the road. The Russians soon ended up having the monopoly of trade along the route, which displeased the Chinese to the extent that they raised the toll so high that the road soon fell into disuse.

The route from Naryn leads over the 2,484m **Kyzyl-Bel Pass** to cross a valley to bypass the small town of **At-Bashy**, which lies just south of the highway, 40km from Naryn. The Chinese frontier is still another 150km away, but this is the last sizeable place before the border, other than a handful of villages such as Kara-Suu, Kara-Bulung, Kyzyl-Too and Kazibek. A few kilometres beyond At-Bashy are the ruins of the citadel of **Koshoy Korgon**, near the village of Kara-Suu.

From Kara-Suu, the highway continues straight as an arrow along the dead flat valley of the Kara-Suu River, which is squeezed between the parallel ranges of the snow-capped At-Bashy mountains to the south and the slightly lower Jaman-Too to the north. It is a largely deserted landscape, apart from occasional herders with their flocks of sheep and a couple of evocatively eroded Kyrgyz cemeteries near the roadside.

Naturally, much of the light traffic heading this way is involved in tourism of one sort or another, ferrying travellers to Tash Rabat and the Chinese border. The remaining vehicles along this road are either large Chinese lorries delivering cheap manufactured goods to Kyrgyz markets, or battered Kyrgyz trucks loaded high with scrap metal and fleeces heading for the Torugart Pass. This obvious two-way commerce brings alive the government statistics that suggest Kyrgyzstan's foreign trade is largely dependent on animal skins and the recycling of ferrous metals.

There is a stretch just west of At-Bashy where the road widens dramatically. This section was constructed as an emergency military air strip in the event of a Chinese invasion years ago; it was never used. After about 3km or so, this unnervingly wide section – a veritable motorway – suddenly reverts to its former width.

Just before Ak-Beit, where a dirt road from Chaek joins the highway, there is a turn-off south to the remarkable caravanserai of **Tash Rabat**, a worthy destination in its own right, whether or not the crossing to China is on the agenda, and a fairly essential side trip for those heading for Torugart. Beyond Ak-Beit the road twists south to climb up over the 3,282m pass, before reaching the Korgon-Tash outer checkpoint 4km further on, which marks the beginning of the border zone. Leaving the checkpoint, the road skirts the western fringe of the At-Bashy range to climb up to the 3,574m **Tüz-Bel Pass**. From here it leads east above the southern shore of **Lake Chatyr-Köl**, a high alpine lake with a marshy shoreline that lies at the far western end of the **Ak-Say Valley**, a high, wide plateau where large herds of yak graze in summer and hunters from At-Bashy come to catch marmots. This is a wonderful area for fully independent hiking and camping but it requires a border permit because of its proximity to China.

Lake Chatyr-Köl, which at 3,530m is the highest of Kyrgyzstan's larger lakes, is protected as part of the Chatyr-Köl Zoological Preserve, one of the three protected areas of the Karatal-Japyryk State Reserve which also includes Lake Song-Köl. The lake has no fish but it attracts some rare migratory birds to breed here, most notably bar-headed goose (*Anser indicus*), the world's highest-flying bird, as well as birds on passage such as cranes. Because of the wet, boggy ground that surrounds the lake it can be difficult to get very close to the shoreline.

Continuing to climb above the lake's southern shore, and passing some roadside railway carriages that serve as basic dormitory hotels, the Kyrgyzstan customs and immigration post is finally reached 50km beyond the outer checkpoint. From here it is another 5km to the first Chinese checkpoint (the main Chinese customs and immigration post is well into Chinese territory, another 70km further on) and then a further 2km to the summit of Torugart Pass. Up until 2002 there was a Chinese archway that marked the border but this has since been removed.

AT-BASHY (АТ-БАШЫ) At-Bashy is an attractive small town set in a highly dramatic landscape 40km from Naryn, a few kilometres south of the main Naryn–Torugart Pass highway. With the near-5,000m peaks of the At-Bashy range looming to the south and a large evocative Kyrgyz cemetery standing on a ridge above the town, At-Bashy's location is quite spectacular, and the town is a good choice for an overnight stay *en route* to the Chinese border, or as a base for day excursions to Koshoy Korgon and Tash Rabat.

The town is a thoroughly provincial sort of place and, as the last settlement of any size before the Chinese frontier, it does have a certain edge-of-the-world feel about it. As the administrative headquarters of the At-Bashy *rayon*, or region, which extends along the valley, it has all the basic ingredients you might expect – a few civic buildings, a park, a small bazaar and odd fragments here and there of a Soviet past.

The town developed on the foundations of a much older settlement that dates from between the 8th and 14th centuries, of which no trace remains today. Formerly there were a number of collective farms in the vicinity, but these were abandoned along with communism, and the town is a markedly poorer place today, with high unemployment.

At-Bashy means 'Horse's Head' in Kyrgyz and a recent addition to the town has been an 11m-high bronze statue of a grazing horse's head. This replica of *Still Water*, a sculpture by Nic Fiddian-Green at Marble Arch, London, was paid for by a wealthy local deputy who wanted to celebrate the town's name. Unfortunately, the statue had already started degrading within a year of its installation in October 2013.

The town's main street stretches east to west, with the bus station at the far eastern end by an equestrian statue, and some concrete yurts selling booze. Close to this stands a very traditional *chaikhana* and a new mosque. Walking west towards the centre is an enclosure where the weekly animal market is held, and a large government building with busts of prominent Kyrgyz leaders in its grounds. The centre, such as it is, is marked by an abandoned cinema and the Kyrgyz Telecom building.

Immediately west of here is a dusty park with a war memorial and gold-painted busts, the Ak Bank and the bazaar. The road that leads north from the Shepherd's Life sign, Aity Suleymanov, is home to the post office and the combined Ak-Say store, café and *gostinitsa*. To reach the Shepherd's Life homestay, walk down here for four blocks and then turn left at the second sign; the homestay is at the end of this road, a large rambling house which is taller than those surrounding it.

Getting there and away
There are three **buses** a day between Naryn and At-Bashy, an occasional *marshrutka* and share taxis for 150som. A taxi taken privately will cost 500som. There are also **share taxis** and **minibuses** to Bishkek. There is no public transport to Tash Rabat from here, but a taxi there and back with waiting time should cost around 2,000–2,500som. Buses and minibuses leave from the bus station, although minibuses will also pick up at the bazaar if they are not already full. Most taxis congregate outside the bazaar, although there may be one or two at the bus station.

Where to stay

Homestay Arpa 25; ☏ 03534 21 944. Homestay accommodation may be found at the comfortable home of Tursan Akayeva, who has a large house in the northwest of the town, just below the cemetery on the ridge. The house, which has an outside toilet in the garden, is unusually large, with an upstairs sleeping area decorated with *shyrdaks*. The atmosphere is slightly shambolic, with a constant stream of local visitors coming & going. The redoubtable Tursan can also organise local taxis & arrange transportation to Tash Rabat or Koshoy Korgon & arrange visits to local *shyrdak*-makers. B&B **$**, meals 200som.

Nomad Yurt Camp m 0555 207 773, 0556 224 733; e nomadsworldtravel@gmail.com; www.nwtravel.kg. On a farm in a beautiful setting 20km from At-Bashy, this remote yurt camp offers yurt stays with hands-on Kyrgyz nomad experiences like horseriding, yurt assembly & *kumys*-making. Also mountain bikes & trekking. B&B **$**, meals 250som.

Where to eat and drink
There are some cafés along the main street towards the bus station. The bazaar has a reasonable range of fruit, vegetables and dairy produce; there is a good *nan* bakery on the main street just to the west of the bazaar. The new-looking **Kadirzhan café** (☏ 03534 22 517; **$$**) almost opposite the bazaar is probably the best place in town. The fancy wooden entrance has what looks like a carved Chinese symbol at the front. The food is, in fact, Russian, with staples like *pelmeni* at low prices.

Other practicalities
The **post office** is on Aity Suleymanov, north of the crossroads by the park. Kyrgyz Telecom is just south of here. There is *very* slow **internet access** in the telecom building.

What to see and do
At-Bashy's splendour is its location and the landscape that surrounds it. Apart from the new horse's head sculpture (see opposite) and the remnants of the Soviet era that survive on the main street – a park with a war memorial, a Lenin bust, a police building that still has red stars decorating the wall – the town's most impressive sight is the large Kyrgyz **cemetery** that stands on a ridge just north of the town. There are actually two separate graveyards, with a tiny Christian cemetery standing in between the two. The views over the town,

valley and the At-Bashy range here are superb in the late afternoon or early evening. Another worthwhile walk is down to the At-Bashy River just south of the town.

On Sunday mornings there is a photogenic **animal market** in the town that attracts villagers from miles around who come and check out the cattle, horses and sheep on sale. It is also a good opportunity to buy fresh fruit and vegetables at knock-down prices.

KOSHOY KORGON (КОШОЙ КОРГОН) Located about 15km from At-Bashy, Korgon is a ruined citadel at the edge of Kara-Suu village which dates from between the 10th and 12th centuries. The structure may well be Karakhanid in origin, although there is also a legend that it was built by Manas as a mausoleum for his friend Koshoy who fell in battle, which gives rise to its name: 'Koshoy's burial place'.

All that is left today is a large section of 2–3m-high crumbling clay walls that delineate the extent of the original building; it is an impressive site nevertheless. Archaeological work was carried out on the site in 2004 and a museum was established in 2007, although it is not always open.

The citadel is reached by turning left after Kara-Suu's mosque and war memorial, and then continuing to the end of the road, where the ruins are found in a field to the right. A taxi from At-Bashy will cost around 500som for the round trip.

TASH RABAT (ТАШ РАБАТ) Tash Rabat is probably Kyrgyzstan's most remarkable monument; indeed, it is one of the most interesting sites in the entire central Asian region and its presence is in complete contradiction to the popular tenet that Kyrgyzstan is all about landscapes rather than historical sites. Tash Rabat is a Silk Road monument *par excellence*: a small but perfectly formed 15th-century caravanserai that sheltered an array of merchants and travellers along one of the wilder stretches of the Silk Road. Its location is even more remarkable: tucked away from sight, half-buried in a hillside, up a valley at 3,530m above sea level.

The building is entirely stone-built, half-sunken into the hillside from which it emerges almost organically like a rocky outcrop. It is a broad rectangle in shape, measuring 36m long but looking smaller from the outside because some of its internal structure lies beneath the hillside. The front entrance leads into a central hall that is surrounded by a network of small rooms, about 30 in all, which were used as bedrooms, prison cells, pantries and prayer rooms. A dome stands above the central hallway and this still bears faint traces of plaster and decorative paintwork. Facing the entrance just beyond the dome is the khan's seat, where the local ruler would have sat, and behind this is a small room that probably served as a gaol, as there are two deep, covered holes, one of which has been subsequently filled in, in which prisoners may have been confined. There is also a well for supplying water. Local rumour suggests that there was a tunnel leading from the building through the hillside to a lookout post on the other side of the hill. It is probable that the building was constructed as a place of rest and Muslim worship, and as protection from both bandit attacks and the sometimes atrocious weather of the region.

The site may have been originally used as a monastery by Nestorian Christians, or even possibly by Buddhists, who lived in the region before the 13th-century Mongol invasions took place, and well before Islam came to the region. There is some archaeological evidence to suggest that the building may have been occupied as early as the 10th century, which would support this theory. Whatever the true historical facts, there is no denying the atmosphere of the place, which seems to be imbued with ghosts of the past and authentically redolent of the old Silk Road. The cold, dank atmosphere inside the building and the altitude-rarefied air both help cement this impression.

The Soviet restoration that took place in 1984 was carried out in an uncharacteristically sensitive way and, apart from some mortar added to cement the stones together, has done little to damage the integrity of the structure, the only gripe being the need to position the car park directly in front of the entrance, thus blighting photo opportunities from this direction.

Part of Tash Rabat's timeless appeal lies in its location in a high, velvet-green valley far away from anything that vaguely resembles civilisation. Another element of its wow factor owes much to the journey taken to reach the site, which lies 125km from Naryn and 90km short of the border at Torugart. After turning off the main road to the border just after the stretch of aircraft runway, it is another 15km along a small but very beautiful valley, the Kara-Kojon Gorge, before the caravanserai is reached. There is an entrance fee of 50som to pay to go inside. The caretaker lives directly opposite and will probably find you first if you arrive by taxi.

Getting there and away Many **tour companies** have Tash Rabat firmly on their itineraries, either as a destination in itself or as an appendage to a trip to China via Torugart. CBT Naryn can organise transport and yurt accommodation for those wishing to make an overnight or longer trip here from Naryn. Individual travellers can organise **taxis** from either Naryn or At-Bashy, which should cost in the order of 2,500som return from At-Bashy or 3,500som from Naryn.

Where to stay and eat There is a fair choice of yurts to stay in if you wish to overnight, either close to the monument or a couple of kilometres back down the valley. The caretaker has a few **yurts** opposite the entrance, which are a little cheaper than CBT's yurts, and there are some private yurts a little further down the valley that offer accommodation and meals to travellers (**$**, *meals 250som*).

All of the above tend to be open in the tourist season only, which here is late May to September. Although yurts usually provide adequate bedding, be aware that it is very cold at night here. Toilet and washing facilities are either rudimentary or non-existent. Do not use the stream for toilet duties of any sort as, understandably, this upsets the locals who use its waters for drinking and cooking.

Hikes from Tash Rabat Tash Rabat is a good base for hikes or horse rides. Horses may be hired from the Tash Rabat caretaker who charges around 150som per hour and who can provide a guide for 1,000–1,200som per day if required. A horse will certainly make it easier on your legs, although perhaps not on other parts of your anatomy.

One **classic hike** or ride from Tash Rabat is the ascent to the ridge of the At-Bashy range that overlooks **Lake Chatyr-Köl**, a tough four- to five-hour climb or seven- to eight-hour round trip. The ridge is at almost 4,000m and so offers wonderful views over the lake and the wide Ak-Say Valley. Naturally, the altitude makes for hard work, and the weather can be very changeable, too, with snow or sleet a possibility at any time of year. The route begins by following the river upstream on the opposite bank to the caravanserai. There will probably be several yurts along this stretch, and herds of yaks in addition to sheep, cattle and horses. After a couple of hours, a gorge on the right leads to up to the 3,968m **Tash Rabat Pass**, a steep, heart-thumping climb. It is possible to descend to Lake Chatyr-Köl in a couple of hours or less from the ridge, although, technically at least, it requires a border permit, as does any further trekking along the Ak-Say Valley. CBT Naryn organise a two-day **horse trek** that follows this route, staying in a yurt on the south side of the lake and visiting a nearby cave, before returning to Tash Rabat on the second day.

The route over the 3,752m Torugart Pass is one of just two roads into China from Kyrgyzstan, the other being the route via Irkeshtam further south in Osh Province. While Chinese trucks regularly trundle along the route (and damage the roads with their 80-tonne loads, according to many Kyrgyz) it is a different matter for foreign visitors, for whom the crossing here is more problematic.

Crossing into China via the Torugart Pass is made difficult by a combination of paperwork, random decision-making and official intransigence. This is not to say it cannot be done – it can – but it is prudent to be aware that there are a lot of factors that may go wrong, and sometimes they do. Having said all of this, the general trend appears to be one of matters easing slightly of late: long delays and turnings-back are less frequent than they were a few years ago and, with the correct paperwork and a fair wind, you should be able to arrive in Kashgar the same day as leaving Tash Rabat or Naryn. What is indisputable is the need for a degree of flexibility, as well as patience and a certain spirit of adventure, but if you did not possess these last two qualities then you probably would not be in Kyrgyzstan in the first place.

The first thing to understand about the Torugart border is that it is what is known as a 'second grade' border – one through which nonnationals are not normally admitted. To allow foreigners to overcome this, special regulations are in place that require those in transit to be met by a Chinese travel representative at the frontier to transport them into China itself. It is imperative that travellers have in their possession the documentation to prove that this transfer will definitely take place.

To take your own vehicle involves far more headaches than suggested here and will take at least two months to organise with a Chinese agency. Similarly, it is very hard to get permission to cycle across the border. Most cyclists heading for China take the Irkeshtam route from Osh, which is far more straightforward.

PLANNING A CROSSING Crossing the Torugart Pass requires a certain degree of prearrangement. It is best organised in advance in Bishkek, with a travel company which will make all the necessary arrangements once a firm date has been agreed. As it is fairly expensive, currently around US$450–500 per vehicle (more than half this from Naryn), most independent travellers either try to find others to join them for the journey, or allow an agency to assemble a group for them. Groups usually consist of four travellers, although some agencies will only allow three because they say room is needed in the car for spare fuel and tyres.

Because an exact entry date needs to be arranged, an organised Torugart passage will slightly restrict the way you spend the rest of your time in Kyrgyzstan, as it is vital you show up on the prescribed date. Choosing a date on which to cross is an important consideration, particularly the day of the week that is selected. Many travellers, wishing to arrive in Kashgar in time for the Sunday market, choose to travel on a Friday. The problem with this is that if anything goes wrong with the crossing on the Friday then there will be a delay of another three days, as the border is firmly closed on weekends (it can be firmly closed at other times, too, but more of this later). Because of this, a midweek crossing is probably a safer bet.

Another very important consideration is to avoid **public holidays** on either the Kyrgyz or Chinese side, as anything that vaguely resembles a holiday will result in one or both of the customs posts shutting up shop. In theory, the border is supposed to be open all year round, but because of holidays it is likely to be closed on the following dates: 1 January (New Year's Day), 7 January (Orthodox Christmas) and 29–31 January; 1–4 February and 23 February (Army Day); 8 March (International

Women's Day), 21 March (Nooruz) and 24 March (Anniversary of the March 2005 revolution); 1 May (Labour Day), 5 May (Constitution Day) and 9 May (Victory Day) – it is best to avoid the first ten days of May altogether; 1 August and 31 August (Kyrgyz Independence Day); 1 October and 7 October (again, best to avoid the first ten days of October altogether); and 7 November (Anniversary of the October Revolution).

Also be aware that those holidays that fall on weekends are normally taken on a Monday or Friday instead. China has holidays on 29 January–4 February, 1–7 May, 1 June, 1 July, 1–2 August, 12 September and 1–7 October. There are also the moveable holidays like Chinese New Year, Orozo Ait (feast at the end of Ramadan) and Kurban Ait (nine weeks after the end of Ramadan). As well as holidays and weekends, bad weather and deep snow can close the pass at any time, even in July or August. Political events may also take their toll: the border was closed in October 2001 for a period as a result of the political situation in Afghanistan, and briefly in 2010 at the height of the riots in Bishkek and the south.

The **precise timing** of the crossing, as in the hour of the day, is also crucial as the two customs posts operate on different time zones, with Chinese time being two hours (three in winter, October–March) later than Kyrgyz time. This is *official* Chinese time, or Beijing time – much of far western China operates on unofficial Xinjiang time, two hours earlier, but the customs post observes the Beijing convention. Because of this, and because of the slow bureaucratic proceedings at customs and the distances to be covered, it is important to arrive at the Kyrgyz post as early as possible – it opens at 09.30 and closes at 17.00; the Chinese post is open, in theory at least, between 10.00 and 17.00 (Beijing time). Both posts observe a two-hour lunch break (sometimes even longer) when very little is likely to happen. It is 100km from the border to the Chinese immigration post and there are bound to be delays, so start early!

As well as **documentation** proving that onward Chinese transport has been arranged, a **Chinese visa** will also be required. This is not available at the border. Chinese visas can sometimes be obtained in Bishkek, but it is much better to apply for them well in advance in your country of origin, as the Bishkek Embassy will probably insist on an invitation from a Xinjiang travel company, which entails more expense and hassle and takes at least a week – in your own country you can simply apply by post. On the application form do not mention Torugart, Xinjiang, Tibet or any overtly politically sensitive areas; just write Beijing, Shanghai, Xian and other obvious non-controversial destinations in eastern China – these will not be mentioned on the visa that is subsequently issued. Once again, this involves some advance planning as you will need to know the date on which you plan to enter China from Torugart.

Normally, Chinese visas are issued for a period of one month, so as long as the visa has become valid by the time the Torugart is crossed there will be no problem. **Border permits** are *not* required providing that the Torugart Pass is approached directly from Naryn (allowing a side trip to Tash Rabat).

TOUR OPERATORS There are a considerable number of tour agencies in Bishkek which will happily arrange the Torugart border crossing for you, either all the way from Bishkek to Kashgar, or just from Naryn. Itineraries may be tailored to individual tastes and many standard tours include a night at Tash Rabat, and possibly a trekking excursion from there, before the pass is traversed.

The agencies will liaise with a Kashgar-based company to arrange the onward transport from the pass, although this portion of the cost is usually paid directly to the Chinese driver in US dollars. The agency should give you written confirmation of the agreed price for this just in case of dispute. On agreeing a fee with an agency, check for any hidden extras: the quoted price should include everything – fuel, the food and accommodation for the driver, as well as that for the clients; the exit tax levied on the vehicle leaving Kyrgyzstan should also be accounted for. Also check the type of vehicle that the agency is providing as, early or late in the season when there may be snow on the ground, a 4x4 is definitely preferred. The driver himself should be experienced with the crossing, not just with the roads leading to the Torugart Pass, but also with the various procedures involved at customs.

Of the **Bishkek travel agencies**, the following companies all have considerable experience of arranging a Torugart crossing: Ak-Sai Travel, Celestial Mountains, Edelweiss, Fantastic Asia, ITMC Tien Shan, Kyrgyz Concept and Novi Nomad (see pages 53–5). In **Naryn**, both CBT and Kubat Tour are expert at organising a crossing. In summer 2014, the going rate was around US$400–450 for all-inclusive transportation from Naryn to Kashgar; from Bishkek, US$500–550. This works out at just a little over US$100 per person from Naryn if a group of four can be put together – most of the agencies will help facilitate this.

TRAVELLING INDEPENDENTLY It is also possible to make your own way to the Torugart Pass and book onward transport on the Chinese side directly with a Kashgar agency such as **John's Information Café** (✆ +86 998 298 1186; e johncafe@ hotmail.com; www.johncafe.net). They would need to send you all the necessary documentation by fax, and the cost of a private vehicle and requisite guide from the border to Kashgar is around US$300.

Crossing the border this way requires finding a taxi in Naryn to drive to the border post at the designated time to meet the Chinese vehicle, which will not be easy to synchronise. The driver will also need a foreign ministry permit stamped into his passport to travel through no-man's land and proceed to the border post. Otherwise, you will have to be dropped off at the customs post to hitch the final 7km through no-man's land to the border, as you are not allowed to walk.

BORDER FORMALITIES At the Kyrgyz post the confirmation of the onward Chinese transportation is shown and the Kyrgyz guards will await radio confirmation that the Chinese transport has arrived. After confirmation, which may take hours if the vehicle is delayed (likely), Kyrgyz immigration will collect customs forms, perhaps inspect your baggage and thoroughly go over the vehicle. Customs being cleared, you drive on 7km to the border zone where the Chinese driver will be waiting. This is still sometimes referred to as the 'arch', although the Chinese arch that formerly stood here to welcome visitors to China was removed in 2002 for reasons unknown. The Chinese customs post, where luggage is x-rayed and possibly searched, is a few kilometres further on. From here it is 100km along sandstone canyons to the Chinese immigration post, where immigration forms are completed and passports stamped. The Chinese guards are exceptionally officious and no English is spoken. If you are carrying a large video camera, video tapes, mobile phone, Sat phone or walkie talkie you may well have them confiscated or sealed until you leave China again. If this happens, do not unseal them yourself. It is a further 60km to Kashgar.

If, for whatever reason, you cannot get through there are very basic places to stay at the pass just before the Kyrgyz post. The border guards on the Kyrgyz side may also let you stay in their decidedly warmer barracks if you pay them directly in cash (US dollars are preferred), and their wives can rustle up a basic meal. The toilet is outside and is little more than a concrete hut surrounding a very deep and smelly pit. The most likely problem, other than closure for an unanticipated holiday, is that your Chinese transport has been delayed for some reason. This is rarely the fault of the travel company themselves but usually down to overzealous customs officials creating problems just to relieve their own boredom. Long, cold waits at the top of the pass and the payment of excessively large bribes on the Kyrgyz side are, sadly, all too common.

NARYN TO KAZARMAN

West of Naryn the Naryn River leads upstream along a wide valley, between the Moldo-Too range which lies immediately south of Lake Song-Köl and the Jaman-Too ('Bad Mountains') range which hems in the northern side of the At-Bashy Valley. It is a landscape of arid badlands and occasional dusty, scattered settlements. The direct road to Kazarman, and subsequently Jalal-Abad, splits into two at the village of Ak-Tal, with the route via Kök-Jar being the shortest in distance. Most traffic takes the longer southern route via Baetov, which has considerably better road conditions. Both of these routes are fairly rough, but they do offer a rugged and reasonably direct option to the very long alternative route via Bishkek.

Unfortunately, the small bus that used to travel twice weekly between Naryn and Kazarman no longer runs and services now only go as far as Baetov (see below). Share taxis to Kazarman can sometimes be found in Naryn, but it is usually necessary to hire a whole taxi for the journey, which will cost something in the order of 5,000som.

Heading west, the first village of note is **Dostuk**, where the At-Bashy flows into the larger River Naryn through a narrow gorge which is dammed and has a hydro-electricity station. The road skirts south of the river for another 60km to reach **Ak-Tal**, a small village which offers potential access to the southern shore of Lake Song-Köl along a rugged, 4x4-only track over the Moldo Pass. Ak-Tal is the birthplace of the famous Kyrgyz poet and *manaschi* Togolok Moldo (1860–1942), who has a street in Bishkek named after him and who also puts in an appearance on the 20som banknote. Heading for Kazarman by means of the shortest route possible, it is important to take the gravel road to the right here that crosses to the north bank of the Naryn River rather than the paved road to the south that leads to Baetov, as the route to Kazarman is much longer this way. The main Naryn–Kazarman route follows the north bank of the river west to eventually reach the village of Kök-Jar, from where it climbs up a steep, switchback road to the 2,839m pass that marks the beginning of Jalal-Abad Province.

A little further north of the river at Ak-Tal on the road to Song-Köl is the village of **Kurtka** (confusingly also sometimes called Jangy-Talap and marked on maps as such). Close to the village is the 13th-century mausoleum of Taylik Baatyr. There is a daily afternoon bus to Kurtka from Naryn's bazaar.

Just west of Ak-Tal, the road plunges south towards **Baetov**, the largest town in the region, which is served by a daily bus service from Naryn, and which has homestay accommodation with the Shepherd's Life programme. From Baetov, a rough 4x4 road leads south along the Terek Valley to link with the At-Bashy Valley and the Torugart Pass, via a 3,268m pass and the tiny settlement of Orto Syrt. Leaving Baetov to the west, the long road to Kazarman follows the course of the Ala-Buka River to the southwest, crossing the river just before reaching the village of Kosh-Döbö. From here, it swings north, away from the river, and soon leaves Naryn Province to enter Jalal-Abad Province over the 2,932m Ak-Moinok Pass. The lacklustre mining town of Kazarman lies another 30km or so to the north (see page 248).

JALAL-ABAD PROVINCE

9

Jalal-Abad Province

Kyrgyzstan's west-central province, Jalal-Abad, with its capital of the same name, is one of the most varied in the country in geographical terms. It has several mountain ranges, lakes and vast areas of broad-leaved woodland, and in the south, where the province lies on the northern fringe of the Fergana Valley, arable farming is extensive. The province covers 33,700km² in total and with a population of a little less than a million it has a population density of 29 per km² overall, slightly above the national average and about the same as West Virginia in the USA.

Its economy is based on agriculture, in which cotton, maize, wheat and tobacco are all important products, and the mining of minerals, coal and metals; oil and natural gas are also important resources, as is water, with the Toktogul hydro-electricity station producing the lion's share of the country's power supply, as well as providing neighbouring countries with electricity. The climate is generally warm and dry in the summer with temperatures peaking above 40°C on occasion. Rainfall is fairly low but adequate, at about 450mm per year.

Jalal-Abad Province has some of the most intriguing and beautiful destinations for visitors in the entire country: the marvellous gallery of 4,000-year-old petroglyphs high on a mountain top at Saimaluu-Tash; the jewel-like alpine lake of Sary-Chelek surrounded by forests of wild fruit trees; and the remarkable walnut forests around the entirely Uzbek town of Arslanbob. In the extreme southwest corner of the *oblast* in the inaccessible Chatkal Valley is the Besh-Aral State Reserve. The provincial capital of Jalal-Abad has a largely Uzbek character and makes for a pleasant stopover *en route* to Osh.

JALAL-ABAD (ДЖАЛАЛ-ЛБАД) *Telephone code: 03722*

Jalal-Abad (sometimes spelt Dzhalal-Abad, Djalalabad, Jalalabad or Jalalabat), the province's capital and Kyrgyzstan's third-largest city, lies at the southeast corner of the *oblast*, very close to the border with Uzbekistan in the foothills of the Babash-Ata mountain range. The city's proximity to the Fergana Valley is reflected in its mixed population, of which the great majority of a total of 89,000 are Uzbek. A branch of the Silk Road used to pass this way to trade with the settlements of the Fergana Valley, and although little evidence of this remains today, Jalal-Abad still has something of a timeless feel, in spite of its modernity.

The city, which takes its name from a 13th-century warrior, Jalal ad-Din, has a bright, relaxed feel that is different from the towns of the north. The streets are wide and well shaded with trees, and many of the houses are typically Uzbek, hidden away behind walls and tall metal gates with rooms that face inwards on to a communal family area with the inevitable grapevine. The city's spirit of gentle

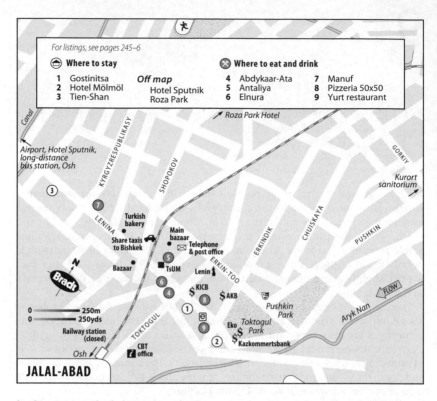

For listings, see pages 245–6

Where to stay

1 Gostinitsa
2 Hotel Mölmöl
3 Tien-Shan

Off map
Hotel Sputnik
Roza Park

Where to eat and drink

4 Abdykaar-Ata
5 Antaliya
6 Elnura

7 Manuf
8 Pizzeria 50x50
9 Yurt restaurant

Roza Park Hotel

Canal

KYRGYZRESPUBLIKASY

Airport, Hotel Sputnik,
long-distance
bus station, Osh

SHOPOKOV

GORKIY

Kurort
sanitorium

③

⑦

LENINA

Turkish
bakery

Share taxis
to Bishkek

Main
bazaar

Telephone
& post office

ERKINDIK

CHUSKAYA

PUSHKIN

Bazaar

TsUM

Lenin

ERKIN-TOO

⑤

⑥

④

① KICB

⑧ AKB

FLOW

Pushkin
Park

Aryk Nan

0 —— 250m
0 —— 250yds

Railway station
(closed)

TOKTOGUL

⑨

Eko

Toktogul
Park

Osh

CBT
office

② Kazkommertsbank

Bradt

N

JALAL-ABAD

liveliness is partly due to its youth: there are several universities based in the town and students throng the cafés around the centre.

Russians first came to Jalal-Abad in the late 19th century when a garrison and military hospital were established here. In 1916 it was connected by railway through the Fergana Valley to Tashkent and Moscow, a conduit to transport the vast amounts of cotton the region produced to European Russia. Later, they developed the town as a health spa, as Jalal-Abad became well known for the various mineral springs found in its vicinity. In the Soviet period several sanatoriums were developed to offer mineral water treatment programmes and warm-weather holiday opportunities for the proletariat. The mineral water business is still going strong and the sanatorium just outside the city continues to receive its share of visitors, although nothing like the old days.

Visitors arriving in Jalal-Abad in July or August will immediately notice how much hotter it is than most places in the north of the country. This is partly because of its comparatively low altitude, but also a consequence of its proximity to the cauldron-like microclimate of the Fergana Valley.

Jalal-Abad was the scene for some of the worst violence in the summer of 2010's rioting and it led to the declaration of a state of emergency. Although the violence has been officially blamed on supporters of ousted President Bakiyev and on inter-ethnic tensions, there are substantiated allegations that the mafia (specifically regional drugs lords) and foreign security forces were also involved. It is estimated that 800 people were killed in the city and many more were injured or fled. Around 330 buildings were severely damaged, of which 291 were completely destroyed. A number of businesses in the city, including hotels, were burned or looted and have not reopened.

British nationals were evacuated from Jalal-Abad on 15 June 2010 and in the following year the FCO was still advising against all but essential travel to Jalal-Abad Province, as well as Jalal-Abad city. This advice was later downgraded to simply one of 'Take care if you travel to the *oblasts* (provinces) of Osh, Batken and Jalal-Abad'. No widespread violence has taken place in the city or region since 2010.

GETTING THERE AND AWAY Jalal-Abad's **long-distance bus station** lies 3km west of the centre at the edge of the town. It is a long walk but can be easily reached by the number 110 minibus, which leaves regularly from outside the bazaar (*10som*). There is a large timetable inside the *avtovakzal* that gives the scheduled bus times, although it is best to confirm times at the ticket kiosk outside. The bus station's spacious interior is given over to billiards and table tennis, but tickets may be bought at the grilles outside or on the bus itself.

Buses leave three times a day for Tash-Kömür (*200som*), as well as for Toktogul (*400som*) along the main Bishkek road, and also for Kerben (*400som*), further west towards the Chatkal Valley. Massy- or Kochkor-Ata-bound minibuses for Bazar-Korgon (*30som*) also leave regularly, where a connection can be made to Arslanbob. **Minibuses** to Osh (*120som*), Ozgön (*60som*) and Kara-Suu leave regularly from here, as do **share taxis** to the same destinations (*Osh, 200som*). Share taxis to Bishkek (*1,100som*) leave from the side of the bazaar in the town centre. It may also be possible to find a shared 4x4 for Kazarman in the bazaar, although this can be arranged with a day's notice through the local CBT (see below). Transport to Osh skirts around Uzbekistan by way of Özgön rather than taking the direct road shown on many maps.

The **train station** has no services these days, although at one time it would have linked with Bishkek via a very circuitous route through Uzbekistan, Tajikistan and Kazakhstan.

The **airport** (✆513 30) is northwest of the centre and can be reached by minibus numbers 1 and 5 from the bazaar. There are daily flights to Bishkek (*2,500–3,400som*) that take about one hour.

TOURIST INFORMATION The **CBT** (*3, Toktogul 20;* ✆ *219 62;* m *0772 376 602;* e *cbt_ja@rambler.ru; www.cbtkyrgyzstan.kg;* ✆ *09.00–17.00 Mon–Fr; at w/ends* ✆ *256 43;* m *0502 376 602, 0502 284 164*) will gladly arrange local homestay accommodation in the city, in addition to organising tours to Arslanbob and horse treks to Saimaluu-Tash. The co-ordinator, Ruhsora Abdullaeva, speaks good English, as does her sister who runs the guesthouse in their Uzbek family home.

WHERE TO STAY *Map, page 244*
As well as the hotels listed below, the CBT office is able to offer homestay accommodation at a number of places around the city (**$$**, *with outside toilet* **$**), either in flats or in traditional Uzbek houses. Some of these are some way from the centre. The homestay of the co-ordinator's sister, Rukiya, in a traditional Uzbek home at Chuiskaya 33, is especially pleasant.

🏠 **Roza Park** (11 rooms) Baltagula 183; ✆730 90; m 0772 260 327; e rozaparkhotel@hotmail. com. Run by an American & his Kyrgyz wife, this new hotel is a contender for the smartest place in town. Pleasant rooms with AC, fridge & satellite TV. Wi-Fi, free parking & restaurant. The main

disadvantage is that it lies at some distance north of the centre. **$$$$**
🏠 **Tien-Shan** Lenina. A brand new hotel & restaurant in 2 separate blocks on Lenina west of the bazaar. **$$$$**

⌂ **Hotel Mölmöl** (50 rooms) Lenina; ☎ 550 59. This is the city's solitary Soviet-period hotel & it is not too bad if you arrive late at night, as at least it is very central. The rooms are worn, the beds squeak & taps drip but it is clean & perfectly adequate. *Sgl* **$**, *dbl* **$$**

⌂ **Hotel Sputnik** (14 rooms) Jany-Zhol, Microdistrict Sputnik; ☎ 509 10. West of the centre, beyond the airport, with dark but clean rooms & decent bathrooms. Rate inc b/fast. *Std* **$**, *lux* **$$**

⌂ **Gostinitsa** Lenina 18; ☎ 210 01. A simple unnamed *gostinitsa* in the centre with reasonable, bargain-priced rooms. **$**

✕ WHERE TO EAT AND DRINK *Map, page 244*

There are numerous *chaikhanas* around the bazaar and a few cafés on the fringes of Toktogul Park. Otherwise, most of the city's restaurants are to be found along Lenina. Those given below are just a selection. These tend to be open throughout the day from around 09.00 in the morning until 22.00 or 23.00 in the evening. The bazaar has tasty fresh bread and local specialities like walnut jam and excellent honey. It also has plenty of delicious fruits and nuts in season, such as peaches, apricots, melons, grapes, walnuts and pistachios. There are also a couple of small cafés in Pushkin Park, which make a pleasant stop for a beer and a breath of fresh air.

✕ **Abdykaar-Ata** Lenina, near junction with Toktogul. A good range of standard Uzbek dishes in a slightly upmarket *chaikhana* which has an outdoor terrace facing on to the street. **$$**

✕ **Elnura** Lenina. Next door to Abdykaar-Ata, this is in a pleasant shady garden terrace with a cooling central fountain. Wide choices of dishes, inc desserts & draught beer. Nicely secluded from the noise & activity of the bazaar opposite & understandably popular with locals. **$$**

✕ **Pizzeria 50x50** Lenina, opposite *gostinitsa*; m 0779 015 050. A rare pizzeria in this city of *shashlyks* & *plov*. Next door to Launch Bar. **$$**

✕ **Antaliya** Lenina. Just back from Lenina near the main square, almost opposite the Abdykaar-

Ata, this is an outdoor café in an enclosed garden which has beer & good *laghman*. **$**

✕ **Manuf** Lenina, junction with Kyrgyz Republikasy. West of the bazaar, this is a traditional Uzbek *chaikhana* with outdoor seating on raised *takhta* platforms. Uzbek staples such as green tea, *plov* & *shashlyk* are served. **$**

✕ **Yurt restaurant** Lenina, junction with Erkindik. Not actually called this, but there is a kitchen yurt that serves a number of tables under the trees here at this establishment. A rather limited selection of dishes is available, but it is a nice location at night. **$**

⬛ **Simit Dunyasi** Lenina. A 24hr Turkish bakery just west of the bazaar.

OTHER PRACTICALITIES The **post and telephone office** is on Toktogul north of Lenina, at the junction with Erkin-Too. There are several **banks** along Lenina – KICB, Credit Bank, Eko Bank, Kazkommertsbank – most of which have functioning ATM cash dispensers that accept Visa. Toktogul also has several exchange offices and small banks. Internet access can be found at a couple of places on Lenina close to the university. For general shopping, as well as TsUM there are a couple of modern department stores like Aigul in front of the bazaar.

WHAT TO SEE AND DO Jalal-Abad has a pleasant atmosphere and a good bazaar but no specific sights to seek out. The central square has a gilded statue of Lenin who, unusually, is in a seated pose. **Pushkin Park** is a green, leafy space to spend a few hours, but the loud amplified music does little to improve its serenity. The 'Kurort' sanatorium, 3km out of town, is worth a visit, if only for the view it offers over the surrounding countryside. There is a café close to the entrance of the sanatorium, Ikram-Ajy, where the panoramic view may be admired. The water for this and the other sanatoriums in the area comes from the Hozret-Ayub-Paigambar spa, whose waters are supposed to cure leprosy. The spa is also the source for many of the bottled water brands in the country, in particular the eponymous Dzhalal-Abad brand.

KAZARMAN TO JALAL-ABAD

This is the toughest part of the difficult but spectacular route taken by travellers who wish to reach Jalal-Abad from Naryn to the east without backtracking through Bishkek. Naryn to Kazarman is covered in *Chapter 8*, page 241. This stretch, an uncomfortable, 160km-long roller-coaster ride up and over the Fergana range, is considerably harder. Unlike the major north–south trunk roads that go from Bishkek to Osh and from Bishkek to Naryn, this road is not maintained in the winter months and it is usually only open between April and October. In some years it may be closed as late as May and as early as September because of heavy snowfall. This seasonal inaccessibility should become a thing of the past in the next few years, however, when the new, Chinese-built Balykchy–Kazarman–Jalal-Abad road is finally completed.

As a destination in its own right, **Kazarman** has little to hold even the most enthusiastic of travellers, but the village serves as a necessary base for a visit to one of Kyrgyzstan's most intriguing and inaccessible sights – the petroglyph galleries at Saimaluu-Tash. Public transport between Kazarman and Jalal-Abad is very rare: there is little habitation along the route and consequently little demand. It is also a challenging road which is only really suitable for robust vehicles like 4x4s, although there is reputed to be an occasional minibus; most ordinary taxis usually refuse to travel this route because of the quality of the road surface. Some improvement work was carried out on the road in 2003 but it remains a difficult drive.

Leaving Kazarman, the road is slow but serviceable at first as it twists west through the village of Aral and past the turn-off for Saimaluu-Tash. It starts to deteriorate further after about 25km, as it climbs up to over 3,000m to top the **Kaldama Pass** in the Fergana range. From the top of the pass there are superb views of the valley south towards Jalal-Abad and the switchback gravel-surfaced road snaking down to the Urut-Bashi River. Descending the pass, the sudden change of scenery is abrupt and almost shocking as the vast green expanse of the Fergana Valley edges into view for the first time.

Eventually, after descending to flatter terrain, the fertility of the valley becomes a reality: the fields are full of tall sunflowers and maize in summer and in late August and early September the road itself is used for drying vast heaps of sunflower heads. There is a tangible feeling that another world has suddenly been entered, not just physically but culturally, too, as the figures along the roadside are no longer the Kyrgyz herders predominant on the far side of the pass but, instead, farming Uzbeks busying themselves with their crops. A line has been crossed and this is Kyrgyzstan's south: an almost alien world for many northern Kyrgyz highlanders, but perhaps less of a culture shock to those visitors familiar with the lowland farming areas of southern Europe.

Just after the sprawling village of **Mihailovka**, there is a road barrier checkpoint where luggage may undergo a peremptory examination. From Mihailovka it is a further 40km to Jalal-Abad through fertile farmland along a relatively good road. Just to the north of Mihailovka, in a large area of walnut and fruit-tree forest similar to that found in the Arslanbob region, is the village of **Ortok**, which has a few CBT homestays and is a good centre for day hikes into the surrounding hills.

This poor, dust-blown settlement in northern Jalal-Abad Province has something of a reputation as a tough mining town down on its luck. Kazarman is situated just to the north of the Makmal opencast gold mine – indeed this is part of its *raison d'être* – but the mine no longer provides the employment opportunities that it used to, and consequently the town suffers with the familiar problems that accompany high unemployment in this part of the world – alcoholism and poverty. To add insult to injury, the climate is uncompromisingly harsh here: Kazarman is relatively low in altitude at just 1,230m above sea level but, like Naryn, it suffers from a climate that is extreme, with hot dry summers and extremely cold winters.

Certainly, it is an unprepossessing place, with a scabrous central square that has the Dom Kulturi and a couple of shops, a poorly stocked bazaar and absolutely nothing to see other than grey Soviet-era apartment blocks. The town – or more accurately, village – is extremely isolated, even for Kyrgyzstan, and is virtually cut off during the winter months when the roads south to Jalal-Abad and east to Naryn are closed by snowfall. There is a small airport but currently no flights. Even in the summer, Kazarman is not a cheerful place and so it is hard to imagine just how dispiriting the village must be during the long, and very cold, winter months; it is hardly any wonder that many locals turn to vodka for escape. The good news is that there is a CBT operation at work here which can facilitate onward transport to Jalal-Abad or Naryn and help organise treks to the unforgettable petroglyphs at Saimaluu-Tash.

GETTING THERE AND AWAY Buses to and from Naryn no longer run and so the only option is a chartered **taxi**, although share taxis (*800–1,000som*) may ply the route sporadically between the two towns. There is no regular transport for the five-hour drive to Jalal-Abad either, although share taxis usually run in the summer months. While saloon car taxis may agree to make the journey, a 4x4 is a better bet. For a 4x4 booked through the CBT, the cost is around 3,000som per vehicle, though you may be able to pay for a single seat.

TOURIST INFORMATION At **CBT** (*Bekten 36;* ✆ *412 53;* m *0777 224 063;* e *reservation@cbtkyrgyzstan.kg; www.cbtkyrgyzstan.kg*). Bujumal Arykmoldoeva can organise horse trips to Saimaluu-Tash from one to three days' duration, as well as day excursions by car and on foot to *jailoos* in the nearby Kargalyk mountain range and visits to Kalmyk burial sites and salt and silver mines. Bujumal can also arrange transport for the trip to Jalal-Abad.

WHERE TO STAY AND EAT The English-speaking CBT co-ordinator, Bujumal Arykmoldoeva, offers **accommodation** in her own large house at Bekten 36, just two blocks from the central square. There are several other CBT options in the village which include Baktygul Chorobaeva at Kadyrkulova 35, south of the centre, who speaks English and has three rooms in her house; and also the homes of Ariet Bolotakunov and Nazgul Idrisova (*all* $ *including breakfast and dinner*).

There are few **restaurants** to speak of in the village, other than a couple of cafés near Dom Kulturi and some fly-blown places near the bazaar; overall, it is probably better to eat at the homestays.

OTHER PRACTICALITIES There is an **Aiyl Bank** with an ATM at Kojalieva 83 in the centre and a branch of **Bai Tushum Bank** on Jeenaliev in the Nur-Jayik microdistrict. The **Saimaluu Tash Park Office** (⊕ *09.00–18.00 Mon–Fri*) is next door to Dom Kulturi.

SAIMALUU-TASH (САЙМАЛУУ-ТАШ)

The name means 'embroidered' or 'patterned stones' in Kyrgyz and this is not a bad description for what is the most remote, and certainly the most spectacular, collection of petroglyphs in the country. Here, high on a lonely alpine plateau, are an estimated 11,000 petroglyphs scattered over the slopes of two glacial moraines that have been named by archaeologists, not very imaginatively, as Saimaluu-Tash One and Saimaluu-Tash Two. The larger of the two, Saimaluu-Tash One, measures 3km in length.

The petroglyphs, which are etched on to shiny basaltic stone, date from at least as early as 2000BC in the Bronze Age, and may well be even older. They most probably represent votive offerings that were brought to this sacred site from the valleys below. The site itself has undoubtedly long been considered to be sacred and it is believed the small pond that lies in the middle of the lower gallery was frequented by shamans.

The Bronze Age tradition of marking this sacred spot with rock drawings was continued by subsequent settlers in the region and one of the most fascinating things about the site is not just the sheer extent of the galleries, or the large number of petroglyphs, but the millennia-long continuity of the site as a place of spiritual activity. The earlier Bronze Age etchings are succeeded by those of the Iron Age from around 800BC onward, and the tradition continued until medieval times when Scythian and Turkic settlers added their own quota.

This continuity of use has afforded the site sacred credentials which are still respected by modern-day Kyrgyz, who recognise Saimaluu-Tash as having spiritual power and healing qualities. Unfortunately, there are a few modern-day visitors who have clearly wanted to make their own artistic mark, too, but thankfully 21st-century graffiti is not very common.

The designs on the stones are various but they tend to fall into categories. The majority are representations of animals such as horses, wolves, lions and, most commonly, ibex. Many more depict hunting scenes in which deer with larger-than-life antlers are stalked by men with bows and spears. Some have scenes that show ploughing and ritual dancing, and many more have solar imagery and wavy patterns that perhaps depict the course of rivers. There are even some highly erotic stones that portray the procreative act.

The intent driving this artwork is as meaningful as its content. The petroglyphs are less the stone pages of a prehistoric sketchbook than they are individual acts of sympathetic magic in which the artist, in physically representing his desire – a successful hunt, a good water supply, sunshine for crops – has invoked the gods to help him: on top of a mountain at 3,200m is not a bad place to summon the spirits.

The site was rediscovered in 1902 by Russians doing mapping work for a road they were building between their garrisons at Jalal-Abad and Naryn – the present-day road through Kazarman. While working on the road, one of the cartographers, Nikolai Khludov, started to pay attention to the stories told by local shepherds of 'painted stones' in the nearby mountains. Khludov decided to organise a small expedition to investigate the site. Although his preliminary findings were reported to the Archaeological Society in Tashkent, who, in turn, organised an expedition, the site was soon forgotten and there was no more academic interest in it until 1950. In that year Saimaluu-Tash was revisited and excavated, and the petroglyphs dated and numbered. Currently the site is under sporadic investigation by the Institute of Archaeology in Bishkek.

VISITING SAIMALUU-TASH Getting to the 'Stonehenge of central Asia', as Saimaluu-Tash is sometimes playfully referred to, is not at all easy. In the first place, it normally requires reaching Kazarman, the village that is used as the base for visits to the petroglyph site, itself a rather isolated and not altogether agreeable place. From Kazarman, it is possible to travel some of the way by 4x4, but the rest has to be done on foot or on horseback. This is best organised with the local Kazarman CBT co-ordinator, or in advance with the CBT office in Bishkek or Jalal-Abad. Arrangements can also be made at the park office in Kazarman, where admission tickets (*100som*) should be bought before visiting the site.

The site lies at 3,200m on top of a mountain and, although it is not technically difficult, the climb up to the petroglyphs is long and slow, and requires a certain amount of stamina. A guide is certainly necessary. There are a few variations on the route to the site, depending on how much time is available.

A very long one-day, or better, overnight, trip to the site can be made from Kazarman. This route entails heading down the Jalal-Abad road for 20km just beyond the village of Aral, where a left turn takes you along a much worse road to the pretty village of Atay, from where the going gets ridiculously difficult. The track from here, which is basically a rough bed of boulders, eventually leads to a small *jailoo* where there are a few tents, horses and beehives. Horses are rented here to make the journey up to the site: a 1,000m ascent along a small glacier to the mountain-top moraine where the petroglyphs are. Before the glacier is reached, the path leads through meadows above a boulder-strewn river – a gorgeously lush landscape that is at odds with the arid badlands seen closer to Kazarman.

It is possible, with an early start, to get up to Saimaluu-Tash and back along the same route in the same day, returning to Kazarman to sleep, but an overnight stay at the top means a much less rushed approach, and you will have time the following morning to make a thorough examination of the site. Petroglyphs or not, it is an idyllic setting and the ascent is worth the effort for the views alone. Those staying overnight at the petroglyph site often return by a different and longer route via the village of Chet-Bulak on the Kazarman to Makmal road. Timing is very important; the site is really only accessible during a narrow window which lasts from early August to very early September. Late in the season, locals may not be willing to rent horses as they worry about them plunging through the melting ice of the glacier (although they do not seem too bothered about hapless tourists doing the same thing!). If this is the case, the site must be approached on foot. On foot to the site from the *jailoo* it is approximately 3½ hours up and 2½ hours down. The slippery surface of the glacier is not much fun in trainers.

Another route that takes a full four days to do it justice is from the village of Kalmak-Kyrchyn in the Kök-Art Valley, which is reached from Mihailovka on the Jalal-Abad to Kazarman road. The route from Kalmak-Kyrchyn leads along a very rough track for 20km, to a honey farm where horses and guides are organised. The trek from here takes a whole day to the site. The logistics of this route can be organised through CBT Jalal-Abad with a little advance notice.

ORTOK (OPTOK)

This village is usually overlooked in favour of other destinations like Arslanbob, which are far better set up for incoming tourism. Although it certainly has potential,

Ortok suffered considerable damage a few years back due to landslide, and many villagers moved away as a result. Like Arslanbob (see below), the village lies in the midst of a large area of relict walnut forest about 60km northeast of Jalal-Abad. The forest, which virtually surrounds the village, is rich with a variety of fruit trees in addition to walnut, and there are *jailoos* which can be hiked to above the village, and a system of caves 6km away in a cliff face. A three-day trek from Arslanbob terminates here, and this could equally be done in reverse with prior arrangement through CBT Jalal-Abad.

GETTING THERE AND AWAY A share taxi leaves Jalal-Abad for Ortok in the afternoon, returning next morning – but please note that the road is in poor condition and the going is slow.

WHERE TO STAY AND EAT There are a handful of homestays (**$**) in the village which can be booked in advance through CBT Jalal-Abad (see page 245) or simply by just turning up.

ARSLANBOB (АРСЛАНБОБ) *Telephone code: 03738*

Arslanbob is central to one of Kyrgyzstan's most remarkable regions – the vast relic walnut forest which stretches east and west of the village to cover a total area of 11,000ha. The large, sprawling village of Arslanbob serves as the market centre for the entire region as well as a summer resort with a gentle climate.

Arslanbob is actually far more than this though: unusually for Kyrgyzstan, the village itself is a highly attractive place with a population that is almost entirely Uzbek, and with gorgeous mountain scenery, friendly locals and a pioneering local CBT group, it is hard to beat as a base for hikes in the hills that surround the village or as a start or end point for more energetic treks deep into the mountains.

The village, which is sometimes referred to as Arstanbap, its Uzbek name, is named after an 11th-century hero known as Arslanbob-Ata (or Arstanbap-Ata), whom legend suggests may have been an Arab, as his name can be interpreted as deriving from *aslan* (lion) and *bab* (gate) in that language, the suffix *-ata* meaning 'father of' in various Turkic languages, so Arslanbob-Ata means 'Father of the Lion Gate'. Another explanation of the name may be due to the tradition in the Fergana Valley at that time of adding *-bob* to someone's name if they were a traveller and explorer.

Arslanbob's actual name was Salman Abdul Rahman, a scientist and military leader who is credited with planting the vast walnut forest central to the region's economy. Legend tells of an honest, hard-working man who had been given the task by the Prophet Muhammad of finding a paradise on earth. He eventually came across a beautiful valley with a swift-flowing mountain river running through it but no trees. Reporting this to the Prophet, he was issued with a bag of walnuts and Arslanbob climbed to the top of a mountain and cast the seed in every direction to create a shady garden, which he tended until he died. The name of Babash-Ata, the mountain peak which dominates the village to the north, reflects this, meaning 'Father of the Garden'.

Beautiful as this legend is, it does not quite match the millennia-long presence of vast walnut forests in the region. Walnuts are known in Russian as *gretchki* or 'Greek nuts' because they were said to have been sent back to Greece from Alexander the Great's campaign to central Asia; whether or not this is true, the forests certainly pre-date the 11th century. The walnuts of the area have always been highly prized and were one of the goods transported west along the Silk Road when it was in its prime.

Arslanbob lies about 70km north of Jalal-Abad and is reached by way of the town of Bazar-Korgon at the lower end of the Kara-Ünkür Valley. The village, which sits at the head of a valley on the lower slopes of the 4,427m-high Babash-Ata Mountain, has a mean altitude of around 1,600m above sea level, although it spreads so far up and down the valley from its centre that upper parts of the village are several hundred metres higher than this, and the lower parts several hundred less. The central square stands at an altitude of 1,430m.

By Kyrgyzstan standards, Arslanbob is considered to be a conservative place due to its isolation, its predominantly Uzbek population and its religious associations – there are several sites in the vicinity of the village that are considered holy by local Muslims. In recent times, there have been accusations of the village being a recruiting ground for the outlawed Hizb-ut Tahrir, an Islamist group that advocates a single Islamic caliphate for the region, but the atmosphere of the village is extremely friendly and relaxed, as long as visitors adopt reasonably modest dress. Many of the older men – the *aksakals* of the village – wear traditional Uzbek clothing and most women sport headscarves, but this cultural conservatism is tempered by traditional Islamic hospitality, which welcomes visitors with a warm smile.

Because of their long association with this mountainous region many of the Uzbek inhabitants of Arslanbob see themselves as a little different from their brothers in the lower reaches of the Fergana Valley. There is a popular belief that they have an input of Kazakh blood in the mix, as one of Arslanbob's grandfathers is said to have married a Kazakh woman. The woman's father, Sultan Bulak, gave his name to the local spring he lived by. Many say that the Uzbeks here look far more Kazakh than those in the nearby lowlands of the Fergana Valley. All of the villagers claim to be descended from Arslanbob, their common ancestor, and say that those living in Arslanbob today represent the 26th, 27th and 28th generations.

What is without doubt is that they are all immensely proud of their village and its distinct traditions. The village's founder, Arslanbob-Ata, did well when he was sent off to find an earthly paradise by the Prophet; looking at Arslanbob, it would seem that his mission was entirely successful. In high summer, though, things can sometimes look a little different when the main village street is choked with dust from the constant stream of jeeps and pick-ups that ferry local Uzbek tourists between the main square and the *turbaza* at the top of the village. But even at peak times like this it is possible to escape the crowds – in Arslanbob you never have to go that far to find a bit of peace and quiet.

GETTING THERE AND AWAY Arslanbob is usually reached from Jalal-Abad by way of a change in Bazar-Korgon. A regular **minibus** from Jalal-Abad to Bazar-Korgon (which may continue to Kochkor-Ata or Massy) takes 45 minutes and costs 30som. A **share taxi** may run the same route for roughly twice the price. From Bazar-Korgon bus station a minibus to Arslanbob (with the destination sign 'АРСТАНБАП' – 'Arstanbap') leaves hourly throughout the day, taking two hours and costing 50som. The 20-seater bus can get *very* full (I counted 48 at one point on one journey) so be prepared for someone to sit on your lap. Some minibuses also run directly to and from Jalal-Abad and there are a couple of direct services to and from Osh each day that leave early morning and mid-afternoon.

In Arslanbob, they stop by the shops in the main square. To reach Kyzyl-Ünkür, the main village in the next valley to the east, from Arslanbob requires changing buses at the village of Oogon-Talaa, where the road to Arslanbob joins the Kara-Ünkür Valley; however, the buses that pass here are likely to be very full.

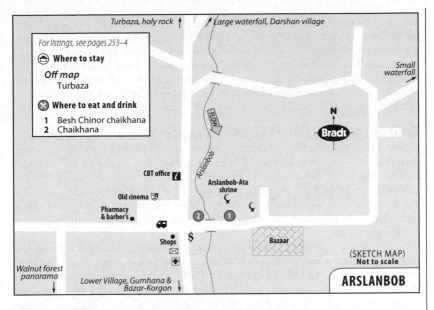

For listings, see pages 253–4

🔵 **Where to stay**

Off map
　Turbaza

❌ **Where to eat and drink**
1　Besh Chinor chaikhana
2　Chaikhana

Turbaza, holy rock ↑

↑ Large waterfall, Darshan village

Small waterfall

FLOW

Arslanbob

CBT office ℹ

Arslanbob-Ata shrine

Old cinema

Pharmacy & barber's

Shops

$

Bazaar

Walnut forest panorama

Lower Village, Gumhana & Bazar-Korgon

(SKETCH MAP)
Not to scale

ARSLANBOB

N

Bradt

GETTING AROUND Arslanbob may be technically a village but it is extremely spread out, covering several kilometres; it is also very hilly, with plenty of stiff climbs to give your calf muscles a good workout. **Taxis** and **4x4s** for hire congregate in the central square, although on weekends in high summer these tend to be in high demand by Uzbek tourists. In the summer months, bench-seat **pick-ups** run up and down the rocky road to the *turbaza* or small waterfall charging 20som per seat each way. Other vehicles – sturdy 4x4s charging 600som per vehicle – convey visitors to as close to the large waterfall as is possible. CBT will generally pay one-way taxi fares to their homestays as a way of compensating for their sometimes far-flung location.

TOURIST INFORMATION Arslanbob's CBT team (m *0773 342 476;* e *arslanbob_2003 @rambler.ru; www.cbtkyrgyzstan.kg*), under the dynamic leadership of co-ordinator Hayat Tarikov, is one of the most forward-looking in the country. Not only are the staff very knowledgeable about the local area and able to offer a wide range of tours centred on the village, they are constantly developing new routes and looking for new attractions for visitors. Good English is spoken by Hayat and most of the staff. The CBT office occupies a small building on the left a little way uphill from the main square. There is a sign on the door but, if no-one is here, try ringing or knocking on the garden gate next door. Alternatively, ask at the barber's shop on the same road just up from the square as one of the CBT guides works here.

🏠 **WHERE TO STAY**

CBT homestays CBT have a total of 18 excellent places to stay around the village. As Arslanbob is so spread out, the homestays tend to be widely scattered too, but usually a longer walk into the centre is rewarded by a better view of the valley, especially if the property is in the upper reaches of the village. Two of the guesthouses are in Gumhana village, which is 5km south of Arslanbob centre.

All of the homestays (**$$**) are good and there is little point making individual recommendations as the ethos of community-based tourism is that the dividends are spread around evenly. Consequently, the CBT office does its best to allocate rooms on a rotating basis. Virtually all the homestays have flower-filled, shady gardens and pleasing views, and although rooms are invariably clean and cosy, bathrooms and showers tend to be outside across the yard. Meals are generally hearty and filling, partially dependent on whatever local produce is available and in season. There is normally a choice of meal for both breakfast and dinner and, unusually for Kyrgyzstan, vegetarians are well catered for.

Turbaza (*Map, page 253*) The *turbaza* was built in 1971 and used to be very busy in Soviet times during the summer months, when more than 10,000 visitors came each season. Now it is quieter and a little run-down, catering mostly for domestic visitors who come for short stays or weekends. Accommodation is in wooden cabins (**$**) set around the 15ha site at the top of the village. Some rooms have hot water and en-suite toilets but most do not. There is a swimming pool and also a disco that tends to shatter the village's atmosphere of peace and tranquillity when it is in operation.

In the summer months, a number of food and souvenir stalls set up near the *turbaza* entrance where pick-ups from the central square drop off and pick up passengers. There is also plenty of (non-CBT affiliated) homestay accommodation (**$**) on offer in the surrounding area, although they are not to CBT standards. For return visitors to Arslanbob who might be wondering whatever happened to the lion statue that used to grace the central square down in the village – it's now here, at the *turbaza*.

✘ WHERE TO EAT AND DRINK   *Map, page 253*
There are no proper restaurants in the village, just simple *chaikhanas*, but this not a hardship as most homestays serve up huge, delicious meals with plenty of fresh produce. The shady **Besh Chinor chaikhana** (**$**) in front of the mosque is where many of the local *aksakals* hang out, and it is a restful place to watch the world go by over a pot of tea. Besh Chinor means 'Five Plane Trees' and it is plain to see why it is so named.

There is another *chaikhana* nearby across the bridge with a rustic terrace over the river, and another basic place selling *samsi* on the other side of the street.

OTHER PRACTICALITIES The **post and telephone office** is just off the main square to the south. There is also a small **bank** at the crossroads by the square, although this does not have an ATM. The square itself has a few **shops** that sell basic staples, a pharmacy, a barber's shop and an old cinema that now serves as a community centre. The bazaar is across the footbridge, over the stream just beyond the mosque. There is a Univermag department store behind the *chaikhana* and in front of Arslanbob's shrine. At the time of writing there was no public internet access available in the village.

WHAT TO SEE AND DO
Arslanbob-Ata shrine The *mazar* or shrine of the village's founder is right in the centre of the village, next door to the *chaikhana* with the large plane tree. The shrine is said to have been around since the 16th century, although the building that stands today was erected in the 20th century. It is entered through a garden and colourful gatehouse next to the *chaikhana*. A flower-lined path leads to the shrine, a small white, brick-built building with a walnut-wood door frame and rams' horns above the entrance. There are tables close to the mausoleum where visitors can sit and

eat, and many pilgrims come to share food here and soak up *baraka*, the spiritual blessings of the shrine. The new mosque next door, which at the time of writing was undergoing considerable expansion to include a *madrasa*, has an elegantly carved ceiling and is also worth a look.

Small waterfall This is easily reached at the northeast of the village. This 25m-high waterfall is a popular spot with visitors and locals alike, and this is borne out by the scraps of material tied to the trees and bushes that stand near it. Even some branches hanging over the waterfall itself have had ribbons tied to them, which must have been a highly hazardous activity for the person doing the tying. At the base of the waterfall there are a couple of prayer caves. One of these, known as 'The Cave of the 40 Angels', used to be frequented by a holy woman whom visitors would come to petition. There's also a stuffed mountain goat next to which you can have your photo taken (done in five minutes, apparently).

To reach the waterfall, walk past the mosque and bazaar and turn left uphill. At the second road to the right, turn right (there is a faded sign for '*Vodapad*' on the wall pointing the way). At a junction of four roads, take the lowest one, which continues uphill past a long line of stands in summer that sell all manner of cheap jewellery, hats, herbs, Islamic paraphernalia, woodcarvings and general tourist tat. If you want an 'I <3 Arslanbob' keepsake then this is the place to buy it. The waterfall is now in sight and reached through a turnstile (*10som*), which leads down past benches and caves to the waterfall.

From the base of the waterfall a path continues up steps on the other side which you can ascend to reach a viewpoint pavilion where ice cream and snacks are sold. Continuing uphill from here, turning left takes you to the top of the falls, while keeping right will bring you to a wide path on the edge of a ridge from where there are fantastic views of the peaks of the Fergana range. Here, away from the tourist clamour at the falls, you will probably just have the sound of the river and birdsong for company.

Large waterfall This much larger, 80m-high, waterfall is a three- to four-hour round trip from the centre of the village. It is a relatively easy walk apart from the last part, which can be tricky underfoot. Do not be tempted to try and climb up behind the waterfall – going up is easier than coming down and you may well end up stuck in a highly precarious position. As with the small waterfall, votive rags have been tied close to the site. As the votive rags attest, the waterfall is attributed with spiritual and magical powers and a visit is supposed to boost fertility.

The large waterfall lies in a cliff face due north of the village. To reach it, walk directly north from the main square, along the main road that lies west of the stream. Continue steeply uphill until there is a fork in the road, with a blue hut in the middle; take the right, not quite so good, road just before the *turbaza*. This eventually reaches a junction at the very northern limit of the village. The left-hand fork leads across boulder-strewn open land, meadows and *jailoos*, uphill to the holy rock (see page 256); take the right-hand fork, which leads along the course of a stream to eventually reach trees with votive rags tied to them. Cross the stream here and continue towards the waterfall, which should have come into sight by now.

Many local tourists come here by 4x4 these days, following a rough jeep track that brings them just a few hundred metres short of the waterfall. Unfortunately, this mode of transport creates a lot of dust and noise and puts a dampener on the pleasure of those energetic enough to walk there.

Holy rock A visit to this sacred site requires a considerable investment of effort, as it lies high above the village on the slopes of Babash-Ata at 2,900m (see page 257). This large, almost cube-shaped rock is closely linked to the legend of Arslanbob-Ata. He is said to have been killed here while praying – betrayed by his wife who informed his enemies of his whereabouts. His bloodstains, footprints and handprints are believed by many to be still visible on the rock. Incongruously, perhaps, there is a metal step-ladder lodged in place behind the rock to enable pilgrims to climb up on top of it.

Ibn Abbas shrine This *mazar* is said to be little more than a ruinous hut in the woods and is hard to find as it lies deep in the walnut forest. If you wish to check it out for yourself then get a guide, or at least precise instructions on how to reach it, from the CBT office.

Darshan village Hardly a village but just a collection of isolated houses at a crossroads in the heart of the walnut forest, this was once a settlement made up of Chechens forced from their Caucasus homeland by Stalin in the 1940s. No Chechens remain today and just a few Uzbek families live here now, eking a modest living from the forest. In late September and early October, the area around the crossroads becomes far more animated when families come to camp here for days on end during the walnut harvest (see page 258).

Walnut forest panorama One easy walk from the village centre, which is particularly delightful in the late afternoon, is to take the narrow road that leads south off the road at the west side of the main square. Follow this, keeping right past two forks, and left at the third one, to descend to a wooden bridge over a stream. Cross the stream to climb up along a steep path through walnut woodland to reach an area of red cliffs. From here, there is a panoramic view over the village, valley and walnut forest to the east. Continuing to the top of the path, a small plateau is reached, which is filled with carefully tended potato and sunflower fields.

Approaching dusk, the path can be quite busy with locals, mostly small parties of women and girls, on their way back to their homes in the village from the fields above it. This is a charming spot to soak up the tranquil atmosphere of the valley and enjoy the play of light on the silvery trunks of the walnut trees as the sun lowers in the sky.

If you don't want to sweat it out all the way to the top, a little way after crossing the stream there is a path to the left next to some large boulders that follows the contour line east to give almost as good views.

ACTIVITIES AND TOURS
Trekking and horseriding The village is an excellent base for many treks on foot or horseback into the surrounding countryside. CBT has many standard tours, and can advise on routes and logistics or devise bespoke tours. They run a number of short tours close to the village that take in the cultural highlights and also organise sunset and sunrise tours that take in panoramic views of the valley at these times of day.

One-day treks to the **large waterfall** and/or the holy rock described above are easily organised with or without a guide. On foot, the round trip to the waterfall takes three to four hours, while the **holy rock** is further and higher and takes 3½–4 hours to reach from the centre. To reach the holy rock it is necessary to follow the road north out of the village, past the *turbaza*, turning left at the junction, where the right road leads to the large waterfall. Follow this track, cross the stream, then take a right fork along a stone-lined lane. When this joins a 4x4 track bear left and continue until you reach a small path that forks off to the right to cross a *jailoo*. The holy rock should be visible on the ridge just below the skyline; look for a large rock that looks a little like a flat-roofed hut from a distance. From here it is cross-country to reach the rock.

After a while, it will start to look deceptively close, but it is not and even when you think that you are almost upon it, it is still a lot further. It is by no means a difficult climb but it does demand stamina, as the rock stands at around 2,900m – an ascent of 1,400m from the village centre. The effect of altitude may be felt in the latter part of the approach. Coming down is easier, of course, and with enough time and energy it is feasible to loop around via the large waterfall on the return trip.

Longer treks may be organised through the walnut forest to the east of Arslanbob to reach the village of **Kyzyl-Ünkür**, by way of Gumhana, Jaradar and the tiny hamlet of Darshan deep in the forest; the last section passes impressive red rock formations before descending to Kyzyl-Ünkür. This is a total distance of about 25km and can be done in a day. A shorter alternative is to head directly to Gumhana from Darshan. Transport can be prearranged with CBT to return to Arslanbob. CBT has a longer two-day horseback variant of this that loops up to Kosh-Terek, north of Kyzyl-Ünkür, in addition to a two-day horseback loop, camping in tents overnight, that takes in the large waterfall. There is a *turbaza* in Kyzyl-Ünkür.

The village of **Üch-Terek** on the shores of **Toktogul Reservoir** may be reached on a four-day, three-night horseback tour, via Kyzyl-Ünkür village, the Kara-Ünkür and Ken-Köl valleys, Shaldyrak Pass, the Kara-Suu Valley and the Kargysh Pass. The last stretch is done on foot. From Üch-Terek it is possible to continue to Jalal-Abad or Bishkek by minibus or taxi.

Probably the most classic trek from Arslanbob is a four-day hike and/or horseback loop to a group of four **holy lakes**, high in the mountains north of the village, which takes in *jailoos*, mountain passes and the holy rock, and is tough but highly rewarding. CBT says that this can be done in just three days but by all accounts this is very demanding and only for the superfit. There are a variety of routes to reach the lakes, most of which require going over passes of at least 3,500m. There is a track that leads from the village by which it is said to be possible to reach the lakes in eight hours on horseback. The lakes, which collectively are called **Köl Mazar**, and which are usually marked as Köl Kupan or Köl Kulan on maps, are a pilgrimage destination for Muslims from Mailuu-Suu (which has partial road access) who come here between June and early September to slaughter a sheep and have a local preacher say prayers for them.

Other trekking and horseriding possibilities include a three-day hike or horse trek to **Ortok**, where there is a CBT homestay programme. Longer tours to Toktogul, Sary-Chelek and Saimaluu-Tash are also possible. CBT can organise a three-day jeep tour or demanding seven-day horse trek to **Saimaluu-Tash**, and there is also the option of a one-day jeep tour (*8,000som per car*) to **Sary-Chelek** and back that leaves early in the morning and returns via Kyzyl-Tuu, where a large colony of storks can be seen at sunset.

Trekking guides cost 800som a day around the village, 1,200som while on tour; horse guides, 1,600som per day, 2,000som on tour. Assistant horsemen, porters and cooks are 600–700som per day. Horses cost 800som per day.

Winter activities Having pretty well reached full capacity for summer activities like trekking and horseriding, Arslanbob CBT is keen to develop its winter options.

There's enormous scope for skiing and snowboarding in the surroundings of the village, and the CBT staff can provide both equipment and local expertise. Such activities are still under development but a good variety of options are already on offer to experienced skiers – both downhill and cross-country – and snowboarders between November and February. Possibilities include skiing through the walnut

WALNUT TIME IN ARSLANBOB

Arslanbob is at the centre of the world's largest expanse of relict walnut forest. The forest, which grows at altitudes between 1,500 and 2,000m on the south-facing slopes of the Fergana range, has a high diversity of trees and shrubs that includes major species like walnut (*Juglans regia*) and various fruit-bearing species in their wild form, such as apple (*Malus siversiana*), pear (*Pyrus korshinsky*) and plum (*Prunus sogdiana*).

During the walnut season, which begins in late September and lasts for about a month, most families in Arslanbob and other villages of the valley are involved in the gathering of the harvest. Walnuts are central to the village's economy; 1,500 tonnes are collected and the majority of families in the valley depend on the harvest of the woods for at least part of their income, which is usually supplemented by the renting of an arable plot for growing crops such as potatoes and sunflowers.

Families generally rent a territory for nut and fruit collecting and wood cutting, for which they pay a percentage to the forestry authority in Arslanbob, the *leshoz*. Five-year contracts are issued for each territory and these come with special responsibilities, such as the planting of new trees and maintenance of old stock. If the conditions of the contract are seen to have been respected then the contract can be extended for a further ten years. It is up to the *leshoz* and its locally appointed representatives to police the forest activities and ensure there is no illegal felling or nut smuggling going on in season.

For the outside visitor, the walnut harvest is a good time to visit, as it is a particularly beautiful season with cool, bright days, clear skies and turning leaves. There is also an upbeat atmosphere about the village, as nut gathering is an essentially social activity which is carried out mostly by family and friendship groups, particularly women and children. Foreign visitors to Arslanbob at this time of year will inevitably find their pockets bulging every time they go for a stroll, as they will be plied with nuts by local collectors delighted to show off their bounty by making a small gift to the visitors they come across. It would be ungracious to refuse.

Walnuts are highly prized and with good reason: they have undeniable health benefits and are a good source of oil, protein, antioxidants and omega-3 fatty acids. They have even been used as currency from time to time: Alexander the Great is said to have brought sacks of walnuts back from central Asia, but had to give them up *en route* as payment to the Greek boatmen who transported his troops. The custom may have passed down into modern times: there is an Iranian film, *Blackboards*, in which impoverished Kurdish tribesmen pay itinerant teachers in walnuts, the only thing they have that is of value to both parties. Travelling to Arslanbob on the bus from Bazar-Korgon, I saw a number of village schoolgirls doing much the same sort of thing as they paid the bus driver … with walnuts.

forest and hiking up to the holy rock and skiing downhill from there (four hours up, one hour down). The CBT can provide special ski covers that grip the snow and enable skiers to walk uphill. Ski hire is around 300som per day; the services of a ski guide, 1,500som per day.

Other activities Mountain biking is another option for which the rugged, mountainous landscape around the village seems tailor-made. CBT has a number of Giant-brand mountain bikes for hire and three standard circular tours of varying difficulty are offered as suggested routes. Individual tours with full back-up can also be devised according to taste. In May, there's an annual downhill ride to Jalal-Abad that energetic visitors can participate in. Bikes cost 800som per day to rent; a mountain bike guide, if necessary, is 2,000som per day.

THE ROAD TO BISHKEK

The main road west of Jalal-Abad goes through an agricultural landscape of maize, sunflowers and cotton to pass Bazar-Korgon and the turn-off for Arslanbob, before reaching Massy and the town of **Kochkor-Ata**, close to the border with Uzbekistan.

During the Soviet period, Kochkor-Ata was famous for its oil wells, but these have since been bought out by Chinese business interests. Apart from a new bazaar building and football stadium there is little to distinguish the town and nothing of interest for visitors. Continuing west, towards Shamaldy-Say and the main route to Toktogul and Bishkek, a turn-off is passed that leads north to Kök-Tash and Mailuu-Suu.

Mailuu-Suu has in recent years become a watchword for environmental pollution, having a large number of unstable uranium dumps close to the town. In Soviet times the town was an important uranium-mining and processing centre, but since independence most of the population of 20,000 have not only been left without work, but also find themselves trapped by poverty in a highly polluted environment.

Due to the large number of unstable uranium tailing pits in the vicinity of the town, radiation levels are high and cancer rates in the town are more than twice the national average. In the period 1946–68, the plant in the town produced and processed more than 10,000 tonnes of uranium in total, some of which was used to make the Soviet Union's first atomic bomb. What is left today is nearly two million cubic metres of radioactive waste that poses an enormous threat not just to the local region but also to the whole basin of the Fergana Valley.

Landslides in 2002 and 2005 caused great alarm because of the possible consequences of large quantities of uranium waste infiltrating the regional water supply. In 2004, the World Bank and the Kyrgyz government signed a US$11.7 million deal aimed at reducing the risk of pollution, but experts insist that a truly effective clean-up operation would cost far more – hundreds of millions of dollars – to be completely effective. In 2006, Mailuu-Suu was listed as one of the ten most polluted sites in the world according to a study carried out by the Blacksmith Institute, a New York-based organisation which supports pollution-related environmental projects.

Older maps show the road west from Jalal-Abad to Shamaldy-Say and beyond weaving between Uzbek and Kyrgyz territories. This used to be the case, but in recent years border formalities have resulted in new stretches of road being built to allow the problematic Uzbek border to be skirted. At Shamaldy-Say, where there is a bus station just outside the town, which many long-distance services

9

stop at to eat, the main Bishkek road veers north to **Tash-Kömür**, a long, thin town which hugs the lower Naryn River for several kilometres on the west bank opposite the highway. Coming from the broad, agricultural plain of the Fergana Valley, the landscape around the town has an almost claustrophobic feel to it; the river, road and railway are tightly enclosed by deeply folded sandstone hills. It is an industrial – or perhaps, post-industrial – landscape where the lines of pylons, slag heaps and deserted factories speak loudly of the unsightly demand for energy.

TASH-KÖMÜR (ТАШ-КУМЫР) This rambling thread of a town has two aspects, neither particularly alluring. Along the main Bishkek–Osh highway stands a line of makeshift kiosks intent on capturing the attention of passing vehicles. Taxis throng this stretch, too, which effectively serves as a roadside service station.

Across the river lies the main part of town, with its shoddy bazaar, blocks of flats and bus station. This part of town gives the impression of somewhere small and provincial, but seen from the main road it becomes clear that Tash-Kömür is an altogether larger place: a Soviet-era coal town whose industry since independence has sadly gone the way of most of the rest of Kyrgyzstan's mining heritage.

Getting there and away The small bus station has early morning **buses** to Jalal-Abad (*200–250som*) and Osh (*300–350som*), as well as later services to Kerben (*100som*) and Kara-Jygach for connections to Arkyt and Sary-Chelek. There is a basic *gostinitsa* next to the bus station that might do if you get stuck here, and a public toilet block between the bus station and the non-functional railway station that is seriously worth avoiding. **Share taxis** to Bishkek (*around 800som*), Osh (*400–500som*) and Kara-Köl (*150som*) leave from the main road across the river near the bridge; a taxi from the bus station will take you to the correct spot.

KARA-KÖL (КАРА-КУЛЬ) From Tash-Kömür the lower Naryn River squeezes through a narrow gorge, with red and purple sandstone cliffs towering above the road. The river here is a series of five dammed lakes – the Nizhnenarynskiy *kaskad* (Lower Naryn Cascade) – which have been constructed along the Naryn River for the production of hydro-electricity. Kara-Köl, the next town reached, heading north, is effectively a dormitory town for workers at the hydro-electricity station. The uppermost dam at Kara-Köl, which is not visible from the main road here, was completed in 1976 after 14 years of construction, an impressive feat of engineering.

Hydro-electricity is a considerable money-spinner for Kyrgyzstan as the electrical power produced here is exported right across the central Asian region. It is not without controversy, however, as there have been arguments with the Uzbekistan government over the Kyrgyz control of water, which the neighbouring country requires in large quantities to irrigate its cotton fields in the Fergana Valley. In reflection of its role as an important source of income, the dam appears on the reverse of the 100som note.

Getting there and away **Buses** and **minibuses** stop at the roadside outside the town for regular connections north to Toktogul (*150som*), and south to Bazar-Korgon (*200som*) and Jalal-Abad (*300–350som*).

TOKTOGUL (ТОКТОГУЛ) This medium-sized town gives its name to the reservoir which lies just to the south. From Kara-Köl, the main Bishkek road sweeps in a wide arc around the eastern end of the large manmade lake, following the southern shore closely to just beyond the village of Üch-Terek, before it doubles back west to reach Toktogul. North of Toktogul, the main road to Bishkek climbs steadily, following the Chychkan River to enter Talas Province and the Chychkan State Zoological Reserve, on the way to the 3,184m Ala-Bel Pass and Chui Province.

Toktogul is a quiet, reasonably attractive provincial town which is not a bad place to break the journey between Bishkek and the south. The town gets its name from the well-known *akyn* (bard) Toktogul Satylganov (1864–1933), who was born here in what was then known as Kushchusu. Toktogul's image appears on the front of the Kyrgyz 100som banknote. The reservoir which lies immediately south of the town was created in 1974 when the Toktogul Dam was completed, displacing 26 communities that now lie beneath the reservoir's waters.

Getting there and away From the *avtobeket* (taxi and minibus station) at the western end of town, share taxis and minibuses leave for Tash-Kömür and other southern destinations. Share taxis leave from here for Bishkek (*800som*) and buses leave from in front of the bazaar at the eastern end of Lenin.

🏠 **Where to stay and eat**

🏠 **Gostinitsa** Lenin. A little further along on the right from Hotel Ak-Jibek, this Soviet-era *gostinitsa* is probably where the British travel writer Colin Thubron stayed when he describes spending the night in a workers' hostel in the town in his book *Shadow of the Silk Road*. **$**

🏠 **Guesthouse** Nabereshnaya/Akimkan 86. This friendly guesthouse, run by Ilyatbue Kuldanbaev, lies immediately behind the grounds of the hospital, at the western edge of the town. Ilyatbue speaks French, as does her son, & her daughter Mirgul speaks good English. The guesthouse is a short taxi ride or a 15-min walk from the taxi & minibus park. From the taxi park, head along Lenin towards the town centre then take the first right. Walk down this road for 10 mins to reach a hospital, which has a couple of pharmacies in front of it; walk straight on through the gate & hospital grounds to reach a tall wall that has gap knocked into it. Go through the gap & No 86 is almost directly across the street. **$**

🏠 **Hotel Ak-Jibek** Lenin. This hotel has received mixed reviews. **$**

🏠 **Kaghan** Israilova 18; 📞 504 43; e azamat@ im-nomad.com. This guesthouse in the centre of town also offers local tours. **$**

What to see and do The Kyrgyz Telecom building is on the right a little further into town than the *gostinitsa*, and beyond this, a 15-minute walk east from the taxi park, is the town's bazaar, the Ay-Tulan restaurant and a large leafy park opposite. A pleasant walk is to go through the park, past the war memorial to reach a sports field with a broken Ferris wheel. From here there is an excellent panoramic view of the reservoir and the mountains beyond contrasted with the flat, green agricultural area in front of the water.

WESTERN JALAL-ABAD PROVINCE

The road that leads west from Shamaldy-Say, hugging the border with Uzbekistan, leads eventually to the small town of Kerben. The road is quite obviously truncated in parts, the old route now curtailed by having to cross Uzbek territory, and in places makeshift road barriers block once-busy side roads to prevent illicit traffic between the two countries. The small town of **Kerben** (or Karavan, its Russian name) sits on top of one of the most northerly meanders of the Uzbek Fergana Valley. It's a crossroads town which sits midway between Jalal-Abad and the lonely Chatkal Valley to the west. For visitors, the town also serves as a jumping-off point for visits to Lake Sary-Chelek to the north. West of Kerben the road twists around the Uzbek frontier on a circuitous, sometimes pot-holed road to reach **Ala-Buka** and the nearby **mausoleum of Safed Bulan**, before continuing to reach the southern reaches of the Chatkal Valley beyond.

KERBEN (KARAVAN) (КЕРБЕН) (*Telephone code: 03742*) Arriving in Kerben from Jalal-Abad to the east, it is immediately apparent that the pace of life here makes even relaxed Jalal-Abad seem frenetic in comparison. This calm façade seems at odds with the recent tragedy in the town, in which six protesters were shot by panicking policemen at an antigovernment rally in 2002, one of the key events that gave momentum to the downfall of the previous Akayev government and the so-called Tulip Revolution (see page 19). There is a monument that commemorates this tragedy at the roadside on the Sary-Chelek road.

Set in a pretty agricultural landscape with lovely views of the mountains to the north, Kerben's day-to-day activity, such as it is, revolves around the crossroads of Frunze and Karl Marx, the town's two principal streets. The crossroads has a cinema, a yurt restaurant, a covered market and a park all gathered around it. Just south of the crossroads on Frunze is a large stone head of Lenin, and beyond this lies the Kyrgyz Telecom building and a hospital.

Walking west along Karl Marx past the TsUM building, there is a small bazaar on the right just before the local bus station. Continuing in this direction over the river and past a petrol station, a larger bus station is reached opposite a newly built mosque.

Immediately to the east of the central crossroads is a steep rocky mound that offers excellent views from the top. If you end up staying the night then it is highly likely you will end up climbing this, as Kerben has few real distractions other than some good *chaikhanas*. The town receives few overseas visitors and so the presence of a foreigner may arouse a little more curiosity than usual, but nevertheless it is a relaxed and friendly place.

Getting there and away There are two bus stations: the **large bus station** at the western end of Karl Marx, which has regular services to Kara-Jygach (for Sary-Chelek) and Tash-Kömür (for Bishkek); Jalal-Abad (four to five hours) three times a day in the mornings; and four buses a day to Ala-Buka. The **small bus station** has crowded snub-nose buses going to local destinations, including Arkyt at 16.00 and Kyzyl-Köl at 16.30.

There are **flights** to and from Bishkek twice a week (three times in the summer) which take about an hour.

🏠 **Where to stay**

🏠 **Homestay of Dilbar Sulaimankulova** Jany-Turmush 5. Dilbar lives in a house with a large, shady garden on the northern outskirts of the town. To reach Dilbar's homestay, walk north along Frunze from the crossroads, pass the bus stop & continue past a large building with a container outside that sometimes opens as a café. After another 5 mins a small road leads left over a little footbridge towards a small shop with a blue door, go left here & follow the road left around the corner on reaching a larger building. The house is then the 2nd blue gate on the left. *B&B* **$**; *meals 200som.*

✗ **Where to eat and drink** There is good home-cooked food at the homestay above. Otherwise there are a few *chaikhanas* and simple restaurants in the town (*all* **$**). There are more cafés along Frunze heading north from the crossroads.

✗ **Ak-Kaiyn café** Between the small bus station & the bazaar. Good for staples.

✗ **Amanbay-Ata** At the crossroads, next to TsUM. This shady & very traditional Uzbek-run *chaikhana* has really good *shashlyk* & is probably the best for atmosphere, coupled with very low prices.

AROUND KERBEN
Padysha-Ata State Reserve North of the village of Kashka-Suu, 15km north of Kerben, a road follows the river gorge lined with birch groves to reach the village of Kara-Bashat, where there is the 18th- or 19th-century mausoleum of Padysha-Ata, a pilgrimage site for Muslims from the Fergana Valley region. The Padysha-Ata State Reserve was established in the region in 2003 and covers 305km² of the lower Chatkal ridge. The reserve office is in Kerben at the Selhoztehnika building (*Umetaliev;* ✆ 225 47).

LAKE SARY-CHELEK (ОЗЕРО САРЫ-ЧЕЛЕК)

Lake Sary-Chelek is one of Kyrgyzstan's true gems – a major draw that is a little difficult to reach but, as all visitors seem to attest, is well worth the effort. Sary-Chelek (literally 'Yellow Bucket') is a fairly small, alpine lake set amid conifer, and relict fruit and nut forest at an altitude of 1,873m. The lake is just one part of the Sary-Chelek Biosphere Reserve which protects more than a thousand species of plants, 160 birds and 34 mammals, including rarities such as bear, lynx and snow leopard.

Sary-Chelek is relatively small: just 7.5km long and 2,280m wide at its broadest point, with a maximum depth of 234m. The lake is fed by the Sary-Chelek River, in addition to numerous other streams and underground sources, and its outflow travels into the Kara-Suu. The hollow in which the lake sits was probably created by earthquake activity hundreds of years ago, although the precise geomorphology of its formation is unclear. The name 'yellow bucket', although hardly romantic, is perfectly apt, as in early autumn the turning leaves of the forest that surrounds the lake positively glow with golden-yellow light that contrasts sharply with the deep blue-green of the water.

Lake Sary-Chelek does not stand alone, as there are other, smaller lakes within the reserve to the southeast, but without doubt it is Sary-Chelek which is the jewel in the crown. Its glorious alpine location among forest and rocky crags is as impressive as the lake itself, and the steep slopes that surround the lake support dense forests of pine, fir and juniper. At slightly lower elevations there are tangled stands of nut and wild fruit trees, including walnut, pistachio, apple and pear. Although they are not strictly supposed to, many locals come to gather the fruits of the forest in this part of the reserve.

GETTING THERE AND AWAY Unless you're planning on hiking over the mountains from the north (which *is* possible), the only routes leading to Sary-Chelek come from the south, either by way of the village of **Arkyt**, which is on the edge of the reserve and serves as its administrative headquarters, or from the Kara-Suu Valley in the buffer zone. The only drivable road to the lake leads from Arkyt, 16km away.

Both Arkyt and Kyzyl-Köl village in the Kara-Suu Valley are connected to Kerben and Kara-Jygach by a daily **bus** service. From Kerben, a bus leaves from the small bus station for Arkyt at 16.00 and for Kyzyl-Köl at 16.30 (*2–2½hrs*). Both buses go via Kara-Jygach, which can be reached by bus from Tash-Kömür by two buses a day which leave in the morning (*2hrs*). Returning from Arkyt there is an early morning bus that goes to Kerben via Kara-Jygach (*1hr, 25som*). The morning bus from Kyzyl-Köl to Kerben leaves at 07.00. There is a morning bus from Kara-Jygach to Tash-Kömür (it will wait for the Arkyt bus to arrive) and another around midday. This takes 2½ hours and costs 150som. There are also share taxis to Tash-Kömür and to Bishkek. On the way to Tash-Kömür, look out for strangely eroded rock formations in the valley. A bus from Tash-Kömür to Jalal-Abad leaves at 12.20 (3½hrs, 200som) and so there is time to make a connection to get back to Jalal-Abad by mid-afternoon.

Coming from either Bishkek or Jalal-Abad, the most direct route is by way of Tash-Kömür and Kara-Jygach, where it is possible to pick up the daily bus coming from Kerben as it passes through to Arkyt or Kyzyl-Köl in the late afternoon. This is quite a long, uncomfortable journey to do in a single day, and a better bet from Jalal-Abad might be to spend a night in Kerben en route, making it an even longer route but at least a more leisurely one. A faster but more expensive alternative to all of this is to hire a **taxi** from Tash-Kömür to Arkyt.

Once in Arkyt, a vehicle may be hired to reach the lake the following day. From Arkyt it is possible to go to Sary-Chelek by share taxi for 150som per person each way. Walking to the lake from Arkyt will take at least three hours, mainly uphill, along the road, although the views are splendid and ever-changing along the way. Even driving, it is worthwhile stopping a couple of times to enjoy the view down over Arkyt and the valley.

TREKKING TO SARY-CHELEK The most northerly of the string of villages along the Kara-Suu River, **Kyzyl-Köl**, is more distant and has no direct road to Lake Sary-Chelek, so it makes sense to come here only if you plan to trek to the lake or wish to go for hikes in the equally attractive buffer zone. You can organise an overnight trek to the lake via Kara-Suu Lake and the Kemerty Pass through the CBT office in Arslanbob or Jalal-Abad (see page 245).There are also four- and five-day combined horseback and trekking circular routes that can be made from Kyzyl-Köl, which take in Sary-Chelek, Kara-Suu Lake and various passes. The Kara-Suu CBT co-ordinator, Bazarkul Jooshbaev (m 0559 549 959; e cbt_sary-chelek@mail.ru), should also be able to help with accommodation and trekking arrangements.

Other **cross-country trekking options** include a seven-day horseback and trekking tour over the Talas range, which begins or ends in Kyzyl-Köl. As this requires some degree of preplanning it is best organised in advance through the KCBTA office in Bishkek. This could be done independently with the right equipment and mountain experience. It begins near Leninopol, west of Talas, and heads due south to the 3,601m Chimtash Pass, before following a valley east over a low pass to the 3,161m Kara-Kulja Pass, where it skirts a couple of the minor lakes to reach Lake Sary-Chelek and then finally either Arkyt or Kyzyl-Köl.

Another possibility is trekking east from the north of the Chatkal Valley along the Aflatun Valley and over the Ashu-Tör Pass, a tough five-day hike.

Several Bishkek companies offer trekking and horseback itineraries to Sary-Chelek and it is worthwhile comparing what is on offer by visiting their offices in Bishkek before heading south. Similarly, the GeoID map shop in the capital may also have 1:200,000 maps that show some of the routes.

DAY HIKES AT SARY-CHELEK A day trip to the lake is all too brief, but it is possible to enjoy a short circular hike close to the lake that passes some of the smaller lakes in the reserve and gives a good flavour of the various landscapes contained by the park.

Starting at the car park by the lake, head right from the keeper's house to follow a track that leads gently uphill, to the east, past some beehives in a meadow. Climb to the top for a great view of the lake, then return to the track that skirts around the back of the hill and descends slightly to a meadow, before climbing again, passing some dead trees on the left, to follow a ridge above an eastern inlet of the lake. The path goes gently uphill through meadows that have large, scattered boulders and then continues towards an enormous scree slope and corrie on the other side of the valley before descending almost to the valley floor.

Follow this until, just beneath the scree slope, the path, which is quite well-defined at this point, veers to the right (south) and downhill. The path descends to a meadow and then leads north again across meadows and around a spur, and then east following a ridge. After approximately two hours' walking, a small lake (Iyri-Köl) comes into view and the path leads along its shore to the left. At the end there is an orchard and a 4x4 track. Follow this to the right to reach a much smaller lake which is more like a pond.

At the southern end of this lake there is a small path that climbs off right from the main track. Climb this up to a steep wooded ridge then continue along the path on the east side of the ridge, which rises and falls with superb mountain views, before descending more steeply through hay meadows. Lake Sary-Chelek suddenly comes into view again and then, shortly afterwards, another lake by the road to Arkyt (Kula-Köl) is viewed. The path stays high above the lake before eventually descending to a small *jailoo* and honey farm. The path continues above the north side of the lake before descending to the road by a bridge just to the south of the starting point. The entire walk should take 3½–4 hours in total.

ARKYT (АРКЫТ)

Arkyt is a very pretty mountain village which follows the course of the river for some distance upstream. The central part of the village has a bus stop, a post office, and the *zapovednik* or park administration headquarters (03742 22 284), with a museum next door which has stuffed animals, examples of local flora and a topographical model of the reserve. Next door is a government guesthouse. A little further downhill is a shop which has a rudimentary café that could probably prepare food if given some notice. There is another shop in the northern part of the village. These both just have basic supplies like biscuits and fizzy drinks, but nothing fancy like mineral water. The bus terminus is in the northern part of the village close to the radio tower. To leave the village to the north and enter the park through the upper barrier beyond the radio tower there is an entrance fee of 500som (100som for locals) to pay per person per day.

WHERE TO STAY AND EAT There are several homestays scattered around the village. In the south of the village is the homestay of **Gulnara Khadirova ($)**. There are a couple more in the centre, at the homes of **Sultan Chukotaev** and **Respek Urmanaliev**. Respek's homestay (**$**, *with evening meal*) is a rambling farmstead, reached by crossing the footbridge just north of the *zapovednik* and following the dirt road as it curves uphill to the right. His house is at the top of the hill on the right-hand side. Respek also has a car and will ferry you to the lake for a negotiated fee. He may also offer to fire up the sauna for you.

The north of the village, towards the radio tower, has another guesthouse which is signed from the street. There is a clean but austere **government guesthouse ($)** next to the park administration building.

There is also a *turbaza* south of Arkyt, at the village of Jylgyn, which has basic wooden chalets to rent (**$**) and a converted *dacha* at the lake itself offering rooms

(\$–\$\$) which should be prebooked at the park administration headquarters. Camping at the lake requires permission, again from the *zapovednik*.

WEST TO THE CHATKAL VALLEY

ALA-BUKA This small town, 50km west of Kerben, is the gateway to the 12th-century **mausoleum of Safed Bulan**, 8km away. Four buses a day run to and from Kerben to Ala-Buka, and a daily bus leaves the town for Jany-Bazar in the southern Chatkal Valley.

Mausoleum of Safed Bulan and Shah Fasil The shrine stands on the outskirts
of the village of the same name. The brick-built mausoleum is said to have been built in the 12th century and still has considerable potency as an important Sufi pilgrimage site in the region. Many Uzbeks from Uzbekistan's Fergana Valley come here, as well as their kinsmen from Kyrgyzstan. Visitors should respect this and dress and behave appropriately.

The *mazar* contains the graves of two revered individuals: Safed Bulan, a pious local Kypchak woman, and Shah Fasil, a warrior and descendant of the Prophet Muhammad. Shah Fasil is reputed to have first brought Islam to central Asia, while Safed Bulan was responsible for burying the heads of thousands of decapitated prisoners captured in battle. There is a mass grave representing these 700m from the mausoleum.

Legend tells that a grandson of the Prophet Muhammad came with an army to the region in order to convert the local populace to Islam. When the Arab army was at prayer the locals attacked the proselytising soldiers, taking 2,700 prisoners whom they proceeded to behead. A woman travelling with the army searched in vain through the carnage for the head of her lover and, although she did not find him, she proceeded to carry out the gruesome task of washing and burying all of the heads of the fallen, before staying on at the village to look after their graves. In gratitude for this pious act of purification, she was given the honorary title *safed*, 'white', and the village was named after her.

Another, altogether more ethnocentric, version of the legend suggests that Safed Bulan had originally been a black woman and that Allah turned her skin white as a reward for her deed. A mausoleum was erected to her when she died and in later years her grave was joined by that of Shah Fasil, who came to the area to avenge the massacre of his father, Muhammad ben Jarir, who had been Safed Bulan's lover. The legend is supported to some extent by archaeological evidence, which suggests that a large battle took place near here.

The mausoleum complex consists of several vaults, a mosque and a large holy stone within a courtyard. Shah Fasil's tomb, although stark externally, has a tall central cupola set in an octagonal base, and a lavishly decorated interior that has fine decorative panels, ornaments and complex Farsi calligraphy depicting verses from the Qu'ran covering every centimetre. Opposite Shah Fasil's mausoleum stands the tomb of Safed Bulan, next to the room that is said to contain the skulls she washed. Pilgrims come from far and wide to parade clockwise around the graves, the standard procedure at any Sufi site. Only women may enter the tomb of Safed Bulan.

CHATKAL VALLEY This highly inaccessible valley in the far west of Jalal-Abad Province is where the road from Jalal-Abad turns to the northeast towards Talas Province. The colder, northern part of the valley climbs up to the 3,302m Kara-

Buura Pass to descend along the Kara-Buura River into Talas Province. There is little contact between the two provinces along this route as the pass becomes impassable during the winter months due to snowfall, and there is no public transport that connects the Chatkal Valley with Talas at any time of year. Even the southern part of the valley is difficult to reach and, with many more easily accessible destinations to tempt visitors, it is no surprise that very few make it this far; those who do tend to come for rugged outdoor activities such as rafting expeditions or trekking. The whole region is, as they say, ripe for exploration.

That the valley has long been settled is evidenced by archaeological finds that date back to the Neolithic period. Metal ores were extracted here in the Bronze Age and bronze vessels have been found in burial mounds from this region that date from the 1st and 2nd millennia BC. It appears that the livestock breeding that still characterises the economy of the region today has been important since the Iron Age and that later, between the 4th and 12th centuries AD, the valley was fairly densely populated by a mixture of settled farmers and nomadic herdsmen.

Trade used to be important, too, and Silk Road commerce along the valley transported silver from Talas and walnuts from Arslanbob to destinations south and west. As with almost everywhere else in the central Asian region, Genghis Khan's violent forays into the region disrupted settled life severely and this, coupled with feudal warring, heralded a sharp decline from the 12th century onward.

The most important centre in the valley today is the small market town of **Jany-Bazar**, which has limited public transport reaching it from further east in Jalal-Abad Province. Jany-Bazar serves as a centre for visiting the Besh-Aral State Reserve and also has the 18th-century Idris Paygambar mausoleum on a hill nearby, which was built for an Arab mystic who came to the region. The brick mausoleums were constructed between the 18th and 19th centuries. There is a guesthouse for pilgrims in the town which has rooms to rent, and it should be possible to find homestay accommodation in the town. A daily bus runs between Ala-Buka and Jany-Bazar, leaving both destinations in the morning.

With adequate preparation it is possible to trek to Sary-Chelek or the village of Kyzyl-Köl from the northern part of the Chatkal Valley, crossing high passes and taking five days. Coming in the opposite direction this can be organised with the CBT co-ordinator in Kyzyl-Köl.

BESH-ARAL STATE RESERVE This reserve of 112,018ha, established in 1979, is the main draw for most visitors to the Chatkal Valley. It covers part of the lower reaches of the Chatkal Valley next to the Uzbekistan border and consists of coniferous and deciduous forest, alpine meadows and steppe. It was created to specifically protect the habitat of certain endemic species found only in the Western Tien Shan, like Menzbier's marmot, endemic species of tulips and other flora that are listed in Kyrgyzstan's Red Data Book. Snow leopards, Tien Shan bear and Turkestan lynx are all present, as are raptors such as lammergeiers and eagles. Most of the reserve can only be reached on horseback, although a car is able to provide limited access. There is an entrance charge of the equivalent of US$10 for foreign visitors (150som for locals) and this should be paid at the administration office in Jany-Bazar on the main street near the park (℡ *03759 212 22, 212 71, 312 66*) where transport, horses and compulsory guides may also be arranged.

SOUTHERN KYRGYZSTAN

CHINA

UZBEKISTAN

TAJIKISTAN

TAJIKISTAN

T i a n   S h a n   R a n g e

A l a i   R a n g e

P a m i r

Z a a l a i   R a n g e

Turkestan Range

Ugyut
Baetov
Naryn
Naryn
Kosh-Döbö
Kazarman
Saimaluu-Tash
Ak-Moinok Pass
2,932m
Kaldama Pass
3,062m
Kyzyl-Ünkür
Kara-Kulja
Kara-Darya
Özgön
Osh
GulCha
Kashgar,
China
Irkeshtam
Kyzyl-Art Pass
4,280m
Murgab,
Tajikistan
Sary-Tash
Kok-Yangak
Mihailovka
Jalal-Abad
Kara-Suu
Kurshab
Taldyk
Ak-Buura
Taldyk Pass
3,615m
Sary-Mogol
Achik-Tash
7,134m
Peak Lenin
Kashka-Suu
Kyzyl-Suu
Kyzyl-Suu
Daroot-Korgon
Eski-Nookat
Aravan
Chil-Ustun
Andijan, Uzbekistan
Fergana Valley
Kyzyl-Kiya
Shakhimardan
(UZB)
Kadamjay
Barak
(KYR)
Dzhangail
(UZB)
Qalacha
(UZB)
Sokh
(UZB)
Batken
Sokh
Ak-Suu
Dushanbe,
Tajikistan
Batken
Vorukh
(TAJ)
▲5,621m
Karavshin
5,509m
Pyramid Peak
Isfara,
Tajikistan
Khojand, Tajikistan
Kainagach
(TAJ)
Sülüktü
Isfana
Bazar-Korgon
Kochkor-Ata
Massy
Mailuu-Suu
Arslanbob
Kok-Art
Ortok
Orok
Kara-Ünkür
Jalal-Abad
Bishkek
Tash-Kömür
Shamaldy-Say
Ala-Buka
Kazarman
Jassy

N

0 ___ 50km
0 ___ 50 miles

Bradt

268

10

Southern Kyrgyzstan

Kyrgyzstan's most southerly region consists of two provinces, **Osh** (Ош) and **Batken** (Баткен), which make up the southern arm of the country that extends westward south of Uzbekistan's Fergana Valley. The southern border with Tajikistan is demarcated by the high ridges of the Turkestan and Alay mountains, the most northern range of the Pamirs, while to the east is China's Xinjiang Province and the Great Game market town of Kashgar (Kashi), accessible from Kyrgyzstan across the border at Irkeshtam. The Batken region used to be part of Osh Province but was awarded provincial status in 1999 to become an *oblast* in its own right.

Osh Province has an area of 29,200km², with a population of around 1,300,000 and a population density of 44.5 per km², the highest in the country apart from Bishkek; neighbouring Batken is almost 17,000km² in area, with a total population of just 400,000, which is less than 24 people per km². Together the two provinces make up just under a quarter of Kyrgyzstan's total land area. The vast majority of Kyrgyzstan's Uzbek minority live in Osh Province, where they are the majority ethnic group in some areas.

The region was badly affected by the ethnic violence and rioting in 2010. Things have settled down considerably since that time, although tensions still exist between Uzbeks and Kyrgyz. The British FCO no longer advises against travel to this region, but it does encourage travellers to 'take care' when visiting.

OSH (ОШ) *Telephone code: 03222*

Although you would not know from looking at it, Osh is Kyrgyzstan's oldest city. As Kyrgyzstan's second-largest city, with a mixed population of around 250,000, it is considered to be the capital of the south and has served as the administrative centre of the *oblast* since 1939. It is a lively city which, despite its smaller size, can seem busier than Bishkek. It has the largest mosque in the country and one of the largest and most crowded markets in all of central Asia. Central to the city is the steep outcrop of Solomon's Throne, which is an important Muslim pilgrimage site, as well as a popular place for locals and visitors alike to enjoy the view over the city. The city has a strong Uzbek presence and in many ways looks westward towards the Uzbek Fergana Valley rather than north to the capital Bishkek. The Uzbekistan border is just a few kilometres from the city, a ten-minute *marshrutka* ride away. However, international wrangling between Kyrgyzstan and its immediate neighbour has meant that from time to time border crossings are not always as straightforward as they might be.

HISTORY The city of Osh, which claims to be 3,000 years old and 'older than Rome', is certainly one of the oldest permanently inhabited settlements in the

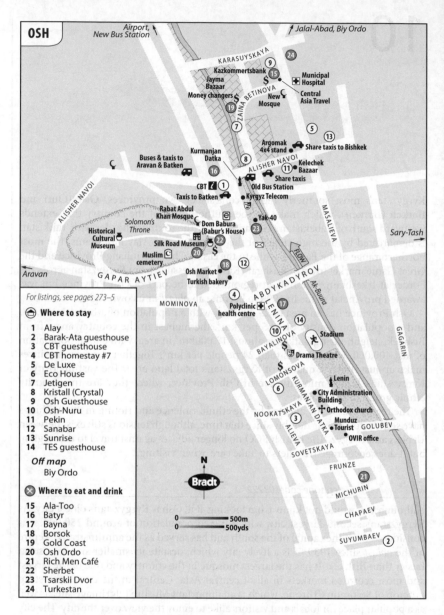

OSH

Airport,
New Bus Station

Jalal-Abad, Biy Ordo

KARASUYSKAYA

Kazkommertsbank
Jayma
Bazaar
Money changers

Municipal
Hospital

Central
Asia Travel

New
Mosque

ZAINA BETINOVA

Argomak
4x4 stand
Share taxis to Bishkek

Buses & taxis to
Aravan & Batken

Kurmanjan
Datka

ALISHER NAVOI

Kelechek
Bazaar

Share taxis
Old Bus Station

CBT
Taxis to Batken
Kyrgyz Telecom

Rabat Abdul
Khan Mosque

Yak-40

Historical
Cultural
Museum

Solomon's
Throne

Dom Babura
(Babur's House)

Silk Road Museum

Muslim
cemetery

Osh Market
Turkish bakery

Aravan

GAPAR AYTIEV

MASALIEVA

Sary-Tash

MOMINOVA

Polyclinic
health centre

ABDYKADYROV

Ak-Buura

GAGARIN

LENINA

FLOW

Stadium

BAYALINOVA

Drama Theatre

LOMONSOVA

Lenin

City Administration
Building

KURMANJAN DATKA

NOOKATSKAYA

Orthodox church

Munduz
Tourist

OVIR office

ALIEVA

SOVETSKAYA

GOLUBEV

FRUNZE

MICHURIN

CHAPAEV

SUYUMBAEV

N

Bradt

0   500m
0   500yds

For listings, see pages 273–5

🛏 **Where to stay**

1   Alay
2   Barak-Ata guesthouse
3   CBT guesthouse
4   CBT homestay #7
5   De Luxe
6   Eco House
7   Jetigen
8   Kristall (Crystal)
9   Osh Guesthouse
10 Osh-Nuru
11 Pekin
12 Sanabar
13 Sunrise
14 TES guesthouse

Off map
    Biy Ordo

✕ **Where to eat and drink**

15 Ala-Too
16 Batyr
17 Bayna
18 Borsok
19 Gold Coast
20 Osh Ordo
21 Rich Men Café
22 Sherbet
23 Tsarskii Dvor
24 Turkestan

central Asian region. Although 3,000 years of history may be an exaggeration, the settlement dates back at least to the 5th century BC. It was known as early as the 8th century AD as an important centre for silk production and as a trade centre at a crossroads on the Silk Road. Legend states that Alexander the Great visited the city on his way to India, but, then again, most legends make some sort of claim for the Macedonian warrior king. King Solomon is also said to have visited and slept on top of the hill that still bears his name – Taht-i-Suleiman ('Suleiman Mountain' or 'Solomon's Throne'). What is more certain is that the founder of the Indian Mughul dynasty and descendant of Tamerlane, Zahiruddin Muhammad Babur, who was born nearby just across the Uzbekistan border in Andijan, came to Osh to visit Solomon's Throne before venturing on to India. Of Osh, he wrote in his memoir, the *Baburnama*:

> There are many sayings about the excellence of Osh. On the southeastern side of the Osh fortress is a well-proportioned mountain called Bara-Koh, where, on its summit, Sultan Mahmud Khan built a pavilion. Farther down, on a spur of the same mountain, I had a porticoed pavilion built in 902 [AD1496–97].

Babur is credited with having built the mosque on top of Solomon's Throne, which even today is still referred to as Babur's House.

The Solomon connection led over the years for Taht-i-Suleiman to become a holy place for central Asian Muslims, and it is even believed that the Prophet Muhammad prayed here. Between the 10th and 12th centuries it was the third of the great cities of the Fergana Valley, but in the 13th century the Mongols came and did their level best to destroy the place. Slowly Osh recovered and rebuilt itself over the next few centuries and the city went on to become part of the Kokand khanate in 1762.

Russians first came to Osh in 1876 during the height of the Great Game era between Tsarist Russia and Britain, when Russian forces overpowered the khanates that hitherto had controlled the city. Following the October Revolution in 1917 the Soviets made their mark on the city and some of this legacy remains today, including a large statue of Lenin in one of the city parks.

In the post-independence period the city became a byword for the inter-ethnic conflict that erupted in 1990 between Uzbek and Kyrgyz factions, although the worst of this took place at the town of Özgön, 50km to the northeast. Fuelled by political meddling and media insensitivity, tensions again spiralled out of control in the summer of 2010, killing at least 400 people and forcing up to 100,000 refugees to flee to the Uzbek border. It was claimed that the violence was initiated by the ousted president Kurmanbek Bakiyev, who was said to have links with foreign jihadists, although clear proof of this has not been forthcoming. Either way, the security services briefly lost control of the city to rioting gangs of young men intent on blood-letting, looting and destruction. Many observers accuse the security forces of being complicit in the violence or, at best, highly ineffective and slow to act. Several years on, many of the refugees have still not returned and a number of issues remain unresolved – few of the more than 5,000 crimes investigated in relation to the violence of 2010 have brought prosecutions. Of those that have been convicted, over 90% are Uzbeks – an anomaly considering that it was the Uzbek community that suffered the majority of deaths. Ethnic tensions still exist in the city although these are unlikely to be noticed by the casual first-time visitor. Those returning to the city, who have seen Osh in the period before 2010, may well notice that its character has shifted noticeably to become more homogenously Kyrgyz than before.

UPHEAVAL

Note: At the time of last update (summer 2014), the city was in considerable upheaval awaiting the large-scale redevelopment of the bazaar area. The wide thoroughfare, Alisher Navoi, was completely dug up and closed to all traffic and access along both sides of this was also limited.

GETTING THERE AND AWAY

By air There are up to five flights a day to and from Bishkek with Air Kyrgyzstan, Avia, Air Bishkek, Tez Jet and Pegasus. The flight takes less than one hour and, on a clear day, is a wonderful way to get a bird's eye view of the country's rugged topography. Most flights leave inconveniently early in the morning. Flights cost between 1,800 and 2,500som one-way, and are sometimes discounted to considerably less than this. Osh is an international airport despite its modest size and facilities, and also has direct flights to Istanbul, Ürümqi and several Russian cities.

The airport is 8km north of the city. *Marshrutka* number 107 runs between the airport and the city centre and charges 9som, otherwise a taxi charges 200–300som.

By bus and minibus Osh has a couple of bus stations, as well as separate taxi and minibus stands.

The **Old Bus Station,** tucked away next to the bazaar and the river on Alisher Navoi, has frequent services in small buses and minibuses to destinations like Özgön (*60som*), Jalal-Abad (*150som*), Aravan (*50som*) and Kara-Suu (*30som*), plus daily minibuses to Gulcha and various destinations in the Alay Valley like Sary-Tash, Sary-Mogul and Daroot-Korgon. Buses for Toktogul and Kerben also leave from here. Share taxis to similar destinations leave from the parking area next door.

The **New Bus Station** is inconveniently located a few kilometres north of the city centre. Direct sleeper buses to Kashgar in China (US$95) usually leave from here at about 19.00 on Wednesday and Sunday evenings.

On **Alisher Navoi**, across the road and a little further along from the Hotel Alay, is another minibus and taxi stand where transport to Aravan, Nookat and Batken can be arranged. Minibuses to Batken via the Uzbek enclave leave in the morning and cost around 300som. A share taxi to Aravan costs 50som.

By taxi A car park at the eastern end of Alisher Navoi, roughly opposite Kelechek Bazaar, has share taxis to Bishkek (*1,200som*) and Jalal-Abad (*250som*). Share taxis also leave from outside the Old Bus Station (see above). Taxis to Batken leave early in the morning from the car park by the GUM department store near the Hotel Alay (*around 600som per seat or 2,400som per car via the Uzbek enclave; 3,000–3,500som to go around it*). Occasional share taxi 4x4s to Murgab (*1,500–2,000som*) leave when full from either Zainabetinova or the Argomak 4x4 stand close to the Bishkek share taxi stand on Alisher Navoi, from where morning minibuses to Sary-Tash (*300som*) and Sary-Mogul (*450som*), and buses to Daroot-Korgon (*300som*), also leave.

Crossing into Uzbekistan The Dostlyk border with Uzbekistan is very close. Kyrgyz taxis are not allowed to cross the border, so a taxi (*200som*) or minibus (*9som*) number 107 or 113 from the Old Bus Station, or 136/137/138 from the Hotel Alay, should be taken to the border post. Apart from sporadic periods when there is marked international tension between the two countries, crossing on foot is usually straightforward and after customs another taxi can be taken onward to Andijan.

GETTING AROUND *Marshrutka* and **bus** number 2 travels north–south through the city centre – along Kurmanjan Datka heading south, and north along Lenina. **Minibus** number 107 serves the airport and the city centre. Minibus 7A runs between the New Bus Station and the city centre, and minibus numbers 7 and 13 operate between the new and old bus stations. The flat fare is 9som.

Taxis, mostly Daewoo Ticos assembled just across the border in Andijan, charge 50–100som for a short journey within the city centre. A taxi to the airport should be 200–250som, although drivers will probably quote more on first asking.

TOURIST INFORMATION The company **CBT Alay** (*Hotel Alay, 2nd floor, Kurmanjan Datka 280;* m *0555 077 621, 0553 985 001;* e *cbtgulcho.mail.ru; www.cbtosh.com*) can organise transport, arrange homestay accommodation in the city and yurt stays in the Alay Valley, suggest trekking itineraries and advise on local sites of interest. They also have a number of newly developed trekking and horseriding tours of between three and six days in the Alay Valley centred on Gulcha and Sary-Mogol, and treks in the Kyrgyz Ata National Reserve.

TOUR OPERATORS

Central Asia Travel Zaynabetdinova 18a; m 0555 657 799; e osh@centralasia-travel.com; www.centralasia travel.com. Covers all of central Asia but can organise trekking in Tien Shan mountains plus trekking & horseriding tours to Lake Sary-Chelek.

Chyngyz Ametov m 0555 030 030, 0773 115 567; e chyngyzametov@mail.ru; www.kyrgyzstannomad.jimbo.com. This multilingual guide & translator offers tours to little-visited parts of southern Kyrgyzstan, as well as various trekking & horseriding itineraries. Also full- & half-day cultural tours of Osh.

Daniyar Abdurahmanov Osh Guesthouse, apartment 8, flat 48 Masalieva; ✆306 29;

m 0772 372 311; e oshguesthouse@gmail.com; www.oshguesthouse.hotbox.ru. Daniyar, who works through the Osh Guesthouse, speaks good English & is able to arrange transport to China via Irkeshtam, or to Murgab in Tajikistan. He can also help arrange GBAO permits & put travellers together to form groups.

Munduz Tourist Kurmanjan Datka 124a; ✆222 76, 550 72; m 0772 345 000; e munduz_tourist@hotmail.com, munduz_tourist@yahoo.com. Offers a wide range of travel services inc air tickets, tours to Sary Tash & Irkeshtam, & Alay Valley climbing expeditions to Peak Lenin and Pyramid Peak. Also GBAO permits & transport to Tajikistan.

WHERE TO STAY *Map, page 270*

Hotels & guesthouses

⌂ **De Luxe** (19 rooms) Alyskaya 35; ✆782 61. A newish, very central hotel across from Kelechek Bazaar. Bright rooms with AC, cable TV & fridge. **$$$$**

⌂ **Sunrise** (50 rooms) Masalieva 25a; ✆728 93. Pleasant, modern hotel with friendly, helpful staff. Clean rooms with AC, satellite TV, fridge & Wi-Fi. **$$$$**

⌂ **Barak-Ata guesthouse** (8 rooms) Ibraimova 22/1; ✆555 32. A small, modern guesthouse south of the city centre with satellite TV, sauna, swimming pool & small business centre. **$$$–$$$$**

⌂ **Eco House** (8 rooms) Lomonsova 25; m 0322 220 945. Attractive rooms with satellite TV, AC & Wi-Fi. Summer terrace & garden. **$$$–$$$$**

⌂ **Kristall (Crystal)** (20 rooms) Alisher Navoi 50a; ✆204 47, 738 96. Kristall is a refurbished

hotel right next to the bazaar. The cheapest rooms share a bathroom. Conference hall, 2 dining halls, casino. There is a possibility that the future of this hotel might be threatened by the redevelopment of the bazaar area. **$$$–$$$$**

⌂ **Pekin** (41 rooms) Alisher Navoi 11a; ✆440 00. Modern Chinese-run (& Chinese-speaking) hotel in centre with decent enough rooms, Wi-Fi & Chinese style b/fast. **$$$**, lux **$$$$**

⌂ **Jetigen** (6 rooms) Jim 1/1; ✆399 10. Near Jayma Bazaar on the ground floor of a high-rise; all rooms come with AC, cable TV & bath. Conference hall, sauna & business centre. **$$$**

⌂ **TES guesthouse** (5 rooms) Say-Boyu 5; ✆215 48, 573 43; e guesthouse@tes-centre.org; www.oshtestravel.com. A small, tidy guesthouse just south of the centre, near the stadium & Delfin. Kitchen & laundry service available. Conference room for 30, outdoor patio, living room with satellite TV, internet access, European b/fast, swimming pool. The guesthouse is popular with NGO workers so book well ahead. **$$$**

⌂ **Alay** Alisher Navoi; ☎577 33; e palvan@yandex.ru. An old, cavernous Soviet-era hotel at the junction of Kurmanjan Datka & Alisher Navoi which was partly refurbished fairly recently. Anonymous spartan rooms, but mostly reasonable enough, with shared bathrooms apart from the 'deluxe' suites. Good value for sgl rooms (**$**), which unusually are half the price of dbls **$$**, deluxe suite **$$$**

⌂ **Biy Ordo** (15 rooms) Saliyeva 39; ☎830 91; m 0556 008 989; e biyordo.hotel@gmail.com; www.biyordo.com. Opened in 2012 & some way north of the centre in the direction of the airport, this has good-value 6-bed dorms, as well as simply furnished sgl & dbl rooms with AC, satellite TV & fridge. B/fast is 150som. Dorm **$**; dbl **$$–$$$**

⌂ **Osh-Nuru** (96 rooms) Bayalinova 1; ☎756 14; http://osh-nuru.kg. This former state-owned Intourist hotel, in a side street between Lenina & Kurmanjan Datka, was fully renovated in 2006. Helpful, English-speaking staff. Pool, bar & Wi-Fi on the first 2 floors. B/fast inc with deluxe rooms. Sgl or dbl without TV **$$**; dbl, lux **$$$**

⌂ **Sanabar** (4 rooms) Gapar Aytiev 9a; ☎254 37. A small, relatively new hotel at the junction of Kurmanjan Datka & Gapar Aytiev, just south of the silver-domed souvenir shop at the base of Solomon's Throne. Plain rooms with bathroom but no b/fast served. **$$**

Homestays

⌂ **CBT Alay** Hotel Alay, 2nd floor, Kurmanjan Datka; m 0555 077 621, 0553 985 001;

e cbtgulcho@mail.ru; www.cbtosh.com. The CBT office can arrange homestay accommodation at a number of locations around the city. A recommended place close to the city centre & Solomon's Throne is CBT homestay #7, hidden away at Mominova 7, which has a large courtyard garden & quiet location. Another good place is the CBT guesthouse at Alieva 133 just behind the city administration building. CBT homestay accommodation in Osh is generally a little more expensive than elsewhere in the country – around US$16 for B&B. **$**

⌂ **Osh Guesthouse** Masalieva, apartment 8, flat 48; ☎306 29; m 0772 372 311; e oshguesthouse@gmail.com; www.oshguesthouse.hotbox.ru. Not so much a guesthouse, more of a crash pad, but cheap, centrally located & understandably popular with backpackers. This is a good meeting place for those wishing to join with others to share transportation. A 4-bed dormitory & 1 dbl room with shared bathroom; also, a common room with cable TV & internet access. Friendly, English-speaking staff, although the place is usually a bit overcrowded. Daniyar, who is based here, can help with transport to China & Tajikistan & help organise share taxis to Bishkek & Tashkent. To find the guesthouse, which is just a Soviet-period flat, walk north on Masalieva from Zaina Betinova & the mosque; go past several restaurants & then turn left down an alley by some kiosks (one of which has the guesthouse signed on its wall). Veer right to reach the middle of 3 apartment buildings (the white one); the flat is on the top floor. Arriving by taxi, ask for 'Aeropag', which is the large shop on Masalieva which has the apartment block behind it. **$**

✗ WHERE TO EAT AND DRINK *Map, page 270*

There is a concentration of traditional restaurants along Masalieva close to the mosque and the bazaar – Ala-Too, Turkestan, Jibek Jolu and others. These all serve excellent *shashlyk* and green tea and have brightly lit terraces which are pleasant places to sit on a warm night (*all* **$**). In the bazaar, along Zaina Betinova, there are several *chaikhanas* like Gold Coast (**$–$$**) that have terraces over the water – not that the sluggish, dirty water of the Ak-Buura River is particularly appealing here.

Lenina, south of Abdykadyrov, has many simple *shashlyk* and beer places like Bayna, while the entrance to Solomon's Throne and the park just to the south of it with the three-storey yurt have a handful of simple places to eat – a good choice for lunch. There is also a Turkish bakery nearby on Kurmanjan Datka, and Borsok, a fast-food restaurant at Kurmanjan Datka 211b, near Osh Market. A vast range of bread and takeaway food, such as *manti*, is sold from stalls near the entrance to Jayma Bazaar along Zaina Betinova. The bazaar itself has every type of food imaginable and even hard-to-find items like ham and yak meat.

Most of the following will be open between 10.00 and 22.00 daily. Places with live music tend to stay open later.

✗ **Rich Men Café** Kurmanjan Datka 60; ☎ 243 03. Quite a long way south of the city centre, with an indoor dining area & outside courtyard, this is one of the choicest places to eat in the city. The English-language menu lists a good range of dishes at reasonable prices inc wide range of cold appetisers & salads, many beef, chicken & fish dishes, & a decent selection of Georgian & Romanian wines. Also 'farinaceous foods', ie: pasta dishes. Service can be slow. There is usually live music after 19.00 (*cover charge*). $$$

✗ **Tsarskii Dvor** Lenina. Set in the shade of trees next to the park in a large, rambling wooden building, this characterful place has swings & a play area for children & a good selection of draught beer for dads. There's a large, outdoor terrace area with booths & scattered tables that have paths winding between them. Good *shashlyk*, live music later in the evening & possibly Wi-Fi (but possibly not). $$-$$$

✗ **Osh Ordo** Gapar Aytiev 11. This 2-storey place has a pleasant, breezy upstairs terrace overlooking Solomon's Throne. Varied, imaginative menu with good *laghman* & salads as well as usual meaty offerings. The more run-of-the-mill Aida-Aka *chaikhana* ($-$$) is next door. $$

✗ **Sherbet** Kurmanjan Datka. Next to the park just south of Solomon's Throne, this is 1 of several places to eat in the park environs, with a cool, shaded terrace & good quality staples like *shorpo* & *pelmeni*. The park has several other places to eat, like Ak-Ordu ($$) & a yurt restaurant ($-$$). $$

✗ **Batyr** Alisher Navoi/Kurmanjan Datka. This large café opposite the Hotel Alay is popular with locals at lunchtime. $-$$

SHOPPING The **Jayma Bazaar** is one of the oldest and busiest markets in central Asia and sells every item imaginable, from fruit and vegetables to cutlery, metal goods, musical instruments, baby cribs, traditional clothing and silk. The bazaar and surrounding areas were severely damaged during the 2010 riots, but 70% of the buildings have now been repaired and trading has resumed. There are a few souvenir stores around the bazaar entrance from the steps off Alisher Navoi by the river. This is a good place to buy a good quality Kyrgyz *kalpak* for 300som. The silver-domed souvenir shop, at the bottom of the walkway up to Solomon's Throne, also has a small selection of items. Prices are generally lower than Bishkek but there is less variety. Osh Market is a well-stocked **supermarket** set back from the road on Gapar Aytiev, close to the junction with Kurmanjan Datka.

OTHER PRACTICALITIES

Health For urgent matters, the **Municipal Hospital** is on Masalieva, opposite the junction with Zaina Betova and the new mosque. The **Polyclinic health centre** on Abdykadyrov is another option.

Money There are many **banks** scattered around the city. Most of these now have ATM machines that will take Visa and issue cash in the form of both Kyrgyz som and US dollars. The Kazkommertsbank ATM on Zaina Betovina outside the Taj Mahal Hotel will also accept MasterCard/Maestro cards. **Jayma Bazaar** has a whole row of money exchange stalls just inside the entrance where Zaina Betinova starts to curve round. These buy and sell Tajik, Uzbek and Chinese money, in addition to the usual currencies. If leaving Kyrgyzstan, it may be a good idea to get a little foreign currency in advance, particularly for Tajikistan along the Pamir Highway, as there are no money-changing facilities until Murgab is reached. All of the exchange stalls seem to offer the same (low) rates.

Communications The main **post office** is on Lenina in front of the park. **Kyrgyz Telecom** is also on Lenina, further north and close to the equestrian statue of

Kurmanjan Datka, the feisty female leader known as the 'Queen of the South' who was instrumental in persuading local Kyrgyz to accept Russian control of the region. **Internet cafés** come and go in the city, but at the time of writing there were several clustered around the top end of Kurmanjan Datka north of Gapar Aytiev. The standard price for internet access across all the cyber cafés is around 40som per hour.

Red tape For visa extensions and registration, the City Administration Building and the OVIR office are at the southern end of Lenina, opposite the park and close to the Osh Ordo Hotel.

WHAT TO SEE AND DO Today, there is little evidence of Babur's residency, or of the city's 3,000-year-old heritage. While the city is an instantly likeable and friendly place there are no 'must-see' sights, although the ageless, if now depleted, Jayma Bazaar and the hill of Solomon's Throne are both well worth a visit. Before the Russians arrived and developed Bishkek as the regional capital, Osh was the largest urban centre in the territory of present-day Kyrgyzstan. With *chaikhanas*, busy mosques, Uzbeks in skullcaps and a bustling bazaar, Osh still feels more authentically central Asian than the upstart capital, although recent troubles have definitely subdued the atmosphere and Uzbek culture is somewhat suppressed.

Jayma Bazaar The bazaar stretches north from Alisher Navoi, divided by the Ak-Buura River, which has a number of traditional *chaikhanas* along its west bank, dishing up *chai* and *laghman* in a relaxed convivial atmosphere. Although somewhat diminished from what it once was, it is still a vibrant, crowded place with a constant stream of shoppers weaving their way through it, dodging out of the path of men pushing loaded carts, who urge 'Bosh! Bosh!' as they inch their way through the crowd. As with any true bazaar, the goods on sale are demarcated in clearly defined zones: money-changers, dried fruit, *lepyoshka* (flat loaves), meat, gold jewellery and so on. The bazaar is open every day, but Sunday is generally the busiest day and Monday the quietest.

Near the bazaar is the Shaid Tepa Mosque, the largest mosque in the country, which was originally constructed in wood between 1908 and 1910, but which served as stables and blacksmiths during the Soviet period. It reopened in 1943 and in recent years has been renovated with Saudi backing.

Solomon's Throne Solomon's Throne or Taht-i-Suleiman is the city's focal point: an arid rocky outcrop which arises abruptly from the city centre above a large Muslim graveyard. The hill is topped by **Dom Babura** (Babur's House), a small but uninspiring shrine that identifies the place where, at the end of the 15th century, the teenage Zahiruddin Muhammad Babur built a shelter for his spiritual retreat from the world while he pondered his future. The original shelter was destroyed in 1853 by an earthquake and its replacement in the 1960s by an explosion. The 'house' today is a small, 1990s steel-roofed structure.

To reach the summit, take the path from the silver-domed souvenir shop near the base on Kurmanjan Datka. There is a small entrance fee (*5som*) to be paid at the gate at the base of the footpath, and from here the path leads through an arch to switchback up the slope along numerous steps to the summit, a 20-minute walk. Babur's House is an important pilgrimage site and many come here to pray or have prayers said for them by the resident holy man. More mundanely, the rocks around Babur's House make an excellent vantage point for enjoying the sunset and it is especially busy with people, mostly families and young couples, in the late afternoon and at dusk.

Just behind the shrine is a smooth, sloping slab of rock where the custom is to slide down feet-first; there is usually a queue of local families lining up to do just this. Sliding down the rock is said to confer considerable health benefits and many believe it also helps with fertility problems, a belief linked to the fact that the hill itself is said to resemble a pregnant woman.

Continuing west along the path from the summit, the **Historical Cultural Museum** (*\229 68; ⊕ 09.00–18.00 Wed–Sun, closed 12.00–13.00; admission 50som*) is reached, housed in a cave blasted out of the holy rock with a rather unfortunate sheet-metal frontage. This has a modest collection of the usual Soviet-period museum accoutrements: pottery fragments, miscellaneous rocks, dusty stuffed animals, photographs of local shamans and, of course, a yurt.

Silk Road Museum (*Alimbek Datka Square, off Kurmanjan Datka; ⊕ 09.00–18.00, closed 12.00–13.00 daily; admission 50som*) This purpose-built museum at the base of Solomon's Throne, also known as the Historical Museum, opened in 2001 to celebrate the Osh 3,000th anniversary event (see page 269) and has a number of archaeological, geological and ethnographic displays, including weapons, pottery and drinking vessels. There are also displays on the Kyrgyz migration from Siberia, the Kokand khanate, petroglyphs from Saimaluu-Tash, traditional handicrafts such as felt and leather goods, and displays detailing the *manaschi* tradition of storytelling. A 1953 map shows the territories of the different Kyrgyz tribes and clans. The interpretive material is in Kyrgyz and Russian only.

Rabat Abdul Khan Mosque This small mosque near the start of the footpath up to Solomon's Throne is the city's oldest mosque, and dates from the 16th–17th century, although the present-day building is mostly a 1980s rebuild. This is a busy, working mosque which may not admit female visitors; ask politely first. Obviously, modest dress is required of both sexes and shoes must be removed before entering.

Other sights Two contrasting historical figures look out over the city from their respective stone plinths – Vladimir Ilyich Lenin and Kurmanjan Datka. Lenin's lofty statue is found in the park south of the stadium, along the street that still bears his name. Close to the park, in wooded grounds on the other side of Lenina, is a small Russian Orthodox church. The equestrian statue of Kurmanjan Datka (1811–1907), the 'Queen of the South', at the junction of Alisher Navoi and Lenina, represents an altogether different sort of hero: a female Kyrgyz ruler who helped to liberate the Fergana Valley from the Kokand khanate in the 19th century and, although at first she opposed it, she eventually persuaded her people to accept Russian rule (see page 34).

The smaller park, closer to the city centre behind the post office, has a grounded Aeroflot Yak-40 for those curious about Soviet aviation. This was once, apparently, a cinema. The Ferris wheel next to the plane provides good, if fleeting, views of the city skyline for just 30som a whirl. West of here, the small park in front of the Silk Road museum has a curious three-storey yurt (⊕ *09.00–21.00 daily; admission 50som*) where you can dress up and have yourself photographed in traditional costume should the urge take you.

AROUND OSH

KARA-SUU (КАРА-СУУ) This Uzbek-majority town, 23km northeast of Osh, sits squarely on the Kyrgyzstan–Uzbekistan border, with its counterpart, Qorasuv, across the river on the Uzbek side. The close proximity of the border is the reason why the town's enormous Turutali market, which takes place here twice a week on Saturdays and Tuesdays, developed to become such a major trade centre.

In Soviet days, Kara-Suu/Qorasuv was a single settlement known as Ilyichovsk, which spread across both sides of the river but, with the coming of independence for both Kyrgyzstan and Uzbekistan, the town's Uzbek population found themselves politically divided for the first time. Despite the newly introduced frontier, a brisk trade continued between the two sides until 1999, when the Uzbek authorities destroyed the bridge across the Kara-Suu River which linked the two closely related communities. The bridge had been a lifeline for many from the Uzbekistan side of the border, who came to Kyrgyzstan to buy cheap Chinese goods and trade fruit and vegetables from the fertile farmland of the Fergana Valley. Despite the best attempts of the Uzbek authorities to curtail it, cross-border trade continued by means of improvised ropeways that brought both goods and people across the river, but this was a hazardous pursuit and each year up to 50 traders died falling into the fast-flowing river. As well as the danger of crossing the river, corrupt Uzbek border guards would also demand bribes to allow the traders to pass. Despite these considerable obstacles, trade continued as best it could.

In 2005, riots broke out in Qorasuv, following the massacre by Islam Karimov's troops in nearby Andijan in which an estimated 500 protesters were killed. Locals attacked government officials, stoned police cars and burned buildings, and within hours of the insurrection the destroyed bridge had been hastily replaced with a number of improvised footbridges. An estimated 6,000 Uzbek refugees streamed across the Kyrgyz border at Kara-Suu to safety before it was sealed by Kyrgyz troops.

The grey market trade at Kara-Suu increased markedly following the Andijan tragedy because of all the improvised bridges that had been built. As a result, many more Uzbeks were able to make a scant living carrying goods back into Uzbekistan. Following the resurgence of the Kara-Suu market, several illegal crossings were set up elsewhere in the area to facilitate cross-border trade. One example of this was at the Uzbekistan village of Suratash, where locals pooled their resources to build an access road and concrete barrier, and collected 100 Uzbek som in 'transit tax' from everyone wishing to cross to the minibuses and taxis waiting on the Kyrgyz side to whisk shoppers directly to Kara-Suu market.

The market is an enormous money-spinner for the regional economy, although the 'grey' wealth generated at Kara-Suu certainly comes at a price – two past directors of the market have been murdered by unknown assassins. There have also been protests at the increasing number of Chinese Uyghur traders setting up shop at the market and some of these have been beaten up, accused of undercutting the prices of the Uzbek traders. The market itself covers an area of around 15ha and, like Dordoi Bazaar in Bishkek, goods are stored in and sold from shipping containers which are piled two high. It is said that there are around 1,500 containers in total and that overall the market trade employs anything up to 15,000 people.

Kara-Suu market is nothing like the traditional bazaars in Osh or Kashgar and is unlikely to have anything that a typical foreign visitor may wish to buy, unless they are on the lookout for a flat-screen television set or a DVD player. Notwithstanding this, it is an impressive place to visit just for its sheer size and spectacle, and makes for an easy half-day trip from Osh. The main road in front of the market is lined with busy *chaikhanas*, and is an unending traffic jam of honking taxis and vans massively overloaded with bolts of cloth, computers and DVD players precariously balanced on roof racks. Facing the market on the other side of the road is a huge hangar which seems to be entirely devoted to the sale of lurid Chinese socks.

Trade at the market has declined dramatically since the ethnic violence of 2010. Once Kyrgyz and Uzbek worked alongside one another amicably here – Kara-Su was always far more integrated than urban centres like Osh or Jalal-Abad – but Uzbek traders and shoppers no longer throng here and stall holders have suffered badly as a result. Whether or not Kara-Suu's border market will eventually recover to anything like its past glory still remains to be seen.

Getting there and away Regular, very crowded, **minibuses** (*30som*) leave from Osh's Old Bus Station and drop off in front of the market. Shared Daewoo Tico **taxis** run the same route and charge just 40som per seat.

ARAVAN (APABAH) The small Uzbek town of Aravan lies 25km southwest of Osh, nuzzled against the Uzbekistan border. Just outside the town is a holy site which pays tribute to the syncretic tradition that suffuses central Asian Islam with earlier pagan beliefs.

The Celestial Horses of Aravan The Celestial Horses of Aravan, as they are known, are petroglyphs which have had an important role in regional folklore and have become a pilgrimage site for Muslims in the Fergana Valley.

The rock carvings, which can be seen with a little patience on a south-facing cliff-face just outside Aravan, are thought to date from the 1st century BC. The horses etched into the rock face are thought to represent the legendary, blood-sweating 'Celestial' or 'Heavenly' Horses of Fergana that were so admired by the Chinese of the Han dynasty at the time, especially by Wu-Ti, the dynasty's ruthless emperor. The site was excavated twice in the 20th century and evidence has been found of animal sacrifices at the cliff-base below the carvings. Today, there is a small Sufi shrine at the site and a shelter for pilgrims.

Visiting the site The carvings and the nearby spring are considered sacred to local Muslims and it should be remembered that this is an important religious site rather than just one of archaeological interest to tourists. It goes without saying that one should dress accordingly and behave in an appropriately decorous manner.

The cliff-face is reached by going through a green gate on the main road, near the hospital, on the outskirts of the town. The gate has a sign above it that says: '*Dul-Dul at Ziyarit Zhai*', which refers to the Sufi shrine found within. A path leads down next to a Russian Orthodox and Soviet cemetery on the left, and then crosses a stream to come to the base of a cliff, where there is a pilgrims' shelter on the left and the small shrine of a Sufi sheikh on the right. The petroglyphs are rather hard to see, high on the cliff above, and slightly to the left of the shrine; they're about three-quarters of the way up, just above the top branches of a willow tree. Binoculars would be a great help, although they're not essential.

Sadly, there is also much modern-day graffiti around the base of the cliff, testament to the popular belief that making one's own mark at a sacred site such as this will bring its own spiritual benefit. Hornets, too, seem common here in late summer.

From Osh, regular share taxis for Aravan leave from the bus stand on Alisher Navoi, just west of the junction with Kurmanjan Datka. The road to Aravan follows the Uzbekistan border so closely that recently erected Uzbek watchtowers and barbed wire can be seen at the roadside. Approaching Aravan, ask to get off at the hospital ('*balneetsa*'); the green gateway is just before the right turn to the hospital and a garage on the left-hand side of the road. Minibuses also run from the Old Bus Station (*50som*).

Chil-Ustun The Chil-Ustun cave system is close to Aravan in the limestone hills above the Ak-Buura and Aravan river basin. The cave system takes its name from the Tajik for '40 columns', a reference to the stalactites found in the cave network. The entrance to the Chil-Ustun system is about 4km from Aravan, high on the southern slope of a 1,460m-high mountain of the same name. The 380m-long main cave has three big chambers connected by narrow corridors, the largest of which is 100m long, 50m wide and 20m high. Numerous stalactites hang from the roof of the cave and the walls bear inscriptions in a variety of languages said to include Sanskrit. Other caves nearby include Sasyk-Unkur (140m deep), Suvli-Kamar (120m), Chil-Mayram (130m) and Teshik-Tash (180m).

Another canyon, in the Tuya-Muyun region 20km south of the Chil-Ustun cave system, has the deepest cave in the entire country, the 240m-deep Fersman Cave.

None of these caves are set up for tourist visits in any way at all, and all require torches, ropes and a knowledgeable local guide to locate them; enquire at tour operators in Osh, or at the Osh CBT office.

ÖZGÖN (ОЗГОН) *Telephone code: 03233*

HISTORY The town of Özgön (also spelled Ozgon or Uzgen; Russian: Узген) lies 55km northeast of Osh, on a clifftop above the wide plain of the Kara-Darya River. These days the town is visited mostly for its well-preserved 12th-century Karakhanid monuments and for its interesting Uzbek-dominated bazaar, but it also has an unfortunate recent past that most would prefer to forget.

In the summer of 1990, the town momentarily became famous for the inter-ethnic fighting that broke out between the town's Kyrgyz and Uzbek communities over issues concerning land tenure. The violence was thankfully short-lived, but the sudden eruption of blood-letting resulted in hundreds tragically losing their lives – an event that still leaves a shadow over the town today. Conservative estimates say that around 300 lost their lives on both sides of the ethnic divide; others claim it may have been as many as 1,000. Both Kyrgyz and Uzbeks alike criticise the Soviet authorities at the time, who seemingly just stood by as the violence unfolded. These days there is no tangible evidence of the event, but with such a comparatively recent event fresh in the memory of most of the town's citizens, coupled with the knowledge of the ethnic violence that blighted Osh and Jalal-Abad in 2010, it does beg the question as to exactly what lurks behind the mask of Özgön's apparently calm exterior.

Özgön is a town with at least 2,000 years of history. It is mentioned by Chinese chroniclers in the 2nd century BC and there are even the usual claims that Alexander the Great passed this way and camped in the vicinity of the present-day town. Özgön went on to become an important Silk Road centre, with an economy based on trade and coin production, and later, during the period of Karakhanid rule, it was further developed as one of the capitals of the Karakhanid state which became known as Mavarannahr. The Karakhanid heyday was during the 11th and 12th centuries, and as the khanate fell into decline in the 13th century, following the raids of Genghis Khan, so did Mavarannahr.

Today the town is mostly an agricultural centre, with sunflowers, tobacco and especially rice all being important crops. Özgön has a university, a brewery and a distinctive bazaar which is very Uzbek in character.

GETTING THERE AND AWAY Regular buses, minibuses and share taxis run between Özgön and Jalal-Abad to the northwest, and Osh to the southwest. A minibus from

Osh's Old Bus Station costs 60som. The bus station is on Manas, a five-minute walk from the bazaar. There are also fairly regular minibus and share taxi services to Bishkek.

🏠 **WHERE TO STAY AND EAT** Özgön is best visited as a half-day trip from Osh or Jalal-Abad, and there is no real need to stay over, which is just as well as the only *gostinitsa* in town, on the corner of Manas and Gagarin, is pretty basic. There are plenty of *shashlyk* and *laghman* places in the bazaar for a meal, as well as slightly more formal restaurants along Manas, between the bazaar and the Karakhanid mausoleum complex, like **Café Roshana**, near the tower, and **Café Islam** close to the bazaar entrance (*both* $). The large, cool dining hall almost directly opposite the bazaar entrance is also quite reasonable for Uzbek staples.

WHAT TO SEE AND DO

Karakhanid mausoleum complex This complex of buildings is reached by turning left out of the market and following the main road, Manas, for ten minutes to come to a park with a silver statue of Lenin. The site is a little further on and can be seen from the Lenin statue.

The complex consists of three adjoining 12th-century mausoleums and an 11th-century minaret (*foreign entrance ticket to minaret & surrounding sites 300som, inc guide & permission to use a camera;* ⊕ *daylight hrs*). The stubby, pepper-pot shaped **minaret** dates from the mid-11th century and, although it has been thoroughly reconstructed, it is considerably shorter than was originally intended, as its upper 7m plunged earthwards during an earthquake in the 17th century. The 20m minaret that remains is of bands of fine honey-coloured brickwork and carved terracotta. The cupola was built in 1923–24 to top the truncated structure. Ruins of a medieval *madrasa* have been found nearby.

The three **mausoleums** all date from the 12th century and two of them are very finely detailed. The most northerly one was built in 1152–53 for Jalal ad-Din al-Huseyn, and is a fine surviving example of early Islamic art. The portico is decorated with delicate terracotta ornamentation and there are inscriptions on the arch in Naskhi script, together with Kufic script above the entrance. The slightly taller, central mausoleum is older, dating from the 11th century, and was probably built for Nasr Ibn Ali, the founder of the Karakhanid dynasty, who died in 1012–13. This is the most reconstructed of the trio and, consequently, the least elaborate in terms of detail. The southern mausoleum was built a little later than its northern counterpart, which it superficially resembles, between 1186 and 1187, for an unknown recipient. This has an even more lavishly decorated entrance than the northern mausoleum, with intertwined floral motifs, inscriptions and terracotta ornamentation.

If the complex already seems strangely familiar it is because the three mausoleums adorn the reverse side of the Kyrgyz 50som note. There are good views of the Kara-Darya River Valley from the complex, and even better ones from the top of the minaret.

AROUND ÖZGÖN

Ak-Terek About 43km northeast of Özgön, the village of Ak-Terek, on the banks of the Jassy River, has a whole range of possibilities for trekking and horseriding in the region, with mineral springs, a nearby gorge filled with walnut trees, and the Kara-Shoro National Park just 40km away beyond the village. CBT Osh (see page 273) organises a four-day tour for experienced horseriders that begins with sightseeing in Özgön, before continuing to Ak-Terek, from where a horse trek is made east along the Jassy River through a gorge and several villages, before climbing up to the Besh-Terek, Kara-Döbö and Baibiche *jailoos*. This continues the following day to Kypchylma Gorge and another *jailoo* camp. From here, the Kara-Shoro National Park is reached on the third day of riding from Ak-Terek.

There is homestay accommodation in Ak-Terek that can be booked in advance from Osh or, alternatively, on arrival in the village. There are daily buses to and from Özgön.

THE ALAY VALLEY (АЛАЙСКАЯ ДОЛИНА)

The M41 highway south from Osh leads to the remote village of Sary-Tash, which is a crossroads of sorts, with the road to Kashgar leading east to the Chinese border at Irkeshtam and the road south struggling over the immense barrier of the Pamir Alay range into Tajikistan's Gorno-Badakhshan Autonomous Region. The road to Sary-Tash is spectacular, and one of the most beautiful drives in the country. The road is in good condition too, having been comprehensively upgraded in recent years.

GULCHA Leaving Osh, the highway climbs slowly out of the fertile plain to follow the Taldyk River on the way to the 2,408m Chyrchyk Pass, before descending down to Gulcha at the confluence of two rivers. CBT Alay in Osh (see page 273) offers two-day trekking and horseriding tours based at a yurt stay at Chyrchyk *jailoo* close to Gulcha. Share taxis running from the Argomak 4x4 stand in Osh cost just 150som and take 45 minutes. There is also a comfortable homestay in the town itself (*Dostuk 1;* m *0552 414 188, 0770 701 131;* e *ainagul04@gmail.com*).

From Gulcha, the highway follows the Alay Valley south through rugged mountains and red sandstone cliffs above the snaking river to eventually climb over the 3,615m Taldyk Pass before descending to Sary-Tash. Just before the village is reached, a roadside sign enthusiastically bids you a 'Harry Journey' as you start to think about leaving Kyrgyzstan for pastures new.

SARY-TASH (САРЫ-ТАШ) Spending a night in this rather unprepossessing village is a necessary evil for independent travellers who wish to travel to China or Tajikistan under their own steam. Whatever its other limitations might be, it cannot be denied that, with the high, snow-spattered ridge of the Pamir Alay looming to the south, Sary-Tash ('Yellow Stone') is located in a natural setting that is undeniably beautiful. However, at 3,173m above sea level, it can get very cold at night.

The village has a couple of shops and a basic café, and as well as a couple of homestays. There is also a guesthouse that can be prebooked through CBT Alay at Osh. Just asking around will no doubt unleash more offers of homestay accommodation.

Getting there and away For individual travellers who have come from Osh and intend to continue south to Murgab in Tajikistan, hitchhiking out of here is said to be very difficult as very little traffic uses this road. Transport to Irkeshtam is generally much better, but it is still possible to get stuck here for hours. Most of the passing vehicles heading for Irkeshtam are big trucks going to China.

To reach Sary-Tash from Osh there is a daily **bus** (*300som*) that continues to Sary-Mogul and Daroot-Korgon and takes four or five hours. **Share taxis** from Osh's Argomak 4x4 stand also run the same route, although they can be hard to find.

SARY-MOGOL (САРЫ-МОГОЛЬ) The Sary-Tash 'crossroads' leads north to Osh, east to China and south to Tajikistan. A little way along the Tajikistan branch, another road leads west along the Alay Valley to the village of Sary-Mogol. At 3,100m above sea level, Sary-Mogol sits in the shadow of Pik Lenina ('Peak Lenin'), a gigantic, 7,134m wall of rock, ice and snow which demarcates the Kyrgyz-Tajik border 20km south of the village. Peak Lenin is purported to be one of the easiest of the world's 7,000m peaks to climb and most of the foreign visitors who come to Sary-Mogol tend to have some sort of business with the mountain.

With no jobs, a harsh winter climate and poor conditions for agriculture, life is immensely tough here, and most of the adult male population has left to seek work elsewhere. However, tourism of a non-mountaineering kind has definite potential here, too, and a CBT network was established in the village in 2007. The CBT co-ordinator is Abdilla Tashbekov (m *0773 505 939, 0556 092 627;* e *sarymogol@gmail. com*), who can arrange transport and accommodation in the village, as well as yurt stays at the 3,500m-high Lake Tulpar-Kul not far from Peak Lenin base camp at Achik-Tash. A yurt stay at Lake Tulpar-Kul gives the opportunity to catch a glimpse of Achik-Tash without the need for a border permit, as the camp is clearly visible from further up the valley. CBT Osh can also help organise horse treks to Lake Tulpar-Kul, as well as camping treks that go over the 4,300m Sary-Mogol Pass to follow the southern Sary-Mogol Valley.

West of Sary-Mogol, the road along the valley continues to Daroot-Korgon and the Tajik border. At the time of writing this route into Tajikistan was closed to foreigners (see page 61).

Getting there and away A daily bus (*400som*) runs between Osh and Sary-Mogol via Sary-Tash in the morning from the Old Bus Station. Any buses running between Osh and Daroot-Korgon also pass through the village. The CBT co-ordinator can arrange transport to Achik-Tash base camp from the village.

Around Sary-Mogol

Peak Lenin Now officially known by its non-Soviet name of Koh-i-Garmo ('Warm Mountain'), this mountain is still referred to as *Lenina* by most locals and climbers alike. At 7,134m, Peak Lenin is the third-highest mountain in the CIS, and has a reputation for being a relatively easy climb. This is not to make light of it, as climbing Peak Lenin is hardly a stroll in the park and many climbers have died attempting to reach the summit. Despite being considered relatively straightforward for a 7,000m-plus mountain, Peak Lenin is by no means a trekking peak and a successful ascent requires all the essential equipment of ice axes, crampons, etc and, most importantly, a great deal of mountaineering experience. The greatest dangers are avalanches and suddenly changing weather. In 1974 an eight-woman team perished on the mountain in a storm, and in 1991 an ice-fall trapped 44 climbers, leaving only one survivor.

Peak Lenin is essentially a broad-based pyramid with a northern face that is far steeper and more difficult than its other slopes. Attempts on the peak are invariably made from the southern, Tajikistan side, although there are many variants of the approach, with 16 different routes to the summit. In keeping with its reputation as a relatively easy 'walk up' summit, Peak Lenin is one of the world's most frequently climbed peaks above 7,000m.

Achik-Tash Achik-Tash ('Open Stone') at 3,600m is the main base camp for climbing Peak Lenin, but it can be visited in its own right for lower-level trekking.

Nearby is Lukovaya Polyana ('Onion Glade'), which is a relatively easy hike from the base camp. The Bishkek-based IMC Pamir trekking company (*http://home.tiscali. nl/imcpamir*) maintains a base camp at Achik-Tash which has accommodation in wooden huts, in addition to tents. The same company organises a 24-day expedition to the peak from Osh that builds in plenty of time for acclimatisation. Other Bishkek companies, such as ITMC Tien Shan, also operate base camps here in the summer months (see pages 53–5). Staying here independently requires total self-sufficiency, so stock up on fuel, food and other supplies in Osh before setting off. Due to altitude and an unpredictable climate, the trekking season here is naturally a fairly short one – from mid-July to early September.

THE IRKESHTAM CROSSING TO CHINA

The road from Sary-Tash to the Chinese border has been massively improved in recent years and the journey now only takes around 1–1½ hours, although it is still prone to blockages by trucks when there is heavy snow. Leaving the village behind, the road slowly climbs up from the Alay Valley over a 3,536m pass, before winding downhill to the river basin which has the dreary hamlet of Irkeshtam and the Chinese border beyond. The Kyrgyz border post is reached at the bottom of the road from the pass. There is a rugged no-man's land of around 10km between the Kyrgyz border post and the first Chinese customs post and, for those travelling independently, it is necessary to hitch across this in whatever transport is available once you have had your passport stamped.

Close to the Kyrgyz border post is a trucker's café and basic *gostinitsa*, which is really not recommended. A little better are some of the trailers further down where a cheap bed for the night is also a possibility. Better still is not to stay here at all.

There is a **checkpoint** a little way uphill from the Kyrgyz post where passports need to be shown before crossing the no-man's land to the upper Chinese customs post, where customs tends to be polite but thorough. Here bags are searched and passports checked but not stamped, as this is just a preliminary check. From here it is a mind-boggling 140km to the main Chinese post at Wuqia (also called Uluqqat). Prearranged onward Chinese transport will pick you up here, otherwise the border police will insist that independent travellers take one of the 'approved' taxis that ply the route and will not return your passport until this is organised. Hitching trucks is not permitted. Approved taxi drivers will take independent travellers between the two posts for about 100–200 RMB (US$15–30) per person depending on whether they travel by car or van and how many there are on board. Cyclists will also need to get a ride and transport their vehicle, as cycling is not allowed between the two posts. Stopping or taking photographs in the long stretch between the two posts is not permitted either.

At the **main post**, luggage has to be taken inside a large, modern immigration building for examination. Kyrgyz luggage is normally more rigorously searched than that belonging to travellers, although great interest is often taken in Western reading material like guidebooks. Maps are sometimes confiscated, so it is best to hide these. Electronic goods like cameras, laptops and iPods are usually very thoroughly scrutinised for anything that the Chinese authorities might regard as suspect.

From Chinese immigration it is about two hours to Kashgar from here. Taxi drivers usually hang around outside to offer onward rides to Kashgar, but they tend to drive a hard bargain. There are money-changers at the border and a hotel and minibus station in Wuqia town centre, a short taxi-drive (15RMB) away, if you get stuck. There is also basic accommodation at the first Chinese checkpoint if you arrive too late to move on.

As with the crossing at the Torugart Pass, problems can arise because of unforeseen circumstances: the road blocked by snow-bound trucks; power cuts that result in Chinese computers not working; extra-long lunch hours and unexpected holidays meaning one or both sides of the border have closed for the day.

Good timing is crucial because of the different time zones that each side operates by. The Chinese authorities observe Beijing time, which is two hours ahead of Kyrgyz time. The Chinese post is supposedly open from 10.30–20.00 Beijing time, but closed for lunch between 14.00 and 16.00 (12.00–14.00 Kyrgyz time). The Kyrgyz border is supposedly open from 09.00–11.00 and 14.00–18.00 travelling in the direction of China. Going through all the border posts can take anything between four to six hours. The important thing is to start early and reach the Chinese customs post before it closes for its lengthy lunch break. Coming from China, it is possible to cross into Kyrgyzstan between 11.00 and 18.00 (Beijing time) apart from during the lunch break period.

The **Irkeshtam crossing** is technically open all year round, although there is the potential for it to be closed by heavy snowfall from time to time. It is closed at weekends and on Kyrgyz and Chinese public holidays (see page 238). If all this seems rather unnecessarily complicated then bear in mind that things – times, customs, border posts, rules and regulations – can change at a whim, although things are easier now than they were a few years ago. The best advice is to plan your crossing as carefully as you can and leave as little as possible to chance. Bring food, drink and warm clothes too.

Considering the problems that can occur with both the Torugart and Irkeshtam crossings into China, the question remains: given a free choice, which is the better of the two? Until recently, there was no choice in the matter as Irkeshtam was closed to foreign travellers until 2002. Unlike Torugart, Irkeshtam needs no special permit or prior arrangement of transport to meet travellers on the other side of the border, and this could be seen as a distinct advantage as it allows for more flexibility of plans. There is no simple answer, but common wisdom seems to dictate that if you have sufficient money but a tight schedule, it may be best to travel to China via the Torugart Pass; with plenty of time at your disposal but less money, take your chances with Irkeshtam.

GETTING THERE AND AWAY Buses running from Osh to Kashgar (US$95) take anything up to 24 hours and usually leave Wednesday and Sunday evenings from Osh's New Bus Station. It is apparently possible to book a seat the day before for 100som, paying the US$95 on the day of departure. This is a Chinese sleeper bus with bunks, and locals will compete for the lower bunks, although the upper ones are fine. The bus is supposed to leave at 19.00 but will more likely depart later than this in order to arrive at the border around 08.00. Border proceedings will take up to six hours in total. Coming the other way, once- or twice-weekly buses from Kashgar's International Bus Station cost US$90–100. There have been incidents in which Kashgar bus station staff have refused to sell bus tickets to foreigners; if this happens a local travel agent can be employed to purchase them.

The main problem with travelling on the bus is that, coming either way, it passes through the best of the scenery in the hours of darkness. A way round this is to travel the stretch between Osh and Sary-Tash in daylight by **minibus** or **taxi** and stay the night in Sary-Tash. Early the next morning, take a taxi or hitch a lift to Irkeshtam, cross the border then, after travelling the 140km between the two Chinese border posts by taxi, take another taxi to Kashgar from the main border post. This is, of course, fraught with a little more uncertainty, but it is certainly more adventurous and may or may not prove to be fun. It is also less expensive as a rule. For some idea of prices: minibuses from Osh to Sary-Tash are 300som, share taxis a little more per seat; transport to Irkeshtam from Sary-Tash is about 300som, although some truck drivers may not charge. Jeeps to Irkeshtam from Osh (from the jeep stand on Alisher Navoi) cost around 10,000som. The Osh Guesthouse can also arrange a 4x4 to the border for this price or less. Trucks across no-man's land between the Kyrgyz customs post and the first Chinese checkpoint probably will not charge anything.

THE ROAD SOUTH TO TAJIKISTAN

Just outside Sary-Tash village is a lonely police checkpoint next to a collection of radar domes. From here, the road makes a beeline south towards what appears to be the impenetrable barrier of the magnificent Pamir Alay. The road climbs gently at first and then steeply along a very rough, rocky road, up to the 4,280m Kyzyl-Art Pass and the Kyrgyz customs post. The air is gaspingly thin here: a reminder that this is the highest road in Kyrgyzstan, and this is not far off its highest point.

The Tajik post is reached shortly after. Even in the summer, it is freezing cold at night here and it feels rather like the edge of the charted world – it almost is. Few travellers visit Tajikistan, and even fewer have the necessary paperwork that allows them to enter the Gorno-Badakhshan Autonomous Oblast (GBAO) and take the Pamir Highway south. To do so is neither cheap nor easy to organise, but it is undeniably one of the last truly adventurous road trips that can be made in the 21st century. It feels like a privilege, and it is. Entering Gorno-Badakshan along the Pamir Highway from the Kyzyl-Art Pass, even southern Kyrgyzstan can start to seem a little touristy.

For a number of reasons, mostly to do with the high-altitude terrain and a very sparse population, there is virtually no public transport along this route, and to enter Tajikistan requires both a Tajik visa and a GBAO permit, which both need to be arranged in advance. The best option is to arrange transport in Osh to go at least as far as Murgab, from where ACTED, a sort of CBT equivalent for Tajikistan, can help organise onward travel to Khorog, either by way of the direct route through the Pamirs or by the spectacular Wakhan corridor along the northern border with Afghanistan.

Interestingly, despite a change of country, virtually all of the population between the Kyrgyz border and Murgab are ethnic Kyrgyz rather than Tajik.

GETTING TO TAJIKISTAN Transport for the two-day trip to Murgab can be organised in Osh, providing a Tajik visa and a GBAO permit have been obtained in advance. At the time of writing this was very easy to organise in Bishkek despite being almost impossible just a few months earlier – these things tend to change periodically, usually because of politics. A robust vehicle is required for the journey – a 4x4 Niva or an ex-army UAZ – and sufficient fuel must be carried, as there will be virtually nothing available until Murgab. Transport can be arranged by asking around at the jeep park, although most drivers tend to quote wholly unrealistic prices for the journey and many of them do not have experience of the route.

Overall, it is easier to make use of an agent like Daniyar Abdurahmanov (m *0772 372 311*; e *oshguesthouse@gmail.com; www.oshguesthouse.hotbox.ru*), who runs the Osh Guesthouse, has plenty of experience of arranging transport along this route and can usually arrange a vehicle and driver within 24 hours. A typical price is US$300 for the vehicle, plus an extra US$15–20 for the driver to sleep over at Karakol, the first village in Tajikistan before Murgab is reached. This is well worth doing, as Karakol is a stark but interesting ethnic Kyrgyz village, high in the Pamirs by a beautiful blue lake. To travel all the way to Murgab from Osh would make for a very long day and the landscape *en route* is so good that you really do not want to rush it. Daniyar can also help put a group together if you are travelling alone. Excess Kyrgyz som should be exchanged for Tajik somani in Jayma Bazaar before leaving Osh.

ENCLAVES AND EXCLAVES: A POLITICAL JIGSAW

Kyrgyzstan's Batken Province has several isolated foreign enclaves within its territory. These eccentric political paint splatters on Kyrgyzstan's national map first came about when Stalin created the jigsaw of interwoven borders which characterise central Asia today. The various borders were drawn up between 1924 and 1936, ostensibly based on political and economic considerations, which attempted to group linguistically distinct populations together. It is all too easy to argue that the creation of such enclaves was part and parcel of Stalin's ruthless divide-and-rule strategy. This, no doubt, is part of the explanation, but it would seem that local politics came into the equation, too, and that a certain degree of bartering of territories took place between local leaders at the time. Such territorial haggling was also probably responsible for predominantly Uzbek areas, such as that in the vicinity of Jalal-Abad, becoming attached to Kyrgyzstan rather than finding themselves belonging to what might appear to be their more obvious natural home in Uzbekistan.

Four of the Batken enclaves belong to Uzbekistan: Sokh, the largest territory at 325km², which paradoxically has a population that is almost entirely Tajik; Shakhimardan, a territory of 90km², which is mostly Uzbek; and two much smaller enclaves that are located to the north of Sokh and north of Shakhimardan, close to the Uzbek border – Qalacha and Dzhangail.

Two more enclaves belong to Tajikistan: Vorukh, a large, 130km² enclave west of the provincial capital which is linked by road to Isfara in Tajikistan, and Kairagach, another tiny settlement north of Sülüktü in the far west.

Kyrgyzstan is not alone in the region in having political enclaves. Uzbekistan's Fergana Valley also has two small enclaves of its own: Sarvak, just 14km long and 500m wide, which belongs to Tajikistan; and Barak, an isolated Kyrgyz village of just 600, which lies 13km from the Kyrgyz border stranded between the Uzbekistan towns of Margilan and Fergana. As Uzbekistan is one of only two double-landlocked territories in the world, that is completely surrounded by territories that are themselves landlocked (the other is Liechtenstein), it must follow that by a unique quirk of political geography both Sarvak (Tajikistan) and Barak (Kyrgyzstan) share the inimitable honour of being the world's only *triple-landlocked* territories.

The existence of these enclaves, which probably did not affect people's lives that much when they were first created, has serious consequences for those who live in them today. Political differences and frequent antagonism between Uzbekistan and Kyrgyzstan has made ease of movement between the Uzbek enclaves and the surrounding territory problematic at times, while Barak, the lone Kyrgyz exclave within Uzbekistan, faces exceptional difficulties in terms of the movement of its citizens to and from the Kyrgyz 'mainland'.

10

Batken Province was created in 1999 from the three most westerly *rayons*, or regions, of what was then part of Osh Province: Batken, Chong-Alay and Kadamjay. This came as a result of more direct and visible governing in the region, following an unstable period in which there had been frequent incursions by militants from the Islamic Movement for Uzbekistan (IMU). A couple of well-documented kidnappings involving Japanese geologists and young American climbers put the region firmly off-limits for several years. Travel to the Batken region was advised against in the period following the 2010 riots, but this advice has since been relaxed by the British Foreign & Commonwealth Office (FCO).

The north of the *oblast* occupies part of the southern Fergana Valley which extends into Uzbekistan, an area of rolling dry hills and semi-desert steppe; the province's southern boundary is defined by two stark, treeless mountain chains – the Alay, which extends east into Osh Province, and the Turkestan range, both subsidiary ranges of the Pamirs. The most remarkable feature of Batken Province's geography, however, is political rather than physical, as the *oblast* is host to no less than six island enclaves that belong to neighbouring Uzbekistan and Tajikistan.

In terms of tourist potential, the province is the least well known in all Kyrgyzstan, partly a result of its isolation and partly because travel was proscribed here until recently. Another considerable problem is the existence of the enclaves that, in theory at least, necessitate visas even for swift transit and create logistical problems for those wishing to travel through the province.

Mountaineering expeditions have long favoured the province, which offers speciality mountaineering challenges like the sheer walls of 5,504m Ak-Suu peak, southwest of Batken, and the sharp peaks of the Turkestan range that have been carved by wind and ice to resemble sharks' teeth.

BATKEN (БАТКЕН) The journey west to Batken from Osh passes through a dreamy agricultural landscape of tobacco and rice, with the stunning backdrop of the snow-capped Alay range ever-present to the south. The road is generally good apart from some of the dusty stretches skirting the Sokh enclave, which are barely more than dirt tracks. Close to Batken, the road itself is used for drying and threshing rice, and piles of rice-straw line the roadside in places at harvest time. The Batken region is also well known for its apricot orchards and the *oruk* (dried apricots) they produce.

The provincial capital is a pleasant enough town and a reasonable place to spend the night *en route* to Khojand in Tajikistan. Batken was awarded city status in 2000, although the place has more of the atmosphere of a large village. Since it became capital of the recently created *oblast* a number of new government offices have been opened. In contrast to the Tajik-populated enclaves of nearby Vorukh and Sokh, Batken's population of around 12,000 is almost entirely ethnic Kyrgyz.

Getting there and away With an Uzbek transit visa it is perfectly possible to reach Batken from Osh by the regular daily **minibus** service (*300som*) or a **share taxi** (*around 600som per seat or 2,400som per car*). Without the appropriate visa, things are more problematic as the direct route goes straight through the Uzbek enclave of Sokh. Some insist that it is possible for the taxi drivers to pay the Uzbek border guards a small 'appreciation' so that they turn a blind eye to the foreigner in their midst; others say that travelling on the minibus Uzbek border guides will just wave any obvious foreigners through without fuss. Of course, all of this is rather uncertain and dependent on the mood of the guards, as if they wanted to cause trouble for a visa-less foreigner they certainly could do. A safer alternative is to take a taxi that goes *around* the Uzbek enclave on rough, dirt roads, thus avoiding the problem altogether. Naturally, this will cost more because of the greater distance travelled. At the time of writing, these dirt roads were being upgraded, and so it is possible the 'detour' route will become more standard in the future. If you are travelling independently, by car or bicycle, then the non-enclave route is a must.

Share taxis to Batken from Osh usually leave fairly early in the morning. Unfortunately, it can sometimes be difficult to find other passengers who want to take the longer route, because the visa requirements do not affect locals in the same way as they do foreign travellers. Going to Batken avoiding the Uzbek enclave should cost in the order of 1,000–1,200som per place. Be sure to ascertain that the driver is going *cherez obyezd* ('via the detour'). By this route the journey time from Osh is around six hours. A cheaper 'safe' alternative is to go first by minibus from Osh to Kadamjay via Kyzyl-Kia (*150som*), then take another minibus (*200som*) or share taxi to Batken, thus avoiding any checkpoints.

Batken's small airport has **flights** to and from Bishkek three times a week. The flight takes one hour and ten minutes, and costs upwards of US$60.

Tour operators Batken Travel Service (m *0772 776 691*) can help with local travel advice as well as organise treks to areas like the Karavshin Valley.

Where to stay and eat

🏠 **Gulnara homestay** Paizullaeva 76; m 0555 277 668. **$**

🏠 **Intourist Hotel** (20 rooms) South of the park & town municipal buildings, this institution has undergone few changes since independence. Best avoided if at all possible. **$**

✗ **Cafe-bar Asylbek** On the main road west of the park and hospital. On the same street is a pleasant, shady outdoor *chaikhana* next to the entrance to the park. **$**

✗ **Café Minim** East of the municipal building. A very friendly place with good food & a pleasant atmosphere. **$**

What to see and do Batken is leafy and pleasant but it does not really have any sights. Fans of Soviet-era statuary can seek out the golden figure of Lenin in hailing-taxi pose, and the gold and red Great Patriotic War memorial in the park. There is also some more modern Kyrgyz-themed sculpture in the park, the work of local sculptor Turgunbay Sadyov.

FROM BATKEN TO TAJIKISTAN Transport to Isfara in Tajikistan leaves from the west side of Batken's hospital. There are fairly regular buses and taxis (*30som*) making the short hop to the border, from where it is another ten minutes on to Isfara. As a rule, border formalities here seem to be astonishingly brief, the Kyrgyz post not even looking at passports and, at the Tajik post, just a cursory examination and a passport stamp is required, without even the need to get out of your taxi. From Isfara there are frequent buses onward to Khojand, and money-changers at the bus station who will change any remaining Kyrgyz som into Tajik somani.

AK-SUU AND TURKESTAN RANGE Southwest of Batken, the mountains of the Turkestan range offer superb opportunities for highly experienced and adventurous climbers. The jagged peaks here are often likened to those of the southern Patagonian Andes and are better described as rock towers than mountains. The whole of the Turkestan range provides unique challenges to climbers in search of sheer rock faces and big wall climbing.

It was in this area that Japanese geologists and American climbers were kidnapped in 1999 and 2000 by IMU militants from over the border in Tajikistan (see page 18). The area appears to be safe now, although this should be verified before travel. As well as advanced climbing skills, a visit to this region requires specialist back-up, and climbing and border zone permits may be required. Contact one of the Bishkek trekking and climbing operators for further details.

Approaches to the range are usually by way of the Ak-Suu, Leilek and Karavshin valleys that lie to the south of the Vorukh enclave. These valleys also offer excellent opportunities for adventurous trekking, although engaging the services of a local guide is highly advisable.

The ultimate challenge for extreme climbers is the north face of the almost perfect pyramid of 5,509m Pik Piramidalny ('Pyramid Peak'), which dominates the upper Leilek Valley and offers the archetypal 'big wall' with its 2km-high sheer rock face. The highest peak in the Turkestan range is 5,621m Pik Skalistiy, which lies a little further east, due south of Vorukh.

Appendix 1

LANGUAGE

Kyrgyz is the official language of state and parliament, although Russian also remains an official language for the time being. Kyrgyz is a member of the central Turkic group of languages and is similar to Kazakh. 'Standard' Kyrgyz is based upon the northern dialect found in Kyrgyzstan, which contains words from Mongolian languages as well as from Russian. Southern Kyrgyz has many words of Persian, Uzbek and Tajik origin. Modern Kyrgyz is written with a slightly modified Russian Cyrillic script: the alphabet below shows the Cyrillic alphabet, its Latin equivalent and a guide to pronunciation.

Cyrillic		Latin		Pronunciation
А	а	A	a	as in 'father' (if stressed), or 'fat' (if unstressed)
Б	б	B	b	as in 'back'
В	в	V	v	as in 'victim'
Г	г	G	g	as in 'good'
Д	д	D	d	as in 'deal'
Е	е	E	e	'ye' as in 'yen'
Ё	ё	Yo	yo	as in 'Yorkshire'
Ж	ж	Zh	zh	as in 'pleasure'
З	з	Z	z	as in 'zoo'
И	и	I	i (ee)	as in 'feet'
Й	й	Y	y	as the 'y' in 'toy'
К	к	K	k	as in 'kangaroo'
Л	л	L	l	as in 'laugh'
М	м	M	m	as in 'map'
Н	н	N	n	as in 'note'
О	о	O	o	as in 'sort'
П	п	P	p	as in 'pen'
Р	р	R	r	as in 'red'
С	с	S	s	as in 'set'
Т	т	T	t	as in 'test'
У	у	U	u	as in 'tool'
Ф	ф	F	f	as in 'father'
Х	х	Kh	kh	as in the Scottish 'loch'
Ц	ц	Ts	ts	as in 'sets'
Ч	ч	Ch	ch	as in 'chop'
Ш	ш	Sh	sh	as in 'shore'
Щ	щ	Shch	shch	as in 'fresh chives'
Ы	ы	Y	y	as in 'fill'
Ь	ь			soft sign, not pronounced on its own

Cyrillic		Latin		Pronunciation
Э	э	E	e	as in 'ever'
Ю	ю	Yu	yu	as in 'abuse'
Я	я	Ya	ya	as in 'yam'

The following adopted Cyrillic characters are also used in Kyrgyz

Ѳ	ѳ	Ö	ö	'ur' as in 'turf'
Ң,	ң,	Ng	ng	as in 'long'
Ү	ү	Ü	ü	'ew' as in 'few'
Т				

he combination Dzh (ДЖ) is usually written as J in Kyrgyz.

BASIC KYRGYZ GRAMMAR
As with other Turkic languages, suffixes are added to fixed stems to indicate grammatical functions, and added to nouns to indicate gender and number. There are six cases: nominative, genitive, dative, accusative, locative and ablative. Sentence order tends to be subject, then object, then verb. As a Turkic language, there has to be vowel harmony within a word, so if a rounded vowel is contained by the stem, it must also be present in the suffix eg: *tüshündüm* – I understand; *tüshündüngüzbü?* – Do you understand?

RUSSIAN
Although most Kyrgyz delight in foreigners' attempts to use their native tongue, Russian is, in many ways, a more useful language, as it's spoken by almost everyone in Kyrgyzstan, including minorities like Uzbeks, and of course ethnic Russians. Russian is also the *lingua franca* throughout the central Asian region. Russian is a notoriously difficult language to learn, with Byzantine rules of grammar, but learning a little goes a long way, and even to just know the basics is invaluable. Bringing along a Russian dictionary and/or phrase book is highly recommended.

The vocabulary below is given in both Kyrgyz and Russian: the Russian words have been spelled phonetically and the stress underlined to help with pronunciation. In Kyrgyz, the stress usually falls on the last syllable.

WORDS AND PHRASES
Essentials

English	Kyrgyz	Russian
Good morning	*assalamu aleykum**	*dobra-ye ootra*
Good evening	*assalamu aleykum**	*dobri vyechyer*
(* literally: Peace be upon you; the response is *Wa aleykum assalam*)		
Good night	*tününgüz beypil bolsun*	*spakoyni nochee* (on going to bed)
		da sveedanya (on leaving)
Hello	*salam*	*zdrasvooytye*
Goodbye	*kosh*	*da sveedanya*
My name is…	*menim atiym…*	*menya zavoot…*
What is your name?	*atëngëz kim?*	*kak vas zavoot?*
I am from…	*men … keldim*	*ya eez …*
… England/Britain	… *anglia* …	… *anglee-ya*
… America	… *amerikadan* …	… *amyereeka*
How are you?	*kanday siz?*	*kak dyela?*
fine	*jakshë*	*kharasho*
not bad	*jaman emes*	*nyeplokha*
please	*chakëruu*	*pazhalsta*
thank you	*rakhmat*	*spaseeba*
Excuse/Pardon me	*kechiresiz*	*eezveneetye/prasteetye*

English	Kyrgyz	Russian
OK	*makul*	*kharasho*
Yes	*oba/oshandoy*	*da*
No	*jok*	*nyet*
No problem	*ech nerse emes*	*nyet prablyem*
Sorry	*kechiresiz*	*eezveneetye*
I understand	*men tüshündüm*	*ya paneema-yoo*
I don't understand	*men tüshünbödüm*	*ya nye paneema-yoo*
Do you understand?	*tüshündüngüzbü?*	*viy paneema-yetye?*
Have a good trip!	*ak jol bolsun*	*sh-chashleevava potee!*

Questions

How?	*kancha?*	*kak?*
What?	*kancha?*	*shto?*
Where?	*kayerde?*	*gdye?*
Which?	*kaysë?*	*kakoy?*
When?	*kachan?*	*kagda?*
Who?	*kim?*	*kto?*
How much?	*kancha turat?*	*skolka eta sto-eet?*

Numbers

1	*bir*	*adeen*
2	*eki*	*dva*
3	*üch*	*tree*
4	*tört*	*chyetiyrye*
5	*besh*	*pyat*
6	*altë*	*shest*
7	*jeti*	*syem*
8	*segiz*	*vosyem*
9	*toghuz*	*dyevyat*
10	*on*	*dyesyat*
11	*on bir*	*adeenatsat*
12	*on eki*	*dvyenatsat*
13	*on üch*	*treenatsat*
14	*on tort*	*chyetiyrnatsat*
15	*on besh*	*pyatnatsat*
16	*on altë*	*shesnatsat*
17	*on jeti*	*syemnatsat*
18	*on segiz*	*vasyemnatsat*
19	*on toghuz*	*dyevyatnatsat*
20	*jëyërma*	*dvatsat*
21	*jëyërma bir*	*dvatsat adeen*
30	*otuz*	*treetsat*
40	*kërk*	*sorak*
50	*elüü*	*pyadyesyat*
60	*altëmësh*	*shesdyesyat*
70	*jetimish*	*syemdyesyat*
80	*seksen*	*vosyemdyesyat*
90	*tokson*	*dyevyanosta*
100	*bir jüz*	*sto*
1,000	*bir ming*	*tiysyacha*

Time

English	Kyrgyz	Russian
What time is it?	azër saat kancha boldu?	katori chas?
it's ... o'clock	... saat	... chasa
today/ tonight	bügün/ kechinde	syevodnya/syevodnya vyechyeram
tomorrow	erteng	zaftra
yesterday	keche	fchyera
morning	erteng menen	ootra
evening	kech	vyechyer

Days

English	Kyrgyz	Russian
Monday	düshömbü	panyedyelneek
Tuesday	seyshembi	ftorneek
Wednesday	sharshembi	sryeda
Thursday	beishembi	chyetvyerk
Friday	juma	pyatneetsa
Saturday	ishembi	soobota
Sunday	jekshembe	vaskryesyenye

Months

English	Kyrgyz	Russian
January	yanwar	yanvar
February	fewral	fyevral
March	mart	mart
April	aprel	apryel
May	may	my
June	iyun	ee-yoon
July	iyul	ee-yool
August	awghust	avgoost
September	sentabër	syentyabr
October	öktöbür	aktyabr
November	noyabër	na-yabr
December	dekabër	dyekabr

Getting around
Public transport

English	Kyrgyz	Russian
I want to go to ...	men ... barmakmën	ya khachoo pa-yekhat f ...
How much is it?	kancha turat?	skolka eta sto-eet?
Is it far?	alësbë?	eta dalyeko?
far	ales	dalyeko
ticket	bilet	beelyet
bus station	vozkal/aptobus ayaldamasë	aftavakzal
railway station	poyuz istansiasë	vokzal
airport	ayeroport	a-eraport
bus	aptobus	aftoboos
train	poyuz	po-yest
plane	samolyot	samalyot
taxi	taksi	taksee
bicycle	welosiped	vyelaseepyet
motorbike	motorsikil	matatsiykl
petrol	benzin	byenzeen
departure	ayrëlüü	atpraviyenee-ye

Directions

English	Kyrgyz	Russian
Which direction?	*kaysë baghëtta?*	*fkak_om napravl_yenee-ee?*
Go straight ahead	*tüz keterberingiz*	*_eta pr_yama*
turn left	*solgo buruluu*	*pavyern_eetye nal_yeva*
turn right	*onggho buruluu*	*pavyern_eetye napr_ava*
north	*tündük*	*s_yevyer*
south	*tüshtük*	*yook*
east	*chëghësh*	*vast_ok*
west	*batësh*	*z_apat*
near	*jakën*	*r_yadam*
far	*ales*	*dalyek_o*

Signs (Russian)

Entrance	ВХОД
Exit	ВЫХОД
Open	ОТКРЫТ
Closed	ЗАКРЫТО
Toilets – men	МУЖСКОЙ
Toilets – women	ЖЕНСКИЙ
Information	СПРАВКИ
Prohibited	ЗАПРЕЩЕНО

Accommodation

English	Kyrgyz	Russian
hotel	*mëymankana*	*gast_eeneetsa*
guesthouse	*konok üy*	*dom dlya pree-_ye-zhikh*
apartment	*bölmö*	*kvart_eera*
cheap	*arzan*	*dyesh_ovi*
clean	*pakiz*	*ch_eesti*
Do you have any rooms?	*bosh bölmö barbë?*	*oo vas yest namyer_a?*
I'd like …	*magha … kerek*	*ya khach_oo …*
… a single room	*… jalghëz bölmö …*	*… adnyam_yesni n_omyer*
… a room with two beds	*… eki kishilik bölmö …*	*… dvukhm_yesni n_omyer*
How much is it per night?	*bir tünösö kancha bolot?*	*sk_olka eta st_oeet fsootkee?*
I am staying for …	*men … tünöyüm*	*ya astanav_eelsa*
… one night	*… bir kün*	*… na adn_oo noch*
… a week	*… bir juma*	*… na ned_yelyoo*
Where is the toilet?	*daaratkanasë kayerde?*	*gdye too-al_yet?*
room	*bölmö*	*n_omyer*
bed	*karawat*	*krav_at*
toilet	*daaratkana*	*too-al_yet*
bathroom	*moncho*	*v_a-naya*
shower	*dush*	*doosh*
I'd like to pay the bill	*men talongho pul tölöymün*	*m_ozhna zaplat_eet?*

Food

English	Kyrgyz	Russian
I am a vegetarian	*vegetaryan min*	*ya vyegeetaree-_anyets (m)*
		vyegeetaree-_anka (f)
I don't eat meat	*et jebeymin*	*ya nye yem myas-_nova*
The bill please	*eseptesheli*	*sh-chot pazh_alsta*
breakfast	*ertengmenki tamak*	*z_aftrak*

English	Kyrgyz	Russian
lunch	*tüshkütamak*	*abyet*
dinner	*kechki tamak*	*oozhin*

Basics

bread	*nan*	*khlyep*
cream	*kajmak*	*sleefkee*
eggs	*jumurtka*	*yitso*
rice	*kürüch*	*rees*
meat	*et*	*myasa*
salt	*tüz*	*sol*

Drinks

beer	*pivo*	*peeva*
tea	*chay*	*chay*
coffee	*kofe*	*kofye*
vodka	*arak*	*votka*
yoghurt drink	*ayran*	*kefir/yogoort*
milk	*süt*	*malako*
water	*su*	*vada*

Shopping and communications

How much is this?	*bul kancha turat?*	*skolka sto-eet?*
I'm just looking	*men jönele karap jatam*	*ya prosta smat-ryoo*
That's expensive	*al këmbet*	*eta doraga*
Is that OK with you?	*makulbu?*	*viy nye vazrazha-yetye?*
OK	*makul*	*kharasho*
cash	*nak pul*	*naleechni-ye dyengee*
credit cards	*ötümdüü kartochka*	*kryedeetna-ya kartachka*
travellers' cheques	*sayakhat chegi*	*darozhni chyek*
receipt	*öjöt*	*kveetantsi-ya*
expensive	*këmbat*	*daragoy*
cheap	*arzan*	*dyeshovi*
bank	*bankasi*	*bank*
post office	*pochtokana*	*pochta*
stamps	*marka*	*marka*
telephone call	*el aralëk telefon*	*zvanok*

Emergency

Help!	*jardam beringiz!*	*pamageetye!*
Call a doctor!	*dokturdu chakërëngiz!*	*viyzaveetee vracha!*
There has been an accident	*al jerde kërsëk bolghon*	*pra-eezashol nyesh-chasni sloochee*
I am injured	*men jarat aldëm*	*menya ranyeni*
I have been robbed	*men tonodu*	*menya agrabeelee*
Go away!	*ket!*	*ookhadeetye!*
Thief!	*ooru!*	*vor!*
first aid	*tez kutkazun*	*pyerva-ya pomash-ch*
police	*milisanë*	*mileetsi-ya*
hospital	*dokturkana*	*balneetsa*
I am ill	*oorup kaldëm*	*Ya bolyen/balna (m/f)*

Health

English	Kyrgyz	Russian
diarrhoea	*ich ötkök*	*pan__o__s*
doctor	*doktur*	*vrach*
nurse	*medsestra*	*myedbr__at__/myetsyestr__a__* (m/f)
pharmacy	*darëkana*	*apt__ye__ka*
painkillers	*ooru toktutuu darësë*	*bolye-ootal__ya__-yoosh-chee-ye*
antibiotic	*antibiotic*	*anteebee-__o__teekee*
antiseptic	*antiseptic*	*anteesept__ee__chyeska-ye sr__ye__tstva*
condoms	*prezervativ*	*pryezyervat__ee__f*
contraceptive	*töröttün aldën alaturghan*	*proteevazach__a__tachna-ye sr__ye__tstva*
I have ...	*men ...*	*oo men__ya__...*
... a pain	*... ooruu*	*... boll*
... a stomach ache	*... ich oorusu*	*...b__a__leet zhiv__o__t*
... a fever	*... temperatura*	*... temperat__oo__ra*
asthma	*astma*	*__a__stma*
diabetes	*diabet*	*dee-ab__ye__t*
I'm allergic to ...	*menim...ge alergiyam bar*	*oo men__ya__ alerg__ee__ya na...*
... antibiotics	*... antibiotikter ...*	*... anteebee-__o__teekee*
... penicillin	*... penitsilin*	*... pyeneetsil__ee__n*

Other

English	Kyrgyz	Russian
black/white	*kara/ak*	*ch__o__rni/b__ye__li*
this/that	*bul/al*	*eta/tot*
fine/wet	*jakshë/nëm*	*khar__o__shi/m__o__kri*
last/next	*ötkön/keler*	*pasl__ye__dnee/sl__ye__doosh-chee*
boy/girl	*bala/kyz*	*m__a__lcheek/d__ye__vachka*
big/small	*chong/kichinekey*	*balsh__oy__/m__a__lyenkee*
good/bad	*jakshë/jaman*	*khar__o__shi/plakh__oy__*
hot/cold	*ëssëk/suuk*	*gar__ya__chee/khal__o__dni*

KYRGYZ GESTURES

To show welcome	Pressing the right hand to the heart
To apologise	Touching right or both hands to chest
To beckon	Hand palm down with fingers curling and unfurling
To show shameful behaviour	Pinching or rubbing own cheek downwards
To stop a taxi	Arm out straight, palm downwards
To attract attention	Raise hand and say 'kechiresiz'.

Appendix 2

GLOSSARY OF KYRGYZ TERMS

aksakal	literally 'white beard', a village elder
Ak-jol	literally 'white road', meaning *bon voyage* or have a good trip!
akyn	storyteller or bard
ala kachuu	practice of bride-kidnapping
ala-kiyiz	unstitched felt carpet
archa	juniper
askhana	traditional café
at chabysh	traditional long-distance horse races
ayran	yoghurt-like drink
aytish	performance competition between two *akyns*
bai	Kyrgyz clan leader
baibiche	respected female elder
batyr	khan or tribal leader
bakshi	shamans
bürkütchü	eagle (or bird of prey) hunter
beshbarmak	'five fingers', a Kyrgyz dish traditionally eaten with the hands
boorsok	deep-fried pieces of dough
bosogo	yurt door frame
bozo	beer-like drink made from fermented millet
bozoy	literally 'grey house', a yurt
chabana	cowboy, herder
chaikhana	traditional tea shop
chapan	traditional Kyrgyz padded coat
chiy	reed mat for rolling *shyrdaks*
chuchuk	horse meat sausages
djigit	young horseback warrior
dostorkon	tablecloth spread on ground for food
eptchi zhak	women's section of the yurt
erz zhak	men's section of the yurt
gumbez	mausoleum
jailoo	alpine meadow for summer grazing
juk	wooden chest for clothes and bedding in a yurt
kajmak	cream made on a *jailoo*
kalama	flat bread
kalpak or ak-kalpak	white felt, triangular-shaped hat worn by Kyrgyz men
kalym	dowry or bride price

kamcha	horse whip
kanat	yurt framework of poles
kerege	trellis wall support of yurt
kok boru	'grey wolf', another name for *ulak tartysh*
komuz	three-stringed guitar-like instrument
kookor	anchor-shaped leather *kumys* container
kurut	dried cheese balls
kuirik	highly regarded tail fat of sheep
kumys	mildly alcoholic drink made from fermented mare's milk
kurak	patchwork
Kurban Ait	holiday and feast nine weeks after the end of Ramadan
kyz-kumay	'kiss the girl' horse game
manap	tribal leader
manaschi	*akyn* who recites from Manas cycle
mazar	tomb or shrine of holy man
nardi	game like backgammon
omin	ritual face-washing gesture at the end of a meal
oodarysh	horseback wrestling
ordo	game played with pieces of animal bone
Orozo Ait	holiday and feast at the end of Ramadan
samagonka	homemade *arak* or vodka
shokulo	tall conical hat traditionally worn by Kyrgyz women
shyrdak	carpet made of felt pieces sewn together in a pattern
temir komuz	mouth harp
tunduk	round, wooden central roof-piece of yurt
tush kiyiz	wall hanging
tiyin enmei	game of picking up a coin from horseback
tyor	the best place in a yurt reserved for honoured guests
ulak tartysh	horseback polo played with a headless goat
upai	game like marbles, played with sheep's knee bones

Appendix 3

FURTHER INFORMATION

BOOKS Although relatively few books concentrate on Kyrgyzstan specifically, there are many that include the country as part of the central Asian region.

History and politics

Anderson, John *Kyrgyzstan: Central Asia's Island of Democracy (Post-communist States and Nations)* Routledge, 1999. A rather out-of-date study of the political development of a country in transition.

Golden, Peter B *Central Asia in World History* OUP USA, 2011. An account of the whole region, from prehistory to present.

Grousset, Rene (author) and Walford, N (translator) *The Empire of the Steppes: History of Central Asia* Rutgers University Press, 1988. An authoritative account of the historical development of the region from the arrival of the Scythians to the last Mongolian emperor.

Hiro, Dilip *Inside Central Asia: A Political and Cultural History of Uzbekistan, Turkmenistan, Kazakhstan, Kyrgyzstan, Tajikistan, Turkey and Iran* Gerald Duckworth, 2011. A wide-ranging account of the politics and social history of the region.

Hopkirk, Peter *The Great Game: On Secret Service in High Asia* John Murray, 2006. A fascinating account of the Great Game as played between the forces of Russia and Britain in the late 19th century. This is more of a page-turner than most historical accounts. Not relating specifically to Kyrgyzstan, but offers excellent background on the way the whole region developed in Imperial times.

Lewis, David *The Temptations of Tyranny in Central Asia* C Hurst, 2008. Contains a detailed account of the 2005 revolution in Kyrgyzstan and examines US policy in the region.

Marat, Erica *The Tulip Revolution: Kyrgyzstan One Year After* The Jamestown Foundation, 2006. A quick-off-the-press account of the political machinations of 2005.

Naumkin, Vitaly *Radical Islam in Central Asia: Between Pen and Rifle* Rowman & Littlefield, 2005. A thorough study of various radical Islamic movements in the region.

Rashid, Ahmed *The Resurgence of Central Asia: Islam or Nationalism?* Zed Books, 1994. A look at the way Islam has resurged in the central Asian region in the wake of post-Soviet independence.

Roy, Olivier *The New Central Asia: Geopolitics and the Creation of Nations (Library of International Relations)* IB Tauris, 2007. A good overall survey of the newly formed central Asian states and their geopolitical position, although it is now rather out of date.

Soucek, Svat *A History of Inner Asia* Cambridge University Press, 2000. A full history of the entire central Asian region from the arrival of Islam until the Soviet period.

Tranum, Sam (editor) *Life at the Edge of the Empire: Oral Histories of Soviet Kyrgyzstan* CreateSpace Independent Publishing Platform, 2012. A fascinating collection of personal histories related by Kyrgyz, Tajiks, Uzbeks, Russians and Jews living in Kyrgyzstan during the Soviet period.

Whitfield, Susan *Life Along the Silk Road* University of California Press, 2001. The history of the Silk Road as told by a series of stories from different characters who might have inhabited the region in the past.

Whitlock, Monica *Land Beyond the Oxus: The Central Asians* John Murray, 2003. A BBC journalist examines the changes taking place in central Asia in the late 1990s, mostly, but not exclusively, focusing on Tajikistan. Currently out of print.

Wood, Frances *The Silk Road: Two Thousand Years in the Heart of Asia* University of California Press, 2004. The entire 5,000-year history of the Silk Road with plenty of photographs by explorers like Stein, Hedin and Mannerheim.

Culture

Antipina, Klavdiya (author) and Paiva, Rolando (photographer) *Kyrgyzstan* Skira, 2007. An expensive, but beautifully photographed, coffee-table book of traditional Kyrgyz costume by a Russian anthropologist and a French photographer.

Baldick, Julian *Animal and Shaman: Ancient Religions of Central Asia* IB Tauris, 2012. A survey of ancient customs and religions of central Asia from the Scythians onward.

Clayton, Sally Pomme (author) and Herxheimer, Sophie (illustrator) *Tales Told in Tents: Stories from Central Asia* Frances Lincoln Children's Books, 2006. A nice collection of stories for children, from the central Asian region.

Harvey, Janet *Traditional Textiles of Central Asia* Thames & Hudson, 1997. A full survey of all types of textiles from the region, including felt and embroidery.

Kalter, Johannes *The Arts and Crafts of Turkestan* Thames & Hudson, 1984.

Knobloch, Edgar *Monuments of Central Asia: A Guide to the Archaeology, Art and Architecture of Turkestan* IB Tauris, 2000. An admirably thorough survey of central Asia's historic sites and monuments, including those of Kyrgyzstan.

Morton, Margaret *Cities of the Dead: The Ancestral Cemeteries of Kyrgyzstan* University of Washington Press, 2014. A photographic survey of the unique architectural grandeur of Kyrgyz cemeteries.

Sahadeo, Jeff and Zanca, Russell (editors) *Everyday Life in Central Asia: Past and Present* Indiana University Press, 2007.

Natural history

Ayé, Raffael, Roth, Tobias and Schweitzer, Manuel *Birds of Central Asia* Princeton University Press, 2012.

Sparks, John *Realms of the Russian Bear: A Natural History of Russia and the Central Asian Republics* Little Brown & Co, 1992. Now out of print but still worth getting hold of if you can, this is a beautifully illustrated volume on the flora and fauna of the former USSR, with a large section on the Tien Shan and central Asia.

Van Der Ven, Joost *Looking at Birds in Kyrgyz Republic, Central Asia* Bishkek, 2002. This is a hard-to-find guide to Kyrgyzstan's birdlife in Russian and English.

Travel

Akchurin, Marat *Red Odyssey: A Journey Through the Soviet Republics* HarperCollins, 1992. A Russian's view of the republics of the central Asian region in the period just before independence. Out of print.

Bealby, Jonny *Silk Dreams, Troubled Road* Arrow Books, 2003. This is the first of several travel books to chronicle a long-distance journey by horse through the region in post-independence times.

Child, Greg *Over The Edge: The True Story of Four American Climbers' Kidnap and Escape in the Mountains of Central Asia* Villard Books, 2002. A rather dry, journalistic account of the kidnapping of young American mountaineers in the mountains of Batken Province in 2000. Controversial at the time, with implications that the much-publicised account did not contain the whole truth, the naïve and none-too-bright climbers do not evoke that much sympathy in the light of this book.

Deakin, Roger *Wildwood: A Journey Through Trees* Penguin, 2008. Although mostly concerned with travels in England this evocative book also contains two delightful chapters on Deakin's travels in the walnut forest regions of Jalal-Abad Province.

Farr, Saffia *Revolution Baby: Motherhood and Anarchy in Kyrgyzstan* Spire Publishing, 2007. This is a humorous account of expatriate life in Kyrgyzstan leading up to and during the revolution of March 2005.

Levine, Emma *A Game of Polo with a Headless Goat* Andre Deutsch, 2003. The title says it all. This has good coverage of the *ulak tartysh* horse game in Kyrgyzstan.

Maillart, Ella *Turkestan Solo: A Journey Through Central Asia* Tauris Parke Paperbacks, 2005. A captivating account of a feisty Swiss woman's solo journey through central Asia in 1932, which included a traverse of Kyrgyzstan's Tien Shan range.

Nazaroff, Paul *Hunted Through Central Asia: On the Run from Lenin's Secret Police* Oxford, 2002. More derring-do in central Asia, as the title suggests. Rather stereotyped characters and also plenty of descriptions of the flora, fauna and geology of the region.

Paine, Sheila *The Golden Horde: From the Himalayas to the Mediterranean* Tauris Parke Paperbacks, 2006. The author visits Kyrgyzstan as part of her fascinating odyssey in search of an amulet.

Stewart, Rowan and Weldon, Susie *Kyrgyz Republic: Heart of Central Asia* Odyssey, 2008. An attractively illustrated overview of historical, cultural and social aspects of the country.

Thubron, Colin *The Lost Heart of Asia* Vintage, 2004. A lyrical account of Thubron's first journey to central Asia in the early 1990s, which included some time in Kyrgyzstan. This is beautifully written prose: rich, deep and thought-provoking.

Thubron, Colin *Shadow of the Silk Road* HarperCollins, 2007. A second journey into central Asia made more than a decade later. Wonderful, expressive writing that does not patronise the reader but quietly impresses with its erudition and Old World sensitivity.

Watson, Claire Burgess *Silk Route Adventure: On Horseback in the Heart of Asia* Robert Hale, 2007. A redoubtable female banker goes on an 18-month, 6,000km horseback trek through central Asia and Mongolia.

Tolstoy, Alexandra *The Last Secrets of the Silk Road: Four Girls Follow Marco Polo Across 5,000 Miles* Profile Books, 2004. Four ex-public schoolgirls go horseriding across central Asia and squabble a lot. No sign of Marco Polo.

Whitely, Leon *Kyrgyzstan: Reflections on a Winter's Journey* lulu.com, 2012. An evocative journey through Kyrgyzstan at a bleak time of year.

Whitell, Giles *Extreme Continental: Blowing Hot and Cold Through Central Asia* Phoenix, 1996. Out of print but highly entertaining description of a journey through the new states of central Asia in the early 1990s, just after independence from the Soviet Union.

Mountaineering and trekking

Maier, Frith *Trekking in Russia and Central Asia* Mountaineers Books, 1997. Long out of print and completely out of date in terms of political geography, this guide is still very useful to browse for a general overview of what the region has to offer for adventurous trekkers.

Literature

Aitmatov, Chingiz *Jamilia* Telegram Books, 2008. A new English edition of one of Aitmatov's best-known works.

Aitmatov, Chingiz *The Day Lasts More Than a Hundred Years* Indiana University Press, 1988. Out of print but easily available secondhand.

Aitmatov, Chingiz *The Place of the Skull* Grove Press, 1989. Out of print but available secondhand.

Rosenberg, Robert *This Is Not Civilization* Mariner Books, 2005. An American-abroad novel based upon the experiences of a young Peace Corps volunteer's stay in Kyrgyzstan.

Language

Krippes, Karl A *Kyrgyz-English/English-Kyrgyz Concise Dictionary* Hippocrene Books, 2003. The only complete Kyrgyz-English dictionary available and currently out of print.

Rudelson, Justin Jon *Central Asia: Languages of the Silk Road* Lonely Planet Publications, 2008. This has brief sections on the Kyrgyz, Uzbek and Tajik languages (but not Russian).

WEBSITES Some of the tour operators listed in *Chapter 2, Practical Information*, and *Chapter 3, Bishkek*, also have useful websites.

www.cbtkyrgyzstan.kg Community Based Tourism in Kyrgyzstan
www.eurasianet.org Regional news website
www.helvetas.kg General information on the country
www.iwpr.net Institute for War and Peace Reporting
www.kgembassy.org Kyrgyz embassy in the USA
www.kyrgyz-embassy.org.uk Kyrgyz embassy in the UK
www.kyrgyzstan.orexca.com General information about Kyrgyzstan
www.silkpress.com Website of a magazine about the central Asian region
www.thespektator.co.uk Online version of monthly *Spektator* magazine
www.times.kg *Times of Central Asia* website

Index

Page numbers in **bold** indicate major entries; those in *italic* indicate maps

311

INDEX OF ADVERTISERS